THE STORY *of*
GARDENING

THE STORY *of*
GARDENING

PENELOPE HOBHOUSE

LONDON, NEW YORK, MUNICH,
MELBOURNE, DELHI

Senior Editor Pamela Brown
Senior Art Editor Ursula Dawson

Editors Penny David, Margaret Mulvihill
Art Editor Murdo Culver

Editorial Assistant Victoria Willan

Senior Managing Editor Anna Kruger
Senior Managing Art Editor Lee Griffiths

Picture Research Emily Hedges
DTP Design Louise Waller
Production Controllers Mandy Inness,
Jane Nower

First published in Great Britain in 2002
by Dorling Kindersley Limited,
80 Strand, London WC2R 0RL
A Penguin company

2 4 6 8 10 9 7 5 3 1

Copyright © 2002, 2004
Dorling Kindersley Limited, London
Text copyright © Penelope Hobhouse 2002, 2004

A CIP catalogue record for this
book is available from The British Library

ISBN 0 7513 3390 5 hardback edition
ISBN 1 4053 0714 5 paperback edition

Colour reproduction by Colourscan, Singapore
Printed and bound in China by Toppan
Printing Co. Ltd.

See our complete catalogue at

www.dk.com

Illustrations

Half-title page: the Blue Steps at Naumkeag,
Stockbridge, Massachussetts, designed from 1926 by
Fletcher Steele; page 2: 17th-century Villa Barbarigo
Pizzoni Ardemani, near Padua, Italy; page 3: roof terrace
designed by Topher Delaney for the Bank of America,
San Francisco; right: path of timber discs in Bob Dash's
garden on Long Island, New York State

CONTENTS

INTRODUCTION 6

Timechart 12

1 In the BEGINNING: the ORIGINS of GARDENING
The records and remains of the gardens and parks of Mesopotamia, Egypt and Persia 16

2 Our CLASSICAL HERITAGE: ANCIENT GREECE and ROMAN GARDENS
The beginnings of botany and herbalism in Greece and design developments in the Roman world 30

3 The GARDENS of ISLAM: HEAVENLY BEAUTY, EARTHLY DELIGHT
The Islamic concept of the "fourfold" garden and its spread from the Middle East to Spain, India and Turkey 56

4 PLEASURE and PIETY: MEDIEVAL GARDENS of CHRISTENDOM
The layers of meaning in the stylized garden of the Middle Ages 96

5 The RENAISSANCE VISION: the FLOWERING of the EUROPEAN GARDEN
The transition from the classical villa gardens of 15th- and 16th-century Italy to Louis XIV's power-gardening in 17th-century France and its translation in Holland and Britain 118

6 PLANTS on the MOVE: BOTANISTS, COLLECTORS and ARTISTS
The early plant enthusiasts who drew, grew and went in search of new species 168

7 A NATURAL REVOLUTION: the ENGLISH LANDSCAPE GARDEN
The 18th-century Landscape Movement, from its birth to its legacy 204

8 The ECLECTIC 19th CENTURY: NOVELTIES, INVENTIONS and REVIVALS
Fashions in European gardening at a time of technogical change 244

9 The AMERICAS: NEW HORIZONS in HORTICULTURE
Gardening's evolution on the American continent from the Inca and Aztec civilizations to the ideals of Frederick Law Olmsted 280

10 GARDENS of CHINA: a TIMELESS TRADITION
The long history of Chinese gardening, and its links with the landscape and painting 318

11 JAPANESE STYLE: SYMBOLISM and RESTRAINT
The essential elements of Japanese design and its influence on the rest of the world 346

12 A TIME of CHANGE: from NATURALISM to MODERNISM 1870–1950
Pioneer voices in America and Europe as gardening goes global 380

13 TODAY and TOMORROW: a WORLD of OPPORTUNITIES
The designers, ecologists and landscape architects who are shaping the way we garden in the 21st century 420

Bibliography and Picture Acknowledgements 454

Index and Acknowledgements 459

INTRODUCTION

THE STORY OF GARDENING, traced through almost three millennia to the 21st century, is not just one story but an infinite number – as many as there have been gardeners. And it can be told in an infinity of ways. In this case the storyteller is a gardener and perhaps, more importantly, a designer too, so the viewpoint is an aesthetic one. My primary interest is in layouts – garden styles – and how and why they came about. But as a working practical gardener, I also feel a perennial satisfaction with plants, how they have been used in the past and might be used in the future. I believe that discovering the way in which gardening has evolved enriches every gardener's life and that seeing how successive periods have influenced each other can help each of us to identify our own aims and look into the future. It is tempting to say that there is nothing new in gardening, that every garden in the making depends on and derives its inspiration from past styles but, in an age when science is likely to spring many more surprises, this may be too great a generalization. However, if it is broadly true, studying the past seems all the more worthwhile. Being able to recognize echoes of previous styles makes it possible to adapt them to our own individual needs and desires, and so I have written this book for the enjoyment of all gardeners, not just those interested in history.

First to define the scope of the book. There have to be limits and I have chosen to confine the discussion to "gardening for pleasure". As a designer, I find aesthetic satisfaction in the rhythmic planting of orchards, vegetable gardens and allotments but have excluded them from the story on the grounds that they get too close to "crops" – agriculture and functional productive horticulture. I have also steered clear of "hobby" gardening – prize dahlias, alpine troughs and bonsai – all fields for the enthusiasms of experts. Mine is a more general history and concerns outdoor gardening, stopping for the most part on the threshold of greenhouse and conservatory. There are, nevertheless, grey areas between "usefulness" and "beauty". A tree can be planted for shade but a grove of trees on a Greek hillside can also be sacred or, as part of a 'Capability' Brown landscape, can help to paint a picture in light and shadow. Although herbs are outside the parameters, I do include descriptions of the earliest herbals and herbalists

Author's territory
Author Penelope Hobhouse (opposite) in her own Islamic-inspired garden in Dorset, and (above) a gardener in his appropriate apparel as envisaged by Nicholas de Larmessin, c.1690.

Delicate symmetry

This charming portrayal of an orchard, painted in 1685 in the Deccani region of India, illustrates the fundamental features of an Islamic layout, which have remained unchanged throughout the centuries.

because they are important in the whole development of botanical science, a necessary part of gardening's evolution. We tend to think that before the 16th century, plants were never considered for their beauty alone – that until then they merely supplied us with our food and other necessities or were used to remedy illness. But garden myths and recorded literature reveal something quite different. From earliest times, Chinese emperors, Assyrian kings and medieval poets were absorbed by the idea of the beauty of gardens while, by the 12th century, Persian poets wrote of roses and nightingales as the measure of a garden's delight.

Gardening soon became an art, not just a collection of useful, sometimes beautiful, plants.

The new relationship with nature, first expressed by Petrarch in the 14th century and expanded by Renaissance humanists, led to a dialogue about the relative values of "art" and "nature" in the garden, a dialogue which continues today between the garden-architect and those more interested in gardening in naturalistic ways. In 16th- and 17th-century Italy the garden-architects resolved this conundrum by inventing a third category, which, put simplistically, was nature "improved" and "expanded" by man's management. The art of gardening is much more than combining plants with designed elements. Plants flourish when managed by a gardener, and the layout also blossoms when its structure is disguised by nature's vegetation. Although the art of gardening may seem to lie in the control of nature, we are nonetheless totally dependent on nature's co-operation if it is to be a collaboration, not a tussle.

The modern sensitivity to ecological needs and naturalism in gardening has sometimes been at the expense of garden aesthetics. But what is gardening if not artifice? In an artificially enclosed area, some manipulation of nature is inevitable: topiary, clipped hedges and ornamental flowerbeds are all a means of subordinating nature. This runs counter to the philosophy behind modern wildlife gardening. Here, the re-creation of nature has become more important than art, with any element of control shunned. Visual satisfaction is sacrificed to a desire not just to imitate nature but to copy it slavishly. There are many valid reasons for this sort of gardening – saving threatened flora and fauna, conserving water and avoiding pollution by herbicides and pesticides – but none is to do with seeing gardening as a fine art.

What is a garden? The English word derives from the French *jardin* and Teutonic roots of the word "yard" – an enclosure, usually walled or fenced, in which the soil has been worked for growing plants of various kinds. The concept goes back beyond the Judaeo-Christian tradition of the Garden of Eden and the imagery derived from it, which the Muslims transformed into a terrestrial paradise, literally a foretaste of heaven to come. This is something rather different from the Persian *paradeisos* – the hunting park of kings in the fertile crescent before the Arab conquest. A garden as a place to grow plants implies water, soil, warmth and light and someone, the gardener, who wants to grow them. For me the equation adds up to a "garden" only when an extra element is added: some kind of choice and control of the layout, decided for aesthetic reasons.

In all countries, but particularly in desert areas, water is the vital ingredient for life, human and plant, and gardeners have long invented ways of using it to add beauty, and pleasure, to the garden in the form of pools, splashing fountains, rills and lakes. The Muslim *chahar bagh* or "fourfold" garden has four water channels, which represent the four rivers of life revealed in the teaching of the Koran. In 16th-century France, Catherine de' Medici staged water fetes and miniature water battles on the chateaux lakes – the ultimate in sophistication at the time – while Renaissance water engineers created all manner of hydraulic tricks to amuse and impress. In the 18th century, placid reflecting lakes became an essential ingredient in the English landscape garden. The sound and movement of water introduces another, more functional, element: in hot climates, fountain sprays controlled insects as well as cooling the air, while, today, rushing water in vast modern fountains on the American West Coast helps to drown the noise of traffic.

Why do we garden? Is the garden a place where we can create our own private oasis, feel the satisfaction of making a pleasing layout and growing plants well? Or, had we the means and the status, is it a place for showing off power and possessions, as it has often been in the past? Some, including emperors of China, have lost their lives after bankrupting their country in pursuit of grandiose schemes. On a more modest scale, others, such as Charles Hamilton at Painshill in Surrey in the 18th century and Prince Pückler-Muskau in eastern Germany in the 19th century, have seen their passion for gardening swallow their family fortunes. Both these aristocrats were forced to sell their properties because of their horticultural overspending. Louis XIV got away with outrageously extravagant gardening at Versailles, though his descendants may have had to pay for it with their lives. His legacy of formality and grandeur has influenced all gardening styles since, if in a sometimes negative way, by showing us what we don't want. Reasons for gardening have been many and various across history and cultures. We may well

want to make the garden a place for entertaining, as it was in Mughal India, an expression of spirituality as in a Japanese Zen garden or a statement of ecological beliefs as in Jens Jensen's Lincoln Memorial Garden in Illinois. During the Renaissance, the gardens of some European plant enthusiasts were the equivalent of a botanical museum of all possible "collectibles", and today, the restoration of an historic garden plays an educational role while preserving layers of the past.

Different people want different things from gardening, and different cultures and climates make people see things differently. Both Sir John Chardin in the 17th century and Vita Sackville-West in the 1920s, travelling in Persia, expressed amazement that the Persians wanted simply to sit in their gardens and not walk about as Europeans have always done. Of course the Muslim garden was a place for contemplation, under a shady portico or spreading plane tree, and, from a practical point of view, not a place to wander in under the hot sun.

It is from the earliest desert gardens, literally oases of vegetation in an arid climate, that we get our idea of the garden as a refuge. For nomads an oasis was a place of lush contrast to the shifting sands, wind and beating sun, a place of seclusion from the outside world. Today, for many of us, the garden is still an oasis, a place apart, though the concept may exist as much in the mind as in reality.

Versailles grandeur
The Bosquet de la Galerie des Antiques *painted by J.-B. Martin the Elder, c.1688. Louis XIV's* bosquets, *carved out of the forest, were designed as places for the king to lay on vast entertainments.*

Natural considerations
At Pensthorpe Waterfowl Trust, in Norfolk, Dutch designer Piet Oudolf, renowned for his naturalistic planting, has used perennials to create seasonal drifts and bold abstract patterns of colour.

Where does this fit with the first tentative attempts by early Renaissance architects to incorporate distant views and "nature" into their garden schemes, and with the ideas of the English 18th-century garden-makers who, after Kent had "leaped the fence", wanted to bring the whole landscape into the garden? In the United States the "wilderness" approach is still relevant, bolstered by an important need to preserve native plants and coincidentally ban exotic aliens which tend to upset natural balance and corrupt plant ecology. At the opposite end of the spectrum from the garden as private retreat is the whole notion of the public park, a place for recreation in densely populated towns and cities or sometimes, as Frederick Law Olmsted described New York's Central Park in the second half of the 19th century, the "green lungs" of the people.

Over the centuries we have been learning how to respect nature and preserve it for the future, how to garden wisely without sacrificing the idea of gardening as a fine art. The story of gardening is a continuing one – just like a garden it is a process not a product. We can, I am convinced, produce the best gardening by letting the past speak to us and re-interpreting its messages for today and tomorrow.

TIMECHART   A brief survey of some of the main

	3000BC	2000BC	1000BC	0

NEAR AND MIDDLE EAST AND INDIA

SUMERIANS develop **HUNTING PARKS,** combining the idea of pleasurable landscape with provision of sport and food

EGYPTIAN GARDENS, as revealed by tomb paintings, usually contain ornamental pools and are planted with trees and flowers. The gardens' rectangular shape is dictated by Egyptian irrigation methods

ASSYRIANS, BABYLONIANS and **PERSIANS** make hunting parks, like the Sumerians before them. A few surviving stone reliefs (*c.*700 BC) show that some **ARTIFICIAL LANDSCAPING** was carried out

HANGING GARDENS OF BABYLON follow an established ziggurat style of construction

In ancient **PERSIA,** Cyrus the Great builds a garden at **PASARGADAE.** Remains reveal a layout organized around a pattern of rectangular pools and water channels

Alexandrian **HYDRAULICS EXPERTS,** such as Hero, create ingenious devices, later to inspire Renaissance water engineers

FAR EAST

CHINESE ideas of gardening derive from the people's animistic beliefs and veneration of nature and the landscape

In **CHINA,** Emperor Qin Shi Huang Di and his successor Wudi both create fabulous **PLEASURE PARKS.** Wudi's has features designed to tempt the Immortals to stay and supply him with the elixir of everlasting youth

EUROPE

ANCIENT GREEK delight in plants is evident from frescoes and pottery decoration dating to *c.*1500 BC

GREEKS develop an intense, almost mystical relationship with their landscape (as described in the 8th-century works of Homer), and an interest in the herbal properties of plants

THEOPHRASTUS classifies and describes over 450 plants in his *Enquiry into Plants* (*c.*300 BC) – the beginnings of botanical science

THE AMERICAS

WORLD EVENTS

• 2686 BC Beginning of Egyptian Old Kingdom

• 2500 BC Sahara region begins to dry out

• 2000 BC Beginnings of Minoan civilization, Crete

• 2500 BC Horse domesticated, Central Asia

• 1792 BC Birth of Hammurabi, founder of Babylonian empire

• 776 BC First recorded Olympic Games, Greece

• 753 BC Traditional date of founding of Rome

• *c.*517 BC Death of Lao Zi, founder of Taoism

• 486 BC Death of Buddha

• 479 BC Death of Confucius

• 221 BC China unified under first emperor, Qin Shi Huang Di

3000BC	2000BC	1000BC	0

trends, gardens and garden-makers of the past 5,000 years

| 0 | 500AD | 1000AD | 1500AD |

Arab followers of the new **ISLAMIC** faith adapt garden layouts such as found at Pasargadae into the basic, spiritual design of the **FOURFOLD GARDEN**, quartered by water channels

MONGOL invaders rule much of the Middle East and, under Emperor Timur, create tent-filled enclosures with flower-decked meadows

Rulers of the new **OTTOMAN** empire in Constantinople create **PLEASURE GROUNDS** and **PUBLIC GARDENS**

ARABS build impressive palace gardens, with sophisticated water systems, on the banks of the Tigris

THE CHINESE begin to develop the tradition of the town garden of the mandarin and the **SCHOLAR'S GARDEN**

IN CHINA Emperor Yangdi landscapes a wondrous **PARK AT LUOYANG**. The Japanese ambassador's reports (607) of this garden have a profound **INFLUENCE ON DESIGN IN JAPAN**

PAINTING AND GARDENING develop a symbiotic relationship in **CHINA** – the garden is designed to resemble a landscape scroll

JAPANESE gardens are largely inspired by Chinese ideas, but in Japan's limited space, garden features become highly **SYMBOLIC** and layouts more **ASCETIC**. Rocks are venerated in both Chinese and Japanese cultures

DIOSCORIDES writes his 1st-century *De Materia Medica*, influencing the work and travels of botanists and plant collectors for several hundred years to come

MEDIEVAL kings and nobles create **HUNTING PARKS**, successors to the ancient parks of the Middle East and forerunners of the 18th-century landscape parks and 19th-century municipal parks

Leon Battista Alberti's *De re aedificatoria* (1485) reawakens Italian architects to Roman and Greek theories of **PROPORTION AND GEOMETRY**, which they now apply to garden design, as at the **CORTILE DEL BELVEDERE** (1506) in Rome. The garden turns outwards to face the landscape

The art of **TOPIARY** is born and is much used in Roman gardens

Images from the **MIDDLE AGES** depict **SMALL, ENCLOSED, INWARD-LOOKING GARDENS**, with a multitude of features such as turf benches and trelliswork

Francesco Colonna publishes his **HYPNEROTOMACHIA POLIPHILI** (1499). Its illustrations will become the model for pergolas, flowerbed patterns and other decorative features

The **ROMANS** garden on the sort of small domestic scale that would be familiar today, as ruins at **POMPEII** reveal. They also develop the **PERISTYLE GARDEN**, a kind of porticoed "outdoor room". The wealthiest among them, the owners of **COUNTRY VILLAS**, create large landscape-like gardens, as recorded by Pliny the Younger, a future inspiration for Renaissance garden-architects

Moors bring **ISLAMIC**, water-dominated ideas of layout to southern **SPAIN**. The finest remaining examples, the gardens of the **ALHAMBRA AND GENERALIFE**, date to the 14th century when Moorish rule was coming to an end

The farming peoples of **PERU** continue to develop sophisticated irrigation systems and horticultural techniques

AZTECS, in **MEXICO**, develop ornamental pleasure gardens and an extensive knowledge of plant cultivation and botany

- 30 Jesus Christ crucified in Jerusalem
- 79 Eruption of Vesuvius
- 105 Paper first used in China
- 117 Roman empire at its greatest extent
- 632 Death of Muhammad
- 711 Moors invade Spain
- 800 Charlemagne crowned Holy Roman Emperor
- 786 Harun al-Rashid becomes caliph of Baghdad, ruler of the Islamic world at its greatest extent
- 1325 Aztecs found Tenochtitlán (now Mexico City)
- 1338 Incas enlarge their empire in Peru
- 1450s First books printed in Europe
- 1453 Fall of Constantinople

TIMECHART continued

	1500AD	1600AD	1700AD

NEAR AND MIDDLE EAST AND INDIA

Babur, descendant of Timur, carries the **ISLAMIC GARDENING TRADITION** from Afghanistan into **NORTHERN INDIA** and establishes the Mughal dynasty

Babur's Mughal heirs, especially Jahangir and Shah Jahan, create beautiful **LAKESIDE GARDENS** in the vale of **KASHMIR**

Shah Jahan builds the **TAJ MAHAL** (1632), most famous of the remaining great Mughal gardens of northern **INDIA**

IN PERSIA Safavid rulers create exquisite gardens including the surviving **CHEHEL SUTUN** (1647), in Isfahan, and **BAGH-E FIN** (17th century), in Kashan

In **TURKEY**, Ottoman sultans' fondness for flowers reaches new excesses under Ahmed III, whose reign (1703-30) is known as the **TULIP PERIOD**

FAR EAST

IN CHINA, the garden, however small, is seen as a **MICROCOSM OF THE UNIVERSE** and the ideals of Chinese gardening remain unchanged over hundreds of years. A concentration of small gardens belonging to mandarins develops in the city of **SUZHOU**

IN JAPAN, Zen-inspired dry landscapes of rock and raked gravel or gardens of moss and rock are designed to aid meditation. Kyoto's **SAIHO-JI**, **DAISEN-IN** and **RYOAN-JI** are classic examples

The **TEA CEREMONY**, a Zen rite, plays a key role in Japanese life and the tea house becomes an important part of the garden

JAPANESE emperors build large stroll gardens at **KATSURA** (*c*.1620) and **SHUGAKU-IN** (*c*.1650). The latter makes use of *shakkei*, or borrowed scenery

Despite severe trade restrictions, European collectors look for **JAPANESE AND CHINESE PLANTS** to export to the West

EUROPE

The great era of **ITALIAN RENAISSANCE VILLAS** and gardens begins, many of them built by members of the Medici family. Some of the best remaining are the **VILLA CASTELLO** (1537) and **BOBOLI GARDENS** (1550), in and around Florence, **BOMARZO SACRO BOSCO** (1542), **VILLA D'ESTE** (1559) and **VILLA LANTE** (1568) near Rome and Viterbo, and **VILLA REALE** (1651), Marlia, near Lucca. Others such as **PRATOLINO** (1569) have been considerably altered or lost. The garden becomes a place of "outdoor living", much as in California today

THE FRENCH begin to adapt Italian concepts, fusing new-style Renaissance gardens onto existing chateaux (as at **FONTAINEBLEAU** and **ANET**), and making them fit into a flatter, more forested landscape. Eventually chateau and new-style garden become fully integrated, as at **SAINT-GERMAIN-EN-LAYE** (1593)

First **BOTANIC GARDENS** are founded at Pisa and Padua (1545) and the great wave begins of plant introductions into western and northern Europe from the eastern Mediterranean, especially Turkey

The newly invented **MICROSCOPE** reveals that plants have male and female organs – scientific plant breeding can begin

ANDRÉ LE NÔTRE puts new theories of optics to dramatic effect at the French baroque gardens of **VAUX-LE-VICOMTE** (1656), **CHANTILLY** (1663) and **VERSAILLES** (from *c*.1670), gardens designed to demonstrate man's power over nature

DUTCH gardens are given a French baroque infusion, as at **HET LOO** (1693). The Dutch-French influence is also seen in **BRITAIN**, most famously at **HAMPTON COURT** (1689)

Reaction against baroque manifests itself in Britain in a new informality in garden design and the start of the **ENGLISH LANDSCAPE MOVEMENT**. Gardens at **CHISWICK HOUSE** (*c*.1731), **STOWE** (*c*.1734), **ROUSHAM** (1737) usher in the new style

LINNAEUS introduces the **BINOMIAL SYSTEM** for classifying plants

THE AMERICAS

SPANISH colonists create the very first mission gardens (with Islamic characteristics) in Florida

European settlers repeat north European models of layout in **SMALL UTILITARIAN GARDENS**. The Pilgrim Fathers sow their first seed (brought with them) in 1621. The settlers also learn about the indigenous flora from American native peoples

Dutch settlers quickly display horticultural talents and the English begin to make **ORNAMENTAL GARDENS** at **WILLIAMSBURG**. Quaker William Penn founds the "garden city" of Philadelphia in 1682

THE GREAT PLANT EXCHANGE between America and Europe begins

IN THE SOUTH, plantation owners sometimes design their gardens around their farming, as at rice-producing **MIDDLETON PLACE** (1742)

WORLD EVENTS

- 1519-21 Cortés conquers Aztec Mexico
- 1532 Inca Peru conquered by Pizarro
- 1526 Babur becomes first Mughal emperor of India
- 1564 Shakespeare is born; Michelangelo dies
- 1517 Martin Luther sets off Reformation
- 1520 Reign begins of greatest Ottoman sultan, Süleyman the Magnificent
- 1603 Japan's Tokugawa era based at Edo (later Tokyo) begins
- 1644 Rule of China's Qing dynasty, lasting until 1911, begins
- 1683 Siege of Vienna by Ottoman forces
- 1687 Newton formulates laws of gravity
- 1620 *Mayflower* sets sail for North America
- 1661 Start in France of Louis XIV's active reign

	1500AD	1600AD	1700AD

1800AD   **1900**AD   **2000**AD

CHINESE Emperor Qian Long builds Yuan Ming Yuan, his magnificent GARDEN OF PERFECT BRIGHTNESS

As JAPAN opens its doors to foreigners, the SEARCH FOR PLANTS to take to the West reaches a new peak

As well as influencing gardens around the world, some Japanese designers, such as SHIGEMORI MIREI, re-examine and REVITALIZE their own TRADITION

Drawings coming out of China of the Garden of Perfect Brightness contribute to the vogue for European CHINOISERIE, as at Sanssouci and Veitshöchheim, Germany, and Drottningholm, Sweden

WILLIAM ROBINSON publishes *The Wild Garden* (1870) and pioneers a more ECOLOGICAL ATTITUDE to gardening

VITA SACKVILLE-WEST creates SISSINGHURST (from 1932), icon of English gardening of the 20th century

'CAPABILITY' BROWN perfects the smooth, green landscape ideal at a host of English park-gardens, including PETWORTH (*c*.1750) BLENHEIM (1764), BURGHLEY (from *c*.1755) and LONGLEAT (1757)

Influx of gardenworthy, hardy PLANTS FROM JAPAN AND CHINA broadens the scope for new planting styles

HUMPHRY REPTON assumes 'Capability' Brown's mantle. His landscapes often combine PICTURESQUE elements and flowerbeds with green parkland, as at WOBURN ABBEY (1802) and ENDSLEIGH (1815). The picturesque style becomes immensely popular in Continental Europe, for example at MUSKAU and WÖRLITZ

Among other feats, JOSEPH PAXTON revolutionizes GLASSHOUSE BUILDING with Chatsworth's Great Conservatory (1836)

The JEKYLL/LUTYENS partnership creates a highly influential architectural and planting style. One of the best examples is HESTERCOMBE (1906). LAWRENCE JOHNSTON'S HIDCOTE (1907) also sets a fashion for the compartmented garden

The fashion for CARPET BEDDING reaches its zenith. South American and African plants (raised in the new glasshouses) bring bright new colours to European gardens

The MODERNIST MOVEMENT makes a faltering pre-war entrance but becomes an important force in the 1980s and 1990s, although designs in northern Europe tend to remain more plant-oriented than those in warmer climates

Thomas Jefferson introduces the INFORMAL STYLE at MONTICELLO (1771)

Andrew Jackson Downing advances notions of the PICTURESQUE

FREDERICK LAW OLMSTED and Calvert Vaux build New York's CENTRAL PARK (1858), a major recognition of the need for urban green spaces. Olmsted also calls for America's WILDERNESS areas to be conserved

JENS JENSEN leads the Prairie School of planting and the movement towards a greater appreciation of American native plants

Modernist designers take centre stage but no one style dominates. Gardens range from the ECOLOGICAL and PLANT-BASED to the MINIMALIST and almost PLANT-FREE

Frank Scott urges the DEMOCRATIZATION of the American FRONT GARDEN by the removal of boundary barriers

THOMAS CHURCH proclaims that GARDENS ARE FOR PEOPLE. His designs in California put the garden at the heart of a new relaxed outdoor lifestyle

- 1775–83 American War of Independence
- 1788 First European settlers arrive in Australia
- 1789 French Revolution begins
- 1768 Naturalist Joseph Banks sails with Captain Cook to South Pacific
- 1835 Queen Victoria begins reign (until 1901)
- 1870s Most western European countries industrialize
- 1853 US forces Japan to "open" to Western powers
- 1845 Texas and Florida become US states; California 1850
- 1825 First passenger railway opened in England
- 1914–18 World War I
- 1939–45 World War II
- 1929 Wall Street Crash triggers Great Depression
- 1969 First men land on Moon
- 1952 Completion of Unité d'Habitation at Marseilles, Le Corbusier's "machine" for living

CHAPTER ONE

In the beginning
THE
ORIGINS
OF GARDENING

WHEN WE FIRST BEGIN GARDENING our learning curve, inevitably, is steep. We need to become acquainted with our plot, understand its soil, rainfall and climate, find out which plants we want to grow, and which, more importantly, will succeed. We can only imagine how much steeper the curve must have seemed to the world's first gardeners in Mesopotamia, Egypt and ancient Persia; what problems of water supply, seed germination and cultivation technique they had to solve. Today, we have all the benefits of the accumulated knowledge of previous generations of gardeners and advances of science. We can seek information at the press of a button or turn of a page. Nonetheless gardening remains a highly personal affair. We value our own individual discoveries. However worldly we might have become, however much science we learn, we can still marvel at the way tiny seeds sprout and become plants, the way the bare earth awakens when warmth or rain spurs the growing season. We share something of the wonder that the earliest gardeners must have felt.

If we succeed in creating our ideal garden, we might perhaps call it an "oasis" because in it we find escape from the stresses of the world outside. It might even be our personal "paradise". These are metaphors borrowed from some of the earliest people to garden. In some ways nothing changes: we are always in their footsteps, and across the millennia can find their first thoughts and responses reassuringly familiar.

Scenes from an Egyptian garden
This tomb painting dating to *c.*1475 BC found at Thebes shows an Egyptian funeral ceremony in the garden of a temple. A canopied barge bears the deceased through lotus-filled waters edged with papyrus, with date palms and sycamore figs in the surrounding beds.

THE BARE NECESSITIES

From the beginning, gardening has always depended upon topography and climate, life itself being sustainable only where water is available. Water makes it possible to grow trees, useful in themselves and also for providing shade for other plants and for gardeners. Gardening has always tended to develop first in warmer climates where water comes as melting snow from mountains or where rivers periodically inundate flood plains. Civilizations learned to harness water – storing it, creating dams, canals and sluices, and finding ways to conduct it to where it will be needed (see page 24). We gardeners who have had water on tap for generations tend to take it for granted. But perhaps we should remember and marvel at the ingenious ways early humankind managed water by utilizing gravity, or defying it with the motive power of animals or slaves. And perhaps, like the earliest gardeners, we should appreciate that it is a precious resource that we can no longer take for granted.

The first gardens must have been primarily useful, with little emphasis on beauty, with orchards of fruit, vegetables for food and herbs for medicines and offerings. They must also have been regular in layout – a side-effect of essential irrigation systems. Still, for many of us, a formal layout with repetitive geometric themes is immensely satisfying, providing the safe logic of an identifiable pattern, pleasing to the eye and understanding. Valuable plants would have needed to be protected from raiding animals and enemies, so gardens became walled or fenced – exclusive. In spite of the undoubted beauties of naturalistic open landscapes, many of us still crave the sanctuary offered by a secure walled retreat, a place in which to create our own idea of paradise.

We can picture the garden-owner gradually beginning to derive pride, status and pleasure from the plot that it was within their power to make fertile and beautiful. They would want somewhere to sit and admire their possessions, and paths to stroll along for viewing. A very early fable relates how a king planted a date palm and a tamarisk in the courtyard of his palace and held a banquet in their shade.

At the same time both garden-owner and labouring gardener were deeply astonished by the mysteries of nature. Any "green" site became sacred, a sign of a mysterious power that ruled the universe. To early agriculturists, water and the consequent vegetation were direct symbols of the mercy of the gods, and it is not surprising that the Egyptian and Mesopotamian civilizations, totally dependent on their respective rivers for survival, invested river gods with the personification of fertility. The palm tree, able to perpetuate itself by producing new leaves as the old ones dropped, had a magical aura of immortality.

FERTILE CRESCENT AND FRUITFUL NILE

The story of Western gardening begins in the countries of the Middle East, Mesopotamia, Egypt and Persia. It begins by introducing two themes we recognize today and that run as a recurring strand through this book. They are the vast landscaped park and the smaller contained garden.

Tree of life
An alabaster relief from Nimrud dates to the 9th century BC and shows Ashurbanipal II and a winged god worshipping a sacred tree. The tree stands for a natural force both feared and venerated by man, but which ensures immortality, the annual rebirth of nature in spring and "death" in autumn.

We think of Western civilization beginning in the foothills of northeast Mesopotamia and the Anatolian plateau where humankind, 8,000 years ago, first evolved from being nomad hunters to settled agriculturists. By 4000 BC these people's descendants, the Sumerians, the world's first literate civilization, descended from the cooler and wetter uplands with forests of scrub oak, planes, box, cedar, cypress and poplar, to the alluvial plains of the Euphrates and Tigris delta. Within another millennium they had constructed canals for irrigation and drainage to turn desert and swamp into rich cultivated lands, the "fertile crescent" of history. Originally only willows grew along the riverbanks with date palms in the deltas, while nothing grew in the swamps between the river basins except the giant reed, *Phragmites australis*. Within a few hundred years their descendants were laying out luxuriant hunting parks with sophisticated watering systems and collecting new plants (as well as animals and birds) from their foreign campaigns. We gardeners can imagine their efforts to provide the new exotics with conditions for growing as close as possible to those of their native habitat. Through all the centuries of plant discoveries every gardener has enjoyed pushing out the boundaries of plant possibilities in the garden, amending the soil, giving protection from hot sun or shelter from cold.

This second agricultural revolution, introducing new varieties of domesticated crops and new techniques, brought about a significant hierarchy of wealth and culture. This is always a key prerequisite of gardening. Non-utilitarian and aesthetic attitudes to horticulture become possible. Wild fruits and flowers, herbs and spices were transformed into domesticated plants, grown for interest and pleasure as well as for offerings to the gods.

The story of Egypt's adaptation of landscape to human ideas and needs runs parallel in time to that of the fertile crescent, but the development of gardens was very much influenced by the particular physical and geographical setting of the Nile Valley. Permanent planting was only possible in small walled areas protected from the floods, so there was no question of developing the large hunting parks favoured by Sumerians and Assyrians. The gardens we know from tomb paintings discovered by 19th-century archaeologists were smaller and walled. They were filled with useful fruits and vine arbours, with a pond and vegetation for wildfowl, and ornamental flowers grown as offerings to the gods and for embalming. Over the centuries the introduction of new trees, herbs and spices from exotic foreign sources gradually increased the range of plants grown in private garden schemes and in the larger temple gardens. In both the propitiation of the Egyptian gods was essential – mainly to ensure the annual floods – with flowers for bouquets and wreaths being an essential part.

By the second millennium BC the Egyptian "idea" of a garden spread to the Levant, through both military conquest and trade, and into Mesopotamia to influence garden development on geometric lines. Later, under Persian domination, the gardens of the great conquerors in the Middle East, documented by Xenophon and Herodotus in the 5th century BC, not only gave us the word *paradeisos*, but established the whole aesthetic of garden enjoyment, their gardens planned for viewing from shady pavilions, with channels of water and flowerbeds

ETYMOLOGY

The word paradise derives from the ancient Persian *pairidaeza*, itself a combination of *pairi*, meaning around, and *daeza*, meaning wall. The word first came to us through Xenophon, who in the 5th century BC saw how the Persian king Cyrus the Younger excelled not only in war but in cultivation: "In whatever country the king resides…he is concerned that there be gardens, the so-called pleasure gardens, filled with all the good things that the earth brings forth, and in these he spends most of his time." He translated the Persian *pairidaeza* into the Greek *paradeisos*. In the first translation of the Old Testament the word *parades* was used for a garden, and in both Jewish and Christian tradition the word paradise became associated with the Garden of Eden.

sunk below the path levels for ease of irrigation, their groves of trees laid out in strict rows to facilitate watering. The 6th-century BC palace of Cyrus I at Pasargadae near Shiraz (see page 58) had a rhythm of water rills opening out into square basins, a forerunner to the "fourfold" or *chahar bagh* gardens of Islam, sacred expressions of the Koran as interpreted by the Prophet Muhammad in the 7th century AD, the garden seen as a new sort of paradise, the terrestrial equivalent of the heaven to come for the devout Muslim.

PARADISE AND EDEN

The idea of paradise as a garden is very ancient, certainly predating the Garden of Eden of the three great monotheist religions, Judaism, Christianity and Islam. It has remained a central theme in garden history. In each age the idea of Eden is reinterpreted to suit current fashion; sometimes it is imagined as a formal layout, at others as a jungle of plants jostling for position.

The first gardens on record were made in Mesopotamia, but the idea of the mythical paradise garden is set in an earlier age. It envisaged a place of perpetual spring where men could live without toil, at accord with each other and with animals, secure of fruits in abundance. Later, in spiritual terms, it became an image of a place of perfect peace and plenty, where ordinary existence became meaningful and its transitory nature acceptable. The nuances of its interpretation change through the centuries but our modern idea of a garden is not so different.

The lack of detail in the Old Testament book of Genesis leaves ample room for speculation on both the nature of the Garden of Eden and its geographical location, although it seems likely that that mythical place was an orchard where deciduous trees flourished in the cool climate among the foothills of northern Mesopotamia. The Greek translation of the Old Testament used the word *paradeisos* for garden, describing that paradise which became identified with the Garden of Eden, where primeval man dwelt in harmony with the Lord. This sacred vision of a garden in Jewish and Christian tradition extended into New Testament teaching and, importantly for the development of the Islamic garden, into interpretations of the Koran, in which the garden paradise gave believers a foretaste of heaven to come.

To the desert-dweller, the water and shade stressed in the *Epic of Gilgamesh* were the essential ingredients of a garden paradise, with fragrance and fresh fruit to further delight mind and body. The Sumerian-Babylonian paradise, or Garden of the Gods, was the idyllic garden of peace and plenty reserved for the immortals, corresponding to Homer's Elysian Fields and the mystic islands dwelt in by the Immortals of Chinese fable.

Image of paradise
Sennacherib's paradise garden outside Nineveh existed in the 7th century BC. This stone relief shows a pavilion on columns overlooking a landscape park with trees, winding paths and streams. The water came from an aqueduct and the swamp, planted with reeds, was a refuge for wild pigs and waterfowl.

HARD EVIDENCE

The first evidence we have of the concept of paradise as a garden was found on the oldest of known cuneiform tablets, the earliest writing known, possibly dating to 4000 BC, unearthed in Mesopotamia. The Sumerian god of water, Enki, had ordered the sun-god, Utu, to create a divine garden by providing fresh water to transform the parched land of Dilmun – a land "pure, clear and bright" whose inhabitants knew neither sickness, violence, nor ageing but had no fresh water – into a paradise with fruit trees, green fields and meadows.

Later Babylonian tablets of 2700 BC reveal fragments of the Sumerian *Epic of Gilgamesh*, an heroic saga in which the warrior Gilgamesh, ruler of the Sumerian state of Erech (modern Warka in Iraq), searched out his enemy Hubaba in his home on a high mountain surrounded by cedars: "In front of the mountain rise the cedars in all their luxuriant abundance; their shade is pure joy" – while shrubs and fragrant plants could "nestle under the cedars". The dramatic epic was popular over centuries, with the figure of Gilgamesh becoming the hero of other folk myths, developing themes of death, immortality and eternal hope. The paradise myth describes a garden in which Gilgamesh wanders:

> And lo, the gesdin [tree] shining stands
> With crystal branches in the golden sands,
> In this immortal garden stands the Tree,
> With trunk of gold, and beautiful to see,
> Beside a sacred fount the tree is placed,
> With emeralds and unknown gems graced…

HANGING GARDENS, HUNTING PARKS

We have descriptive records rather than archaeological evidence of the great hunting parks and of another type of garden layout – the ziggurat – constructed by the Sumerians, with Babylon, established in 2250 BC as their capital. No plans (or definite archaeological identifications) exist of actual garden layouts before the second millennium BC, but scholars interpret the Mesopotamian ziggurat as a sacred building, a stepped terrace representing mountains, as the bond between heaven and earth. These are the architectural prototypes for the famous Hanging Gardens of Babylon constructed so that trees could grow on the terraces. Early stone reliefs of stylized plants include palms, pine trees, cypresses, phragmites and vines, as well as the Egyptian palmette and rosette patterns. In a Sumerian walled city, such as Ur to the west of the lower Euphrates, fruit trees and vegetables were grown in the spaces between inner and outer fortifications and may well have been grown on the various levels of the ziggurat.

From 1350 BC the Assyrians, followed by the Babylonians and Persians, were in turn to establish great empires. They made large hunting parks in the thickly wooded landscape of the north, where the climate would allow a wider range of trees and flowers. Inspired by the vegetation of these northern domains, the

Babylon's Hanging Gardens
The famous Hanging Gardens of Babylon, attributed to Nebuchadnezzar II (605–562 BC), grandson of the leading Babylonian conqueror, were constructed for his wife Amyitis, daughter of the King of the Medes. Living in the flat river delta, she missed the hills and meadows of her native country to the north. Described by the Greek Diodorus 500 years later, when already in decay, the gardens were composed of a series of terraces raised on vaulted brick, the beds probably irrigated from the River Euphrates by a screw system. Hollow brick columns, filled with soil, held the roots of the larger trees. In this way a considerable range of exotic plants could flourish above the rooftops of the city itself. Today, lightweight compost in large planters and electric pumps facilitate this sort of terrace and roof gardening, "greening" our inner cities.

Assyrian landscape design
This stone bas-relief is one of the earliest portrayals of a managed landscape. Dating from *c.*715 BC, it shows Sargon II's park at Khorasabad, northeast of Nineveh, depicting soldiers, a small temple with Doric columns and an artificial hill densely planted with trees, possibly cypresses. Evidently quantities of earth have been moved and shaped to define new contours, showing that Sargon, besides understanding the need for reliable irrigation, also had an appreciation of the visual elements in landscape design.

Assyrian kings also began to lay out hunting parks and gardens on the banks of the upper Tigris, harnessing river waters for irrigation.

When Sargon II made his park at Khorasabad, to the northeast of Nineveh, he must have been one of the first to change the lie of the land to suit his own purposes, to create a designed landscape, moving and shaping huge amounts of soil to define new contours. A bas-relief of *c.*715 BC clearly shows a man-made hill planted with a grove of trees. Today, with vast earth-moving machines, this kind of hard landscaping has become the norm; in pre-industrial England, and earlier in both China and Japan, it depended on a large relatively cheap labour force. When Sennacherib (704–681 BC) moved his palace to Nineveh he too laid out parks, diverting mountain water for irrigation and planting cotton bushes, vines and olive trees. Sennacherib was especially pleased with his complex system of irrigation canals that made his tree-growing possible: "To dam up the flow of water I made a pond and planted reeds in it…at the command of the gods, the gardens with their vines, fruit, sirdu wood and spices waxed prodigiously. The cypresses, palms, and all other trees grew magnificently and budded richly."

It is difficult for us to distinguish between afforestation, farming and horticulture, but these were certainly "managed" landscapes, dependent on adequate water and soil preparation. Sennacherib's successor Esarhaddon (680–669 BC) planned another great garden emulating the vegetation of the Amanus mountains in the land of the Hittites on the Black Sea. Records of his reign describe the detail of a temple garden in Babylon with fruit trees and burgeoning vegetable beds irrigated with channels of water, presumably to provide fresh produce as offerings to the gods.

Various stone reliefs dating from around this time depict scenes in a garden setting. However, many are stylized and it is difficult to identify plants. Some are obvious: the palm tree, associated with the gods and with royalty, and the sacred lotus, offered in gifts and sacrifice throughout the Middle East and Egypt, as well as pine trees and cypresses, with lilies (almost certainly *Lilium candidum* and *L. chalcedonicum*). Abstract flower-type designs, such as the palmette and the rosette, appeared in architecture and in craftwork, on clothes and on carpets, incorporated into Mesopotamian art from Egypt.

From the 9th to the 4th centuries the Achaemenians and Medes established their own empire in Persia, on the high plateau in the lands east of Mesopotamia. The emergence of the Persian empire, its borders reaching to Egypt and Greece in the west and China in the east, begins with Cyrus the Great and his victory over the Medes in 550 BC. Within 10 years he had consolidated his empire by subduing the tribes of eastern Iran and conquering the Babylonians, bringing to an end the Mesopotamian dominance of the known world. In this new civilization gardens such as that of Cyrus the Great at Pasargadae assumed great importance. It is the pattern of the Achaemenian gardens, with their "fourfold" theme, rills, fountains, and pavilions, that was to be adopted by the Muslims in the 7th century AD (see Chapter 3).

EGYPT REVISITED

The ancient gardens of Egypt, visually familiar from tomb paintings, have a particular interest for gardeners today. The functional irrigation system that the Egyptians perfected, using the flood waters of the Nile, inspired the garden patterns found throughout the emerging civilized world. By the second millennium BC the Egyptian idea of a garden had spread to the Levant, through both military conquest and trade, and into Mesopotamia, influencing garden development on geometric lines.

Relatively isolated from foreign influence, with an agricultural economy confined to the Nile Valley, the delta and the Faiyum area, southwest of Memphis and modern Cairo, Egypt developed its own garden culture during its dynastic history. Between the foundation of the Old Kingdom in *c.*3050 BC and Alexander's invasion in 330 BC, Egypt was exceptionally stable politically, reflecting its isolation from its neighbours. Excavations and hieroglyphics written on papyrus or on clay reveal an almost static situation, with garden styles portrayed in tomb paintings remaining almost unchanged over a thousand years.

From the earliest days the rulers had planted groves of trees around the pyramids and later pharaohs made extensive funerary gardens in and around temples such as those at Deir-el-Bahari in Thebes and Amun in Karnak. Although royal gardens were not represented in tomb paintings, those of high-up court officials and landowners portrayed the Egyptian idea of a garden, with features intended to

Ashurbanipal's arbour
The Assyrian King Ashurbanipal (668–627), grandson of Sennacherib, and his queen, are depicted on a stone relief at Nineveh, feasting under an arbour of grapevines flanked by palms and pine trees. Ashurbanipal introduced many new trees from countries he conquered.

WATERING THE DESERT

BOTH THE EGYPTIANS and the Persians proved remarkably innovative in their quest to get water to their crops and gardens. Rainfall in the Nile Valley is negligible but, with careful management, the river's annual inundation ensured enough water for growing crops and the irrigation of increasingly sophisticated gardens, keeping them luxuriant through the droughts of summer. Three seasons – inundation, bringing a concentration of silt, followed by winter and summer – controlled all plant growth. After the floods, between July and October, Egypt was a "black cloth of mud", according to the Arab poet Masudi. From January to March it was a "green cloth", with germinated seeds in the fields and gardens making a rich haze; and from April to June, the country was a ripening "nugget of gold".

As a result of these seasons, two characteristics emerged in Egyptian gardens. Firstly, any permanent tree planting or studied gardening had to be above the level reached by the Nile in flood. Trees with deep questing taproots were most likely to succeed, and many were planted in pits surrounded by a wall made of plastered mud for ease of watering. Secondly, water was collected in pools and canals by a series of dykes, and many of the richest citizens had wells and reservoirs in their gardens. Water was drawn up from an elaborate system of dams, terraces and sluices with the aid of a *shaduf*. The irrigation system perfected by the Egyptians, with canals parallel to each other and at right angles, also allowed the periodic flooding of planting beds.

High on the Iranian plateau, the ancient Persians had to find a different method of bringing water to their plants. Their solution was to exploit oases of natural springs and water supplies from melting snows in the high mountains for their agriculture and horticulture. To avoid evaporation, they introduced an elaborate network of underground aqueducts known as *qanats*.

Shafts were sunk to the permanent subterranean water level at the base of the hills; from these, water was propelled by gravity through mined underground tunnels to be saved in reservoirs or distributed in open channels, or *jubes*. At intervals of 15m (50ft) or so, the conduit's path was marked on the surface of the ground by a series of shafts, dug for removing spoil and to provide air to underground workers. In areas where the soil was particularly porous, tunnels were lined with stone or tile.

For orchards and avenues of trees the *qanat* method was augmented by the use of *jubes*, these channels allowing water seepage to the plants' roots. Together with planting beds sunk below the level of the surrounding ground, which could be watered by flooding with a system of sluices, these made domestic gardening a possibility.

Working the *shaduf*
The stored flood waters from the Nile were drawn up using a shaduf. *This invaluable device consists of a long pole balanced over a stand, with a bucket of mud attached to one end as counterpoise, and at the other, an empty jar for collecting the water. The* shaduf *is still used today.*

Jubes are still evident in cities such as Isfahan and Shiraz.

Ancient *qanat* lines, dug with the simplest of tools, could run for many miles and have been discovered all over the Middle East and on the desert route to Samarkand and into Afghanistan, the shafts sometimes proving a hazard for caravans. Until the recent construction of dams and mechanized wells enabled commercial concerns to draw off water and make many of the *qanats* run dry, these ancient water ducts made the very sustenance of life possible throughout much of rural Iran.

Where water was more easily available from wells, rivers and canals, waterwheels, or *norias*, could be used to raise and store it. In later centuries, the Arabs, masters of hydraulic technology, perfected their use, employing camels, bullocks or donkeys to work them, and, at Samarra, even ostriches.

propitiate the relevant gods observing certain artistic conventions. The gardens were set inside walls, with the quite rigid geometric pattern of canals and pools, pavilions and fruit trees evolving as a basic concept.

Tending the garden was hard work. Such was the skill acquired by the Egyptian garden labourers working in difficult circumstances that by Hellenic times they were as much in demand throughout the Mediterranean world as Scottish and Kew-trained gardeners were in the 19th- and 20th-century world of Western international horticulture. The garden labourer had a tough life, transporting soil, watering, building up dams with sand and mud, removing sand blown in from the desert and digging and fertilizing. According to a contract found inscribed on a pot, in the evening after his other duties were over he had to make baskets for carrying soil. A fragment of verse describes a gardener's life thus:

> The gardener carries a yoke
> His shoulders are bent as with age:
> There's a swelling on his neck
> And it festers.
> In the morning he waters vegetables,
> The evening he spends with his herbs,
> While at noon he has toiled in the orchard.
> He works himself to death
> More than all the other professions.

It must have been brutal labour; a landlord admonishes his workers: "Take great care, hoe all my land, sieve with sieve; hack with your noses in the work."

A labourer's life
In the Egyptian tomb of Sennadjem a 13th-century BC painting shows Sennadjem and his wife tilling and sowing in the fields in the Valley of the Nobles at Thebes. In real life, rather than as shown in this symbolic painting made for the tomb, this kind of work would have been done by skilled labourers who had an arduous workload, toiling over the soil with only the most basic of equipment to help them.

The DATE PALM

Although there is a vast number of palm species, many of tropical origin, it is the date palm, *Phoenix dactylifera*, with which we are most familiar. It has been cultivated for 6,000–8,000 years, its generic name, phoenix, coming from the mythical bird said to dwell in the Arabian desert, which reinvents itself through an ordeal by fire every 500 to 600 years. The economies of the emergent civilizations of the fertile crescent and Nile delta were dependent on the palm. Its fruit was a staple crop for much of the year and, according to an old Arabic

PHOENIX DACTYLIFERA

saying, its uses are as many as the number of days in a year; fibres from the leaves and bark were used in rope- and basket-making and woven with camel hair to produce cloth for tent-making.

Originally portrayed in wall paintings of gardens in Egyptian tombs (sometimes with the doum palm, *Hyphaene thebaica*, from which it can be distinguished by the doum's branching habit), *Phoenix dactylifera*'s single stem makes it a decorative tree in any suitable climate. However, its ability to survive in very hot climates, with its roots in saline sub-soil, has led to its particular favour in desert reclamation schemes in countries such as Israel and Jordan.

Phoenix dactylifera is dioecious – its male and female organs are found in separate flowers on separate plants – but one male plant can pollinate 100 females. Grown mainly in orchards, palms, along with pines and pomegranates, assumed a certain symbolism and special rites took place under them. *Phoenix dactylifera*, in Arabic *nakhl* or its plural *nakhil*, with its fruit called *tamar*, is mentioned 20 times in the Koran, and a date palm garden is called *nakhilstan*, which also means oasis.

The oldest record of an Egyptian garden dates to the Old Kingdom when in the reign of Sneferu (*c.*2600–2576 BC) Methen, the governor of the northern delta district, inscribed the detail of his life's achievements on the walls of his tomb. Most hieroglyphics are pictures and many represent stylized plants, particularly papyrus, different tree varieties and lotus. His garden, with the house and pool, was the core of his estate, a hectare (2.5 acres) in extent, with a further vineyard of 405 hectares (1,000 acres). It had in it a "very large lake" and "fine trees". The actual inner garden area probably resembled that of a garden layout dating to *c.*2000 BC. This carved wooden model of doll's-house dimensions (see opposite), found buried under the floor of the tomb of Mekutra, chancellor to Mentuhotpe II, and now in New York's Metropolitan Museum of Art, shows a walled garden including a fishpond shaded by sycamore figs (*Ficus sycomorus*) painted a bright green. The portico columns appear as if made from papyrus canes. Plants such as the date palm (*Phoenix dactylifera*), the native blue water-lily (*Nymphaea caerulea*) and the palmetto (*Chamaerops humilis*), as well as papyrus (*Cyperus papyrus*), were already used as architectural motifs in buildings and temples. Stories written on papyrus before 1600 BC tell us of an earlier king who boated on his pool – which was large enough to allow 20 beautiful ladies clad only in nets to row him. In a further series a crocodile lurks in a pool to catch the queen's lover.

TEMPLE GARDENS

In about 1470 BC the formidable Queen Hatshepsut, "for whom all Egypt was made to labour with bowed head", was the first Egyptian recorded as introducing exotic trees. For the journey from Somalia – known to Egyptians as the Land of Punt – their roots were protectively balled in baskets. Among them were "lovely plants from the god's country and heaps of myrrh resin and myrrh trees, with ebony and genuine ivory…with fragrant wood". Frankincense (*Boswellia sacra*) or the equally desirable myrrh (*Commiphora myrrha*) would provide valued incense for the temple of Deir-el-Bahari in western Thebes, built in honour of sun-god Amun-Re. Unfortunately, as with many early plant introductions, the trees did not survive, but they are illustrated by reliefs in the temple with an inscription describing their journey back to Egypt. Her co-monarch and successor Tuthmosis also collected plants on his campaigns in Asia Minor – "all the growing plants, all the flowers that grow in god's world" – but we cannot tell if they flourished after planting. Journeys would have been long and arduous, sometimes lasting months if not years. Seeds and bulbous plants had a greater chance of success than living trees, just as they did later during the 18th-century transatlantic plant exchange. The dried herbarium of later botanists, useful for scholarly identification, did not yet exist but Tuthmosis had his court artists make drawings of the exotic plants, carving the reliefs on the walls of the temple at Amun in Karnak to leave for posterity the oldest herbal in the world. Fortunately, the sands have preserved foundations of temples, houses and gardens and also at Deir-el-Bahari, excavations of the earlier mortuary temple of Mentuhotpe I, built *c*.1975 BC. Trees were arranged quite formally to frame the entrance ramp, the tree pits confirming three rows of seven sycamore figs and tamarisks planted in a continuous line, perhaps the earliest avenue to be recorded. The king's statues were shaded by the figs and there were separate geometrically arranged flowerbeds. Part of the temple garden plan was sketched on a floor slab, confirming the root patterns discovered in the 20th century.

By 1425 BC Sennufer, mayor of Thebes, had a picture painted for his tomb, showing the walled garden of the temple at Amun as it looked in his day. Laid out next to a canal, the garden has four ponds, with trees, plants and buildings shown in elevation, all arranged symmetrically as was the Egyptian custom, establishing a formal rhythm that was to influence the development of all future gardening styles. Even today the pattern evolved in these rectangular Egyptian gardens could be successfully copied. Walls were an essential attribute, designed mainly to keep out animals (including the domesticated goat), but also to keep out drifting sand. The threat from wild animals is confirmed by a garden owner at Thebes during the Late Period between 732 and 712 BC promising to carry a spear and sword when visiting her garden because of wolves and hyenas.

TOMB PAINTINGS

The paintings found on walls of tombs of rich private individuals, dating from the expansionist times of the New Kingdom (about 1600 BC), almost certainly portray a combination of scenes from a real garden, possibly belonging to the deceased who would have still been alive at the time of the painting, and contemporary scenes of agriculture, hunting and fishing which did not actually take place in a real garden. The paintings also had religious overtones not always easily understood. In the tomb painting of a scribe of the granary called Nebamun (*c*.1380 BC) a female figure emerging behind a tree is Hathor or Nut, the sycomore fig tree goddess, bearing provisions for the use of the tomb-owner during the hereafter. Fruiting trees and flowers provided sustenance as well as offerings to the gods, all of whom had mystical associations with the fertility of the earth. Flowers and fruiting trees were particularly associated with the sun-god Amun-Re.

Garden in miniature
One of the earliest indications of how a garden may have looked comes from Thebes, *c*.2009–1998 BC. A small wooden model of a house and garden found in the tomb of Mekutra, Mentuhotpe II's chancellor, is painted and gessoed and the fishpond, lined with copper, is flanked by sycomore figs. The pillars of the house are sculpted to resemble bunched papyrus canes.

It is possible that tomb paintings give a false impression of what actual contemporary gardens looked like. It is not easy to disentangle artistic symbols and established conventions used for portraying scenes with religious connotations from more mundane realities of ordinary life. All had to be included in the picture. Sometimes painters portrayed harvest scenes in order to ensure the perpetuation of the seasonal cycle rather than to imply a particular scene in a particular garden. A pool painted as if suspended between date palms signifies a holy place and may not relate to the owner's garden. Any certain identification of all the plants is difficult, as in many of the paintings a sycomore fig was adopted as a determining shape for all trees. Plants could be painted as if viewed from above or from the side. Most of the artistic conventions had already been arrived at by the period when the great pyramids were being built during the 4th Dynasty before 2000 BC and were then maintained for the following 1,500 years.

All the gardens, enclosed by high walls and mostly containing rectangular or T-shaped pools, were laid out geometrically, with trees in rows and beds in symmetry. This formal arrangement almost certainly arose from the need for irrigation, with sluice gates controlling periodic flooding. Twin groves of trees, twin trees and twin pools are frequently found in the illustrations and in excavations. Inside a grand gateway framed by pillars, entered from a side canal, would be an open courtyard, then a wall and another doorway leading into a wider open but walled space containing trees to provide fruit and shade and possibly a vegetable garden patch with a vine pergola shading the entrance to the house.

The decorated tomb

This wall painting from the tomb of Nebamun found at Thebes dates to *c.*1380 BC. It shows a garden and ornamental pool with ducks and fishes swimming among the sacred lotus. Palms with single stems and branched doum palms grow against the walls, while the sycomore fig tree goddess is arranging fruit as offerings in the hereafter. The papyrus planted round the pool is a symbol of rebirth and was often used as a decorative motif on capitals and columns in ancient Egypt.

In another tomb painting the portrayal, although nothing like so complete, is likely to be a real garden rather than an idealized concept. Imeni, in charge of the building operations for Tuthmosis I (1528–1510 BC), was a collector of trees. A view of his house with the garden behind, including a rectangular fishpond with water-lilies, is depicted in his tomb. Although the painter did not make a complete plan, a selection of trees are shown in rows, with a plant inventory of his orchard.

THE PLANTS OF ANCIENT EGYPT

Gardening in Egypt probably began with the cultivation of grapes, forms of *Vitis vinifera*. Vines are illustrated even more frequently than date or doum palms, with vine cultivation being portrayed in at least 24 of the Old Kingdom tombs. In earlier times vines were grown on forked props, laced through neighbouring trees, but in the paintings they are shown on curved or flat pergolas, creating shade for the garden as well as producing fruit – a feature we can identify with today.

In a love poem written on papyrus a young girl brings her garden to life:

I belong to you like this plot of land
That I planted with flowers
And sweet-smelling herbs.
Sweet in its stream
Dug by your hand
Refreshing in the north wind.
A lovely place to wander in
Your hand in my hand.

Egyptians grew flowers for bouquets and wreaths, for offerings in temples and for use in embalming and medicine. Information about the plants grown has come from excavation and analysis of roots, seeds, pollen and carbonized remains, as well as from manufactured items such as furniture and weaponry that were placed in tombs at the time of burial. Many are represented in paintings, on papyrus and with hieroglyphics. A whole flora of ancient Egypt can be compiled listing plants used in gardens, for religious rituals, for embalming and as vegetables and crops for the field. Some flowers had religious and ritual roles. Of these, the sacred blue-flowered lotus water-lily, *Nymphaea caerulea*, found in the Delta and the symbol of Upper Egypt, was the most important, although the Egyptians also used the white *N. lotus*. The rhythm of the lotus, disappearing in winter to be renewed in spring, symbolized resurrection after death. In early summer, the pools of palace and temple gardens would be transformed into a sea of blue and white flowers.

Most gardening as shown in tomb paintings and in landscaping activities around temple sites during the times of the pharaohs had a symbolic and religious significance. The trees known and grown by the Egyptians were dedicated to different gods: the date palm to Re and Min, the doum palm to Thoth, the syco-more fig to Hathor and the tamarisk to Osiris, trees which are often portrayed in the tomb paintings and which framed temple buildings to create sacred land-scapes. Similarly the activities which took place in both the imaginary tomb gar-dens and temple landscapes all had a symbolic significance, rituals concerned with the burial and cult of the dead and with the various deities.

The early gardeners of Egypt, ancient Persia and Mesopotamia had to solve many of horticulture's fundamental problems. In particular, they developed a remarkable expertise in water management that was to benefit generations to come. The patterns of irrigation they introduced have had a profound influence on garden layouts ever since, East and West, large and small, while the hunting parks were to be a model for the royal parks of medieval Europe, from which the 18th-century landscape park developed and, eventually, the city park of today.

CHAPTER TWO

Our classical heritage
ANCIENT
GREECE
and ROMAN
GARDENS

MANY OF THE PLANTS WE GROW in our herb and flower gardens come from Mediterranean countries. They would have been familiar to the ancient Greeks and the citizens of Rome, and were recorded in the first Greek herbals, by Pliny the Elder in his *Naturalis Historia*, and in the Roman manuals of agriculture. But it is not only with plants that we are concerned. In Western civilization the classical tradition is embodied in our culture. It informs our language – incidentally giving us the vocabulary of botany – and it shapes the names and nature of our institutions. Greece and Rome have provided the architectural idiom for our grand buildings and cityscapes.

In gardening, structures and ornaments can also be traced back to classical influences. Yet the Greeks were never gardeners, and the sophisticated Roman gardens were forgotten for centuries after the fall of the Roman Empire – centuries during which the Arabs developed medicine and botany, their scholars translating Greek and Latin texts while most of Europe was illiterate. But the humanists and philosophers of the Renaissance looked back to both Greece and Rome for intellectual and artistic stimulation, and brought about a "rebirth" in classical style. Here we explore that original "naissance" – sometimes using as our storytellers the Renaissance scholars and garden-builders who discovered and disseminated the ethos of the earlier classical world.

Hadrian's villa
The Roman Emperor Hadrian incorporated many distinctive Hellenistic elements into his villa at Tivoli, such as the canopus. Laid out between AD 118 and 138, the villa was so vast in concept it more closely resembled a small rural city. Parts of it were later to inspire the 17th-century Isolotto garden in the Boboli in Florence and a 20th-century feature at Renishaw in Derbyshire.

The Greek landscape
Although the Greeks have never
been gardeners in the accepted sense
of the word – the high mountains
and lack of rain making sustainable
horticulture almost impossible –
the romantic countryside, with
mountains, groves of trees and wild
flowers, is itself a natural
"landscape". It was the visual
inspiration for the garden-makers
of the 18th-century Landscape
Movement. Edward Lear's
watercolour of the Greek island of
Corfu, c.1862, demonstrates the wild
beauty of the countryside and the
spirit of Homer's poetry, where
forests become the secret abodes
of mythical gods.

GREECE AS A GARDEN

If the Greeks were neither gardeners nor pioneers in garden style, they have contributed to the way we garden today in other important ways. Firstly, the Greek countryside embodies the idea of beauty, with sites of ancient temples and theatres chosen for their scenic splendour and awe-inspiring panoramic views. These views and sacred groves became the backdrop to later portrayals of Greek myths and created an awareness of the beauty and mystery of natural scenery. Through the paintings of Claude (1600–82) and Poussin (1594–1665) the Greek and Roman countryside became the models for the 18th-century English Landscape Movement.

Secondly, the scientific study of plants begun in the Greek classical period formed a core of botanical knowledge that was not superseded for the best part of two thousand years. Even in the 16th and 17th centuries, botanists and collectors from northern Europe were still studying Dioscorides's great herbal, the *Materia Medica*, struggling to identify the herbs he described growing at the eastern end of the Mediterranean during the 1st century AD.

Thirdly, although the mountainous terrain and lack of water renders Greece unsuitable for sustained horticulture, with much of the land deforested by man and goats long before Homer described it in his 8th-century poetry, nevertheless its flora is extremely rich. Greece has more than six thousand species of flowering plants and ferns – a greater number than any other European country. These pro-

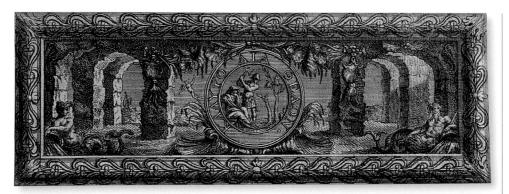

Pope's *Odyssey*
Like the idealized paintings of the
Greek and Roman landscape by
Claude and Poussin, classical works
of literature were highly influential
on the development of the
Landscape Movement in 18th-
century England. It is no
coincidence that Alexander Pope's
translation of Homer's The Odyssey
was also published at this time.
Among William Kent's illustrations
for it was one of Calypso's cave
(left), based on Pope's own grotto
at Twickenham.

vided the first herbalists with specimens for medicinal use, and later enriched the gardening palette of other countries. Archaeology records some gardening on the islands of Crete and Santorini (modern Thira) before the first millennium and there are hints of the peristyle gardens later developed by the Romans in Hellenic times, but on the whole ancient Greek garden layouts have no important historical significance.

The Greeks possessed a keen awareness of the plants and landscape around them, and had an ability to communicate their vision. At first it was the useful plants that were noticed. Aristotle was the first to study plants scientifically in the 4th century BC, followed by his pupil Theophrastus — studies that culminated in Dioscorides's *Materia Medica*. This was translated into Arabic before the first millennium and was still a subject of great interest to people like John Sibthorp who botanized in Greece at the end of the 18th century — by which time ornamental plants had become as interesting as useful ones to both botanist and gardener. The Greeks did, in fact, praise flowers for their beauty. They spoke of Athens as "crowned with violets" (they actually meant violet-coloured anemones, the native *Anemone coronaria*) and sited their sacred temples and shrines in places of scenic beauty. Homer described only useful plants, yet his poetry makes their beauty implicit.

HOMER AND THE LANDSCAPE

"Ungardenable" mainland Greece was so arid and mountainous that green and shady places, especially where water flowed, became imbued with a rich mythology. These magical landscapes, lived in by mythical gods and archaic heroes, were revealed in the 8th-century works of Homer, who wrote about sanctuary gardens dedicated to Apollo, Athena or Aphrodite, and idyllic scenes of groves and meadows watered by streams. In Book V of *The Odyssey*, the cave of the nymph Calypso, where Odysseus was held captive, was deep inside a copse of poplars, willows, alders and tall cypresses, with a vine which "ran riot with great bunches of ripe grapes" trailing around the cavern's entrance. There were four springs "with four crystal rivulets, trained to run this way or that". This must be the first description of a grotto or nymphaeum.

In Homer's poetry, trees and bushes personify gods; caves, grottoes and springs are the dwelling places of nymphs and dryads; and herbs with

Floral fresco
A fresco in the Minoan palace of Knossos, *c.*1600 BC, restored by Sir Arthur Evans during his excavations in Crete in the 1920s, portrays a warrior prince and a stylized representation of lilies. Other flowers shown included irises, the sea daffodil, roses, and useful plants such as papyrus and date palms, probably imported from Egypt.

Among the red lilies
Frescoes on the island of Thira
(ancient Santorini), now in the
National Museum in Athens, were
painted before 1500 BC when the
island was almost destroyed by an
earthquake and a volcanic eruption.
They show swallows swooping
among red lilies, probably *Lilium
chalcedonicum*, growing in the rocks.

magical powers provide an evocative background to both *The Iliad* and the travels in *The Odyssey*. The "silver trickle" of water over a cliff, the "black wind" on the sea and "the meadow of asphodels, which is the dwelling place of souls, the disembodied wraiths of men" all convey something of the drama of the Greek mountains and herb-scented valleys.

Homer wrote about what he saw in contemporary Greece. *The Odyssey* contains two actual garden descriptions – those of Alcinous's luxuriant enclosed garden of fruit trees (Book VII) and the carefully tended garden of Odysseus's father, Laertes (Book XXIV). Between them we find all the elements of garden topography, with abundant fruit trees for sustenance and shade, neat flowerbeds, vineyards and channelled water supplies – all already standard in contemporary Middle Eastern and Egyptian civilizations.

SHARDS OF EVIDENCE FROM CRETE AND SANTORINI

Concrete evidence of the Greeks' enjoyment of plant forms is first revealed in the decoration of pots, vases and frescoes, executed the best part of 4,000 years ago. Flowers, including irises, lilies and the autumn-flowering sea daffodil (*Pancratium maritimum*), which grows on the shores of many Mediterranean islands, are depicted in frescoes in the Minoan palace at Knossos. Potentially "useful" plants, such as the date palm from Egypt and the marsh-loving papyrus from the Nile delta, suggest trading interests. These early second millennium BC frescoes also give us the earliest known representation of a rose – perhaps the Abyssinian rose (*Rosa* × *richardii*) from the Upper Nile regions, brought by trade with the Egyptians, the single dog rose (*R. canina*), or the cabbage rose (*R. centifolia*) from Macedonia. By the end of the Classical period roses were cultivated intensively on the island of Rhodes, hence its name, but these were probably grown as a commercial crop rather than in gardens.

Lilies feature in Minoan sculpture as well as in frescoes; a vase in black soapstone (*c.*2000–1800 BC) shaped like reflexed lily petals was probably used in funerary rites. Red lilies – probably *Lilium chalcedonicum* – in bud and in flower were beautifully depicted slightly later in a fresco found on the island of Santorini. A fresco in an adjacent room shows women collecting the stamens of the saffron crocus (*Crocus sativus*), a bulb native to northeast Iran: but we should perhaps remind ourselves that this is a scene of harvesting, and that the crocus counts as a crop not an ornamental plant.

As surviving artefacts become less rare, hard proof of the ancient Greeks' aesthetic pleasure in plants becomes increasingly evident. Wreaths of ivy and swags of myrtle, friezes of grapevine and periwinkle, were all painted on pottery. Plant forms also ornamented architecture. The acanthus (see page 37) remains the symbol that identifies Corinthian capitals, while fluted columns were modelled on wild angelica stems.

Yet archaeological evidence does not reveal gardens. The siting of the palace at Knossos, on the side of a valley, cool in summer and sheltered from wind, must have been ideal for gardening, but there is no indication of a garden layout. We do know that the Minoans grew plants in containers, in much the same way as we do today. Excavations have found the remains there of lines of terracotta plant pots watered by irrigation channels. They could have been planted with shrubs such as pomegranates or myrtles, or with roses, lilies or irises from Asia Minor. A similar arrangement dating from Hellenistic times was discovered alongside the 3rd-century BC Temple of Hephaistos in Athens, probably planted with laurel and pomegranate. Shattered terracotta pots in square root pits have been discovered in excavations. Plant branches would have been layered straight into pots for rooting and the pots broken up at planting time – a practice described by Cato a century later in his *De re rustica*.

Archaeology also confirms that trees and shrubs were planted around the sacred places of the Archaic and Classical Greeks. Black poplars, cypresses, plane trees and arbutus would provide shelter and shade for the sanctuaries of the gods. Today, visiting the ancient temples and theatres, we still find trees, and the sites, carefully fenced against goats and sheep, have become a haven for wild flowers, ensuring their preservation. But in mainland Greece, land suitable for farming was scarce enough to preclude any ornamental planting; that outside the city was reserved for agriculture. Market gardens, including orchards, vegetables and useful herbs, formed a green belt; the gardens were to be worked on, like the field crops, during the day, owners and slaves returning to the city in the evening. In Athens, for example, distribution of property was planned to allow equal divisions, the city laid out so that each house or block of houses took up an entire plot, leaving no room for an urban garden. In the 5th century BC both Aristophanes and Demosthenes allude to small domestic gardens (*kepoi*) adjacent to town houses belonging to the wealthy, but in the main, scarcity of water precluded any attempt at ornamental gardening, except in public places such as the open market places, "green" spaces confirmed by excavation (*agora*).

By Classical times, in the 5th and 4th centuries BC, groves of trees could be found in city sanctuaries and in the *agora*. In the *agora*, root pits and water channels confirm that olive trees and bay laurel (*Laurus nobilis*) shaded the altar of the Twelve Gods. By now such archaeological finds are endorsed by contemporary writers. Plutarch gives the Athenian statesman Cimon credit for planting plane trees (*Platanus orientalis* from Asia Minor – the *chenar* of Persia) to shade the *agora* in the 5th century BC, as well as in Plato's Academy in the valley of the Kephissos outside the western walls of Athens, turning it into a "well-watered grove with trim avenues and shady walks". Cimon also provided an irrigation system for the Academy, allowing elms, poplars and olive trees to grow with the planes. Aristophanes described the valley as: "All fragrant with woodbine and peaceful content and the leaf which the lime blossoms fling/When the plane whispers love to the elm in the grove in

Painted palms
This Minoan earthenware amphora from the palace of Knossos is decorated with date palms, evidence that trade existed between Egypt and Crete by 1500 BC, before the palace was destroyed.

The ACANTHUS

In both ancient Egypt and Mesopotamia plants were used as motifs in architectural decoration, but it is the wild Greek acanthus, either *Acanthus mollis* or *A. spinosus*, that was moulded into capitals for Corinthian columns during the 5th century BC, which is most familiar. Acanthus is a genus of herbaceous perennials that thrive in relatively mild climates and go dormant either from winter cold or summer heat. *Acanthus mollis* is from northern Greece, while *A. spinosus* is found throughout the south and is therefore the most likely to have inspired the architects at Corinth. The leaves of spiny acanthus, known colloquially by gardeners as bear's breeches, are distinctly fretted with spiny margins, while those of *A. mollis* are less indented, wider and shiny green. Both bear racemes of white flowers with pinkish-purple bracts on tall stems.

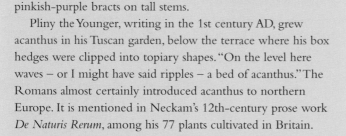

ACANTHUS MOLLIS

Pliny the Younger, writing in the 1st century AD, grew acanthus in his Tuscan garden, below the terrace where his box hedges were clipped into topiary shapes. "On the level here waves – or I might have said ripples – a bed of acanthus." The Romans almost certainly introduced acanthus to northern Europe. It is mentioned in Neckam's 12th-century prose work *De Naturis Rerum*, among his 77 plants cultivated in Britain.

the beautiful season of spring." Pupils in Plato's Academy and Aristotle's Lyceum, walking among the *peripatoi*, the shaded avenues of plane and poplar, olive and laurel, became known as the "peripatetic" philosophers. In the hot summers the shade and humidity brought by the vegetation must have been a welcome relief. Nearby was the small garden of Epicurus (341–270 BC), one of the few private gardens mentioned, a vegetable garden cultivated by Epicurus himself to give practical expression to his moral and social philosophy. Later in Hellenistic times came the planting around the Temple of Hephaistos mentioned above.

THE WRITTEN RECORD

By the 4th century BC, Aristotle (384–322 BC) was turning Homer's mythological and economic attitude to plants into a more serious study, based on reflection, observation and research in the living world. Curiosity about plants originated in concern as to their use for food or medicine, and not with any evaluation of their decorative value. On the island of Cos, Hippocrates (460–370 BC) developed practical medicine, liberating its study from the speculation of treatment linked to the worship of the gods. The root-diggers of archaic times had become serious rhizotomists who developed a lucrative business providing pharmacists with medicinal herbs. The naturalist Theophrastus (*c*.370–*c*.287 BC) succeeded Aristotle at the Lyceum. Until this point, herbal lore had been transmitted verbally and memorized. In his *Enquiry into Plants*, Theophrastus cleared away much of the so-called mystery of the "miracles of nature", his studies establishing the greater part of the modern disciplines of botany. Theophrastus classified plants according to their sap, roots, leaves, buds, flowers and fruits. In all he described over 450 plants, assessing contributions given him by country people engaged in age-old pursuits such as woodcutting, beekeeping and collecting medicinal plants. Although the majority of the 450 plants described by Theophrastus are useful, he does list flowers cultivated to make crowns or garlands – including rose, carnation, sweet marjoram, lily, thyme, bergamot, calamint and southernwood. He was especially interested in exotics, including in his herbal the descriptions of plants seen abroad by Alexander the Great's generals and by special observers sent with the expeditions. Alexander arranged for seeds and roots of some exotic trees, such as peach (*Prunus persica*) and lemon (*Citrus limon*) to be sent to Theophrastus from Asia, the first record of attempts to grow these plants in Europe. There were also plants

Capitals and columns

According to legend, the sculptor Kallimachos adapted the acanthus leaf for his design for column capitals (above), in the 5th century BC, after seeing how an acanthus growing on a Corinthian girl's grave had woven its leaves through a fisherman's basket. Another plant, Angelica sylvestris (inset), was the model for the fluted columns (left) used in many buildings. Markedly ribbed stems are typical of angelicas and sculptors and architects would undoubtedly have been familiar with this angelica that grows wild over the Greek hillsides. A good example of fluted columns can be seen at the temple of Apollo Epicurius at Bassae in the Peloponnese.

A philosophical plantsman
In the 3rd century BC, naturalist and philosopher Theophrastus's *Enquiry into Plants* laid the foundations for the modern science of botany. In it he described some 450 plants. They were useful rather than decorative, although he included those cultivated for garland-making such as rose, lily, bergamot and carnation.

The digging of roots
In the German version of the *Apuleius Platonicus Herbarium* (*c.*1200 AD but first put together from Greek material in the 5th century AD and containing elements of Dioscorides's work), ancient Greek root-diggers – the rhizotomists – are shown gathering herbs for use by apothecaries. To the right of the scene, a physician is weighing out drugs.

from Egypt, especially those from "rivers, marshes and lakes", or "plants special to northern regions" from Macedonia or beyond, deserving study for their different habitats – shadowing the modern gardener and botanist's interest in ecological matters. In his own garden Theophrastus had a shrine dedicated to the Muses and his own funerary monument. He left his whole garden to his slaves, who were to be freed on condition they maintained it. Its site on the north side of Constitution Square was recently revealed in excavations, but we have no confirmation that it was laid out in any systematic order.

Theophrastus's botanical work was not immediately followed up: it was not until the reign of the Roman emperors Nero and Vespasian in the 1st century AD that Dioscorides further extended the study of herbs and their remedies. Meanwhile, Greek literature contains many references to plants besides those of the botanists and of physicians such as Galen (AD 129–99). Writers including Hesiod, Xenophon and Herodotus left their observations.

If they were not gardeners by instinct, the Greeks evidently responded with pleasure to the idea of the garden as amenity – like modern tourists who enjoy visiting gardens but would not dream of making a garden themselves. Before Alexander the Great's time, Greeks had brought home descriptions of the great *paradeisoi* parks of the Persian kings. The Spartan King Lysander visited Cyrus the Younger's garden at Sardis in Lydia (western Turkey) 70 years before Alexander's conquest. He described its geometric layout to the Greek general Xenophon, who recorded it in his *Oeconomicus* on his return to Greece in 394 BC – incidentally expressing Lysander's surprise at finding the king gardening, germinating seeds and putting in plants with his own hands. In the slave society of mainland Greece such manual labour by a member of the ruling classes was anathema.

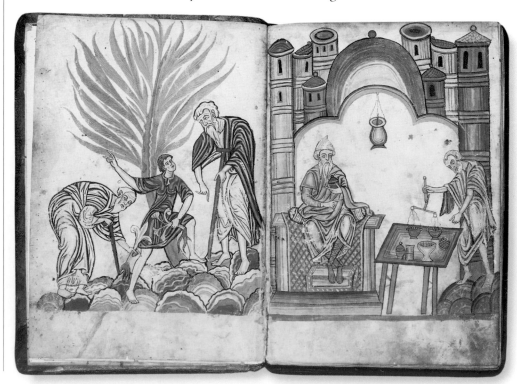

The year 334 BC marked the end of the ancient Persian empire, as Alexander defeated Darius III and took possession of the palaces of Babylon, Susa and Persepolis. Alexander's troops inherited the well-maintained network of roads that had bound the vast empire together, and as they journeyed east discovered the far-flung oasis gardens in which groves of trees were laid out in formal order with aromatic shrubs and well-watered gardens. Plants travelled back to Greece with Alexander's generals from as far as India to be examined and categorized by Aristotle and his pupil Theophrastus.

After Alexander's death the lands he had conquered were divided into several large kingdoms ruled by his friends, Hellenistic aristocrats who adopted Eastern habits and copied and adapted Persian ideas. In the Nile delta the Ptolemaic kings established large productive estates. These were predominantly agricultural, consisting of a network of fields and gardens looked after by agricultural labourers and by professional gardeners. However, they also incorporated pleasure gardens, and here these Hellenistic Ptolemies rivalled the eastern potentates in splendour. Courtyards were paved with elaborate mosaics and planted with aromatic shrubs and flowers. In Thebes and Alexandria, in Italy and Sicily, cities began to boast public parks with fountains and grottoes. Tomb gardens – already a feature in Classical times – became popular not only in Greece but also in Asia Minor and Egypt. Important citizens could be honoured in cemeteries outside the city walls, their graves marked by groves of trees, normally cypresses, which are used in churchyards and burial plots in Greece today. Gardens around tombs in the suburbs of Alexandria were rented out for five-year periods and planted with fruit trees and vegetables, the tenants growing melons, lettuces, figs, cabbages, asparagus, leeks, grapes and dates. This practical aspect of these "garden" spaces is reminiscent of the allotment plots that still flourish on the fringes of towns and cities in Britain today.

More and more examples of garden features – of which, sadly, only the descriptions remain – give glimpses of the emerging Greek taste for gardens, and presage ideas that we associate more strongly with Roman traditions. The gardening prowess of the Alexandrians was specially commended by Walafrid Strabo, a medieval monk writing in the 9th century. Water was harnessed to provide motive power for fountains and to play organs. Aristotle had first toyed with similar inventions, but it was left to two Alexandrians, Ctesibius and Hero, to turn his abstractions into practical reality. Hero describes the construction of a fountain adorned with singing birds which were silenced by the appearance of a mechanical owl, a contrivance repeated in the late 16th-century Villa d'Este at Tivoli and admired there by John Evelyn on his 17th-century travels. On Rhodes one garden had rock-cut steps, benches and grottoes – a prototype for later Romantic landscapes. The tyrant Dionysius (430–367 BC), ruler of Syracuse, is said to have created a Persian-style pleasure park in the Greek colony. Another expatriate, Hieron (269–221 BC), more like an oriental potentate than a Greek, laid out a sumptuous garden on his boat in Syracuse, with flowerbeds watered by an ingenious system of invisible lead pipes. Ivy and grapevines, their roots in casks of earth, provided shade. On the island of Delos villas with "peristyle" gardens,

BEGINNINGS OF BOTANY

The word botany derives from the Greek *botane*, meaning "pasturage for cattle" in Homer's time, but later translated as "weed, herb plant". In the Classical age, the study of botany grew out of a need to study medical remedies and research into plants remained linked to their curative properties until the 15th and 16th centuries. The first European botanic gardens, founded in the 1540s at Pisa and Padua, were gardens of simples attached to universities to aid medical students in the identification of plants they would use. By the end of the 16th century plants were being studied for all their qualities and the old "useful" herbals were superseded by illustrated florilegia.

THE LEGACY OF DIOSCORIDES

GARDENERS STILL GROW some of the plants described by Dioscorides in the 1st century AD and use his nomenclature (although not always in the same way that he did), and scientists (now employing state-of-the-art techniques) still investigate the pharmaceutical properties of his herbs. More comprehensive than any previous herbal, and incorporating material from other works now lost, Dioscorides's *De Materia Medica* remained the most respected herbal until the Renaissance, when it helped to inspire the new quest for plant knowledge in Europe. Every botanist of the 16th century was concerned with the identification of the 500 plants described in its five volumes. The aura of the great Dioscorides continued to hover over botanical discovery for another two or three centuries as travellers and botanists sought to rediscover the original plants he mentioned.

Manuscript copies of *De Materia Medica* also became sought-after objects. The work has survived in at least 23 copies from different periods. The most impressive of these is the *Codex Vindobonensis*, made in Constantinople for a Byzantine princess, Juliana Anicia, in about AD 512. In addition to botanical paintings in colour, it contains several illustrations of a more general nature, one showing Dioscorides receiving a mandrake plant.

The naturalism conveyed in the illustrations in the *Codex Vindobonensis* suggests that they were copied from an earlier age – probably from at least as early as the 2nd century: contemporary 6th-century Byzantine images would have been much stiffer. Lost for nine centuries, the codex reappeared in the early 15th century, being rebound by a monk in the Prodomos Monastery in Constantinople. At that time it belonged to a Jewish physician at the court of Süleyman the Magnificent after the Muslim conquest of 1453. Turkish, Arabic and Hebrew names were added to the original Greek text. In 1562 Ogier Ghiselin de Busbecq (1522–92), ambassador from the

Dioscorides the teacher
A scene from an Arabic version of Dioscorides's De Materia Medica *by Yusuf al Mawsili shows Dioscorides holding the famous mandrake plant (Mandragora officinalis), the root of which was thought to have magic powers, to show to his disciple.*

Emperor Ferdinand to the Sublime Porte, discovered the manuscript. When his offer of a hundred ducats was refused, he used all his influence to induce the emperor to acquire it: "On account of its age the manuscript is in a bad state, the outside being gnawed by worms, that hardly anyone finding it in the street would trouble to pick it up." It finally arrived in the Imperial Library in Vienna in 1569, purchased by Ferdinand's successor, Maximilian II, making Vienna a place of pilgrimage for later plantsmen.

By the 16th century the compilers of printed herbals, although still dependent on Dioscorides, included a wider range of plants from northern Europe and further afield. Pierandrea Mattioli (1501–77), the most renowned of the woodcut herbalists, in his *Commentarii in sex libros Pedacii Dioscorides* published in Prague, identified many of the original plants. Pierre Belon (1518–63) journeyed in the Levant between 1546 and 1549, his primary purpose, besides collecting new plants for acclimatizing in France, being to identify Dioscorides's plants. He was followed by the German physician Leonhardt Rauwolf in 1573, another Dioscoridean pilgrim.

In 1784 John Sibthorp broke his journey in Vienna to examine the great *Codex*, on his way to the Levant to gather material for his *Flora Graeca*. He was also able to see another surviving illustrated Dioscorides manuscript, the 7th-century *Codex Neapolitanus*, which was later returned to Naples. Sibthorp took Ferdinand Bauer, a Viennese artist, with him to Greece in 1786 to illustrate the plants. They were the first naturalists to reach the summit of Mount Parnassus, where they discovered the Greek shepherds still

using Dioscorides's names for plants growing on the mountainside: "my Pastoral botanist surprised me not a little with his Nomenclature; I traced the names of Dioscorides and Theophrastus somewhat corrupted indeed in the pronunciation…but many of them unmutilated and their virtues faithfully handed down in the oral tradition."

Although Dioscorides listed only the "useful" attributes of medicinal plants, many of those portrayed or described in *De Materia Medica* have since become garden plants grown for their beauty, some (such as aristolochia, anemone and anagallis) even retaining their ancient names. Many of the later herbalists followed Dioscorides in including practical hints that still ring true. These included recommendations on gathering herbs in fine weather and

Voyage of discovery
The frontispieces from Volume VI (above left) and Volume IX (above right) of John Sibthorp's Flora Graeca, *a work that was published in 10 volumes between 1806 and 1840, with plates by the horticultural artist Ferdinand Bauer. Sibthorp's journey to Greece, begun in 1784, was inspired by the desire to identify Dioscorides's original plants.*

always noticing the changing development of plants from when they "first shoot out of the earth, when they are fully grown, and when they begin to fade". Dioscorides also advised on how to store herbs after gathering, how and when to collect roots, bark, petals and juices, and the manner of preserving them. "Flowers and sweet-scented things should be laid up in dry boxes of Lime-wood", he wrote.

designed as inner spaces surrounded by columns in the interior of each house, were constructed in the 2nd century BC, predating the characteristic peristyle gardens made by the Romans at Pompeii and in the Campania by the 1st century AD, and later found in many regions of the Roman Empire.

ROME AND THE GRAMMAR OF GARDENING

Although the gardens of classical Rome crumbled to ruin with the Empire, their legacy remained as inspiration. The great architects of the Renaissance studied and measured the ruins of the Roman villas, copied the patterns of the layouts and pilfered the statues to ornament their "new" garden plans. With the help of 16th-century mathematics they were able to grasp the mysteries of classical proportion. Their villas and gardens, based on Roman precepts, are among the greatest in the world. Their influence on developing garden styles through the succeeding centuries is impossible to measure or to overrate. The Italian garden with its Roman overtones, as an architectural concept, dominates the whole future development of European and American garden styles; its rules provide the "grammar" of all good Western garden design. More indirectly, the Roman garden also influenced the next great gardening evolution, that of the English Landscape Movement. Englishmen making the Grand Tour in the 17th and 18th centuries brought back not only Renaissance visions. Their cultural interest went deeper, to the villas of classical Rome, Pliny the Younger's villas, Virgil's farming in the *Georgics* and Ovid's tales of metamorphoses. All these strands were drawn together with their impressions of Italy to prepare the way for a new vision of landscape, a fusion of philosophy and poetry dependent on a knowledge and appreciation of Classical Rome, with a timely spicing of contemporary politics.

PRIVACY AND PERISTYLE – THE DOMESTIC ROMAN GARDEN

Recently, increasingly professional archaeological investigations have revealed the secrets of the smaller Roman gardens in cities such as Pompeii, destroyed by the eruption of Vesuvius in AD 79, as well as the grander Roman gardens both at home and also in more far-flung regions of the Empire. The gardens of classical and imperial Rome were not all grand architectural conceptions, although towards the end of the period an increasingly wealthy society had turned their estates into vast pleasure gardens, so much so that agriculture was neglected and provisions had to be imported. From the earliest days of the Roman Republic, gardens were an integral part of a private house in the city and in the country. Excavations at Pompeii, Herculaneum and the surrounding Campania have revealed the pattern of domestic architecture over a period of at least four hundred years up to the moment in AD 79 when the volcanic eruption buried cities and villas. The covering of lapilli (pumice pieces about the size of peach stones) has preserved a whole civilization at that moment, allowing detailed studies of the architecture and authentic reconstructions of public spaces and individual gardens.

Although of course unknown during Renaissance times, these Pompeian gardens, in a confined space, contain many of the features expanded upon by later Romans when they made their grander compositions, from which in turn architects of the Renaissance drew their inspiration. Charming as were the Pompeian gardens, their size and scale bore as little relationship to those of wealthy Romans as the smaller country house in England does to a Chatsworth or Blenheim, the palaces of the very rich. But because of their size, these smaller gardens may have a new relevance for us today. The gardens were arranged on a central axis with the house, so that house and garden were inextricably linked. From the entrance portico there was a direct view through the house down the centre of the garden, the view often further prolonged by painting a garden perspective on a wall at the far end. But the domestic garden was also an integral part of the life of a house or of a country villa and, with its accepted formulaic layout developing over centuries, dictated how the house was used and lived in, in a way that has a direct relationship to 20th-century Californian gardening styles. In both cases the garden has become a "room outside". In Pompeii houses with a rear garden date to the late 4th and early 3rd centuries BC, their subsequent extension to the more luxurious contained "peristyle" garden can be traced right up to the Vesuvius eruption. Interpreted as the *hortus*, and primarily an enclosed yard for fruit, vegetables and herbs, the early garden did not differ functionally from the Greek market garden except in its location adjacent to a house, rather than in the green belt surrounding the city. The private garden developed from the early *hortus* to a family pleasure garden. Surrounded by porticoes it became a "peristyle" garden, providing a walking area in shade, as well as a central garden for flowers, a fountain and pool.

To dedicated scholars of Greece, Roman culture and architecture have often seemed secondhand, imitations of other civilizations rather than innovative. In gardening matters the Romans drew their inspiration from the known garden topography of the Greek and Hellenistic world, incorporating into their schemes the idea of sacred landscapes, urban promenades and meeting places for philosophical discussion. By the 2nd century BC they had penetrated into Asia, to reproduce at home the opulent *paradeisoi* parks of the Persian kings. They took ideas from the Egyptian gardens of the Ptolemaic period, many of which had also been influenced by Eastern gardens, incorporating canals and *euripes* – channels of moving water – in their gardens, as at Hadrian's Villa. The Romans, affluent from the spoils of conquest, were able to build luxuriant palaces and villas, often pillaging statues from Greek or Egyptian sites, or having them copied. In 62 BC the general and statesman Pompey built a theatre in Rome, in front of which he planted trees for shade. The oriental plane brought from the East or Greece was planted everywhere – in spite of health warnings from both Dioscorides and Galen that its pollen affected breathing and the lungs. From the end of the 2nd century BC there were a great number of private parks, described in contemporary texts and inscriptions. In 63 BC in the Republican period, the consul Lucullus, who had an extensive knowledge of plant lore, retired to his villa on the

Pliny at his studies
The frontispiece of a 15th-century manuscript copy of Pliny the Elder's *Naturalis Historia*, primarily a picture book, shows the writer himself, a contemporary of Dioscorides, with dividers and an astrolabe. The *Naturalis Historia* was an encyclopaedic compilation of the known natural world and remained the great dictionary of knowledge throughout the Middle Ages. The Loeb Classical Library Edition, in 10 volumes with parallel Latin and English texts, is well worth reading, both as an introduction to the 1st-century mind and for its information.

THE PAST PRESERVED AT POMPEII

WHEN VESUVIUS ERUPTED in AD 79 the living cities and thriving country and seaside villas around it in the Campanian plain were preserved exactly as they were at the moment of destruction. Owing its fertility to the volcanic soils, the plain was so rich that even today it can bear four crops a year, and with its incomparable climate attracted many wealthy Romans. The elder Pliny, who lost his life in the eruption, called it "the fairest of all regions, not only in Italy, but the whole world".

The town of Herculaneum was covered with lapilli to a depth of 12–20m (40–70ft), making archaeology difficult. Further away the covering was less deep, and at Pompeii excavations over centuries have uncovered the city, revealing the details of both public and private garden planning. Most of the gardens were in private homes, those at the centre of the building complex

The outdoor room
The garden of the Villa Julia Felix at Pompeii may well have been used as a dining room, where diners ate lying on couches by the pools.

sometimes with walls frescoed in *trompe l'oeil* to make the garden seem larger. In the paintings flowers and shrubs grew in profusion, behind a low dado, backed by trees and fountains too large for the actual garden space: today these are a

valuable source of information about the flowers, birds and animals of the time. Views of wilder mountain landscapes indicate an appreciation of nature. Religious shrines and statues of gods and goddesses had their place; an ancient vase found at Pompeii was inscribed: "Fill me with pure wine, then may Venus who guards the garden love you."

Recent archaeological techniques can reveal the identity of plants. Sometimes soil contours, carbonized or preserved stems or roots, pollen, seeds, fruit, bacteria and even insects can be accurately identified. Larger root spaces can be emptied of lapilli, reinforced with wire and filled with cement, to produce moulded shapes to compare with roots of modern plants. Double rows of root cavities in one garden suggest nut or fruit trees; in another garden the root cavities were of a fig tree. Plants were also grown in pots, probably as the root cuttings or layers suggested by Cato, who recommended rooting figs, olives, pomegranates, quince, bay laurel, myrtle and plane trees in this way, in baskets or pots with holes, the pots being broken at planting out time. This method was especially useful for evergreen shrubs such as citron (*Citrus medica*) and lemon (*C. limon*), probably grown at Pompeii in the peristyle garden of the House of Polybius excavated in 1973. Lemons are shown in many of the wall paintings, so

Planting picture
A fresco (of which this a detail) from the House of the Marine Venus at Pompeii shows myrtle, ivy, oleander – which kept away mosquitoes – southernwood and roses, plus oriental planes, bay laurel and strawberry trees in the background.

we assume they were known, as well as the citron introduced earlier. In the same garden, nail holes in the walls indicate espaliered fruit.

In some gardens planting was more informal, probably from an earlier time when water was scarcer, with large tree holes in the corners and smaller holes suggesting a pergola of grapevines. Obviously the gardens at Pompeii developed at an accelerated pace after an aqueduct built in the time of Augustus (d. AD 14) provided easily accessible water for fountains and pools as well as flowers. Water features, large central pools and fountains became more common. A garden room – or

dieta – decorated with exceptionally informative and fine garden paintings has been found at the House of the Wedding of Alexander. In the foreground a bubbling fountain shelters delicate white camomile and small-flowered chrysanthemum backed by a canopy of plane trees. Madonna lilies (*Lilium candidum*) next to opium poppies (*Papaver somniferum*), a young date palm and white morning glories (*Calystegia sepium*) are the first of their kind found at Pompeii. At Oplontis, near the sea, a luxurious villa – possibly belonging to Poppaea, wife of the Emperor Nero – includes 13 spectacular gardens, varying in type

between informal and formal peristyle and courtyard gardens, perhaps the first compartmentalized garden on record. Porticoed exterior gardens stretch out towards the sea and towards the mountains in the rear, with views through the house. Avenues of trees, probably planes, and statues backed by citron or lemon bushes and oleanders decorated a sculpture garden, with a pool 17 × 65m (56 × 210ft) to its west.

The peristyle garden
This elaborate courtyard at the House of Vetti, decorated c.AD 60–70, is typical of a peristyle garden, with a pool and fountains. Its sculptures have been kept in situ. Many Roman garden statues were copies of original Greek works.

Pincian Hill, immediately above the Spanish steps in Rome. The villa became renowned for its magnificence and resemblance to an eastern park. There is no record of the overall garden plan, but enough remained in the 16th century for the Renaissance architect Pirro Ligorio to make a study of its terraces and steps, incorporating their design in drawings which established one of the greatest of Renaissance themes, the architectural transformation of a rising site into a series of stairs and ramps traversing the main axis of the garden. Later when constructing the Villa d'Este at Tivoli, Ligorio surveyed the layout of Hadrian's abandoned villa nearby, "borrowing" sculptures and statues to embellish the cardinal's garden.

COUNTRY RETREATS

The development of country estates as both farms and gardens – the true meaning of a villa – was inspired by contemporary poetic themes praising the bucolic

Virgil and the Muses
A 3rd-century Roman mosaic shows Virgil and the Muses. Virgil celebrated country life, encouraging patrician retirement to a villa lifestyle made possible by great wealth. Having been brought up in the country near Mantua, he valued the actual working of the soil. The idealization of the countryside in his writings was to be influential on the 18th-century English gentleman's relationship with his estate.

life. Cato in 160 BC in *De re agricultura*, Catullus, Cicero, Horace and Virgil in the *Eclogues* and *Georgics*, showed a love and appreciation of nature and the countryside, inspired by the Epicurean creed preaching contentment in withdrawal from public life. During Virgil's lifetime the Italian peninsula ceased to be self-sufficient, with farming no longer profitable unless done by the slaves of rich men. The small farms were disappearing, to be replaced by great estates. For the rich owners, the *villa rustica* encouraged the experience of *otium*, a life of leisure where "surrounded by nature man became the master of his own destiny" – its opposite being *negotium*, the busy city life of politics and commerce. The rural villas of the rich Romans provided a mould for the 16th-century villas of the Veneto strung out along the Brenta canal or clustered around Vicenza, and were echoed in 15th- and 16th-century Italy when the Medici put together large properties at the expense of small farmers. A later parallel occurs in 18th-century England when the wealthy and classically educated landowners consolidated their land holdings by Acts of Enclosure, depriving villagers of rights to common land to make their landscape parks. These English gentlemen interpreted the Roman country villa and its garden anew to suit prevailing fashions.

The antithesis of the enclosed peristyle gardens of cities, the Roman country villas had views of distant mountains, rolling hills and vineyards, a classical concept incorporated by Leon Battista Alberti in his influential 15th-century publication *De re aedificatoria*. He advised finding a site for a country house "that overlooks the city, the owner's land, the sea or a great plain and familiar hills and mountains…in the foreground there should be a delicacy of gardens". Continually quoting the practices of "the ancients", Alberti actually lifted his instructions almost word for word from the classical authors.

In the *Eclogues*, Virgil (70–19 BC) laments the loss of the farm near Mantua where he was brought up; in the *Georgics*, written between 38 and 29 BC, he

PLINY'S VILLA IDEAL

PLINY THE YOUNGER'S TWO VILLAS, at Tusculum and Laurentium, have been the subject of much speculation. Since the 16th century scholars have studied the descriptions in Pliny's letters and made frequent attempts to re-create them in drawings. The details of architecture, garden arrangements and named plants give by far the most telling accounts of any Roman villa. But Pliny's importance to garden development goes beyond topographical detail. It lies in his ideas, nurtured and expanded first by Renaissance scholars and afterwards by many distinguished architectural historians.

Pliny's writings on his villas were lifted almost verbatim by Alberti in the 15th century, in particular as regards the siting of villas in the landscape, and influenced the new generation of Renaissance builders. Pliny's words to Apollinaris on the situation of his Tusculum villa sum up his requirements: "Imagine to yourself an amphitheatre of immense circumference…a wide extended plain is surrounded by mountains…my house, although built at the foot of a hill, has a view as if it stood upon the brow. The ascent is so gradual and easy that you find yourself on the top almost before you feel yourself ascending. Behind it at a distance, is the Apennine mountain range." The countryside around appears, from a height, "not as real land but as an exquisite painting". He adds: "The heat in the summer is very moderate…there is always some air stirring abroad…To this I attribute the number of our old men." Sadly Pliny himself was not to live to old age in Tusculum but died in his fifties on official business near the Black Sea.

Recommendations from Pliny (and Alberti) were also followed by Andrea Palladio (1508–80) in siting his famous Villa La Rotonda outside Vicenza in an amphitheatre of hills, its four identical façades with different views. Archaeological scrutiny of the still-existing ruins of Roman villas, combined with modern mathematics, allowed the Renaissance architects and their patrons, such as the Medici, to discover the secrets of classical proportion.

Pliny's Laurentium villa lay close to the sea, thus having a private and a public face, the latter with access to the road from Rome. Both his villas were carefully oriented to make use of cooling breezes, with colonnades to provide shade from the midday sun. Pliny's happy detailing of observing the crops and the rotation of seasons conveys all the joy of being a landowner, as well as the pleasure he found in retiring to the country to pursue his writing. He insists on a close interdependence between garden and villa, giving more specifics of his garden

features and planting schemes than he does of the architecture. In the poor soil of his Laurentium villa he grows only figs and mulberries, with hedges of box interspersed with rosemary.

In Tusculum the garden possibilities are greater. Below the main colonnade "figures of animals cut in box face each other", while on the level below is a bed of acanthus. A path is hedged with bushes trained into different shapes, and an oval drive contains various box figures and clipped dwarf shrubs. The riding ground is "planted around with ivy-clad plane trees, green with their own leaves above, and below with ivy…which links tree to tree as it spreads across them. Box shrubs grow between the plane trees, and outside there is ring of laurel bushes which add their shade to that of the planes." Tall cypresses shade one corner and roses grow in the more open areas.

In Pliny's dining room water gushes from pipes to be held in a polished marble basin, regulated to remain full but not to overflow. The lighter dishes "float about in vessels shaped like birds or little boats". At the 16th-century Italian Villa Lante, the architect Vignola must have had Pliny in mind when he introduced an open trough with running waters to cool bottles of wine.

Robert Castell's *The Villas of the Ancients Illustrated*, published in England in 1728, reflected contemporary interest in setting new landscape philosophies inside the classical tradition and also referred to Pliny. Some of the illustrations in Castell's book show reconstructions of Pliny's villa gardens, proving his relevance to the new informality in English gardening.

PLINY THE YOUNGER

celebrates the actual working of the earth as "a happy compulsion that makes labour sweet". He makes no secret of the efforts required to produce agrarian bounty – labour done by servants, leaving the wealthy patrician free to realize Virgil's idealized life in the countryside, a recurrent myth surviving from Roman times until the present day. Virgil's labourers, however, led a fulfilled if hard-working life, following Virgil's calendar of seasonal work.

While Virgil wrote about the countryside and native plants, including cultivation of orchards, another writer has become the most reliable source for descriptions of a garden's close relationship to the villa and for the details of its topography and planting. In his letters written between AD 97 and 107, Pliny the Younger (*c.*61–113), nephew and heir to the naturalist Pliny who was overcome by fumes in the Vesuvius calamity of AD 79, describes his two gardens in Laurentium, on the coast near Ostia, and at Tusculum in Tuscany, in the upper valley of the Tiber (see previous page). The attractions of both villas are still resonant today.

The grand "open" garden like those of the younger Pliny and of the Emperor Hadrian became a home for buildings, pools, columns and porticoes, pavilions and statues – elements composing a whole landscape. The ruins of Hadrian's villa (see page 31), set among the olive groves of the Aniene valley, occupy some 60 hectares (150 acres). Hadrian (born AD 76 in Spain) was a cultivated man, with knowledge of painting, music, poetry, architecture and especially Greek culture and he incorporated several elements of Hellenistic garden art such as the Canopus canal from Alexandria, flanked by caryatids copied from the Erechtheum on the 5th-century BC Parthenon at Athens. Many of these artefacts, each a theme with a complete entity, have since entered the language of garden design. The island nymphaeum, known as the Marine Theatre, a circular building surrounding a pool and island, inspired the Isolotto garden in the Boboli in 17th-century Florence. In Nero's time (AD 54–68) the garden of the Golden House in Rome, on the banks of a lake and later the site of the Colosseum, with a juxtaposition of buildings with small-scale woods and meadows reduced to a human scale, was a complete panorama. In further outposts of the Empire the design of palace and villa gardens would be adapted to the prevailing climate and soil conditions. Where summers were hot the villa opened out to provide shady porticoes and to allow cool breezes through the garden courts. In colder places the gardens would be enclosed, sheltered from the prevailing winds. Pliny's letters amply demonstrate the importance of aspect. Provincial villas in the Iberian peninsula would have had much the same layout as those in Italy.

PRACTICAL GARDENING: THE MANUALS

The Romans may have exploited ideas from other cultures but they knew how to do it successfully. One of the most obvious reasons that their garden art developed so rapidly was improved technology. Their management of water is a case in point. The Greeks, lacking the river economies of Mesopotamia or Egypt, were dependent on spring water – we notice how often fresh springs are praised in their literature. The Romans, on the other hand, introduced aqueducts and plumbing, making possible both pools and fountains and enabling a far greater range of plants to be grown. Their sophisticated irrigation techniques have been discovered during the course of many excavations.

They were also good at summarizing and disseminating their knowledge. Practicalities of cultivation were described by a number of writers in a series of important manuals – four of them, each confusingly entitled *De re rustica* – which have, if anything, grown in importance in the two millennia since they were written. They survived and were copied in monasteries and other centres of learning throughout the Dark Ages. The advice of these agronomes (see right) was often reiterated verbatim by medieval authors, such as Albertus Magnus in 13th-century Germany and Pietro de' Crescenzi in 14th-century Italy, and after the invention of printing their ideas were still widely circulated in translations. Today, they provide a valuable window into a lost age. Among the "rustic matters" with which they were concerned was the management of estates for agriculture and horticulture, but it is, of course, the gardening aspects that interest us.

Cato's *De re rustica* is episodic rather than arranged coherently, but contains much practical information: we have already come across his instructions on layering plants (see page 44). Varro's schedule of yearly work advises when to plant lilies, crocus and roses. He writes about flowers but is concerned less with gardening than with farming (which, he stresses, should be managed for both profit and pleasure). He describes laying out commercial beds for growing roses – the rose gardens of Paestum and the Campania were already renowned – and deplores the unprofitability of violet farms, where beds formed by heaping up soil were frequently washed away. Varro does give one tantalizing glimpse of his own garden, where we find that he built an aviary with a domed casino in which a table "revolved so that everything to eat or drink is placed on it at once and moved round to all the guests", an early version of a dumb waiter or lazy Susan.

Columella, as a country gentleman, has a lively feeling for gardening as the extension of farming. His tenth volume, written in verse, is an evocative ode to the workings of nature in which he discusses the whole layout of the garden, its water supply, the plants suitable for growing and their culture. The eleventh volume returns to prose to include specific instructions for choosing a site, enclosing it, the preparation of soil, use of fertilizers, and choice of herbs and vegetables. His description of how best to establish a new hedge composed of brambles, roses and Christ's thorn (*Paliurus spina-christi*) was incorporated almost word for word into Thomas Hill's 16th-century *The Gardener's Labyrinth*: "the seeds of these briers must be picked as ripe as possible and mixed with meal of well-ground bitter vetch…sprinkled with water [and] smeared either on old ship's hawsers or any kind of rope…these are dried and put away in an attic…when midwinter is passed…the ropes…are uncoiled and stretched lengthways along each furrow and covered up in such a manner that the seeds…may be able to sprout." Winter pruning of vines and hedges is discussed at length. In February, poplars, willows, elms and ash should be planted before they put forth their leaves, and new rose beds planted. In early March, "broadcast of the berries of laurel and myrtle and other evergreens in beds". He even lists several tasks to be accomplished in the dark days of November and December. One was to sharpen

ROMAN AGRONOMES

Cato the Elder (234–149 BC), statesman, consul and censor, was the first of the four influential Roman writers on rural matters to publish his ideas. His treatise (written in the form of a notebook, and called, like the others that followed, *De re rustica*) is the best known, although his work on agriculture and horticulture is largely ignored. The second of the four, Varro (116–27 BC), wrote his version when already over 80. Begun as a manual for his wife, who had recently acquired a farm, he concentrates on cultivation on a commercial scale.

Columella's treatise, written between AD 60 and 65 and often quoted by Pliny the Elder, runs to 12 volumes. The tenth volume, written in response to Virgil's invitation in the *Georgics*, is in hexameter verse, and the eleventh is full of practical advice. Palladius, who wrote his version in the 4th century AD, drew heavily on Columella's work. His book was one of the first of the manuals to be translated into English early in the 14th century. Although perhaps the least worthy, Palladius's was the most widely read of the Latin treatises. His list of plants from AD 380 is useful for comparison with later medieval catalogues.

Roman precision (right)

The Roman garden at the Getty Museum in Malibu, California, is inspired by classical paintings and texts, which suggest that fantastic sculptures were as much a part of the ancient topiary repertoire as simple geometric shapes and squared hedges. Box (*Buxus sempervirens*) was popular with Roman topiarists (*topiarii*), specialist gardener-slaves who, typically, hailed from Greece, and used single-handed shears, sickles and sharp knives to create their works of art.

Levens Hall survivors (above)

The triumph of the informal, landscape garden in England spelled defeat and destruction for the orderly formal garden of the 17th century of which topiary was a major element. The outstanding display of beech hedges and shaped yew trees at Levens Hall in Cumbria – some of which were planted between 1689 and 1712 – is one of the few early English topiary gardens to survive the change in fashion.

Japanese barque (right)

Photographed around 1905, this stately "cloud-pruned" pine tree was growing in a courtyard of Kyoto's Kinkaku-ji (Golden Pavilion). In the interests of control and a certain solemnity – as opposed to geometry and symmetry – trees and shrubs may be strictly pruned and trained in traditional Japanese gardens.

Green walls of Castellazzo (below)

Laid out early in the 18th century, the garden of the Villa Castellazzo in northern Italy boasted some spectacular pieces of topiary. Although this contemporary engraving exaggerates the height of Castellazzo's hedge "walls", they were famously tall. The tunnel arbours and towering evergreens of the formal garden provided visitors with shaded areas for sitting outdoors and for strolling at their leisure.

Art of topiary

Topiary – the pruning and training of trees and shrubs into geometric and fanciful forms – dates back to ancient times. Its place in the pleasure gardens of the classical Mediterranean world may have owed something, originally, to the availability of topiary-friendly trees, such as cypress and yew. In his *Naturalis Historia*, Pliny the Elder describes cypress trees that have been cut and trained to represent hunting scenes, ships at sail and indeed "all sorts of images". Other Roman texts refer to edgings or hedges formed of intricately clipped box.

More than a thousand years later, when the garden-makers of the Renaissance were seeking to re-create the landscapes of antiquity, they resorted to extensive topiary schemes. Blocks, rows, columns and pyramids of green imparted definition and structure to garden designs. This architectural use of topiary was to reach its apogee in the grand formal gardens of 17th- and 18th-century France. At the court of Louis XIV topiary was so "in", it came to a famous ball. To celebrate his son's wedding in 1745, Louis hosted the Ball of the Clipped Yew Trees, at which he appeared in a costume designed to resemble one of his own topiarized yews.

The French grand style, of which topiary is such a key element, duly conquered the great gardens of Europe, as well as a small corner of China. Although many fine English displays were destroyed under the impact of the Landscape Movement, topiary lived on in the grand gardens of Continental Europe and the cottage gardens of ordinary folk. Indeed, topiary has never lost its popular appeal and fun has often played as great a part in its long and lively history as fashion and philosophy.

Versailles pattern book (above)
Evergreens clipped in all manner of guises, a selection of which is illustrated in this 18th-century album, enlivened the gardens of the French king at Versailles, where no expense or skill was spared. Topiary specimens, often combined with flowers, were a feature of the borders surrounding parterrres. Planted in containers, they lined walks.

English clouds (below)
For good or for ill, topiary has been associated with formal garden designs. The sinuous, almost organic sweep of these hedges at Saling Hall in Essex shows how, with a relaxed approach and some inspiration from Japan, the art of "clipped greens" can provide structure without being a matter of cones, globes, boxes and pyramids.

tools and make handles for them of the best wood, with holm oak, hornbeam (described by Pliny as "yoke elm") and ash being preferred, in that order. Columella is well worth reading today.

Palladius drew heavily on Columella's original text and copied Columella in arranging his 4th-century manual in calendar form, giving hints for each month of the year – a formula of "topical tips" that is perennially successful. Palladius's work was being copied as late as the 12th and 13th centuries and translated into English early in the 14th century.

GARDENING TECHNIQUES

The encyclopaedia *Naturalis Historia* written by Pliny the Elder (*c.*23–79), the younger Pliny's uncle, in 37 volumes is extremely comprehensive. Almost contemporary with Dioscorides's *De Materia Medica*, the immense compilation drew on at least 500 sources, many of them Greek. Scouring earlier literature, Pliny accepted – or at least recorded – superstitions, as well as practical advice given by gardeners, adding gardening ideas gleaned from his own experience. Pliny covers a range of topics, including land, seas, rivers, animals, birds, trees, insects, flowers, herbs, medicine and precious stones, as well as the art of painting and sculpture. In spite of difficulties in identifying species, Pliny's work still makes fascinating reading. He wrote of the plane tree, first brought to Sicily from the Ionian Islands but originating in northern Persia. He refers to the forcing of fruit in some sort of hothouse. Although the manuscript did not survive, a copy was available in England in the 8th century, owned by the Venerable Bede, and a fine illustrated copy was produced in Italy in the 15th century.

The grafter's craft
A page from the 15th-century Italian manuscript of the *Naturalis Historia* of Pliny the Elder shows a man grafting trees in an orchard. Pliny's opus still makes fascinating reading. It includes superstitions as well as practical advice, based either on his own experience or that of other gardeners.

Cato and Varro list a number of useful tools including billhooks, sharp knives for cutting the vines, and metal forks. Spades were mostly made of wood but sometimes of metal, or fitted with a metal shoe. Although metal examples of tools and terracotta pots have been excavated – the pots usually in pieces but reconstructed they show the shapes – neither wood nor wicker survives. A mattock had a long handle and a pointed or straight-edged blade. Cultivators for loosening soil had tines, one with two tines being called a *bidens*. There were rakes, hurdles and baskets for gathering fruit and flowers, and watering pots or *nassiterna*. Collections of tools, often depicted in frescoes and mosaics, demonstrate how little useful implements changed until quite recent times.

Gardening techniques are described in most of the manuals as well as in Pliny's *Naturalis Historia*. Cato advises on cuttings and layering, and Pliny recommends growing plants in raised beds contained with wooden edges. Columella protects sowings from frost by using "low trellises…constructed with reeds, and rods…thrown in and straw on top of the rods, and thus the plants are protected"[3]. Columella also discusses the merits of different sorts of manure for fertilizing, including ash and cinders as well as kitchen waste, and using green manures such as lupins and vetch. Soil drainage was improved by using stones or potsherds at the bottom of a planting bed. There was also "companion" planting to control pests and diseases, bitter vetch protecting turnips and chickpeas deterring caterpillars from eating cabbages. Compounds containing lees of olives or soot, and the juice of wormwood (*Artemisia*), horehound or houseleek, controlled spread of disease, and heliotrope was recommended to protect plants from ants.

Most of these tools and techniques of gardening, documented in the texts or illustrated in mosaics and frescoes, survived in use almost unaltered to the end of the Middle Ages in Europe, some of them until the present day. Even the mattock has recently been reintroduced to Britain. In modern ecological planting schemes chemicals to combat pests and disease are being increasingly discarded to be replaced with more biologically friendly natural methods, many of which were pragmatically employed by the earliest gardeners.

CLASSICAL COMPOSITION

Besides the core of useful manuals there were other Latin authors who instructed their contemporaries and, suitable for expansion into the new humanist idiom, were studied for inspiration in both building and gardening in the 15th and 16th centuries. Vitruvius's work on architectural principles (*De Architectura* of 30 BC) includes discussion of the art of landscape painting. While paying little attention to gardens, he first explained a relationship between theatrical and garden design. A backdrop composition of trees, caverns and mountains could imitate a land scape, while in turn those creating gardens could borrow theatrical elements. This is a subject to be returned to in Renaissance times and after.

Hero of Alexandria's *Pneumatica* (1st century AD) on hydraulic devices and technology, useful and experimental in its own time, was expanded in Arab textbooks on engineering and in Renaissance Europe to include elaborate water organs and the water jokes so much enjoyed in Italian gardens.

Then there was sculpture. Sites such as Pompeii, undisturbed for centuries, reveal garden sculptures still *in situ*. In most other Roman gardens statues were the first things to be removed for incorporation into new Renaissance garden schemes, or of course simply destroyed over the centuries. Many Roman statues were copies of Greek originals. Often the sculpture combined functions of religion and decoration. Altars in the form of a small pedestal, or in reliefs or frescoes, were often accompanied by statues of relevant gods or goddesses, indicating use in a sacred enclosure or at least some form of worship. Sometimes they were framed by serpents, commonly believed to ward off evil. In wealthier properties, such as the gardens of Servilius in Rome, works of famous Greek sculptors such as Praxiteles and Scopas would be displayed (as described by Pliny the Elder), while at Pompeii smaller marble stone reliefs known as *pinakes*, heads on columns called herms and animal statues such as those of fawns, greyhounds and hares were all found. Often figures were linked with a particular divinity and with a theme – Flora usually crowned with flowers, Pomona presiding over an orchard, or Venus often associated with water. Hercules leaning on his club, Diana as a huntress, Apollo as god of prophecy and healing, and Bacchus with an entourage of revellers – associated with the grapevine – were all popular. Herms or busts of

A model for today
For the pool at Sotogrande, the modern Spanish designer Fernando Caruncho has taken his inspiration from the Roman gardens at Conimbriga (modern Coimbra), in Portugal. Caruncho's water jets, arching elegantly above clipped boxwood hedges, are reminiscent of the Conimbriga gardens, which were constructed in the time of Septimus Severus (AD 146–211). The gardens contained elaborate water parterres and fountains (inset), and flowerbeds, created within watertight containers, were made to look like floating islands.

philosophers were deemed suitable for an academy-style garden (such as in the 18th-century English landscape garden at Stowe). Cupid and Psyche, whose love affair took place in a garden inspired by tales of the orient, were often portrayed. All these allegorical themes were re-adopted in Renaissance times.

THE ROMAN PLANTING PALETTE

Plants in Roman gardens were mainly those native to the provinces within the Empire or at least those areas in contact with it. New fruit introduced to the Roman Empire included peaches, melon and citron, and if archaeological evidence from Pompeii is to be believed, the lemon. In their turn Romans were, of course, responsible for taking their Mediterranean plants and others from further east to their northern outposts across the Alps.

For their own garden flora we can turn to Pliny the Elder's *Naturalis Historia* together with Dioscorides's herbal as useful sources for identification. The original Latin and Greek names have been brought up to date by modern scholars. Plants mentioned in Pliny that we use today in ornamental flower gardens (as opposed to useful herbs and spices) include acanthus, anthyllis, box, cerinthe, citron, cornflower, crocus, cyclamen, cynoglossum, germander, European heliotrope, hesperis, hyacinth, iris, ivy, bay laurel, lavender, lilies, myrtle, narcissus, oleander, periwinkle, pomegranate, poppy, rosemary, southernwood, strawberry trees and violets. The twice-flowering roses of Paestum (probably *Rosa* × *damascena* var. *bifera*, a form of the autumn damask *R. damascena* var. *semperflorens*), praised by Virgil in his *Georgics*, were grown for garlands and their scented petals. Other roses known in Roman times were *Rosa gallica*, *R. phoenicia*, *R. canina* and *R.* × *alba*. Violets were highly scented and grown commercially. Evergreen shrubs – arbutus, bay laurel, myrtle, cypress, ivy and box with aromatic leaves – were staples of the Roman garden in winter and could be clipped into required shapes. Plane trees were introduced from Greece through Sicily, and a native, the nettle tree (*Celtis australis*), is praised by Pliny.

Cato mentions vegetables for Roman gardens, mainly varieties of cabbage, which he maintained could treat many ailments; other *hortus* plants would have been specifically for medicine. Mustard cured snake bite, mushroom poisoning,

toothache and stomach ailments, and could ease asthma. More familiar to us today are plants recommended for providing nectar, not only for honey but to ensure that bees performed their essential function as fruit pollinators. Columella included rosemary and trefoil as essential for a bee's health, but we can turn to Virgil's *Georgics* for a poetic version of instructions as to where to place the hives, and what plants and flowers were essential: "To make a proper job of it, a beekeeper must be a gardener too. He must collect wild thyme, pine seedlings from the hills, and flowering shrubs, and plant them with his own hands and keep them watered."

All the knowledge about plants and gardens acquired by the ancient Greeks and Romans was to be of little use during the next 500 years in western Europe. Here, during the Dark Ages, it lay dormant until medieval times. The centre of gardening activity instead travelled eastwards into the world of Islam.

CHAPTER THREE

THE GARDENS OF
ISLAM

Heavenly beauty, earthly delight

THE GARDENS OF ISLAM ARE AMONG the most sublime in the world, soothing, refreshing and spiritual. But the followers of the Prophet Muhammad did not invent the principles of layout that all Muslim gardens share. With water and symmetry the essential features and water channels dividing the garden into four, they had originated much earlier in the desert countries. The 6th-century BC garden of Cyrus the Great is one of the earliest which can still be identified on the ground.

Through a history that is like a series of intertwining tales (as in *The Arabian Nights*) we learn how, as the new faith spread, the fundamental "fourfold" design travelled with it. As the concept developed and matured in its Middle Eastern heartland, it also moved through north Africa westwards to Spain (and hence to Hispanic America), to the Ottoman empire in Turkey and eastwards to India with the Mughal rulers. From its original quadripartite form it expanded to include six or eight or 10 divisions with a multiplicity of dividing water rills, water chutes and viewing pavilions. Islam's gift was not one purely of design: the gardens also had a spiritual content, a terrestrial interpretation of future paradise as revealed in the Koran.

Some of the most impressive of these Islamic gardens still exist – they are among today's wonders of the world. A more intimate record has been left to us by the Persian miniaturists. Their exquisite paintings capture the Islamic garden's very essence, depicting it as a place of romance and pleasure, enclosed and secluded from the harsh rigours of the world outside.

Mirror image
The Court of the Myrtles in the Alhambra, built by the Nasrid rulers *c.*1370, and remaining in Moorish hands until 1492, is the best preserved Muslim garden surviving in Europe. The elaborate stucco arches at both ends of the enclosed court are perfectly reflected in the water.

HISTORICAL SETTING

At the time of Muhammad, power in the Middle East was divided between two great empires, Sasanian and Byzantine. The Byzantine empire controlled modern Turkey, Syria, Greece, much of Egypt and part of Italy, while the Sasanians held the reins in modern Iran and Iraq, spreading east into Turkmenistan and Afghanistan. Their capital in AD 637 was Ctesiphon (modern Baghdad). The Sasanians, and before them the earlier Achaemenian dynasty, had originally come from Fars, or Pars, in southwestern Iran, from which the name Persia derives.

The ruins of Pasargadae
The site of Cyrus the Great's palace and gardens, dating from the 6th century BC, lies in the plain north of Shiraz. Nothing remains of the garden, where Cyrus grew fruit trees sheltered by tall silver-stemmed poplars and dark cypresses, except some water rills and rectangular basins, marking out a geometric pattern dividing the garden into four parts. The water was brought from the mountains by an aqueduct.

THE PATTERN IS FOUND

When Muhammad's Arab followers swept through western Asia and defeated the Sasanian Persians in AD 637, they discovered a style of gardening that had existed for at least 1,000 years. At Pasargadae, in 559–530 BC, the Achaemenian Emperor Cyrus the Great had built a complex of palaces and pavilions with colonnaded porches to give shelter from the burning midday sun. The main inner garden was patterned into a network of narrow gravity-fed limestone watercourses, or rills, which opened at 15m (50ft) intervals into square basins, each cut from a single stone. The pattern of rills divided the garden into four parts – the earliest known remains of the "fourfold" garden, or *chahar bagh* as it came to be known. Planted with orchard trees and possibly ringed with protective cypresses, this was the form of layout that was to inspire the future gardens of Islam. At Ctesiphon (today's Baghdad), scene of the decisive battle in 637, the invaders found another example of this gardening tradition, the most famous of all Persian garden carpets, known as the Spring of Khosrow. Woven from silk and measuring 26 × 11m (84 × 35ft), its pattern represented a royal garden, divided by rills into flowerbeds in much the same way as at Pasargadae. The carpet would have been spread on the ground in the audience hall of the king's palace. Its makers had used golden threads to represent earth, shimmering crystal for the rills, and pearls for the gravel paths. Fruit trees in the geometric plots had trunks and branches shaped in silver and gold with precious stones representing flowers and fruit. Sadly, the carpet no longer exists – the conquerors cut it up and divided it out as booty – but the tradition of garden carpets continues with patterns today still representing garden layouts with water channels, pools and plants.

The new Islamic religion, with its abstract concept of God and descriptions of paradise, adapted and spiritually embellished the ideas that underpinned the gardens the conquerors found. They turned the purely physical, earth-bound garden into the celestial paradise that awaits the righteous after death – a paradise that, reveals the Koran, "shall be abounding in branches, therein fountains of running water, and of every fruit there shall be two kinds. The

believers shall find themselves reclining upon couches lined with brocade, the fruits of the garden nigh to gather; and will find therein maidens restraining their glances…lovely as rubies, beautiful as coral…green, green pastures, therein fountains of running water, fruits and palm trees, and pomegranates…"

The development of the Islamic garden was an integral part of the interpretation of the Muslim faith, which filled the whole life of a believer. In Islam, art, designed to inspire the righteous, took on a new meaning; architecture, painting, calligraphy and decoration reflected the essential unity that permeates the message revealed by the Koran. Ornamentation and abstract geometric patterns and arabesques (developed from the twining branches of vines), as well as elegant calligraphy, often quoting directly from the Koran, expressed the intellectual and spiritual world of Islam. This ornamentation was applied to all surfaces and objects, from the most humble to the most holy, a reminder of heaven in all aspects of life.

Islamic culture developed at a time when northern Europe had descended into barbarian chaos. Baghdad and, later, Cordoba in Andalusia became recognized centres of scholarship in the known world; the Arabs established universi

Carpet tradition

The Arabs swept into the delta of the Tigris and Euphrates in AD 637, destroying the Sasanian Palace of Taz-i-Kisra, Ctesiphon. The ruins (top) show the great iwan, or audience hall, where the Spring of Khosrow carpet would have lain. Nothing remains of this fabled carpet, but the tradition of garden carpets has endured, many of them clearly showing the fourfold garden layout as in this 18th-century Persian example from Kerman (above).

The fourfold garden
This Mughal miniature *c.*1610–15, painted during the reign of Jahangir, shows a central platform at the meeting of the four "rivers" in a typical *chahar bagh* garden where the enclosing walls convey a sense of refuge, implicit in the Koranic description of paradise. Flowerbeds, edged with slender cypresses, are sunk below the walkways.

ties, studied botany and medicine; their gardening knowledge and expertise – especially their hydraulic systems – in Spain, Sicily and southern Italy helped to prepare the way for the classical Italian garden of the 15th and 16th centuries. Even the 18th- and 19th-century Spanish mission gardens established as oases in the hot, dry western states of North America owe their origins to the Islamic ideal.

Plants introduced from the East to Spain and Sicily gradually augmented the limited Mediterranean and north European flora available to medieval gardeners. By the end of the 16th century, with diplomatic relationships established with the Ottoman sultans (ultimate successors to much of the Byzantine empire), the trickle of plants became a flood as new bulbs, corms and rhizomes, many already cultivated in gardens in the Orient, were brought to Europe via Constantinople. During the next few centuries the Ottoman empire spread through the Balkans and as far as the gates of Vienna, bringing with it the Turks' enduring delight in flowers and gardens.

THE SIMPLICITY OF THE FOURFOLD GARDEN

The Islamic garden contains certain recognizable elements which, with minor deviations and extensions dependent on local conditions, have remained constant over the centuries. From the beginning, the square or rectangular shape, enclosed within walls pierced by a monumental doorway, would be divided into four by intersecting watercourses which represent the four rivers of life, "rivers of water unstaling, rivers of milk unchanging in flavour, and rivers of wine – a delight to drinkers, rivers too, of honey purified". The term *chahar bagh* (*chahar* means four and *bagh* means garden) describes this fundamental Islamic pattern. The point where the watercourses met would be marked by a central pool, mausoleum or pavilion.

Water was the essential element in all Islamic gardens (or earlier oasis gardens): it was literally the source of all life. When the Arabs invaded Persia, they inherited the *qanat* irrigation system, a network of underground tunnels capable of carrying water from melting mountain snows long distances to desert areas (see page 24). As well as the garden's main watercourses or rills, bubbling fountains and sparkling jets provided sound and movement, designed not only to soothe the senses but also to cool the air and discourage insects. In Kashmir, especially,

Symbols of loss and hope

This piece of Persian satin damask (left) dates to the 16th or 17th century, and the Persian velvet (below) to the 16th century. In both centuries the decorative arts flourished under the Safavids, reaching the greatest heights during the reign of Shah 'Abbas I in Isfahan. Carpets and some sumptuous silks, velvets and satins were designed with themes taken from the garden. These themes were also illustrated in Persian poetry and, of course, in Persian miniatures. A favourite portrayal was of the dark cypress, the symbol of death and mortality, clasped by the flowering almond, symbol of spring and rejuvenation, often surrounded by meadow flowers, birds and deer.

ABBASIDS AND UMAYYADS

In AD 750 the Abbasids overthrew the Umayyads of Damascus, who had been in power since *c*.660, and massacred nearly all members of the Umayyad family. One, however, escaped from Syria to Cordoba. He established the city as a centre of learning for the whole of Europe and brought the Islamic garden-making tradition to Spain. The Abbasids, who made their capital in Baghdad, reached the zenith of their power during the caliphate of Harun al-Rashid (786–809), the caliph of *Arabian Nights* fame.

the *chadar*, or sloping water screen, developed as a further feature just as, more recently, rushing water cascades and complicated fountain layouts have become an essential tool in helping today's city planners reduce traffic noise and provide areas for rest and refreshment (for instance, the Ira Keller complex at Portland, Oregon, see page 87). If the garden was built with sufficient slope, the water, held in a tank, would flow with gravity to work the fountains. Water runnels, edged with pathways, were decorative as well as functional, with flowerbeds, sunk below path level, flooded at intervals for irrigation, an arrangement that created the sensation of walking on a carpet of flowers. Stately plane trees (*chenars*) provided dense shade, and were often planted in a pattern of four around a pavilion or fountain just as they were later planted around springs and grottoes in 16th-century Italian gardens. Fruit trees cast lighter dappled shadows to contrast with the dark columns of cypresses.

To these basic elements were added ornamental architectural detail: beautiful glazed tiles, intricate mosaic paving patterns, lotus-shaped marble basins. Such features, old and new, are still to be seen in the courtyards of Cordoba and Isfahan: modern craftsmen continue to be inspired by the traditional designs. The *chabutra*, a stone or marble platform, about 60cm (2ft) high and often placed over the meeting point of the four main water channels, could serve as a place to rest, catch the breeze and view the garden. The sound of water rippling over patterned channels or cascading over *chadars* delighted the senses still further. At the time of the Arab invasion, the enclosed Persian garden was called a *bustan*. The term *chahar bagh* was probably not in common usage until at least AD 1000.

Most of these features appear in Persian miniatures and in the patterns of "garden carpets", as well as being evocatively described in poetry and manuscript memoirs. In both the miniatures and carpets spring-flowering almond trees are portrayed clasping a spire of cypress, the almond a symbol of spring and renewed life, the cypress of eternity and death. That they clasp signifies love. Although gardens would be filled with fruit blossom and scents to bring delight, for the devout Muslim there was at first no special emphasis on rare or new plants since it was the beauty of the plant as a sign of God's creation that was most important. However, in many regions, especially the Iberian peninsula, collections of new fruit later became greatly sought after, initially grown in gardens and later planted in commercial orchards.

THE EARLY YEARS OF ISLAM

Within a hundred years of the Prophet Muhammad's death in AD 632, the Arabs had formed the initial core of their empire – a vast area that included Sasanian Persia and Egypt (and incorporated the lands of the ancient civilizations of Sumeria, Babylon and Assyria). They were able to inherit many of the sophisticated traditions of their new subjects and it was the cultured Persians, newly converted to Islam, who became most influential in government.

The Arabs also brought a new attitude to conquest. Islam taught that it was man's duty to preserve and protect all nature, which had a divine source. From the beginning the first caliph, Abu Bakr (632–34), was dedicated to spreading the new religion rather than ravishing the countryside. He ordered that no palm trees or orchards were to be cut down and no cornfields burnt during the victorious progress. By 762 – backed by the refined and luxury-loving Persians, able administrators whose ways the Arabs partly adopted – the early Abbasid caliphs had developed the new city of Baghdad, laid out in a circular pattern on the banks of the Tigris. It quickly became a centre of scholarship and creativity, carrying on garden traditions first established centuries earlier in the delta of the Euphrates and Tigris by the Assyrians and Babylonians, who had enclosed pleasure grounds and created fabulous hunting parks and menageries.

In their gardens, the Persians cultivated fruit trees and flowers, some introduced from eastern Asia. On the plain around Fars they grew red roses, exporting the attar (the essential oil produced from them) to India, China, Egypt and the Maghreb. And in the fertile valleys and uplands of Persia, the Arabs, from further west, discovered a wealth of wild flowers new to them, many of them spring-flowering bulbs. These were to travel westwards with the Muslim religion, through north Africa and into Spain, to be catalogued by Arab botanists in the 11th century. Many carried by pilgrims and travellers found their way across the mountains into northern Europe.

ERUDITION AND FANTASY IN BAGHDAD AND SAMARRA

Islam not only expanded the horizons of garden architecture: early Islamic scholars pushed out the boundaries of contemporary plant studies. In the late 8th and 9th centuries, in an era of religious and political tolerance under Harun al-Rashid, the new city of Baghdad became famous for its pursuit and dissemination of knowledge, as well as playing an important role as a commercial centre. Greek and Latin texts on medicine and plants were translated into Arabic, including Dioscorides's 1st-century herbal *De Materia Medica* (see pages 40–41). This was to become as much a standard reference work throughout the Arab world as it was in medieval Europe, and 13 copies were made between the end of the 11th and 15th centuries. Although Muslims put restrictions on image-making, it was permissible to make pictorial representations of floral and vegetable motifs for scholarly purposes and to use plant motifs in architectural decorations. New studies in botany were undertaken by Abu Hanifah al-Dinawari (*c.*820–95), the so-called father of Arab botany, who collected together all known written material from earlier encyclopaedias and poetry and from the Bedouin stories that were transmitted orally. In the 11th century al-Biruni (who died in 1030) began to note the particular arrangement of flowers, while studying the medicinal properties of plants, remarking on the strictly geometric alignment of flower parts and petals, part of nature's "logic".

Excavations of the city of Baghdad, built over many times in successive centuries, have failed to reveal the foundations of any gardens from the Abbasid era. But the *Arabian Nights* tales tell of garden fantasies, follies of the imagination, a reminder that wealth, combined with a taste for

Dioscorides translated
After the collapse of the Roman Empire, when northern Europe was in chaos, Baghdad, and later Cordoba, became centres of scholarship, including plant study. Many Greek and Latin texts were translated into Arabic, including Dioscorides's *De Materia Medica*. By 983 the Umayyad sultan's physician Ibn Juljul had added a supplement incorporating plants known in Spain. *Rosa sempervirens* and henna (*Lawsonia inermis*) are shown here in an Arabic version (987–90).

costly and glittering materials, can carry an accepted style into a different realm. In 917 two Byzantine ambassadors sent from Constantinople were impressed by the splendour of palace gardens on the banks of the Tigris: "The new kiosk is a palace in the midst of two gardens. In the centre was an artificial pond, round which flows a stream in a conduit…that is more lustrous than polished silver. This pond was thirty cubits in length by twenty across and round it was set four magnificent pavilions with gilt seats adorned with embroidery…all around extended a garden with lawns and palm trees…their number was four hundred and the height of each five cubits…All these palms bore full-grown dates…ever ripe and did not decay." Elsewhere, in a Roman-style hippodrome, mechanical silver birds, worked by hydraulic devices of the sort studied in Alexandria in earlier Hellenistic times, perched on golden trees and sang and whistled in the breeze. Another more sober-minded Abbasid ruler grew orange trees from Basra and rare trees from Oman and India in his garden where "fruits gleamed yellow and red, bright as the stars of heaven in a dusky night".

In 825 the capital moved from Baghdad to Samarra, on the east bank of the Tigris 110km (68 miles) further north, where it remained until 892. The foundations of palaces with distinctive garden layouts have been discovered in the sand-covered ruins. Writing in 889, the geographer al-Ya'qubi reported that the whole land was converted to gardens "for the upper class", with palaces, halls, and playgrounds for riding and polo, the latter a national pastime.

Harnessing water for irrigation had to be a priority before any garden could be laid out. The city's founder revolutionized the water supply, introducing an irrigation system by digging underground canals some 40km (25 miles) up the river. Waterwheels, sometimes powered by ostriches – an exotic touch – pumped the water through smaller canals. As a result every garden could have ornamental pools. Those in the caliph's palaces were vast, up to 200m (219yd) square. The court poet al-Buhturi described the Samarra palace called al-Sabi:

> And the stream being replenished with gush-
>   ing water, glittering like a luminous sword
> When it burst into the middle of the
>   beautiful pond its marble colours the water
>   would assume
> And the waterwheels rotate with no animal
>   or plough but with ostriches
> These gardens make us long ardently for
>   Paradise and thus we eschew more sins and
>   shun evil deeds.

Although the magnificence of Samarra was short-lived, its influence on garden architecture was considerable. The palatial 10th-century garden

Survivor in the sand
Although no actual gardens remain in the city of Samarra, founded in 825, the great mosque and spiralling minaret still survive in the desert. Excavations have revealed the foundations of palaces and garden layouts in the sand, the most important being the Balkuwara Palace, with vast water tanks overlooked by arcaded buildings.

city of Medina Azahara (see overleaf) outside Cordoba, in Spain, was in part modelled on the garden of Samarra's Balkuwara Palace, with arcaded pavilions facing large water tanks.

During the 10th century Abbasid control crumbled and the caliphs retained only a symbolic authority. Real power passed to local rulers and a new dynasty gained control in western Persia. Weakened by internal feuds, the region was ripe for invasion when the Golden Horde Mongols descended in the 13th century under Genghis Khan. Their story is picked up again later in the chapter (see page 71), but at this point the centre of gardening activity moves to Spain.

THE ISLAMIC GARDEN IN SPAIN

Southern Spain was first colonized by Muslim raiders, Berbers from north Africa, in the early 8th century. By 756, the Umayyad dynasty, founded by the survivor of a massacre in Damascus, had established itself in Cordoba, its territory extending to Toledo and Seville and incorporating the city of Granada, a far greater area than modern Andalusia. The Moors (as the Muslims became known in Spain) inherited a garden culture, with irrigation systems that had survived from Roman times, and incorporated it into their own vision to produce the most exquisite gardens yet seen in Europe.

The powerful Umayyads made the first of the great Andalusian gardens. They planted exotic fruits and flowers, many brought from the eastern end of the Mediterranean and from as far afield as Persia, India and China, their botanists recording both Iberian natives and newly introduced plants. During the next few centuries, Arab scholarship, including considerable botanical expertise, was gradually absorbed across the Pyrenees, with bulbs, seeds and roots of plants carried by travellers and pilgrims returning to northern Europe. (By 902, other Arabs from North Africa had conquered Sicily. Their architecture and the parks they created, "disposed round the town [Palermo] like a necklace", were subsequently to inspire the Norman invaders who took over in 1091 and, in turn, provided yet another route by which Islamic culture spread to other parts of Europe.)

To some degree, the Islamic gardens of Spain varied in style depending on their size and function. On the grand scale was 'Abd al-Rahman III's extraordinary garden city of Medina Azahara. There were simple orchard gardens, like the *bustan* of Persia (identical to the spring-flowering enclosures seen in modern Iran), in which both common and exotic fruits were grown. And there were courtyard gardens, large and small. The courtyard of orange trees, the Patio de los Naranjos, at Cordoba's magnificent Grand Mosque, may be Europe's oldest surviving garden. Building of the mosque was started in the 780s by the first Umayyad ruler, 'Abd al-Rahman I, with many enlargements being made over the next two centuries. The mosque's 19 naves (now enclosed) originally opened onto the courtyard, the forest-like rhythm of their rows of columns repeated in the ordered rows of orange trees outside. On a much more intimate scale are the small flower-filled courtyards, glimpsed through iron grilles from the street, which have been a feature of the city ever since. With much of their planting in pots, they are an inspiration for today's urban gardener.

MEDINA AZAHARA

Abd al-Rahman III started building Medina Azahara in 936. Sheltered under the southern slope of the sierra near Cordoba, 7km (4 miles) northwest of the

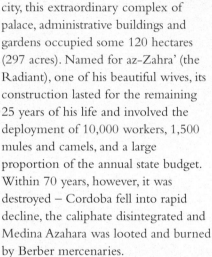

A RESTORED AREA OF THE GARDENS

city, this extraordinary complex of palace, administrative buildings and gardens occupied some 120 hectares (297 acres). Named for az-Zahra' (the Radiant), one of his beautiful wives, its construction lasted for the remaining 25 years of his life and involved the deployment of 10,000 workers, 1,500 mules and camels, and a large proportion of the annual state budget. Within 70 years, however, it was destroyed – Cordoba fell into rapid decline, the caliphate disintegrated and Medina Azahara was looted and burned by Berber mercenaries.

The chief architect, inspired by the art of Byzantium, used 4,000 locally quarried blue and pink marble columns, placing them alternately in the main buildings, which were built from blocks of white limestone. Other columns were brought from Greek or Roman ruins around the Mediterranean. In the Dar al-Mulk, or Royal House, decorated stucco arches depicted tree-of-life themes showing Byzantine influence. The twining branches, leaves and flowers of such themes were later to develop into the arabesque, or *islimi*.

The complex was built on three great stepped terraces, with the main palace on the highest terrace in the centre, and, on the lowest level, a mosque, markets, barracks for the 12,000 soldiers of the caliph's private guard, gardens with pools and fountains, and cages for wild beasts. The main gardens were on the second terrace in front of the great reception rooms of the palace, with an immense tank of still water opposite the entrance. Water for the garden, as well as for the vast throng of courtiers and servants, was brought 15km (9 miles) by aqueduct from the neighbouring hills to the north. Legend has it that quicksilver was used to fill a pool in the royal reception room, an idea possibly taken from the fabled gardens of Baghdad. When the quicksilver was made to ripple, the walls would be covered with dancing patterns of light. In the garden's heyday, avenues of cypress, and groves of bay laurel, pomegranates and orange trees were intermixed with sunken flowerbeds for roses and lilies, with a separate area reserved as a botanical garden for the rarest exotics.

Contemporary reports record that visitors to Medina Azahara were dazzled by its splendours, and today, wandering in the partly excavated ruins, it is still possible to grasp something of the extent and magnificence of the interlinked palaces and gardens. These may have been the inspiration, seven centuries later, for the layout of the Red Fort, at Agra, in India, built by the Mughal emperor Shah Jahan.

Echoes of past grandeur
The ruins of the 10th-century Medina Azahara still convey some of the awesome scale of the vast garden palace.

OF SMUGGLED FIGS AND SUPERIOR POMEGRANATES

One of the earliest gardens in Muslim Spain (not surviving today) was the Arruzafa of Cordoba, a palace with a cemetery, gardens and poplar groves built, like the Grand Mosque, to the order of 'Abd al-Rahman I. It was an experimental garden for both useful and purely decorative plants newly imported to the Spanish peninsula. After trials, the stones, seeds or rooted cuttings of improved or rare fruits, including citrus, figs and pomegranates, could be distributed throughout Moorish Spain for cultivation in orchards, fields or flower gardens. Sometimes specially prized varieties were jealously protected in the countries where they were already cultivated and a degree of skulduggery was needed to bring them to Spain. A Cordoban ambassador smuggled a coveted variety of fig, the *donegale* fig, from Byzantium in the 9th century by unravelling the cords used to strap up his books, placing the seeds inside and resewing the cords.

'Abd al-Rahman I spoke of the garden in a plaintive poem he wrote expressing his yearning for his native Syria: "the lonely palm tree in the midst of Arruzafa, here in the west, far from its land…let the morning rain from the scurrying clouds fall upon you, their waters spilling upon you, and let the stars weep their tears upon you". He also helped to introduce the Syrian pomegranate, "the best type of pomegranate for its sweetness, smooth texture, juiciness and beautiful shape", getting his friend Safar to grow plants from seed in his garden near Malaga before transplanting them to Arruzafa. It is still known as the *zafari* pomegranate.

Other, more splendid, gardens were to follow. Medina Azahara was built by 'Abd al-Rahman III, who, in 929 proclaimed himself caliph of the western Islamic empire, and under whose reign Cordoba was to reach new heights of splendour and prosperity. Within a hundred years, however, both Medina Azahara and Arruzafa were destroyed when Berbers captured the capital in 1010. Soon afterwards Muslim Spain broke up into different states, the most important centred on Toledo and Seville.

BOTANISTS AND POET GARDENERS AT TOLEDO AND SEVILLE

After the fall of Cordoba, Toledo became the hub of horticultural activity. A palace garden, the Huerta del Rey, was founded by physician and botanist Ibn Wafid (999–1075) for the Sultan al-Ma'mun, "the lover of gardens". Here, excavations have revealed that waterwheels were used to raise water from the River Tagus to fill a pool. In the chronicle of Al-Maqqari, Ibn Madrun relates that "King al-Ma'mun of Toledo ordered the construction of a lake, in whose centre stood a crystal pavilion; water was lifted to its roof, and from there it ran down on all sides, like artificial rain, into the water below." On one side of the palace there was a water clock, worked by two vessels which alternately filled and emptied. Ibn Wafid travelled widely, collecting and identifying plants, visiting Sicily and Egypt, Mecca and Khorasan in northeast Persia. He experimented with growing oranges (the bitter orange *Citrus aurantium*), figs and vines. In his writing he concentrated on agriculture but he also included information on flowering and aromatic plants.

Traveller from Asia
Melia azerdarach, known as Persian lilac, Pride of India and, most frequently, the Chinese bead tree, is mentioned in Ibn Bassal's 11th-century *Book of Agriculture*. It originally came from northern India and China, so would have been brought to Spain by the Arabs as they moved through north Africa.

After Ibn Wafid's death, the Huerta del Rey was maintained by Ibn Bassal until the Christian reconquest of 1085 forced him to seek sanctuary in Seville, where he carried out improvements in the royal gardens. Ibn Bassal's *Book of Agriculture* (the Arabic text was only rediscovered in recent times but an incomplete Castilian translation was made *c.*1300) is really a gardening book, hardly touching on field crops. Divided into 16 chapters it deals with practical matters: water, soil, manure, the choice of ground and its preparation, as well as trees and methods of planting. Fruit trees are given a major treatment and include almond, apricot, citron, date palm, fig, olive, orange, peach, pistachio, pomegranate, apple, cherry, pear, plum and quince. Other trees mentioned include arbutus, ash, *Melia azedarach*, bay laurel, cypress, holm oak, chestnut, hazel and walnut. Flowers include roses, wallflowers, stocks, violets, lilies, narcissi, hollyhocks, camomile and wormwood. He even includes advice to discourage slugs: "Form your beds, strew on them an inch of ashes from the Public Baths, then lay on your manure and sow the seed: thus the animal mentioned, on leaving the earth in search of plants, will meet with the ashes and retire confounded."

A hundred years later Ibn al-'Awwam drew heavily on Ibn Bassal's work but broke new ground in suggesting some design principles. His 12th-century *Book of Agriculture* (consulted by Victorian gardening expert J.C. Loudon in the first half of the 19th century) included many more species in cultivation, the numbers doubling between 1080 and 1180. Al-'Awwam recommended planting cypresses to mark corners and as avenues along the main walk. Cedars and pines could be used for shady alleys, with citrus and bay laurel in more open sites. Jasmine was trained on walls or trellis, while pools and watercourses could be shaded by pomegranates, elms, and willows and poplars (known as black and white elms). Hedges might be of box and bay laurel. He also suggests a very modified form of wild gardening, using bell-ivy (probably *Calystegia sepium*) and ivies to climb and hang on trees, as Pliny the Younger had recommended in his gardens. Among the new fruits listed were jujube (*Ziziphus jujuba*), lemon and medlar. Ornamental trees and shrubs included the plane tree, acacia, hawthorn, ivy, jasmine, Judas tree, lavender and oleander. For the flower garden there were mallows, colocasias, hibiscus, hollyhocks and iris species.

Many of the original Arab manuscripts, including local floras, were lost, but the value of some was recognized in Christian Spain. The translation of these works into Castilian, initiated by Alfonso X, was among the first to be made into the vernacular rather than into Latin.

Under the Moorish Ta'ifa kings the constant territorial warring between factions allowed the unification of the Christian kings in the north, who reconquered Toledo in 1085 and Seville in 1248. The rest of Muslim Spain fell into Christian hands, leaving Granada isolated as a tiny sultanate that survived until 1492. This period, however, saw the creation of two of the most famous and exquisite gardens in Granada, the best preserved of all Islamic gardens in Europe. The gardens of the Generalife, the summer residence of the sultans, belong to the time of Isma'il (1315–25) and those of the Alhambra to Muhammad V, 25 years later. Granada finally fell in 1492.

Glories of Granada

A lotus-shaped basin lies at the end of the central water rill in the Patio de la Acequia (right) in the gardens of the Generalife. Alterations over the years have included the 19th-century addition of water jets and the raising of the beds, which were originally below the level of the paths. The ground plan of the Generalife (below) comes from *The Arabian Antiquities of Spain*, published in 1815. In the painting (bottom) of the 14th-century Court of the Myrtles in the Alhambra, from *Souvenirs de Grenade*, 1836, the garden can be seen before the 19th-century introduction of myrtle hedges to flank the water.

THE GARDENS OF THE ALHAMBRA AND GENERALIFE

Enclosed and intimate, refreshed by flowing water and cooled in summer by breezes from the snow-covered Sierra Nevada, the gardens of the Alhambra and Generalife seem almost to represent the Islamic dream of paradise to come. They were built for the Nasrid rulers of Granada, Spain's last Moorish state, and are the best examples of the Arab-Hispanic garden in Andalusia. The upper garden of the Generalife was laid out *c.*1319. The Court of the Myrtles in the Alhambra was built for Yusuf I (1333–54) and the royal apartments, including the Court of the Lions, for his son Muhammad V soon after his accession. Today, much of what we see is reconstruction.

The most important part of the Generalife is the inner garden, the Patio de la Acequia. This fourfold garden is divided by a water rill and backed by high walls. The original flowerbeds were 50cm (20in) below the present levels and irrigated by periodic flooding. The water spouts seen today are a 19th-century introduction. Unfortunately, although excavated after a fire in 1959, the flowerbeds have been returned to their pre-1959 higher level, and modern summer-flowering annuals have replaced the aromatic shrubs and flowers that would have been grown in Moorish Spain. The rest of the Generalife garden is orchard, with the water supply channelled diagonally in a rill across the steep hillside and along the tops of the walls flanking the steps down to the inner garden. In the 1730s, William Kent designed a snaking water rill in the gardens at Rousham (see page 215), and Francis Cabot has designed similar water channels beside descending steps in his modern garden at Les Quatre Vents, in Quebec.

Today in the Alhambra, myrtle bushes (*Myrtus communis*) line the pool in the Court of the Myrtles (Patio de los Arrayanes), part of a 19th-century restoration instigated by the American writer Washington Irving, who lived in the Alhambra for a time, but possibly an original theme. At one end, the pool reflects the Comares, the sultan's official residence, a delicate structure with stuccoed inter-woven arabesques; Charles V's Renaissance palace dominates the other end, built in the early 16th century after Granada had been captured from the Moors. The Court of the Lions (Patio de los Leones) has an extremely simple planting of orange trees in the four corners.

EFFECTS OF THE MONGOL INVASIONS

The invasion of the Mongol hordes under Genghis Khan in 1220 obliterated much that was sacred and beautiful in the Eastern world, with cities in Afghanistan and eastern Iran destroyed, plundered and depopulated. With the irrigation systems damaged, the fields could not be cultivated and they returned to desert. It was common practice for raiding parties to fill their enemies' wells with sand. Further west, Baghdad was pillaged by Genghis Khan's grandson, who broke down canal banks, turning the deltas into malarial swamps and bringing famine and disease to the fertile land so carefully irrigated and cultivated since ancient times.

But the Mongols were not always the destroyers that popular history usually portrays; they were also builders. Ghazan Khan (reigned 1295–1304) created a great park called the Bagh-e 'Adalat (Garden of Justice) to the west of his capital Tabriz. A square area enclosed by a wall was made into a meadow for the emperor, with cisterns for water storage. Avenues planted with willows provided a passage for people to walk around the periphery, while the central part was reserved for the Golden Pavilion and Golden Throne.

Existing Persian gardens were used by the Mongols for royal encampments, the tents and awnings set on lawns of rough grass and clover, as described by visitors to the court of Timur in Samarkand in 1403. Timur declared himself heir to

Far pavilions
This Mughal-style illustration from an Islamic book published in 1560 shows a scene in a walled garden, with a ruler on a raised dais greeting delegates. Palms and cypresses grow in the outer landscape.

TIMUR'S COURT IN SAMARKAND

Ruy González de Clavijo was one of the first Western observers to visit Timur (better known in the West as Tamerlane) at Samarkand. He had been sent, in 1404, as ambassador by Henry III of Castile and Leon. After long months of travel the Spanish party reached Kash, beyond which the fertile plains stretching to Samarkand yielded yearly crops of corn, cotton, grapevines and melons. Clavijo noticed that "so numerous are the gardens and vineyards surrounding Samarkand that a traveller who approaches…sees only a mountainous height of trees, and the houses embowered among them remain invisible". In one garden, the House of Flowers, Ibn Arabshah, writing in 1436, describes "a carpet of emerald, on which are sprinkled diverse gems of hyacinth", where tents and awnings were erected for festivals.

By the end of August the party finally reached Samarkand, where they were received in the orchard enclosure Timur had created for receptions and festivities. "We found it to be enclosed by a high wall which in its circuit may measure a full league, and within it full of fruit trees of all kinds, save only limes and citron trees which we noticed to be lacking…Further there are six large tanks for a great stream of water flows from one end of the orchard to the other. Five rows of very tall and shady trees have been planted beside the paved avenues which connects the pools and smaller paths lead out of these avenues to add variety to the design."

At the next garden enclosure, known as Dilkusha (or Heartsease), Clavijo found Timur in his palace. The emperor, now 70 and nearly blind (he died the following February), was drinking wine from a golden cup and reclining on silken cushions on a raised dais, attended by a daughter-in-law and handmaidens. In front of him a fountain sprayed jets of water into a basin on which floated red apples. Clavijo notes various diversions at the feasts, including demonstrations by weavers, parades of elephants and horses, and numerous hangings of criminals on specially built gallows. Timur subsequently entertained Clavijo in two other gardens, the Plane Tree Garden and one entered by a majestic gateway ornamented with tiles in blue and gold. A hundred years later the gardens were still there and visited as a young man by the Mughal Emperor Babur (a descendant of Timur). They are thought to have inspired Babur's love of gardens (see pages 82–83), and it is his descriptions that have helped fill in some of the details for us today.

Clavijo, although from Castile in Christian Spain, may have seen the Moorish gardens, the Generalife and Alhambra, which would have just been reaching their peak. He might also have read the texts of Arab botanists Ibn Wafid and Ibn Bassal from Toledo, translated into Castilian under Alfonso X. He would have been familiar enough with the idea of bubbling fountains and canals as features but might have been surprised to see the vast lawns planted with grass and clovers and wild flowers. They suggest the kind of flowery mead more commonly associated with the gardens of medieval northern Europe.

The mighty Timur
An imaginary picture shows Timur seated on a central dais. On either side are the Mughal Emperor Babur (whose mother was descended from Timur) and Babur's son Humayun. The picture was painted c.1630 during Emperor Jahangir's reign. It stresses the importance of the Turko-Mongol ancestry, which establishes the Mughal emperors' right to rule.

Genghis Khan, seizing power in Samarkand in 1369. He eventually extended his empire to include the whole of Iran, some of India and part of Russia, with cities such as Tabriz, Baghdad, Damascus, Aleppo and Delhi under his control, destroying the old trade routes of the Iranian plateau on which prosperity had depended.

GARDENS OF THE PERSIAN MINIATURES

Timur's descendants were to become the most cultivated rulers in central Asia and India. His son Shah Rukh moved the capital to Herat in Afghanistan, where he created a garden with pools, red tulips and roses, covering 40 hectares (99 acres). This, like the gardens of Samarkand, was to inspire the Emperor Babur, who used its design as a prototype for his own gardens around Kabul and in northern India.

Shah Rukh's glittering court became a centre for 15th-century science and artistic achievement. Delicate miniatures illustrated the manuscripts of epic poems, with scenes often set in imaginary gardens before the 13th-century Mongol invasion – tales such as Firdausi's *Shah-nameh* (*Book of Kings*) and Nizami's 12th-century poems about the love of Khosrow for the Christian Princess Shirin. The tales are full of the imagery of gardens – flowers and birds, roses and nightingales, and shade trees providing refuge from the blazing sun. These poetic concepts of the earthly garden derive directly from the garden paradises described in the Koran, often linked with the idea of spring and the happiness it brings. "O gardener, the smell of spring comes to me from the garden. Give me the key to the garden, for tomorrow I will need it. At night the flowers in the garden are like a gardener's lantern…and now each lover takes wine in hand and strolls toward the garden with a seductive beauty," wrote Farrukhi in *Divan*. In the *Shah-nameh* rhyming couplets recount legends of Persian dynasties and set scenes of courtship in gardens: Zal visits Rudab "whose cheeks are like pomegranate blossom, she hath cherry lips, her silver breasts bear two pomegranate seeds, her eyes are twin narcissi in a garden".

With the artists often drawing from nature, working in the shade of pavilions or under cool awnings, the miniatures provide a source of practical information about contemporary garden layout, the watercourses, pavilions, flowerbeds and planting. Later Persian miniaturists (some of whom fled to the Mughal court after religious persecution) portrayed scenes from the gardens of northern India. Courtly owners recline on cushions while gardeners work against a backdrop of almond blossom, emblem of spring and renewal, or statuesque cypresses, symbols of mortality, plane trees and poplars. Flowers such as the rose, day-lily, poppy, hollyhock and peony were favourites in poetry and in painting and native

Lovers' tryst
In the *Shah-nameh* (*Book of Kings*), an epic describing the myths, legends and history of Persia's pre-Islamic past, Zal was abandoned by his father at birth and brought up by the mythical bird Simurgh. Here, in a 16th-century manuscript, Zal climbs a balcony to his lover Rudab, in a walled garden dominated by a magnificent vine.

END OF EMPIRE

Scant evidence remains of the dozens of royal gardens made in the valley of Herat. In 1933 Robert Byron visited the one built by the last Timurid ruler, and wrote in *The Road to Oxiana*: "On the way home the landau stopped at Takht-e Safir, the Traveller's throne, a terraced garden all in ruins whose natural melancholy was increased by…the first whistle of the night wind. From the empty tank at the top, a line of pools and watercourses descends from terrace to terrace. This pleasance of Hussein Baikara was built by forced labour; for when his subjects over-stepped even his broad limits of the morally permissible, they had to help with the Sultan's garden instead of going to prison."

bulbous plants such as iris, hyacinth, tulip, narcissus, anemone and lily were frequently portrayed. After Timur's death in 1405 Mongol power declined and disintegrated. In the western part of the empire, Persia, which had long been in a state of flux, was reunited under the Safavids, who gradually consolidated its borders. By the early 1500s, Babur, one of Timur's descendants, began to build his own Mughal empire in northern India.

THE GLORIES OF PERSIA

From 1500 a new dynasty was establishing itself in Persia – the Safavids. They made the Shi'a branch of Islam Persia's official religion and, under the great Shah 'Abbas I (1587–1629), extended and made secure the country's borders. 'Abbas I undertook vast public and private building programmes, renewing contact with the outside world, and welcoming foreign emissaries and traders, many of whom told of the magnificence of the new capital, Isfahan. On a plateau, 1,590m (5,300ft) high and ringed by mountains, the city became world famous as a centre of culture and commerce.

In 1626 Thomas Herbert accompanied Charles I's British ambassador, Sir Dodmore Cotton, to Persia to wait on Shah 'Abbas. Summoned by the shah to join him on the shores of the Caspian Sea, Herbert travelled north across Persia but on the way was able to appreciate the new city of Isfahan: "Gardens here for grandeur and fragour are such as no City in Asia outvies: which at a little distance from the City you would judge a Forest, it is so large, but withall so sweet and verdant that you may call it another Paradise; and Agreeable to the old report, *Horti Persarum erant amoenissimi* [the gardens of the Persians were most delightful]."

Shah 'Abbas had made the ancient city beautiful with the glittering domes of mosques, lined with tiles of floral arabesques and calligraphy, towering over wide shaded avenues. Spacious terraced gardens were watered by an extensive irrigation system with stone-lined canals. The central water channel of the main Chahar Bagh avenue, faced with onyx, was intersected by secondary rills and flanked with eight rows of stately plane trees and tall poplars shading beds of poppies and roses. Six canals, called *maddi*, remain, one running through the courtyard of the 17th-century Madraseh-e Shah. Herbert speaks of the Hazar Jarib gardens having terraces leading up to a 12-sided reservoir with fountains. He also describes a garden at Tajabad where, with water ensured by a clear stream fed from a *qanat*, "Damask roses and other flowers, plentie of broad spreading Chenar trees (which is like our beech), with Pomegranats, Peaches, Apricokes, Plummes, Apples, Peares, Chesnuts and Cherries" were a paradise of plenty after the desert, "rich in nothing but Salt and Sand".

In a poem written in honour of Shah 'Abbas's garden of Sa'adatabad at Qazvin, in northeast Iran, the poet Ramzi praised the fragrant narcissi, violets, hyacinths, sweet sultan (*Centaurea moschata*), poppies, anemones, larkspurs, irises, tulips, white and gold lilies, damask and musk roses with red and yellow petals, white jasmine, sweet basil, marigolds, and hollyhocks. Marvels of Peru (*Mirabilis jalapa*) and tuberoses (*Polianthes tuberosa*) had been brought from Europe, where

they had been newly introduced from the New World. The garden, divided geometrically, was built to precise plans, including a square with covered pavilions, other buildings and pools.

In the north of the country, Shah 'Abbas enjoyed the entirely different, subtropical climate around the Caspian Sea, where the annual rainfall of 100–150cm (40–60in) is some five times the average for the country. The pleasure gardens at one of his summer palaces there were terraced with luminous water chutes. Sir John Chardin, the Anglo-French jeweller and traveller, visited the area in the 1670s and found himself enchanted: "the whole country is nothing but one continued Garden or a perfect kind of Paradise as the Persians call it," with causeways and highways flanked with "many Alleys of Orange-Trees, bordered on either side with fine Parterrees and flowery Gardens". Today, sadly, much of the southern Caspian shore has lost its romance, with rice fields, tea plantations and ribbon development.

Two pavilions in Isfahan survive: the Chehel Sutun (Forty Pillars), built in 1647 by 'Abbas II, and the Hasht Behesht (Eight Paradises), built during the reign of Süleyman I in 1669, in 'Abbas I's Garden of the Nightingales. The Chehel Sutun's name comes from its 20 supporting wooden pillars which, when seen reflected in the large rectangular pool, double to 40. The Westphalian physician and botanist Engelbert Kaempfer came to Persia in 1685, one of the countries he visited on his way to Batavia and Japan (see page 370). He spent over a year waiting for permits, but used his time profitably to make measured drawings and a map of

The gardens of Isfahan
This late 17th-century engraving is taken from the *Voyages du Chevalier Chardin en Perse, et autres Lieux de L'Orient* by Sir John Chardin (1643-1713). Published in 1811, it shows the Hezar Jarib at the far end of the Chahar Bagh avenue in Isfahan, across the river. One of Shah 'Abbas's gardens, it had 12 terraces and a view of the city to the north. At the top of the slope, the palace of Jahan-Nameh (Garden that Displays the World) is visible. Today, a main road to Shiraz and the university occupy the site. In the foreground is an even larger garden, the Farahabad (Abode of Joy), which was made in 1700 by Shah Soltan Hosayn and included pools with islands on which were built summerhouses.

Reflections in the water
The palace of Chehel Sutun, or
Forty Columns (left), was named for
the reflection in the canal in front of
the 20 wooden cedar columns
which support the porch or *talar*.
Still one of the great sites of Isfahan,
the palace was built in 1647 as a
pavilion for the Safavid emperors to
stage their entertainments.
Originally part of the complex of
royal gardens behind the royal palace
in the maidan (the central piazza),
today it houses a collection of
paintings and faded frescoes,
illustrating the Safavid period of
power. Plane trees and elms shade
alleys at right angles to the pool
(inset, below) and evoke some of the
spirit of that earlier age when the
Persian garden had escaped the
narrow confines of the walled *chahar
bagh* to celebrate wider horizons and
become a site for lavish festivals.

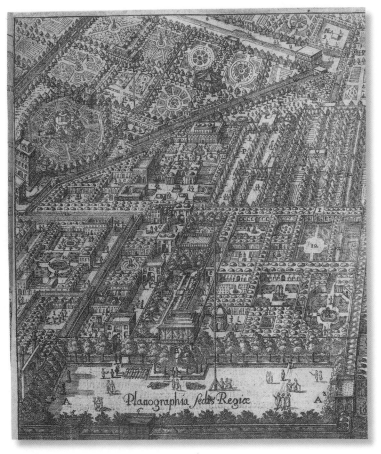

Kaempfer's map
This plan of Isfahan appeared in the *Amoenitates Exoticae* (1712) by Engelbert Kaempfer, the German botanist and physician who visited Isfahan in 1685. It shows the maidan (the central piazza in the foreground) and palace of Ali Qapur with the stables and royal gardens stretching behind, including the Chehel Sutun. The Chahar Bagh avenue is at a diagonal angle in the background. Few of the numerous gardens and pavilions built during the 17th century still survive.

Isfahan. His engraving was published in *Amoenitates Exoticae* in 1712. He described the garden of Hasht Behesht as having a pavilion located in the middle of a courtyard covered with square pavers and a waterway running around it. Two north–south avenues planted with plane trees led to the pavilion, while water ran in east–west channels to a basin filled with swans and ducks.

One of the few gardens remaining almost untouched from the time of Shah 'Abbas I – and one of the most beautiful of all Persian gardens – is that of the Bagh-e Fin at Kashan, on the edge of the great salt desert south of Tehran. It is one of the oldest and most important Safavid gardens to survive in Iran, although it has been altered at various times since the 17th century and was restored in 1935. Approached by a wide avenue and contained by a high wall pierced with a monumental gateway, the garden covers more than 2 hectares (6 acres). A spring (the Fin) and a *qanat* from the mountains feed the reservoir that provides the water, whose force is entirely dependent on gravity. It is skilfully maintained under pressure to keep it flowing and working the bubbling jets. In the centre, a 19th-century Qajar-period pavilion, built on the foundations of a Safavid pavilion, covers a square pool. The resin scent of the garden's 400-year-old cypresses waft a fragrance of antiquity.

VOICES OF DISSENSION AND UNDERSTANDING

Not every traveller appreciated the Persian way of gardening. Some found themselves quite baffled by the notion that the greatest pleasure is to be found from sitting in, not walking around, a garden. Sir John Chardin, fulsome in his praise for the Caspian region, travelled in Persia during the 1660s and 1670s, and was an informed critic. "I have found it to be a general rule that where nature is most easy and fruitful, they [the Persians] are very raw and unskilful in the art of gardening…The most particular reason one can assign to this is that the Persians don't walk so much in their Gardens as we do but content themselves with a bare prospect; and breathing the fresh Air: For this End, they set themselves down in some part of the Garden…and never move their Seats until they are going out of it." Flowers were to be enjoyed largely in spring, when they were plentiful; in summer there were disappointingly few to be seen. Some plants took his fancy. One rose bush, he says, "bore upon one and the same branch, Roses of three colours, some Yellow, others Yellow and White, and others Yellow and Red". Elsewhere he speaks of the tulip, already a much prized flower: "When a young man presents a tulip to his mistress he gives her to understand by the general colour of the flower, that he is on fire with her beauty, and by the black base, that his heart is burned to coal." Chardin finally retired to England, where, having become a friend of John Evelyn, he died in 1703.

Perhaps Vita Sackville-West, travelling in Persia in the 1920s, best sums up a Westerner's view of the Persian garden. "Ever since I have been in Persia I have been looking for a garden and have not yet found one. Yet Persian gardens enjoy a great reputation. Hafez and Sa'di sang frequently, even wearisomely, of roses. Yet there is no word for rose in the Persian language; the best they can manage is 'red flower'…'Garden' we say and think of lawns and herbaceous borders, which is manifestly absurd. There is no turf in this parched country; and as for herbaceous borders, they postulate a lush shapeliness unimaginable to the Persian mind. Here, everything is dry and untidy, crumbling and decayed; a dusty poverty, exposed for eight months of the year to a cruel sun. For all that there are gardens in Persia. But they are gardens

The living past
In the walled garden of Bagh-e Fin, outside Kashan, the main water rill, with turquoise tiles, is shaded by 400-year-old cypresses. Developed by Shah 'Abbas I in the 17th century, this is the oldest living garden in Iran. With water brought by a *qanat* to supplement a spring, the bubbling fountains in the garden operate by gravity.

of trees, not of flowers: green wildernesses. Imagine that you have ridden in summer four days across a plain; that you have then come to a barrier of snow-mountains and ridden up the pass; from the top of the pass you have seen a second plain, with a second barrier of mountains in the distance, a hundred miles away…and that for days, even weeks, you must ride with no shade, and the sun overhead, and nothing but the bleached bones of dead animals strewing the track. Then when you come to trees and running water, you will call it a garden. It will not be flowers and their garishness that your eyes crave for, but a green cavern full of shadows, and pools where goldfish dart, and the sound of little streams. That is the meaning of a garden in Persia, a country where the long slow caravan is an everyday fact, and not a romantic name." Later she calls the garden a place of spiritual reprieve, as well as a place of shadows. "As a breeze at evening after a hot day, as a well in the desert, so is the garden to the Persian."

THE MUGHAL GARDENS OF INDIA

When Babur turned towards India to extend the bounds of his empire he took the Islamic-style garden with him and it was he and his successors, the great Mughal emperors, who dominated India for two centuries, who made the most spectacular gardens of all. In very different locations, on the inhospitable plains around Delhi and Agra, and magically on the shores of Lake Dal in Kashmir, where cedars clothed the mountain slopes and willows and poplars fringed the water, they created gardens encapsulating the idea of paradise.

The seclusion of gardens
Palace life in the *zenana* or women's quarters, Kangra, northern India, painted *c.*1790 (above). Although often highly influential, women only emerged heavily veiled and could only be visited by close relations, their whole life revolving around the paradise pleasure gardens where they were free to roam and picnic.

Family portrait (opposite)
In an 18th-century gouache, after an earlier 17th-century miniature, the Empress Nur Jahan is seen entertaining her husband, the Emperor Jahangir (descendant of Babur), and his son, the future Shah Jahan, in a garden in front of a pavilion. Nur Jahan, from Persia, had her own garden in Kashmir and introduced the manufacture of attar of roses to the Indian Mughals.

BABUR, THE EMPEROR-GARDENER

THE CULTURED EMPEROR BABUR – poet, musician and lover of plants and the natural world, and founder of the Mughal dynasty in India – managed to combine his conquests with prolific garden-making. Born in 1483, he visited Samarkand and Herat as a young man, and never forgot the gardens he saw, particularly one called the White Garden, with its "sweet little abode" built in two storeys. His memoirs reveal his joy in nature. He wrote of the beauties of wooded slopes and of fruit growing in the meadows that lay near the crest of the Hindu Kush. Babur loved to find flowers in the wild and twice recorded making a collection of tulips. Of Kabul itself, where Babur made his early gardens, he wrote in the *Babur-nameh*, his manuscript memoir: "If the world has another [place] so pleasant, it is not known."

His favourite garden near Kabul was the Bagh-e Vafa (Garden of Fidelity). An entry in his diary during October 1519 reflects on its autumnal beauty: "Those were the days of the garden's beauty: its lawns were one sheet of trefoil: its pomegranate trees yellowed to autumn splendour." He noticed as well "a few purslane [poplar] trees in the utmost beauty" and by November found one young apple tree so beautiful that "it was such that no painter trying to depict it could have equalled it". He planted pomegranates, oranges and citrons in the garden and later added plantain bananas, other fruit trees and sugar cane. The garden was laid out on rising ground with, in the middle, a mill stream that "flows constantly past the little hill on which are four garden plots". A Mughal artist illustrated the Bagh-e Vafa, *c.*1595, for the *Babur-nameh*. The painting shows a fourfold garden of intersecting streams, within an imposing entrance portal, the four plots being prepared for planting by his gardeners. Kabul's climate was excellent for gardening, with hot days followed by cool nights.

Today, in another of Babur's gardens called Nimla, 40km (25 miles) from Jalalabad, slim cypresses and ancient plane trees line the dry water channels and orange trees still thrive in

BABUR READING, A WATERCOLOUR BY
BISHN DAS, *c.*1615

the garden plots. In 1505 Babur described how he brought cuttings of sour cherry and plane trees to a garden already planted with willows, setting them above a large circular seat.

Babur continued his garden-making when he led his troops into northern India although he complained bitterly about the flat, parched terrain and lack of running water. At Agra, in spite of finding the prospect of the plains "so bad and unattractive we traversed them with a hundred disgusts and repulsions", he constructed a palace, the Ram Bagh, which was later completed by his son Humayun. Waterwheels were needed to raise water from the River Jumma. The Ram Bagh can still be seen today.

Characteristically, Babur managed to find time for his collecting, despite his other activities. He ordered that the new plants he discovered in India – mangoes, bananas, banyan trees, red oleanders, oranges and lemons – be sent home to Kabul, while arranging the import of his old familiar favourites to enhance his new Indian gardens.

A plantsman's priorities

Babur's favourite garden – the Bagh-e Vafa (Garden of Fidelity) – in Afghanistan was a typical walled chahar bagh *with watercourses meeting to empty into a pool. Babur describes finding wild tulips in the mountains and the glories of his garden in autumn, when all had turned to gold. Here, he is seen directing his gardeners and his garden architect, complete with a plan on a grid system, while envoys at the gate await an audience.*

These Mughal gardens were geometric, with a central water channel crossed at right angles by smaller channels, each containing flowerbeds. The earliest were in the plains of Hindustan where Babur reigned (until his death in 1530), followed by his descendants, Humayun, Akbar, Jahangir, Shah Jahan and Aurangzeb. Babur disliked the flat landscape and its lack of water, but nevertheless started building a palace and garden at Agra (whose completion fell to his son Humayun), and made notes about the new flora he found in India. Humayun (1508–56) was keen to expand other arts such as painting and poetry but left further garden development to his son Akbar (1542–1605), who consolidated the Mughal empire, demonstrating his assimilation of Hindu culture by marrying two Rajput princesses (one the mother of Jahangir).

Akbar built the Red Fort at Agra, its design inspired by the almost legendary Medina Azahara at Cordoba, before moving his capital to Fatehpur Sikri and laying out another complex of palaces and gardens, importing quantities of trees and flowers with which to decorate it. When he visited Kashmir, in 1586, Akbar had river palaces and floating gardens prepared in his honour. He was entranced by the scenery of shimmering Lake Dal and treated Kashmir as his private garden, enjoying watching the harvesting of the saffron and rice crops and walnuts in the orchards, and the quiet reflection of poplar trees in the water. To reach the vale of Kashmir, the emperor had to negotiate narrow mountain passes. This made the fertile valley, once attained, seem even nearer to heaven. On the lake carved wooden houseboats floated among green islands of vegetation and pink lotus flowers. The first garden palace he built was that of Nasim Bagh.

Jahangir (1569–1627) inherited Akbar's love of Kashmir and with his own son, Shah Jahan, built the finest of the Kashmir gardens, the Shalimar Bagh. In Jahangir's time there were no less than 700 gardens around Srinagar on Lake Dal, all with water as their dominant theme. Built on a vast scale, the wide, gently flowing canals, fountains, waterfalls, cascades and chutes, with small palaces and pavilions, were dwarfed only by the surrounding tree-clad mountains. At Nasim Bagh a few of the giant plane trees survive out of the original 1,000 that were planted by Akbar on the lake shore, and an avenue

The incomparable Taj

The Taj Mahal, Shah Jahan's mausoleum for his wife Mumtaz Mahal, was built between 1632 and 1654. Flanked by symmetrical buildings, it rises on a high terrace at the end of the garden above the River Yamuna, its image perfectly reflected in the central canal. Originally the garden extended beyond the river to the Moonlight Garden and an octagon pool – now being restored – which reflected the white marble mausoleum on the south bank. The mausoleum, instead of being in the centre of the garden, as in a traditional *chahar bagh*, was placed to receive cool river breezes and be visible from boats on the river and from the opposite shore. On the building, besides verses of the Koran, there are raised marble reliefs and inlays of semi-precious stones – the famous *pietre dure* which may have been inspired by Florentine work – portraying the flowers loved by the emperor and his family.

Moving water

Beads of brightness and light (above)
Water falls as a crystalline curtain over the Fountain of the Oval at the Villa d'Este in Tivoli. An aqueduct and a diverted river fed the astonishing water displays of this Renaissance villa, where the water-powered "special effects" once included bird song and dragon noises.

Clarity of purpose (below)
The concept, form and fabric of William Pye's contemporary sculptures – including this Triangular Fountain at Antony House in Cornwall – are inspired by the sights and sounds, and geometry, of moving water in natural landscapes.

No Islamic garden worthy of the name was without the sensory joys of pure water. The paradisiacal element reposed in lotus-filled canals and flowed along rills. It coursed through the marble chutes called *chadars* (from a word for a shawl or sheet), and rose in bubbles and sprays from jets and fountains. But whereas, in the gardens of Islam, the art and science of moving water was focused on the element itself, the water that emerged in sheets, swathes and sprays in the grand gardens of 16th- and 17th-century Europe was all about show.

Water rather than plants flowered in the gardens of Renaissance Italy's princes and prelates, where lavishly ornamented fountains acted as "stations" along river-like trails leading to a final, stupendous spectacle. At the Villa Lante, the Fountain of Rivers – personified by massive statues of the Tiber and the Arno – were linked by a "chain" of water (see page 131) to the primal Fountain of the Deluge. The *fontanieri*, the engineers who designed these waterworks, saw themselves not so much as inventors as rediscoverers of the hydraulic technology of the ancient Mediterranean world, but there was much that was innovative about their expertise. At Castello in Florence water-powered organs were concealed beneath statues of primordial beasts, and their "music" was as strange as it was diverting. Elsewhere, pools were animated by automata that appeared to move or make music, and unwary guests were surprised, and sometimes drenched, by ingenious hidden mechanisms (*giochi d'acqua*). There was little room for these unashamedly artificial spectacles in the private landscape gardens of the 18th century. But the public spaces of cities and towns all over the world continue to be graced by fountains and jets descended from wonders performed by the water wizards of the Renaissance.

Spectacle for the Sun King (left)
For sheer variety and extravagance there was nothing to beat the Great Fountains of Versailles, which needed 5,000 cubic metres (1,100,000 gallons) of water to be pumped up from the Seine each day and were "programmed" to come on just before Louis XIV arrived on a garden tour.

An emperor's last garden (below)
Babur, the first Mughal emperor, was an enthusiastic gardener and lover of the natural world as well as a leader of men. In this 19th-century painting of Bagh-i-Babur Shah – the garden around his tomb in Kabul – sparkling water cascades down a stone avenue or *chadar*.

Refreshment and leisure (below)
The Ira Keller Fountain, a full square block of flowing streams and pools, provides the citizens of Portland, Oregon, with a secluded and refreshing resting place. It is designed to be the "experiential equivalent" of the cataracts in the nearby mountains.

Romantic cascade (below)
Tumbling water provides the drama in this 18th-century view of Hestercombe, a recently rediscovered English landscape garden in Somerset. It was created in the 1750s, when natural water features, as opposed to gravity-defying ornamental waterworks, were fashionable.

The OPIUM POPPY

A native flower of the Mediterranean and the Middle East, *Papaver somniferum*, or the opium poppy, probably came to northern Europe with the Romans. Well known in the Arab world, it spread eastwards into Mughal India, where the emperors used it to concoct a drink which gradually drove their rivals insane. Frequently grown in Muslim gardens, flourishing in the sunken beds under fruit trees, the opium poppy is also portrayed in the raised marble carvings on the outside of the Taj Mahal. In spite of all efforts to ban its cultivation, it is still grown commercially in Afghanistan and elsewhere, its juice being used to produce heroin, the mainstay of the drug trade.

PAPAVER SOMNIFERUM

A self-seeding annual, over centuries it has been bred with sumptuous double peony flowers – whose seeds, according to Parkinson, originated in Constantinople – with whitish-pink to almost black petals. From classical times this attractive poppy was spoken of as the flower of sleep and oblivion, and described in herbals for its medicinal qualities. The seeds, mixed with wine and honey, were given to athletes preparing for the Olympic Games, and are still used for flavouring. According to classical mythology, *Papaver somniferum* was created by Somnus, the God of Sleep, to ease Ceres in her care of the corn crops. Its generic name comes from the Latin *pappa*, meaning milky juice, and its specific name, *somniferum*, from its sleep-inducing qualities. It was one of the 500 plants described in Dioscorides's *De Materia Medica*, written in the 1st century AD and translated into Arabic in Baghdad in the 9th century by a Nestorian Christian, banished from Europe for heretical views.

of silvery poplars reinforces the straight lines of canals at the Shalimar gardens.

Shah Jahan was also a great builder of gardens and palaces. Under his patronage painters were encouraged to make life-like representations of flowers, birds and animals. Although there are few portrayals of actual gardens there are many exquisite Persian and Mughal miniatures showing the quadripartite concept as well as portraying colourful flowers and fruit trees. Painters did not show the world as it is, but aspired to show it as it should be – a harmoniously ordered sublime paradise. The most ordinary garden scene is transformed into a luxuriant oasis of exquisite beauty.

The Taj Mahal at Agra is Shah Jahan's masterpiece. Built from 1632 to 1654 in white marble as a mausoleum for his wife Mumtaz Mahal, it is a symbol of his great love as well of paradise. Richly adorned with verses from the Koran, it is a sacred Muslim site. Perhaps its most significant garden feature is the reflecting canal that mirrors the Taj's famous dome. The garden is quartered with a raised marble platform at the central junction of the great canal with its smaller lateral branches.

The Flower-loving Ottomans

When the Frenchman Pierre Belon (1517–64), an observer and collector, explored the Levant between 1546 and 1549 to identify Dioscorides's plants (see pages 40–41) and collect those suitable for acclimatization in France, he expressed admiration for the gardens he saw and the Turks' appreciation of flowers: "There are no people who delight more to ornament themselves with beautiful flowers, nor who praise them more, than the Turks. They think little of their smell but delight most in their appearance. They wear several sorts singly in the folds of their turban; and the artisans have often several flowers before them, in vessels of water. Hence gardening is in as great repute with them as with us; and they grudge no expense in procuring foreign trees and plants, especially such as have fine flowers." Belon also noted the Turkish addiction to floral themes in miniatures, poetry, embroidery and ceramics.

The Turkish Ottomans, originally nomads from central Asia, were absorbed into Islam from the 10th century onwards. As they moved westwards (taking nearly three centuries and following in the wake of other Turkish invaders), they came into contact with the tradition of the Persian pleasure parks and gardens before encountering the culture of the Byzantine world. After capturing Constantinople (modern Istanbul) in 1453, they established an empire that grew within two centuries to dominate an area from the Crimea to Asia Minor, Egypt, Greece, the Balkans and Hungary, reaching the gates of Vienna for the second time as late as 1686. Their civilization was to survive for six centuries, its cultural heritage drawn from the East and from Greek, Hellenistic and Roman sources. Reflecting this inheritance, Ottoman gardens represent a fusion of Eastern and classical art, with a strong emphasis on the love of flowers and the open air.

Until the spread of Islam in the 7th and 8th centuries, the Byzantine world had remained largely Roman in spirit, but from then on manners and lifestyles of the Eastern world were frequently adopted. In the garden, however, only the rudiments of Eastern design were incorporated. This usually meant a walled enclosure containing water features and probably a pavilion – called a kiosk by the Turks – rather than the true fourfold garden. Fountains and pools were installed in city and village streets as well as in gardens. Many gardens were laid out around palaces and mosques in Bursa and then in Adrianople (modern Edirne). Water was not a scarcity as in the desert and the Turks were natural gardeners, "taming" the wild species that bloomed on the mountain slopes and in the valleys. They loved flowers so much that they even took potted plants on their campaigns, and at the second siege of Vienna in 1686 Kara Mustafa Pasha planted a garden in front of his tent for the duration. This and a love of being outside has remained a Turkish characteristic.

A BURGEONING BULB TRADE WITH THE WEST

The wild flowers of the eastern Mediterranean and Persia drew the attention of several Western plant enthusiasts and collectors. Pierre Belon noticed that many were already cultivated as garden plants and, in his *Les Observations de Plusieurs Singularitez et Choses Mémorables* (1553), noted that Constantinople's merchants had already built up a considerable export trade in bulbs. He was the first to describe cherry laurel (*Prunus laurocerasus*) and recorded seeing the lyre-shaped tulips, which he called "lis rouges", that were later gathered by Ogier Ghiselin de Busbecq and sent to the botanist Clusius in Vienna (see page 178). In 1573 the German physician Leonhardt Rauwolf visited the area in search of plants and noted the Turks' delight in flowers of all sorts, and their habit of wearing them in their turbans. He took 800 different plants back to Europe, among them wild rhubarb and a "pretty sort of tulip" with yellow stripes. Some of these are still preserved in the herbarium at Leiden, in the Netherlands.

The political and trading contacts established between the West and the Ottoman sultans, just 20 years after the Turks had besieged Vienna for the first time in 1529, made possible an astonishing influx of strange new plants into European gardens in the second half of the 16th century. The arrival of this exotic

Floral tiles

These two earthenware tiles date to *c.*1483 (below) and *c.*1520–50 (bottom). Glazed tiles originating in Turkey and Syria in the 15th century under the Ottoman sultans often portrayed flowers such as tulips, poppies and peonies, with decoration in dark blue, black, purple and green. By the time of Mehmed II, between 1469 and 1473, the *cini-i-iznik* pottery had a distinct Chinese look. It was the forerunner of the great Iznik wares of the 16th century.

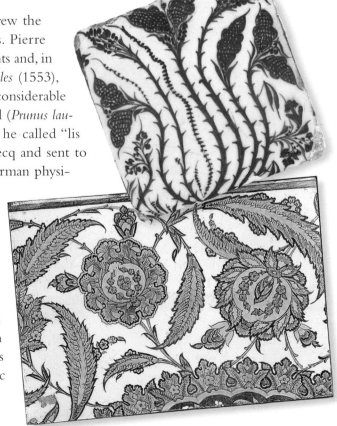

Sultan's delight
After his conquest of Christian Constantinople in 1453, Mehmed II moved his capital there from Bursa. The sultan built "large and lovely" pleasure gardens throughout the city and around his palace, the Topkapi Saray, where he housed his harem in pavilions. There was abundant water and a tradition of fruit and flower gardening inherited from both Persia and Samarkand.

THE WRONG NAME

The tulip, it seems, should never have been called the tulip. Legend has it that ambassador de Busbecq was astonished by the fields of hyacinths, narcissi and tulips he saw blooming in winter on the road from Adrianople. Searching for a name, he pointed enquiringly to a single tulip in a man's turban. "*Tulipand*" replied the man, giving the Turkish word for turban. De Busbecq applied the name to the flower and tulips have been tulips ever since, though in Turkish they are called *lâle*.

flora gave an impetus to the study of scientific plants in Europe and the development of botany. Among the imported horticultural wonders were a plethora of bulbs, including tulips, crown imperials, irises, hyacinths, anemones, turban ranunculi, narcissi and lilies, many of them the product of a high degree of garden sophistication. Stories of the tulip's introduction to Europe are numerous, with most believing that the ambassador from the imperial court of Ferdinand I, the cultured de Busbecq, whose tour of duty began in 1554, should have the credit. By the 1630s commercial speculation in tulip bulbs led to the famous Dutch "tulipomania", in which huge sums of money were staked against the breeding of new cultivars, and fortunes made and then lost when the market crashed in 1637.

ROYAL DECREES AND POPULAR DELIGHTS

After the conquest of Constantinople in 1453 by Mehmed II, there was an explosion of creativity, using ideas taken from both Persian and Western cultures. A series of palace gardens was created in Constantinople, Adrianople, Bursa, Amasya and Manisa, filled with fragrance and colour. Large trees provided shade, there were gazelles and sauntering peacocks and the air was sweetened by the sound of songbirds. In Constantinople Mehmed made pleasure gardens around the newly built Topkapi Saray, his palace on one of Constantinople's seven hills. They contained a series of enclosures with flowerbeds and trees of all kinds, the whole area surrounded by a high wall. A rose garden or *gülhane* was added later on the eastern slopes facing the Sea of Marmara.

The Turks maintained the Eastern tradition of outside living. Great public gardens were laid out by the seashore and along riverbanks which were used by the people for picnicking, a national pastime. Beautiful floral rugs would be laid out on the ground for lounging and feasting. Similarly fruit gardens could be visited and the produce picked for a small admittance fee. Plums, cherries, raspberries, blackberries and figs were all available when ripe. Mehmed's vizier insisted that gardens and fruit should be provided for "the delectation and happiness and use of many". Houses nearly always had small interior courtyards where gardening on a small scale could be carried out. The urban aspect of Constantinople was of a "green" town with luxuriant trees shading walled courtyards.

Early records tell of large-scale cultivation of bulbs and roses in the last quarter of the 16th century in the gardens of Adrianople and Constantinople. In May 1593 Murad III ordered 50,000 white and 50,000 blue hyacinths from the administrator in Maras in southern Anatolia to be dug from the mountains and highlands. "Dispatch youths who are knowledgeable in flowers into the region…to gather the above amount of hyacinth bulbs with all haste. Once obtained, hand them to ones dispatched under my orders and bring the bulbs to the castle gate of the town…those who wrought bulbs can demand payment according to the numbers brought. Strive to make efforts and be careful. Avoid sloth or carelessness." These statistics, from the historian Ahmet Refik's records (published in the 1930s), detailing the enormous numbers of bulbs collected at the time, must have a bearing on the rarity or extinction in the wild of certain parent species.

In September of the same year rose trees for the gardens at Adrianople were ordered by weight: 400 *kantar* of red roses and 300 of white, making a total of nearly 40 tonnes of rose bushes. Roses, also grown for making perfumed rose-water and for flavouring cool drinks, were almost as popular as bulbs, and were also considered sacred. A Guild of Gardeners looked after all the imperial gardens,

A ROYAL PASSION FOR TULIPS

IN THE EARLY 18TH CENTURY, under Ahmed III (1703–30), Turkey developed its own particular form of tulip enthusiasm. Ahmed's sultanate was famous as the *Lâle Devri* or Tulip Period. The new shapes of many of the tulips bred in Europe aroused tremendous interest in Constantinople. Ahmed's extravagant tulip parties, illuminated by tortoises wandering among the flowerbeds with lighted candles on their backs, helped lead to his downfall, brought about largely by his overspending. The grand vizier, his son-in-law, organized nightly entertainments in the flowering season, with tulips mounted on towers and pyramids with lanterns and songbirds in cages. Guests were required to dress in clothes to match the tulips.

Before the 11th century only one tulip was known in Constantinople, the *Sahra-e Lâle*, but wild tulips, in a variety of shapes and colours, were constantly collected from eastern and central Asia and brought into garden cultivation, giving rise to new forms. Different tulip shapes were

FROM *THE BOOK OF TULIPS*, 1725

prized in different eras. In the 15th and 16th centuries, collectors favoured elegant waisted blooms, while by Ahmed III's time the preferred flowers were elongated and slender, with thin pointed petals.

The tulips available in Turkey in the 16th century were painted in a mural on the walls of a Tulip Kiosk, overlooking the Bosphorus, and

specialist florists competed to produce the required favourites. Selim II ordered 50,000 bulbs to be sent to Syria for the imperial gardens, presumably species gathered *en masse* from the wild. The historian Hodja Hasan Efendi, accompanying Murad IV (1612–40) on his expedition to the East, brought back seven distinctive kinds of tulip from Persia to raise in his own garden in Constantinople. Mehmed IV, sultan from 1648 to 1688, established an official tulip list with a description of each flower and the name of the grower who had bred it. He also set up a council with its own research laboratory where new cultivars could be assessed. The home-grown tulips that filled Ahmed III's royal gardens and palaces were reared in the Sipylus mountains above Manisa.

The tulip, whose Turkish name *lâle* when written in Arabic uses the same letters as Allah, was often used as a sacred symbol, and by the 16th century was continually used as a decorative motif on buildings and fountains, portrayed on Iznik tiles and other ceramics, and embroidered on sumptuous silks.

THE OUTDOOR LIFE

On 1 April 1717 Lady Mary Wortley Montagu wrote to Alexander Pope: "For some miles around Adrianople the whole ground is laid out with Gardens, and the banks of the River set with rows of Fruit Trees, under which all the most considerable Turks divert themselves every Evening: not with walking, that is not one of their pleasures, but a set party of 'em chuse out a green spot where the Shade is very thick, and there they spread a carpet on which they sit drinking their coffee."

Tulip dish
This Iznik basin (a detail of which is shown here), dating to the 16th century, is decorated with black tulips.

Days of pleasure (opposite)
The gardens of the Kâgithane (the Sweet Waters of Europe) were the site of festivities and entertainments, as depicted in this late 18th-century manuscript painting. Created by Ahmed III (1703–30), the gardens in the meadows of the Kâgithane were used for camping and picnicking, a Turkish custom described by Lady Mary Wortley Montagu in her letters to Alexander Pope. Elegant kiosks and pavilions enhanced the pleasure grounds, where men and women mingled freely. Sadly, the site was ruined by industrial pollution, although restoration is now in hand.

growing vegetables as well as flowers, any surplus being put on sale in the market. The gardens at the Topkapi Saray sold roses, violets and vegetables, so perhaps the desire for profit led to the bulk ordering.

Evliya Celebi, a celebrated Turkish traveller who wrote a 10-volume book of his journeys, gives an account of the gardens he saw in Constantinople and Adrianople in 1631. Every royal garden was encircled with cypress or pine trees. Within the gardens there were geometric flowerbeds filled with roses, hyacinths, violets, tulips, jasmine, jonquils, narcissi, lilies, stocks, peonies, carnations and sweet basil, each set in its own private triangle or square. The tulips in the meadows of Kâgithane, where two streams run into the Golden Horn, were, he says, "intoxicating". He also describes kiosks wreathed in honeysuckle and jasmine, terraced fountains and bright garden paths of shells or coloured pebbles. In 1638 he witnessed a review of the 1,001 guilds in front of Murad IV. Among them were the gardeners, holding their hoes, spades and saws, with oxen drawing their watering machines. Sporting elaborate floral creations on their heads, the gardeners tossed flowers to the crowd. The Guild of Grafters balanced plates of fruit on their heads and carried their knives, saws and other grafting equipment.

By the 18th century it was not only plants that Turkey was exporting to the West. Highly decorative Turkish-style pavilions and tents became fashionable features in European gardens in the picturesque style, such as Haga Park in Sweden and Painshill in England. Schwetzingen, in Germany, acquired a Turkish mosque, as did London's Kew gardens.

The favourite garden of Süleyman the Magnificent was on the Asian coast between Harem and Salacak, with a view of the Sea of Marmara, the Topkapi Saray, the Golden Horn and the Bosphorus. The gardens were given to Sinan, Süleyman's architect, who contributed 400 buildings in Constantinople in the 50 years between 1538 and 1588.

THE ENDURING ISLAMIC TRADITION

The enclosed spiritual and sophisticated garden developed by the Muslims had its origins in the oases used by nomad tribes, life-sustaining places of refreshment and greenery in expanses of desert. Even today, much of the appeal of the Islamic garden still lies in its separateness from the surrounding countryside. In this it is quite unlike the modern environmental garden, which takes its natural surroundings as its guide.

The Islamic garden exists still in its simplest form in Iran where, in spring, clouds of blossom cover the walled orchards, a total contrast to the tawny-brown tones of surrounding hills and desert; almonds, plums, quince, apricots, pears and apples flower in turn in the spring season, their nuts and fruits providing a vital part of the rural economy. In remote villages, the walls protect groves of pomegranates from marauding sheep and goats. Gardens with more sophisticated layouts are marked by tall cypresses, umbrella pines or soaring poplars framing

Quiet seclusion (opposite)
The garden designed for Her Majesty Queen Elizabeth The Queen Mother at Walmer Castle, in Kent, was a gift from English Heritage. Planned by Penelope Hobhouse and Simon Johnson, it has a distinctive feeling of an enclosed Muslim garden, with a central pool, flanking yews (instead of cypresses) and a viewing pavilion where Her Majesty could sit undisturbed.

A view to distant hills
At Les Quatre Vents, Francis Cabot's garden in Quebec, Canada, a stylish wooden arch inspired by Mughal architecture (left) frames a view into the Laurentian mountain country beyond. Les Quatre Vents contains a number of atmospheric architectural features and buildings from different cultures, recalling different periods of garden history.

watercourses and pathways. In Isfahan elms, still untouched by the disease that has destroyed elms in northern Europe, form alleys, their pale green leaves refreshing in the heat, while in Shiraz orange groves and roses perfume the air.

Today, gardeners in search of refreshment and contrast from the business of ordinary life can be inspired by the sense of seclusion it is possible to create inside a walled space, whether in an urban or rural setting. Shade from hot sun, murmuring water to cool the air and muffle sound and the scent of flowers and leaves combine to offer an inner haven. The ordered pattern of the Islamic layout adds to the feeling of security; all is logical and geometric. Many people have already created such gardens without having analysed the reasons. An enclosed garden will provide a secluded world for spiritual contemplation and enjoyment. For many of us it is what gardening is all about.

CHAPTER FOUR

Pleasure and piety
MEDIEVAL GARDENS
OF CHRISTENDOM

FOR A THOUSAND YEARS, between the collapse of the Roman Empire and the beginning of the Renaissance, we have little knowledge of gardening activity in Europe.

During this period, while Islam perfected its gardens and advanced its knowledge of plants, we are left to explore the scant evidence left by our so-called Dark Ages. If the concept of gardening for pleasure barely survived during centuries of chaos it has left few records. As a more ordered world emerged, the picture of its gardens must be pieced together from isolated fragments and incidents.

What became of our Roman heritage in northern and western Europe – the sophisticated irrigation systems, the urbane gardens depicted in frescoes? Even the plants the Romans successfully acclimatized in colder colonies were almost forgotten until they were reintroduced by travellers as a new kind of gardening civilization became established.

Gradually, like stars in a clearing night sky, specks of information increasingly begin to relieve the gloom. There are written accounts and portrayals in surviving manuscripts and miniatures. Instead of frescoes we find a new kind of visual clue – the Christian icon. Stylized and imbued with spiritual significance, these jewel-like images present an especially rich record to be deciphered to discover what medieval gardens were really like, and what grew in them.

Symbolism in the flower-spangled meadow
The tapestry series of the Lady and the Unicorn in the Musée du Moyen Age in Paris, woven *c.*1484–1500, shows the Virgin and legendary unicorn on an island of flowers, silhouetted against a paler background in which more flowers and small animals are scattered. To viewers today these scenes typify the medieval flowery mead which we emulate in our modern meadows. The allegorical scenes of religious significance portray the unicorn, symbol of purity, who is lured to his death by the Virgin and then reborn in Christ.

Saintly delights

The Garden of Paradise, painted by an unknown Rhenish artist *c.*1410–20, shows the Virgin Mary surrounded by saints in a *hortus conclusus*, a highly idealized form of an enclosed walled garden. Although the painting may have lost much of its symbolic religious significance for today's viewer, the plants growing in profusion in the flowery mead are recognizable enough. They include flag iris, rose campion, Madonna lily, leucojum, lily-of-the-valley and peony, all plants grown in northern Europe through the Middle Ages. Hollyhocks and sweet rocket were introduced by the 13th century.

DARKNESS AND ILLUMINATION

The medieval period loosely covers a thousand years. Following the fall of the Roman Empire, with much of Europe returning to the wilderness of the Dark Ages, there must have been little, if any, chance to practise gardening for beauty alone. Survival in a brutal age precluded aesthetic considerations, and the concept of creating a garden for enjoyment was lost. Or is it merely that evidence of gardening activity is lacking?

The later centuries of the Middle Ages show no lack of glorious visual imagery. Religious paintings were produced throughout the late 14th and the 15th centuries as altarpieces and in the various illuminated prayerbooks produced as calendars for grandees. Other painted gardens served as illustrations to the poems and romances written from the turn of the millennium. In these we can trace the main patterns of gardens that emerge. In essence they comprise the small, enclosed garden nestling within the precincts of a building, the larger orchard designed for pleasure as well as fruit production, and the more extensive hunting park. These colourful depictions are matched by vivid descriptions in literature. This was an age of faith, and whether religious or secular in intent, all

these images of gardens are highly idealized and rife with symbolism, yet they give us more than a hint of how gardens may have looked and how they were enjoyed. Then came the "professional" garden writers. Albertus Magnus first described a pleasure garden in the middle of the 13th century and provided practical advice, and less than a hundred years later the Italian Pietro de' Crescenzi expanded the theme.

Unlike the Islamic garden with its inspirational overall pattern, and the Roman gardens of classical times, the medieval pleasure garden of Christendom made no profound impact on subsequent garden design. With no coherent message to follow, a chronological analysis of medieval gardening becomes a series of incidents rather than a developing narrative. A thousand years can be encapsulated in a study of individual garden features and events. However, what is interesting is tracing the concept of the pleasure garden from being almost forgotten in 800 to its importance in both secular and monastic gardens by 1500. The quest begins with a search for archival or archaeological evidence of any kind, a quest rewarded first by a little flurry of documentation from around the time of Charlemagne. Later, when sumptuous depictions of gardens are plentiful, the challenge becomes that of interpretation: what was the gardening reality behind the ideal?

GARDENING IN OBSCURITY

Nowadays the term Dark Ages is considered a misnomer because it disregards the continuing progress made in scholarship after the fall of the Roman Empire. However, to those of us who are interested in the practicalities of garden history the obscurity of the period between the retreat of the Romans and the dawn of the Renaissance is real enough. Few records survive for much of northern and western Europe – Britain, modern France, Germany, Switzerland, the Netherlands, southern Scandinavia, northern Italy and Austria, and that part of Spain not occupied by the Moors – areas united by a common Christian heritage, with Latin as the learned language and later with French spoken in court life and in commerce. The fragments of knowledge that we have of gardens in this period include no complete layouts, although modern archaeological methods are now beginning to reveal many more man-made landscape features and garden patterns – traces of walls and planting beds, some ancient trees and evidence of managed woodland. The only remains of medieval gardens still extant in western Europe are the Hispano-Arabic gardens in the Iberian peninsula representing Islamic culture (see Chapter 3): in the damp and cold of more northerly climates, gardens were too ephemeral to survive.

A handful of documents begin to record the existence of European gardens towards the end of the first millennium, around the time of the Emperor Charlemagne. Plans can be roughly reconstructed from verbal descriptions, but there is one unique survival, a single drawing of a garden layout. This is the famous proposal for a monastery garden (if it was ever made, or where, is unknown) which was found in the library at St Gall in Switzerland and dates from about AD 820. This plan includes a cemetery for the monks and functional areas for growing herbs and medicinal plants. Possibly there were flowerbeds in an area

THE MIDDLE AGES

Originally this was the cultural period in European history identified by Renaissance humanists between the fall of the Roman Empire in the West and the classical revival of their own day – that is *c.*500–1500. Sometimes, however, the term is applied only to the four or five centuries after 1000. The years from *c.*500 to 1000 have been dismissed as the Dark Ages, when some three hundred years of chaos prevailed in northern Europe.

CHARLEMAGNE'S DECREES

Charlemagne, the King of the Franks (771–814), subdued and Christianized neighbouring kingdoms and was crowned Holy Roman Emperor by the Pope in 800. With his empire encompassing most of Christian western Europe, he consolidated his rule with firm laws, promoting education and the arts, and encouraging agriculture, trade and industry by means of edicts. One of these was the *Capitulare de villis*, which instructed citizens what plants they should grow.

Plucking the herbs
The salvia shown in this medieval illustration is the ordinary cooking sage, *Salvia officinalis*, which was included in Charlemagne's *Capitulare de villis*. The five illuminated manuscripts of the *Tacuinum Sanitatis*, in which the illustration appears, have texts derived from Arab botanical and medical treatises and date from the late 14th to early 15th centuries. All the plants portrayed have useful medicinal properties or are grown for their fragrance.

labelled "paradise", with flowers grown for altar decoration. The names of the vegetables inscribed in the rectangular plots are familiar to us today – though the cultivars we grow are doubtless very different – among them are celery, parsnips and members of the onion family. These were all included in the list of a hundred vegetable crops that Charlemagne recommended to be grown throughout his empire in his decree concerning towns – the *Capitulare de villis* – an indication that by the early 800s a more orderly civilization was becoming possible.

That gardens and their fruits offered pleasures and sensual delight as well as produce is confirmed by the monk Walafrid Strabo of Lake Constance, not far from St Gall, writing a generation or so afterwards. His poem *De cultura hortulorum* echoes Virgil's *Georgics* and the "sweetness of labour" and is a clear expression of delight in both gardens and garden work. Strabo dedicated the work to one Father Grimaldi, whom he pictured sitting in a remembered orchard of his childhood:

> Under apples which hang in the shade of lofty foliage,
> Where the peach-tree turns its leaves this way and that
> In and out of the sun, and the boys at play,
> Your happy band of pupils, gather for you
> Fruits white with tender down and stretch
> Their hands to grasp the huge apples…

Strabo's poem is a song of praise to gardening in both practical and pleasurable senses. His mouth-watering description of cutting melons in summer could hardly be less vivid: "When the iron blade strikes to its guts, the melon throws out gushing streams of juice and many seeds. The cheerful guest then divides its bent back into many slices." In a more practical vein, Strabo encourages spreading manure, routing moles and attacking nettles armed with "mattock and rake".

THE NEED FOR WALLS

The enclosed garden, an area separated from the wild, was not only a practical necessity but an essential to the medieval mind, as it had been in the earliest years of civilization in the desert. Any notion of finding comfort and beauty in a rural setting, any appreciation of natural scenery, as described by Virgil and Pliny the Younger in the 1st century AD, had vanished; in the material and social conditions prevalent in the early years of the Middle Ages it was an idea the contemporary mind found impossible to grasp. Besides this, the early Christian teachers believed that the ancient pagan gods lurking in the forest were not only dangerous but evil spirits akin to the devil, who could seduce man from his Christian beliefs. The humanist Greek mentality, in which a grove of trees in a beautiful landscape came to personify a deity, was a dangerous heresy for a Christian. The early Christian fathers who withdrew to the desert were considered to be testing their belief against the forces of evil.

Very gradually, over centuries, a new appreciation that beauty might exist in nature began to dawn, finding its expression in the humanist thinking of the

A haven from worldly cares

This Flemish illustration to *Le Roman de la Rose* (c.1485) by the Master of the Prayer Books shows a noble pleasure garden of the 15th century, complete with a spouting fountain, trelliswork garden divisions, raised beds, turf benches and roses grown along the railings. In the story the lover and Dame Oyeuse are waiting to go into the garden.

This scene could also represent a setting for Boccaccio's *Decameron*, in which the characters sought refuge from the plague in an elaborate garden.

Renaissance, and further developed in the 18th century in the philosophy behind the Landscape Movement. A glimmer of this change was signalled as early as the 14th century, when the poet Petrarch astonished his contemporaries by climbing Mont Ventoux in Provence just for the view, anticipating by a hundred years the beliefs of the humanist Pope Pius II, who extolled the beauties of the natural countryside in his *Commentaries*.

THE PLEASANCE, HERBER OR ENCLOSED GARDEN

In any age it is the great gardens, whether secular or sacred, which set the tone and later provide records for historical research. Indeed, the humble gardens of the Middle Ages would have been very roughly tilled plots for vegetables, which would be supplemented by fruit and nuts from the wild. The small enclosed garden (which might or might not have echoes of the sacred *hortus conclusus*, see

ELEMENTS OF A MEDIEVAL GARDEN

Alley or tunnel
Tunnels of fruit trees, vines or roses, trained on wooden frames, provided shady walks for exercise and blossom and fruit in season.

Estrade
Shapes made of wood over which plants were trained were used in gardens as if they were living topiary pieces. A typical *estrade* would be a series of concentric circles trained in tiers, the size decreasing with height.

Flowery mead
An idealized meadow of flowers portrayed in contemporary manuscripts, tapestries and as a foreground in religious paintings. By the end of the 15th century the

flowers were painted more naturalistically and could be identified.

Fountain
As in the Muslim garden, water, the symbolic fount of life, was an essential element and fountains, placed in the centre of small enclosed gardens, assumed increasingly elaborate Gothic shapes.

Gloriette
A word of Spanish origin used to describe a pavilion, usually placed at the centre of a garden to mark the intersection of pathways or avenues. In the Middle Ages the gloriette often provided accommodation.

Raised bed
While in desert countries flowerbeds were sunken for irrigation purposes, in the wetter climate of northern Europe, raised beds, surrounded by boards or woven willow as already suggested in the Roman manuals, improved drainage.

Trelliswork
Built with strips of hazel or willow, trelliswork for fences or arbours on which roses could be grown was a feature throughout the Middle Ages.

Turf bench
Often seen in medieval illustrations, the bench's frame of stout willow, or even brick, was packed with soil in which grass

TURF BENCH

or scented herbs were grown. Pietro de' Crescenzi recommended using sods of turf rather than sowing grass seed.

Viridarium
From the Latin, the word was originally used for a plantation of trees. In late medieval times it was applied to the pleasure garden or orchard as distinct from the more useful *herbularis*.

FLOWERY MEAD

page 104), as described by Albertus Magnus in 1260, is our idea of the medieval garden. This pleasure garden was not a grand idea; as part of a great household it was generally small and adaptable, constructed close to the castle walls if not inside its curtilage. We glean such knowledge from 14th- and 15th-century illustrations seen in the background to religious altarpieces or in the lavishly painted prayerbook scenes by painters such as Pol de Limbourg, whose *Très Riches Heures* incorporated seasonal agricultural activities as well as more domestic pleasure garden scenes.

In these early illustrations perspective had still to be invented; balance, symmetry, proportion and contrast, classic elements of the architectural garden of the Renaissance, had still to be discovered or adapted from Islamic sources. Without conscious design or geometry, a modest pleasance could be fitted into a castle complex to become a luxury partner to the more functional vegetable, herb and medicinal garden, the essential component of any monastery complex. Trellis fences or arbours served for division and privacy. A degree of formality would follow naturally from the shape of the site. Paths running parallel to boundary walls would tend to take a rectangular course, and perhaps a fountain as the main structural item would be centrally placed.

Most of us can recognize some of the more obvious elements, small conceits which, readily and perhaps rustically constructed, can enliven a modern garden without sounding an anachronistic or discordant note. Indeed, some modern fashions, such as topiarized herbs and fruit bushes, so popular in a small garden, have a medieval ring without necessarily medieval authenticity. These features were found in the small enclosed garden of the Middle Ages, or in its spiritual extension the *hortus conclusus*, although larger buildings, such as the gloriette, may have been further removed from the castle or house, in the parkland.

GARDENING ADVICE FROM ALBERTUS MAGNUS

Albertus Magnus was one of the first to describe a medieval pleasure garden as a place of delight. His treatise *De vegetabilibus et plantis*, written in about 1260, did not neglect the more practical nature of gardening, much of which he culled from the classical Roman manuals. But he added a chapter emphasizing the agreeableness of an ornamental area set aside for recreation and repose.

Born Count of Bolstädt, *c*.1206, in Swabia, the aristocratic Albertus Magnus joined the Dominican Order as a young man and became its Provincial. His gardening ideas were not exactly new, but he was able to articulate them, condensing concepts and descriptions of the previous two centuries. He dealt mainly with gardens of the great belonging to bishops and archbishops, abbots and monastic houses. Many of these were in Normandy and England, made by Normans who had possibly been inspired by Arab gardens they had seen in Sicily.

Albertus Magnus's outline of a herber, called a *virgultum*, "a green place and merry with green trees and herbs", came in part from Bartholomew the Englishman (1200–60), who had incorporated a section in his encyclopaedia of 1240 on plants in *de orto*. Less than a century later this chapter of Albertus Magnus's was copied almost verbatim by the Bolognese lawyer Pietro de' Crescenzi in Book

THE HORTUS CONCLUSUS

TODAY THE WORDS *hortus conclusus* are translated literally to refer to any enclosed medieval garden (and most contemporary illustrations do, indeed, show walled or fenced enclosures), but this simple definition was not the original interpretation. The term was once charged with a profound religious resonance that is not easy for us to grasp. It no doubt contained far greater meaning and significance for the medieval mind, but even so it remains a complicated concept in a period when Christian beliefs and dogmas, particularly with reference to the importance of the Virgin Mary, were changing and developing.

Like the Islamic garden for the Muslim, the *hortus conclusus* had a sacred meaning for the Christian. In both religions the origins of the idealized garden or Garden of Eden were encapsulated by the Old Testament Song of Solomon, the Song of Songs (4:12): "A garden locked is my sister, my bride; a garden locked, a fountain sealed…" In Christian interpretation the locked garden stood for the Church and the sealed fountain for baptism. The interpretation was eventually extended so that the enclosed garden became the symbol of the Church in each individual and the sealed fountain blessings for those who believed in the virgin birth. In New Testament terms the enclosed garden, often set within a larger garden space, was associated with the Virgin Mary, and became a symbol of Christ and the Holy Church, bearing "fruits of the spirit". The *hortus conclusus*, seemingly a place of luxury and ease, with paths and beds laid out to a pattern around a fountain, was translated into Christian symbolism. As early as the 7th century the Venerable Bede had described the Madonna lily as the Virgin's emblem, the white petals representing her purity and the golden anthers the glowing light of her soul. Roses, once sacred to Venus, also became Mary's special flower (red roses representing the blood of martyrs), while the modest violet reflected her humility. By the 12th century the Virgin

Purity and luxury
This illustration from the Grimani Breviary *of c.1510 shows a* hortus conclusus — *a place of luxury but also, with the white lily and the rose growing in it, a symbol of the Virgin Mary.*

The lily as emblem
In paintings of the Annunciation the angel is portrayed presenting a white lily, the symbol of purity, to the Virgin. This detail is from a 15th-century painting by Filippino Lippi.

Mary was identified as the "beloved" of Solomon as well as the new Christian Church. Mary becomes a garden because of what grows within her; she is a closed garden because she is fruitful to God alone. At the same time she is the fountain in a spiritual sense, providing the water of life, from its source, sealed against impurities.

From the early Middle Ages the presence of lilies and of the angel Gabriel in a religious painting identified the theme of the Annunciation, usually taking place in an inner room or loggia. By the early 1400s, instead of being set indoors, an Annunciation scene was more often depicted in a richly flowering garden with Mary surrounded by various objects, all imbued with biblical associations and theological interpretations of her role in Christian salvation, sometimes even including a white unicorn symbolizing Mary's virginity.

A MEDIEVAL THEME PARK AT HESDIN

IN WHAT IS NOW Pas-de-Calais in northern France, Robert of Artois created a vast park which embraced villages, menageries, a banqueting pavilion, bridges, water-operated automata and even a labyrinth. He may have been partly inspired by a visit to Palermo, Sicily, and the park made there by Islamic engineers for the Normans (who captured the island from the Arabs and ruled there during the 12th century). Hesdin was created from 1288 and some of the Hesdin gadgetry –

water engines, surprise jets and showers, and an automatic owl – coincides in date with the publication of the Arabic *Book of Mechanical Devices* (1290). However, no connection is proven. Besides, as well as the *burladores* or water jokes, many items such as the gloriette, menagerie for lions and leopards, tree-house, aviaries and fishponds were already recognized features of Western medieval parks.

The park in the forest of Hesdin enclosed over 810 hectares (2,000

acres), and was similar in size to the splendid royal parks at Clarendon and Woodstock in England, but 10 times the size of an average deer park. Nothing today remains on the ground the park; it was finally destroyed by Charles V in 1553. Fortunately for us, however, documentation is plentiful up to 1536, when the French seized Hesdin. Detailed financial records listing income and expenses run from 1288 to the middle of the 14th century, when Artois became part of Flanders. Weekly expenditures are available from 1294 to the same period.

The park was also recorded in a literary sense as the setting for Guillaume de Machaut's poem *Remede de Fortune* (composed before 1342). Later in the 15th century it was owned by Philip the Good, Duke of Burgundy, when we know that it included an enclosed pleasure garden and a banqueting pavilion set on islands among meadows and orchards. Guests were greeted by bobbing marionette monkeys covered in badger skins and operated by ropes.

Hesdin's role in literature as the setting for poems and tales is undisputed. It seems certain, too, that the cultured Robert of Artois, who owned a considerable library, introduced various physical creations into the park to satisfy his own literary imagination. Was he perhaps even deploying his panoply of features, plants and animals in an attempt to create on earth his own idea of the Garden of Eden, or at least the medieval image of an earthly paradise?

The wedding party
The marriage of Philip, Duke of Burgundy, to Isabel of Portugal, painted by Jan van Eyck in 1430, takes place in a large pleasance which may well resemble the park at Hesdin.

Magnificent record
The *Très Riches Heures*, illuminated by Pol de
Limbourg for Jean, Duc de Berry in the early
15th century, provides precise visual
information on buildings and landscapes in
northern Europe at the time.

Orchards were incorporated into the larger hunting parks of royalty and wealthy landowners along with whole villages and managed forests. Although few illustrations exist before 1400, written descriptions of parks are plentiful. Few parks were as grand as Hesdin but their accounts often detail planting projects for woodland. The great tracts owned by kings, courtiers and princes of the Church were in essence landscape parks on the lines of Eastern "paradise" hunting enclosures, of direct descent from opulent Hellenistic layouts introduced to the Roman Empire by generals who campaigned in the Middle East. From descriptions these seem to have been composed of incidents, taking advantage of natural water features and woodland, rather than constituting a planned landscape. Their informality lacked the coherent design of the 18th-century English landscape park, but combined usefulness of tree-planting and land management with occasional flights of design fancy derived from earlier and different cultures. Recent archaeological studies of medieval garden sites begin to reveal traces of man-made water features and planted woods that confirm literary references. Inside the park, and distinguishing it from wild forest, trees and orchards were coppiced to provide breeding places for wildlife and deliberately controlled rather than allowed to grow free, providing timber for both building and firewood. One of the earliest parks in northern Europe was that of Geoffrey de Montbray, Bishop of Coutances from 1059 to 1093, who started his planting in Normandy before William's conquest of England, after returning from southern Italy. He planted a coppice and vineyard and surrounded his park with a double ditch and palisade, sowing acorns and filling the park with deer from England.

By the end of the 15th century plenty of records indicate the existence of areas of parkland beyond the castle curtilage as well as the smaller and intimate gardens within it. Both Van Eyck's *Adoration of the Lamb* at Ghent and Benozzo Gozzoli's painting for the Medici Palace chapel in Florence show processions moving through a sophisticated managed landscape, the former through a Burgundian park, the latter based in northern Italy. Though idealized, the tended forests composed of rows of trees and orchards show evidence of the extent to which a man-made landscape was valued.

The ROSE

Grown and cherished since ancient times, the first depiction of roses dates back to the Minoan period. The Egyptians preserved the petals of *Rosa × richardii*, the holy rose from Ethiopia, in their tombs, and the rose was later associated with the Romans' pagan excesses. The rose also became a symbol of purity for Muslims, while, in the Middle Ages, Christians associated it with the Virgin Mary.

But roses truly flowered in medieval art and literature, with

ROSA GALLICA

the rose window at Chartres Cathedral and illuminations in manuscripts. The rose also figured in gardens of the imagination. The 13th-century poem *Le Roman de la Rose*, translated into English by Chaucer, was almost certainly inspired by the red *Rosa gallica*. The medicinal apothecary's rose, *Rosa gallica* var. *officinalis*, may have been introduced to northern Europe by the Romans, but a more popular tradition dates its arrival to the Crusades of 1239–40 when the King of Navarre, Thibault IV, brought it back from the Levant. It came to England by 1279 in the hands of the Earl of Lancaster, Henry III's son and second husband to Thibault's daughter-in-law. This rose – the red rose associated with the Wars of the Roses – became the badge of England in spite of its Saracenic and French descent.

With a semi-double red (more truly magenta pink) flower, *Rosa gallica* and its famous cultivar *R. gallica* 'Versicolor' (formerly *R. mundi*), a sport with striped petals of pink and white, are among the oldest cultivated roses. There are many 19th-century *R. gallica* hybrids. Among the most desirable is the velvety 'Tuscany Superb'.

THE ROLE OF THE MONASTERIES

The monastery garden catered for the needs of inmates and travellers. The monks who built and maintained them were sometimes familiar with the Roman manuals (and occasionally copyists of some of the great herbals) but had no special botanical expertise other than the knowledge handed on from generation to generation. Early monasteries do not seem to have had a specific healing role, but by the later Middle Ages a herb garden for curative plants was an essential attribute. Cassiodorus in his 6th-century *Institutions* had a chapter entitled *De medicis* in which he urges his monks to specialize in healing and to understand the nature of herbs. The great 12th-century Abbess Hildegard of Bingen detailed their many medicinal uses and also established categories for plants, dividing them into ornamental, wild and useful. Her ornamental plants included roses, white lilies, violets, irises and bay laurel. As monasteries developed into serious centres of learning, medical treatises from classical times were preserved and copied. The abbot would often have a thorough knowledge of medicine and be skilled in the preparation of remedies. Once medical schools had been established at Montpellier and Salerno – both through Islamic influence – monks were forbidden to practise medicine, even if familiar with the early medical works.

The "useful" gardens were usually separated into plots for the *herbularis* (situated close to the infirmary) and the *hortus*. Their layout followed the lines recommended in the Roman manuals of Varro, Cato, Columella and Palladius (see page 49), though their makers always tempered the practical advice of the "agronomes" to allow for the climatic differences found in more northerly latitudes. (From the 9th to the 13th centuries, northern Europe enjoyed a warmer and drier period in which mean temperatures were several degrees higher than those of today.) These Roman works survived widespread illiteracy and were thinly distributed throughout the monasteries of medieval Europe, to be reworked and re-interpreted extensively even after printing was invented and as late as the 17th century.

Monks would have been at the forefront of technological development, becoming experts in drainage, marling, soil enrichment and land reclamation, besides the

Ecclesiastical practicalities
This plan shows the elaborate water supply system for Christ Church, Canterbury, *c*.1165. The herb garden – the *herbularis*, with rows of plants and a trellis fence – lies north of the church and east of the great cloister, while a vineyard and orchard – the *viridarium* or *pomerium* – are outside the precinct between the city walls and the open fields in which the monks may well have grown crops. Monasteries would often have had copies of the Roman manuals useful for both horticulture and agriculture, and the monks would have been experts in all sorts of land management.

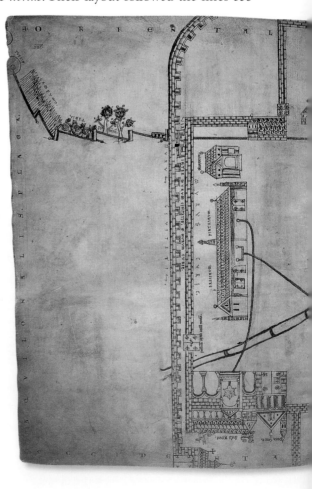

cultivation of vineyards and orchards and managing woodland, with agricultural and horticultural skills and tools hardly distinguishable. For religious orders the enclosed gardens around the monasteries were planned for self-sufficiency. There was an emphasis on fruit and vegetables besides culinary and medicinal herbs, but the gardens also often included a mill, an oven for baking, beehives and, of course, a fresh water supply and fishponds. A *hortulanus* was in charge of the garden and a *vitiscapicerius* was the vineyard keeper. Judging from the St Gall plan, flowers would have been grown for altar decoration and scent. The gardens were also recognized as places for refreshment and for exercise. A detailed contemporary account of the first abbey of the Cistercian Order, founded by St Bernard in 1115 at Clairvaux, mentions a "wide level area containing an orchard of many different fruit trees, like a little wood…as a solace for the monks, a spacious promenade for those wishing to walk and a pleasing spot for those preferring to rest".

Monasteries also owned farmland in which they grew cereal crops and grazed livestock, although the Cistercians often rented out agricultural land, receiving produce or money in return. The 6th-century St Benedict inspired the cloister life in western Europe, ordering that his monasteries should all have water and gardens and that his monks should work in the garden as part of their spiritual dedication. The cloisters, next to the monastic church, were intended for the monks' recreation and in spite of "reconstructions" of herb garden layouts in old cloisters there is no evidence to support the idea of a cultivated garden. There might have been a central fountain and cross paths with four squares of turf, or, in southern Europe drought-tolerant herbs may have replaced grass.

By the Middle Ages monks could express their pleasure in the beauties of nature, a far cry from the early ascetics who felt morally obliged to seek out "thorny and desert regions to have an opportunity to practise abstinence and to

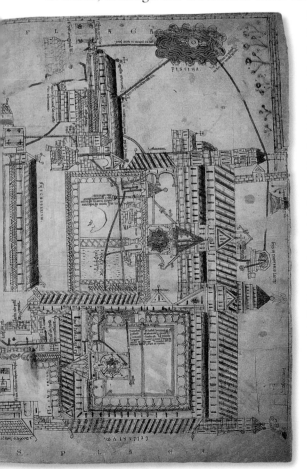

The monastic ideal
At the famous Certosa di Pavia in northern Italy, founded in 1397 but taking over 200 years to complete, monks had individual cells with small attached gardens. The actual cloisters were rarely cultivated but remained an open space with a central fountain and cross paths.

A MEDIEVAL GARDENING MANUAL

PIETRO DE' CRESCENZI'S BOOK *Liber ruralium commodorum*, written between 1304 and 1309, was very much a "how to" manual with a month-by-month calendar of agricultural labours appropriate to each season. Its strong popular appeal ensured that the work had a long shelf-life lasting well over a century.

Two parts, the first on the herb garden in Book VI and the second on the pleasure garden in Book VIII, deal with ornamental gardens. Illustrations from these are among the best known portrayals of medieval gardening (see below). Fenced-in gardens with raised beds and irrigation channels show gardeners working among the plants and bushes, sometimes in a country setting and sometimes in an urban area. To text derived from Albertus Magnus, Crescenzi adds a section in his Book VIII on the "medium-sized" garden of about half to one-and-a-half hectares

(1–4 acres), its perimeters enclosed by mixed hedges of fruit trees, thorns, roses and vines, often with interlaced branches. He also encourages this method for making tunnel arbours. His suggestion of mowing only twice yearly seems optimistic even if much of the turf was meadow. His larger gardens, about 5 hectares (12 acres), were fit for a king and walled about for extra security. In these a spring would ensure the viability of fishponds and trees could provide shelter for deer and game. Trees planted in radiating avenues would allow wildlife to be seen. In a final section he advocates arbours made with thin wooden laths covered with vegetation or formed by plants with their branches intertwined, a very common practice by his time, and one that continued into the early years of the Renaissance. Trees in the leafy bowers provided "cover without rain" for the king and queen; other trees

were trained and clipped to the shape of towers or crenellations.

In format *Liber ruralium commodorum* almost exactly resembled the 12 books of Columella's *De re rustica*, omitting the poetic rendering of the garden intended as a supplement to Virgil's *Georgics*. Although Crescenzi also drew on the work of Albertus Magnus, he was no mere plagiarizer. Much of his text was garnered from his own extensive experience of travel and observation throughout Italy as a Guelph exile from Ghibelline Bologna during the 13th-century conflicts. Crescenzi was not innovative, but he described what he saw in contemporary gardens. In his sensitivity to aesthetics, with an emphasis on an ideal site as well as on scents and textures of foliage and the quality of gentle breezes, Crescenzi foreshadows the 15th-century writer Leon Battista Alberti.

Within little more than a hundred years Crescenzi's work was translated from the original Latin into Italian, French, Polish and German; after the invention of printing, 15 separate editions were issued in Latin and countless in vernacular languages. Illustrations from the various editions are useful guides to customs in the different regions, sometimes showing features not mentioned by the author but known to the local illustrator. Crescenzi's descriptive writing allows for generous interpretation of his text.

The well-ordered plot
In a French manuscript translation of 1485 of Crescenzi's 14th-century work (entitled Livres des proffits ruraux*) this illustration shows a scene in an enclosed garden, in which an elaborate* estrade *is being tended by one of the ladies. Small square beds are planted with herbs and carnations are grown in a pot.*

Love blossoms
This French miniature, *c.*1415, from a French manuscript of the poems of Christine de Pisan (1364–1430) shows a pair of quite grand lovers leaning on a rose-covered trellis, their feet in a carpet of flowers, the medieval flowery mead. The white rose on the left may be *Rosa × alba* and the striped roses on the right *R. gallica* 'Versicolor'. Turf benches can be seen in the background.

avoid distracting the soul with worrisome occupations". The writer of the above, the Cistercian Gilbert of Hoyland, states that the fertile landscape can "revive a dying spirit, and soften the hardness of a mind untouched by devotion". For the inmates of a secluded monastery, garden imagery could provide an incentive to develop some spiritual theme such as the *hortus conclusus*, the contrast accentuated between a harsh life and the amenities and sensual pleasures of a garden in spring. Medieval monks thought of the Garden of Eden as the first paradise, most beautiful of all earthly gardens planted by God himself, lost to humanity when Adam and Eve were expelled. The earthly paradise of Eden became an image of the Church, in which the redeemed had access to Christ and the monastery could become the image of paradise. Even planting an evergreen tree in the enclosed cloister garden became a reminder of the Tree of Life and a symbol of Christ. The medieval monk could begin to understand the meaning of the biblical paradise, which, although lost to man, could still, as an idea, refresh his soul on earth and be an intimation of the paradise to be enjoyed in heaven.

Healing by the act of gardening or by being in a beautiful place is not a modern idea. Medieval monks believed, as we do today, that experiencing nature

The lover finds his rose

The idealized garden of love created in the poem *Le Roman de la Rose* in the 13th century, besides being one of the great monuments of French medieval literature, remains a potent influence on our conception of the medieval garden. Guillaume de Lorris expounded the idea of courtly love in the allegorical poem. The lover dreams of a walled garden belonging to Pleasure, the garden of love and the home of the Rose.

Dream sequence (opposite)

By 1400 the French miniature illustrations to *Le Roman de la Rose* show the walled garden as circular, with animals and birds among the trees, suggesting that it may have been a game park. Having gained admission, the lover Amant sees his beloved in a reflection in the Pool of Narcissus and falls hopelessly in love. His trials follow as the Rose is protected by Jealousy. Amant lies asleep below reminding the reader that it is all a dream.

could be beneficial not only to the mind but also to the body. The Venerable Bede, who never left 7th-century Northumbria, was aware of the value of landscape – the pleasant place or *locus amoenus*, praising the situation of a monastery for its closeness to the woods and sea. A survey of monastic literature reveals a diversity of attitudes to the merits of various sites for religious communities, but almost all stress the beneficial effects on the infirm of a lovely prospect. The medieval Cistercians chose sites suitable for agriculture with ample water and fertile soil and by clearing the land and managing forests improved the land's appearance, to be enjoyed by all, as distinct from the secluded gardens within the monastery walls. The 16th-century monks at Melrose Abbey in Scotland were forbidden to possess private gardens and instructed not only to share the produce but also allow free access between the plots. The Carthusian monasteries, founded in 1084, concentrated on education and preparation for the afterlife. The communal life was restricted and monks lived alone in separate cells or houses with individual gardens, similar to those to be seen in the central courtyard of the Certosa outside Florence. By the early 16th century monks had begun to garden for themselves, tending their own plots with gardens, trees and violet beds, but this was discouraged. Louis of Blois (known as Blosius), and Abbot of Liessies, writing in 1530, admonished his monks in the *Statuta monastica*, aimed at reforming his monastic community, to enjoy the pleasures of gardening but without ownership and by doing so use the beauties of nature as avenues by which the souls could be led to God:

> May the beauty of flowers and other creatures draw the heart
>   to love and admire God, their creator,
> May the garden's beauty bring to mind the splendour of paradise…

It is a point of view not so very different from the Muslim appreciating his earthly garden as a foretaste of heaven to come.

IDEALIZED GARDENS OF ART AND LITERATURE

While documentary evidence exists for gardens in the 8th and 9th centuries, the visual evidence is drawn from later centuries and is based mainly on religious paintings and on artistic interpretation of romances and poetry. This means that the gardens are somewhat idealized. What we see is gardens of the imagination rather than gardens of reality. This is equally true in illustrations to contemporary literature. The writer or poet has a vision which is depicted by an artist. The garden portrayed will contain many features of contemporary gardens, but their purpose will be to illustrate the story rather than to be a faithful rendering of a real garden for historical assessment. It is from these "unreal" gardens that we have acquired our visual image of the medieval garden. In art the garden had a symbolic meaning, its overtones richly endowed by a conception of a garden as paradise. The Christian garden, as represented in the calendar

A ms sont apres bien apparant
Et en pris bien tenu apparant
En actour ami et non mauaise
A mi ne tint pas sauues alobee
A moie descript la vision
Aum amur du roy et pinon
A inconques cuide neqin de
Que soit follour ne mensonge
De croire que songe auenure
Qui que voudra pour fou metenue
Car endroit moy ay je fiance
Que songes sont signifiance
Des biens aus gens a de anuis
Que les plusieurs songent de nuis
Maintes choses couuertement

Quites qui ne diront que sauue
Na se fable non z mensonges
Mais on puet tels songes songier
Qui ne sont mie mensongier

pages of various books of hours showed the *hortus conclusus* with Mary and/or saints represented by various flowers or symbols, with turf-topped benches, fountains, trellis and arbours, orchards and parklands, but also illustrated the gardens through the seasons. In paintings gardens appeared as backgrounds to New Testament events, with lilies, roses, potted plants or topiary identifying events or individuals and triple-tiered *estrades* symbolizing the Trinity. By the 15th century architects had created foliage-symbolism in stone carving and weavers were reproducing the flowery mead in tapestry colours.

Even in secular literature, where themes of courtly love proliferated with imaginary adventures taking place in romantic garden settings, the garden retained its religious symbolism. The *hortus conclusus* became the garden of love, a private place that provided the setting for conversation and dalliance. In medieval literature from *Le Roman de la Rose* to Boccaccio and Chaucer, the garden proper is envisaged as a magical enclosed space, but there are always references to the outer garden, that *locus amoenus* of woodland glades or flower-filled fields, where the garden was unstructured and free. The famous love story of *Le Roman de la Rose*, begun by Guillaume de Lorris in 1237 and finished by Jean de Meun 40 years later, took place in an allegorical garden setting with individuals personified as Love, Idleness or Mirth. The lover Amant, after a period of wandering through flowery meadows, enters the garden in search of the symbolic rose. Translated into English in the time of Chaucer, it was successively illustrated between 1400 and 1500 in French miniatures. Boccaccio's *Decameron*, written in 1348, gives us a verbal picture of a nobleman's garden into which Boccaccio's aristocrats escape from the city during the Florentine plague. Its layout has all the familiar characteristics of the medieval garden – a flower-studded lawn, a central fountain, vine pergolas (as suggested by Crescenzi), citrus trees and roses. Its imagery of descending terraces opening into a "gentle landscape" presage Alberti's *De re aedificatoria* of 1452, and the joys and beauty of nature already praised by Petrarch, Boccaccio's contemporary.

PLANTS AND TECHNIQUES

For enlightenment in horticultural matters we can turn most usefully not only to literary sources but also to accounts of actual gardens made by contemporaries or compiled later from hearsay. In these gardens gardeners really did train fruit bushes, construct trellis walls and graft fruit trees for improved varieties. Although the main flood of new plants did not arrive in Europe until the last half of the 16th century, a steady trickle found its way north from the

Easing man's load

A Flemish *Book of Hours c.*1500 shows a wheelbarrow being pushed with a vast pot containing a single red carnation. Wheelbarrows are first mentioned in the West in the 13th century, although they were already in use in China in the 3rd century BC. The carnation was only introduced from Valencia in Spain to northern Europe – where it was first grown in France and known as *oeillet* – in the 1470s. The gardener's wife seems to be taking the strain.

Mediterranean through the previous centuries. The limited list of mainly useful plants amounting to roughly 100 in Charlemagne's *Capitulare de villis* of AD 800 expanded to 250 by the early 15th century. By the 13th and 14th centuries decorative plants came into their own. Writers such as Albertus Magnus (and the slightly earlier Bartholomew the Englishman) encouraged readers to enjoy plants for their beauty and scent. Although dried rosemary flowers were known in northern Europe earlier, the first rosemary plants arrived in the 1300s. The Countess of Hainault sent a plant to her daughter Queen Philippa of England in 1338, and Henry Daniel (*c*.1315–85), a Dominican friar with a botanic garden in Stepney, London, translated an Arabic treatise on its culture for the queen. At the end of the 14th century a Parisian householder included a description of how to root cuttings of rosemary in *Le Ménagier de Paris*, a treatise he wrote for his young wife. He also provided instructions on how to send rosemary plants on a journey "wrapped in waxed cloth sewn up, smeared with honey and powdered with wheaten flour".

The seed is sown
This illustration shows gardeners at work in a walled plot with a series of square beds, as described in *Livres des proffits ruraux*, the French translation of Pietro de' Crescenzi's 14th-century work. Crescenzi's *Liber ruralium commodorum* was translated from its original Latin into French within a hundred years of publication and became readily available after printing was introduced. Although Crescenzi borrowed freely from earlier authors, his work remained one of the most important textbooks for agriculture and horticulture up to and beyond Renaissance times.

The hollyhock, known as Rose of Spain (although originally from the Orient), reached England from Spain with Eleanor of Castile in 1255. One of the most interesting gardens was that of the Hôtel de Saint Pol in Paris, an 8-hectare (12-acre) garden made in the 1370s for Charles V of France. Drawing heavily on advice from Crescenzi (already translated into French by 1373), the makers of the garden incorporated features such as tunnel arbours, living topiary walls, trelliswork with intertwined plants, turf seats and a labyrinth, and flowerbeds filled with roses, lavender, rosemary and wallflowers. It was restored in 1398 after neglect, and a complete inventory exists of the replanting at that date. Friar Daniel's 14th-century garden in London, in which he grew 252 different kinds of plants, was almost the first early botanic garden in Europe. Learned in all the old herbals, Daniel was ahead of his time in his detailed examination of plants and their habitats.

The Muslims, of course, were there even earlier. The Huerta del Rey in Toledo (see page 68) was built 300 years before Daniel studied his collection. Scholars from the Spanish gardens were responsible for translating early pharmaceutical and botanical treatises from Greek to Arabic and ultimately from Arabic to Latin to become available to Christian Europe. New plants travelled with the Arabs to Spain from as far afield as Persia, and a trickle gradually found their way with returning pilgrims across the Pyrenees to survive in northern gardens. Other Arab influences came through Sicily, where they were absorbed by the Normans into their architecture and gardens. These concepts eventually travelled north and influenced the development of large landscape parks such as Hesdin.

CHAPTER FIVE

THE
RENAISSANCE
VISION

The flowering of the European garden

IN 15TH-CENTURY ITALY, in the hills around Florence, the garden took a major shift in direction. The enclosed, inward-looking garden of the Middle Ages turned outwards to face the world beyond. Architects embraced new ideas of proportion and perspective where house and garden worked together as an entity and were linked to the landscape in a way that had been impossible during turbulent medieval times. In this time of "rebirth", inspired by the classical ideals of the past, man took a new delight in the natural world and his role within it. The garden became a place for "outdoor living", for social pleasures and philosophical debate.

As these new ideas began to spread, first within Italy and then through northern Europe, they were adapted to suit different landscapes and existing architectural features. During the 16th and 17th centuries simple Renaissance styles expanded into more baroque forms with flowing movement and a more linear approach. In flatter, forested, northern France, the relationship with nature also changed as gardeners sought to subdue it, rulers became ever keener to display their power, and optical illusion was added to the tricks of the designer's trade. Nowhere were these elements more convincingly combined than at Versailles. Designed to radiate Louis XIV's splendour, it was the envy of every other monarch and the garden they most wanted to copy. England during this period was a follower rather than a setter of fashion. Nevertheless, on some of the smaller estates, a few independent-minded enthusiasts were cultivating a love of gardening that was to bear fruit in centuries to come.

The sparkle of a new era
The famous Organ Fountain at the 16th-century Italian Villa D'Este, near Tivoli, was completed in 1661. It is worked by the manipulation of water pressure, ingeniously controlled according to the theories of 1st-century architects and water engineers from Alexandria.

ALBERTI'S THEORIES

Leon Battista Alberti had completed his 10-part *De re aedificatoria* by 1452, but it was not published until 1485. The first printed book on architecture, it followed his study of Vitruvius and classical Roman architecture, and in it Alberti evolves a theory of beauty in terms of mathematical symmetry and proportion of parts. In an earlier work on painting, *Della pittura*, Alberti had given the first description of perspective construction. Italian poet, mathematician and engineer, Alberti was a typical humanist and "Renaissance man", and exemplified his own belief that "men can do all things".

PRINCIPLES OF RENAISSANCE DESIGN

As we move into the Renaissance our story arrives on firmer ground. Unlike the gardens of the Middle Ages, which survive only by hearsay or in pictorial depiction, many of the greatest Renaissance gardens still exist: the study of Western garden history can begin "on site".

Of all the innovative periods of garden design, this is the most exciting. Its elements (together with those of the Islamic tradition) remain the inspiration of all Western gardening. The principles of geometrization of space introduced by Renaissance designers have given us a classic formula that, in spite of vast changes in technology and materials, is as valid today as it was in 1500. It is remarkable how much of the work of modern designers (such as Russell Page, Sir Geoffrey Jellicoe, Thomas Church, Fernando Caruncho and Jacques Wirtz, to name but a few) contains references to this period. Even those designers who blanch at the idea of "formality" often use ways of organizing the space in a garden that stem from the Renaissance, though they may disguise the geometry, right angles and axial lines by natural-looking, curvaceous planting.

Using new-found rules of mathematics and linear perspective the early Renaissance builders created gardens where nature and art could co-exist. These rules, many of them derived from classical sources, were set out by Leon Battista Alberti in *De re aedificatoria*, a treatise that was to become the bible of Renaissance architects. Alberti used it to expound theories of proportion relating not only to building but also to music, nature and the idealized human body. When these were applied, harmony would prevail.

The Renaissance garden was all about manipulation of space. Its distinctive geometric composition was based around a central axis leading from the centre of the house that was then intersected by a number of cross axes. In this way a series of garden rooms and ascending or descending terraces could be created. The central axial line of sight was the most exacting characteristic which, by the time of the great baroque gardens of

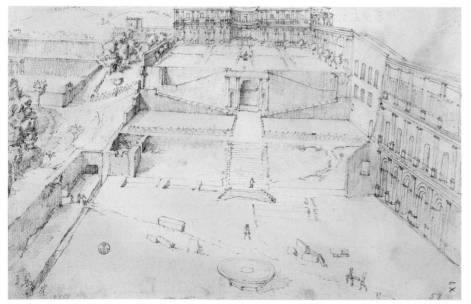

New directions
The Cortile del Belvedere, in the Vatican in Rome, was designed by Donato Bramante in 1506. His revolutionary design, with a strong central axis incorporating staircases and ramps to adjust levels on a sloping site, reflected his study of Roman antiquity.

the 17th and early 18th centuries, had been extended past the ordered layout surrounding the house into "wilder" groves and orchards in the countryside or, in the case of French gardens, deep into the forests, terminating at some topographical or artificial feature or at the horizon (see pages 153–55).

The early Renaissance gardens were subdivided into separate but regular parts by pergolas and hedges, in a grid system defined by perspective. There were trees in rows and clipped topiary pieces. A knowledge of mathematics and the effects of perspective from different viewpoints were as essential for creating the

new gardens as they were for architecture and painting. The garden "outside" was an architectural extension of the "inside". In terms of actual living the Renaissance garden was used in many of the same ways as a modern garden in California.

At the early 16th-century Cortile del Belvedere, in Rome, designer Donato Bramante's dominating central axis, which traverses the terraces at right angles, linking them by a series of stairs and ramps, was typical of 15th-century ideas and new architectural precepts that were to influence all future garden development. Later, by the middle of the 16th century, the gardens of the High Renaissance were intended for viewing from above. On a sloping site, a succession of horizontal planes made by terracing allowed perspective views. These sometimes necessitated a massive amount of earth-moving and feats of water engineering. Water jets could either soar above a flat surface or, as a cascade, link descending levels. Symmetry and harmony, balance and proportion between buildings and garden remained the basic tenets. The mannerist gardens of the late 16th century (such as Pratolino, page 126, and Bomarzo, page 124) were more contrived, breaking out from the strict Renaissance conventions with romantic grottoes, rocks, giants and secret water devices.

Throughout the whole period gardens were designed for pleasure and amusement, even though they also often functioned as sculpture galleries, museums and encyclopaedias of living plants. The early humanists (whose leaders first met at the Platonic Academy founded by Cosimo de' Medici the Elder in the

Paradise restored
The garden of the Villa Barbarigo (today known as the Villa Barbarigo Pizzoni Ardemani), designed in the 17th century, was planned on two axes with hedged alleys, water canals, a maze and a rabbit island, in an amphitheatre formed by the Euganean Hills south of Padua. Majestic stepped ponds, rockworks and cascades lead from the Portale de Diana. Designed by Zuane Francesco Barbarigo, a Venetian senator, the allegorical landscape represents the Garden of Eden regained on earth. Today, admirably restored, the garden is among the most beautiful in Italy.

Medici munificence
This portrait of Cosimo I, Grand Duke of Tuscany (1519–74), was painted by Alessandro Allori two years before his death. A notable patron of the arts, and a member of the powerful Medici family, the grand duke built the gardens of the Boboli behind the Pitti Palace in Florence from 1549 and those at the Villa Castello, near Florence, at the end of the 1550s.

The quincunx
Giovanni Battista Ferrari's *Hesperides*, published in 1646, was the first book completely devoted to the cultivation of oranges, lemons, citrons and limes. This plan of a section of the Horti Farnesiani on Rome's Palatine Hill shows citron trees arranged in a series of quincunxes, a planting pattern that gives maximum light and air to each specimen.

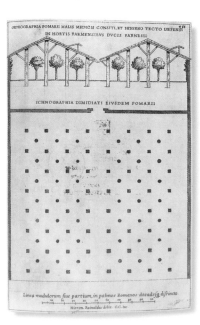

middle of the 15th century) included an interest in garden layout in their study of ancient classical learning, literature and history, the *humanae literae* from which they took their name. Cosimo, for one, liked to prune his own vines. These Florentines were fired by a love of nature and gardens, which they used to provide a setting for philosophical discussion and music, a place to cultivate the soul.

LANDSCAPE AND SETTING

The Italian Renaissance gardens, especially in Tuscany, although remarkable for their new and sophisticated design were also rooted in an agricultural landscape. Linked with the countryside, broad garden terraces reflected the ancient layout of olive groves and vineyards cultivated for centuries. Indeed, some new gardens incorporated vineyards or olive groves into their layouts, often using a traditional quincunxial arrangement by which each plants could receive as much light and air as possible. (A basic quincunx is formed from five trees, four making a square with the fifth in the centre.) In other countries local features played similar roles: ornamental canals in Dutch gardens were decorative extensions of drainage ditches in the polders.

The lunettes painted for the Villa di Artimino by the Flemish artist Giusto Utens towards the end of the 16th century show gardens owned by the Medici family, and illustrate how agricultural patterns were adapted for fruit and flowerbeds. Utens's portrayals are like maps, recording garden divisions, terraces and patterned flowerbeds, and the position of fountains and statues. Utens shows how the layouts of the earliest 15th-century country villas were actually set into farming spaces, although subsequent designs, such as those at Castello and Petraia, nearer the centre of Florence, were more complex. At Pratolino, the most complicated of all the Medici villas, Grand Duke Francesco transformed a mountain slope into a "garden of miracles".

The architect, as stressed by classical writers, had to consider the relationship of the villa and garden to the surrounding landscape and its function as a place for the owners to walk in, enjoy the fragrance of lemon blossom and other flowers, find shade under trees, pergolas or loggias in the hot summers, listen to the sound of falling water and feel the coolness of water sprays. The best site provided the right sort of conditions for the plants – terraced slopes, for instance, improved the drainage for tender exotics and citrus bushes.

In his suggestions for a hillside site for a villa, Alberti borrowed extensively from classical sources when he wrote in *De re aedificatoria*: "I would have it stand pretty high, but upon so easy an ascent, that it should hardly be perceptible to those that go to it, till they find themselves at the Top, and a large prospect opens itself to their View. Nor should

there be any Want of pleasant Landskips, flowery meads, open Champlains, shady groves. Or limpid Brooks, or clear Streams and Lakes for swimming...with all other Delights of the same Sort...to be necessary in a Country Retreat, both for Convenience and Pleasure...I would have the Front and whole Body of the House perfectly well lighted, and that it be open to receive a great deal of Light and Sun, and a sufficient Quantity of wholsome Air". He echoed Pliny the Younger's descriptions of his two functional villas (see page 47) when he went on to explain how the "ancients" planned their sites so that loggias should be filled with winter sun, but shaded in summer, and so arranged as to give shelter from winter winds.

It was not only the garden that was changing; the villa itself, instead of being an inward-looking fortress with views onto an enclosed courtyard, turned outwards to incorporate the prospect of landscape and light. Except for the entrance used by Cardinal d'Este himself, the original approach to the Villa d'Este at Tivoli

A villa in its landscape
This fresco (1574–76) in one of the pavilions in the Villa Lante, near Rome, shows the garden soon after it was laid out with its original Italian parterres, which were later replanted in French baroque scrolls. The original entrance was through the park to the east, so that visitors would descend the garden from the grotto, with views and fountains unfolding before them.

THE MANNERIST GARDEN

The term mannerist is applied, at its most specific, to a movement in Italian art from about 1520 to 1600 (between High Renaissance and baroque), in which style became a preoccupation and was sometimes taken to extremes. All over Europe, mannerist gardens were characterized by their artificiality and fantasy and made much use of symbolism and hydraulic intricacy. In its enthusiasm for decoration and drama, mannerism is sometimes likened to the postmodernism of the 20th century. Gardens typifying the style include Pratolino (see page 126), Bomarzo (see below) and Hellbrunn in Salzburg, Austria.

Mind games
The gardens of Bomarzo, near Viterbo, now known as the Sacro Bosco, contain extraordinary statues of allegorical monsters carved from stone, as well as buildings which have iconographical interpretations. Much of the fantasy could be understood by contemporary Italians, who read Aristotle, Virgil and Dante. The gardens were laid out from 1542 by Count Vicino Orsini.

(now through the villa at the top of the steep slope) was from the plain below. It led through orchards and covered *berceaux*, and up the ramps and staircases, from where the visitor could watch, as the French philosopher and essayist Montaigne did in 1581, the spray of sparkling fountains produce ephemeral rainbows. It was impossible to appreciate the full exploitation of the site until the visitor had climbed through the garden and looked back across the Roman Campagna.

NATURE AND ARTIFICE

The most basic ingredients of the Renaissance garden were evergreen plants, stonework and water – permanent, rather than ephemeral, materials. There were dark groves of ilex or cypresses – at Castello a circular cypress grove formed a labyrinth – pergolas, arbours and topiary, as well as the stonework of terraces, stairways, sculpture and pavilions. Caves were made into grottoes, while water might be contained in still pools, or sent tumbling down cascades or shooting high from fountains. Making tree houses, building mounts (see page 129) and laying out flowerbeds in patterns were all part of this manipulation of nature. It is the organic quality of such features that differentiates a living garden from a purely architectural concept, and the manipulation of nature which distinguishes it from nature itself. In a garden, it has been said, art imitates nature by repeating artificially what nature put there naturally, and if nature is conceived as ordered, a reflection of cosmic order, as was believed in this period, then imitations of nature also had to have a basic pattern. Art, the Renaissance designers felt, must imitate not only nature's outward appearance but also

LOVE'S TROUBLED DREAM

THE EXTRAORDINARY allegorical romance the *Hypnerotomachia Poliphili*, by a young Italian prince, Francesco Colonna, was written at almost the same time as Alberti's *De re aedificatoria*. It was completed in 1467 and published in Italy in 1499 (and soon afterwards in France and then England, although with much

A PERGOLA, ILLUSTRATED IN THE
HYPNEROTOMACHIA POLIPHILI

reduced text). Its title was compounded from three Greek words, *hypnos* (sleep), *eros* (love) and *mache* (strife), and translated as *The Strife of Love in a Dream*. Although engaging in its unreality, the story itself – the hero Poliphilus's pursuit of the nymph Polia – was of less importance in influencing the development of garden design than the woodcut illustrations of classical ruins, arbours and pergolas that portrayed Colonna's ideas about garden architecture.

These show an amphitheatre and a peristyle garden with antique reliefs, statues, herms and altars being used as decoration. At one point the hero and heroine wander through a landscape of classical ruins. Colonna's references to mythological and historical statues, as well as to fountains, grottoes and living plant features, such as groves of cypresses and labyrinths, inspired the

allegory and symbolism of the Mannerist gardens of the 16th century. The elaborate parterres and planting details were essentially derived from contemporary 15th-century gardens and closely resembled those described in Pietro de' Crescenzi's 14th-century treatise *Liber ruralium commodorum* (see page 112), with pergolas covered in intertwined climbers and hedges of mixed plants. Colonna's knowledge of plants and gardening practice was considerable. His flowerbed patterns were among the earliest to be published. Just as Alberti had declared that "every fine fruit that exists in any country" should be planted in a garden, so Colonna wanted it to contain "all the delights that were scattered throughout the universe, so that one could come to know all that had been created".

its underlying if elusive preordained order. At the same time nature could be improved by the gardener's art.

Even in the 15th and 16th centuries, part of a garden, to contrast with the architecturally contrived areas near the villa, were more naturalistic *boschetti* with paths winding through the woodland, very much as might be prescribed in a modern layout. This "naturalism" was especially appealing to the 17th- and 18th-century Englishmen on the Grand Tour. The woodland grove at the Villa Lante through which a visitor could ascend to reach the grotto and fountain at the top of the main garden, so making a progression from relatively uncultivated nature to triumphant sophistication, is an example of just such a juxtaposition. As the gardens of the 16th century evolved into grander and grander creations, nature's materials were manipulated almost to a point where nature became entirely subordinated to art.

OF MYTHOLOGY AND METAMORPHOSIS

Some Renaissance gardens, especially from the middle of the 16th century, were more than pleasure gardens. They were an expression of an individual's splendour.

PRATOLINO: A GARDEN OF MIRACLES

AN UTENS LUNETTE of 1599 shows the Villa Pratolino. The southern portion of the thickly wooded gardens were laid out for the Medici grand duke Francesco I by the architect Bernardo Buontalenti from 1569. Almost 10km (6 miles) north of Florence, in the foothills of the Apennines, the original setting was "wild by nature, surrounded by mountains and full of woods", a site chosen by the duke, it was said, in order that he could demonstrate his mastery over nature.

The garden was among the most sophisticated of its time. Below the villa, the lunette shows a main axis, 15m (50ft) wide, intersected by a series of straight avenues, some at right angles to it but others at an acute angle (a regular grid system would have been difficult in the terrain). A series of irregularly shaped pools on either side of the villa meander down the hillsides in a deliberately natural way, with water flowing from one to another as they descend. The trees are densely planted, some to look natural, others in serried rows, with two formal circles of fir trees and a quincunx, perhaps of fruit trees, near the mount. Reports speak of labyrinths of bay laurel and open meadows sprinkled with wild flowers. Overall Pratolino was a generous mixture of art and naturalism, "ordered" nature and "natural" nature. Some areas displayed the genuine wonders of nature itself; others showed how nature could be imitated.

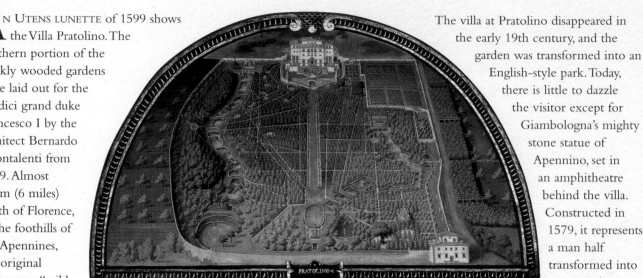

Pratolino plan
This lunette of the Villa Pratolino was painted by Giusto Utens as one of the famous series showing the Medici gardens. The lunettes, originally for the Villa di Artimino but today in the topographical museum in Florence, demonstrate garden styles evolving through almost 100 years.

The gardens were especially famous for their elaborate waterworks, and it was the surprise fountains, grottoes and hydraulic miracles rather than the beauties of nature that most enraptured Michel de Montaigne when he visited the villa in the 1580s. Fynes Morison, writing 10 years later, was equally intrigued by the hydraulics. Water, it seemed, might shower you at every other step. The grottoes were inlaid with semi-precious stones, coral from the Red Sea and pearls. A "pergola" of arching water jets spanned part of the central axis, and water was harnessed to make figures and birds play instruments, controlled by an elaborate system of gears and pulleys. Statues of Apollo, the Muses and Pegasus were brought to life by the unearthly music of a water organ installed inside the mount.

The villa at Pratolino disappeared in the early 19th century, and the garden was transformed into an English-style park. Today, there is little to dazzle the visitor except for Giambologna's mighty stone statue of Apennino, set in an amphitheatre behind the villa. Constructed in 1579, it represents a man half transformed into a mountain or a mountain transformed into a man.

The marvels of Pratolino, which by the end of the 16th century was one of the most celebrated gardens in Europe, were imitated far and wide: at Rudolph II's garden at Prague, Maximilian II's Neugebaude at Vienna, Henri IV's Saint-Germain-en-Laye in Paris and Henry, Prince of Wales's Richmond Palace, near London. These have all disappeared. The garden at Hellbrunn, however, built for the Archbishop of Salzburg by Santino Solari between 1613 and 1615, has survived, its automata still in working order. With grottoes lined with sponge and shells, ornamental singing birds activated by pneumatic bellows, an avenue of water jets and other similar Pratolino tricks, Hellbrunn, though much altered over the centuries, is one of the few remaining Renaissance gardens left in northern Europe.

Man and mountain
Giambologna's colossal statue of Apennino at Pratolino, created in 1579 and 11m (35ft) high, still remains as an indication of the scale of the "garden of miracles".

But to "read" them, as the humanists would have done, required an understanding of mythology, the classics and contemporary politics. Travellers from northern Europe who came later to admire these gardens would have benefited from the same sort of explanatory guidebook that is provided for today's visitor to English landscape gardens such as Stowe or Rousham.

The Medici gardens at Castello and at Boboli conveyed their "messages" in carefully devised iconographical programmes intended to trigger certain responses in visitors. At Castello the fountains and statuary celebrated the rise of the Medici and the greatness of Florence. The statue of Hercules and Antaeus by Bartolemeo Ammannati represented the Rivers Arno and Mugnone, with Giambologna's statue of Venus emerging from the waters, an allegory of Florence. On the upper terrace Giambologna's giant bronze in the oak wood symbolized winter and the Apennines but was also the fount of water for the whole garden, an allusion to the hills and springs of Florence. At Pratolino a gigantic stone statue personified the Apennines. And at the Boboli gardens, Cosimo I wished to emphasize the dynastic pretensions of the Medici family. The great fountain of Oceanus, carved by Giambologna in the 1750s, symbolized the family's power and control over water by celebrating the building of a new aqueduct bringing water to Florence. Originally an amphitheatre, the statue became the centrepiece of the Isolotto Basin in 1637.

At the Villa d'Este, the architect Pirro Ligorio incorporated an allegorical theme comparing

Fabled terrace
The double Terrace of One Hundred Fountains at the Villa d'Este at Tivoli was part of the great design by Pirro Ligorio for Cardinal d'Este from 1559. A series of terracotta reliefs, based on Ovid's *Metamorphoses*, back a formal promenade which traverses the garden. Here, a 17th-century view in Giovanni Battista Falda's *Le Fontane di Roma* (above) compares with a modern photograph (right).

the harnessing of water for display to Hercules' labours and in particular to the cleansing of the Augean stable. A further theme linked Venus with profane love (an easy path leading to her statue), and Diana with chastity (her grotto defended by a steep ascent). Hercules not only represented power but through his mythical association with the Garden of the Hesperides, from which he had stolen the golden apples, he was a highly suitable figure for garden decoration at a time when citrus-growing was all the rage. There was another connection with Hercules: Cardinal d'Este's given name, Ippolito, is Hercules in Italian.

Within the orderly and symmetrical arrangements of trees, fountains, flowerbeds and statues, a fascination with ancient mythology provided the symbolic themes of many of the sculptures and grottoes. A popular source of garden motifs was Ovid's *Metamorphoses*, a Latin poem as familiar to Renaissance contemporaries as it was in its own time. At the Villa d'Este, in 1645, John Evelyn found the Terrace of a Hundred Fountains to be "a long & spacious Walk, full of Fountaines, under which is historiz'd the whole Ovidian Metamorphosis in *mezzo relievo* rarely sculptured". Today, the sculptures, worn by water and weather for more than 300 years, are almost obliterated by moss and maidenhair fern. Buontalenti's grotto in the Boboli Gardens also takes its theme from Ovid, with a transformation of architectural material into natural rock as you enter and, inside, scenery representing both men and animals emerging out of or changing into stone, a scenario of impending disaster as described by Ovid.

WATER TRICKS AND TREATS

Water was not merely a characteristic feature of Renaissance gardens but an essential tool, giving life, movement and sound. It enlivened the architectural stonework and sombre evergreens, its transformation from a slow-moving murmuring stream to the noisy splashing of fountains part of a demonstration of the owner's power and magnificence. Using complicated hydraulic systems, water organs and water jokes became ever more commonplace as technology improved. Water is the dominant theme on the steep slopes of the Villa d'Este and, at the Villa Lante, the whole garden scheme is linked from the grotto at the top through pools and gentle cascades and fountains which descend to broaden out into the great water parterre.

Water was used ingeniously to drip down walls, to arc over sitting areas or create a pergola from its sparkling beads, and to replicate the sound of music or chirruping birds. It was also used as a diversion. Trick water jets (*giochi d'acqua*) produced surprise showers to soak unsuspecting spectators, who found themselves sprayed yet again when they tried to escape. Fountains and nymphaea were, along with grottoes, important features, designed with symbolic undertones. Invoking classical precedent, a stream's source would be implied by featuring a statue of a river god pouring water from an urn and the planting of plane trees.

On the mount

Artificial constructions of Mount Parnassus, showing the winged horse Pegasus and the nine Muses, introduced the idea of the pagan earthly paradise into Renaissance gardens. This Parnassus is from a drawing by the Dutch artist Nicolas Visscher, engraved by Johannes van den Aveele, *c.*1700. Famous Parnassus constructions include one at 16th-century Pratolino, near Florence, and an 18th-century island fountain at Veitshöchheim in Bavaria. Mounts allowing views to the countryside outside a garden were medieval in origin but also one of the elements of Renaissance gardens, as evidenced in the garden at the Villa Medici in Rome.

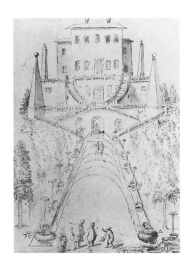

Walking under water
The Pergola of Water at Pratolino, drawn by Giovanni Guerra in 1604. The sprays arching over the broad avenue below the villa were one of the garden's "miracles", and were, according to John Evelyn, wide enough for a man to ride on horseback beneath. Water in all its forms was an essential element in Renaissance gardens, just as it had been in the earlier desert gardens. By the 16th and 17th centuries hydraulic engineering experts, often inspired by 1st-century Alexandrian theories, were introducing elaborate technical feats of water display.

A fine joke
The Fountain of Venus from Falda's *Le Fontana di Roma,* drawn by G.F. Venturini, shows garden visitors escaping a soaking from the sprays of *giochi d'acqua,* or water jokes, a popular feature of later Renaissance gardens.

Throughout history garden forms have originated from natural phenomena, and Renaissance ideas are still adapted for gardens today, just as they were by the English landscapers in the 18th century. Grottoes (see pages 132–33) were intended to represent caves in their savage state, although "improved" to demonstrate the superiority of human endeavour over nature, while maintaining the mystery of the underworld. Just as wildernesses were the garden versions of the wild wood, cascades and fountains were inspired by natural water features. The Fountain of the Organ at the Villa d'Este resembled a mountain waterfall, and the water chains (*catena d'acqua*) of the Villas Lante and Farnese, Caprarola, near Rome, were artificial versions of streams descending a hillside.

In order to put some of these ideas into practice, Renaissance engineers delved into classical sources and studied the works of Archimedes, Aristotle, Vitruvius and Hero of Alexandria. Their interest was not only in garden irrigation and decorative devices but also in finding efficient methods of land drainage and irrigation. Mechanics was first introduced into the curriculum at Padua University in the 1560s.

The ideas of the inventor Agostino Ramelli, published in his *Le diverse et artificiose machine* in 1588, include 110 devices for raising water. Ramelli also gives specific designs for water organs and for fountains with singing birds and moving parts, as seen at the Villa d'Este and at Pratolino. These hydraulic devices were inspired by Hero of Alexandria's *Pneumatica*, written in the 1st century AD and translated from the original Greek into Latin in the 15th and 16th centuries. Hero's "playthings", operated by air, water and steam, were constructed by contemporary engineers to amaze the many visitors – among them, in the 1580s, Montaigne, who was excited by moving statues, unexpected sprays triggered by springs or levers and crashing noises of artillery. A German architect, Heinrich Schickhardt, made a neat series of drawings of the gears and pulleys that controlled the automata in the grotto at Pratolino.

PLANTING AND DESIGN

Alberti recommended formal patterns for use in the garden: "Circles, semi-Circles and the like, and surrounded with Laurels, Cedars, Junipers with their branches intermixed and twining into one another…the trees ought to be planted in rows exactly even, and answering to one another exactly in straight lines…let the walks be lined by evergreens". Porticoes and vine-covered arbours could offer shade and cypress trees could be draped with ivy. Much of Alberti's work derives from classical literature – he quotes Theophrastus on plants and may even have read Lysander's description of how the Persians planted trees in regular lines. He recommended that attention should be paid to the "accuracy of the spacing, the straightness of the rows, the regularity of the angles". His practical gardening experience was rooted in Pietro de' Crescenzi's 14th-century *Liber ruralium commodorum* (see page 112), long available in manuscript form but not printed in Italian until 1471.

Other Renaissance planting schemes came from Crescenzi's 16th-century successors Girolamo Fiorenzuola, whose *La grande arte della agricultura* came out in 1552, and Giovanvittorio Soderini's *Trattata della Cultura* in the last decade of

Fluid links

The water chain at the Villa Lante, near Rome, with its shapes of crayfish, is a pun on the name of Cardinal Gambara, for whom Vignola built the garden in the 1560s. Enclosed by tightly clipped hedges, the water cascade, or *catena d'acqua*, descends from the grotto to the Fountain of the River Gods. At Lante, water, moving and still, is one of the most important elements of its design.

Grottoes

When the distinguished families of Renaissance Italy endowed their gardens with cave-like buildings they were proclaiming their affinity with the civilizations of ancient Greece and Rome. These grottoes were animated by statues of antique deities and heroes, and veneered with *grottesca*: mock stalactites and fantastic forms made of tufa (waterworn limestone), flint, pebbles and shells. According to Alberti, this "grotesque" style of ornamentation was in accord with antique taste, for the ancients had dressed their imitation caverns with "all manner of rough work".

More than a hundred years later, in 18th-century England, Alexander Pope decorated the interior of his riverside grotto with real stalactites, which his friends had shot down off Cheddar Gorge. The poet liked to sit inside and, with the aid of mirrors, watch the world go by. But whereas in Italy grottoes served as retreats from summer heat, in cooler, wetter Britain, as Samuel Johnson declared, "a grotto is a very pleasant place – for a toad".

Even so, by the mid-18th century, a garden grotto was as desirable as a swimming pool is today. One house-for-sale advertisement of the period mentions a "Merlin's Cave, in shellwork, composed of over a thousand beautiful shells". Shimmering with scallops, periwinkles, mirrors and mother of pearl, such grottoes were labours of love, often involving the ladies of the house. The Duchess of Portland is said to have killed a thousand snails for her grotto at Bulstrode.

Stourhead's river god (above)
A cave facing the exit of the grotto at Stourhead, in Wiltshire, is the home of the river god Peneus, mythical ruler of the waves and the nymphs who inhabited his river. Made of painted lead, this powerful statue was erected in 1751 and captioned with a quotation in Latin from the poet Ovid. Like every other British gentleman of his day, Henry Hoare, the creator of Stourhead, was well versed in classical literature.

A model grotto (below)
The wealthy French patrons of landscape designer François-Joseph Bélanger were keen to enliven their gardens with follies and grottoes. In the 1770s Bélanger had toured the gardens of England and his sketches with designs for grottoes featured in the influential volumes of engravings, *Des Jardins Anglo-Chinois*, produced by George Louis Le Rouge and J.C. Kraft.

A pattern of scallops (left)
The shell house at Ballymaloe in County Cork, Ireland, is lined with the treasures of the seashore. These breathtaking mosaics required thousands of shells, considerable artistry and months, often years, of dedication, but created an effect more magical than melancholic.

The view out (right)
Within the lifetime of its owner and designer, Charles Hamilton, Painshill, in Surrey, became one of the most popular pleasure gardens in England. Its grotto – a glinting spectacle of crystal spar, water and stalactites – was probably the work of cave specialist Josiah Lane.

Performance art (left)
The "special effects" at the grotto at Castello, in Florence, villa of Cosimo I, Grand Duke of Tuscany, enthralled the French writer Michel de Montaigne, an early visitor. An ensemble of primal beasts, he said, spouted water "some by the beak, others by the wing, some by the nail or the ears, or the nostrils".

Unearthly beings (above)
Strange forms and faces are discerned in the most splendid of Italy's surviving 16th-century grottoes, La Grotta del Buontalenti at the Boboli gardens, Florence. The creator of this fantasy underworld, architect Bernardo Buontalenti, was also responsible for the wonders of Pratolino.

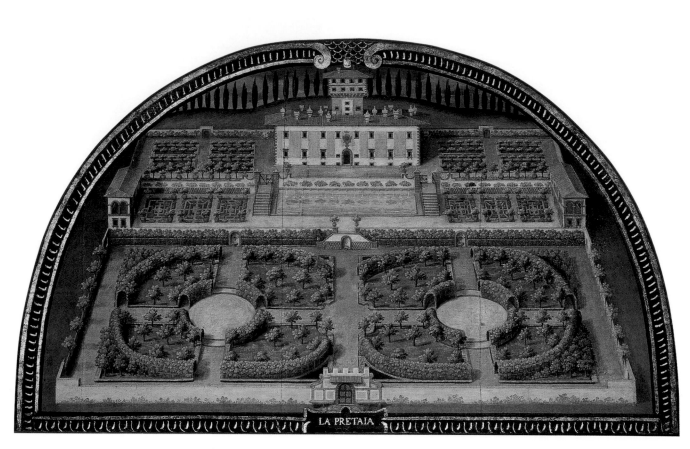

Symmetry at Villa della Petraia
This lunette by Giusto Utens shows the Villa della Petraia, near Villa Castello. It was renovated by Ferdinando de' Medici from 1591 to 1597, after he became Grand Duke in 1587. He terraced the sloping site and laid out the garden in contemporary fashion beside and below the original villa. The symmetrically arranged terraces, either side of the house and the large fishpond, have identical squares planted with fruit trees. On the flat lower level the trees are contained by curving pergolas. Perhaps because water was diverted to embellish the fountains of the Villa Castello next door, the Petraia plan reflects a simplicity of approach for actual living rather than demonstrating Medici power and prestige.

the century, both of whom recommended very similar plants. Earlier classical literature – the Roman manuals of agriculture, Pliny the Younger's letters about his two gardens and Virgil's *Eclogues* and *Georgics* – could also be consulted. To all intents and purposes, practical horticulture had hardly advanced since the time of Columella and Palladius.

It is possible to identify plants in Renaissance gardens from descriptions and contemporary paintings. In the early years, low hedges of mixed shrubs, such as myrtle, box, lavender and rosemary, marked out garden divisions, although by the middle of the 16th century box was more frequently used on its own. For taller hedges there were almonds, apricots and quince, as well as citrus fruit, pomegranates, myrtles, laurustinus and jasmine, a mixture of broad-headed trees and thick-growing shrubs. Walls were frequently covered with trellised vegetation, and early gardens often contained "green" pergolas that channelled or obscured views. Citrus might be espaliered against walls or grown in pots and removed to shelter in a *stanzone* (special room) for the winter. Fiorenzuola especially recommended dwarf fruit trees, grown on quince stock. These were popular in the Boboli Gardens by the end of the century.

In the flowerbeds familiar herbs were grown. It was not until the early 17th century that new imports – tulips, narcissi, anemones and hyacinths, for example – were regularly planted, and then mainly in the beds of botanic gardens or in the gardens of wealthy plant collectors. Often they were displayed as if in a museum rather than part of a living, growing garden. These novelties from the Levant, bulbous plants flowering in spring, could be followed for the summer months by Mexican tuberoses, amaranthus, celosias, sunflowers and marvels of Peru (*Mirabilis jalapa*). By the middle of the 16th century there were basic "recipes" for flowerbed patterns, many of which were replicated in different gardens (see pages 138–39). Mainly square, they were based on geometric subdivisions that can be readily adapted in our own gardens today.

THE TRADITION OF THE GRAND TOUR

Long before the Grand Tour had become an accepted ritual for the sons of noblemen, travellers had begun arriving in Italy from all over Europe. William Thomas, whose *Historie of Italie*, published in 1549, was the first book written in English about Italy, had plenty to say about the gardens at a time when many were still being constructed. He describes the six terraces, "one above another" of the Palazzo Doria at Genoa and the just completed Villa Imperiali outside Pesaro. Others followed: the French philosopher and essayist Michel de Montaigne visited Italian gardens in 1580–81, praising their ingenuity; and Englishmen Fynes Morison, in the 1590s, and Thomas Coryate, in 1608, were both keenly interested in the new garden styles. In the 1640s John Evelyn (see page 188), one of the most influential English garden writers and theorists of the 17th century, appreciated the collaboration of art and nature and commented on the architectural features, statues, grottoes, water features and plants, visiting among others the Palazzo Doria in Rome, Castello and the Villa d'Este. He even took home to England a "winter garden", or *hortus siccus*, of dried plants specially prepared for him in the botanic garden at Padua.

The LEMON

We still cannot be sure when *Citrus limon*, the sweet lemon, was first grown in Europe, nor are we certain of its country of origin. The Chinese have been growing members of the genus for at least 3,000 years, but the lemon itself – along with the citron, *Citrus medica* – probably came to China from tropical east India a little later, and was used in the hybridization programmes first described in Han Yanzhi's *Ju Li* in 1178. In fact, the lemon is probably a hybrid of *Citrus medica* and an unknown parent.

CITRUS LIMON

We know that the citron was grown in Roman gardens at Pompeii. By Renaissance times citrus fruit, brought to Spain, Sicily and southern Italy by the Arabs, was grown extensively – by the 1550s there were 200 varieties at the Medici villa at Castello. The earliest illustrations ever produced with the aid of a microscope contributed to G.B. Ferrari's *Hesperides*, published in Rome in 1646. Engravings of the sweet lemon (above), grown in Italy and Portugal, were made from drawings and watercolours by Vincenzo Leonardi (active 1621–46). These watercolours were in the famous Paper Museum of Cassiano dal Pozzo, a collection made in the early 17th century specifically to help classify the natural world. (Many are now in England, in the Royal Library at Windsor.)

During the 17th century, European horticulturists developed considerable expertise in growing citrus fruits, devising winter shelter and heating to coax them into flower and fruit. Today, one of the most popular lemons is a compact dwarf variety called *Citrus* × *meyeri* 'Meyer', which, in cold climates, can be cultivated in conservatories. The scented flowers and fruit are often carried in the same season.

These 17th-century travellers returned to northern Europe with their minds alive with new ideas for both garden layout and decoration. But by the early 18th century, the real age of the Grand Tour, Italy was less prosperous and the gardens were already declining: much of the dazzle and colour was gone and flowerbeds, previously filled with exotic introductions, had vanished. Travellers from then on could, and certainly did, appreciate the design concepts but they carried home a rather faded picture to emulate in their own gardens: the manipulated spaces with moss-covered stonework, crumbling statues and water features, planted with evergreens, were all that remained. The Grand Tour of Italy and its gardens still goes on. There is no better way to study the art of garden design.

THE RENAISSANCE IDEAL TODAY

FOR THE 21ST-CENTURY garden visitor, two of the most atmospheric and educative gardens are at Villa Gamberaia and Villa la Foce. Although almost modern creations, they beautifully illustrate the whole Renaissance formula. In both, the axial principles and use of space are easily recognizable as Renaissance-inspired – indeed, they are nearly exaggerations of the real thing. The "restoration" of Villa Gamberaia at Settignano, on the slopes above Florence, dates to the turn of the 19th century, when it was given a new water parterre and contemporary planting. The gardens of Villa la Foce, south of Siena, were laid out for Iris Origo from 1924 by an English architect, Cecil Pinsent. Today, it is easier for us to grasp the idea of the Italian garden in these two living gardens than in some of the grander public spaces.

At Gamberaia, where much of the layout was established in the 16th century, an awkwardly shaped site and a much-restored 15th-century villa are tied together by a series of axes and vistas. A main bowling alley unites the garden stretching from one end to the other, its cross-axis leading to a wooded *giardino segreto* from which double stairs rise to the lemon garden above, with box-edged beds beside the *stanzone*. Gamberaia was Sir Geoffrey Jellicoe's favourite Italian garden where "all the various aspects of the individual mind find their counterpart in physical environment". The garden presents, inside a limited space, a complete design vocabulary in which the disposition of the "outside rooms" around the two axes, the treatment of levels, and the contrast of sunlight and shadow, together with the setting and view to Florence below, complete the composition. The arcades of cypress, layers of box and the water parterre are Edwardian conceits.

As a young man, Cecil Pinsent worked with Geoffrey Scott, author of *The Architecture of Humanism*, and like Scott he looked back nostalgically both to the classical Roman period and to the Renaissance. At la Foce, Pinsent developed the sloping site into a series of level terraces and cross axes, a *viale* of cypresses taking the eye up to the hilltop. Although the main garden compartments are geometric, winding pathways follow the contours of the hill, and luxuriant planting by Marchesa Origo softens the "bones" of the high walls and stiff box hedging. Native brooms, pomegranates and cyclamen grow on the hillside. It is a Renaissance garden in which modern flowers and gardening provide scent and colour.

View from Villa Gamberaia
At Gamberaia (right), a long bowling alley, part of the original 16th-century layout, stretches the length of the garden. This view looking east shows the edge of the 1900s water parterre.

Vista at Villa la Foce
The fountain pool designed by Cecil Pinsent, in the lower garden at la Foce, is the centrepiece of an enclosed area by the house. Situated on the shoulder of a hill, with views to the harsh eroded countryside of the crete senese, la Foce had fallen into decay when the Marchesa Origo and her husband began its reclamation in the 1920s.

FLOWERBEDS, PARTERRES AND KNOTS

BASIC RECIPES FOR flowerbed patterns, probably in manuscript form, existed in Italy from the mid-16th century. The geometric beds, often arranged in compartmental squares, were separated one from another by sand or gravel paths. Designs produced by Sebastiano Serlio were available from 1537 and became familiar throughout Europe, with versions appearing in an engraving of the Padua Botanic Garden and in John Parkinson's *Paradisus* of 1629. Though more intricate than the very early recipes, many of Serlio's patterns are nevertheless still composed purely of elementary triangles and semicircles. These beds were intended for a place near the house and for viewing from the house windows or from a higher terrace.

Rails and low trellis around beds, common in medieval gardens, were replaced by low hedges during the Renaissance. These hedges were often of mixed plants such as rosemary, myrtle, lavender and privet. Box was not generally approved of as a continuous hedge until after 1600. Sometimes, a group of beds would be further enclosed by an outer pergola or "living tunnel", which would provide a shady walk as well as a screen.

In France the word parterre at first indicated the whole flower garden, but as designs began to get ever more elaborate the flowers started to disappear. In 1546 the translation into French of Colonna's *Hypnerotomachia Poliphili* seemed to encourage designers to experiment but it was not until 1595 that the first *parterre de broderie* in box was created at Saint-Germain-en-Laye. Here, royal gardener André Mollet

Dutch hybrid
The Dutch garden at Huis ten Bosch, illustrated by Jan van der Groen in Den Nederlandtsen Hovenier, *1669, has a strong Italian flavour but also shows French-style scrolls.*

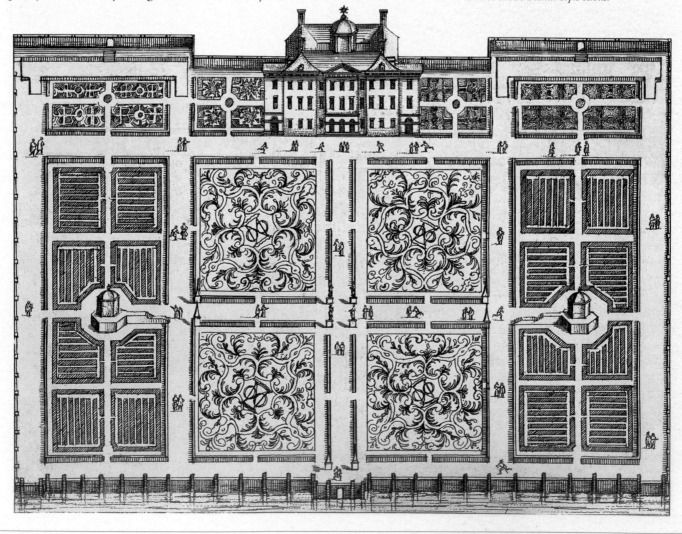

Pattern by Mollet
A design by André Mollet (below), from
Le Jardin de Plaisir, *shows a highly
complicated* parterre de broderie *using
flowing lines of box. The use of dwarf box
made such curvaceous patterns possible.*

(see page 149) persuaded Henri IV to
let him make beds using the new dwarf
box, *Buxus sempervirens* 'Suffruticosa'. Its
low, neat habit of growth allowed
Mollet to "embroider" the parterre
with the tightly clipped scrolls,
arabesques and palmettes that became a
hallmark of French baroque patterns.
These swirling lines were adopted
enthusiastically in the great Dutch
gardens, such as Het Loo, at the end of
the century.

    In Tudor Britain, less sophisticated
knot gardens, with interweaving lines of
herbs and box, were common. Almost
certainly of medieval origin, a knot
garden was a general term applied to
any intricate design that replaced the
functional oblong, symmetrical
flowerbeds arranged around a central
well or fountain. English versions put
an emphasis on pattern-making as
found in embroidery for carpets and
clothes, in plaster or strapwork, in
leather book-bindings and elaborate
jewellery. By 1594 Thomas Hill, in *The
Gardener's Labyrinth*, incorporated
French embroidery embellishments,
using "trayles" resembling plant tendrils
in the corners or centres of designs.

Austrian swirls
*The elaborately scrolled patterns that typify French
baroque were enthusiastically taken up in other
countries, as shown above in this Austrian garden.*

Two knot designs
*The knot garden pattern (right) for box appeared in
William Lawson's* The Country Housewife's
Garden, *published in England in 1638. In recent
years, knot gardens, particularly effective in small
spaces, have again become popular. Rosemary Verey's
design at Barnsley House (below) is based on plans
found in Lawson and in Stephen Blake's* The
Compleat Gardener's Practice *of 1664.*

THE ITALIAN MODEL MOVES ON

Italian art and architecture dominated the European scene throughout the 16th century, with Italian garden style being adopted as a model in northern countries beyond the Alps. By the end of the century its main stylistic features of symmetry and geometry had been established all over Europe, although few of these gardens survive to demonstrate how the new ideas were implemented. Gardens are easy to destroy and subject to whims of fashion. In France some of the most famous, such as Fontainebleau, have been remade many times, reflecting changing mores. In northern Europe, many early Renaissance gardens were either obliterated in religious wars – the Thirty Years' War ending in the Peace of Westphalia in 1648 left few in reasonable condition – or were later overlaid by grand French-style baroque layouts. Although many English gardens were destroyed during the Civil War yet more suffered from the development of the Landscape Movement in the 18th century. In its turn, the French Revolution brought about the ruin and despoliation of many chateaux and their gardens, which were often abandoned to be reconstructed and replanted in a different style.

THE JOURNEY TO FRANCE

When Charles VIII of France captured Naples from the Aragonese in 1494, he and the whole French court were seduced by the villa and garden at Poggio Reale, overlooking the Bay of Naples. "An earthly paradise", as Charles recalled, it had been built for Alphonso II by the Florentine architect Giuliano da Maiano in an opulent almost oriental style. The garden no longer exists but reconstructions based on early 16th-century unscaled sketches reveal some of its secrets. The humanist poet Giovanni Gioviano Pontano, one of Alphonso's tutors, in his poem *De splendore*, had described the "ideal" garden for a Renaissance prince as a place "for walking, or for banquets, as the occasion demands. The garden will have

French adaptation
Fontainebleau, illustrated by Jacques Androuet du Cerceau in 1570 (see page 142), was François I's favourite residence. François laid out the trapezoid lake as the focus of the Cour de la Fontaine, with the tapering ground further west as the Jardin des Pins. The gardens north of the palace, partly enclosed by moats, had figured flowerbed patterns decorated by statues. This illustration shows the lack of symmetry of the French chateaux, and how gardens had to be fitted in with existing walls and moats. The grounds at Fontainebleau were later to be much altered by Henri IV, and again in the 17th century by André Le Nôtre.

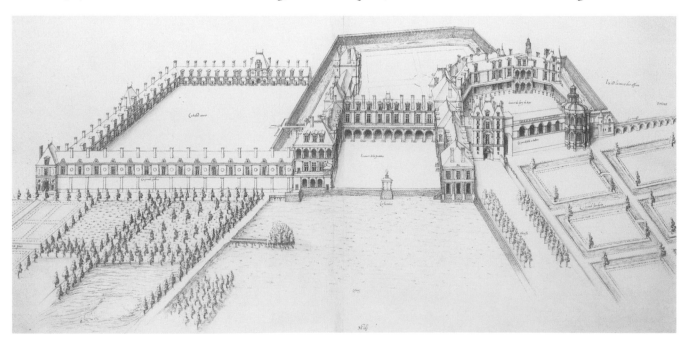

exotic plants and excellent little trees, very artificially and properly arranged." The garden would also demonstrate a prince's power and consequence.

After only five months, Charles's army returned to France carrying with them a quantity of Italian "marvels": tapestries, paintings and sculpture. And, most importantly, the French took Italian craftsmen to decorate their own chateaux – Amboise, Blois, Gaillon and others in the Loire valley and near Paris – in the new Italian style. Many of the gardens – all recorded in the drawings of Jacques Androuet du Cerceau (see overleaf) – remain, but most were substantially altered in the 17th century with Le Nôtre-style parterres or later with landscape-style planting. After Charles's death, the new king, Louis XII (Charles's cousin), completed building at Amboise and began the enlargement of his ancestral home at Blois. Louis also married Charles's widow, Anne of Brittany. The two of them shared an interest in plants and gardening and today her *Book of Hours*, decorated by Jean Bourdichon, is a major source for period flower identification.

The first plans for implementing the Italian idea in France were hampered by the irregular shapes of the existing medieval chateaux, which seldom lent themselves to axial alignments and an easy integration of building and garden. The new gardens, as we see from du Cerceau, were laid out on a horizontal plane to the side of the chateaux with no obvious link to the main buildings. Amboise and Blois show few Italian characteristics, and nothing of the magical ambience of Poggio Reale. At Blois the main walled gardens to the west of the castle had a central axis which divided the 10 squares, five on each side, laid out in flat geometric patterns. Described by Don Antonio de Beatis in 1517, these were edged with low green railings, and each pattern was planted differently. Some were filled with fruit and flowers, others contained box and rosemary cut into the forms of horses, ships and birds, or were used to mark out coats of arms, mottoes or labyrinths. The garden was entirely surrounded by galleries "wide and long so that horses can go there; they have a fine wooden vault covered with trellis".

ITALIAN THEORY, FRENCH PRACTICE

Italian principles had to be adapted to France's topography and climate, as well as to its Gothic architecture. Unlike the Italian landscape, with its intensely cultivated plains, valleys and hills terraced for vines and olives, the French countryside was flatter and densely wooded, its hardwood forests punctuated only by the occasional cluster of village houses and a small area of farmland surrounding them. The forests seemed unwelcoming and even fearsome. These and the almost hostile French attitude to nature affected garden development. In the 17th century, gardens were to occupy whole landscapes, with great avenues stretching into the distant woods, demonstrating power and conquest over organic nature, rather than sympathy with it. Although the

The key to control
Louis XIV's gardener, Jean de la Quintinye, published his *Le Parfait Jardinier ou Instruction pour les Jardins Fruitiers et Potagers* in 1690. The most comprehensive manual on fruit growing and pruning, it is still an inpiration to interested fruit-growers. It was translated into English by John Evelyn in 1693 as *The Compleat Gard'ner*, his last important undertaking.

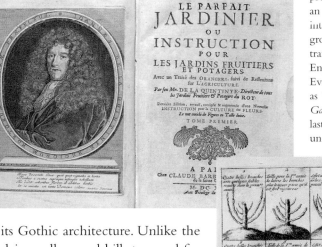

DU CERCEAU'S ENGRAVINGS

BESIDES BEING THE best existing record of 16th-century French gardens, the engravings of Jacques Androuet du Cerceau played an inspirational role. His portrayals of features such as galleries, fountains and ornaments have been used continuously as models by architects and gardeners from the great age of French baroque right up to the present day. Elaborate Edwardian trelliswork galleries have their roots in du Cerceau's drawings.

An architect and engraver, du Cerceau (born *c*.1515) travelled in Italy between 1534 and 1544 studying antiquities in Rome. On his return he established himself at Orleans as an engraver. He published the first of his architectural handbooks in 1539, and the second, which included designs for fountains, pavilions and garden ornaments, in 1561. In *Monuments Antiques* (1560) he included reconstructions of Roman gardens. Other publications show gardens much in the style of the Dutch designer Vredeman de Vries and a collection of knot designs, called *entrelacs* in French. His best-known work, *Les Plus Excellents*

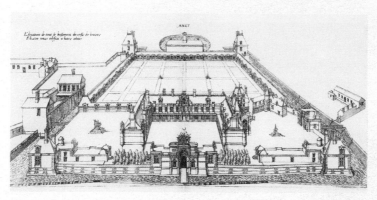

The plan at Anet
This drawing of Anet by du Cerceau from Les Plus Excellents Bâtiments de France *shows a view from the south. The architect Philibert de l'Orme worked at Anet between 1548 and 1553. In the gardens he introduced a style of double semicircular steps for which he became famous.*

Bâtiments de France – published in two volumes in 1567 and 1579 and dedicated to Catherine de' Medici, wife of Henri II – presents a comprehensive picture of architectural evolution in 16th-century France. It shows the transition from Gothic to Renaissance, under Louis XII, followed by the trend towards increased classicism in the reigns of Henri II and Henri III. As in Italy the gardens at this time became distinctly linked to the chateaux themselves. The drawing of Gaillon, begun in 1502 for Georges d'Amboises,

is the first of du Cerceau's works to show a new integration between castle and garden.

Two of du Cerceau's own designs in the 1570s, for Verneuil and Charleval, demonstrate a much more Italian-inspired ethos. The elaborate terraces he envisaged for Verneuil, set high on a hill, were never built, although in influence they may have anticipated the vast terraces of Saint-Germain-en-Laye. At the end of the main walk at Charleval (designed for Charles IX around a hunting lodge south of Rouen) an oval space is lined with a double row of trees, resembling the circle of cypresses in the garden at Medici villa at Castello. That, together with the decoratively shaped parterres, gave a first hint of the curvilinear complexity of baroque, although very little of the palace had been built by the time of Charles's death in 1574.

The shape of trellis to come
A view by du Cerceau from Les Plus Excellents Bâtiments de France *shows an arcade or pergola at Montargis. This style of French trelliswork has had a lasting influence, and, over the centuries, has been adopted for use in numerous gardens around the world.*

gardens of Amboise, Blois and Gaillon had escaped from the cramped confines of the castle walls, they still reflected an unease with the natural world and lacked the vistas with which the Italians "called in" the countryside beyond.

The French idea of gardening as it developed its own sophistication during the 16th and 17th centuries was to subdue nature. This extended to the clipping of trees, shrubs and fruit bushes, the tall hedges, *palissades* (hedges clipped like walls, sometimes containing arches) and *berceaux* (arching arbours) of hornbeam, beech and lime, and the rigid layout of the great box parterres. Over the years the concept of formality has become synonymous with French garden style. The French have also become acknowledged experts in topiary and the pruning and training of trees, shrubs and fruit.

Water was another problem in certain parts of France, a problem never satisfactorily solved even by Louis XIV at Versailles, where fountains could only be activated for the king as he progressed round the garden. Because the style of water features used in the steep hillside gardens of Italy were mostly unsuitable for a flat terrain, the French developed the idea of using a moat, originally a defensive feature, as an ornamental canal, also serving the practical purpose, as in Holland, of draining marshy ground. Vast water layouts around the Loire valley have created a whole landscape, stretching for hundreds of miles, that dominates the topography in much the same way as the 18th-century landscape park changed the appearance of the English countryside. One of the first canals, 800m (2,640ft) long and 20m (70ft) wide, was dug in the 16th century at Fleury-en-Bière, west of Fontainebleau. It inspired Henri IV to construct the Grand Canal at Fontainebleau itself, 1,200m (3,960ft) long and 40m (130ft) wide.

Although Italian garden-architects could gain inspiration from the ideas of classical Rome through the works of Alberti and the *Hypnerotomachia*, little was set down about how to develop the principles. Theories tended to be formulated on the evidence of the "finished product", after a garden had been created, rather than the other way round. This was especially true of the mannerist gardens which, with their emphasis on symbolism and the intricacies of hydraulics and grottoes, were spontaneous productions by men of genius. The "classical" French garden, however, was to develop from architectural theory. A number of principles were established early on that were to remain central to the evolution of garden design in France.

WRITING SOME RULES

When François I came to the throne, he encouraged a second immigration of Italian artists to France. After his defeat at Pavia in 1525, and imprisonment in Spain by Charles V (Holy Roman Emperor), François abandoned the chateaux on the Loire to reside near Paris, especially favouring Fontainebleau in the forest to the south of the city. By 1526 he was employing the Italian designers Primaticcio, Vignola and Sebastiano Serlio, and the painter Il Rosso, to indulge his interest in sculpture and ornament and create grottoes to rival those in Italy. A French interpretation of the Italian style, the Grotte des Pins at Fontainebleau, attributed to Primaticcio, was one of the earliest to be built in France in the Italian style.

Heidelberg: an iconic garden

The Hortus Palatinus at Heidelberg was designed by Salomon de Caus, grandson of du Cerceau, between 1618 and 1621 for the young Elector Palatine, Friedrich V, and his English bride, Princess Elizabeth Stuart, daughter of James I. One of the few "Italian" gardens to be built north of the Alps, it was never completed and only survived a few years before being half-destroyed during the Thirty Years' War. It was damaged further during Louis XIV's campaigns. Today, only some giant terraces are a reminder of its magnificence. De Caus himself recorded the building in his book *Hortus Palatinus*, published in 1620. Features included giant retaining walls above the River Neckar, terraces divided by hedges and pergolas, a maze, gazebos, grottoes and basins, and allegorical statuary. The waterworks, de Caus's speciality (see page 160), were so spectacular and complicated that the short-lived garden was hailed as "the eighth wonder of the world". This illustration by J. Fouquires was made before 1620 and may include features that were planned but never completed.

CATHERINE DE' MEDICI'S EXTRAVAGANZAS

WITH HENRI II'S DEATH in 1560, his widow Catherine de' Medici took over Chenonceaux from Diane de Poitiers (the mistress for whom Henri had acquired the chateau), developing the gardens for her famous entertainments, the forerunners of Louis XIV's extraordinary fetes in the *bosquets* at Versailles.

In March 1560 she celebrated the arrival at Chenonceaux of her son, the young François II (who was king for just one year and died aged 16), and his bride, Mary Stuart, by erecting a triumphal entrance arch of ivy and ornamenting the park with tunnels, green rooms – called *cabinets* – little theatres made of turf and other fantasies. Further displays were held in 1563 and 1577, including fireworks, a water fete and a masque.

At Fontainebleau she organized festivals to celebrate the peace between the Huguenots and Catholics in 1564. The Valois Tapestries in the Uffizi Gallery in Florence depict the scenes, and also those of the entertainments held in the Tuileries to welcome Polish ambassadors who offered the future Henri III the Polish crown. Structures for these festivities, such as Apollo and the Muses on Mount Parnassus, often became permanent features. After Catherine introduced the French palate to sorbets, ice houses were installed in the gardens.

Catherine spent a fortune on the gardens at Fontainebleau. She employed Primaticcio to surround the whole area of the king's private gardens north of the Cour Ovale with a moat, install a painted gallery and add parterres and statuary. Other additions included setting up a menagerie with cattle and a dairy where she could retreat in the summer. Even the latter, far from simple, was painted and gilded like the main buildings.

Spectacular showmanship
Catherine is especially remembered for her lavish garden displays, some of the most dazzling being those staged on water with fantastical nautical tableaux and fireworks.

Another at the Tuileries (built for Catherine de' Medici) was decorated by Bernard Palissy with polychromatic ceramics representing gods and goddesses as well as animals and reptiles.

Sebastiano Serlio's *Tutte l'opere d'architettura*, published in five volumes between 1537 and 1547, was one of the few practical titles to set out Italian theories. It was translated into French almost immediately by Jean Martin, with its fourth volume containing the first designs for ornamental parterres to be printed in France.

In 1597, Philibert de l'Orme provided the French answer to Serlio's book with his *Le premier tome de l'architecture*. After studying the antiquities in Rome (where he met Serlio) between 1533 and 1536, de l'Orme, the son of a master mason at Lyon, had adjusted his version of classical architecture to the topography of France and the need to adapt existing buildings rather than construct new ones. A skilful engineer, he founded his designs on sound principles using a delicacy of invention and harmony which was to be the foundation stone of French classical architecture until at least the 18th century. His earliest publication was *Nouvelles inventions pour bien bastir et à petis frais* (1561).

Henri II, who followed his father François I to the throne in 1547, put de l'Orme in charge of all royal buildings and gardens. Henri had married Catherine de' Medici, daughter of Lorenzo the Magnificent, in 1533, but it was for his mistress, Diane de Poitiers, that Henri commissioned de l'Orme to design at least two gardens, at Anet and Chenonceaux. De l'Orme designed Anet around an iconographical scheme based on the huntress Diana, relating to Diane de Poitiers. Henri II's sudden death in 1559 left de l'Orme unemployed when Catherine, regent until her third son Henri III became king in 1574, reinstated Primaticcio and the Italian school.

GLIMPSES OF THREE LOST GARDENS

Although the golden age of French garden design was not to come until the latter half of the 17th century, the early years saw a series of gardens that are important landmarks in French garden development. Instead of being designed as adjuncts to existing chateaux, each of the gardens at Saint-Germain-en-Laye, the Luxembourg Palace and Richelieu formed part of an integrated plan and complemented a purpose-built house.

Almost nothing remains today to remind us of the brilliance of Saint-Germain-en-Laye, the most Italianate garden of all, begun in 1593 for Henri IV but already outlined by Philibert de l'Orme for Henri II. Built 80m (280ft) above the Seine on a steep rise, with panoramic views over the river winding towards Paris, the gardens were spectacular. Designed by Etienne Du Pérac, with a succession of eight steep terraces, they were reminiscent of both the 16th-century Cortile del Belvedere in Rome and the Villa d'Este in Tivoli. The terraces were laid out with new *parterres de broderie*, one of the earliest examples of Claude Mollet's use of dwarf box to create elegant, curving arabesques, which were set off by coloured earth or sand. The Italian hydraulic engineers, the Francini brothers, who had worked at Pratolino, installed the automata.

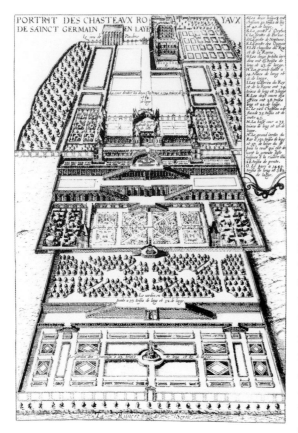

The Italian connection
Saint-Germain-en-Laye was the most Italian in style of all the French chateaux. Built for Henri IV from 1593, its terraced gardens descended to the Seine, and its grottoes with automata by the Francini brothers emulated those at Pratolino.

THE INGENIOUS FRANCINIS

Apart from working at Saint-Germain-en-Laye, brothers Thomas and Alexandre Francini also created water wonders at Fontainebleau; for Cardinal Richelieu at Rueil; and, in 1623, engineered an aqueduct to bring water to the Luxembourg gardens. Thomas's son François designed the fountains at Versailles, where he faced immense difficulties in providing a sufficient water supply for the displays.

Both Louis XIII and Louis XIV spent much of their childhoods at Saint-Germain-en-Laye, but even by 1618 the grottoes were in need of repair, the great terraces collapsing through neglect of the water systems rather than from unstable building. They were partly restored by Louis XIV after 1660, but little now remains except the upper terrace, redesigned and extended by Le Nôtre to make a wide 2.5km (1.5 mile) walk on the escarpment.

Marie de' Medici began laying out the Luxembourg Palace and gardens in 1615, the *allées* of elms having already been planted in 1612. She wanted to emulate the Pitti Palace and Boboli gardens of Italy, where she had spent her childhood, but was restricted by the configuration of the site and, in the event, the parterre shaped like an amphitheatre proved almost the only element that she could copy. John Evelyn visited in 1644 and described the walks of limes, elms and hornbeam hedges, as well as the box parterres, as "so rarely designed and accurately kept cut, that the embroidery makes a wonderful effect…'Tis divided into four squares, and as many circular knots, having in the centre a noble basin of marble nearly 30 feet diameter…a dolphin that casts a girandola of water nearly 30 feet high, playing perpetually, the water being conveyed from Arcueil by an aqueduct of stone built after the old Roman magnificence." Jacques Boyceau was probably responsible for the parterre patterns and Thomas Francini for the waterworks.

Not all the great 16th- and 17th-century gardens belonged to the royal family, but all were meant to impress as symbols of social status, power and wealth. Vistas into the forests, canals stretching across the flat terrain, on a scale not seen before, and vast *parterres de broderie*, which needed an equally vast labour force to maintain them, were all part of French pomp. But they were only the forerunners of the schemes implemented later in the century. Cardinal Richelieu (1585–1642), who unified France during Louis XIII's minority and laid the foundations of absolute monarchy, emphasized the advantages of comprehensive organization of space. By the end of the 1630s his gardens in Paris were the largest after the royal gardens of the Luxembourg and the Tuileries. In Touraine, his property Richelieu, which comprised not only gardens and park but also a new Renaissance town, reflected the cardinal's desire to demonstrate his own importance, and through that the supreme power of the king. His architect, Jacques Lemercier, planned an axial approach through the forecourts of the house which revealed the gardens as a surprise climax. Building was begun in 1631 and completed in 1639. Three radial avenues of elms converged on the circular entrance court, part of which survives to this day. At the time the gardens of Richelieu had an unprecedented collection of fine statuary. Today, although most of the gardens' glory has vanished, it is still possible to grasp something of the scale of their vast grid-like layout. The chateau was demolished in the 1820s, leaving only the walls and pavilions of the circular courtyard.

THE MOLLETS: A DYNASTY OF ROYAL GARDENERS

THE MOLLET FAMILY provided at least four generations of outstanding gardeners, whose technical virtuosity helped prepare the way for the genius of Le Nôtre. The Mollets are particularly associated with the development of planting styles in parterres, working in the royal parks and gardens in and near Paris. The first, Jacques Mollet, worked at Anet for the Duc d'Aumale, but it is his son and grandson, Claude and André, who are the most important.

Claude, author of *Le Théâtre des Plans et Jardinages* (published posthumously in 1652), also spent time at Anet but worked principally for Henri IV at Saint-Germain-en-Laye and other royal gardens. He claimed that, while at Anet in 1582, Etienne Du Pérac had taught him to make a garden in the form of a single compartment divided by walks rather than the repetitive squares of different designs that had been used through most of the 16th century. "These were the first *compartiments en broderie* which have been made in France," he wrote. "At the time...box was still rarely used, because very few people of rank wished to have box planted in their gardens." Instead Claude Mollet used several kinds of plants which could not long survive the French climate. Eventually, in 1595, Henri IV allowed him to plant the garden of Saint-Germain-en-Laye all in the new dwarf box (*Buxus sempervirens* 'Suffruticosa') that Mollet had been assembling in his own nursery, and to use box in a small garden at Fontainebleau. This allowed Mollet to develop the kind of sophisticated swirling patterns and flowing lines that were almost impossible to achieve with a mixed

CLAUDE MOLLET, AS HE APPEARED IN HIS BOOK *THÉÂTRE DES PLANS ET JARDINAGES*

planting. He also used ordinary species box to make higher hedges in the gardens of the Tuileries. (Later, his son André, working in the colder climate of Sweden, recommended using red whortleberry, *Vaccinium vitis-idaea*, instead of box.) In *Le Théâtre des Plans et Jardinages*, Claude Mollet describes how to lay out parterres, space *allées*, and make "walls" and *palissades* of both beech and hornbeam. He stresses the "relief" effect of tall clipped *allées*, rows of trees, arching *berceaux* and sharply cut hedges when used to act as backdrops to the parterres – as necessary today in modern flower gardens as in the 17th century. It is not often appreciated that the Mollets (and Le Nôtre) always recommended planting more relaxed flowerbeds adjacent to the great parterres with shrubs and a mixture of bulbs and summer flowers.

In *Le Jardin de Plaisir*, written in Sweden while working for Queen Christina in 1651, André Mollet went beyond the practicalities of growing plants to discuss theory and perspective, many of his ideas deriving from Italy. He defined the scope of pleasure grounds in this way: "The Garden of Pleasure consists in ground works, Wildernesses, choice trees, Palissades and Alleys or Walks, as also in Fountains, Grotto's and Statues, perspectives, and other such like Ornaments."

André Mollet stressed that those features most remote from the eye "ought to be drawn of a larger Proportion than those that are nearer so that they thereby appear more beautiful". He felt that definite rules should determine the progression of garden features as the garden becomes more distant from the house. "Groundworks" near the chateau, he said, should not be concealed by any "Trees, Palissades or other high Work". *Parterres de broderie* should be followed by turf parterres, and the whole should be divided by a grid system of *allées* and walks, arranged symmetrically about a central axis. Avenues, hardly mentioned before the 16th century, should be extended in lines perpendicular to the façade of the house. He also recommended cypresses as feature plants. Wildernesses, known as *bosquets* in France, were also essentially to be formal, with tall hedges of hornbeam, lime, beech, phillyrea or cherry laurel. *Palissades*, formed by plants trained head-high on a framework of thin lathes, could make shady walks and mark out labyrinths in the outer area.

Besides France and Sweden, André Mollet worked in England for Queen Henrietta Maria before the Civil War, and in Holland, returning again to England after the Restoration to advise Charles II on St James's Park.

ORDERED PERFECTION: THE AGE OF LE NÔTRE

The French formal garden – clipped hedges, straight *allées* and geometric planning – is celebrated as the pre-eminent expression of French rationalism, in which knowledge of the world could be gained by the use of reasoning. Controlled and logical, these French gardens, punctuated by wide pools reflecting the sky, stretched out into the distant forests and beyond to the horizon. Today, this remains the most cogent image of French gardening. One of the guiding principles, as described by the Duc de Saint-Simon (writing of Versailles), was "to tyrannize nature". The French influence was to spread throughout the courts of Europe, and to Britain after the Restoration of 1660. In Holland, Germany, Spain and Russia, French spatial theorems and the concept of power over nature were imposed on simpler Italian styles.

Above all, architectural theories – culminating in Le Nôtre's exploitation of aerial perspective to carry the eye into infinity – played a dominant role in France, with "ordered" rows of plants populating the gardens in prescribed patterns and regimented lines of trees or hedges confirming the geometry. But the great practitioner Le Nôtre himself added another dimension to the gardens, one based on optical illusion. Dezallier d'Argenville's *La Théorie et la Pratique du Jardinage*, published in 1709, is generally considered a codification of Le Nôtre's practice, and as such provided the means whereby contemporary and future owners and designers could exploit the principles in their own sites. It provided mainly "how-to" advice such as planting instructions and the techniques of surveying and terracing but contained relatively little information about the Cartesian principles which had led Le Nôtre into devising his theatres of optical illusion and false perspective.

Descartes understood that perspective views would vary according to where they were viewed from, thus confirming that any perception of reality was an illusion based on the idea of a fixed viewpoint. Le Nôtre followed these prinicples and exaggerated the proportions of garden features to accommodate not only a single viewpoint from the entrance of a garden or from the chateau, but also a variety of perspectives taken from various points around the garden. He so modelled the land that on a tour of the garden all the perspective views appeared as he had planned, and the visitor could be deceived into believing that the proportions and dimensions of the garden were different from what they were in reality. Even if Le Nôtre's optics are not understood by most amateur gardeners, all modern landscape architects can usefully study his theories, which can be verified on the ground, especially at his masterpiece, Vaux-le-Vicomte.

Chantilly's mirror effects

This view of Chantilly, the "garden of mirrors", by Adam Perelle, 1680, was painted from the north. It shows the grand canal excavated in the valley of the Nonette in 1671–72, the chateau to the right with Mansard's Orangerie, two identical water parterres with basins and fountains, plus the long view to the south. Chantilly, with its water reflections and manipulation of perspective, is considered by many to be Le Nôtre's finest achievement, even more impressive than Vaux-le-Vicomte.

Du Cerceau had originally designed the layout in 1570, and the gardens had remained almost unaltered until 1662, when the Prince de Condé called in the services of Le Nôtre. His plan imposed a new regularity by means of a giant axial arrangement with the main existing terrace as its centre. Chantilly's magic lies in its celebration of water effects, with canals hidden by various levels in the garden, but uncomplicated by fountains and statues. Still water pools create reflections that enhance a spectator's perceptions – not by doubling the buildings, as in an Islamic garden, but by mirroring the sky, the clouds and surrounding nature.

Entertainments Versailles-style
Jean Cotelle's view of the Bosquet
du Théâtre d'Eau shows one of the
most ingenious of the Versailles
water spectacles, constructed
1671–74. Other *bosquets* also
depended on dramatic fountain
displays, ironic when one remembers
the chronic shortage of water at
Versailles. When Louis XIV toured
the garden, gardeners had to hurry
ahead to turn on the fountains as the
king approached as those behind
were switched off.

Laid out for Louis XIV's finance minister, Nicholas Fouquet, Vaux was completed by 1661 in time to stage an elaborate celebration in honour of the king. The lavishness of chateau, garden and statuary – only the best craftsman had been employed – was Fouquet's undoing. Within a few weeks of the festivities he was arrested and Vaux sequestered, its trees and statues plundered by the king for Versailles. Vaux remained neglected until restored by Achille Duchêne in the early 20th century.

The gardens of Vaux, although designed to be seen from the windows, are entered today from the rear of the chateau, where, from the centre of the steps, the whole garden seems to be revealed in a perspective view. The topography of the gently sloping and rising land allowed Le Nôtre to create a whole landscape of deception. A central path is flanked by symmetrical rows of trees, lawns, gravel paths, flowerbeds, fountains and statues. One can see a rectangular pool with statues in niches, beyond which is a lawn sloping upwards, towards a vanishing point. The central path slopes slightly down towards a pool that, from a distance, appears to be oval, but is in reality a circle. From there not only does a further transverse canal appear but the central path proceeds at a lower level, both features invisible from the original viewpoint at the chateau. The second pool, when reached, turns out to be square not rectangular, statues in the niches are more visible, and prove to be on a lower level than the pool and separated from it by another wide transverse canal, separating the pool and final slope.

Le Nôtre achieved his results by studying Euclid's *Optics*, Descartes and the general laws of linear perspective. These demonstrated the effects of distance on perceived heights as viewed from a static position at the entrance compared to the changing views which appear on traversing the terrain. At Vaux, the space, the levels and angles were all carefully measured. When the viewer glances back from the other side of the square pool, the chateau is exactly reflected in its surface.

Versailles and Vaux seem to be the epitome of French garden style, with a vast ground plan based around a formal central axis and a vanishing point at the horizon where the garden seems to disappear to infinity. But Le Nôtre's work is less successful at Versailles. The garden is on such a large scale and scattered with so many distractions that no visitor could expect to complete the whole tour in one session. Although it has a strong central axis and distant focus, the garden lacks sufficient coherence to dictate a route. Louis XIV's own guide, *La Manière de Montrer les Jardins de Versailles*, can be a useful starting point. Designed for his own glorification as the Sun King, the gardens, in spite of the many symbolic reminders, seem to have lost their point without his presence.

IN THE GARDEN OF THE SUN KING

Versailles was built at a time when Louis XIV's power in Europe was unprecedented. The chateau, originally used by his father Louis XIII as a hunting lodge, was first used by Louis XIV for entertainments. Following his visit to the unfortunate Fouquet's Vaux-le-Vicomte, he commanded that Versailles be made suitable for staging the same kind of elaborate spectacle. A medieval tournament, the Carrousel, performed in June 1662 before 15,000 spectators, highlighted his heliotropic symbolism and his theme for Versailles. Finally, between 1668 and 1671, he enlarged the chateau, making it the court's chief place of residence and the seat of government. His own private retreats were at Marly and Trianon. Using Fouquet's team of craftsman the first construction was of the Orangerie, with a vista over it to the south – the main axis of the garden until 1668. The design of the Orangerie was altered by Hardouin-Mansart between 1682 and 1688 and a wider parterre and a huge rectangular lake called the Pièce d'Eau des Suisses were added. Many members of the Swiss Guard employed in the lake's excavation died from the marsh gas released during the digging.

Le Nôtre's Parterre de Latone, with a horseshoe terrace leading to the Fountain of Latone, was the first step towards creating the dominant axial development to the west, the view into the setting sun. This western vista, ranging over pools, basins, fountains and canals to the poplar trees on the horizon, the Pillars of Hercules, has come to symbolize the reign of the Sun King and his association with Apollo. The Bassin d'Apollon itself was installed in 1670. The main vista, a canal called the Allée Royale, was enlarged in 1667; it stretched 1.5km (0.9 miles) to the west and had branches to Trianon to the north and the Ménagerie to the south. It was finally completed between 1668 and 1672.

The site at Versailles, in marshy ground, was inauspicious, but the canals, designed to be seen from the chateau, helped ensure adequate drainage. The entire formal framework was carved out of the forest, through which secondary *allées* were cut. Along these rides a variety of *bosquets*, set pieces decorated with fountains and statues, were carved out as "green" rooms for entertainments. There were 17 original *bosquets*. Facilities for banquets, fetes, theatre and dancing, all arranged as temporary "furnishings", were gradually replaced by more permanent constructions of fountains and basins, all much altered during the years up to 1713. One, the Labyrinthe, long since vanished, was designed by Le Nôtre

The Sun King
Although we may judge Versailles primarily as a setting for Louis XIV to display his power and importance, the king (painted here by Jean Petitot) was genuinely interested in his gardens and plants, demanding flowers at all times of the year. He ordered tender tuberoses from Provence, which arrived in wagons each spring to perfume the flowerbeds.

The view to infinity (overleaf)
Pierre Patel's perspective of Versailles from the east, painted in 1668, gives an idea of the scale of the garden. By 1682 Versailles had become the official seat of the government and changes to the original hunting lodge as well as to the garden, including the *bosquets* planned for festivities, totally changed the character of the whole complex.

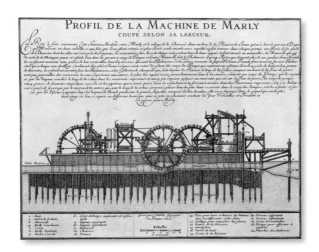

PROFIL DE LA MACHINE DE MARLY
COUPÉ SELON SA LARGEUR.

Marly's water machine
The gardens of Versailles were always short of the water necessary to make the fountains function. At nearby Marly, where, after 1679, Louis XIV did his more private entertaining, a machine, operated by a series of waterwheels, raised water from the Seine. Used to feed the royal fountains at Versailles, the water was carried 6km (3.7 miles) across the hill by an aqueduct, with three reservoirs excavated along the route.

between 1664 and 1667, then redesigned after 1669 to contain 39 fountains and statues from Aesop's fables. Another, the Bosquet Le Marais, suggested by the king's mistress, the Marquise de Montespan, contained a central tree surrounded by reeds, all made of metal, which spouted jets of water, some emerging from the tips of the branches. The elaborate waterworks were the king's pride. The water supply, however, was always short of requirements. A team of gardeners using whistles were needed to turn each fountain on and off as Louis made his royal progress. And the cost of bringing water to the park was vast. A monumental project for raising water 162m (520ft) up from the Seine involved 14 waterwheels, each 12m (40ft) in diameter, powered by a series of pumps.

The garden incorporated most, if not all, the planting ideas expounded by the Mollets – tall tightly clipped hornbeam hedges, used for *palissades* or *berceaux*, and elaborate *parterres de broderie* of box. Flowers were not neglected. Louis was passionate about them, encouraging botanizing explorers to bring back plants to be cultivated first in the Jardin du Roi (established in 1625 in Paris and later to become the Jardin des Plantes) or, if of doubtful hardiness, in Montpellier. In 1672, 10,000 tuberoses (*Polianthes tuberosa*), only introduced from Mexico in 1629, were grown in Provence and transported across the mountains in wagons to supply the gardens at Versailles. Louis insisted that Le Nôtre should see that the gardens were stocked with flowers "even in winter". Other flowers, including bulbs from the Levant and more familiar plants from the Mediterranean, were planted in the box-edged beds of the Grand Trianon.

DUTCH BAROQUE AND THE SPLENDOUR OF HET LOO

In the early 18th century French baroque, as epitomized by Vaux and Versailles, was to be emulated by the courts of Europe and beyond. Each country expressed the style in a slightly different way. Some had already absorbed earlier Italian ideas, helped by pattern books such as those of Serlio and Vredeman de Vries. During the 17th century the young Dutch republic became extraordinarily wealthy, and Netherlanders travelling abroad discovered the Renaissance gardens of Italy as well as the work of Mollet and Le Nôtre in France. After the Revocation of the Edict of Nantes in 1685, many French Huguenots fled across the border and settled in Holland. Among them was the engraver and designer Daniel Marot, who was to play such a large part in the development of Het Loo.

In Holland all designs had to be adapted to the unforested but flat landscape and to smaller estates. There was a more open approach, with vistas running into the countryside to disguise the actual perimeters of the garden. Avenues flanked canals to distant perspectives and plants in pots and topiary were used to decorate the restricted spaces. Statues and water features, including gushing fountains adapted from vast French gardens, were less successful in the smaller spaces.

Het Loo, conceived in 1686, was one of the great French-Dutch-style gardens of the late 17th century. Between 1807 and 1809 the famous baroque sunken

garden was buried in sand by Louis Napoleon, its terraces levelled for the construction of an English-style landscape garden;
so Het Loo became a victim of the fashion for 18th-century
naturalism. Fortunately the story of the garden does not end
there. Between 1979 and 1984 both garden and palace (now a
museum) were completely restored, their regeneration the result
of skilled, meticulous research, both of architectural details and
of planting. It is one of the most authentic restorations of all time.

The gardens were constructed for William of Orange and
Mary Stuart to accompany the palatial hunting lodge built by
Jacob Romano. Daniel Marot designed the whole garden and
was responsible for much of the detail of the decoration inside
the palace. Raised terraces, which continued all round the
garden, surrounded a sunken Lower Garden reached by lavish
fan-shaped steps. Arranged as eight square beds, there were four
central *parterres de broderie*; in the outer beds flowers surrounded
a central statue. Around each square a narrow flowerbed or *plate
bande* was edged with box and planted with single specimens of
rare plants, displayed as if in a museum. Water was an important
feature in the design, both for its beauty and for its soothing
sound, in the form of cascades, basins and fountains. The king's
garden was located under his apartments on one side of the
palace, the queen's on the other, the latter having a tunnel of
hornbeam trained over wooden trellis, reminiscent of those
shown in Vredeman de Vries's engravings.

A hybrid between Renaissance and baroque, Het Loo's
layout is reminiscent of the Luxembourg Gardens with its semicircular termination. Others see it as a Dutch layout with
French decoration. Two main sources of information about
contemporary plants were used when restoring the garden:
Jan van der Groen's *Den Nederlandtsen Hovenier* (*The Dutch
Gardener*) of 1669, and a manuscript held in the Uffizi Museum,
the *Codex Hortus Regius Honselaerdicnesis*, in which plants grown at Honsholredyk,
where van der Groen was gardener, are illustrated.

Parterres of Het Loo
Built from 1685 to 1686 by Jacob
Romano as a hunting lodge for
William and Mary, Het Loo became
a royal palace after 1689. The
sumptuous gardens were designed
by Daniel Marot in Renaissance
style, but the flat terraces below the
main building were decorated with
intricate French-type box *broderie
arabesques* set in gravel and earth.
Narrow *plates bandes* around the
parterres gave space to plant newly
introduced perennials and annuals
between a series of upright junipers.

DEVELOPMENTS IN ENGLAND

In England, where we need to step back again to the 16th century, gardens,
especially royal gardens, were mainly inspired by those of France and Holland.
This was particularly so under Henry VIII, who considered the French king,
François I, his main cultural rival. (The two had met famously on the Field of the
Cloth of Gold and tried to outshine one another in their splendour.) The detail
of gardening was transmitted, often by French and Dutch craftsmen, through
France and the Netherlands and a familiarity with the drawings of du Cerceau,
the theories of Philibert de l'Orme and the pattern books of Vredeman de Vries.
In Henry's time, English travellers were familiar with the royal Valois court at

Fontainebleau and drew inspiration from the French chateaux of Gaillon and Anet sooner than they did from Italy. But many Englishmen also travelled to Italy and studied the gardens there. A distinctive French influence was evident after the Restoration in 1660.

By the end of the 16th century the highly educated courtiers had become interested in Italian garden philosophy and its origins in classical Rome. They were reading books on architecture, such as those by Alberti, Colonna, Serlio and Palladio. These, with classical texts, became their sources for ideas on architectural features, iconographical programmes and garden entertainments. Reports from travellers, especially after the middle of the century, gave detailed descriptions of the great allegorical gardens recently constructed in Florence and Rome. Nevertheless early attempts to introduce the Italian style in England were piecemeal. Rather than create a whole garden on the scale of the Villa d'Este, which few Englishmen could manage, elements of the Italian gardens – terraces, grottoes, fountains, waterworks and statuary – were used to summon up the Italian idea. Such features appealed to the English imagination, but did not necessitate making over a whole garden to new orderings of perspective based on an integration of house and garden. The first complete Italian-inspired garden came much later in 1631, when Wilton House, in Wiltshire, was entirely remodelled by Isaac de Caus for the Earl of Pembroke.

In England's Tudor and Jacobean gardens, medieval ideas and attitudes still lingered on. Typical features were heraldic symbols, knot gardens, mounts, fountains and obelisks, banqueting houses and beds of old-fashioned scented flowers and herbs associated with the countryside and Shakespeare. Masques and festivals were organized to celebrate Elizabeth, the Virgin Queen. In universal terms, the English 16th- and 17th-century garden had little to add to the ordered ideas originating in Italy. But it seems highly likely that the English interpretation

Whitehall scheme
This bird's-eye view of Whitehall Palace from the Thames, by Anthonis van der Wyngaerde, _c_.1557–62, shows the Great Garden centred on a large fountain laid out in knots. We know from _The Family of Henry VIII_, painted _c_.1545 and showing a view of the garden, that there were raised beds surrounded by rails, painted in Tudor colours of green and white, with heraldic beasts on posts.

of these European theories, adapted to the English countryside and English mind, became a preparation for the 18th-century English Landscape Movement and its return to a classically orientated pastoral theme.

Unlike Continental Europe, and in particular Italy, France and Holland, no representative English garden made between 1550 and 1660 remains to yield clues (although this lack is now being made up for in part by recent archaeological discoveries). Most gardens of the period disappeared during the Civil War or, as at Hampton Court and Hatfield, had their original appearance disguised under new layers of history. Others disappeared during the 18th-century landscape revolution. The spirit of these earlier gardens, however, can be found in letters, poetry and prose, as well as in tapestries, etchings and paintings. Until relatively recently little attention had been paid to the tales of splendid gardens being laid out to set off the newly built mansions of wealthy courtiers, in which terraces, grottoes, statues and water features began to rival contemporary constructions in Italy and France. Twenty years ago Sir Roy Strong redressed this balance in *The Renaissance Garden in England*, in which he explored their extent, and other historians continue to illuminate the period.

Tudor ornamentation
Heraldic beasts, here sitting atop Henry VIII's pavilion at the Field of the Cloth of Gold, were favourite Tudor decorative devices and much used in gardens, as in the Great Garden of Whitehall Palace.

TUDOR GARDENS

Under Henry VIII it is only the royal gardens that are of note: Hampton Court, which he took over from Cardinal Wolsey in 1525; Whitehall (another Wolsey property); and Nonsuch in Surrey. At first, under Henry, gardens were arrayed with painted heraldic symbols conveying Tudor importance and illustrating the lineage of the royal house, together with a series of heraldic beasts. Under Elizabeth I the gardens came to symbolize the queen's prestige, often with each flower seen to mirror one of her regal virtues, the whole an emblematic representation of the queen herself.

Descriptions given by travellers to Hampton Court, even if viewing the gardens 50 years after their construction, are especially vivid. A German, Thomas Platter, visited the gardens in 1599 during Elizabeth's reign. He refers to the squares in the Privy Garden as being laid out in a pattern with red brick dust, white sand and grass to resemble a chess board, and goes on to describe strange topiary figures representing a great array of shapes: "men and women, half men and half horse, sirens, serving maids with baskets, French lilies and delicate crenellations all round made from dry twigs bound together and…evergreen quick-set shrubs, or entirely of rosemary, all true to the life, and so cleverly and amusingly interwoven, mingled and grown together, trimmed and arranged picture-wise that their equal would be difficult to find".

The great gardens of Nonsuch Palace, constructed by Henry VIII between 1538 and 1546 to rival François I's Fontainebleau, reached their peak in the 1580s after Mary Tudor had sold the palace to Lord Lumley. Lumley's alterations brought Nonsuch into the forefront of garden development, its Italianate facelift making it the first mannerist garden in England. The gardens declined after 1649 and were finally destroyed in the 1680s, leaving virtually no trace.

Stylish centrepiece
The Susanna Fountain at Wilton House, in Wiltshire, was designed by Isaac de Caus after 1632. Four *compartiments de broderie* in clipped box were centred on four fountains, including the Susanna, which was sculpted by Nicholas Stone. The fountain still survives there, although damaged.

THE DE CAUS BROTHERS

Two French brothers were to have a remarkable impact on European gardens. Salomon de Caus (*c.*1576–1626) visited Italy and studied hydraulics at Pratolino before coming to England, where he worked for James I's queen, Anne of Denmark, at St James's Palace and Wimbledon House, as well as for Henry, Prince of Wales. He was the most extravagant and ambitious of all the water wizards. His *Raison des Forces Mouvantes* (published 1615, second edition 1624) was an astonishing treatise on "unnatural" ways with water, many of them based on the works of Vitruvius and Hero of Alexandria. Little remains of his most impressive garden design, the Hortus Palatinus at Heidelberg (see pages 144–45), which was destroyed by war. His brother Isaac, meanwhile, brought a mannerist style and various of his own water tricks to Britain with his designs for Wilton House.

Although Henry's royal gardens all seem to have kept one foot in the past, the Elizabethan courtiers, familiar with the French court and French gardening and also well read in the Italian architectural theses and classical texts, were much more innovative. Lord Lumley's work at Nonsuch may have been partly inspired by that at Theobalds. There, near Ware in Hertfordshire, William Cecil, Lord Burghley, began a vast building programme in 1575, to be completed in 1585. As Theobalds grew it became a popular venue for Elizabeth on her frequent "progresses". In his Great Garden, Burghley introduced changes of level with steps, loggias and a wilderness grove, although his garden departments remained independent units. Nine square gardens were laid out as knots, one "planted with choice flowers", the rest either with armorial knots, or more simply with "all grass knots handsomely turfed in the intervalles or little walks". In a summer-house "twelve Roman emperors in white marble" helped to persuade Continental visitors that there was a distinct Italian resonance, as did the little wood and labyrinth which surrounded the Mount, called the Venusberg, possibly a tribute to the queen as the Goddess of Love. In 1600, Baron Waldstein (a visitor from Moravia whose diary gives glimpses of these early gardens) describes the garden's water jokes, which sprayed unwary passers-by, an overhanging rock or grotto "made of different kinds of semi-transparent stone", and wooden watermills in the corners of the ornamental pool, resembling that of Pratolino.

At Wimbledon House, built on a hill south of London and another Cecil property, begun in 1588, there was a distinctive Italian approach at the front of the house, with a series of courtyards with stepped terraces divided by two grand staircases sheltering grottoes beneath them.

ITALIAN-STYLE SCENES AND SCHEMES

After 1600 the Italian influence became more evident. By 1615 Inigo Jones had completed his Italian journey with Lord Arundel, and was remodelling Arundel House in London as a setting for antique statuary, and also providing stage scenery for court masques based on Italian buildings and landscape. Gardens acquired symbolic meanings, their creation, a combination of art and nature, a metaphor for the shaping of human society into an equally harmonious order. In *Luminalia*, a court masque devised in 1638, a scene of disruption and chaos was exchanged for a delightful and serene garden within which Queen Henrietta Maria herself was discovered, thus associating royal presence with the arts of government and social harmony. Inigo Jones's scenery, although costly to create, was much less expensive than real gardens, and opened the eyes of contemporaries to new garden ideas. Jones's Italian experience led to his reproducing scenery to resemble many features he had seen: the grotto at Pratolino, various versions of Mount Parnassus including those at Aldobrandini and Pratolino, Fame blowing her conch on the top terrace at Villa Garzoni near Lucca, and many other elements which could be gathered together in one theatrical scene.

The French hydraulics engineer Salomon de Caus, with his brother Isaac, introduced mannerist themes that could be exploited in the royal gardens. Salomon designed schemes for Henry, Prince of Wales (James I's eldest son, who died in 1612 aged 18) at Somerset House, Greenwich and Richmond Palace. His book of 1615, *Les Raisons des Forces Mouvantes*, showed a design for a huge statue of a reclining giant planned for Richmond. At Somerset House he proposed a fountain grotto, another copy of the Parnassus at Pratolino, with his own addition of river gods and water to flow over the sides of the mountain. After Prince Henry's death, Salomon went to Heidelberg, where he laid out one of the most spectacular of European gardens, the Hortus Palatinus, for Friedrich V, Elector Palatine, and his wife Elizabeth Stuart, daughter of James I. Isaac meanwhile continued to work in England at Moor Park for Lucy Harrington, Countess of Bedford, and at Wilton.

The epitome of Italian gardening in England, Wilton, in Wiltshire, created in the 1630s, was divided into three parts, with a broad walk up the middle. The first division of four "Platts, embroidered" with four "Fountaines with Statues of Marble" in the middle and flowerbeds on either side, was to be viewed from a low terrace. The second part consisted of groves of trees with walks cut through them – a wilderness – with symmetrically placed statues of Bacchus and Flora on either side of the main walk. Rounded pergolas or tunnels of vegetation ran down the outer edge. The River Nadder in its natural course meandered through the groves. In the final section, under a high terrace, the shape of a Roman hippodrome was marked out with fruit trees, while more "covered Arbours" ran along the edge. Behind, the hillside was shaped into an amphitheatre with the alley into the woods terminating with an equestrian statue of Marcus Aurelius (cast from its original at the Capitol in Rome). A cascade was embellished with a Pegasus, a familiar Italian motif for water. The grotto, under the terrace arches, was paved in black and white marble and furnished with Italianate hydraulic machinery introduced by de Caus to work the *giochi d'acqua*.

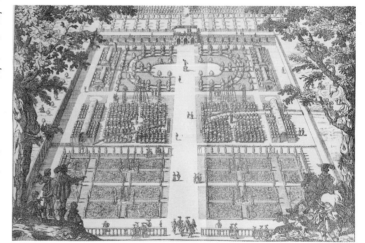

Plan for Wilton
Of all the gardens of England from the period before the Civil War, those at Wilton House, designed by Isaac de Caus between 1631 and 1635, have the most Italian look. The formal parterre squares and total symmetry are broken only by the meandering line of the River Nadder, which crosses the garden, and some formal "wildernesses" and groves of trees. De Caus's most famous feature at Wilton was the grotto.

WATERY DELIGHTS

Ponds for breeding and storing fish had been integral to monastic and secular estates all through the medieval period, but although recognized as a source of pleasure, they were seldom designed as part of an enclosed garden. The French adaptation of moats to make ornamental canals inspired the English to incorporate water to provide settings for fetes and other entertainments, with mirror pools to reflect the sky. Originally defensive, Lord Leicester's moat at Kenilworth was developed as a place to hold a spectacle for the queen's visit in the 1570s. At Holdenby, in Northamptonshire, Sir Christopher Hatton had water brought by pipes to supply his garden pond "out of the feylde adjoyninge on the west, quarter of a myle from the same house". In fact there were numerous Holdenby ponds, including a geometrical arrangement below the terraced Privy Garden. Paul

AN ESSAY FOR OUR TIMES

Sir Francis Bacon's garden has gone, but his essay, *Of Gardens*, published in 1625, a year before his death, remains a source for study in any attempt to encapsulate the aura of Tudor or Jacobean gardens. Although clearly disapproving of knots – "you may see as good sights many times in tarts" – and of topiary figures – "they be for children" – he recommends broad walks, low hedges and pyramids, decorative wooden columns and a 10m (30ft) high mount topped by a banqueting house, all features which date back to gardens such as Theobalds or even Kenilworth. In his striving to discover the ideal garden, Bacon vacillates between the approval of a "natural wildness", with thickets of sweetbriar, honeysuckle and wild vine, and a desire for ordered lines, a broad gravelled walk and views from mounts "to look abroad into the fields". In some ways he reflects a quite modern approach to gardening, in which the desire for nature and "wild" gardening is given a structured framework to set it off.

Hentzner (another of the foreign visitors whose descriptions have added to our knowledge of the period) visited Holdenby in 1598 and mentions the pleasure of rowing in a boat in a ditch between the shrubs in the labyrinth. By 1600, Baron Waldstein describes the more complex arrangements by which water was brought a distance of 3km (2 miles) and raised 24 steps by gravity in order to feed the ornamental pool.

Water became an even more important element in early Jacobean gardens. Italian-inspired fountains and elaborate grottoes were constructed by engineers who had learnt their art in Italy. By 1608, Robert Cecil, forced by the king to exchange Theobalds for a new palace at Hatfield, Hertfordshire, was employing Salomon de Caus to devise cascading fountains in the east garden. The Dell at Hatfield was a water parterre in a square moated garden, bisected by a natural stream to make two triangles. A visiting Frenchman, Monsieur de Sorbière, describes an evening at Hatfield in 1613: "We dined in a hall that looked into a Green plot with two fountains in it and having espaliers on the side…and from this Terrass you have a prospect of the great Water Parterre…you have also in those places where the river enters into and comes out of the parterre, open sorts of Boxes, with seats around, where you may see a vast number of fish pass to and fro in the water, which is exceedingly clear and they seem to come in shoals to enjoy all the pleasures of the place."

Sir Francis Bacon seems to have consulted his cousin Robert Cecil as early as 1608 on the possibility of turning a pond into a place of pleasure. He inherited his father's house at Gorhambury in 1601 on the death of his brother. After the accession of James I, Bacon's political fortunes rose rapidly, but his great career ended in 1621 with charges of corruption and a short spell in the tower. From then until his death in 1626 he devoted himself to writing. His prose includes the essay *Of Gardens*, which begins with the words: "God Almighty first planted a garden. And Indeed it is the purest of Human Pleasures."

Bacon's water garden, recorded in a manuscript in the British Museum, like Robert Cecil's Dell, was to be square, surrounded by a wall and a terraced walk 8m (25ft) broad, above a stream, which acted as a moat, to a further terrace and lake with a banqueting hall in the centre. Although mentioned by John Aubrey in 1656, the ponds at Gorhambury might have been abandoned even during Bacon's lifetime. In *Of Gardens* he advises: "For fountains, they are a great beauty and refreshment; but pools mar all, and make the garden unwholesome, and full of flies and frogs."

RESTORATION GARDENS: THE FRENCH AND DUTCH INFLUENCE

With the Restoration in 1660, Charles II brought with him from exile in France the French style of gardening, which had reached its fullest expression of baroque splendour under Louis XIV. In England, most of the earlier gardens, and especially royal ones, inspired by Italian or French Renaissance principles, had been destroyed in the Civil War. Royal gardening had to begin again, and it was the Le Nôtre-style gardens which became most fashionable. Having worked in 1640 for Charles's mother, Queen Henrietta Maria, at Wimbledon House (which had been purchased for her from Cecil), André Mollet came back to London within a few months of Charles's return, supervising the digging of a canal in St James's Park and overseeing work at both Whitehall and Hampton Court. At the latter, an even more magnificent canal, flanked by avenues of lime trees stretching to the horizon, marked the beginning of the new age. Planned to celebrate the arrival of Catherine of Braganza from Portugal to be Charles II's queen, the canal and avenues were part of the view from the new queen's gilded balcony. At Greenwich Charles had ambitions to rival French grandeur, asking Louis XIV's permission to invite designs from Le Nôtre himself. Plans, never to be completed, were sent by Le Nôtre in 1662 for a parterre with fountains directly behind the Queen's House, with 12 steps (already in place) leading the eye up the hill to a new elm avenue which disappeared over the crest.

The next 30 years were to see "improvements" of estates all over the country, with the English baroque format typified in the familiar bird's-eye views of Kip and Knyff published in the 1720s. After the Glorious Revolution, with William and Mary on the throne, the Dutch influence, itself strongly French in origin, was in vogue. Its greatest example is Hampton Court, where Charles II's ambitious plans were finally executed after 1690. On the whole, the highly organized French layouts, with great axial avenues reaching from a house's approach to an axis behind it and into the distance, and ornamental parterres surrounded by terraces under the house windows with a wilderness or orchard beyond, were the most common arrangements. Grottoes were often hidden in the terraces. The most successful results were achieved when the estate was vast and where the topography could reconcile the ordered geometry. Orangeries for tender plants and plants in tubs arranged around pools or along canals were very much Dutch features. The gardens of Westbury Court in Gloucestershire, begun in 1696 by

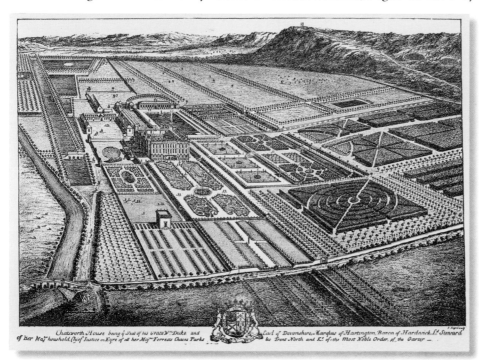

Chatsworth's splendour
This Kip and Knyff engraving of Chatsworth in Derbyshire was made in 1707 and shows the gardens as they were in 1699. Leonard Kynff (1650–1751), a Dutch painter and draughtsman, worked with the engraver Johannes Kip (1653–1722) to produce a series showing French-style English gardens, with avenues radiating into the countryside. They were published in *Britannia Illustrata* and in *Le Nouveau Théâtre de la Grande Bretagne*. The park at Chatsworth was later "naturalized" by 'Capability' Brown, although much of the inner formal gardens remained to be further improved by Joseph Paxton in the 19th century.

FOREIGN INFLUENCES AT HAMPTON COURT

WILLIAM III AND QUEEN MARY made extensive alterations to the old gardens at Hampton Court in a French-Dutch style brought with them from Holland. According to Daniel Defoe: "King William fix'd upon Hampton Court; and it was in his Reign that Hampton Court put on new Cloaths and being dress'd gay and glorious, made the Figure we now see it in." The gardens are important since they demonstrate the differences between French and Dutch styles, with small sectionalized spaces for fashionable box parterres contrasting with the longer French avenue vistas. Shortage of land and a network of canals meant that, in Holland, the Dutch had to contain their parterres in a prescribed space while, for the French, there was no obstacle to driving avenues deep into the forests.

There were two distinct phases of work, the first from 1689 until Queen Mary's death in 1694, after which William lost heart in what had been their joint project, and the second phase after the fire at Whitehall Palace in 1698, when William's interest in Hampton Court was reawakened.

In the first phase Sir Christopher Wren's new east front was decorated by lime avenues planted at a diagonal to Charles II's first avenue and the Long Water. The gates were to be designed by Jean Tijou. The new parterre by Daniel Marot, inside a vast semicircle of trees, had long scrolls of *broderie* edged with dwarf box. An array of pools and fountains proposed in a sketch by

Power and prestige
This detail of an engraving by Johannes Kip from Survey of London *shows the east front with lime avenues radiating diagonally to make a* patte d'oie *around the central Long Water.*

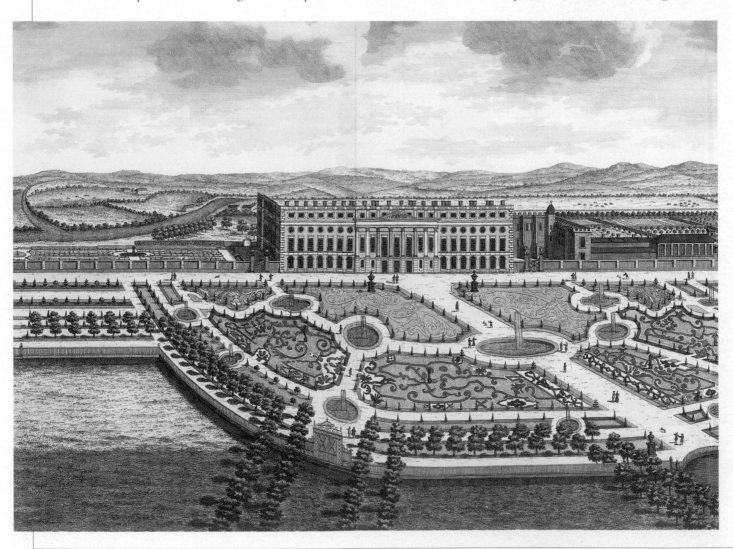

Marot in 1689 was later to be proved impractical. Clipped evergreens, including 304 yews as obelisks and 24 silver hollies as globes, were planted alongside the paths. Celia Fiennes visited, but not until 1712, and wrote: "there is a long Canall…and a large fountain next the house in the first garden with a broad gravell and a cross which cutts the grass plotts into four, which are cutt into flower deluces [fleur-de-lys]".

Although the Privy Garden under the south front was extensively altered *c*.1690, work was not completed until 1702, with Tijou's screens installed at the river end in 1701. The *c*.1690 alterations included widening the side terraces of the Privy Garden, and replacing the old banqueting house and towers by Queen Mary's Bower on the west terrace. The lower portion of the palace became an orangery, with citrus and tender plants arrayed on the terrace during summer. In the Pond Garden, Queen Mary established a botanical collection of interesting plants. North of the palace there were new avenues to Bushy Park and a wilderness, a geometric network of paths between high clipped hedges.

In the second Hampton Court phase, from 1698, much that had been

The gardens restored

Restoration of Hampton Court's Privy Garden has been carefully researched and executed. The gazon coupé design, with grass cut out in geometric shapes, was originally planned by Henry Wise, who, with George London, was one of the most famous designers of the day.

planned 10 years earlier was completed. The Privy Garden was lowered by 3m (10ft), to give the king a better view from the orangery, and laid out in *gazon coupé*, turf with geometric shapes cut out and filled with coloured earth or gravel. Henry Wise was responsible for the design. Statuary decorated the parterres throughout the garden.

Maynard Colchester, with wide T-shaped canals framed by topiary yew hedges, box-edged beds and lawns, are another superb example surviving today.

THE 17TH-CENTURY GENTLEMAN GARDENER

Not all the new English gardens were of baroque or Dutch design, nor did they necessarily display the pomp and circumstance of the estates illustrated by Kip and Knyff in *Britannia Illustrata*. Some were quite modest, with classical features absorbed from Italy by owners who felt no need to impress with copies of grand grottoes and complicated water features laden with allegorical meaning. John Evelyn's gardens at Wotton and Albury (see page 188), Sir William Temple's garden Moor Park, near Farnham, designed between 1680 and 1690, and the simpler Canons Ashby in Northamptonshire (recently restored by the National Trust) retained an English flavour somewhere between the early Tudor gardens and later 17th-century extravaganzas. At Canons Ashby there were simple terraces contained within high walls, and views to the countryside were framed by gate piers. Topiary yews occupied a green compartment behind the house, and four square flower gardens, with a simple pattern of beds and sundial, were all low key.

At Moor Park, where only the site remains, William Temple devised a garden for the English climate, its walls built expressly for the protection of flowers and fruit. He maintained that just as gardens in a southern climate were properly designed to be cool oases providing "shade of trees, frequency of living streams and fountains, perspectives and statues", so in England (and Holland) they should be enclosed. Already he esteemed the English speciality: "the fineness and almost perpetual greenness of our turf, and the gravel of our walks". In his essay *Upon the Gardens of Epicurus*, written in 1685 but not published until 1692, Temple makes one of the first allusions in English garden literature to the possibility of irregularity affording an alternative basis for design. "The Chinese scorn this [formal] way of planting…Their greate reach of imagination is employed in contriving features where the beauty shall be…without any order or disposition of parts, that shall be commonly observed: yet though we have hardly any notion of this sort of beauty, they have a particular word to express it…they say the *Sharawadgi* is fine or admired…whoever observes the best India gowns or the painting upon their best screens or porcelains will find their beauty is all of this kind of order." Although he goes on to advise that *sharawadgi*, translated as "the art of not being regular", was too difficult for a Western mind, Temple may have made an attempt. In a corner of the Moor Park design there is a wilderness with winding walks without any semblance of order. Likewise some watercolours by John Aubrey, the antiquarian and literary garden critic, show his own garden at Easton Piercy, in Wiltshire, designed in a very simple way.

TOWARDS A NEW LANDSCAPE

During the second half of the 17th century a constant stream of English visitors to Italy – the successors to William Thomas, Fynes Morison and Thomas Coryate – learned to appreciate not only the Italian gardens, the most famous still just reaching completion, but the whole Italian landscape, still redolent with clas-

sical ruins and nuances. John Raymond, travelling, like the famous diarist John Evelyn, in the 1640s, was able to see and envy the sophisticated gardens. Richard Lassels' *The Voyage of Italy*, written as a guide book and published posthumously in 1670, first used the term the Grand Tour to describe the progress of young aristocrats sent abroad with a learned tutor for their artistic education. To Lassels Italy seemed one vast garden, "a world of stately palaces and gardens". Unlike painting, gardens were a complete three-dimensional experience, more like architecture but both artificial and natural. A fourth dimension, time, needed for planting to develop, was also an essential element in the garden's. Those gardens with a classical allusion were of real importance in the developing English Landscape Movement in the 18th century.

The Italian experience is explored further in the next chapter, when the travels of some of the earliest advocates of the Landscape Movement are discussed. Scholars such as John Dixon Hunt have pointed out that the appreciation of the dual role of nature and art in laying out gardens, which was to become such a part of English landscape garden theory, was one imbibed from Italy. The dream of the classical gardens of Rome and the Italian countryside was absorbed into the new era of William Kent and 'Capability' Brown.

Embroidered simplicity

The Stoke Edith needlework tapestries, now in the new British Gallery at the Victoria and Albert Museum in London, show a formal English garden in the late 17th century. An orangery overlooks a simple parterre where evergreens are cut into slim topiary shapes, citrus fruit is grown in tubs to be brought in to shelter in winter and tulips are lined up in narrow beds surrounding symmetrical grass panels. A *palissade* of slim cypresses separates this garden from another formal area where four parterres surround fountain pools much as seen at Wilton House in the 1630s.

CHAPTER SIX

Plants on the move

BOTANISTS, COLLECTORS and ARTISTS

SOMEWHERE IN THE WAKE OF THE RENAISSANCE the relationship between people and plants underwent a major shift. Long before they began to reshape people's gardens, plants began to change people's lives. New professions were created: botanists studied and described them; authors and printers circulated information about them; artists depicted them; collectors searched them out; nurserymen propagated them – and armies of gardeners grew and tended them. Individual "Renaissance men" sometimes combined several of these roles with careers as physicians, diplomats or scholars.

Collectors and connoisseurs of all ranks succumbed to a passion for plants. Some of the stories entail real drama, as when tulip speculation bankrupted families in the Netherlands or plant hunters were beset by pirates or plague in faraway places. In others plants play a much more subtle role. Today, we grow aubrieta and fuchsia, lobelia, matthiola (or stocks) and monarda, robinia and tradescantia in our gardens. But what do we know about the artists, botanists and collectors for whom they were named – Claude Aubriet, Leonhart Fuchs, Matthias de l'Obel, Pierandrea Mattioli, Nicolas Monardes, Jean Robin and John Tradescant? This chapter tells the story of some of the people behind the plants.

The floral canvas

This study of flowers was painted by Girolamo Pini *c.*1614. He included a list of the names of all the bulbous and perennial plants illustrated, many of which can be quite easily identified. Pini painted another very similar picture at about the same time, the only two flower paintings for which he is known.

SPREADING THE WORD

The world in 1562 was one where an Antwerp merchant, receiving some bulbs with a consignment of cloth from Turkey, cooked and ate them assuming them to be onions. They were in fact tulip bulbs, a new discovery for western Europeans, and soon to be worth their weight in gold as a commodity. The consumption of those bulbs is symbolic; a package of imported plants, it suggests, had some obvious use (Romans, for example, mashed lily bulbs to make corn plasters). Nowadays we might look up an unfamiliar plant in an encyclopaedia. But the few books on plants available in the mid-1500s would have been herbals, indexed by ailment rather than by plant species: earlier writers looked only to the usefulness of plant material. Besides, new and unfamiliar plants were appearing at a rate that made it hard to keep up. Within a hundred years of the 1560s, 20 times as many plants entered Europe for the first time as during the preceding two thousand, providing not only studies for the new academics, but a huge potential for a new type of gardening.

To counterbalance the prevailing ignorance, this changing world was peopled by a new breed of enthusiasts keen to supply the missing information. Fired by the Renaissance spirit of enquiry, they began to look at plants in new ways. Physicians and scholars began to question the assumptions of their hallowed predecessors and started to observe plants with a new scientific curiosity. The recently invented microscopes helped them to analyse and classify the novelties that were flooding in. The academics' improved powers of scientific observation were already being reflected by artists, who began to draw plants directly from nature. Along with the expansion of botanical science came extraordinary developments in the aesthetic and technical portrayal of plants. Moreover, illustrations could now be reproduced in printed form. Books were to remain for a long time the preserve of the privileged few, but at least the communications revolution had begun. Any idea or image could now reach a far wider audience than ever before.

The main focus of the revolution in the way plants were perceived seems to have been firmly based to the north of the Alps: in the Low Countries and along the Rhine. It was here that printing technology first developed, and that some of the finest flower painters and botanists worked. It is perhaps no coincidence that the Netherlands is still today the centre of the floriculture industry. Manuals of practical gardening provided advice on planting and management, and to exploit the new plants there was a rapid expansion in the number of nurserymen and horticulturists who experimented with techniques of cultivation. By the 1600s florilegia (illustrated plant anthologies), with increasingly life-like watercolours and metal engravings of plants including their flowers and botanical parts, introduced the reader to the whole range of known plants, even if they (plants and images) were not all immediately available to the ordinary gardener.

It was some time before the new vision of plants percolated through to have a real impact on the appearance of gardens. The Renaissance and baroque gardens developing in Italy and France (and imitated in neighbouring states) emphasized formality and concepts of design over plant content. However, even where design theory ostensibly ruled, an undercurrent of plant collecting

Arrival from Peru

One of the earliest florilegia, the manuscript *Camerarius Florilegium*, lost almost since its completion in 1589, was only rediscovered in the 1990s. It contains 473 portrayals of plants growing in the garden, during the last half of the 16th century, of the physician Joachim Camerarius (1534–98), leading German botanist of the day and friend of Clusius. The quality and naturalism of the flower paintings matches those in Besler's famous *Hortus Eystettensis* (see pages 181–84). Many of the plants are indigenous Europeans but the manuscript also includes the new rarities, such as tulips, crown imperials, Persian fritillaries, lilac and this illustration of Indian cress, a form of nasturtium introduced from Peru in the 1580s.

by enthusiasts can be detected. New introductions were made by every country that had overseas contacts.

THE NEW PLANTSPEOPLE

By 1600 plant exploration had become a purposeful pursuit for serious botanists and collectors rather than being left to haphazard acquisition by ambassadors and merchants. Explorers' books and diaries logged the plants' arrivals, the new academic botanists classified and described them, and gardeners catalogued and displayed them. They were cared for and observed in botanical gardens attached to universities and in gardens belonging to wealthy individuals. Botanic gardens, established after 1545, published catalogues with plants marked on garden grid systems for ease of identification. Plants were exchanged between collectors, motivated (as gardeners are today) by pure interest, or one-upmanship, or the simple urge to acquire a complete collection of all known variants. The horticultural world of botanists and plant connoisseurs was a narrow one. Most of its figures would have been familiar with one another and with their respective con-

Garden of rarities

In a connoisseur's town garden in Ulm in Germany, tulips, fritillaries and other rare specimens are grown in pots, sunken in the earth, arranged in serried ranks like works of art in a museum. Joseph Furttenbach was one of the first German-speaking architects to produce designs for gardens and his *Architectura Privata* included plans for specially prepared beds of newly introduced plants. His brother Abraham provided a list of some 40 plant species suitable for this sort of display.

tributions in the world of plants. Botanists – the earliest ones almost always trained as physicians – were appointed to the courts of Europe, where emperors and kings wished to be in the forefront in establishing not only opulent gardens but also important scientific collections. Other botanists were subsidized by wealthy patrons and were able to prepare sumptuous illustrated books with scientific comments.

PLANT DISCOVERIES IN THE OLD WORLD

Celebrated botanists such as Clusius embodied the more scientific approach to the plant world, but many adventurous and enquiring individuals played their part in the quest for plants. The career of Pierre Belon makes an exciting example. Sponsored by a rich patron, René du Belay of Le Mans, Belon travelled in the Levant between 1546 and 1549 observing and collecting plants, and making notes of different gardening practices that were new to him. His specific mission was to identify the original plants in Dioscorides's 1st-century herbal *De Materia Medica* (see pages 40–41). Belon was also interested in discovering trees and medicinal plants suitable for acclimatization in France. He admired the plane tree of Hippocrates on Cos, found papyrus in Egypt, saw bananas and sugar cane and praised the "exquisite greenery" of the sycomore fig. Unfortunately most of the plants he collected were lost when pirates attacked his homeward-bound ship. In Turkey, Belon saw tulips and observed merchant ships trading in Turkish bulbs for export to Europe, which seems to confirm Clusius's story of tulip bulbs reaching an Antwerp merchant in 1562 along with bales of cloth from Constantinople. (This was the recipient who, thinking they were onions, roasted some; fortunately he planted others in his garden, from where they were rescued by a more discriminating merchant.)

With the plants of Dioscorides as his starting point, to an extent Belon still lived in a world of legend, imprisoned by the vague approximations of ancient science. Yet he also represented the new breed of inquisitive botanist/gardener who studied the problems of acclimatizing exotics brought from widely differing habitats. He attempted, for example, to grow tender cork (*Quercus suber*), holm oaks (*Q. ilex*) and *Arbutus unedo* in his own experimental garden in France.

More than a hundred years later, in 1700, Louis XIV dispatched Joseph Pitton de Tournefort (1656–1708) on another mission in search of Dioscorides's plants. Tournefort, Professor of Botany in Paris, was not merely a theoretical botanist. The story of his travels in the Greek Islands, the Levant and Turkey with the artist Claude Aubriet shows indefatigable energy and perseverance. In Constantinople they teamed up with a pasha returning to Erzurum, taking a boat along the Black Sea to Trebizond (now Trabzon). Climbing away from the sea into the snows of the Pontic Mountains, they discovered a new terrain "full of so many fine plants, so different from what we had been used to, that we knew not what to fall on first". He records finding the purple-flowered *Rhododendron ponticum*, a dangerous weed also found in Spain, as well as *R. luteum*, the scent of which gave him a headache. This plant was the source of pollen for the bees whose honey drove the

Proud display
This view of the garden flowerbeds at Count Nassau's castle at Idstein, near Frankfurt, comes from *Similacrum Scenographicum* by Johan Jakob Walther, *c.*1654–70. Just as Basilius Besler had recorded all the plants belonging to the Prince-Bishop of Eichstätt for the famous *Hortus Eystettensis*, Walther composed a florilegium or catalogue recording the plants at Idstein, 133 flower studies plus views of the gardens.

Precious tulips (opposite)
These two beautiful blooms were painted by Joris Hoefnagel in Prague for Rudolph II, *c.*1590. Catalogues from French tulip dealers in the middle of the 17th century describe some 400–500 varieties. Grown from seed, tulips could give rise to unexpected combinations of variegated flower colours; or a "breeder" tulip, attacked by a virus, might burst into extravagant double or triple colouring. In Holland, in the 1630s, this led to Dutch "tulipomania", in which vast speculative sums were invested in these chance blooms, resulting in bankrupty and debt for many when the market collapsed in 1637.

African exotic

Pierandrea Mattioli's *Commentarii in sex libros Pedacii Dioscoridis*, first published in 1544, was in its subsequent various illustrated editions the finest of the woodcut herbals. The plants were drawn by Giorgio Liberale of Udine and translated into woodcuts by the German Wolfgang Meyerpeck. Although restricted by the confined spaces of the page, the artists portrayed nature as realistically as possible. Although the *Commentarii* contained many of Dioscorides's original plants, mostly of Greek origin, it also included other European plants, introductions from the New World and this aloe from Africa, named in the text as *Aloe sine floribus*.

Greeks mad as they reached the sea on their epic march of "the ten thousand". Even by the end of the 18th century, not all Dioscorides's plants had been identified. Plant collector John Sibthorp and artist Ferdinand Bauer visited Greece in the 1780s. (Most early plant collectors took with them an artist who could record their discoveries.) After a journey in which they faced malaria, pirates, an earthquake, swarms of locusts and risk of bubonic plague – besides all the other usual discomforts of travel in underdeveloped regions – they returned home from Patras in 1787 with drawings and specimens of over 2,000 plants, 300 of which were new to science. Sibthorp's finds were published in his *Flora Graeca* (see page 41).

PLANT NEWS FROM THE NEW WORLD

Portuguese explorers brought back spices from the coast of Malabar and India as early as 1498, but their discoveries made little contribution to gardening. It was left to the Spanish to introduce to Europe the wealth of gardenworthy plants discovered in the New World. By the 16th century American plants – marigolds (*Tagetes*), marvels of Peru (*Mirabilis jalapa*), sunflowers and tobacco plants – were already being grown in Europe and were soon planted in oriental gardens. Letters from the Spanish conquistador Hernando Cortés describe the marvellous beauty of the gardens of the Aztec kings and their "botanic gardens" laid out as order beds (see page 283).

One of the first publications describing American plants appeared in two parts in 1569 and 1571. Written by Nicolas Monardes, a doctor from Seville born in 1493, it was translated into English by John Frampton in 1577 with the pleasing title *Joyfull Newes out of the Newe Founde Worlde*, and subsequently translated into Latin by Clusius. Based on information received from navigators, it described tobacco, sunflower, sassafras and 25 medicinal species. Philip II of Spain, already interested in the healing possibilities of plants in his new empire, dispatched his palace physician Francisco Hernandez on a seven-year scientific expedition in 1570. Over the period Hernandez completed descriptions in seven volumes with numerous drawings. He named many plants in the Mexican language as well as giving valuable information on medicinal traditions and the botanic gardens created by the Aztecs.

SEEING PLANTS: THE ARTIST'S EYE

We learned in Chapter 4 how, even as early as the 14th century, writers such as Petrarch and Boccaccio showed a reawakening of interest in the natural world. Reflecting this, by the 15th century, naturalistic paintings of flowers began to appear in the borders of prayer books and living flowers growing in gardens appeared in the background detail of religious paintings. Leonardo da Vinci's 15th-century drawings of flowers and trees and Albrecht Dürer's watercolours of wild flowers and grasses near his native Nuremberg in the early 1500s were forerunners of the new naturalism. Dürer recommended studying nature diligently: "be guided by nature and do not depart from it, thinking that you can do better yourself. You will be misguided, for truly art is hidden in nature and he who can draw it out possesses it." Dürer's introduction of a new note of accuracy to his watercolours of flowers anticipated future botanical rigour, although he was not portraying individual plants for identification purposes. Painters and illustrators began to draw plants from the wild, with attention to both aesthetics and analytical detail, rather than copying images already distorted over the years.

The invention of printing in the middle of the 15th century revolutionized the spread of shared knowledge. The old herbals, laboriously hand-copied and recopied throughout the centuries in monasteries or by Arab scholars from Greek and Latin texts, could now be superseded by the printed word. In the 16th century the old stylized plant paintings were replaced by drawings from life translated into decorative black-and-white woodblocks. Printing had made it possible to reproduce these illustrations, which were set up side by side with the text. By the 1600s, etchings and metal engravings, which allowed greater accuracy and detail, and which could be hand-coloured at a later date, largely superseded the woodcut. In a hundred years the drawing of flowers was transformed into the art of modern botanical illustration, a product of close collaboration between artist and scientist.

The Birth of Botany and Botanic Gardens

Until the second half of the 16th century collections of plants were primarily used as tools for the education of physicians, but gradually a wider, more scientific approach to the study of plants began to be adopted. Students of botany started to extend their knowledge of native plants by examining them in the field, and to make collections of dried specimens to supplement the living ones. Botany became an official subject in 1550 in the medical faculty of the old University of Montpellier, under Guillaume Rondelet, and a stream of young physicians (some of whom, like Clusius, would later become esteemed botanists) examined plants in the countryside as part of their studies. The more learned among them were employed in categorizing newly introduced plants and experimenting in growing them.

The new realism
Albrecht Dürer's *The Large Piece of Turf* (*Das Grosse Rasenstuck*), a watercolour painted in about 1503 near Nuremberg, displays a new naturalism in plant portrayal. This detailed study shows meadow grasses, dandelions and plantains on a dull day growing beside water.

16TH-CENTURY WOODCUT HERBALS

The appearance of three great woodcut herbals in the 16th century, their authors all physicians, heralded a new era in botanical illustration. All three gave detailed descriptions and their illustrators, working from life, depicted the whole plant, including its roots. The first herbal, published in Strasbourg in the 1530s, was *Herbarum Vivae Eicones*, with text by Otto Brunfels and illustrations by Hans Weiditz. It was followed in 1542 by *De Historia Stirpium*, published in Basle. Written by Leonhart Fuchs, the herbal included drawings by Albrecht Meyer and large woodcuts that were the work of Veit Rudolf Speckle. The third – and most beautiful – was Pierandrea Mattioli's *Commentarii in sex libros Pedacii Dioscoridis*, first published with full illustrations in Venice in 1565. Giorgio Liberale and Wolfgang Meyerpeck designed the delicate woodcuts. This herbal became the standard work on medical botany for European physicians, going into 60 editions. New plants portrayed included lilac, horse-chestnut, auricula, datura and sea holly. For modern readers the work has its flaws, as the names reflect pre-Linnean nomenclature: the picture labelled narcissus is actually a tulip.

The career of the Flemish botanist Rembert Dodoens (1517–85), or Dodonaeus as he was also known, marks a sea-change in the way plants were perceived. When he published his herbal, the *Crüÿdeboeck*, in 1554, it contained an index arranged by ailment rather than by plant species. Fourteen years later, his *Florum et coronarium odoratarumque nollullarum herbarum historia* "paid no heed to the question of ailments and plants as remedies". It is one of the earliest scientific studies of flowers considered as botanical subjects and as a source of "honest pleasure and refreshment of the soul".

Dodoens, Lobelius (Matthias de l'Obel) and Clusius were the three great Flemish botanists of the day. Their works were printed in Antwerp by Christophe Plantin, with illustrations probably taken from a common pool of woodblocks, those for the Dodoens herbal having already been published in an earlier work by Leonhart Fuchs, *De Historia Stirpium*. Carolus Clusius (see page 178), botanist *par excellence*, was the first to describe plants in a scientific and systematic manner. His work dominated European botanical development through his position at the imperial gardens of Hapsburg Vienna, and through his vast correspondence with other botanists and explorers, until his death in Leiden in 1609.

From their foundation botanic gardens, generally attached to universities, were laboratories for medical and botanical research. The first was established at Pisa in 1543, followed within a few months by one at Padua. Then came Florence in 1545, Bologna in 1567, Leiden in 1587, Heidelberg and Montpellier in 1593, Oxford in 1621 and Paris (now the Jardin des Plantes) in 1626. Although conceived as an aid to students acquiring first-hand knowledge of plants used in medicine, these botanic gardens quickly became something more. The unfamiliar new plants introduced from abroad were soon being grown and classified even when they had no obvious role to play in medicine. At the same time, paintings of plants, a collection of dried plants or *hortus siccus* and other natural curiosities were gathered in adjacent galleries. In true Renaissance style, the whole world of nature and natural history became the object of study, with animal, mineral and plant kingdoms displayed together.

In order to provide centres for scientific experiments and teaching, the new botanic gardens had, inevitably, to sacrifice design appeal to practical requirements, as can be seen by comparing the plans for Padua in 1545 and those for Oxford in 1621 (see page 180). Seen with 21st-century hindsight, the gardens laid out as order beds (in which plants are arranged by genera), with a grid system for ease of identification, have great charm – especially if we recollect the excitement with which contemporaries must have awaited the identification and planting of new arrivals. In most cases complex geometric beds gave way to simple rectangles surrounding a central well, much as prescribed in Roman man-

Leonhart Fuchs

Considered one of the great figures of German botany, Leonhart Fuchs (1501–66), for whom fuchsias were later named, published his *De Historia Stirpium* in 1542. This Latin herbal (see opposite) deals with 400 native German plants from the area around Tubingen, where he was professor.

Pierandrea Mattioli

Mattioli (1501–77), from whom stocks get their botanical name, *Matthiola*, first published his *Commentarii in sex libros Pedacii Dioscoridis* (see page 174) in 1544. It was translated into many languages and appeared in many editions, and included not only Disocorides's original plants but all those known to Mattioli.

Matthias de l'Obel

Matthias de l'Obel or Lobelius (1538–1616), for whom lobelias are named, studied at Montpellier, coming to London in 1569. With Pierre Pena he published the *Stirpium Adversaria Nova* in 1570–71, for the first time distinguishing different groups of plants by the character of their leaves.

uals (and like the layout usual in medieval monastic gardens). A typical botanic garden was divided into four quadrants by two intersecting paths, each quadrant divided again into two halves containing several pillow-like beds called *pulvilli*.

THE ENGLISH HERBALISTS

The introduction of printing in the 15th century led to a greater exchange of ideas between all European scholars, but because England had failed to establish any teaching gardens in the 16th century, it lagged behind the Continent, although William Turner's *The Names of Herbs*, in Greek, Latin, English, Dutch and French, with common names that herbalists and apothecaries used, somewhat redressed the balance. The first authoritative work with the English names of plants, it was published in 1538. Turner, a physician and botanist, was involved in the religious disputes of the day and spent several years exiled abroad. He became a friend of Conrad Gesner, the Swiss naturalist, and studied botany under Luca Ghini at Bologna. After the accession of Edward VI in 1547, he was appointed physician and chaplain to the Duke of Somerset at Syon House, where he planted some mulberry trees, still growing there. His *chef-d'oeuvre*, his *New Herball* of 1551–68, earned him the title of father of English botany. In this pioneering work he condemned superstition in science in an age when legends abounded – such as that concerning the mandrake root. (A spirit, it was thought, lived within the mandrake's root which would kill the hapless person who pulled it from the ground.)

THE HORTUS SICCUS

Italian botanist Luca Ghini (*c.*1490–1556), who taught at Bologna and Pisa, was one of the first to establish a *hortus siccus*, a collection of dried plants and the forerunner of the modern herbarium. Such collections made study possible at any time of the year and because of this were sometimes known as "winter gardens". John Evelyn was presented with a *hortus siccus* on the occasion of his visit to the Padua Botanic Garden in the 1640s.

CLUSIUS: EUROPE'S LEADING BOTANIST

CHARLES DE L'ECLUSE (1526–1609), known as Carolus Clusius, was an all-rounder, a Renaissance man who spoke eight languages and studied law, philosophy, history, cartography, zoology and numismatics. Clusius was one of the most important of the new academics who based their botany on personal observation rather than on a study of the works of Dioscorides or Pliny the Elder. In his final years as praefectus horti at the new university at Leiden he ensured that the garden, as seen from the *Index Stirpium* of 1594, would embrace all plants as a *hortus botanicus* rather than being solely a *hortus medicus*. Clusius was always more than an academic; he grew plants himself, becoming one of the first to gain expertise in managing and flowering the new bulbs flooding in from the eastern Mediterranean.

CAROLUS CLUSIUS

Clusius studied medicine and natural history under Guillaume Rondelet at Montpellier, where he familiarized himself with the flora of southern France. He was excited by Rondelet's approach and later explored Spain and Portugal for plants, taking notes as he had been taught. In 1571 Clusius visited London in order to acquire some of the new plants from America, including sassafras, sunflowers, tobacco and the potato, playing a considerable part in the popularization of the last two. He translated Nicolas Monardes's *Joyfull Newes* into Latin. From 1573, during his time as prefect of Maxmilian II's Imperial Botanic Garden in Vienna, he studied the flora of the Pannonian plain (in what is now modern Hungary). In 1574 he was joined in Vienna by Dodoens, who became physician to the emperor. Clusius published his *Rariorum aliquot Stirpium per Hispanias* on the Iberian flora in 1576, and his work on the Pannonian flora in 1583.

In an appendix to the former he included a list of plants he had received as bulbs or seed from the Levant from Ogier Ghiselin de Busbecq, Ferdinand I's ambassador to the sultan in Constantinople. The list included tulips, anemones and ranunculi. By the end of the 1550s diplomatic relations had been established between Süleyman I and the imperial court, only 30 years after the Turks had been at the gates of Vienna. Many new plants now found their way to Europe, not only to Vienna and the imperial gardens in Prague, but also to the Medici gardens of the grand dukes of Tuscany and to the Netherlands. Clusius also received cherry laurel, horse-chestnut, lilac and philadelphus from eastern Europe. Between 1587 and 1593 he was based in Frankfurt, advising Wilhelm IV, Landgrave of Hesse, on the botanical garden founded there by his friend Joachim Camerarius, for which he had supplied many of the original plants.

Clusius was already 67 when he accepted the post of praefectus at the Leiden Botanic Garden in 1593. He took some of his tulips there with him, but many were stolen during the first winter. He was among the first to observe the phenomenon of tulips "breaking", in which a "breeder" tulip of a single colour develops a much sought-after variegation in its petals. Now known to be caused by a virus, this peculiarity was to lead to the speculation in bulbs, the Dutch "tulipomania" of 1634–37. Clusius published his *Exoticum libri* in 1605.

A tulip for Clusius
Clusius was first given a bulb of this charming tulip, a native of Iran, by Florentine plant enthusiast Matteo Caccini. Tulipa clusiana was later named in his honour.

Gerard's *Herball*, published in 1597, in spite of its imperfections and plagiarizing, has since become the best-loved English herbal of all time. John Gerard was a barber surgeon in London by trade, but a gardener by inclination. A list issued in 1596 shows that in his own Holborn garden he grew all the interesting plants of the age. He also supervised Lord Burghley's London gardens in the Strand and at Theobalds in Hertfordshire.

Much of Gerard's *Herball* was taken from Dodoens and a Dr Priest who had partly translated Dodoens's work. It contains about 1,800 woodcuts, most of them used before. The illustration showing the potato was new (it was the first published figure of the plant), although it is wrongly described as native to Virginia. Gerard sometimes failed to couple the woodblocks with the appropriate plant descriptions, and Matthias de l'Obel was brought in by the printer to correct Gerard's blunders in botanical identification. In 1632 Gerard's publisher commissioned Thomas Johnson, a London apothecary and botanist, to produce a new edition of the *Herball*, improving the original text and illustrating it with 2,766 woodblocks from Plantin's publishing house.

The last English writer who ostensibly belonged to the herbalist tradition was John Parkinson (1567–1650). Parkinson's own garden was in Long Acre, in London. The title of his book, *Paradisi in Sole Paradisus Terrestris*, published in 1629, is an allusion to paradise as a park and also a pun on his name (park-in-sun). As much a florilegium as a herbal, it contains descriptions of "A garden of Pleasant Flowers" as opposed to the single-minded categorization of useful plants, and gives reference to plants for the flower garden, the kitchen garden and the orchard. With a nostalgic touch of medievalism, Parkinson describes the unicorn as living "farre remote from these parts, and in huge vast Wildernesses among other fierce and wilde beastes", and his famous title page shows the legendary "Tartary Lamb" growing on a stalk in the Garden of Eden.

Strange fruit
Gerard sometimes took various unlikely legends on trust, in particular his often quoted account of the "Goose" or "Barnackle" tree. He claimed to have observed a tree bearing geese himself, and included this illustration in his *Herball* of 1597.

Gerard's first edition
The woodcut illustrations in Gerard's *Herball* were mainly from a collection of engraved blocks established in Antwerp by Christophe Plantin and had already been used by the botanist Tabernaemontanus in his *Eicones* of 1590. A few new woodcuts portrayed plants such as the recently introduced potato. The *Herball*, in spite of Gerard's plagiarism, is a useful reference, especially in determining which plants were already grown in England by that year. Thomas Johnson's edition of 1633 has the more useful text. The plants shown here are European native white and yellow water-lilies.

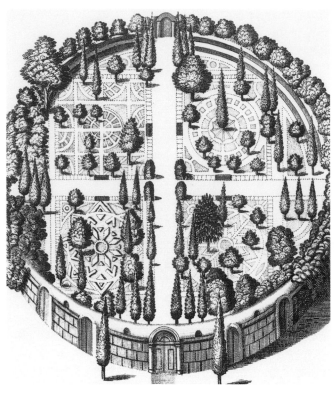

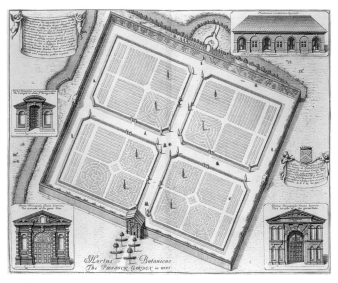

Glorious Florilegia

By the early 1600s new florilegia began to appear, illustrated with beautiful and true-to-nature woodcuts, etchings and engravings, which could be hand-coloured at a later date. These were of real relevance to the new botanists and also highly attractive to the new collectors and amateur gardeners who were entranced by the delicacy of the productions and who appreciated their accurate rendering. The florilegia were equivalent in usefulness to the glossy catalogues of modern nurserymen. Unlike the old herbal, the florilegium had little descriptive text, revealing only the beauty of each flower rather than documenting its botany. The invention of the microscope at the beginning of the 17th century allowed an increasing emphasis on accurate renderings of minute phenomena. These florilegia were themselves destined to become collector's items of immense value today, sometimes fetching up to a million pounds.

One of the most important artists who originated the genre of the florilegium was Jacques Le Moyne de Morgues (1530–88), a French Protestant who divided his time between France, England and the Americas. He joined the disastrous French Huguenot expedition to set up a colony in Florida in 1564 as recording artist and cartographer (the colony was overrun by the Spanish a year later but he escaped). Unfortunately none of Le Moyne's paintings of North American plants survive. His watercolours of flowers are immortalized in his *Clef des Champs*, published in Blackfriars in 1586, and reflect his work as a refugee in England after 1572. His last known work, it is illustrated with woodcuts of flowers, animals and fruit, and was intended to serve as a model for other artists.

The most popular florilegium was that of Crispin van de Passe, the *Hortus Floridus*. Divided into seasonal sections showing flowers in spring, summer, autumn and winter, its meticulously produced copperplate engravings were an inspiration to artists and scientists. Garden scenes are also shown. Van de Passe came from a family of engravers and was still only 25 when the *Hortus* was pub-

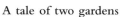

A tale of two gardens
The botanic garden at the University of Padua (above) – sharing with Pisa the honour of being the oldest in Europe – was founded in 1545 to ensure that medical students could study living plants. Its layout established a relationship between mathematics and architecture, with a circular wall containing the four quadrant order beds, in which plants were first divided between four continents. The botanic garden at Oxford, founded some 75 years later in 1621 by Henry Danvers, is the oldest in Britain. A high stone wall still surrounds the garden, with a main gateway designed by Inigo Jones. The illustration above right is from David Loggan's *Oxonia Illustrata* of 1675. The first catalogue was issued in 1648 by the keeper Jacob Bobart. By the 1720s a professorship was endowed for the German botanist J.J. Dillenius. John Sibthorp, renowned for his *Flora Graeca*, held the chair at the end of the century.

Paintings as teaching tools
In the early 1600s a whole new genre of Dutch oil painting was invented, the flower still life. Artists such as Jan Brueghel the Elder (1568–1625) portrayed decoratively arranged collections of flowers in vases. These defied nature in that the plants depicted could not have bloomed at the same time, each flower having been painted from life in its own flowering season. These everlasting bouquets had a use for identification and teaching, although, of course, parts of the plant other than the flower were not shown. This sumptuous arrangement of roses, tulip, bluebell, anemone, aquilegia, marigold and crocus was painted by Ambrosius Bosschaert the Elder (1573–1621).

lished in 1614. Written in Latin, it was translated into English the following year. Many of the flowers, especially in the spring section, were among the recently introduced new varieties coming in from Constantinople and its hinterland. Summer flowers included gladioli, irises, lilies, peonies and roses, while autumn flowers included cannas, marigolds, marvels of Peru (*Mirabilis jalapa*), morning glories, sunflowers and tobacco plants from the Americas.

One of the most beautiful florilegia ever published was the *Hortus Eystettensis* of 1613. It was commissioned in 1600 by the Prince-Bishop of Eichstätt, Johann Conrad von Gemminger, a connoisseur of flowers, who made an extensive collection of plants in his luxuriant terraced garden surrounding the hilltop castle at

Besler's masterpiece (overleaf)
The *Hortus Eystettensis*, one of the finest of all florilegia, was published by Basilius Besler in 1613 for the Prince-Bishop of Eichstätt. It catalogued the bishop's extensive collection of plants growing in his terraced garden on the hilltop in Eichstätt. The book is divided into illustrations of plants representing the different seasons. Shown overleaf are illustrations of *Cyclamen hederifolium* flanked by blue- and white-flowered forms of French lavender, *Lavandula stoechas*, and (on the right-hand page) the orange lily, *Lilium bulbiferum* var. *croceum*, generally found in the western Alps or the Juras.

III.
Spica vulgaris flore cæruleo.

I.
Cyclamen Roma num.

II.
Spica vulgaris flore albo.

II.

Lilium purpureum maius Do-donei.

Scapus cum bulbo.

CREATING NEW EDENS

In the 16th century, the account of the Garden of Eden in Genesis was still accepted as a complete truth and, long before the founding of the first botanic gardens, private plant collectors sought to establish their own encyclopaedic version of mythical Eden, in which every known plant was cultivated. This endeavour reflected the idea of the re-creation of the earthly paradise in existence before the fall of man. The urge to collect plants seems to be a primitive and competitive one, still prevalent today among some gardeners. In 1613, when Gaspard Bauhin brought out his comprehensive *Pinax theatri botanici*, there were 3,000 species of known plants listed; it still seemed possible to be able to grow them all. A century later there were 10,000, far too many for one ordinary gardener to contemplate growing.

A plan for plants
An engraving by Giovanni Battista Falda, published in 1665–69, shows the layout of the Horti Farnesiani in Rome. Originally laid out by the architect Vignola at the instigation of Pope Paul III in the middle of the 16th century, terraces descended from the top of the Palatine Hill to the Forum. The collection of plants was catalogued by Pietro Castelli as the *Horto Farnesiano Rariores Plantae Exactissime Descriptae* in the 1620s.

Eichstätt. The garden was under the supervision of the apothecary Basilius Besler (1561–1629), who was responsible for the florilegium, choosing and cataloguing all the plants. Besler himself executed some of the original drawings, but many other artists and engravers were also involved. More than 1,000 plants are represented, including wild and cultivated species (600 botanical species and over 400 varieties), making the magnificent florilegium an extremely valuable reference for the plants already known by the early 17th century. The various botanists cited in the text include Dodoens, de l'Obel, Bauhin, Clusius and Camerarius. Each plate shows several plants arranged decoratively to display patterns of flowers, leaves and roots.

PLANT CONNOISSEURS

By the end of the 16th century, an international trade in sought-after rare flowers developed, leading to their multiplication and a rapid increase in the availability of plants for more ordinary gardeners. Interest in flowering plants exploded in 17th-century Europe, encouraged by the availability of exquisite florilegia. Rare and beautiful flowers, first grown in the gardens of the wealthy, became available to pharmacists, botanists and amateur collectors who were connoisseurs of flowers, and to the collectors and growers who became known as *jardiniers fleuristes*. Known in England as florists, these people were not purveyors of cut flowers as in the term's modern connotation but serious growers with a keen interest in all aspects of horticultural life. Many of the *jardiniers fleuristes*' treatises took a very serious attitude to gardeners learning the place of origin of each plant and the climate and type of soil it required. They also considered plants' compatibility, anticipating modern ecological gardening ideas.

Ideas, information and plants were liberally exchanged among these early enthusiasts. Matteo Caccini, a Florentine, and Emmanuel Sweert, a Dutchman

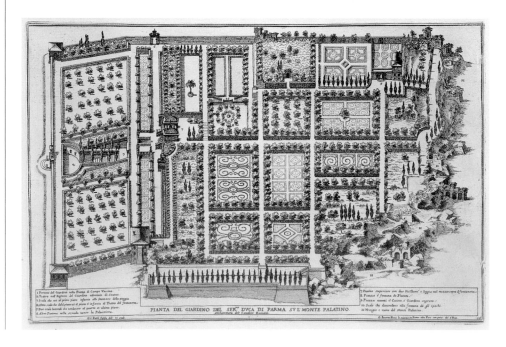

THE TRADESCANTS AND THEIR ARK

THE MOST FAMOUS English plantsmen of the first half of the 17th century were the royal gardeners John Tradescant the Elder (*c.*1570–1638) and his son John the Younger (1608–62). Their south London garden, with a celebrated museum popularly known as the Ark, was open to the public at a charge of sixpence (it was probably the first public museum in England). The natural history collection from the Ark was the initial foundation of the Ashmolean Museum in Oxford.

Both Tradescants, succeeding each other as gardeners to the king at Oatlands Palace, were responsible for the introduction of many new plants as well as growing them, obtaining them from abroad and from colleagues and passing them on to other plant lovers.

Father and son
The two Tradescants were buried in London, at St Mary's in Lambeth. Today, the church has, fittingly, become the site of the Museum of Garden History.

John the Elder was also gardener to Robert Cecil, first Earl of Salisbury, and his likeness is carved on a newel post on the Grand Staircase at Cecil's Hatfield House in Hertfordshire.

Between 1610 and 1615 John the Elder travelled to the Netherlands where he obtained Provins roses, cherries, quinces and medlars for the Hatfield gardens, as well as a selection of fritillaries, tulips and gillyflowers (which can mean either varieties of matthiola stocks or pinks and carnations, but in this instance were almost certainly the latter). Later he went as far as Russia and north Africa, where he collected a purple clover. The Tradescants had shares in the English Virginia Company, through which they obtained plants from North America. In 1638, the year of his father's death, John the Younger made the first of three visits to Virginia, bringing back, among other plants, the tulip tree (*Liriodendron tulipifera*).

The Tradescants' reputation as plantsmen and growers of exotics is deserved, and their influence on English gardening profound. John the Elder made a list of plants he had received from abroad between the years 1629 and 1633, which he recorded in his own copy of Parkinson's *Paradisus*. In 1634 he published his own catalogue, *Plantarum in Horto Iohannem Tradescanti Nascentium Catalogus*, which contained more than 7,150 plants and a number of fruit trees. In 1656, John the Younger published a more substantial volume, which described the plants in Latin and English.

T. 3. Nº 18.

LIRIODENDRON tulipifera. TULIPIER de Virginie

Tradescant treasures
The Tradescants introduced several North American plants to Britain, among them Tradescantia virginiana *(left, a detail from a study of a collection of plants painted by Alexander Marshal, 1625–82), and (far left) the tulip tree (*Liriodendron tulipifera*), painted by Henri Louis Duhamel du Monceau, c.1760.*

FLORISTS' SOCIETIES

Certain of the newly introduced or newly bred plants were grown by a new band of enthusiast – the florist. Drawn from all ranks of society, from gentry to tradesmen, florists appreciated the exquisite detail in the flowers of anemones, auriculas, hyacinths, pinks, ranunculi, tulips and Provence roses. The florists formed their own societies where they could show their prize plants in competition. Flemish weavers, fleeing persecution, and Protestant refugees, mainly Huguenots, escaping from France after 1685 undoubtedly brought plants with them to England and helped found the societies.

Already skilled illustrators of 15th- and 16th-century books of hours and great religious painters and tapestry makers, the Flemings also led northern Europe in practical gardening and, as exiles and refugees, introduced other Europeans to horticulture. Some Flemings moved only as far as the United Provinces (a Dutch republic at the time) for security where, as flower painters and horticulturists, they were labelled as Dutch. Societies of flower-lovers were formed in Ghent in 1648, in Brussels in 1650 and in Bruges in 1651, all dedicated to St Dorothea, the patron saint of floriculture. Guilds of St Dorothea still existed in Flanders in the 18th century. By the end of the 18th century the florists' societies had become the preserve of factory workers, who bred flowers for a perfection determined by a rigid set of rules, a pursuit quite outside the ordinary run of garden practice.

employed by Rudolph II in Prague, were both traders in plants, with Sweert publishing his own *Florilegium* in Frankfurt in 1612, a form of catalogue for his clients' information. Caccini sent a box of day-lilies, ranunculi and the newly discovered marvels of Peru to Clusius in Leiden. He discovered *Tulipa clusiana* in Crete, which he sent to Clusius to be named. Clusius in return sent many bulbs to Florence, besides a painting of a green tulip. Another great naturalist, Ulisse Aldrovandi, founder of the botanic garden in Bologna, kept notes for over 30 years of his correspondence with botanists and plantsmen of the time, including members of aristocratic circles who were keen amateurs. He also kept lists of seeds and plants received and sent.

Louis XIII's gardener Jean Robin, who had his own collection in Paris in the early part of the 17th century, also exchanged information and plants with contemporary gardeners. It is still a question of dispute whether *Robinia pseudoacacia*, the black locust or false acacia from northeast America, was received first by Jean Robin or the Tradescants: it was named for Robin *c*.1630. In 1651, Parisian nurseryman Pierre Morin published his own *Catalogue de Quelques Plantes*, many of its plants originally obtained from Robin. In Morin's flower garden, later copied by John Evelyn at Sayes Court, a central oval in the form of a flower was surrounded by a series of smaller beds in the shapes of petals. Here Morin grew "Tulips, Anemonies, Ranunculus's, Crocus's & etc" which "were held for the rarest in the world".

By the beginning of the 17th century the most sought-after flowers were varieties of *Hyacinthus orientalis*, narcissus and iris, and especially anemones and tulips. Francesco Caetani, Duke of Sermoneta, had a passion for both the latter. In his garden in Cisterna he grew beds of tuberoses, sunk in flowerpots so that they could be easily watered. He also had white narcissi from Constantinople, dwarf orange trees and white-flowered broom. He owned 15,000 tulips, but anemones came first in his estimation – especially the downy variety called in Italian "*di velluto*". He acquired 29,000 of 230 different kinds. One called *Anemone* 'Sermoneta', "all scarlet and pale yellow", was grown by Sir Thomas Hanmer in his Shropshire garden in 1659.

Hanmer (1612–78) was one of a handful of English 17th-century amateur enthusiasts whose passion for plants we can identify with today. He was a staunch royalist who spent the Civil War years in France, returning later to his home in Bettisfield, on the Welsh border, to get on with his gardening. During his time in France he evidently picked up useful tips on cultivation as well as a good many plants, but he remained unmoved by the current trends in garden design, laying out his garden in a conservative and functional way, with rectangular tulip beds near the house. His great interest was in plants, and between 1644 and 1652 he met all the French horticulturists of the age.

Hanmer's ideas are eloquently recorded in his *Garden Book*, transcribed from the original manuscript of 1659, but published only in 1933. Besides being an avid collector of new bulbs Hanmer was one of the first writers in England to plan his garden to accommodate new plant introductions and he lists his extensive collection – anemones, cyclamen, fritillaries, irises, narcissi and tulips, mainly

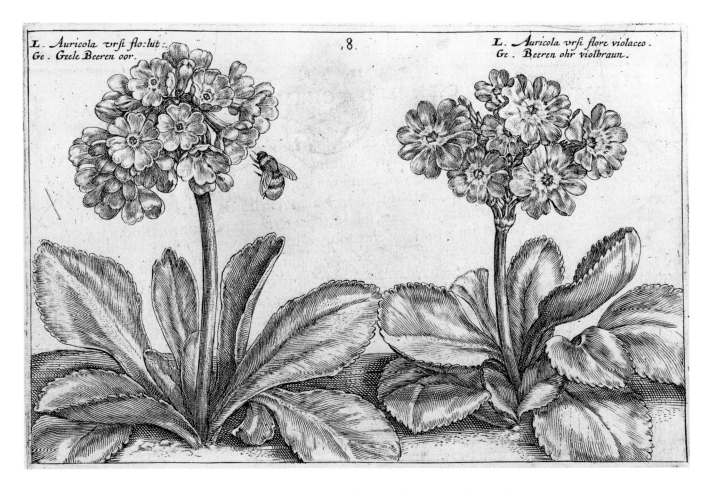

L. Auricola ursi flo:lut.   .8.   L. Auricola ursi flore violaceo.
Ge. Geele Beeren oor.   Ge. Beeren ohr violbraun.

obtained from French sources – and recommends methods of growing them. Tulips, "the Queene of Bulbous plants whose Flower is so beautiful in its figure and most rich and admirable in colours and wonderful in variety of markings", were to be lifted every third year and offsets grown on. Hanmer grew his tulips in beds slightly raised at the centre, which must have improved drainage. He also grew plants from North America, including the brilliant scarlet *Lobelia cardinalis*.

Renowned gardener John Rea dedicated his book, *Flora* (1665), to Hanmer, his friend and neighbour. Another gardening contemporary was the Parliamentary General Lambert at Wimbledon, who collected tulips. In 1655 Hanmer gave him "a very great mother-root of Agate Hanmer". This fine tulip with three distinct colours – crimson, white and pale "gredeline", a greyish-purple – was described later by John Rea. Hanmer gave the same tulip to his friend John Evelyn, for his garden at Sayes Court in Deptford.

In a slightly different league as a plantsman was Henry Compton (1632–1713), son of an earl and Lord Bishop of London from 1675 until his death. During his incumbency he made the gardens of Fulham Palace famous for exotic trees and

Double vision
Auriculas (above), members of the primula family, were popular florists' flowers during the 18th century. They were probably brought to Britain by Huguenots by 1700, their natural home being the upper pastures of the Alps and Dolomites. This illustration is taken from Crispin van de Passe's *Hortus Floridus*. Emmanuel Sweert portrayed the blue-flowered *Scilla peruviana* (left) in duplicate in his 1612 *Florilegium* – a form of catalogue. This scilla comes from the western Mediterranean and was named for the boat which first brought it to Holland, not its place of origin.

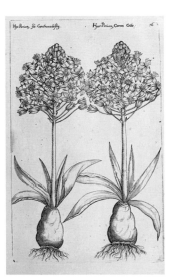

JOHN EVELYN: ERUDITE PLANTSMAN

B Y FAR THE MOST important and influential English writer on gardening, garden history and planting in the second half of the 17th century was John Evelyn (1620–1705) – diarist, tree expert, translator and a founder member in 1660 of the Royal Society, in which he continued to play a prominent role.

Born in Surrey at Wotton, an estate which he would finally inherit from his brother in 1699, Evelyn played a leading part in the development of contemporary horticulture and arboriculture. His writings incorporated the latest scientific and empirical enquiries concerning all matters pertaining to a modern garden. From 1642 until 1647, during part of the Civil War, he travelled abroad discovering the gardens of France and Italy. His *Sylva, or a Discourse of Forest Trees* of 1664 was published at a time when re-afforestation and encouragement to plant oaks for shipbuilding was of prime importance. It remained the standard English work on trees for over a century.

Before his travels on the Continent, Evelyn had helped to design the garden at his family home at Wotton for his brother. On his return he completed a terraced mount with a temple. In 1666 he designed a canal, terraces and tunnel through a hillside for the third Earl of Arundel at Albury, also in Surrey. Each of these gardens had a distinctly Italian resonance in its composition and features. By the time of his death Evelyn had come to disapprove of the ostentatious landscapes in the French style which had been made in England since the

A man of letters
John Evelyn's interests ranged far and wide. Besides horticulture and forestry, he wrote books on atmospheric pollution in London, the art of copper engraving, and his famous Diary *with lively portraits of his contemporaries.*

Restoration, much preferring gardens inspired by Italian layouts.

John Evelyn's most important and ambitious work was the unpublished *Elysium Britannicum* (still uncompleted at his death after four decades of writing), in which he aimed to include all aspects of garden thought and practice. Begun as a description of all the skills necessary in planting a noble garden, but never intended as a pragmatic "how-to" manual, Evelyn's *magnum opus* grew to be a philosophic discourse on the pleasures and virtues of gardens. He removed parts of the *Elysium Brittanicum* and incorporated them into his *Sylva*.

When Evelyn moved in 1652 to Sayes Court, in Deptford (his wife's

ancestral home, which had been sequestered during the Commonwealth), he began a massive programme of improvement and planting. His plan was to replicate Pierre Morin's Paris garden, which he had twice visited and admired both for its planting and design, including its central oval flowerbed (see page 186).

He encountered problems growing the cypresses Morin had used to surround the French garden, storms and hard winters decimating many he had laboriously grown from seed. Most of his more unusual plants were grown from seed, often obtained from his father-in-law in Paris. The garden contained a grove and a "formal" wilderness of standard trees crossed by eight main diagonal walks. Terrace walks and *palissades* of holly and berberis finished off that part of the garden. A broad walk on the west led between a banqueting house and a moated island, where he grew fruit and asparagus. In February 1653 he planted an orchard when the moon was waxing, following the belief that this would promote growth.

After Evelyn inherited Wotton from his brother, Sayes Court was rented out to Tsar Peter the Great. One of the tsar's pleasures was to be pushed about in a wheelbarrow by the gardeners, damaging the holly hedge in the process. After inspection by Sir Christopher Wren and nurseryman George London, repairs of £55 were granted to cover the replacement of three wheelbarrows as well as many of the best plants – hollies, phillyreas and fruit trees – that had been broken.

shrubs, many of North American origin. As Bishop of London, Compton had jurisdiction over the Americas, and he instructed his clergy to add botanizing to their duties. One of the most fruitful was John Banister, who acquired several new species from Virginia besides "saving the souls" of American Indians.

ADVICE ON PRACTICAL MATTERS

In any age contemporary herbals, florilegia, plant lists and catalogues reveal the range of plants available. The more practical manuals or gardening books, useful at the time, are invaluable in helping a modern reader grasp the then existing state of garden design, horticultural knowledge and technical advance. The earliest English book on general gardening for the common man, a practical manual rather than a theoretical thesis, was *A most briefe and pleasaunte treatise, teachyng how to dresse, sow and set a garden* written by Thomas Hill between 1557 and 1559. Much of its information was gathered from other sources – including the Roman authors such as Columella – but it has enough practical suggestions to make it popular. An illustration of a square garden surrounded by a paling shows wide walks and narrow paths surrounding a central pattern of beds for plants. His second book, *The Gardener's Labyrinth*, was published in 1577 after his death under the pseudonym of Didymus Mountain. Although it contains little new information about gardening or plants, Hill provides down-to-earth advice for contemporaries. His book also gives an idea of the contents and management of a small Elizabethan garden, a useful source in the understanding of the technical possibilities and limitations of the age.

The first publication in the north of England on general gardening was William Lawson's *A New Orchard and Garden* in 1618. Among its illustrations is one of a typical manor house of the period with a moat and river, and a garden divided into six sections, each allotted a different role. A topiary garden contains

The English scene
Woodcut illustrations from Thomas Hill's *The Gardener's Labyrinth* (1577) portray the garden as a place of horticultural and social activity as well as displaying a typical layout of the day. In this scene, gardeners are busy at their everyday chores, which include using a contemporary watering device, while two gentlemen discuss matters in a quiet corner.

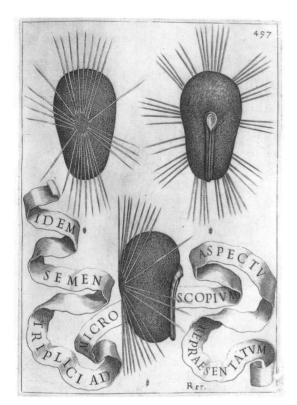

The view through the lens
The seeds of the exotic Chinese rose (*Hibiscus rosa-sinensis*), observed through a microscope, were illustrated in Giovanni Battista Ferrari's *Flora*, published in Rome in 1638. With the invention of the microscope at the beginning of the 17th century, scientists could observe minute phenomena invisible to the naked eye and thus note differences and similarities much more accurately.

realistic figures of a man and a horse; there is an orchard – with fruit trees planted in a quincunx – a complicated and a simple knot and an even simpler design of rectangular beds, probably for vegetables. William Lawson also recommends "comely borders to the beds, with roses, lavender and the like". Parkinson's *Paradisus* also covered practical matters. Its first chapters, called "The Ordering of the Garden of Pleasure", dealt with amending soils, designs of arbours and walks, flowerbeds and their arrangement in knots and what flowers to put in them.

USING PLANTS IN ENGLAND

Inevitably the flood of plants reaching Europe from the Levant and from the New World during the 16th and 17th centuries transformed the appearance of European gardens. By the end of the period the new trees, shrubs, flowers and bulbs added an exotic element to the geometric layouts, with flowerbeds specially designed to display them to best advantage. But the new plants mainly added ornamental detail, with the underlying structure still entrusted to tried and tested favourites. In Italy juniper, cypress, *Viburnum tinus*, bay, yew, phillyrea and box could be topiarized and, until the 16th century, were commonly planted to make mixed hedges. Flowerbed edging was of mixed herbs, including (but never exclusively) box. Santolina, rosemary, myrtle and hyssop were equally popular. In northern Europe evergreens were less predictable, hardy junipers and yew replacing the tender Italian cypress. During the second half of the 16th century, more sophisticated gardens utilized single varieties for hedging to conjure up uniform, manicured effects. Cypress and bay laurel were tightly clipped to make dark hedges; topiary yew was an indispensable feature in the great French gardens; twiggy hornbeam was planted for hedges, *palissades* and *berceaux*, often cut into fanciful finials or other ornamental shapes. In England juniper and the slightly tender bay laurel and phillyrea were at first preferred to yew but, by the end of the 17th century, yew, popularized by John Evelyn, had become the favoured subject for topiary and hedges. Hornbeam and holly, although very slow growing, were also used to provide structural elements. Most importantly, as was seen in the previous chapter, box became the edging plant *par excellence*.

Collecting rare plants became a fashionable and often competitive game between royalty, wealthy churchmen and rich merchants who could afford to obtain them. At first the rarities were grown in serried ranks for admiration exactly as if they were in a museum or picture gallery. Later, ordering them in flower-garden patterns became a new discipline.

By the 1700s, the trees and shrubs arriving from the northeast of America were to alter the appearance of European gardens, their introduction playing a part in the establishment of a new style of gardening. In this, nature itself had a greater role than before, and the clipping and ordering of traditional hedging and topiary plants became less fashionable. At first, the protagonists of the Landscape

Movement mainly used indigenous material with which they were familiar, but gradually more and more American trees and shrubs as well as exotics from other continents, allowed to grow as specimens, were found to fit into the ethos of the new parks.

NURSERIES OF INNOVATION

From the early years of the 18th century, London nurseries were able to introduce a whole new range of plants. These had first to be classified and grown experimentally before customers could be found. Nurserymen led the field in disseminating knowledge about plants through their books and catalogues; they also had to keep abreast of the latest botanical classification. In 1725, 20 of the leading London gardeners and nurserymen established the Society of Gardeners. This association met monthly to discuss plants, including those recently introduced, and attempt some clarification and regulation in their nomenclature.

In order to make best use of the new trees and exotics it was necessary to study the plants and establish their horticultural requirements. Spurred by the challenge (and the prospect of commercial success), the more enterprising nurserymen rose to the bait. The specialists in growing new plants, mainly from seed, both for open ground and for heated houses, encouraged experimental planting in large estates as well as in smaller or city gardens. Among their number was Thomas Fairchild, a scientifically minded London nurseryman. Fairchild's nursery in Hoxton, established in 1690, became well known both for its fruit trees and its exotics, many of which had been sent from North America by Mark Catesby, who worked in the nursery while preparing his *Natural History of Carolina, Florida, and the Bahama Islands* (see page

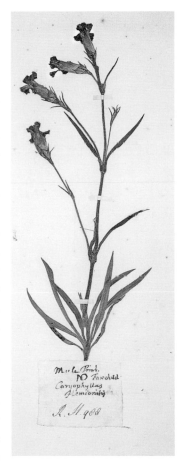

296). Fairchild's *The City Gardener*, published in 1722, recommended plants capable of surviving London pollution. An example offered in his nursery that serves the same purpose today is the hybrid London plane (*Platanus × hispanica*) then a new cross between the oriental *P. orientalis* and the American *P. occidentalis*, which with its defoliating bark will survive a polluted atmosphere.

The nurserymen were of necessity keen communicators. Their publications were intended to promote their plants, but today we find them invaluable as records of the latest developments. The Society of Gardeners (of which Thomas Fairchild was a member) issued the *Catalogus Plantarum*, of which only one part was published in 1730. The catalogue was compiled with the help of Philip Miller (see overleaf), in charge of the Chelsea Physic Garden since 1722; Part I covered trees and shrubs. Two other members of the Society of Gardeners, the nurserymen Robert Furber and Christopher Gray, had purchased part of Bishop Compton's plant collection at Fulham after his death, and both their nurseries became famous for exotics. Furber achieved publicity for his nursery in Kensington Gore with his publication of a series of plates entitled *Twelve Months of the Year*, issued in

Fairchild's mule

Although the Chinese had been hybridizing plants for centuries by transferring pollen from the stamen of the male to the pistil of the female plant, this skill and knowledge was unknown in the West. Thomas Fairchild (1667–1729) was one of the first Europeans to apply the newly discovered knowledge that plants have male and female organs, making it possible to breed a planned hybrid. Hitherto, innovations had depended on chance seedlings, selection of good plants for vegetative propagation or introductions from abroad. Fairchild took the pollen of a sweet William (*Dianthus barbatus*) and placed it on the pistil of a carnation (*Dianthus carophyllus*), the first hybrid cross. By gathering the seed to germinate the following season he produced "Fairchild's mule". In succeeding with this, Fairchild surpassed John Ray, Marcello Malpighi from Bologna and Nehemiah Grew, all of whom had, before the turn of the century, become convinced that plants were equipped with sexual organs.

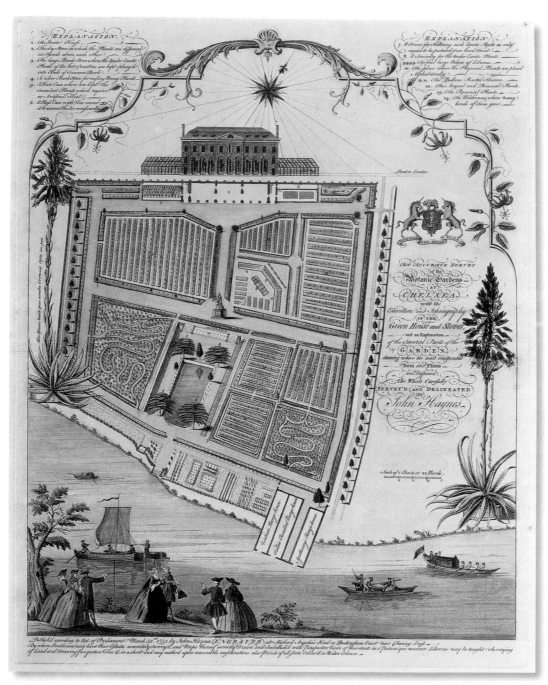

A garden for healing

London's Chelsea Physic Garden was founded by the Society of Apothecaries in 1673 for the purpose of displaying medicinal plants. It remains on its enclosed walled site by the Thames in Chelsea to this day (though separated now from the river by the Embankment). When it ran into financial straits, it was rescued in 1722 by Sir Hans Sloane, a successful Irish physician as well as plant collector and philanthropist, who bought the Manor of Chelsea and the freehold of the

Apothecaries' garden. Sloane was elected to the Royal Society in 1685. He rented the garden to the Apothecaries for an annual £5 and the stipulation that the Royal Society should receive 50 dried specimens of newly cultivated plants each year. Under Philip Miller (see opposite) the Chelsea garden became famous both for its collections and for its generosity in making plants available to a wider public. Sloane's own collections became the nucleus of the British Museum. This

painting of 1751 shows rectangular order beds (in which plants are arranged by genera) and irregular winding walks in the new style of naturalistic gardening. Two cedars of Lebanon planted towards the end of the 17th century were the first recorded *Cedrus libani* planted in England.

the form of nursery catalogues between 1730 and 1732. Each month was appropriately illustrated with a painting, with a key identifying the plants. Gray's catalogue in English and French of trees and shrubs, compiled to sell the American plants discovered by Mark Catesby, was issued in 1737.

PLANT COLLECTING IN NORTH AMERICA

The second major influx of plants into Europe, as important in changing the appearance of English gardens as the 16th-century bulb invasion, were trees and shrubs from America. Until now the main woody introductions (which quickly became quite commonplace in gardens) had been horse-chestnuts, lilacs, Portugal and cherry laurel, phillyrea and philadelphus – all of which had been catalogued by botanists by the end of the 16th century. Tulip trees (*Liriodendron tulipifera*) and black locust (*Robinia pseudoacacia*) arrived from Virginia, and cedar of Lebanon arrived in the 17th century. But by the 1700s plant treasures were pouring in, to be catalogued by Philip Miller for the Society of Gardeners and for inclusion in his *Dictionary*. The story of two Quakers, the American naturalist and plant-hunter John Bartram (1699–1777) and the English merchant Peter Collinson (1694–1768), best exemplifies the whole spirit of 18th-century expansion. Debarred from public appointments and from Oxford and Cambridge Universities, Quakers seemed to develop an affinity with the natural world, perhaps perceiving it as a manifestation of God's handiwork, with a disproportionately large number becoming involved in botany and gardening. This was the era of a great exchange of plants and correspondence between Europe and America.

The link between Collinson and Bartram lasted over 30 years, from 1733 to 1768, and between them they played a major role in changing the appearance of the European garden. The American plants, grown as specimens, fitted easily into the more "natural" styles that were becoming increasingly fashionable. Bartram, exploring the woods of the northeast of America, sent at least two hundred new plants to England, to several recipients including Collinson, who lived first at Peckham and then at Mill Hill, where he cultivated many of the rarities. Collinson's *Hortus collinsonianus*, discovered only in 1809, confirms his responsibility for at least 42 new introductions. By giving a vivid description of the plants' native habitats, Bartram ensured that they might be grown with success. Collinson shared plants and seeds with fellow naturalists in England and on the Continent. The most notable taxonomists of the day – Linnaeus in Uppsala, Gronovius at Leiden and Dillenius at Oxford – all studied Bartram's plants. Linnaeus even went so far as to call him "the greatest natural botanist of his time". By 1765 Bartram, through Collinson's recommendation, was appointed king's botanist. Self-taught, Bartram had to rely on his own observations, his learning at first coming from standard books of the day such as Culpeper's *English Physician*, Turner's early *Herball* and Parkinson's *Paradisus*, none of them a resource for American plant identification. In due course he received copies of Philip Miller's *Dictionary* and Linnaeus's works. Bartram laboriously combed the woods of North America to enrich the gardens of Europeans, but the exchange system worked well with Bartram receiving seeds of plants in European cultivation in

PHILIP MILLER AND HIS DICTIONARY

The *Gardener's Dictionary* compiled by Philip Miller (1691–1771) ran into eight editions between 1731 and 1768. During this period the number of plants in cultivation  multiplied fivefold – not least due to Miller's own avid collecting and his contacts in North America, the West Indies, the Cape of Good Hope and Siberia. His *Dictionary* was the 18th-century bible for a generation and more of plant enthusiasts, clocking the arrival of new plants for cultivation as well as offering both practical and aesthetic advice. Miller was an active participant in syndicates formed for financing the introduction of new plants. John Bartram of Philadelphia was one of his correspondents. In his third edition (1760) Miller included the *Garden Kalender*. At first reluctant to adopt Linnaeus's methods of classification and the binomial system of plant nomenclature, Miller did follow Linnaeus in his final edition. His publications have given him a lasting importance in English gardening. Forced to retire at the age of 79, having grown obstinate and impertinent ("his vanity…so raised by his voluminous publications that he considered no man to know anything but himself"), he died in the following year. Partly self-taught in the schools of botany of Joseph Pitton de Tournefort and John Ray, Miller was not only an able botanist but also an immensely successful horticulturist whose scientific approach enabled him to cultivate plants from very different climates.

Peak of perfection
A drawing of a pomegranate flower and fruit by Georg Dionyius Ehret, the greatest of the botanical illustrators. Even before the invention of the Wardian case in the 1840s, plants were being transported with a high degree of skill. Philip Miller pointed out that "Oranges, jesmines, capers, olives and pomegranites are annually brought from Italy and, if skilfully managed, very few of them miscarry, not withstanding they are three or four months out of the ground."

return. Many of the native plants growing in his own garden, the first botanic garden in America, were models for Mark Catesby's illustrations in his _Natural History_. Bartram's seeds destined for Europe from 1736 were collected from the stock plants established in his nursery near Philadelphia. They were distributed in "five guinea boxes" to subscribers, among whom were Philip Miller at Chelsea, Lord Petre at Thorndon in Essex and the Duke of Richmond at Goodwood, Sussex.

THE TREE PATRONS

Eighteenth-century plant introducers still needed patrons, as in earlier times, to grow on their plants on a large scale. At Thorndon, in Essex, Lord Petre – who contributed 10 guineas a year to Bartram's collecting – grew both American and European trees from 1732 until his death in 1742. He also established stove houses for growing and fruiting tropical plants; his was the first _Camellia japonica_ to flower in England. It was early days for the new landscape style, but Petre studied Batty Langley's _New Principles of Gardening_ (1728) with its idea of "regular irregularities" (see page 209). Inside a quite ordered plan, serpentine paths could meander more aimlessly through woodland, the perfect setting for American shrubs and trees. Lord Petre, in his Octagon Plantation, grew only American plants received as seed from Bartram. Peter Collinson described Thorndon as a mixture of trees and shrubs: "about 10,000 Americans mixed with about 20,000 Europeans and some Asians", established between 1740 and 1742. Elsewhere Collinson suggested that England was being "turned upside down and America transplanted heither" through the prodigious influx which, by the second half of the century, was transforming the appearance of landscape gardens and encouraging the establishment of American gardens with specially prepared soil. Bartram's painstaking descriptions of native habitats gave adequate instructions for creating suitable conditions.

Such was the frenzy of tree collecting that, after Petre's death, the Duke of Bedford employed Philip Miller to value the thousands of trees at Thorndon. He purchased those suitable for planting at Woburn, where acid soil made it possible to succeed with many "Americans", including conifers such as the Balsam fir and Virginia pitch pine. By the 1760s seeds were entering the nursery trade and being sent in quantity to European countries, but many still proved difficult to germinate and grow. Many North American trees thrive best in continental climates where there are extremes of hot and cold, rather than in more temperate Britain.

The Duke of Richmond, with an American wood, an evergreen grove and some fine magnolias. Richard Pococke describes the duke's park at Goodwood as

LINNAEUS AND THE NAMING OF PLANTS

CARL VON LINNE, later known as Linnaeus (1707–78), dominated 18th-century biology. After training as a physician at Uppsala, in his native Sweden, he spent time travelling in northern Europe, meeting the distinguished botanists of the day. He also published two early works, his *Systema Naturae* (1735) and, in 1738, the *Hortus Cliffortianus* (prepared for George Clifford, a director of the Dutch East India Company who had an extraordinary collection of exotic plants, plus menagerie, in his Haarlem garden). At this stage, Linnaeus was already working on his ideas for the classifying and naming of plants, animals and minerals, driven by a desire to arrange the natural world into tidy groups. In 1736 he visited England but by 1741 he was back in Sweden as Professor of Natural History at Uppsala.

Until Linnaeus devised his method of classifying plants, botanists had been struggling to establish principles of resemblance that might logically justify certain groupings. The work of the Italian Andrea Cesalpina (*c*.1524–1603) had been followed by the 1704 publication of the English naturalist John Ray's *Historia Plantarum Generalis*, which offered a tentative exploration and explanation of the sexuality of plant life. This furnished later botanists, including Linnaeus, with a theoretical basis for some of their assumptions.

Linnaeus's sexual system of classifying plants was based on the number of stamens and stigmas found in a flower. The

The power of names
Linnaeus, painted here in his wedding finery, made it possible for botanists and gardeners around the world to speak the same language.

more natural system introduced by Jussieu and de Candolle early in the 19th century superseded Linnaeus's sexual system, but his binomial method of naming plants and animals in place of the long-winded, multi-word descriptions used hitherto was revolutionary.

Linnaeus's essential task was to provide the means of identifying and naming all the organisms then known. The naming of plants by genera and species in a universal Latin-based botanical language unites botanists and gardeners across all frontiers. The work, first published as *Species Plantarum* in 1753, became the starting point for all future botanical naming. Plant names published before 1753 have no standing in modern nomenclature unless they were adopted by Linnaeus or by subsequent botanists.

In 1783, James Edward Smith (later to edit John Sibthorp's *Flora Graeca*) was breakfasting with Sir Joseph Banks in Soho Square when the latter received a letter offering him, for 1,000 guineas, all the collections and library that had belonged to the famous Swedish naturalist. Smith bought the collection, which later became the nucleus of the Linnean Society in London, founded in 1788. The Linnean Society, now housed in the Royal Academy courtyard at Burlington House, still flourishes.

The finer details
The "Tabella", Ehret's watercolour illustration of the sexual system for the classification of plants, was published in Linnaeus's Systema Naturae.

having 30 different kinds of oak and 400 American trees and shrubs. Just as the Duke of Richmond obtained seeds from Bartram, the Duke of Argyll may have obtained seeds or plants from Mark Catesby for his estate at Whitton in Middlesex. Certainly, by 1748, American pines, firs, cypresses, thujas and many other American natives were well established there and described by Pehr Kalm, the Finnish botanist. After the duke's death in 1761 many of the trees were transferred to the gardens at Kew House by his nephew, Lord Bute, where they became the nucleus of the Royal Botanic Gardens' collection.

André Michaux (1746–1803) was sent to North America by Louis XVI in 1785, his mission – couched in diplomatic terms – to find suitable trees that might be acclimatized in France to replenish the Gallic forests depleted by shipbuilding, as well as to introduce new orchard varieties and ornamental species for gardens. He was also to prepare herbarium specimens for the Jardin du Roi (which changed its name at the Revolution to Jardin des Plantes). Michaux had previously toured England and been impressed by the new American exotics. His first visit to America was to John Bartram's garden in the spring of 1786. Although he was always hampered by a shortage of money, particularly during the years of the French Revolution, his first priority was to establish a nursery so that he could germinate seeds and grow plants on until they could survive the long sea voyage home. This he did in Hoboken, outside New York, and in Charleston, South Carolina. Disappointingly many of the plants he sent to France were neglected and lost during the troubled times following the fall of the Bastille. Michaux also imported foreign plants into America. He introduced the Japanese camellia – the old camellias at Middleton Place in South Carolina are believed to be Michaux introductions – and *Rhododendron luteum*. His monograph on oaks, published as the *Histoire des Chênes de l'Amérique*, and his *Flora Boreali-Americana*, the first of its kind, both illustrated by Pierre-Joseph Redouté, were seen through the press by his son after his death.

PLANT RICHES OF THE ORIENT

As well as the influx of American plants into Europe, the 18th century also saw a vast increase in introductions of exotics from other countries. By the 1770s official collectors were being sent out by botanic gardens and sponsored by private enthusiasts. Gardeners will recognize many of them in the names of plants in our gardens today. The Swedish physician Carl Peter Thunberg (1743–1828), a pupil of Linnaeus, went to South Africa from Holland to botanize and spend four years perfecting his Dutch, in order to tackle Japan in the service of the Dutch East India Company. Only the Dutch had a foothold in the Land of the Rising Sun. He sent seeds, bulbs and plant specimens to Amsterdam, Leiden and Sweden.

Sir Joseph Banks chose a Scottish gardener, Francis Masson (1741–1806), to travel to South Africa to augment the Royal Botanic Gardens' collection at Kew.

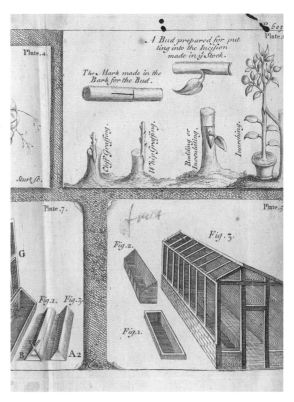

Degrees of control
The stove houses at Thorndon, Essex, allowed Lord Petre to maintain different temperatures and were similar in design to those shown here in an illustration from Richard Bradley's *New Improvements of Planting and Gardening* (1717). Bradley later became Professor of Botany at Cambridge.

Rosebay and laurel (opposite)
This portrayal of the rosebay, or American rhododendron, *Rhododendron catawbiense*, with the narrow-leaved mountain laurel, *Kalmia angustifolia*, seems to have been the combined work of Mark Catesby and Ehret. Catesby's great work, *The Natural History of Carolina, Florida, and the Bahama Islands*, was the first major study of the flora and fauna of the British colonies of North America, finally completed in 1747.

Plant transport

Once his precious finds had been delivered to a suitable port, the pre-Victorian plant collector's mission was far from over as only a fraction of plants survived long sea voyages. No matter how ingeniously packed they were, or how scrupulously their light and water requirements were attended to, growing plants were still perilously vulnerable to salt water spray and variations in temperature. The infamous *Bounty* was carrying 1,000-odd breadfruit seedlings from Tahiti to the West Indies when mutiny broke out and one of the mutineers' first acts was to throw the plants overboard. For the crew, Captain 'Breadfruit' Bligh's valuable plant cargo had been tedious work. The breadfruit seedlings were kept in racked pots below deck and their leaves had to be sponged with fresh water whenever they returned from a "turn" in the light and air above deck.

The invention of the Wardian case, which made life very much easier for sailors and long-haul plants, was a happy accident. In 1829 Nathaniel Bagshaw Ward, a London doctor and a keen naturalist, placed the chrysalis of a hawk-moth in damp soil within a sealed glass jar. The moth duly emerged but, even more interestingly, so did some seedling grasses and ferns. When the entombed plants continued to thrive without fresh air or water for more than three years Dr Ward realized that the glass jar was working as a self-contained microclimate. Water transpired by the plants condensed as droplets on the glass, and fell on to the soil at night, where it was re-absorbed by the plants' roots.

By the 1840s, the Wardian case was the accepted method of transporting plants over long distances, and its inventor was praised on all shores. The migration of tea, rubber and quinine plants had a huge effect on industry and empire, but gardens were also beneficiaries.

A Wardian case and its inventor (above and below) In 1833, Dr Nathaniel Bagshaw Ward made two miniature greenhouses, filled them with ferns, grasses and flowering plants, and shipped them to Australia. Four months later they reached Sydney, where one of the plant pioneers, a primrose, aroused such interest that its glass home had to be guarded. For the return trip to Britain, native Australian plants were put into the "Wardian cases" and they arrived "in the most healthy and vigorous condition". Dr Ward lived until 1868, by which time his cases had been the means of introducing more new garden plants to Europe than any of the stratagems of the whole previous century.

Future investments (left)
New arrivals at the seed bank of Britain's Royal Botanic Gardens. Air transport means that seed can be moved with less risk to its viability than in the days of long sea voyages. Then, seed was coated in beeswax and wrapped in waxed cotton and paper, or "bottled" and packed in boxes of salt.

Clever carriers (above and below left)
Before the advent of the Wardian glass case, plant collectors used a variety of devices and materials for transporting plants and protecting them from the ravages of salt water. For his botanical booty, the 18th-century French plant-collector Jean-François Gallup de la Perouse resorted to ingeniously shaped baskets (above), and beehive-like cabinets (below left).

Well-travelled tulip (right)
Early in the 17th century, the tulip – from Turkey – was the rarest, most alluring flower of northern Europe. For carrying such a luxury import to its new site, without damage to the precious stem and bloom, an enterprising French manufacturer offered this "necessary instrument".

Palm for the Crystal Palace (below)
In 1854, 32 horses drew a gigantic palm tree from Loddiges's nursery in London's East End to the Crystal Palace in south London. The superb *Latania borbonica* had spent its youth in the exotic plant collection of the French Empress Josephine at Fontainebleau. After a day on the road, it reached Crystal Palace during the evening.

Fonthill Abbey from the American Plantation.

Americans abroad
With so many North American
plants requiring a deep acid loam, it
became customary to prepare special
beds where these, and plants
requiring similar conditions, could
be grown together. Whether called a
wilderness, shrubbery or woodland
walk, areas in the big estates were set
aside for magnolias and dogwoods,
kalmias and rhododendrons to be
grown under a woodland canopy,
which might also be composed of
tulip trees, swamp cypresses and
liquidambars. Lord Petre's North
American thickets and the Duke of
Richmond's American Wood in the
1740s may have been an expression
of this understanding, or simply an
encyclopaedic collection of
American plants. The term
American garden came into general
use later in the century and was
gradually extended to include a
lower layer of planting in which
ferns, lady's slippers, trailing arbutus
(*Epigaea repens*) and other small
woodlanders would thrive in half
shade in a rich, black, turf-like soil.
By the turn of the century
Humphry Repton was adding
American gardens to many of his
plans. At Fonthill Abbey (above)
William Beckford created an
American plantation (painted here
by James Storer), discussed by J.C.
Loudon in 1822 in his *Encyclopaedia*.

Masson travelled to the Cape with Captain Cook, who was setting out
on his second voyage of exploration. His salary or "recompence" was £100,
to be paid only on his return, plus £200 for expenses. He was worth every
penny. At first he travelled with the volatile and overconfident Thunberg.
The list of plants Masson sent to Kew finally far exceeded Thunberg's
acquisitions and included pelargoniums, heaths, arctotis and lobelias.

From South Africa Thunberg went on to Japan travelling on a Dutch
trading ship that came with the south–west monsoon in August and
returned in November with the north–east monsoon. As physician he
joined a settlement of warehouses on the island of Deshima, off the port
of Nagasaki, where Engelbert Kaempfer had held the same post 80 years
earlier (see page 370). The fifth section of Kaempfer's *Amoenitates Exoticae*, published in 1712, had introduced its European readers to a vast new
array of trees, shrubs and flowers previously unknown. Thunberg was
almost exclusively a botanist rather than a general observer, yet his *Flora
Japonica* of 1784 had nothing like the impact of Kaempfer's book. Philip
Franz von Siebold (1791–1866), from Wurzburg, held the same Dutch
East India Company post 50 years later, but by that time the chances to botanize
and collect were much greater.

Less well known are some of the French plant collectors, often working as
Jesuit missionaries, who were active in China in the 17th and 18th centuries. The
Peking Mission, an expedition that took two years to reach China, was composed
of a group of Jesuits – Guy Tachard, Louis Le Comte, Père d'Entrecolles,
Dominique Parennin and Pierre d'Incarville. Parennin accompanied the Chinese
emperor on trips to Manchuria, and was to describe the beautiful violet flowers
of *Wisteria sinensis*. This did not reach Europe, however, until the following century. D'Incarville managed to raise the tree of heaven (*Ailanthus altissima*), oriental thuja and the Chinese aster from seed while in China between 1740 and 1756.
Peter Osbeck, a pupil of Linnaeus, collected plants in Canton (Guangzhou) from
1751 to 1752, but within three years China was all but closed to foreigners. Lord
Macartney's appointment as ambassador to the court at Peking in 1792 was an
attempt at infiltration. He took with him George Staunton, an amateur botanist,
as his second-in-command. Among the plants they brought back was the evergreen Macartney rose, *Rosa bracteata*.

THE GENESIS OF THE GARDENING MAGAZINE
The stories in this chapter began with one media revolution – the invention of
printing – and come to a close with another significant change, the rise of gardening journalism. The proliferation of periodicals from the 19th century
onwards marks a general increase in the population's ability to read and – in gardening terms – the expansion of a mass market for horticultural information.

In England one of the most interesting and lasting publications was *The
Botanical Magazine: Or Flower Garden Displayed*. Its first issue was produced in
1787 by William Curtis (1746–99), an outstanding naturalist and proprietor of a
botanic garden. It claimed to illustrate and describe "The Most Ornamental For-

SIR JOSEPH BANKS AND KEW GARDENS

Sir Joseph Banks (1743–1820), a wealthy naturalist and explorer, President of the Royal Society from 1772 until his death, and patron of gardeners, plant collectors and botanists, was the most important figure in British horticultural circles for over 40 years, with an international reputation. As scientific adviser to George III he was (from 1771 until he died) the unofficial director of the Royal Botanic Gardens at Kew, whence he sent out collectors specifically to look for both ornamental and economic plants.

As a young man of 25, Banks accompanied Captain Cook on his voyage around the world on the *Endeavour*, taking with him a team of scientists. Among them was Daniel Solander, a pupil of Linnaeus but by then an assistant in the embryonic British Museum, and Sydney Parkinson, a draughtsman who had already drawn specimens for Banks after his earlier expedition to Newfoundland and Iceland. The primary purpose of Cook's voyage was to observe Venus's transit over the disc of the sun, due in June 1769, from a point in the southern hemisphere such as Tahiti. Its secondary purpose, in which Banks was to play the part of leading naturalist, was the exploration of the great southern continent lying in the South Pacific. The highly successful expedition visited New Zealand and the east coast of Australia, in particular Botany Bay, and the Great Barrier Reef. Among the Australasian plants brought back were

JOSHUA REYNOLDS' PORTRAIT OF BANKS

banksias, named in Banks's honour, bottle brushes (*Callistemon*) and New Zealand flax (*Phormium tenax*). In terms of human mortality the voyage was a disaster, with Banks losing six out of his eight-strong team, including Parkinson, all victims of various fatal sicknesses. Banks had Parkinson's drawings finished and engravings made of 550 plates with text written by Solander. These were finally published in 1973.

Banks played a key role in the development of the Royal Botanic Gardens at Kew, which evolved from

George III's amalgamation of two neighbouring estates. Richmond gardens had been landscaped for the king by 'Capability' Brown after 1760, while the gardens at Kew House had been developed for Princess Augusta. After her death in 1771, George III merged the two. The Kew House gardens already included a small botanic garden under the charge of William Aiton. The king invited Banks to become his unofficial horticultural adviser, but Aiton remained in charge at Kew. His catalogue of 1789, *Hortus Kewensis*, listing 5,600 species growing there, is the most useful reference work for establishing dates of introduction of plants into Britain.

Aiton's son, also William, worked at Kew from 1793 and was one of the seven men who met in Hatchard's bookshop in 1804 to found the Society for the Improvement of Horticulture, which, in 1861, became the Royal Horticultural Society. After Banks's death, Kew went into decline until resurrected in 1841 as a serious national scientific and horticultural institution, with Sir William Hooker in charge.

The landscape at Kew
Before their amalgamation with the Richmond gardens, those at Kew House already contained several buildings by William Chambers, notably his Great Pagoda, as seen in this view of 1763.

AN EMPRESS AND HER ARTIST

PIERRE-JOSEPH REDOUTÉ (1759–1840), probably the most famous of all botanical illustrators, was, with Nikolaus von Jacquin, one of the last great exponents of the florilegium, in which an unsystematic miscellany of cultivated plants was presented in a grand format. From the Belgian Ardennes, Redouté first started to paint flowers in the Jardin du Roi from 1782, taking tuition from Gerard van Spaendonck, and he was inspired to develop a scientific attitude to plant portrayal by the French amateur botanist Charles Louis l'Héritier de Brutelle. Surviving the Revolution, in spite of having enjoyed royal patronage, Redouté reached the height of his fame working for Josephine Beauharnais, who had married Napoleon Bonaparte in 1796 (becoming empress in 1804).

She acquired Malmaison in 1798. Josephine, a passionate gardener, employed Etienne Pierre Ventenat (1757–1808) as her botanist until his death (when he was replaced by Aimé Bonpland), and Redouté as her botanical artist to record her collection.

Josephine's taste for botany was far more than a caprice, and vast sums were spent on acquiring plants – as much as 3,000 francs on a single bulb – in laying out the garden and having her plants illustrated. Many exotics new to France, including tender plants recently arrived from Australia, New Zealand and South Africa, were acclimatized in the greenhouses, while hardier trees and shrubs from Asia and the Americas were planted in the garden along with European natives. Her rose collection came from the German rose garden and

nursery at Wilhelmshoe in Kassel, established by the Landgrave Friedrich II after 1766. Josephine was one of the first to cultivate dahlias (already grown in the botanic garden in Madrid), receiving seed of new varieties from both Aimé Bonpland and Alexander von Humboldt direct from Mexico.

Inspired by the English-style Bagatelle installed by Thomas Blaikie in Paris before the Revolution, Josephine developed a taste for the romantic *jardin anglais* with groves of trees and luxuriant lawns interspersed with temples, ponds and rustic bridges. Louis Berthault was her designer at Malmaison. During the Napoleonic Wars, two London growers, James Lee and Lewis Kennedy, continued to supply her with many new exotics from their Vineyard Nursery at Hammersmith. Kennedy was even issued with a special passport to allow him and any plants he carried to get through the blockades. After their divorce, Napoleon uprooted many of Josephine's "English" plants, although his new empress, Marie Louise, also showed an interest in gardening.

Redouté's *Les Roses* (1817–24), completed after Josephine's death in 1814, is his most famous work, but his *Les Liliacées* (1802–16) is the more sumptuous. Illustrated with watercolours reproduced by stipple engraving and colour printing, it was published in eight volumes and contains 508 magnificent plates.

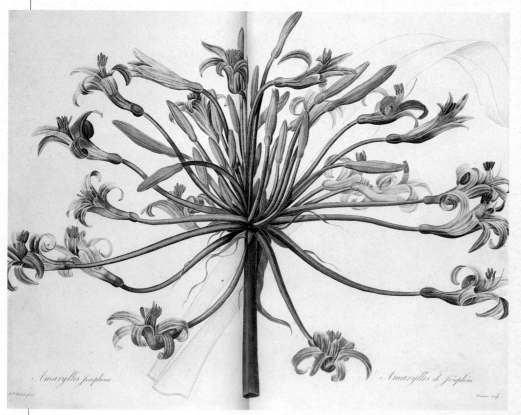

Amaryllis josephinae

Amaryllis de josephine

Josephine's flower
The magnificent Amaryllis josephinae, *named after the empress, was one of the 508 plants painted by Pierre-Joseph Redouté for his* Les Liliacées.

eign Plants, cultivated in the Open Ground, the Green-House and the Stove" and give information about their culture. After many vicissitudes, it is still published today under the name *Curtis's Botanical Magazine*. Illustrations were always made from a living plant and coloured as closely "as the imperfection of colouring will admit". Its appearance marked the beginning of a healthy number of enormously influential general and specialized magazines, which were to multiply during the 19th century. William Curtis had also made a study of the wild plants growing around London, producing his *Flora Londonensis* in the first two parts in 1770 and 1787, but at a financial loss. Realizing that the public had little interest, he abandoned the project in favour of describing the extravagant exotics that appealed more to the gardeners who already

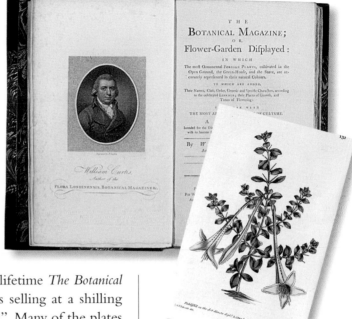

subscribed to his own botanic garden. During the author's lifetime *The Botanical Magazine* was published monthly, its two thousand copies selling at a shilling each, making enough to keep Curtis "in easy circumstances". Many of the plates were by James Sowerby, botanist and artist, and Sydenham Edwards. The latter started a rival magazine, *The Botanical Register*, in 1815. Sowerby himself compiled an ambitious work, a complete *English Botany*, published in 36 volumes between 1790 and 1814 and containing 2,500 plates.

As the 19th century progressed, the printing presses were destined to roll ever faster. As can be seen in Chapter 8, it was not many years before John Claudius Loudon founded his horticultural publishing empire, producing a host of gardening magazines and books designed to appeal to a greatly expanded and newly affluent readership.

Journal of influence
Named after Mark Catesby, this *Catesbieae spinosa*, or wild-thorn, drawn by Sydenham Edwards, was published in William Curtis's *Botanical Magazine* in 1790. The magazine, first issued in 1787, with a portrait of Curtis on the title page (top), proved to be one of the most lasting publications, illustrating recently introduced foreign plants through the next two centuries.

CHAPTER SEVEN

A natural revolution
THE
ENGLISH
LANDSCAPE
GARDEN

OUR STORY'S SPOTLIGHT NOW FOCUSES ON Britain in the 18th century for in this period just one style dominates — that of the English landscape garden. Its grassy meadows, serpentine lakes, gently contoured hills and artfully arranged clumps of trees seem the very model of Englishness, almost indistinguishable from the "real" countryside. And for many, the work of just one designer, Lancelot 'Capability' Brown, represents the style at its finest.

Yet Brown was not without his critics. Exactly how far a garden should or should not resemble a painting caused much heated debate. Nor were the Landscape Movement's roots entirely English. They lay, rather, in the hunting parks of Mesopotamia, the deer parks of Norman England and the gardens of ancient Rome and Renaissance Italy. Other influences came with the huge changes that were taking place in agriculture, science, and philosophical and political thinking.

From these disparate elements the 18th century's garden-makers created an art form, one that has had an enduring effect. They introduced a naturalism into garden design that was completely new to the West, added "landscape gardener" to the language, and indirectly gave us the public park. The private sanctum of the 18th-century landowner has today become the city-dweller's green breathing space.

An eye towards pleasure
This view of West Wycombe Park, Buckinghamshire, by William Hannan, *c.*1752, shows Sir Francis Dashwood's earliest improvements to the grounds which he began in 1739, one of the first of the new landscapes. The river was dammed to create a "rococo" cascade and lake.

Pope's wisdom
Alexander Pope, poet, satirist and enthusiast for changing early 18th-century attitudes to the natural world, became extremely influential in matters of gardening taste. Pope's famous maxim "In all, let Nature never be forgot…Consult the Genius of the place in all", provided a basis for all future environmental planning. The grotto that Pope made in his Thames-side garden was drawn by William Kent, and used to illustrate Calypso's cave in Pope's translation of Homer's *Odyssey*.

OPENING SALVOS AND SOUND DICTUMS

At the beginning of the 18th century, the formal garden still reigned supreme. In Britain two of the style's greatest exponents were George London and Henry Wise. London was one of the era's most sought-after designers while Wise eventually became master gardener to Queen Anne. They not only drew up plans but also supplied the plants needed to create the fashionable gardens of the day. At their prestigious Brompton Park Nursery, which they ran in partnership for many years, they grew the elms, limes and horse-chestnuts for the great radial avenues depicted in Knyff and Kip's topographical bird's-eye views (see page 163), the yews, hornbeams and hollies essential for the precision-clipped *allées* and exaggerated topiary shapes, and the box for parterres and flowerbed edgings. They also bred the sweet-smelling Brompton stock that perfumes gardens today.

This style of gardening and its rigid rules was famously satirized by Joseph Addison in his essays in the *Spectator* and by Alexander Pope in the *Guardian*. In "The Pleasure of the Imagination", Addison condemned straight lines and fanciful topiary, suggesting that parks could be integrated with rural scenery: "For my part I would rather look upon a Tree in all its Luxuriance and Diffusion of Boughs and branches, than when it is thus cut and trimmed into a mathematical Figure: and cannot but fancy that an orchard in Flower looks infinitely more delightful than all the little labyrinths of the most finished Parterres."

In the *Guardian* in 1713, Pope urged a return to the "amiable simplicity of unadorned nature", and in his imaginary catalogue for a sale of topiary, "Catalogue of Greens to be disposed of by an eminent Town Gardener", ridiculed what he saw as an abuse of natural form: "Adam and Eve in Yew; Adam a little shatter'd by the fall of a Tree of Knowledge in the great storm…St George in box; his arm scarce long enough, but will be in a Condition to stick the Dragon by next April…a pair of Giants, stunted, to be sold cheap."

By 1719 Pope was advising the Princess of Wales on her new garden at Richmond Lodge, which in 1728 he describes in a letter to Joseph Spence, Professor of Poetry at Oxford and a writer on landscape gardening. In the letter he expands on his ideas: "In laying out a garden, the first and chief thing to be considered is the genius of the place", which will reveal which assets should be enhanced and which deficiencies remedied.

In his poetry Pope had always expressed a sensibility to natural landscape. He believed that "All gardening is landscape painting. Just like a landscape hung up." As the friend of Lord Burlington and William Kent and others who developed the Landscape Movement, he was the inspiration behind many of the ideas adopted by the Movement. His essential belief that "Gardening is…nearer God's own Work, than Poetry" echoed Francis Bacon's "God Almighty first made a Garden" of a century earlier. By 1731, in his *Epistle* to Burlington, who had by then (together with Kent) embarked on the third phase of his garden at Chiswick, Pope proclaimed what was to become the cardinal rule for the rest of the century: "In all let Nature never be forgot…" The poem continued:

Consult the Genius of the place in all;
That tells the Waters or to rise, or fall,
Or helps th'ambitious Hill the heav'ns to scale,
Or scoops in circling Theatres the Vale;
Calls in the Country, catches opening glades
Joins willing woods, and varies shades from shades,
Now breaks, or now directs, the'intending lines;
Paints as you plant, and as you work, designs.

THE REDISCOVERY OF NATURE

Addison's and Pope's satires demonstrate a reaction against the extreme manifestations of French formality. The prolonged wars with France had also perhaps bred a general distaste in Britain for strict French style while, at the same time, a more liberal attitude in politics and the arts inspired a new freedom of thought in the garden whereby nature could be regarded as a delight to be explored, respected and studied.

As early as 1681, John Worlidge, in *The Art of Gardening*, had deplored the loss to gardening of many beautiful plants through a slavish subservience to formal parterre planting. Then in 1692, Sir William Temple mooted the idea of an irregular, informal style in *Upon the Gardens of Epicurus*. Although he had never been to China, he describes this freer style as that suggested by the Chinese *sharawadgi*, a term Temple coined himself, in which "Beauty shall be great and strike the Eye, but without any order or disposition of parts, that shall be commonly observed." And by 1700 Timothy Nourse in *Campania Felix*, his book on the country house, is recommending an estate on gently rising ground with a river in the

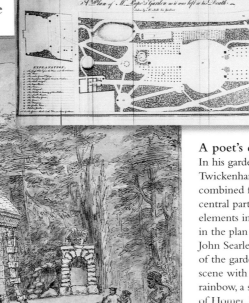

A poet's design
In his garden by the Thames at Twickenham, Alexander Pope combined formal features in the central part with more natural elements in outlying areas, as shown in the plan above by his gardener John Searle. William Kent's drawing of the garden (left) shows a classical scene with gods at the end of a rainbow, a sacrificial altar and a bust of Homer. Pope's dog Bounce and Kent himself, his arm around Pope, complete the scene.

Chiswick's changing times

The gardens at Chiswick House had already probably been worked on by Charles Bridgeman in 1716 before Lord Burlington built his Palladian villa in 1725. Later, from 1731, both Alexander Pope and William Kent much influenced developments, with Kent modifying the formality of the earlier layout. He softened the straight lines of the existing canal to produce a more natural-looking lake and designed a romantic cascade for its head. The view here, painted by Pieter Rysbrack, shows the earlier phase in which Burlington planted a three-armed *patte d'oie*, its thick hedges backed by groves of trees. Focal points included the Domed Temple, already built by 1716, the three-storey Bagnio and a sculpture of Samson slaying the Philistine. By 1733 this view was much altered with the disappearance of Samson and the third alley giving a view to the Rustic Arch.

distance, an open prospect terminated by hills. He speaks of planting banks and hillocks with wild flowers and making a wilderness of shrubs.

Less concerned with practical matters, Anthony Ashley Cooper, third Earl of Shaftesbury, demonstrated in his poetry an enthusiasm for nature that foreshadowed that of Wordsworth a hundred years later, linking aesthetic appreciation with morality: "I shall no longer resist the Passion growing in me for Things of a natural kind; where neither Art, nor the Conceit or Caprice of Man has spoil'd their genuine Order, by breaking in upon that primitive State."

Although the wish to break with French formalism may have exaggerated the pace of change in the 1720s and 1730s, the idea of working with nature can also be traced back to 17th-century Italy where an informal style was often combined with a geometric layout. The desire for naturalism looked back, too, to classical Rome and Roman ideology, with its emphasis on a retreat to bucolic country life.

The well-educated young English mi'lord – the typical landowner who would one day want to "improve" his estate – was thoroughly versed in the pastoral theme of Virgil's *Georgics* and Pliny the Younger's letters (see page 47) celebrating the delights of rural living. His knowledge of the works of Ovid would have enabled him to decode all the allegorical messages contained in the gardens of the Renaissance villas that he visited on the Grand Tour. This, the finishing touch to his education, would also have introduced him to the Italian landscape. From here it was but a small step to appreciating the possibility of developing similar landscapes in England's greener setting. By the time William Kent and Lord Burlington returned from their stay in Italy in 1719 they were poised to dissolve geometry and straight lines into more sensuous curves. A year later an album of engravings of Chinese gardens brought back from China by Father Matteo Ripa came into Burlington's hands – today, the album is in the British Museum. In it could be recognized the prototypes for Temple's *sharawadgi*.

An irregular arrangement
There were already voices besides those of Addison and Pope encouraging the new garden-makers. Both Batty Langley and Stephen Switzer introduced the idea of "irregularity" into garden theory. Langley (1696–1751) worked as an architect as well as a garden designer but is better known for his many books, including *New Principles of Gardening* (1728), from which this plan is taken. He thought that a garden "should consist of regular irregularities" and deplored "a stiff regular garden...fluffed up with trifling flower Knots". He also considered elaborate French *parterres de broderie* unsuitable for the English climate and best replaced by grass parterres.

Green sculpture

The amphitheatre and lake at Claremont, in Surrey, painted by an anonymous artist *c.*1750. Charles Bridgeman designed the extraordinary sculpted amphitheatre for the Duke of Newcastle in the 1720s. Recently restored by the National Trust, it shows how Bridgeman, designing in the transitional period between the two extremes of French-style formality and 'Capability' Brown's smooth expanses, combined geometry with a broad vision of the landscape. It also demonstrates his skill in moulding a steep grass slope into precise terraces without the benefit of modern earth-moving machinery. By 1750, Kent had softened the outline of Bridgeman's circular lake and given it an island temple and grotto.

A NATURAL PROGRESSION

As a broad generalization, there are three evolving phases of development in 18th-century landscape gardening. The innovators of the first, from the 1720s to 1740s, were Charles Bridgeman and William Kent, the latter very much under the influence of Alexander Pope. Bridgeman's and Kent's gardens mixed elements of the formal and informal and gave views into the countryside. Statues, temples, pavilions and other garden buildings were an essential ingredient, especially in Kent's designs.

The second phase was dominated by Lancelot 'Capability' Brown and his followers, their main masterpieces produced between 1750 and the 1780s. For many connoisseurs the simple beauty of Brown's parks epitomizes the English landscape style. Grass, trees, sky and reflecting water were its main elements. No longer seen as an architectural support system for the house, these "green" gardens flowed from the house walls into the whole landscape. The land was moulded into naturalistic contours, with deep serpentine valleys watered by lakes or rivers. From 1788 to 1818 Humphry Repton continued to produce Brownian landscapes but reintroduced the flower garden around the house.

Meanwhile, the ideas that Bridgeman and Kent introduced in the early stages at Chiswick, Stowe and Rousham greatly influenced the third phase, the Picturesque Movement. Champions of the "picturesque" criticized Brown's and Repton's tameness and called for a genuine romantic wildness typified by asymmetry, distant moors or mountains, rushing torrents and crumbling ruins.

A POLITICAL MANIFESTO AT STOWE

Gardens of the 18th century often had vivid links with contemporary politics, poetry and painting. This was particularly so in the gardens at Stowe, where it is impossible to grasp their full meaning without an appreciation of the relationship between Lord Cobham, the gardens' creator, and the Whig prime minister Sir Robert Walpole. Cobham, fervent Whig and supporter of the Hanoverian kings, fell out with Walpole and George II in 1733. He retired from active politics and became part of a Whig faction critical of the government. Instead of writing a barbed political diary, as he might today, Cobham chose his Buckinghamshire garden as the place to draw attention to what he saw as Walpole's political moral shortcomings and to publish his own Whig manifesto. He created some eight lakes and 36 temples, and commissioned

The Temple of British Worthies

about 90 statues and busts. Some features were designed to make particularly pointed comments. Inside the Temple of Modern Virtue, built as a ruin, he placed a headless statue to represent the current state of public life.

During the course of the 30 years or more that it took to create Stowe, successive designers contributed different ideas. Cobham first started work on the gardens in 1714, employing

Sir John Vanbrugh and Charles Bridgeman, but keeping a firm hand himself on stylistic developments. In 1734, after his withdrawal from active politics, he called in William Kent for naturalistic improvements. 'Capability' Brown was appointed head gardener in 1741 and continued for 10 years until after Cobham's death.

Stowe's temples, the Temple of British Worthies (a collection of Whig heroes), Palladian Bridge, Elysian Fields and Grecian Valley are stupendous but not easily understood and without a guide or good background knowledge the gardens' complexity can produce a feeling of disorientation. This is relieved, though, by the way in which the beautiful buildings, smooth meadows and lofty plantations present a series of enchanting landscape pictures.

The Rotunda, painted by J. Rigaud, c.1733

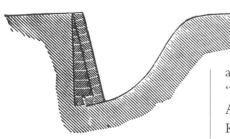

The significance of the ha-ha
The ha-ha, a sunken wall and ditch, played a key role in the development of the naturalistic park. Built at the edge of the pleasure grounds surrounding a house, the ha-ha made an invisible barrier that kept the cows and sheep in their pastures yet allowed uninterrupted views from house into park or from park into distant countryside. It meant that pleasure grounds, park and landscape could seamlessly become one. It is probably French in origin. Charles Bridgeman is generally credited with its introduction, but in fact a ha-ha had already been installed at Levens Hall in Cumbria in 1689.

Few of the great gardens of the century belonged simply to one phase or the other. In many cases an estate was worked on by a succession of "improvers", each leaving his distinctive mark. At Claremont, Bridgeman was succeeded by Kent and then by Brown, and the same trio worked consecutively at Stowe, while Repton was frequently called in to advise and suggest alterations to Brown's parks.

ENTER THE IMPROVERS
Charles Bridgeman and William Kent, working for wealthy patrons, were the earliest protagonists of the more informal approach – the first to consult Pope's "Genius of the place". Bridgeman, a practitioner rather than a writer, played a crucial role in the transitional period between the geometric layouts and great radial avenues portrayed by Knyff and Kip at the turn of the century and Kent's freer landscapes. Bridgeman first came to prominence in 1709 while working for George London and Henry Wise. By 1714 he was already involved with Lord Cobham in Cobham's changes to Stowe, where he installed a ha-ha, and by 1720 was also working at Wimpole Hall, in Cambridgeshire, for the Earl of Oxford. After Wise retired in 1728, Bridgeman became royal gardener to George II and Queen Caroline until his death in 1738.

It is to William Kent, however, that Horace Walpole (vocal gardening and architectural commentator and son of the prime minister Robert Walpole) gives the credit for founding the English landscape tradition. In his essay *On Modern Gardening*, written between 1750 and 1770, Walpole says of Kent: "He leaped the fence and saw all nature was a garden." During the 1720s and 1730s the designs for the main part of a garden retained their structured formality, with curving lines and meandering paths taking the place of the symmetrical "wilderness" that had often been introduced into the outer areas in preceding years. By 1738 at Rousham, Oxfordshire, however, Kent was interpreting Addison's idea of "a whole estate thrown into a kind of garden" and exploited Pope's invitation to call in the surrounding countryside.

The painted landscape

When 18th-century garden-makers were seeking inspiration, it was to the canvases of painters such as Claude Lorraine and Nicolas Poussin that they turned. The Arcadian scenes of distant hills, groves of trees and classical ruins, as seen here in Poussin's painting *Landscape with a Man Washing his Feet at a Fountain*, c.1648, depicted just the sort of romantic composition they wished to emulate. It is worth noting that Henry Hoare, the maker of the landscape garden at Stourhead, in Wiltshire, himself owned two Poussin paintings. A detail in Poussin's most famous painting *Et in Arcadia Ego* was incorporated in the early 1750s as a marble relief in the Shepherd's Monument at Shugborough, Staffordshire, by the designer Thomas Wright.

The façade that William Kent built
in a meadow opposite Rousham is
the perfect example of the
architectural device known as an
eye-catcher. Generally seen in
silhouette and often placed at a
garden's boundary, an eye-catcher
was particularly used to draw the
gaze into the countryside, so
blurring the distinction between
garden and natural landscape
beyond.

THE WORKS OF WILLIAM KENT

Painter, architect and theatre and landscape designer, William Kent (1685–1748)
came from a poor family in Yorkshire. While working as an apprentice coach
painter, Kent's talents were spotted by some wealthy patrons and, with their spon-
sorship, in 1710 he travelled to Rome to study painting. He stayed some nine
years, also visiting other Italian cities, and during this time was introduced to Lord
Burlington. On his return in 1719, Burlington became his patron and by 1731
had employed Kent to redesign his garden at Chiswick – already laid out with a
canal and radiating avenues (see page 208) – in a more naturalistic style. Kent also
worked on several other celebrated designs including those for Claremont,
Rousham and Stowe.

Kent, although not a successful painter, used his visual talents and spatial
understanding to become the foremost garden designer of the day, gradually free-
ing gardens from all traces of formality. He expanded on his friend Alexander
Pope's dictum that "all gardening is landscape painting" to make three-dimensional pictures with light and shade and architecture – creating gardens that
resembled as nearly as possible the idealized romantic landscapes of painters such
as Claude Lorraine and Nicolas Poussin. Throughout Kent's career, the drawings
of his proposals for both landscape and buildings show how influenced he had
been by his time in Italy. The cascade at Rousham seems to have been inspired by
that at Valsanzibio, in the gardens of the Villa Barbarigo Pizzoni Ardemani.

Rousham, beside the River Cherwell in Oxfordshire, remains Kent's masterpiece, his most complete and celebrated work, with both house and garden still
almost as he left them. He worked here between 1737 and 1741 (and possibly
during the early 1730s while still at Stowe). Horace Walpole found it the "most
engaging" of his gardens, preferring it to Stowe, and drew attention to its modest
scale: "the garden is Daphne in little; the sweetest little groves, streams, glades porticoes, cascades and river imaginable; all the scenes are perfectly classic".

Kent achieved great variety in a small and awkward space at Rousham,
indulging his talent for stage design by manipulating the different views, with the
whole ensemble in the pastoral valley extending successive vistas out across the
river into the surrounding fields and hedgerows. An eye-catcher and ruined
Temple of the Mill across the river acted as focal points. Terraces above the river
were smoothed to make a concave slope on which was placed Scheemakers'
marble group of a lion mauling a horse. Each woodland walk and open glade was
terminated by an architectural feature designed to come as a surprise. The Praeneste, a massive arcade that is never seen as an elevation but is approached diagonally, is Kent at his best. The Cold Bath and Octagonal Pool in the woods provide
the source of water for the slender masonry rill which winds downwards to the
Great Pond, following the kind of sinuous course that was to become commonplace in 18th-century landscapes. Although Bridgeman had worked at Rousham
in the 1720s, making basins, an alley, a theatre and a serpentine walk, which provided a framework for the garden, it is Kent's overlay and general softening effects
which firmly predominate today. Bridgeman's formalistic basins were naturalized
into a chain of ponds joined by rustic cascades.

OTHER PATHS OF INSPIRATION

Kent's ideas soon began to influence other garden-makers and, by the 1740s, four English gardens marking a new step in garden design were already in the making, their inspirational owners indulging their own highly individual tastes and sensibilities. Henry Hoare at Stourhead (see page 219), Charles Hamilton at Painshill (see page 234), Philip Southcote at Wooburn Farm and the poet William Shenstone at the Leasowes (see page 232), in their different ways, all introduced new trains of thought in the development of a more natural approach and its evolution into the "picturesque" ideal at the end of the century. The design of Stourhead tells just one story, although it is one that interweaves the life of a Roman hero with that of its maker, Henry Hoare. Painshill has no literary plot but reveals its owner Charles Hamilton's particular interest in plants. And at both Wooburn Farm and the Leasowes, Philip Southcote and William Shenstone took a different route from most of their contemporaries in creating a blend of landscape, pleasure garden and farm – the *ferme ornée*. This not necessarily very practical combination was to inspire a number of gardens on the Continent. Although the 18th century's most enduring legacy is its landscape parks with smooth grassland and trees predominating, flowers and shrubs were by no means abolished from the scene, as we see later in this chapter. Indeed, the new plant discoveries now arriving from the Americas deserved special attention and some gardens, such as Painshill, were specifically designed for their inclusion.

NATURE IMPROVED AND PERFECTED

By the middle of the 18th century, the softening of geometric outlines had evolved into a new ideal from which all formality and symmetry was banished. Nature was "improved" to such an extent that the great new landscape gardens so resembled a natural scene as to be almost, if not wholly, indistinguishable from it.

Between the 1750s and 1780s the Landscape Movement's most famous practitioner, Lancelot 'Capability' Brown, extended the emphasis placed

Rousham's masterpieces (below and overleaf)
At Rousham, William Kent created some of his finest work. Here, Kent imposed his own more natural vistas on a semi-formal Bridgeman landscape. Today the garden remains largely as he left it. A serpentine rill descends from the Octagonal Pool high in the woods to water the Vale of Venus. The valley is overlooked by a seven-arched stone arcade, the Praeneste (overleaf), the garden's focal point.

THE EFFECTS OF ENCLOSURE

The enclosure of common land, which had already started in previous centuries, intensified during the 18th century. Between 1730 and 1820 some 3,500 separate Acts of Parliament were passed. Enclosure created a new underclass of landless, dependent agricultural labourers and much social deprivation and unrest. But it also meant that new improved agricultural methods could be introduced that greatly increased the food supply for a rapidly growing population. Enclosure facilitated the creation of the new landscape parks, although it was often possible to use marginal fields and unproductive land.

on nature's role. By encircling an estate with perimeter woods, he was able to turn a park into a private sanctum with undulating green pastures, contoured land masses, curving lakes or rivers winding through the valleys, and clumps of majestic trees silhouetted against the sky. On an old estate Brown would destroy the traditional gardens around the house and break up the lines of French-style avenues to form groves of trees. Flowers and utilitarian kitchen gardens were banished from sight across the park. In Brown's hands these Arcadian landscapes became such perfect replicas of an ideal that it was almost impossible to distinguish the separate roles of nature and art. Today a surviving 18th-century park fits so easily into the English countryside that the designer's role in "perfecting" nature has almost been extinguished. These pastoral idylls, planned to stress man's relationship and interdependence with nature and to stimulate moods and emotion, are often regarded as the epitome of 18th-century rationalism.

The development of the Landscape Movement coincided with the passing of the Acts of Enclosure. The appropriation and enclosure of common land and the creation of a more comprehensive field system made it possible for landowners to arrange their estates to exploit the new landscape ideals (and also run their estates more profitably by taking advantage of new farming methods). In so doing they changed the face of England. Sometimes whole villages were moved to satisfy an owner's desire for a private elysium. Lamenting the social and economic problems that were a direct result of enclosure, Oliver Goldsmith's *The Deserted Village* depicted such landowners not as improvers but as destroyers of a whole way of life. The fate of "Sweet Auburn, loveliest village of the plain" sums up his attitude:

> The sports are fled and all thy charms withdrawn:
> Amidst thy bow'rs the tyrant's hand is seen,
> And desolation saddens all thy green…
> The mournful peasant leads his humble band;
> And while he sinks, without one arm to serve,
> The country blooms – a garden and a grave.

Goldsmith's "sweet Auburn" probably refers to Nuneham Courtney on the Thames near Oxford, a village which the first Earl Harcourt moved a mile after he built his new Palladian villa in 1756, with a fine prospect over the river and to the distant spires of Oxford. (The flowerbeds introduced later in the century at Nuneham were to become an outstanding example of a combination of pleasure and landscape garden, see page 237.)

BROWN'S FORCE OF GENIUS

Lancelot 'Capability' Brown is, without doubt, the best known of all English landscape designers, famously having been given his nickname because of his habit of exploring an estate to assess its potential or "capabilities". Brown is rare in that he achieved recognition within his lifetime, being praised by Horace Walpole in *On Modern Gardening* as "a very able master", a worthy successor to William Kent. Indeed so successful was his work (and that of his contemporaries)

STOURHEAD'S VIRGILIAN SETTING

Banker Henry Hoare made his allegorical garden at Stourhead, in Wiltshire, between 1745 and 1783. Inspired by Virgil's epic poem the *Aeneid*, Stourhead depicts the story of Aeneas and the Trojan survivors and their voyage to Rome. To convey his message, Hoare developed Kent's notion of a peripheral itinerant walk on which "incidents" – temples, grotto, hermitage and bridge – were revealed in turn in a carefully devised series of views across the lake.

The buildings, tracing Aeneas's descent into the underworld, and statues, such as that of Hercules, symbolize the choice between pleasure and virtue. But they can also be read as themes of husbandry, love, death and triumph over death, recalling events in Hoare's own life. Before creating the garden he had lost two wives, his mother and several children within a short period, the final blow coming in 1752 with the death in Naples of his eldest son, Henry, aged 21.

The irregular-shaped central lake, originally constructed by damming the end of the deep valley below the chalk downs, was planned to reflect temples, trees and hanging woods in the style of a Claude painting. The garden tour culminates with the Temple of Apollo, set high above the lake, its dome designed to receive the rays of the afternoon sun. From the Temple the whole itinerary around the lake becomes visible, representing not only Aeneas's struggles but also man's journey through life.

Hoare, who early acquired the habit, as he put it, "of looking into books and the pursuit of that knowledge which distinguishes only the gentleman from the vulgar"

travelled widely in Europe and was a friend of Lord Burlington, and through him aware of Kent's landscaping activities. He became a patron to the architect Henry Flitcroft, who had begun his career under Kent and was to design many of Stourhead's buildings, including the Temple of Apollo.

Today, with the 19th-century addition of tall dark conifers from northwest America and a collection of rhododendrons, the woods are even denser, intensifying elements of surprise on the circuit walk. At the time the mainly deciduous woodland, even though it was underplanted with cherry laurel, would have taken a number of years to acquire the necessary density.

Hoare's personal vision, realized over more than 30 years, produced a masterpiece that can be enjoyed on every level. Horace Walpole described Stourhead as "one of the most picturesque scenes in the world". In Hoare's own time connoisseurs flocked to see it, including the painter Copleston Warre Bampfylde and the Swedish landscape designer Frederik Magnus Piper. They went on to create their own versions of the scenes: Bampfylde in his Georgian pleasure garden at Hestercombe, Somerset (recently restored, it neighbours the later formal Lutyens/Jekyll design) and Piper at Haga Park and Drottningholm in Stockholm. Later both Turner and Constable drew the landscape.

Stourhead's creation spans a period when Kent was in decline (he died in 1748) and 'Capability' Brown had yet to dominate the natural revolution with his blander schemes. By the time of Hoare's death the Picturesque Movement, with more exaggerated gothic overtones, was in the ascendant.

Perfect composition
The finest view of Stourhead, painted by an unknown artist, shows the Pantheon (right), the Palladian Bridge and the Temple of Apollo, the climax of the garden.

Entrance statement (below)

Stowe's Doric Arch provided a formal entrance to the Elysian Fields and framed a view of the Palladian bridge. It also delighted George III's aunt, Princess Amelia, in whose honour it was erected in 1770. "The chief entertainment of the week, at least what was so to the Princess, is an arch...erected in her honour in the most enchanting of all picturesque places."

Serene prospect (right)

The Pantheon at Stourhead was designed to be the focal point of the "prospect" from the hillside near the main house. It is a homage to the original Pantheon in Rome, which Henry Hoare, the garden's founder-owner, regarded as "a pattern of perfection". Stourhead's buildings and sculptures contribute to a "programme" celebrating the arts and virtues of ancient Rome.

Chinoiserie at Sanssouci (right)

In 18th-century Europe tea and porcelain were luxuries best enjoyed in garden pagodas and pavilions. Frederick the Great's drum-shaped tea house at Sanssouci in Potsdam is animated by life-sized "Chinese" figures, talking and playing musical instruments. It was the envy of Frederick's sisters, who persuaded their royal husbands to build them tea houses of their own – at Bayreuth, in Germany, and Drottningholm, in Sweden.

Picturesque latticework (left)

In pattern books of the day, designers could let their imaginations run riot. This idea for a banqueting room, from 1758, seems to be something of a Chinese-gothic cultural fusion.

Temples of delight

No landscape garden was complete without a selection of architectural eye-catchers. Temples, obelisks, bridges, pagodas, grottoes and ruins lent atmosphere and interest to the "living picture". At Castle Howard they were widely distributed across the landscape; at Stowe, Rousham and Stourhead they marked stages in circuit walks. At Painshill Charles Hamilton treated himself and his guests to a Roman mausoleum, a famously fanciful Turkish tent, a temple of Bacchus and a hermitage, as well as a gigantic grotto (see page 133). Stourhead's circuit was enlivened by a re-erected medieval market cross, a temple of Flora, grotto, Palladian bridge, rustic cottage and temple of Apollo. These buildings were focal points and theatrical sets in the self-contained world of the aristocratic pleasure garden. They enshrined personal philosophical, historical, literary and mythological themes. In commissioning Stowe's 40-odd buildings, Viscount Cobham was amusing himself and living up to his family motto: *Templa Quam Delicta*, or "How delightful are thy temples!"

From the beginning of the 18th century exotic Chinese-style pavilions and pagodas with fanciful latticework and sweeping rooflines were popular in England, but in Germany and France the fashion for chinoiserie (see pages 342–43) did not take off until the middle of the century. In form and function European variations on Far Eastern themes were a far cry from the real thing, about which there was little first-hand information. In China, garden pavilions were not designed as eye-catchers or playhouses. The scholar's garden pavilion was his library and study, and other garden buildings were designed for activities such as music, chess, poetry and meditation.

Fabric of the folly (above and below)
Besides offering shade and shelter, buildings such as this extravagantly embowered German temple (above) were used to entertain high society. When the aim was fun, as opposed to sublime thoughts or moral instruction, follies need not be made to last. The Queen of Sweden's first "Chinese" kiosk, the Kina Slott at Drottningholm, was made of wood (and proved so popular with the Swedish court it was replaced by a permanent brick and stone pavilion). Many an 18th-century Turkish tent was made of canvas. The stylish design (below) by Tom Stuart-Smith for the Chelsea Flower Show follows this playful tradition, and now takes the role of an arch in his own Hertfordshire garden.

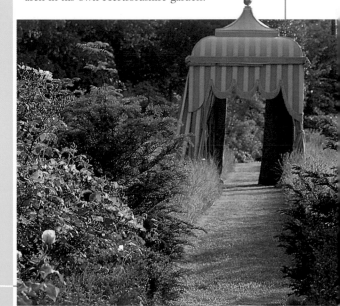

After Sir Joshua Reynolds.

A horticultural skirmish
Chief of 'Capability' Brown's critics
during his lifetime was the architect
Sir William Chambers (above). By
the late 1750s Chambers (1723–96)
had become HM Surveyor General
and treasurer of the Royal Academy,
although he is more famous today
for buildings such as his pagoda at
Kew (see page 343). He condemned
Brown's work for its lack of variety
in content and in features likely to
stimulate the mind. He accused
Brown of a lack of imagination with
his "common meadows" – an
unflattering hint at Brown's lack of a
classical education – asserting that
"whole woods have been swept
away to make room for a little grass
and a few American weeds". Horace
Walpole and the poet William
Mason both sprang to Brown's
defence, with Mason's satirical *An
Heroic Epistle to Sir William Chambers*
attacking the whole character of
Chambers' work.

Brown at Blenheim (overleaf)
'Capability' Brown retained
Vanbrugh's bridge at Blenheim
Palace, in Oxfordshire, but, by
damming the River Glyme, formed
two vast lakes joined by a neck of
water at the bridge.

in reproducing nature's effects that it has only recently been appreciated how much of England's rural scenery is due to these 18th-century designers. Sir William Chambers complained in 1772 that Brown's gardens "differ very little from common fields, so closely is nature copied in most of them".

Pastoral in intent, repetitive and perhaps a little bland, Brown's parks did not depend on literary allusion or allegory. Instead, working on a grand scale, his ideal was to improve the roughness of nature, blotting out any imperfections, and retaining those elements producing the sensation of beauty, as defined by Edmund Burke in his *A Philosophical Inquiry into the Origin of our Ideas of the Sublime and Beautiful* (1757). Brown's landscapes induce a gentle serenity rather than evoking any sort of visual excitement.

One of Brown's most remarkable achievements was his ability to plant for posterity. Even as a young man he was putting in the beeches, oaks and chestnuts that were to be the staple of his "belting, clumping and dotting" as he rearranged parks all over England. During his lifetime these landscapes must have had a certain stiffness, as the bulk of his planting would have been young saplings, probably obtained at 1–1.2m (3–4ft) in height. These would have needed protective fencing against cattle, sheep and deer and even in 30 years would hardly have fulfilled his ambitions. Often "nursed" by soft wood conifers to be removed later, many of these trees have taken more than 200 years to reach maturity.

During his lifetime Brown had few detractors but after his death his reputation soon went into an eclipse. Inept imitators brought Brown's principles into disrepute. Only his successor Humphry Repton defended Brown's "force of genius", and few of the critics were aware of the timescale necessary for Brown's parks to mature. A campaign of ridicule and denigration directed during the 1790s by the advocates of the picturesque attacked both Brown and Humphry Repton for their "perfectly composed" landscapes. Sir Uvedale Price and Richard Payne Knight insisted on the importance of a relationship between a building and landscape creating a picture enlivened by variety and condemned Brown's work for its lack of excitement.

REPTON AND HIS RED BOOKS

After Brown's death Humphry Repton (1752–1818), the first to claim the title of "landscape gardener", became his successor in public esteem (and in some ways prepared the way for a return to formalism in the 19th century). By the 1790s he overshadowed all Brown's contemporaries, working in more than 50 country estates throughout England, employed by landowners such as the Cokes (at Holkham Hall, 1788–89), the Duke of Portland (at Welbeck Abbey, 1789, and Bulstrode, 1790) and the Duke of Bedford (at Woburn Abbey, 1806, and Endsleigh, 1811).

Repton embarked on his new career in 1788 – after a series of false starts in various others – at the age of 36. He was a year older than Brown had been when

LANCELOT 'CAPABILITY' BROWN

LANCELOT BROWN was born in 1716, in the village of Kirkharle in Northumberland. Aged 16, his first job was at Kirkharle Tower where Sir William Loraine was undertaking a vast improvement of his estate in "planting and enclosure". There, under an enlightened employer, with new methods of agriculture, drainage and reclamation and the possibility of growing newly introduced trees and shrubs, Brown embarked on the career that was to make him a household name. For a young man he seems to have been given considerable authority and a chance to develop his eye for shaping contours, forming lakes and transplanting mature trees, all on a large scale. Perhaps the natural beauty of the Northumberland hills and valleys moulded his developing taste.

'CAPABILITY' BROWN, c.1770–75

In 1739 he moved south, visiting estates and carrying references from his employer. Two years later he found a post as head gardener at Stowe, working for Lord Cobham under William Kent (Charles Bridgeman had died the previous year). Here, he was to be in charge of the next extension in the Grecian Valley, supervising the removal of 17,600 cubic metres (23,000 cubic yards) of earth and the demolition of Bridgeman's terrace and the creation of the south lawn. Gaining Cobham's confidence, Brown became a general clerk of the works, in charge of building as well as landscaping operations, and studying architectural works in Stowe's library. He remained at Stowe until 1751, two years after Cobham's death, but even before then had embarked on other commissions.

By the 1750s Brown had proceeded to remould many of the greatest parks of England. At Croome Court, where he was consulted on the building of a new house as well as landscaping the park, his abilities were confirmed when he created a grotto and lake in what had been described as "as hopeless a spot as any in the island". Commissions received during the next few years included Petworth, Burghley, Longleat, Bowood and Syon House. Work on some of his projects lasted for as many as 20 years. In the 1760s he rearranged 800 hectares (2,000 acres) at Blenheim and the parterres and park at Chatsworth. Brown continued to "improve" properties for the rest of his career, occasionally being involved in building or rebuilding, as at Claremont and Fisherwick. In 1764 he received a degree of royal recognition when he was made master gardener at Hampton Court, a job that brought with it a house in the grounds for himself and his family. During the 1770s he worked at Berrington Hall, Sheffield Park and Ditchley Hall.

Although always in demand for his parks, having taught himself a competency in architecture, Brown was able to offer clients a combined service, especially important when the composition depended on the integration of landscape and ornamental buildings.

Brown died, lamented by many friends, in February 1783. A remarkable self-made man, he is described as having "wit, learning and great integrity", and was said to be an "agreeable pleasant companion but a genius in his profession". After 30 years of work on the English landscape he was able to refuse the Duke of Leinster's offer of £1,000 to go to Ireland, excusing himself on the grounds that he had "not yet finished England". By the time Brown's parks had reached maturity, in Victorian times, their creator was almost forgotten his name and achievements coming back into prominence only during the twentieth century.

Sylvan setting
The temple at Harewood House, where Brown first worked in 1758, is seen here romantically framed by trees. It was painted by Thomas Girtin c.1798.

Repton remembered
Nineteenth-century writer J.C.
Loudon was at first not among
Humphry Repton's admirers. But
later he came greatly to appreciate
Repton's ideas and wrote: "The
possibility of turning to advantage
that natural taste for improving the
beauties of scenery, which had
formed one of the dearest pleasures
of his rural life, suggested itself to his
mind one night when anxiety had
driven sleep from his pillow. This
scheme, which at first seems to have
entered his imagination with almost
the vague uncertainty of a dream,
assumed a more substantial form
when, on the return of day, he
meditated upon its practicability.
With his usual quickness of decision,
he arose the next morning; and, with
fresh energy of purpose, spent the
whole of that day in writing letters
to his various acquaintances, in all
parts of the kingdom, explaining his
intention of becoming a 'Landscape
Gardener'; and he lost not a moment
in bending his whole mind to the
acquisition of such technical
knowledge as was necessary for the
practical purposes of such a
profession."

he started designing and lacked Brown's years of practical apprenticeship at
Kirkharle and Stowe. Repton had to depend on his studies of the principles
of taste through the works of contemporary artists and writers and on his
observance of landscape during his youth. Just as the Northumberland hills
had influenced Brown so the East Anglian countryside, with its wide skies
and distant views, was to remain an important part of Repton's vision.
Although he had no technical qualifications, he had one great advantage
over most of his rivals (and over Brown) in his ability to draw and paint,
which allowed him to use his imagination in visualizing effects. Better educated than Brown, Repton was also an able writer. During his career he
advised at some 330 gardens. At first, the gardens were mainly those of the
great landowners but, by the early 1800s, he had acquired a new class of *nou-
veaux riches*, clients with estates more limited in scale, the owners of the suburban villas that were to be described by gardening guru John Claudius
Loudon in the 1820s. Loudon, who in 1806 was one of Repton's foremost critics, in 1840 rescued him from comparative obscurity by republishing his five
major works on landscape gardening.

For his first commission, Repton made use of a professional surveyor and
established a working relationship with the draughtsman-turned-architect
William Wilkins of Norwich. Unlike Brown, Repton did not do his own con-
tracting so charged a daily fee (five guineas by 1790, as reported by Jane Austen in
Mansfield Park, and two guineas for drawing at home) plus expenses. However, his
fees soon had to be increased with the onset of inflation and high taxes after the
outbreak of war with France. From some clients, where work continued for
several years, he received an annual salary, although this seldom worked to his
advantage. From 1794 to 1799 he entered into a business partnership with the
architect John Nash; they undertook their first joint project at Corsham Court, in
1796. Repton and Nash also continued to work independently, with Repton's
two elder sons, John and George, both working at one time or another as Nash's
assistant.

The details of Repton's financial affairs, at a time when his profession was a
new one, make interesting reading; his problems in charging a set fee or a per-
centage of work done differ little from those of designers today. His earning
capacity fell off in the first years of the new century, and from 1811 he suffered
further difficulties caused by a carriage accident. The injuries he received seriously reduced his mobility for the rest of his life.

An important feature of Repton's design work was the production of his
famous Red Books. These were prepared for each client, showing views of the
estate, painted in delicate watercolours, before and after his suggested improvements. An overlay or flap when lifted revealed the completed transformation. A
discursive text accompanied the paintings. Bound in red morocco these handsome books, often put on display by a client, served as excellent advertisements
for his work. They are also a marvellous record to which we can still refer today.
Because of their expensive production, however, Repton found it necessary to
charge for the books, his *chef-d'oeuvre* of Antony House in Cornwall costing £31.

REPTON'S WAY OF WORKING

During the 1790s Repton followed Brown in designing parks that seemed to fit seamlessly into the surrounding countryside. When called in to work on a landscape created by Brown, he would usually make only limited alterations and understood that Brown had intended that some trees should be felled as the main specimens grew. Repton occasionally even retained avenues from earlier periods. Sometimes, as in 1800 at Harewood in Yorkshire, where Brown's planting was by that stage 30 years old, he restricted himself to designing a new carriageway and gateway. One of his specialities was a winding drive, which, having allowed a glimpse of the house immediately after entering the gates, then took a circuitous route so that hills or trees hid the mansion until the final moment of arrival. This dramatic effect made a property look larger than it was. Instead of Brown's hilltop plantations, Repton's groves cascaded down slopes, with shrubby underplanting giving them a more solid appearance.

While still following Brown's lead in the more distant parkland, Repton felt that a house needed a formal link with its grounds and often introduced terracing rather than allowing grass to straggle up to the front door. He also recognized that his clients sometimes wanted a more decorative garden near the house, and introduced areas for growing flowers and other ornamentals, including many of the new introductions now arriving from America and elsewhere. At Woburn Abbey, for the Duke of Bedford, he designed a flower corridor, a rosary, an American garden, a Chinese garden and a menagerie. One of Repton's last commissions, also for the duke, was at Endsleigh, near Tavistock in Devon. Here he landscaped the beautiful Tamar valley around a *cottage orné*, a sporting lodge built by Jeffry Wyattville in 1810. Wyattville's

The present View to the Westward.

Before and after
Repton's captivating sketches added a whole dimension to his designs. His Red Book for Woburn Abbey, one of his commissions for the sixth Duke of Bedford, shows the view (above) to the westward before Repton's suggested improvements, and (left) afterwards, revealed once the viewer had lifted a flap. Repton worked for the duke during the last 10 years of his career.

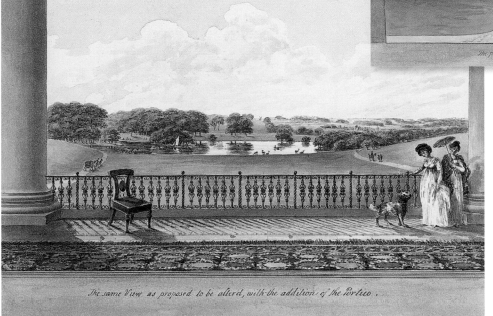

The same View as proposed to be alter'd, with the addition of the Portico.

design, a horseshoe shape of irregular buildings, was planned to allow views to the delightful landscape from many of the windows. Due to his deteriorating health, Repton made few visits to the site and the Red Book, completed towards the end of 1815, was his last. It shows views of the cottage, including Wyattville's charming design for a children's garden to which Repton planned to add a pool on a raised ledge where boats could be sailed. Appreciating the ideas behind Wyattville's design, Repton endeavoured to avoid any planting in front of the cottage that might obscure views to the river and the new woodland on the opposite bank. He also took care not to allow over-domestication to spoil the picturesque character of the place. A weir of stepping stones over the river provided a crossing place for carriages, and the smoke rising from the chimney of a distant cottage added suitably picturesque animation to the scene. Plans also included a formal lawn giving a vista east to a quarry and grotto, and a glass conservatory or "winter garden" for sheltering tender plants.

In 1813 at Ashridge Park, in Buckinghamshire, where James Wyatt was building a gothic pile for the Earl of Bridgewater, Repton was content to restrict himself to the pleasure grounds south of the house, where he proposed an intricate series of 10 gardens including a rosary. He wrote enthusiastically in *Fragments on the Theory and Practice of Landscape Gardening* (1816): "...of all the subjects on which I have been consulted few have excited so much interest in my mind as the plan for these gardens...it being the youngest favourite, the child of my age

A harmony of purpose
The coastal scenery and woods at Sheringham Park, in Norfolk, inspired Repton to create one of his most pleasing landscapes. He produced a Red Book in 1812. Although Repton had no real training or experience, he was supremely confident: "In every place in which I was consulted, I found that I was gifted with the peculiar faculty of seeing almost immediately the way in which it might be improved."

and declining power; when no longer able to undertake the more extensive plans of landscape. I was glad to contract my views within the narrow circle of a garden independent of its accompaniment of distant scenery."

THE PICTURESQUE DEBATE

By the time Humphry Repton emerged as heir-apparent to 'Capability' Brown, reaction against Brown's 30-year domination of gardening style had reached new heights. Brown's critics deplored the smoothness and uniformity of his landscapes and demanded instead that a picturesque aesthetic be applied in which "wildness" characterized the terrain, accentuated by the ruins of castles and crumbling abbeys. Purists required that a landscape, rather than being made to resemble a painting, should have the kind of romantic, rugged aspect that would immediately appeal to a painter.

Endsleigh revived
At Endsleigh in Devon, one of Repton's last commissions, he landscaped the valley of the River Tamar for the sixth Duke of Bedford during 1814. The Red Book shows the romantic landscape and Repton's "improved" version, with a broad terrace walk and conservatory. This photograph shows the terrace as it looks today, after its recent restoration.

Although earlier in the 18th century there had been plenty of discussion on the merits or otherwise of the "tamer"' or "wilder" aspects of "place-making", it was not until the Reverend William Gilpin published his *Observations Relative to Picturesque Beauty* in 1789 that the term picturesque came to be firmly associated with a specific visual quality in scenery where nature was seen in unkempt mode (very different from Brown's compositions, which lacked irregularity and the bold roughness of nature). Already words such as romantic and sublime, interpreted from Edmund Burke's *A Philosophical Inquiry into the Origin of our Ideas of the Sublime and Beautiful*, referred to the appearance of unassisted nature. With Brown in eclipse, the Picturesque Movement gained momentum. The preparation of Repton's *Sketches and Hints on Landscape Gardening* (published in 1795) spurred an attack by Richard Payne Knight in the form of *The Landscape,* a didactic poem addressed to Uvedale Price. This was followed by Uvedale Price's *Essays on the Picturesque*. Both were published in 1794, leaving time for Repton to include a hasty reply in his own book. Knight and Price were both improvers of their own Herefordshire estates at Downton and Foxley respectively. Knight added a gothic tower and battlements to Palladian Downton and cultivated gnarled trees hanging over swirling water and tumbling jagged rocks to achieve his picturesque ideal. It was hardly a genuinely wild scene but one that would appeal to the artist. For adherents of the picturesque, composition could be enlivened by variety, movement, asymmetry and architecture of almost any period or style – Greek revival, Chinese, Turkish, Tudor or gothic.

Untamed nature
The wild and savage scenes of the
Italian romantic painter Salvator
Rosa (1615–73) perfectly expressed
the tastes of the followers of the
Picturesque Movement. They
favoured crumbling ruins, mossy
terraces and unkempt woodland
over the blandness of Brown's and
Repton's tame landscapes. The Rosa
painting seen here is entitled
*Mountain Landscape with Figures and a
Man Bathing.*

The tirade of criticism against Brown and Repton was aimed mainly at
Brown, whose soft undulating green slopes and trim plantations were abhorred
by proponents of the picturesque as "false beauty" since they lacked any semblance of the desirable, almost grotesque, qualities they so admired. Repton
replied by stressing that landscapes were not to be laid out with a view to their
appearance for a painting but should be composed for enjoyment and use. He
fully appreciated the picturesque quality of romantic scenery but felt it should not
be injured by too much interference from art. Nor did he destroy buildings that
were no longer fashionable or build sham ruins, although he allowed picturesque
cottages for estate workers.

Taken up by magazines and reviews, the picturesque controversy became the
subject of lively discussion for many more years, with Repton returning to
Brown's and his own defence both in his *Observations on the Theory and Practice of
Landscape Gardening* of 1803 and in *An Inquiry into the Changes of Taste in Landscape
Gardening* in 1806. In 1804 J.C. Loudon, still a young man, endorsed Knight and
Price at Repton's expense, commenting on Repton's landscape gardening as
being both "puerile" and "pretty". In later years, however, and as editor of *The
Gardener's Magazine* from 1826, Loudon was to appreciate the quality of Repton's
work and his contribution to 18th-century gardening. By 1840, when he pub-

lished Repton's writings, he was to praise Repton as one of the instigators of the "gardenesque" style (see page 249), which he was the first to analyse and describe.

FLORAL DECORATIONS AND DIVERSIONS

Although many of the enclosed flower gardens of earlier periods disappeared during the 18th century, having been dug up or planted over with grass, the idea of the flowerless English landscape park is largely a myth. Thanks to recent pioneer research by garden historians such as Mark Laird and Fiona Cowell, another picture emerges. Not only did shrubberies and flower gardens survive during the 18th century but designers, including 'Capability' Brown, continued to install them. New exotics from America and elsewhere augmented the parkland plantings within and beyond the ha-ha or, where the whole scheme was designed around a carefully contrived circuit – as in the *fermes ornées* of Wooburn Farm and the Leasowes – they were planted along the path.

While the grander landscapes became the model for our public parks, these more intimate 18th-century plantings, which combined new arrivals with traditional plants, hold particular interest for today's gardener who works in a relatively modest-sized plot with beds and borders of mixed shrubs, perennials and bulbs.

In the pleasure grounds, protected from grazing livestock by a ha-ha, flowering shrubs and flowers became important features. This area of the garden became the natural home for many of the woodland shade-loving plants arriving mid-century from eastern North America – exotics such as Virginian fringe tree, *Chionanthus virginicus*, dogwoods and rhododendrons introduced by John Bartram through Peter Collinson (see page 193) and becoming available in nurseries. In

Picturesque vision
Richard Payne Knight, the great advocate of the picturesque, published his poem *The Landscape* in 1796, addressed to his neighbour Uvedale Price of Foxley. In it he attacked both the Brownian and Reptonian schools and suggested his own version of an ideal landscape. This engraving shows the three essential characteristics of the picturesque: roughness, sudden variation and irregularity.

THE ECCENTRIC CHARMS OF THE FERME ORNÉE

As early as 1715, gardening writer Stephen Switzer had suggested mixing the useful and profitable parts of an estate with those used solely for pleasure. The "ornamented farm", or *ferme ornée* as it came to be called throughout Europe, was a style that combined this idea with that of the peripheral walk as used at Stourhead.

The first *ferme ornée* was that of Philip Southcote at Wooburn Farm, near Chertsey in Surrey. Here, in 1735, he created a walk through just under a quarter of his estate, leaving the greater part for farming. The walk itself became a whole garden, with flowering shrubs decorating the plantations and flowers blooming in the hedgerows. A pioneer in transforming a rural working farm into a landscape, Southcote incorporated farm buildings into his walk as well as allowing views inwards to the pasture and arable land and

RURAL IDYLL AT THE LEASOWES

outwards to Windsor and the Thames. Advised by his friend Joseph Spence, he devised a sophisticated planting plan which showed an appreciation of how dark evergreens and the lighter tones of deciduous shrubs and trees could control distance and dimension.

Wooburn Farm was to inspire the poet William Shenstone, who created a *ferme ornée* at the Leasowes, in Warwickshire, which he worked on from 1743 until his death in 1763.

Although less than 60 hectares (150 acres) in extent, the topography was very varied, with wooded valleys, rushing streams and hills allowing views to the local Clint Hills and the Wrekin. Shenstone, an eccentric and reluctant farmer, although only possessed of a small income of £300 a year, was able to turn his domain into a whole landscape, a personal realization of his own rather high-flown verse, where you could imagine his fanciful forest nymphs amusing themselves in the melancholy pastoral setting. During a

ORNAMENTATION AT WÖRLITZ

prescribed route, his visitors were presented with a grotto, bridges, a hermitage, cascades and waterfalls, and a ruined priory. Latin inscriptions invoked classical associations (as they do today at Ian Hamilton Finlay's Little Sparta, see page 445).

William Shenstone, like Henry Hoare (who was making Stourhead at the same time), believed in a strong iconographical programme, with literary associations predominating, but his creation had an originality all its own. The results of his fertile imagination sometimes astonished friends and tourists, although he considered he was only adorning the natural landscape. According to Dr Johnson, the Leasowes became "the envy of the great, and the admiration of the skilful; a place to be visited by travellers, and copied by designers". Always restricted by lack of funds, Shenstone's artefacts were often improvisations, and many had disintegrated within 10 years of the poet's death.

By the end of the century the term *ferme ornée* was expanded to include specially designed ornamental farm buildings. Prince Franz von Anhalt-Dessau laid out his whole Wörlitz estate at Dessau, now known as the Gartenreich, in the landscape style and incorporated agricultural areas and appropriate buildings into the parkland, making a *ferme ornée* on a grand scale. Likewise, at the end of the 18th century at Veltrusy, north of Prague, Count Chotek built a small chain of buildings and monuments on a farm in a bend of the River Vltava, each building providing a focal point on walks through the fields and woods.

summer shrubberies provided shady walks near the house and acted as a relief to dull flat areas of gravel and grass. As parterres were gradually replaced by avenues and lawns to allow full views into the park, shrubberies were put at the side of the house or designed as features, mixed with flowers, to be discovered on a circuit walk. By the end of the century, Hartwell, in Buckinghamshire, and Nuneham Park, in Oxfordshire, had become famous for their original style of flowerbed planting, while at Audley End, in Essex, and at Deepdene, in Surrey, flower gardens once again appeared under the house windows.

The pleasure grounds around the house with manicured lawns (cut by scythe or cropped by sheep), ornamental trees and shrubs, often mixed with flowering perennials – what Humphry Repton was to call "embellished neatness" – provided the variety lacking in the park itself.

THE ARRIVAL OF THE SHRUBBERY

In 1822 J.C. Loudon defined the shrubbery in his *Encyclopaedia* thus: "By a shrubbery, or shrub garden, we understand a scene for the display of shrubs valued for their beauty of fragrance, combining such trees as are considered chiefly ornamental, and some herbaceous flowers. The form or plan of the modern shrubbery is generally a winding border, or strip of irregular width, accompanied by a walk, near to which it commences with the herbaceous plants and lowest shrubs, and as it falls back, the shrubs rise in gradation and terminate in the ornamental trees, also similarly graduated." Other contemporaries such as Henry Philips, in his *Sylva Florifera* (see below), and William Cobbett, in *The English Gardener* (1829), stressed shrubbery design.

As the natural style developed, shrubbery or wilderness planting assumed different patterns, varying between schemes in which blocks of evergreen and deciduous shrubs were either firmly segregated or mixed together to produce contrasts. The shrubbery was known at first as a "plantation" or "border", and even as late as 1770 by Thomas Whately as "thickets" or "groups" of shrubs; the word shrubbery itself was not used until later in the century. Apart from a lack of geometry, its main difference from the old wilderness was its openness as opposed to the hedged enclosures current in French-style gardens. At Rousham in the 1740s, Kent used mixed schemes with yews, hollies, lilacs and roses all together, very much as proposed by Henry Philips more than 70 years later in his *Sylva Florifera: The Shrubbery Historically and Botanically Treated*, published in 1823, but other designers used various schemes through the rest of the 18th century. William Chambers, in his *Dissertation on Oriental Gardening*, emphasized the importance of choosing trees and shrubs suitable in size, habit and foliage rather than planting indiscriminately with too great a variety of

Home pleasures

This illustration entitled "The Luxuries of Gardening" from Humphry Repton's *Fragments on the Theory and Practice of Landscape Gardening* (1816), almost certainly depicts Repton himself in a bath chair after his accident. Raised beds, probably for rarer exotics, a hooped pergola and plenty of gardening activity reflect Repton's interest in the more intimate garden. By the time he wrote *Fragments* he admitted that he enjoyed the improvement of houses and gardens much more than the demands of "parks or forests, landscapes or distant prospects". He encouraged the combining of pleasure ground and kitchen garden, and especially recommended the training of fruit trees as "espaliers on hoops over walks to make shady alleys; or covered *berceaux*, from which apples, pears and plums may be seen hanging within our reach".

PLANTING FOR MIND AND MOOD AT PAINSHILL

THE RECENTLY RESTORED landscape park at Painshill, in Surrey, was conceived by the Hon. Charles Hamilton, youngest son of the Earl of Abercorn, in 1738, on his return from his second Grand Tour of Italy. The infertile, inhospitable land was described by the novelist Samuel Richardson as too poor to grow anything except heath and broom. Hamilton improved it by burning the heath and growing turnips to feed sheep, which in turn manured it. He continued working on the 40-hectare (100-acre) garden (the whole estate, including woodland, covered twice this extent) and installing new features until he ran out of money and was forced to sell in 1773.

Unlike Stowe or Henry Hoare's contemporary Stourhead, Painshill does not have an allegorical or literary programme. Instead it is a collection of unconnected incidents or episodes, which appeal to different emotions and conjure up different moods. These features are joined together by winding paths through woodlands and flowering shrubberies. The circuit of the garden is largely determined by the lake, created by an ingenious mechanical device which raised water 5m (15ft) from the River Mole. Apart from the imaginative

THE RECONSTRUCTED TURKISH TENT

buildings, many probably designed by Hamilton himself, Painshill's interest lies in Hamilton's early use of American exotics, his methods of planting shrubberies and his matching of plants and atmosphere: dark yews were used to induce melancholy on the approach to the Mausoleum, pines evoked the wildness of mountain slopes and flowerbeds introduced a pastoral idyll in the Elysian Plain, an open smooth lawn to contrast with the wild woodland. The Gothic Temple, built on a slight grassy slope, was admired by Sir Arthur Young in 1768: "in point of lightness, few buildings exceed this temple". Other ornaments or buildings were set back into dark glades, revealed in distant vistas or took the visitor by surprise.

At first Hamilton's interest seems to have been mainly horticultural: he cleared existing woodland in order to plant as many of the newly introduced North American plants as possible in his acid soil. When Loudon visited in 1837 he admired the specimens: "among the trees…are some remarkably fine silver cedars, pinasters, and other pines, American oaks, cork trees, and ilices, a tupelo, tulip trees, acacias, deciduous cypress, Lombardy poplar and other poplars…some of the first rhododendrons and azaleas introduced into England". The amphitheatre, now restored with the help of garden historian Mark Laird, has evergreen and deciduous shrubs arranged in a tiered gradation of heights, as recommended by the poet Joseph Spence. In the Elysian Plain Laird has introduced oval flowerbeds. Sir John Parnell noted in his journal of 1763 that it "was dressed and clumped with flowering shrubs, sweet trees and flowers". In the western part of the park Hamilton created wilder planting, in an attempt, as Walpole said, to produce "an Alpine scene, composed wholly of pines and firs, a few birch, and such trees as assimilate with a savage and mountainous country".

In a remote spot Hamilton installed a hermit in a hermitage but he lasted only a matter of weeks, finding the conditions too onerous. Nothing remains of Painshill's most distinguished building, the Temple of Bacchus, nor of the Doric Temple except its foundations, but the Turkish Tent has been reconstructed according to drawings made by the Swedish garden designer F.M. Piper in 1779. The Painshill Trust has further plans for restoration of this remarkable landscape.

THE GOTHIC TEMPLE

VIEW OF PAINSHILL WITH THE LAKE

The MAGNOLIA

The large-flowered, evergreen *Magnolia grandiflora* (painted here by Georg Dionysius Ehret) is one of the greatest of all magnolias. It arrived in Europe from North America in 1734, having been discovered in South Carolina by the great Quaker traveller and collector John Bartram (see page 193). He consigned it to another Quaker, the London collector Peter Collinson, in Peckham. In its homeland in the southern states, it is known as bull bay or laurel magnolia.

MAGNOLIA GRANDIFLORA

Magnolia grandiflora was one of the important acquisitions from East Coast America that revolutionized planting possibilities in European gardens. This new species was especially suitable for landscape projects. With dark, glossy, leathery leaves, often reddish-brown beneath, *Magnolia grandiflora* grows into an elegant pyramidal shape as a specimen, or, in cold climates, it can be rigorously trained against a high wall. Its fragrant creamy flowers open in July and August. Magnolias were named for Pierre Magnol (1638–1715), Professor of Botany at Montpellier.

Magnolia grandiflora first flowered in Europe in the garden of Sir Charles Wager, First Lord of the Admiralty, in Fulham, in 1737. The painter Ehret wrote that he daily covered three miles from Chelsea in order to observe the development of the bud from a button until it unfolded into full flower. Then he "drew every part of it in order to publish a perfect botanical study". Ehret sent the painting to his patron, Christopher Jacob Trew of Nuremberg, who published a report on it in *Commercium Litterarium* (1738), mentioning that, known as the laurel-leaved tulip tree or *Laurus carolina*, it had also flowered in Germany.

new exotics. He also stressed the different conditions that might be required by trees and shrubs: "many…thrive best in low moist situations; many on hills and mountains, some require a rich soil; but others will grow only on clay, in sand, or even rocks; and in the water; to some a sunny situation is necessary but for others shade is necessary".

In general, the English, given the advantages of a temperate climate, attempted to grow too great a variety of different plants together, prompting Henry Philips to remark, "A shrubbery should be planted, as a court or stage dress is ornamented, for general effect, and not for particular and partial expression." When the German landscape designer Friedrich Ludwig von Sckell (1750–1823) visited England, he commented on the indecisiveness of the English gardener: "Amidst the disproportionate abundance of his materials, he knows not which to take first: one is scarcely chosen, when he is attracted to another; then to a third, a fourth, and so on. Each tree, and each shrub, has some particular charm to recommend it, and finally, that none may be lost, he grasps them all…Thus I found the English gardens a real chaos of unconnected beauties." With the new "gardenesque" schemes introduced in the 1820s and 1830s (see pages 249–51), the English desire for excessive variety (exacerbated by the favourable climate) was to descend to new depths.

By the 1800s, there were basically two sorts of shrubbery planting, clearly defined by Loudon. There was "mingled" or "common", in which tiers of shrubs and trees were planted in rows, the tallest at the back, or the "select" or "grouped" manner, in which one species or variety was planted in a mass to produce a powerful effect, with this sort of grouping repeated throughout the planting. Perennials would be planted at the front of the shrubs, mixed in the mingled scheme, or as one kind massed together in the grouped manner. Obviously the scale of the garden could dictate which method should be used, the larger pleasure grounds being best adapted to the massed effects, a small garden needing the variety of the mingled. William Cobbett in *The English Gardener* describes as common practice the gradation of tall trees at the back to smaller shrubs in the front, while John Nash, the architect, attempted more massing. Prince Pückler-Muskau, who had already introduced the English style into his estate in Silesia and was an admirer of Repton, studied Nash's work in Regent's Park and St James's Park during a visit to England in 1826. He commented on the close massing of shrubs which allowed grass to disappear and camouflaged all bare earth. He later incorporated these ideas into his own book *Andeutungen über Landschaftsgärtnerei* (*Hints on Landscape Gardening*) published in 1834.

THE CHANGING FORTUNES OF THE FLOWERBED

Although most of the evidence of 18th-century flowerbed planting, as opposed to shrubberies with flowers, comes mainly from three gardens created in the last quarter of the century – Audley End, Nuneham Park and Hartwell – it is clear that flower gardens near the house often continued to exist throughout the century. By 1750 the beds were more likely to be set to one side of the house than beneath its windows or developed in a separate self-contained garden on a circuit walk. In town gardens where space was severely limited some sort of axial arrangement of geometric beds continued to be used throughout the period.

Hartwell, Nuneham and Audley End are among the best known because they were among the best documented. Some of the plants that were used can be identified in plans, descriptions of layouts and contemporary paintings. The Elysée flower garden at Nuneham (begun in the early 1770s soon after Oliver Goldsmith's *The Deserted Village* lamented the removal of the original village to make way for the first earl's park) was inspired by the philosophical writings of Jean-Jacques Rousseau, expressing his love of nature. It was planned and planted by the second earl, Lord Harcourt, before he inherited, and the poet William Mason. It is remembered through Mason's verse and was illustrated in two watercolours by Paul Sandby in 1777 (available to contemporaries as engravings). The flower garden was developed in an informal asymmetrical space enclosed by thick shrubberies and separated from the rest of the garden, although the main beds were arranged around an axial view focused on the Temple of Flora. Edged with box, pinks or thrift, the beds were circular or oval or even irregular in shape and some shrubs were dotted in the grass. A plan of 1785 (see overleaf), nearly 10 years after its inception, reveals a circuit walk, a lawn studded with flowerbeds, or "clumps" as they were known, and a generous ensemble of architectural and sculptural features, arranged to represent a poetic and moral programme based on Rousseau's ideas and evoking the Garden of Eden and Homer's Elysian plain at the "bounds of the earth". Shrubs and flowers, revealed by a key, are in separate beds, with no flowers shown in the front of the main shrubberies.

By 1778, after his father's death, Lord Harcourt had introduced some changes, including a bust of Rousseau. By 1794 there is a new overall plan differing little from the original except that some of the smaller clumps seem to have merged to form fewer and larger planting spaces, with plants spilling over the edges of beds in an increasingly informal fashion. The planting of the beds would have corresponded with recommendations found in Nathaniel Swinden's *The Beauties of Flora Display'd*, published at the same time as Sandby was painting the scene: "the lowest plants being placed in front, and rising gradually in height from the edge upwards, will form the appearance of plants placed in a Greenhouse, or

Planting circles at Hartwell

The detailed planting plan (right) for a circular flowerbed at Hartwell House is one of 16 sketch plans dating to 1799, now in the Bodleian Library. Laid out by Lady Elizabeth Lee, the garden was inspired by Nuneham Park's flower garden. The plan shows 36 different flower types arranged in four concentric tiers, with the taller plants, phlox and sunflowers, in the centre.

Nuneham's circuit walk

The original flowerbeds at Nuneham Park – the creation of Lord Harcourt (before he inherited the title) and the poet William Mason – are shown here in a plan dating to 1785. The painting shows the evolution of the garden in its overall view, with a lawn studded with beds, and an ensemble of architectural and sculptural features, dotted along a circuit walk.

seats in a Theatre; and by the colours being diversified will have a most agreeable and pleasing effect", in other words "theatrical" planting.

The Elysium Garden at Audley End, in Essex (whose parkland had largely been landscaped by 'Capability' Brown) lay hidden in woods at some distance from the house. Laid out by Richard Woods in 1780, with design and planting improved by Placido Columbani within the decade, the garden was painted by William Tomkins in 1788. Two views show the crescent-shaped informal canal from different directions, the first looking north in evening light towards a Palladian tea house designed by Robert Adam, and the second looking south in mid-morning towards a cascade designed by Woods. The garden as portrayed by Tomkins shows a gentle scene of encircling shrubbery, with a foreground planting of flowers, some strolling visitors on the circuit gravel path and floating swans on the calm water. A blue and white tent, backed by exotic potted plants, is a feature in the southern view, presumably a place to take tea before the homeward stroll to the house, whose towers appear above the shrubbery screen.

The garden at Hartwell House in Buckinghamshire, made by Lady Elizabeth Lee, sister of the second Lord Harcourt, drew much of its inspiration – as well as many of its plants – from Nuneham Park. Detailed plans from 1799 for 16 flowerbeds have been found in the Bodleian Library at Oxford. Each bed shows a sort of concentric arrangement with the taller plants in the centre, schemes

Pavilion proposals
Humphry Repton's design for the Royal Pavilion at Brighton comes originally from his Red Book of 1806 (now in the Royal Collection at Windsor). Virtually all Repton's architectural designs for the pavilion were based on buildings portrayed in Thomas Daniell's *Oriental Scenery* with appropriate flowers of "gothic" or "Grecian" appearance. The designs were never executed, however. To Repton's great disappointment the commission went finally to John Nash, whose flowerbeds contained massed planting of new oriental exotics and only a few American plants.

which included French beans and tomatoes (perhaps the sort of mixed decorative and vegetable planting that we might appreciate in the small garden of today). Lady Elizabeth had married into a horticultural family. Her husband's father had implemented schemes with architectural hedges and radiating alleys, painted in 1738 by Balthasar Nebot, and Sir William himself had before his marriage in 1759 ordered collections of flowering shrubs from Richard Woods. However, Sir William died in 1799 and it was Lady Elizabeth who implemented and tended the new flowerbeds, placed below the windows of the house, until her death in 1811.

THE ENGLISH GARDEN ABROAD

By the end of the century grand English parks such as Longleat and Blenheim and the more intellectual literary layouts of Stowe, Rousham, Painshill and Stourhead had become models to be interpreted anew in Europe as the j*ardin anglais* or *jardin anglo-chinois*, the *englische Garten* and the *giardino inglese*. Not all the foreign adaptations of the English landscape park were entirely successful – a confirmation that much of its success at home depended on the climate and terrain. The Continental versions were often dependent for their effect on outlandish but pale reflections of the originals, or sometimes conceived just as an extension of an existing baroque layout. In many ways it is the later 19th-century interpretations as public parks, the *style paysager*, which are most reminiscent of the English ideal.

Monarchs in countries as far afield as Sweden and Russia demanded the new English style of flowing lawns, groves of trees, contoured valleys, curving lakes, temples and follies

Planting in Poland
This plan of a Polish flowerbed dates to 1808. It shows an English-style garden with very similar planting patterns to those of Hartwell and Nuneham Park, although the shrubby evergreens, periwinkle and juniper, mixed with roses and hollyhocks, would give it a significantly different appearance in winter.

A RUSSIAN INTERPRETATION AT PAVLOVSK

THE PALACE of Pavlovsk, near St Petersburg, was built in the 1780s for Catherine the Great's daughter-in-law, Princess Maria Fyodorovna, wife of the Grand Duke Paul (crowned tsar in 1796). Standing on high ground above the 600-hectare (1,500-acre) park, the palace's classical design, by Charles Cameron, was altered by Vincenzo Brenna after Paul became tsar. The garden near the house was laid out in formal style by Cameron, who also developed the English-style garden along the wooded slopes of the River Slavianka in the valley. Cameron built the classical buildings – the Temple of Friendship, a domed rotunda with Doric columns, and the Apollo Colonnade (now a picturesque ruin) – developing the theme of the park as a sanctuary, with Apollo offering protection for the valleys and groves, as at Stourhead.

The princess herself had a sentimental taste for more rustic vernacular buildings, and a thatched dairy, hermit's cell and charcoal burner's hut were added. The Peel Tower, by the river, was also thatched and painted to look like a ruin.

A keen plantswoman, the princess was in charge of the garden's botanical development over a period of 40 years. Brenna's alterations included creating a central clearing, the Old Sylvia, with a statue of Apollo from which 12 paths radiate. He arranged statues of Mercury, Venus, Flora and the nine Muses around the circumference of the clearing, in the spaces between the radiating rides. In the 1820s an Italian stage designer, Pietro Gonzaga, landscaped an area called the White Birches as an idealization of the meadow and forest landscape of northern Russia with theatrical clumps of trees and receding side-screens (which acted as the wings in a theatre). Gonzaga also added the old Parade Ground, where he introduced water features and groups of trees combined for their harmonious forms, colour and mood.

THE TEMPLE OF FRIENDSHIP

(especially Turkish tents and Chinese tea houses). Catherine the Great was a determined fan: "I now love to distraction gardens in the English style", she wrote to Voltaire in 1772. Others, throughout Europe, forgot about the more stately features and, often in quite confined spaces, indulged in an orgy of winding paths, bridges and ruined buildings more akin to the picturesque aesthetic. Writers and politicians such as Rousseau, Goethe and Thomas Jefferson (who visited English parks during 1785), the German landowner Prince Franz von Anhalt-Dessau from Wörlitz and Prince Pückler-Muskau from Silesia all spread the word, encouraging the construction of large gardens as English parks. Sometimes the relaxed gardens planned as botanic collections, such as those at Empress Josephine's Malmaison (see page 202) and the English Garden at Caserta, Naples, were the most successful.

Many of France's own garden writers accepted some irregularity of design as a contrast to the more formal French features, and recommended layouts not differing greatly from those illustrated by Batty Langley. In his *Théorie des Jardins* of 1776, Jean-Marie Morel went much further, urging naturalistic designs, especially for country gardens, although he allowed the merits of some geometry in both town gardens and public spaces. But some of the French gardens in the English style were a travesty of all that 'Capability' Brown stood for, with no emphasis on tree planting or broad sweeps of landscape.

The first *jardin anglais*, interpreted as the opposite of a *jardin régulier* in the style of Le Nôtre, was made by Baron Montesquieu, the historian and philosopher, at La Brède, in the Gironde, from 1731. Although he visited England in 1729, his design must have been the result of an interchange of ideas rather than the influence of existing gardens. Kent's "improvements" at Chiswick, for example, did not begin until after 1731. At La Brède, Montesquieu extended the grass beyond the moats and opened vistas across the farmland, making the castle a focal point in the landscape.

With Britain and France at war during much of the century, information tended to be secondhand. However, some liberal-minded Frenchmen much admired the development of agricultural techniques in England, appreciating the importance of land as a basis for social order. One of these was the anglophile Marquis de Girardin, who visited England in 1763 and toured William Shenstone's the Leasowes. Girardin's park at Ermenonville, Oise, laid out between 1766 and 1776, was entirely naturalistic and incorporated a number of disparate buildings, including Rousseau's sarcophagus on the Ile des Peupliers. The Duc de Chartres employed Louis Carrogis to create the Parc Monceau on the outskirts of Paris during the 1770s, its picturesque landscape filled with ornaments and decorative buildings. The Scottish landscape gardener Thomas Blaikie (1758–1838) reworked the layout just before the French Revolution, and it became a public park in the 1860s, when Haussmann, town planner *extraordinaire*, was building his boulevards and reorganizing vast tracts of the city. Blaikie also designed the gardens at Bagatelle, in the Bois de Boulogne, in 1775 for the Comte d'Artois (the future Charles X), working with architect F.-J. Bélanger. One of the first *jardins anglais*, it consisted of picturesque scenes ornamented by rocky outcrops and cascades. (The park was subsequently owned by Napoleon, before being returned to d'Artois as Charles X in 1815. It was then acquired by an Englishman in 1835 and sold to the city of Paris in 1905, after which the magnificent rose garden, designed by J.C.N. Forestier, was installed.)

By the 1770s French interpretations were encouraging, in the main, the creation of small-scale English gardens, frequently attached to an existing formal layout and distinguished by a plethora of exotic buildings, ruins or rocks connected with winding paths – fantasies of the rich. These were often called *jardins anglo-chinois*, from a belief fostered by contemporary literature that English gardens perfectly resembled those in China. The French, familiar since 1743 with the Jesuit Father Attiret's reports of the Chinese emperors' gardens (see page 341), read Chambers' *Dissertation* and Thomas Whately's quotes from it. These were enough to convince them that the English landscape parks owed their entire conception to China. Perhaps they preferred to believe that the English could not have invented something they admired and Attiret's descriptions of pavilions and grottoes, winding paths and serpentine water, menageries and fishponds confirmed for them the style's Chinese provenance.

THE LANDSCAPE MOVEMENT'S LEGACY

In England, private arcadias continued to be made throughout the 19th century. They also inspired the idea of parks and cemeteries as places for public recreation in the rapidly expanding, industrially polluted cities. Joseph Paxton's Birkenhead Park, designed in 1843 with Edward Kemp, stimulated Frederick Law Olmsted to present his innovative plans for Central Park in New York. Copied, modified, adapted and sometimes misunderstood, the English landscape garden, with its own roots to be found in ancient hunting parks of the Middle East as well as in the Norman forests of England, and in the classical gardens of Rome and Renaissance Italy, has gained worldwide recognition as an art form, perhaps Britain's greatest contribution to the world of art. What seems today like an essential "Englishness" in the countryside is in reality a man-made landscape in which nature has been moulded and altered to facilitate farming, with the 18th-century parks sanctuaries designed not only to delight the eye but also to attune the mind to harmony with the rhythm of nature.

As an historical subject the 18th-century landscape "idea" may have been overdone, almost to the point where intellectual enquiry into its origins and nuances has become of more importance than the product. Whatever its intellectual origins, the best examples speak for themselves. It is the feelings that they evoke that are important. The English park has a timeless quality of serenity, its basic ingredients – grass, water, trees, sky and buildings – so moulded as to pro-

Arcadian Weimar
A view of Johann Wolfgang von Goethe's garden house at Weimar, Germany. Like other writers of the period, Goethe was inspired by the freedom of the English parks and their relationship with the natural world. Fired by a visit to Wörlitz, he created his Park an der Ilm at Weimar in 1777–78, and in turn inspired Prince Pückler-Muskau. Goethe's house, where he lived for six years from 1776, on the edge of his Arcadian valley, has been restored with a planting of the roses and perennials that he grew or mentioned in his writings. Goethe developed an interest in natural evolution while in Italy, in 1786, when he first saw the fan palm, *Chamaerops humilis*, in the Padua Botanic Garden, the start of his search for the "primal plant".

duce a series of naturalistic pictures. Nature was trimmed and tidied to make it as fascinating as possible. Ambiguous arguments and distinctions between the followers of 'Capability' Brown and the advocates of the romanticism of the picturesque now seem of little importance. The question of Chinese influence also faded when, with a greater European knowledge of China, it became obvious that almost fortuitously the English style shared the common roots of poetry and landscape painting with the ideal of Chinese gardening, with nature seen through the mind as well as through the eye.

Whatever its real origins, the Landscape Movement revolutionized garden theory. Until quite recently, historians tended to see the history of garden development in the West as a steady progression, which separated into two traditions in the 18th century. The one was totally formal, predominantly Italian and French in origin with art dominating nature. The other, the informal, was epitomized by the English landscape park, in which nature takes the leading role. These opposing garden theories have often been simplistically accepted as almost mutually exclusive styles. The reality makes nonsense of this. Most gardens contain elements of the formal and informal which are usefully complementary, with the most formal garden benefiting from meandering paths in the outer areas and the most naturalistic landscape improved by some architectural elements near the house.

The 18th-century development led to a revaluation of the aims and means of gardening – a new assessment of its function and significance in relation to other arts. Until then garden design had existed primarily as architectural support for the house. The new movement, instead of being a logical evolution from the formal tradition, manifested itself as a reaction against it.

In memory of Rousseau
The tomb of philosopher Jean-Jacques Rousseau on the Ile des Peupliers became a famous feature in the Marquis de Girardin's garden at Ermenonville, in France, and was later copied at Wörlitz, in Germany. In making his garden, Girardin drew on the ideas of the poet and gardener William Shenstone at the Leasowes (see page 232), but it was Rousseau who truly inspired him. Rousseau's body was disinterred during the French Revolution and reburied in the Pantheon in Paris. However, the tomb, sheltered by a semicircle of Lombardy poplars, still bears the inscription: "Here lies the man of Nature and of Truth."

CHAPTER EIGHT

THE ECLECTIC
19th CENTURY

Novelties, inventions and revivals

THE STORY OF 19TH-CENTURY HORTICULTURE in Europe is so vast and confusing that it seems sensible to pick out the most important stylistic trends by selecting a few main gardens and some dominant personalities to represent the leaps and strides of change. Horticultural developments of this period in the Americas and parts of Asia are discussed in the three chapters that follow.

Besides places and people, the next most valuable consideration, and one of immeasurable influence, was the growth in the number of gardening books and magazines that became available to an increasingly wide audience. The periodicals themselves recount the history of the age and give us very clear records of changing gardening fashions. From the new rhododendrons and conifers that brought darker tones to woods and shrubberies, through a growing catalogue of hardy shrubs and perennials, to new palettes of bright summer bedding, people made use of planting to bring a new look to their gardens. Arranged in patterns of contrasting purples, yellows, blues and scarlets, flowerbeds were certainly eye-catching, if not garish to modern eyes. Behind this last fashion in particular lay some of the technological innovations and skills that characterized the Victorian age. Nothing seemed beyond the means of the wealthy garden owner. In 1870, however, a move towards a new naturalism came to the fore. This chapter, therefore, concentrates on the century's garden-makers, commentators and gardening styles up until that point.

An Italian touch
Trentham Hall painted by E. Adveno Brooke was published in the *Gardens of England* in 1857. Sir Charles Barry began the garden in 1840, to accompany the vast Italianate house, constructing broad terraces and a distant lake, with gondola and gondolier brought from Venice.

Gardenesque approach
The frontispiece to Charles
M'Intosh's *Practical Gardener* (1828)
perfectly demonstrates the
characteristics of the gardenesque
style, as analysed by John Claudius
Loudon and his contemporaries.
Isolated features, specimen plants
and trees, and circular flowerbeds in
the lawn gave a cluttered, seldom
very pleasing, effect.

DIVERSE STYLES AND DOMINANT PERSONALITIES

The grandest styles of the 19th century, at least until 1870, were
hardly new or original. They were mainly "makeovers" of past innovations, with fashions changing repeatedly during the century. Landlords and garden owners sometimes set styles themselves, but most
employed experts to achieve the effects they required. In the great
gardens, the architect Sir Charles Barry and the parterre expert W.A.
Nesfield personified a return to Renaissance geometry and architecture. Often this formality was imposed on an 18th-century landscape,
with the park and lake beyond the terraces retained as a prospect. The
flat terraces, next to the house, provided the ideal opportunity for
bedding, the seasonal changing of plants that extended the period of
interest and was so much a part of the Victorian style.

In contrast to the artifice of bedding, a more eclectic Gardenesque
Movement developed in the smaller properties, the suburban villas
belonging to a new middle class. The desire to display plants for their
own merits began as an extension of the "natural" movement, but by
the 1840s the availability of new exotics had given most of these collectors' gardens an artificial appearance, although one where considerable diversity and personal choice was possible.

Just as Sir Joseph Banks (see page 201) dominated late 18th-cen-
tury horticultural matters, so two or three personalities dominated
19th-century developments in Britain, in particular John Claudius
Loudon and Sir Joseph Paxton – the lives of whom are traced in
some detail in the course of this chapter. Both Loudon and Paxton
epitomize their age in their rise from obscurity to fame, if not fortune, for both came to exert an extraordinary influence on gardening.
Their careers touch on so many key aspects of Victorian horticulture
that their biographies are the story of much of 19th-century gardening. Both were involved in the explosion of gardening periodicals
giving instruction and advice about plants old and new and the
means of growing them successfully using innovative techniques.
William Robinson, another upwardly mobile character who wrote
extensively, is the third personality of the century, but since his main
period of influence came after 1870 he is discussed in Chapter 12.

There were, of course, gardens that developed their own individ-
uality with little attention to fashion. These either depended on the interest of
wealthy owners backed by a team of skilled gardeners, or were made by genuine
plant enthusiasts, often amateur botanists, who laid the foundations for 20th-century
mixed garden schemes based on the cultivation of hardy plants. Elvaston Castle
garden, laid out between 1830 and 1850, was one of the most eccentric of the
grander properties, while Canon Ellacombe's garden at Bitton, near Bristol (see
page 269), created in the last half of the century, had an interesting mixed planting, one of which became a prototype for fashions in the 1900s. Ellacombe's *In a
Gloucestershire Garden*, published in 1895, in which he describes plants and his gardening season, is still a classic for practicalities and scholarship.

Elvaston's garden rooms

The "compartmental" idea was tried at Elvaston Castle, in Derbyshire, during the 1840s, where manicured, hedged enclosures all had different stylistic themes with fancy names. Mon Plaisir, with its hornbeam tunnels, galleried openings and serpentine scrolling modelled on a Dutch 17th-century design by Daniel Marot, was one. Another compartment was called the Alhambra, although it contained no obvious Moorish features except for its colonnades of yew, intended to resemble staccato cypresses. An Italian garden contained urns and vases, another compartment had lawns decorated with specimen pines and firs, and in another monkey puzzle trees – only just available as seedlings from South America – were used as dot plants. These garden rooms, also a feature at Biddulph Grange (see overleaf), where they are almost equally eccentric, have a strong Victorian flavour, different from our modern interpretation of "compartmental" gardening, as exemplified by Hidcote and Sissinghurst, where each enclosure has coherent cottage style planting and a distinct colour theme. Elvaston Castle's Mon Plaisir, as seen here, was painted by E. Adveno Brooks, *c.* 1857, and appeared in his book *The Gardens of England*.

BATEMAN'S CABINET OF CURIOSITIES

BIDDULPH GRANGE, near Stoke-on-Trent in Staffordshire, is one of the most interesting of the eclectic Victorian gardens. Its owner, James Bateman, an early president of the Royal Horticultural Society, was both an amateur landscape designer and a plantsman with a wide range of botanical interests. At Biddulph, during the 1850s, he provided the growing conditions and picturesque settings for a variety of themed plants, arranging them in separate areas in a series of what we might today call "compartments". He had some useful help in his schemes, including the marine painter Edward Cooke, an expert in rockwork.

One of the settings at Biddulph, called China, came as a carefully orchestrated surprise to the visitor. Hidden from the rest of the garden by a tunnel, it contained a Chinese temple, elaborate rockwork scenes, a joss-house

A SPHINX IN THE EGYPTIAN GARDEN

and a dragon parterre. A collection of Chinese plants – mainly those introduced by Robert Fortune – gave it an extraordinarily authentic spirit. Stone sphinxes framed the Egyptian Court, and a topiary pyramid was

buttressed with clipped hedges. There was a rhododendron ground, a stumpery, a glen for naturalistic planting, a pinetum and an avenue of wellingtonias (*Sequoiadendron giganteum*) – all concealed from each other by elaborate hedges, tunnels and covered ways designed to make the garden both mysterious and romantic.

During his studies at Magdalen College, Oxford, Bateman had developed an interest in orchids – for which he became famous – and the way in which the biblical account of creation could be reconciled with differing geological conditions. This he determined to illustrate in his own garden by growing plants with a range of soil requirements. He also collected and arranged fossils to demonstrate the range of rocks that had developed through the ages, and to encourage students of geology and paleontology. Guided tours were highly educational.

Garden designer and journalist Edward Kemp visited Biddulph in 1856, and wrote about it enthusiastically. He praised the elaborate preparations "of a suitable and congenial home for nearly all the hardy members of the great plant family which the curiosity or taste of man has discovered or cultivated". After 1928, the garden fell into disrepair. However, in 1988 the National Trust acquired the property and undertook an exciting restoration programme. Perhaps because of its lack of unity, on an intimate level Biddulph can sometimes fail to charm, but in its astonishing diversity it remains a spectacle.

The view to China
A glimpse of the Chinese garden from its entrance tunnel, a device designed to surprise the unsuspecting visitor.

A few other large gardens, all of which can be visited today, developed their own 19th-century eccentricities and follow no particular style. The Earl of Shrewsbury's extraordinary garden at Alton Towers baffles all attempts at classification. Its terraces were heavily planted, which helped disguise some of the multiplicity of features. Loudon's report of 1836 stresses "the labyrinth of terraces, curious architectural walls, trellis-work arbours, vases, statues, stairs, pavements, gravel and grass walks, ornamental buildings, bridges, porticoes etc with views to seven gilt glass-domed conservatories". From its inception during the Napoleonic Wars (1800–15), Alton Towers was almost a theme park – which it now is, with some of the original garden and buildings restored. Another garden which brought together a curious mixture of styles and influences was James Bateman's Biddulph Grange (see opposite).

THE GARDENESQUE OR PLANT-BASED GARDEN

Less structured ideas of gardening, more suitable for the smaller suburban villas, concentrated on displaying an assortment of plants. By the end of the Napoleonic Wars, a new and affluent commercial middle class had emerged. Living in suburban villas on the outskirts of manufacturing towns, these people did not have sufficient ground to create a park, nor did they necessarily follow the trend towards re-introducing Renaissance styles. In attitude they were like Humphry Repton's clients who had welcomed the return of more intimate gardens around the house. With limited space at their command, they nevertheless wished to exploit the new plants and horticultural techniques. This was a public that had been educated and informed by instructional books and periodicals. They developed

GARDENESQUE DEFINED

"The Gardenesque style", wrote John Arthur Hughes in 1866 in *Garden Architecture and Landscape Gardening*, "is distinguished by the trees and shrubs, whether in masses or groups, being planted and thinned in such a manner as never to touch each other; so that viewed near, each tree or shrub would be seen distinctly, while from a distance they show a high degree of beauty...Grace rather than grandeur is its characteristic." Although this style of gardening, as portrayed in contemporary periodicals and described by J.C. Loudon, seems cluttered and formless to modern tastes, because of its scope for displaying plants it has remained popular with all those passionate plantspeople who rate plants higher than design.

A taste for the exotic
In his writings, J.C. Loudon recommended using exotic plants whenever possible, or at least a rare or unusual form of some indigenous specimen. Weeping willows and poplars, cut-leaved alders and American species of birch were all to be preferred over native or ordinary species. This illustration is from *The Gardener's Magazine* in 1838.

Patriotic parterre
Lewis Kennedy and his son George constructed elaborate steps and terraces at Drummond Castle in Perthshire, Scotland. In the flat area below, they created a vast parterre in the shape of a St Andrew's cross, embellished with symmetrical planting patterns. Originally, it was planted with rhododendrons and heathers "like an immense Carpet of brilliant Colours". Fortunately, the planting is now much more attractive, with massed perennials and silver-leaved anaphalis.

plant-based gardens typified by a scattering of specimen trees and rare plants exhibited for appreciation individually, and grouped collections of flowers – perennials and annuals from similar habitats – in flowerbeds in the lawn.

As the century grew older, new features were incorporated into these suburban villa gardens. In addition to a range of conservatories and greenhouses, the villa gardener could create elaborate rock gardens, ferneries, pelargonium pyramids and achieve coloured foliage effects. The resulting designs were seldom part of any cohesive scheme and, carried to an extreme, expressed no common purpose; in fact, they were often a recipe for chaos. Gardening experts were keen to promote "the art of the gardener – the individual beauty of trees, shrubs and plants in a state of cultivation", and to encourage technical advance, as well as the proper use of glasshouses and the kitchen garden. It was Loudon who first codified this style as "gardenesque" during the 1820s, in his search for a definition of contemporary trends.

GRAND ARCHITECTURAL GARDENS

As in every age, the history of gardening in the 19th century tends to emphasize the development of themes in the grander estates. We are conditioned to think of the ornamental Victorian garden in terms of Italianate terraces and elaborate bedding schemes, such as those at Drummond Castle, Cliveden and Bowood, backed by an army of gardeners with a complex of greenhouses at their disposal. The strong architectural elements provided the setting and patterns of parterre like stone- or box-edged beds provided the frames for seasonal planting. Skilled head gardeners produced the half-hardy plants – often recent arrivals from overseas – from seed and cuttings to enrich the design with colour. More austere plans, closer in spirit to 17th-century French baroque parterres, were composed only of box and coloured gravels. If, in the 18th century, the landscape garden had seemed to mark a new, changed attitude to nature, design developments in the 1800s restored the architect's decisive role in garden creation. Victorian gardening emphasized the triumph of art over nature. While making use of the astonishing new array of available plants, in all their bright, bold colours, and exploiting new techniques and technologies, the 19th-century architectural garden looked back to the past.

LOUDON: THE MOST INFLUENTIAL HORTICULTURIST OF THE DAY

In his writings and periodicals, John Claudius Loudon (1783–1843) provided a link between Humphry Repton and the development of the Victorian suburban garden. Loudon's talents were extraordinarily diverse, and many of the trends in the first half of the 19th century were a direct result of his influence. Through his writings in treatises, encyclopaedias and periodicals, he was in the forefront of horticultural development, chivvying, bullying and hectoring in order to carry his audience with him. He had an extraordinary grasp of the practical side of gardening in the new technical age, was an expert on all horticultural and agricultural matters, including greenhouse construction and management, and was also a knowledgeable plantsman.

Having visited most of the great gardens of England and Continental Europe, Loudon had absorbed an understanding of the historical development of gardens and the progress of current garden design and horticulture. In general terms, he recommended that every gardener should acquire at least a modicum of historical knowledge to help him decide on the style or school "best calculated for the situation, climate and circumstances in which he is placed". From the 1820s he developed a theme that remains one of his most enduring contributions to environmental planning – his advocacy of public parks for recreation and the enjoyment

Team photograph
It was the duty of the head gardener and his team of gardeners, under gardeners and apprentices to produce the dazzling array of plants that were the hallmark of the grand Victorian garden. With complicated planting combinations and colour schemes to plan, technologically sophisticated glasshouses and heating sytsems to manage, and a host of staff to supervise, the head gardener became more and more powerful, if not spectacularly well paid. Even Joseph Paxton, working for the Duke of Devonshire in 1830, received only £70 per annum, plus a cottage. Here, the gardening staff at Erddig, in Wales, line up to be captured for posterity.

LIFE WITH THE LOUDONS

THE SON OF A FARMER, John Claudius Loudon was born in Scotland in 1783. He began work in a nursery aged 14, but his interests ranged far beyond gardening matters and he learned both French and Italian. In 1803, Loudon travelled south to London where he began his journalistic career with the publication of *Observations on the Laying out of Public Squares*. This was quickly followed by a treatise on hothouses, in which he recommended ridge-and-furrow glazing, a method later taken up by Joseph Paxton, and another on country residences. He was elected to the prestigious Linnean Society when only 23.

For a while Loudon took a lease on a farm in Oxfordshire, which he sold at a profit in 1812. Next he embarked on a tour of northern Europe, visiting palaces and gardens of any note, sometimes recording the Continental superiority in providing parks for public access. He completed the first stage of his European travels in France and Italy, continuing to gather

JOHN CLAUDIUS LOUDON

material for his famous *Encyclopaedia of Gardening* (1822). In 1828, he once again returned to the Continent. Two years later, Loudon met and married Jane Webb, who, although much younger, was already a published author. She was to become a prolific garden writer herself following her husband's death.

Loudon's constant aim was to better the human condition through greater knowledge, and he published some 66 million words to that end. Ever high-minded, with a streak of Calvinistic zeal, he sought to educate both employers and their gardeners and to find ways of improving the working conditions of the latter. *The Gardener's Magazine*, first produced in 1826, was a survey of contemporary domestic and foreign horticultural affairs, including book reviews and educational articles for gardeners. It also provided Loudon with an organ for his own personal and trenchant opinions. Approbations and

JANE LOUDON'S *GARDENING FOR LADIES*

condemnations were freely bestowed, with the management of the Royal Botanic Gardens at Kew and the "illiberal system of management" of the Horticultural Society of London both heavily criticized. At first published quarterly, then every two months, and finally monthly until his death in 1843, the magazine sold more than 3,000 copies of each issue until the advent of a number of competing journals, bringing in an annual income of £750.

The *Encyclopaedia of Gardening* went through nine editions in Loudon's lifetime. This comprehensive book covers all aspects of horticulture. It remains a valuable work, both for its historical content and for its instructive suggestions. Loudon's *Encyclopaedia of Plants* (1829) was another *tour de force*, invaluable when first issued and useful today in providing a list of plants known at the time, with dates of introduction and provenance. (Loudon employed John Lindley to write the descriptions of the plants.) Among his other important works that have stood the test of time is the eight-volume *Arboretum et Fruticetum Britannicum* (1838), an extraordinarily scholarly and meticulous work.

In spite of his success, by the end of his life Loudon's income could not support his family, and he died barely solvent. Jane, with the help of their daughter Agnes, enjoyed notable success with gardening books written for women gardeners – *Gardening for Ladies*, a four-volume *Ladies' Flower Garden* and *The Lady's Country Companion*. Her *Amateur Gardener's Calendar*, a guide to what to avoid as well as what to do, was revised by William Robinson in 1870 and is still a model of concise information and advice.

of nature. Impressed by the parks he had seen on his Continental excursions, he became a fervent advocate for the establishment of green spaces in the burgeoning cities, and extended his ideas to cemeteries and botanical collections. At a time when the pleasure gardens of the 18th century were open to subscribers only, and not to *hoi polloi*, Loudon, like the American Frederick Law Olmsted, the designer of New York's Central Park, believed that they were essential breathing spaces for city workers. He designed the Birmingham Botanic Garden in 1831 and in 1839 laid out a new arboretum in Derby with 1,000 different species and varieties of trees and shrubs.

Loudon's criticisms of how some of the British estates were being run must have made him enemies among landowners, but some were anxious for his advice. He was the accepted authority, and his commissions as landscape consultant were numerous. As a young man, he belonged to the more naturalistic school, backing advocates of the picturesque rather than those who favoured Brown's or Repton's calmer scenes. His tours on the Continent in 1815 and 1819 opened his eyes to other practices. He appreciated the tree-lined avenues in public parks, the beauty of symmetry and order and, in particular, the "spick-and-span" maintenance of many Continental gardens compared to those at home.

Loudon was stimulated by reading the *Essai sur l'Imitation* (1823), in which the "champion of classical aesthetics", Quatremère de Quincy, condemns the English landscape garden as being too perfect an imitation of nature and therefore not art, stating that "Any creation, to be recognized as a work of art, must be such as can never be mistaken for a work of nature." Loudon gradually moved towards accepting the necessity of a predominance of artistry in gardening, and with it, when appropriate, a return to the more old-fashioned styles of geometry. Although he was the first to define the principles of gardenesque, he did not originate the idea but endeavoured to give it rules and significance.

Loudon summarized his own ideas best in his *Remarks on Laying out Public Gardens and Promenades* (1835). Here he recommends being faithful to certain principles: first, the principle that "every garden is a work of art", and the result should never be mistaken for nature itself; second, that of "unity of expression", by which he meant that whatever meets the eye in a single scene must be composed as a picture, a unified composition; third, variety – perhaps the most dangerous of all his commitments; and, fourth, what he termed relation or order, the sequence of scenes in a landscape garden viewed as they unfold before the visitor.

In the *Suburban Gardener* (1838), Loudon describes suitable gardens for suburban villas, classing them as first-, second-, third- and fourth-rate. He criticizes those who condemn straight walks as deformities, pointing out that the geometric or regular manner is a natural style for gardens bordered by straight lines. He also seeks to express the difference, as he saw it, between the picturesque and the gardenesque. The former, he states, was "the imitation of nature in a wild state, such

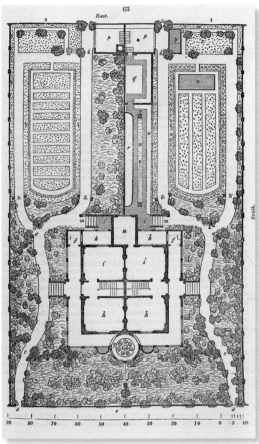

Loudon's own plot

At Porchester Terrace, Bayswater, in London, Loudon's own garden reflected his tastes. His house, built in 1823, before his marriage, was semi-detached with entrances on the side; the Loudons lived on the south side. The garden's most prominent feature was a glass, iron-domed conservatory, filled with camellias, on the west front, which extended to a glass-roofed veranda. The curving pathways penetrated a thick planting of trees and shrubs, a mixture of exotics and natives, so that on the approach it gave the impression of one garden. At the back, Loudon raised the garden levels, using soil excavated from the cellars, in order to create experimental beds where he could try out exotics new to him.

A PROLIFERATION OF PERIODICALS

THE DEVELOPMENT of cheaper methods of printing and reproducing colour illustrations made larger editions of relatively inexpensive magazines and books available to a wide audience. At first the periodicals were

LOUDON'S FIRST PERIODICAL

dominated by horticultural editors who, as well as providing a vast range of information, indulged in intensely competitive price wars and a certain degree of plagiarism. By the middle of the 19th century, however, the periodicals became a medium through which an emergent group of highly skilled and educated head gardeners could communicate and argue with their contemporaries, often laying down new laws of plant association, colour theory and even style.

When Loudon published *The Gardener's Magazine* in 1826, several gardening journals already existed. The oldest was William Curtis's *Botanical Magazine*, founded in 1787, with each monthly issue containing three hand-coloured engravings of plants newly introduced to cultivation. (In a state of decline by the 1820s, it was rejuvenated under the editorship of William J. Hooker.) In 1815, the celebrated nursery firm of Loddiges in Hackney established the *Botanical Cabinet* as a monthly illustrated periodical and catalogue to its vast collection of plants,

probably the greatest in Europe. Another publication, the *Botanic Garden*, was no serious rival, but Joseph Paxton's *Horticultural Register and General Magazine*, later overtaken by *Paxton's Magazine of Botany and Register of Flowering Plants*, provided more competition.

By the 1840s and the decline of Loudon's influence, the establishment of a number of publications continued to provide Victorians with plenty of topical information and to influence current developments. They included the *Gardeners' Chronicle* (1841), which continues as *Horticulture Week*, the *Journal of the Horticultural Society of London* (1846), today published by the Royal Horticultural Society as *The Garden*, and the *Cottage Gardener* (1846–61), which continued as the *Journal of Horticulture* to 1905 and after that under various names. A careful study of these journals could reveal the whole history of garden development during the 19th century.

---

as the painters love to copy", while the gardenesque was "the imitation of nature, subjected to a certain degree of cultivation or improvement, suitable to the wants and wishes of man". However, this hardly clears up the matter, and on another page Loudon improves his description. The irregular or picturesque was best adapted for grounds of considerable extent, while the gardenesque was "more suitable for those persons who are botanists, rather than general admirers of scenery, because it is best calculated for displaying the individual beauty of trees and plants, and the high order and keeping of lawns, walks etc". This may seem a great deal of explanation about a not very attractive style, but it is one that has had lasting influence – if not, by any means, always for good.

THE ITALIANATE GARDEN

It was not surprising that, coexisting with the development of the gardenesque, there was a movement back to designs dominated by architecture in the more imposing landscapes. In an age of wealth and expansionism, structured terraces, steps and fountains made the perfect setting to showcase not only the lifestyles of rich owners but also the myriad plants unavailable to previous generations. The impressive Italianate manner, adapted and modified for country houses and public buildings (and still often adopted for gardens accompanying monumental buildings), is part of our classic heritage. The Victorians used its solid architectural elements and vast terraces for showing off the new exotic plants and their skill in displaying them. Today, in any quite modest garden, it is possible to adapt similar ideas using plants to give the necessary structural features. In appearance, however, the Victorian "makeovers" of earlier styles were significantly different from the originals, and the term "Italianate" came to embrace all revivalist gardens. Though imitative in style, the gardens developed in almost unrecognizable ways, as designers and gardeners made use of the huge variety of plants now available and put into practice new horticultural and scientific techniques. Whether invoking French or Italian styles, or harking back to a form of sentimental medievalism, the Victorian head gardeners fully exploited the plant possibilities in outrageously ostentatious displays. A collection of flowerbeds gathered together on a terrace could as easily be called an Italian garden as a Dutch garden, while box-edged gravel patterns had more of a French feel. An Old English garden contained topiary and simple flowers, often laid out in an accompanying herb garden with strong medieval connotations. Such gardens were the antithesis of the 18th-century pastoral landscape.

The MONKEY PUZZLE TREE

ARAUCARIA ARAUCANA

The conifer *Araucaria araucana*, the monkey puzzle tree or Chile pine, was a Victorian favourite for its outlandish and prickly appearance. It is the only one of the 18 species of this southern hemisphere genus that is hardy enough to be grown outdoors in cool climates, and one of the few South American trees to grow in the British Isles.

The monkey puzzle was first discovered in 1782 by Francisco Dendariarena, a Spaniard, who left his companion, the more famous botanist Hipólito Ruiz Lopez, to travel on his own. In its natural habitat in southern Chile – where it grows in large forests clinging to the lower slopes of a coastal range adjacent to the Andes – it reaches 15–45m (50–150ft) in height. In 1795, Archibald Menzies, surgeon, botanist and plant collector, visisted the coast of Chile with Captain George Vancouver and procured a few seeds which he sowed on board ship. He gave the five seedlings he brought home to Sir Joseph Banks at Kew. One of these survived there until 1892, and was reported by Loudon in 1832 as having reached 4m (12ft). It was not until 1844 that the plant collector William Lobb, who had been sent to South America by the firm of Veitch, obtained viable seed in any quantity. This was to produce some of the finest trees in Britain. At the time, monkey puzzles were planted extensively in many of the country's great estates, sometimes as avenues, as at Bicton in Devon and Castle Kennedy in Scotland. At Biddulph, James Bateman used the tree as a feature in parterres.

Country houses and public buildings epitomized the trends in revivalist architecture. With classicism and the Palladian villa now despised as foreign, the multitude of new styles in Britain included gothic, Tudor, Jacobean, Italian and even Scottish baronial, and there was a smattering of French-style chateaux by the end of the century, all of which encouraged the adoption of similar matching garden styles. As examples of absurdity, the layout for the 16th-century Italian Villa d'Este at Tivoli became a model for the reconstruction of an English Elizabethan garden, while Repton's design at Ashridge, Buckinghamshire, included a gothic garden around a fountain, but was more closely allied to the 16th century than to any earlier style.

Design solution
At Trentham Hall, in Staffordshire, Sir Charles Barry built a pergola to give height and substance to the terraces. It was covered with roses, honeysuckle and grapevines, while classical herms (sculpted busts on pedestals) representing the four seasons ornamented its niches.

Cliveden's planting patterns
On the great flat terrace below the house at Cliveden, Buckinghamshire, Barry made two borders of wedge-shaped parterre beds leading to a great circular bed (inset right). The planting in 1862, mainly of annuals, was done by John Fleming, who had also worked with Barry at Harewood in Yorkshire. Besides becoming an expert on colour, Fleming was an innovator, planting wild bulbs in the meadows and, later, planting tropical bedding schemes. At Cliveden today (far right) the terrace planting, restored by Graham Stuart Thomas for the National Trust in the early 1970s, is an elegant layout of purple-flowering sage, clipped santolinas, senecio and catmint, with accent points of conical yews – much more labour-saving than Fleming's colourful bedding.

BARRY'S TERRACES

By the time of Humphry Repton's death in 1818, the architectural mantle for both house and garden had fallen on Sir Charles Barry (1795–1860). Barry had made a tour of Italian villas and gardens after 1815, and it was he who introduced, or re-introduced, the so-called Italian style. Translated in monumental terms, it reflected the ingenuity of the architect for geometric schemes and, in Barry's case, demonstrated his knowledge of the real thing, as well as providing ideal level spaces on which the head gardeners could display their skills.

The first house and garden to reflect Barry's study of the Italian Renaissance was Trentham Hall in Staffordshire, which he designed for the Duke of Sutherland. Here, he was determined to introduce some form of terracing into the flat terrain. He excavated the swampy ground between the house and lake to create two terraces, each separated by four steps. On the upper level there was a circular fountain: on the lower, two rectangular parterre panels with yews and cypresses to give vertical accents. Barry placed a balustrade at the edge of the lake and introduced a gondola and gondolier from Venice to give a suitably Italian atmosphere. Ambitious plans to build a baroque island reminiscent of the garden of Isola Bella on Lake Maggiore, were never completed. However, there were plenty of other features: corner pavilions, Portugal laurels trimmed to resemble orange trees, and magnificent long ribbon borders planted with bright primary colours – blue nemophilas, yellow calceolarias and scarlet geraniums. George Fleming came as head gardener in 1841, in time to execute Barry's grandiose plans. He had all the technical skills required for managing essential drainage, glasshouse ranges and heating systems. His innovations in bedding schemes made Trentham famous. Fleming planted a rivulet of forget-me-nots in blue and white to meander stream-like through the pleasure grounds and down to the lake, a spring planting scheme that might be attempted today. He must have replaced the forget-me-nots with summer bedding plants to create the same effect in subsequent months.

Barry again worked for the Duke and Duchess of Sutherland at Cliveden, Buckinghamshire, where from 1849 he was employed to Italianize the house and grounds. The head gardener – another Fleming, but this time called John – laid out an impressive parterre below the house to surround a central group of rhododendrons. Each bed was edged with privet or spruce kept clipped to a height of about 20cm (8in). An additional 2,000 bedding plants were used annually as extra decoration, including anemones, silene, *Limnanthes douglasii*, forget-me-nots and tulips. In 1896 Lord Astor, then the owner of Cliveden, acquired the famous 17th-century balustrade from the

Italianate Bowood

The terrace at Bowood, in Wiltshire, was redesigned in 1851 by George Kennedy, whose work we have already seen at Drummond Castle in Perthshire. It is Italian in style – although this was first called "French". Pencil-slim Irish yews were used to resemble Italian cypresses and tall pelargonium-filled vases on the balustrade gave vertical height to the rather flat and elaborate parterres and panels of grass.

Here it is seen as portrayed by E. Adveno Brooke in 1856. Until quite recently, the beds, much simplified, contained "bedding" roses, but the designer Arabella Lennox-Boyd has now introduced box-hedged beds and massed planting – a great improvement.

Villa Borghese in Rome, an addition which no doubt would have pleased Barry. John Fleming also worked at Harewood, near York, where Barry created a substantial balustraded terrace with views southwards across the county. Here Fleming planted the stone-edged beds on the terrace with scrolls of yew, heather and dwarf oak, but Barry's plan for a scheme in the shape of an "H", devised in conjunction with W.A. Nesfield, was not carried out.

The architect's favourite garden, Shrubland Park, not far from Ipswich, remains the most important model of the Victorian Italianate garden. The main terrace ran along a 20m (70ft) escarpment for almost 1.5km (1 mile), the whole divided into a succession of gardens, which included a French fountain and Swiss cottage. A main axis linked the house above, and its vast terrace, to the lower level, with 137 steps forming a dramatic, steep staircase flanked by clipped box, red pelargoniums and staccato cypresses and opening out into a crescent with a loggia as a viewing point. On the upper terrace the gardeners created panels of bright annuals in a series of intricate patterns. Shrubland Park's head gardener, Donald Beaton, had decided views on the use of colour (see page 266) and planting schemes, and went on to become a forceful voice in garden journalism.

In these schemes, clipped Portugal laurels in urns took the place of lemon trees, and tender annuals, many newly introduced from South America, were raised from seeds or cuttings under glass for the extensive flowerbeds. Slim Italian cypresses, out of scale with the massive architectural effects, often proved unreliably hardy and were replaced by other columnar conifers, used as dot plants in panels of grass to emphasize the Italian look. More successful were the solid Irish yews.

Barry always created a series of architectural stages between the top platform, on which the house was set, and the more distant parkland, the stages making the ideal transition between formalized art and nature. Sometimes there was a major parterre scheme sunken below the house in order to allow uninterrupted views to the park scenery beyond. But Barry's great schemes, brutally imposed on the gentle countryside, often failed to capture the organic spirit of the Italian garden, in which the garden seemed to evolve from surrounding olive groves and vineyards. Perhaps, after all, Barry's gardens were designed to impress, rather than for enjoyment and atmosphere.

The sheer topographical extent of Victorian formal gardens and the range of plant material are worthy of much admiration, even though charm seems to have been sacrificed to a form of ostentation – a good example of "more equals less". Too much money and too much skill led to over-decoration. However, at the beginning of the 21st century we can look back nostalgically on the amazing range of seasonal plants available in the middle of the 19th century, and the armies of skilled gardeners who could install them in the flowerbed schemes.

NESFIELD'S PARTERRES

William Andrews Nesfield (1793–1881) trained as an army engineer and land-scape painter. After his sister married the architect Anthony Salvin, Nesfield began his horticultural career by designing character gardens to go with a variety of pseudo-gothic, Elizabethan or Renaissance buildings. He was a copyist rather than an originator, finding much of his inspiration in earlier gardening literature. Like that of his brother-in-law Salvin, Nesfield's research was always thorough, and his designs matched the period of the house. Unlike Barry's formal designs, his work did not extend into the adjacent parkland; rather, he confined his role in parkland to recommending tree planting and some informality.

From the 1830s, Nesfield revived formal French-style *parterres de broderie* on house terraces. Low-growing box (*Buxus sempervirens* 'Suffruticosa') and different-coloured gravels – reminiscent of schemes thought up by the Mollet family in 17th-century France, or by Daniel Marot at Het Loo in Holland – were often centred on a vast sculpted fountain. As in the originals, these sophisticated schemes were designed both for the pleasure of those on the terraces and for appreciation from the upper floors of the house.

An early task in the 1830s was a commission from the 16th Earl of Shrewsbury to rationalize the eclectic garden at Alton Towers, laid out by the earl's father, and to lay out a box parterre in the shape of a giant "S". In Nesfield's scheme for

Nesfield's floral chains
In 1863, W.A. Nesfield and his son Markham designed a broad Italianate avenue in the centre of London's Regent's Park. The avenue was part of a never-to-be-completed scheme originally conceived by the Prince Regent for a walk between Carlton House Terrace to the park via Regent Street. Nash's terraces were included in the proposed layout. The Nesfields' design continued the line of the walk with a sequence of Italianate statuary, with floral borders in concentric circles creating chains of colour. The Regent's Park garden has recently been restored.

Worsley Hall in Lancashire, his parterre pattern was taken from Dezallier d'Argenville's *La Théorie et la Pratique du Jardinage* (1709), the book that had set down many of Le Nôtre's ideas.

Nesfield became better known when commissioned to landscape around the Palm House at the Royal Botanic Gardens at Kew between 1844 and 1848, while it was under construction to Decimus Burton's and Richard Turner's designs. For the next 20 years or so his advice was "sought for by gentlemen of taste in every part of the country", reported *The Gardener's Magazine*. He worked with Sir Charles Barry on the parterre at Harewood at about the same time, and the plan, although not carried out at the time, has recently been implemented. Although he designed an Italianate garden at Grimston in Yorkshire, by the 1850s Nesfield was moving on from the great baroque parterres, using even fewer plants for display in his patterns and becoming interested in the emblematic nature of Elizabethan gardens. He installed monograms outlined in box separated only by coloured gravels and crushed minerals, introducing winter colour into the garden in the Elizabethan and Jacobean mode. Sometimes the gravel was painted, as at Eaton Hall for the Duke of Westminster, to set off extremely narrow scrolls of box. In the East Garden at Eaton Hall, in Cheshire, Nesfield's monogrammed designs of 1852 uncharacteristically included several sorts of flower. In E. Adveno Brookes's *The Gardens of England* the scrolled beds are described as containing "verbenas, calceolarias, geraniums and various other sorts of gay flowering character, whose rich tints harmonize so well with several features of the place. Lines of lavish yew...with box trees cut in spherical form are interspersed at regular intervals, the whole being surrounded by a stone balustrade, thickly studded with shields, bearing the numerous heraldic devices of the family."

The Parterre Garden that Nesfield designed at Broughton Hall, near Skipton in Yorkshire, survives today. Here, in 1857, he used dwarf box, cut to about 10cm (4in) high, to outline his scroll and feather design, accompanied by bright crushed yellow spar and crushed tiles in red, white and blue. But Nesfield's ideas could sometimes backfire: lead poisoned the box plants at Stoke Edith, where he worked for Lady Emily Foley.

When he died in 1881, Nesfield was already a forgotten man, his gravel and box parterres largely out of favour, both with plantsmen and head gardeners who wanted floral displays, and with the new generation of more naturalistic gardeners who despised that kind of artificiality. William Robinson, the advocate of "wild" gardening (see page 384), in commenting on Nesfield's death in his journal *Garden*, complained of "the utterly unsatisfactory character of [his] style of gardening, formal to weariness and only potent in preventing vegetation growing or being arranged in any graceful or natural way". The austerity and dullness of Nesfield's box and gravel schemes at a time when annuals were so much in fashion spelt out the speedy demise in their popularity: their reinstatement had to wait more than a hundred years. As the celebrated gardener and journalist Donald Beaton wrote as early as 1852, "here, with our moist climate, and our superabundance of half-hardy and fine-leaved plants, we need not resort to such extremes", although they were common and more suitable on the Continent. Like 'Capabil-

PLANTING TO IMPRESS

In the middle of the century, Ernest Field, head gardener to Alfred de Rothschild at Halton in Buckinghamshire, reported that rich people used "to show their wealth by the size of their bedding plant list: ten thousand for a squire, twenty for a baronet, thirty for an earl and forty for a duke." Rothschild himself had 41,000. At Waddesdon Manor, the grandest of the Rothschild estates, whole schemes could be changed during the night by armies of gardeners to astonish awakening visitors the next morning. The gardeners of such grandees would have produced their own plants, but today we can obtain them (albeit in a more limited range) through garden centres and the nursery trade, making it possible for the humblest gardener to have summer displays.

ity' Brown's idyllic but flowerless landscapes, Nesfield's baroque twirls and gravel parterres had limited charm for plant-obsessed English gardeners of the time.

However, by the end of the 20th century, box and gravel-patterned parterres were having a fashionable resurgence. Sometimes genuine restorations were inspired by historical precedent, as at Castle Ashby in Northamptonshire, but as often they were driven by the necessity of cutting down on maintenance. The simplicity of upkeep of gravel and box patterns is appealing to modern gardeners – gravel can be spread over an impermeable weed-suppressing membrane, which reduces all the work to annual or twice-annual box-clipping, a job that can be completed successfully by the relatively unskilled. The parterre at Castle Ashby, first laid out in the 1860s, is very much in Nesfield's style, although it was probably designed by the Marquis of Northampton himself. Initials and heraldic devices were interplanted with an array of pelargoniums, lobelias and verbenas to form complex figures.

Nesfield not only made parterres but also liked to arrange the landscape near the house with imposing stone steps and statuary framed by evergreen shrubs and lawns connected by winding gravel paths. The grass was peppered with specimen trees, semi-natural landscapes that may have inspired the drab green shrubberies we associate today with Victorian parks and villa gardens. His schemes also extended into shaping the further landscape. For this his style was formal without necessarily being rectilinear; his repertoire included mazes, bowling greens and arboreta, used as devices to link his parterres with the outer pleasure garden. Viewed on plan, his schemes have a distinct resemblance to the innovative meandering schemes first shown in Batty Langley's *New Principles of Gardening* (1728), in which a number of irregular pathways were introduced inside a conventional layout containing all the old formal elements.

Although Nesfield's parterre schemes were soon out of fashion – and few survived the two World Wars – you have only to look at a list of the great houses where he worked to get a measure of his importance among his contemporaries. Whether he worked in the French 17th-century manner or in the earlier Tudor genre, the patterns he used were authentic, although he was content to use plants with more licence – decorating with all the recently introduced annuals and tender plants. In his wider landscapes he showed considerable botanical interest, encouraging owners to collect new and rare trees and establish arboreta. Nesfield valued the strong textural patterns he could create, seeing his parterres partly as an extension of the inside of the house, and also as the architectural geometrical foreground to the much softer picturesque landscape of the park beyond and the even wilder natural countryside in the distance. This classical formula for the garden – the formal, the informal and then the wild – is as valid today as in any earlier epoch.

THE BEDDING SYSTEM

Both Sir Charles Barry's Italianate terraces and Nesfield's early parterre patterns provided the impetus for an increased use of low-growing plants suitable for seasonal bedding. The 1840s, 1850s and 1860s saw the climax of bedding skills in Britain, with stone- or box-edged beds filled with half-hardy annuals and tender plants, raised under glass from seed or cuttings and arranged in sophisticated colour associations.

There was nothing new about the idea of seasonal planting for short-term effect. Since the 16th century, spring-flowering bulbs had been replaced by summer-flowering plants, mainly from the New World. In 17th-century Italy, Francesco Caetani grew a selection of anemones and ranunculi in his flowerbeds at Cisterna; and in England in the 1680s, John Rae and his son-in-law, the Reverend Samuel Gilbert, were recommending a number of summer-flowering plants such as amaranthus and marvel of Peru (*Mirabilis jalapa*) to take the place of earlier-performing tulips. Antirrhinums had been grown in England since Norman times, and marigolds – both *Tagetes erecta* and *Tagetes patula* from Mexico – were included in Parkinson's 1629 *Paradisus*. As well as filling clients'

THE GARDENS AT MUSKAU BEFORE THE INTRODUCTION OF BEDDING

THE CHANGE BROUGHT BY PRINCE PÜCKLER-MUSKAU'S NEW SCHEMES

flowerbeds with his own strain of scented stocks, Henry Wise, of the Brompton Park Nursery, used the annual burning bush (*Bassia scoparia* f. *trichophylla*) and scarlet runner beans. Philip Miller urged 18th-century gardeners to plunge their tender exotics, housed all winter in dark fume-filled greenhouses, into flowerbeds for summer display. Even Humphry Repton advocated using pelargoniums (introduced from the Cape of Good Hope) for the summer beds at the Royal Pavilion at Brighton.

Zinnias, dahlias and heliotrope were all in Europe by 1800, with South American begonias, calceolarias, petunias, verbenas and the flamboyant Mexican *Salvia splendens* all arriving by the late 1820s. *Verbena chamaedrifolia*, from Peru, was reported by Jane Loudon to be on every balcony in London by 1844. The plant collector David Douglas (1798–1834) also introduced many garden-worthy plants from West Coast America into Europe, to be listed and quickly distributed by Loddiges nursery. Of these, only a few, such as clarkia, mimulus and the blue-flowered *Phacelia tanacetifolia*, could match the brilliance in colour of the annuals brought from South American countries. By the mid-19th century, the number of suitable plants had expanded to give even greater opportunities, with many tender shrubby plants also used for summer show. Techniques had improved with the increased use of glasshouses – faciliated by the removal of the glass tax in the 1840s – and with an improvement in breeding skills. Inspired by educational

Transformation scene
The German landowner and landscape gardener Prince Pückler-Muskau redesigned the garden near his castle at Muskau in the 1820s, removing a bridge over a moat and installing a pattern of low-growing foliage plants – anticipating the "carpet bedding" of the 1860s. At the same time, he removed some trees from the formal line of his lime avenue to produce a more picturesque effect.

A craze for carpet bedding

By the late 1860s, foliage had begun to assume great importance and bedding out moved into a new and subtler phase. Dwarf subtropical and succulent plants such as echeverias, sempervivums and iresine, which gave a variety of coloured and textured foliage, were massed into elaborate patterns resembling mosaics in some of the grand gardens. These could be monograms – such as the giant "HS" devised by head gardener John Fleming at Cliveden for Harriet, Duchess of Sutherland – or patterns of abstract or a more realistic design. George Thomson, superintendent of the Crystal Palace park, created six beds coloured as different species of butterfly. Carpet beds, sometimes laid out on mounds to remove the impression of flatness (as in this 1870 scheme in the gardens at Kew, illustrated in the *Gardeners' Chronicle*), were referred to as embossed, jewel, tapestry, mosaic or artistic bedding. Foliage plants generally lasted longer than half-hardy flowering annuals, the petals of which were often damaged by wind and rain. The comparative neutrality and subtlety of the colouring of most of the small foliage plants came as a welcome relief after the years when primary hues were all the rage. Perhaps because carpet bedding is particularly suitable for laying out as mottoes, coats of arms or other emblems as well as lettering, it has remained with us and is often adapted today to portray the names of towns, make floral clocks or spell out a welcome. Such designs, however, require considerable skill in their management.

periodicals there was a new breed of dedicated head gardeners able to produce exotic plants in quantity and to implement complicated geometric schemes which had no pretension to appear natural.

For winter bedding effects, gardeners primarily used hardy evergreen shrubs such as variegated hollies, clipped box or phillyrea and Portugal laurel topiary, accompanied by aucubas, cotoneasters, skimmias and mahonias – all plants used for permanent schemes. Shrubs were often sunk in tubs into the ground, but their benefits complicated seasonal changeovers, as their winter presence prevented the preparation of a spring display.

In spite of the 19th-century vogue for tender or half-hardy plants, perennials were never entirely neglected. All fair-sized gardens maintained a decent herbaceous border and more modest-sized gardens – without teams of gardeners and a glasshouse – probably never indulged in the fashionable bedding but stuck to perennials and old-fashioned annuals grown in the soil in spring, or the hardy annuals that could overwinter outside. Mixed flower planting in display beds was never popular, although one of Donald Beaton's schemes called "shot silk", in which variegated scarlet geraniums were interplanted with *Verbena venosa*, scored considerable success, and was described in an 1850 issue of the *Cottage Gardener*.

By the 1850s, those actually working in horticulture preferred their flowerbeds in simple shapes arranged in a symmetrical fashion. They disliked the intricate management needed for the fanciful figures designed by contemporary architects to go with gothic-style country houses, or suggestions by writers for complicated interlocking circles, hoops and rings. The first ribbon borders were serpentine, perhaps to give the impression of a meandering stream, but by the 1850s they tended to be arranged along a walk to give a geometric linear impression. Some ribbons, as at Enville Hall, were seven colour strands wide, but more generally they were in threes, often in the patriotic colours of red, white and blue. George Fleming, who had become famous for his spring "streams" of blue and white forget-me-nots at Trentham, was an adventurous exponent of the ribbon border. He used all the latest summer-performing annuals to create continuous parallel lines of colour extending the whole length of a flower border.

Standard shrubs and pyramidal pelargoniums were also frequently used in place of low, evenly sized bedding plants, and with ingenuity almost any of the more dwarf bedding hybrids could be planted into a vertical cone to give three-dimensional effects. Other effects to give height were achieved by making pin-cushion beds with the earth banked up towards the centre. Gardening writer Shirley Hibberd also suggested plunging pots containing plants already in flower direct into the soil to extend the flowering season, something that must have been done in every era to ensure a continuity of display.

COLOUR THEORIES

Purple heliotropes, yellow calceolarias, blue lobelias and scarlet geraniums arranged concentrically in their contrasting colours were an eye-catching (if garish to modern eyes) and typical example of contemporary taste. As Gertrude Jekyll remarked later in the century, "it was not the fault of the geranium" that it was used in such ugly ways. In fact, many schemes showed a more thoughtful approach to both colour and design.

As tender South American plants arrived in Great Britain, one of the first experiments in their use for summer ornament was in Phoenix Park in Dublin, an event reported in one of the first articles in Loudon's *The Gardener's Magazine* for 1826. At first, the schemes were a mixture of plants rather than the massing effects that became more fashionable later, when some advocates even maintained that "massing" was more akin to a natural scene. By the end of the 1830s, colour schemes for flower gardens had become almost an academic study, with John Caie, head gardener to the Duke of Bedford at Bedford Lodge in Kensington, London, taking the lead in advising "clean, simple, and intelligible" concepts of solid colour masses inside a bed. Writing in *The Gardener's Magazine* in 1838, and again through to the early 1850s, Caie advised that colours should be arranged for direct contrast rather than planned for harmonies of shared pigment colours, with beds in simple circles rather than in complicated patterns. By the 1850s, it was generally agreed that colours widely separated on the spectrum should be placed next to one other to produce maximum contrast, and those with the brightest

Floral feast
This colourful arrangement decorated the frontispiece of *Floricultural Magazine and Miscellany of Gardening*. The magazine was published between 1836 and 1842 by Robert Marnock (who was also responsible for giving William Robinson work at Regent's Park in 1861 after Robinson left Ireland).

ALL IN A MORNING'S WORK FOR PAXTON

Sir Joseph Paxton's description of his arrival at Chatsworth shows the measure of his business-like approach and self-assurance: "I left London by the Comet Coach for Chesterfield and arrived at Chatsworth at half-past four o'clock in the morning of the ninth of May 1826. As no person was to be seen at that early hour, I got over the greenhouse gate by the old covered way, explored the pleasure grounds and looked round the outside of the house. I then went down to the kitchen gardens, scaled the outside wall and saw the whole of the place, set the men to work at six o'clock; then returned to Chatsworth and got Thomas Weldon to play me the water works and afterwards went to breakfast with poor dear Mrs Gregory and her niece, the latter fell in love with me and I with her, and thus completed my first morning's work, at Chatsworth, before nine o'clock."

Chevreul's colour wheel
Following in Goethe's footsteps, the French chemist Michel Eugène Chevreul, who worked for the Gobelins tapestry works in Paris, wrote his own theory of colour behaviour, published in 1839 and translated into English in 1854. Writing in order to improve the use of dyes, Chevreul studied the effects adjacent colours had on each other. His famous colour wheel demonstrated his theories of colour harmonies and simultaneous contrast.

hues were the most often planted. Breeding skills had improved, and many of the new plants lent themselves to hybridization, so that the whole bedding range could cover the six main colour groups: yellow, purple, scarlet, blue, red and white.

By the 1850s, Donald Beaton and John Fleming had become the chief exponents of colour theories for bedding plants. At Cliveden, as well as using 2,000 plants in the parterres every summer, Fleming planted anemones and wallflowers, alyssum and daisies, forget-me-nots and pansies, and tulips, hyacinths and narcissi, with a permanent edging of crocus for the earlier season, publishing an account of his experiments as *Spring and Winter Gardening* (1864). His only problem was bareness in autumn when the ground had to be kept clear for bulb planting. (Today, this problem is solved by growing groups of bulbs in plastic sleeves or containers, overwintering them in cold frames and putting them out in spring to replace evergreen bedding plants.) In 1863, Fleming introduced a ribbon scheme of white forget-me-nots and blue pansies. While head gardener at Shrubland Park, Beaton had introduced colour shading, in which rows or groups of plants in very similar colours were planted to grade into each other, with very sophisticated results.

Although spokesmen for their generation on bedding and colour theories, neither Beaton nor Fleming took a dogmatic stance on the best methods or on the rights or wrongs of colour effects, but rather encouraged continual experiment. Controversy was kept alive in the garden periodicals, leaving room for a diversity of opinions. Educational tomes that became the essential references for aspiring artists, such as the German poet Goethe's *Theory of Colour* (translated in 1840) and the French scientist M.E. Chevreul's *Principles of Harmony and Contrast of Colours* (translated in 1854), were more theoretical. John Lindley, at first assistant secretary to the Horticultural Society and finally secretary, and Joseph Paxton, a founder of the *Gardeners' Chronicle*, strongly supported Chevreul's theories on complementary colours applied to horticulture. Beaton considered Chevreul's work mere speculation by a colour theorist with no garden experience. The theories ignored the general background effects of green from which flower colours could not be isolated. Unfortunately for the theorists, any colour scheme could only be thought of in the abstract; implementation had to pay regard to many variables, such as light, prospect, the degree of shade and, of course, atmospheric effects. In the humid grey temperate climate of Britain, bright colours could seem garish, while paler tints, which faded to nothing in harsh sunlight, could glow in the heavier atmosphere.

THE PRODIGIOUS JOSEPH PAXTON

Sir Joseph Paxton was another of the great figures of Victorian horticulture. Like Loudon, he was the son of a farmer. He started work as a gardener at Battlesden, in Surrey, and then in 1823 was fortunate enough to move to the newly opened gardens of the Horticultural Society of

London in Chiswick, on land leased from the sixth Duke of Devonshire. Within two years, the "bachelor duke", as he was known, invited the 23-year-old Paxton to become head gardener at Chatsworth in Derbyshire. The garden had been much neglected in previous years, but in Paxton's capable hands it was to achieve new heights and deserved fame.

Paxton remained at Chatsworth until the duke died in 1858. During that time he became the latter's friend and confidant. Entirely self-made and educated, Paxton became gardener, forester, glasshouse designer and landscape architect. He designed rock gardens and installed the spectacular Emperor Fountain with, at the time, the highest jet in the world. He sent out plant collectors on behalf of the duke; John Gibson returned with the scarlet-flowered, sacred *Amherstia nobilis* from Burma, collected for him by Nathaniel Wallich, director of the Calcutta Botanic Garden. Paxton accompanied the duke on visits abroad in 1838, during which he saw many of the greatest gardens in France and Italy. Paxton had been put in charge of forestry in 1829, and in 1835 began the arboretum – 16 hectares (40 acres) planted with 1,670 different specimens arranged by family. He also built a glasshouse for the giant water-lily *Victoria amazonica*, and was the first to bring it into Britain. His design, inspired by the structure of the ribs of the water-lily's leaves, showed his mastery of buildings constructed in glass, iron and wood.

The garden at Chatsworth had outstanding 17th-century features installed by the first duke, including the Cascade and Great Canal at the end of the South Parterre. It also had a Brown-style landscape constructed after 1760, which fortunately spared these main features, although it swept away elaborate patterned gardens, terraces, topiary and avenues. In the 1820s, with Jeffry Wyatville working on a new North Wing, it was Paxton's duty to re-interpret the landscape near the house in a more formal and fashionable mode. The duke, "bit by gardening" after Paxton's arrival, empowered Wyatville to build a new orangery to protect tender plants, including orange trees saved from the Empress Josephine's collection at Malmaison. Paxton reconstructed the West Garden in 1826, relevelling the ground made to slope by Brown and restoring the 17th-century pond. A new parterre was laid out on a plan inspired by Chiswick House.

By the 1840s Paxton was designing for other clients, although still remaining at Chatsworth. His public park at Birkenhead in 1843, its grounds dedicated to the free recreation of local residents, so impressed Frederick Law Olmsted that it inspired him to present the winning proposals for the design of Central Park in New York. By 1850, Paxton was a recognized authority on the construction of glasshouses. He may be best remembered for his design for the Crystal Palace for the Great Exhibition of 1851, for which he later received a knighthood. After the palace's removal to Sydenham, in southeast London, between 1852 and 1856 Paxton designed very grand Italianate terraces in a baroque style to complement its façade. The *Gardeners' Chronicle* reported in 1852 that "50,000 scarlet Pelargoniums have been contracted for", while in 1854 the *Cottage Gardener* mentions in addition calceolarias, lobelias, petunias, verbenas, gaultherias, alyssum, nemophilas, salvias and heliotrope, interspersed with plantings of dwarf rhododendrons and azaleas. There was an accompanying English landscape of lakes, temples and

Public persona
Sir Joseph Paxton (1803–65), knighted after his contribution to the Great Exhibition of 1851, later became a Member of Parliament and was much involved in metropolitan improvements. Best remembered for his sterling work at Chatsworth, he was also responsible for a large number of public parks: Prince's Park, Liverpool (1842); Birkenhead Park (1843), visited by Frederick Law Olmsted before proposing his plan for Central Park in New York; Coventry Cemetery (1843); People's Park, Halifax (1855); Hesketh Park, Southport (1864); but above all the grounds of the Crystal Palace on Sydenham Hill (1852–56). Paxton almost certainly died of overwork.

On a grand scale
One of Joseph Paxton's outstanding achievements at Chatsworth was the Great Conservatory, built between 1836 and 1840 and measuring 83 × 37 × 20m (290 × 125 × 70ft). Paxton used the ridge-and-furrow technique for the glass, as advocated by J.C. Loudon earlier in the century. Decimus Burton, later to design the Palm House at Kew, assisted Paxton in the construction of the Chatsworth conservatory. The biggest glasshouse in England had room inside for two carriages to pass on the main thoroughfare, and stairs hidden by rocks leading to a gallery from which the highest branches of the exotics could be studied. The Great Conservatory was demolished in 1920, many precious plants having died of cold and neglect during the First World War.

cascades, and islands on which concrete dinosaurs were displayed in life-like poses. It all sounds a bit much.

Paxton was also a journalist: he edited the *Horticultural Register* from 1831 to 1834 and *Paxton's Magazine of Botany* from 1834 to 1849; and was one of the founders of the *Gardeners' Chronicle* in 1841. He became Member of Parliament for Coventry in 1854 and director of the Midland Railway. Paxton died in 1865, probably worn out by overwork, like Loudon 20 years earlier and his contemporary John Lindley, who died in the same year. The Duke of Devonshire, who had come to rely on Paxton more and more as the years went by, appreciated him for his talents, his management skills, his enthusiasm for the beautiful and marvellous in nature, and a judgement faultless in execution. Paxton seems to have remained modest throughout his great success, exciting, according to the duke, "the goodwill and praise of the highest and the lowest, unspoiled and unaltered". Through his designs for gardens and glasshouses and in his journalism, Paxton proved to be almost as influential as Loudon. He was, however, more fortunate in his career, and personifies the successful Victorian head gardener who rose from quite a humble background to have a lasting influence on horticultural developments.

THE TREND TOWARDS MORE NATURAL PLANTING

Even while artificiality triumphed on the terraces of the grandest gardens, there was always an appreciation of more natural scenes and native wild flowers. At the same time, a sophisticated group of gardeners gardened with skill and taste and experimented with new plants. At Cliveden, John Fleming anticipated William

Robinson's *The Wild Garden* (1870) by creating "wild" banks of bluebells, primroses and wood anemones in open vistas in the woodland in the 1860s. In the middle of the century, books by Shirley Hibberd (1825–90), predating Robinson by a decade, were full of basic common sense, recommending the main extravagance of bedding only for the larger or municipal gardens and suggesting the creation of settings without the need for a parterre. For those who had to have a parterre, Hibberd is worth quoting: "In planting the parterre it is as easy to make mistakes as in designing it." He suggested experimenting with neutral tints rather than using only eye-catching primary colours. "The stereotyped repetition of scarlet geraniums and yellow calceolarias is in the last degree vulgar and tasteless and the common disposition of red, white and blue are better to delight savages than represent the artistic status of a civilized people." Of course, like Robinson later, Hibberd's views are subjective, and he liked to exaggerate. He chose to highlight the worst features of contemporary fashions at a time when tastes were already shifting towards a more natural approach and the use of hardy plants. Nevertheless, his writings drew attention to the subject, leaving it to the publicist Robinson to turn it into a crusade.

In laying out borders, Hibberd recommended a repetition of plants or colour groups to hold the overall design together, something that seems as appropriate today as it was in Victorian times. Again, Hibberd is worth quoting, particularly as what he says is entirely relevant to gardening in the 21st century. "The hardy herbaceous border is the best feature of the flower garden, although commonly regarded as the worst. When well made, well stocked and well managed, it presents us with flowers in abundance during ten months of twelve…while the bedding system is an embellishment, the herbaceous border is a necessary fundamental feature." By the end of the century, Shirley Hibberd's ideas had been expanded by William Robinson and orchestrated by Gertrude Jekyll in ways that might well have brought satisfaction to both Hibberd and Beaton.

HORTICULTURAL EXPERIENCE AND EXPERTISE

Plants were now classified in an internationally agreed binomial system and new introductions could be quickly identified, named and then distributed by the increasing number of nurseries. The unfamiliar plants also needed to have their cultural requirements analysed so botanists, as well as being taxonomists, needed to understand how plants functioned. Systematic plant breeding had been a hit-and-miss affair all through the 18th century, with new garden hybrids mainly appearing by accident in seedlings rather than being bred intentionally for specific qualities. Pelargoniums were one of the few exceptions: by 1714, *Pelargonium zonale* had already been crossed with *P. inquinans* to produce zonal

The eclectic clergyman
Canon Henry Nicholson Ellacombe (1822–1916) spent most of his life at Bitton in Gloucestershire, where he followed his father as rector in 1850. He belonged to a group of scholarly gardeners, plantsmen who were also parsons, who did not follow the fashions but, in their own way, collected rare and unusual plants. Often classically educated and knowledgeable in plant lore, they had gardens full of interest. By the 1890s, Ellacombe's garden had become a mecca for those keen on growing hardy plants. His friends included the famous Ellen Willmott and the rosarian the Reverend Wolley-Dod. Among Ellacombe's treasures were plants of *Ferula communis*, the true Mediterranean fennel, seen here soaring to 4m (12ft) above the canon's head.

Under glass

Before there were glasshouses there were orangeries: the rather splendid and extravagantly heated buildings with immense south-facing windows to which orange, lemon, myrtle, pomegranate and bay trees were removed during harsh northern European winters. These plant palaces were the winter playgrounds of the rich, the setting for concerts and balls as well as ranks of ornamental and fragrant trees in tubs.

The increasing contact between 18th-century Europe and the non-European world, and the growth of interest in botany, made for changes in the scope and content of the orangery. As bananas, palms, orchids and scented acacias began to compete with the old hothouse favourites, the orangery evolved into the glasshouse or conservatory. By means of the conservatory, the drawing rooms and libraries of Britain's grand country houses flowed out into the garden, and vice versa.

The minor miracle that was the Victorian conservatory was made possible by industrial technology. Gardening under glass was revolutionized by the invention of plate glass, by efficient hot water systems and by frost-resistant, waterproof cast iron, and one of its foremost champions was Joseph Paxton. After building Chatsworth's Great Conservatory, Paxton went on to design the Crystal Palace, the sensational home of the Great Exhibition of 1851. Erected in five months, the Crystal Palace was a huge success. "We shall be disappointed," *Punch* magazine told its readers, "if the next generation of London children are not brought up like cucumbers under glass." In Britain, where sheet glass was now free of a crippling tax, the Crystal Palace gave rise to thousands of greenhouses and conservatories on a more domestic scale, their manufacturers advertising their wares in the building and gardening magazines of the day.

Palaces of pleasure (above and below)
The Crystal Palace (above), built to house the Great Exhibition, was high enough to accommodate some of the tallest elms in Hyde Park, but there were fears for public safety. It was said that the glass might not withstand the droppings of 50,000,000 London sparrows and that the panes would shatter at the sounding of the royal salute at Queen Victoria's opening ceremony. As a precaution, sections of the interior galleries were built on the ground and tested by having workmen jump on them. In the event, the Great Exhibition was a phenomenal success, attracting thousands of visitors and inspiring exhibitions and glass-covered "winter gardens" all over the world, including Vienna (below).

Lazy California afternoon (left)
San Francisco, 1897, and the Conservatory of Flowers shimmers in the afternoon sun. This palatial glasshouse was brought from Europe and assembled in Golden Gate Park in 1878.

A place of shelter (right and below right)
Until the mid-19th century glass was so heavily taxed in Britain that glasshouses tended to be small and narrow (right), and often attached to grand houses. But soon after the abolition of the tax, and the triumph of the Crystal Palace, the prefabricated components of glasshouses and conservatories began to appear in building supply catalogues. The year-round cultivation of exotic and tender plants was now open to the amateur horticulturist in his greenhouse (below right).

A new-style Eden (left)
The year 2001 saw the opening in Britain of the world's largest greenhouse in Cornwall. Sited on a former clay pit, the Eden Project is dominated by two gigantic geodesic conservatories called biomes. The Humid Tropics Biome accommodates a majestic rainforest, while the Warm Temperate Biome is host to the plants, fruits and flowers of the countries around the Mediterranean, South Africa and California. Snaking boardwalks take visitors through this high-tech paradise, which is designed to be a thrilling reminder of the ongoing interdependence of plants and people.

pelargoniums, the ancestors of bedding geraniums. However, a more scientific approach was gathering momentum.

Following the introduction of the yellow Banksian rose in 1792, there were more exciting China rose introductions. By the 1850s, their new colours were being combined by hybridization with the vigorous old European roses to produce hybrid perpetuals, which flowered on and off through the summer rather than for one season. Thomas Andrew Knight, the brother of Richard Payne Knight, the rather tiresome advocate of 18th-century picturesque (see page 229), was an early fruit specialist raising new and improved orchard fruits for commercial use. Long before Gregor Mendel conducted his famous experiments into inherited characteristics of peas, in 1795 Knight presented a paper on the characteristics of dominance and recessive behaviour to the newly formed Royal Society.

THE SEARCH FOR GIANT CONIFERS

Many of the trees introduced to the West in the 19th century played a part in radically changing the appearance of gardens and landscapes originally composed mainly of broad-headed deciduous trees, besides being used for forestry development. Established parks such as Stourhead assumed a new aspect and recently planted arboreta or pineta often made the collecting of new conifers a priority. While all through the 19th century many missionaries and explorers were also naturalists, there were professional plant hunters too, often trained as botanists, who were sent out collecting with specific instructions from botanic gardens, nurseries and private subscribers. The developing gardens at Kew sent foragers all over the world in search of exotics for practical and scientific use, while those sent by the Horticultural Society of London (from 1861 the Royal Horticultural Society) and nurseries were looking for ornamental plants for house and garden.

David Douglas, a Scotsman, was employed by the Horticultural Society to explore the remote northwest of America, where the climate was very similar to that of the British Isles and where giant conifers – pines, firs, larches and redwoods – dominated the landscape. A group of Russians had staged an exploration in 1741, but few "finds" survived to make their way back to St Petersburg. In 1791, a Spanish expedition with a team of botanists led by the Italian sailor Alessandro Malaspina visited the Pacific Coast. One of the botanists, Haenke, from Prague, gathered specimens of the huge coastal redwood (_Sequoia sempervirens_), but it was not among the seeds later germinated in the botanical garden in Madrid. Archibald Menzies also found specimens of the tree, but neither he nor Douglas managed to bring seed home. The German naturalist Theodor Hartweg, also working for the Horticultural Society, is credited with its introduction within a few years of Douglas's expedition. Others believe that the tree was finally introduced to Britain via Russia only in 1843. Among Douglas's trophies, acquired on three expeditions, were the handsome Douglas fir (_Pseudotsuga menziesii_), the noble fir (_Abies procera_), the sugar pine (_Pinus lambertiana_) and the Monterey pine (_P. radiata_), the latter from warmer California, later to naturalize in parts of Australia. All were trees destined to alter the appearance of many landscape parks both in Britain and Europe.

A NEW FASHION FOR FOLIAGE

BY THE LATE 1840s, experimental head gardener George Fleming had already grown plants with decorative leaves at Trentham Hall. Books solely on ferns had appeared by the 1830s, and the invention of the Wardian case in the 1840s, as well as ferns' shade tolerance, made it possible to grow them inside as a drawing-room amusement – where ivies and moss were also popular. Outside, hardy utilitarian plants such as rhubarb, kale, in all shades from purple to white, and plain and variegated maize added foliage interest.

In Germany, by the 1850s, more exotic plants were being used – tropical cannas and marantas from South and Central America, both with highly decorative striped and patterned leaves, were particularly popular for summer bedding. Donald Beaton recommended such schemes in England in 1860.

In Paris, where summers were hotter, Jean-Charles-Adolphe Alphand and the horticulturist Jean-Pierre Barillet-Deschamps added to the range using coleus, caladiums, dieffenbachias, phormiums and philodendrons. In the Parc Monceau, tender tropical and subtropical plants were chosen for their exciting leaf shapes and colours. There was no attempt at ecological gardening in the summer beds: drought-tolerant desert plants freely associated with those from tropical rainforests in a glorious botanical free-for-all, which in England came to be called "picturesque bedding". In 1867, William Robinson visited the Parc Monceau and admired beds planted with variegated *Arundo donax*,

ADMIRING A NEWLY ARRIVED EXOTIC

Lobelia speciosa and *Ficus elastica*, their bases improbably disguised by mignonette. This was eclectic Victorian gardening, where the most eccentric associations were permitted as long as the results were picturesque.

By 1864, John Gibson, the superintendent of Battersea Park on the south bank of the Thames, had decided to rival the French in the use of tropical and subtropical foliage plants to convey exotic effects. Gibson created shelter from wind by breaking up the margins of the beds with deep indentations and mounding earth so that the more tender and rare specimens, such as wigandias, could be surrounded and protected by other plants, providing sun, shade and drainage as required. An irregular lawn was studded with specimen tree ferns (forms of *Dicksonia*) and palm-like dracaena, with some beds of solanums and cannas.

During the late 1860s, Robinson devoted parts of three books to the exciting possibilities of tropical bedding, but by the 1870s he condemned Gibson's use of tender plants, suggesting instead hardy varieties such as bamboo, pampas grass, ivy and the giant hogweed (*Heracleum mantegazzianum*), with very different effects.

Battersea's tropical bedding
At London's Battersea Park, John Gibson rivalled Paris's Parc Monceau with his use of tropical and subtropical foliage plants.

Many of Douglas's introductions have proved particularly suitable for the British Isles. Also from California, the giant redwood or wellingtonia (*Sequoiadendron giganteum*) was introduced by William Lobb for Veitch's nursery, from where seedlings, at 12 guineas a dozen, must have been obtained by Bateman for his avenue at Biddulph – which, sadly, did not survive. Fortunately, by the end of the century, although the native stands on the Pacific Coast were threatened with devastation by lumbermen, conservationists led by the Scotsman John Muir had the trees put under public protection. The monkey puzzle (*Araucaria araucana*), from Argentinia and Chile, quickly gained popularity after it was distributed by Veitch, and added an exotic touch to many a Victorian garden (see page 255). Another conifer from the Pacific Coast, which, in its various forms, has become common in gardens is Lawson's cypress (*Chamaecyparis lawsoniana*), its seed first introduced to Lawson's nursery in Edinburgh in 1854. Batches of seed often yield differing forms. Leyland's cypress (× *Cupressocyparis leylandii*), a bi-generic hybrid between a chamaecyparis from further north on the West Coast and the Monterey cypress (*Cupressus macrocarpa*), originated as a seedling in Wales in 1888, and became the fastest-growing conifer in the British Isles.

Foreign looks
By the middle of the 19th century, Henry Hoare's 18th-century landscape at Stourhead had been transformed by the planting of conifers, many introduced from America's Pacific Coast. Hybrid rhododendrons were added in the 20th century.

Branching out (opposite)
The arboretum at Westonbirt, in Gloucestershire, was laid out by Robert Holford from 1829 as a fine collection of trees. Many of the newly imported North American conifers were planted in the succeeding years. The mature arboretum is now one of the finest in the Western world.

DISCOVERIES IN THE EAST

Woodland gardens were particularly affected by the flood of rhododendron introductions that began in 1815, with the Nepalese seeds of *Rhododendron arboreum* successfully packed for travelling in tins of brown sugar by Nathaniel Wallich, at the Calcutta Botanic Garden. There was soon a spate of rhododendron hybridizing to produce varieties such as the Ghent azaleas, first of the many deciduous azaleas. On acid soils, the seedling rhododendrons thrived to produce a new sort of woodland, bright with colour in spring but dull for most of the year. Rhododendrons and azaleas were also used in parterre patterns, but to no great effect.

In India, the British East India Company helped Victor Jacquemont to collect for the Jardin des Plantes in Paris. His notebooks, with descriptions and details of the habitats of 4,700 plants, were returned to Paris after his early death in 1832. After China's defeat in the Opium Wars in 1842, Robert Fortune (1812–80) travelled for the Horticultural Society of London with a brief to collect hardy plants for gardens, if possible including blue peonies, yellow camellias, double yellow roses, azaleas, lilies, oranges, peaches and various types of tea. The first two items proved impossible to find, but he did discover the double yellow rose in a

nursery. On his second expedition in 1848, he was requested by the East India Company to obtain the finest varieties of tea plants. In this he succeeded, making it possible to establish plantations in the Indian provinces of Assam and Sikkim. Tea became one of India's main exports in the second half of the 19th century. Fortune also introduced many good plants from nurserymen in China, some already in garden cultivation. He discovered the mourning cypress (*Cupressus funebris*) and the lacebark pine (*Pinus bungeana*), besides many hardy shrubs such as winter-flowering honeysuckle and jasmine, and *Rhododendron fortunei*. In 1860, Fortune was at last able to explore in Japan. His collection of *Cryptomeria japonica*, mahonias and Japanese anemone was outshone by his compatriot John Gould Veitch from the famous nursery, who, collecting in Japan at the same time, was able to introduce 17 new conifers, including pines, chamaecyparis and *Larix kaempferi*, as well as magnolias and lilies.

IDEAL HOMES

One of the earliest tree collections was Sir Robert Holford's Westonbirt Arboretum, established in 1829, laid out in a geometric grid system with radiating forest rides. Later in the century, the newer arboreta became idealized nature parks depending on groupings of plants from similar habitats. The "American gardens" of the 18th century (see page 200) had already stressed the necessity of providing conditions similar to a plant's native habitat. Now, with increasing new tree and shrub introductions from the West Coast of North America and from Asia, this became even more important. Rhododendrons, maples and magnolias requiring acid soil were surrounded by drifts of both American and Japanese woodland and bog plants.

In the 1830s and 1840s, as Professor of Botany in Glasgow, Sir Joseph Hooker realized the possibilities of growing tender trees and shrubs on the Scottish west coast, where the Gulf Stream provided perfect conditions of high humidity and rainfall combined with little frost. Soon new tree collections were also established in Cornwall and the west of Ireland, where many of Hooker's later rhododendron collections, with a sprinkling of camellias, could thrive. Today, Himalayan rhododendrons and magnolias flourish beside Chilean and New Zealand introductions within shelterbelts created by Monterey pine and macrocarpa cypress.

VICTORIANISM REVILED THEN REVIVED

In gardening, as in the other arts, fashions come and go. 'Capability' Brown's landscapes were vilified within a few years of his death for their lack of "picturesque" interest and later by historians for the loss of the structured gardens of earlier eras that were swept away in order to create them. In much the same way, Victorian artificiality was condemned throughout most of the 20th century – only to figure again in recent turn-of-the-century recreations. The great parterres on the terraces of the French-style chateau at Waddesdon, originally created in the last quarter of the 19th century, have been returned to their intricate glory, while the parterres of perennials have been restored at Audley End, and countless Nesfield restorations are in process. Victorian public parks, long neglected and overgrown,

THE ROCK GARDEN

ALTHOUGH THE ELABORATE grottoes of Renaissance times and the picturesque ruins, caves and arches of late 18th-century gardens were forms of Western rockwork, the rock garden as we know it today did not exist until the end of the 18th century. (In China and Japan, rocks were always vital elements of the garden.)

In 1775, Thomas Blaikie was sent to the Swiss Alps "in search of rare and curious plants" by botanist Dr John Fothergill. It was a successful trip: Blaikie sent home 440 seed packets, some of the contents of which were growing at Kew by 1789. In England, the first recorded rock garden for alpine-type plants was made in the 1780s at London's Chelsea Physic Garden using lava brought from Iceland by Sir Joseph Banks's 1780 expedition.

Gradually, rock gardens became more realistic, with layers of native rock assembled as they would appear in nature, providing deep pockets of soil for the questing roots typical of alpines. However, there were different, sometimes bizarre, ways of imitating nature.

In 1838, at Hoole House, Lady Broughton reproduced the Chamonix valley in miniature at the end of her lawn, while Paxton's spectacular rock garden at Chatsworth, built between 1842 and 1848, was on a grand scale, with waterfalls and huge rock piles. The Biddulph Grange rock garden of the 1850s was a more genuine attempt to provide suitable growing conditions for demanding alpine plants, although the required intense light and moisture with adequate drainage were difficult to achieve.

By 1848, rockery enthusiasts could choose between real rocks and James Pulham's Pulhamite stone – Portland cement moulded over rubble – and Backhouse's York nursery had begun to specialize in rockery plants.

Frank Crisp, at Friar Park near Henley, had, by 1900, created the most extraordinary of all rock gardens, a scale model of the Matterhorn, topped with alabaster snow. Some 4,000 tons of stone had to be hauled from the Thames valley on a specially built railway. But despite its bizarre appearance Crisp's rock garden was intended for the serious cultivation of alpine plants, and provided the right sort of home for some 2,500 species. This desire to grow such plants as they would grow in the wild, together with Reginald Farrer's classic books on the rock garden, was to influence the growing of alpines in the next century.

The Alps in miniature

Lady Broughton's rockery at Hoole House, where spiky masses of rock towered to 8m (25ft), with grey limestone, quartz, spar and white marble to resemble snow, was much admired by J.C. Loudon.

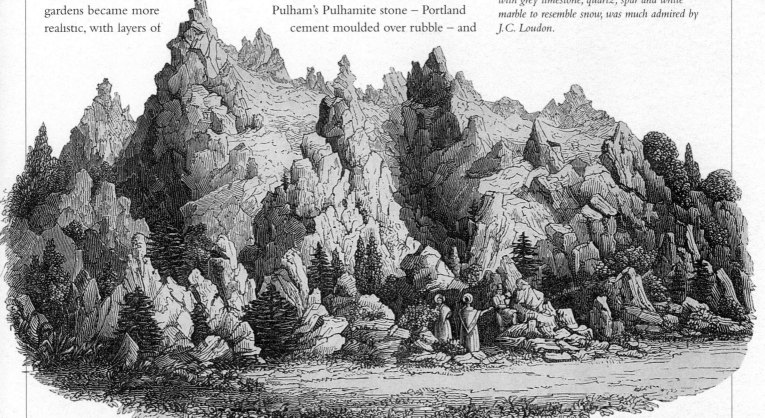

have recently received grants of public money for the authentic restoration of Loudonesque tree planting and full-blown bedding-out schemes. Even private landowners are restoring terraces, parterres and bedding-out schemes that were abandoned during the period of austerity that followed the Second World War. Such is the public interest in history that these gardens bring in a handsome visitors' contribution to maintenance. Among the most important re-creations is that of the intricate terrace parterre at Harewood House, originally designed by Barry and Nesfield but never implemented. Recent restoration work at Tatton Park in Cheshire included Joseph Paxton's fine fernery, a partially restored gardenesque area with small beds showing off specimen plants and W.A. Nesfield's imposing fountain of Perseus and Andromeda.

The grand terraces at Sydenham, in south London, that Joseph Paxton and his protégé Edward Milner developed around the re-erected Crystal Palace in the 1850s are now being restored. This vast complex, with canals and side fountains, which disgusted William Robinson, was possibly inspired by Versailles. And Loudon's Birmingham Botanic Gardens, landscaped in 1829, are still full of botanical interest and today fulfil Loudon's wish that they should become a popular public park.

During the second half of the 20th century, many gardeners reared on a diet of the more naturalistic and subtle planting ideas of Gertrude Jekyll and William Robinson came to despise the bright colour schemes typical of mid-Victorian gardens. For the *cognoscenti*, seasonal flowers in primary colours arranged in concentric circles were out, and permanent, and if possible self-sustaining, hardy perennials were in. Robinson's planting was not only ecologically sound but also economical, doing away with the need to heat greenhouses in winter and to execute twice-yearly changes in planting. Fortunately, in the last few decades, where authentic historical restorations or reconstructions are under way, there has been a renewed interest in experimenting with seasonal planting schemes, especially in areas with a true continental climate of hot summers and cold winters. The re-establishment of some of Barry's and Nesfield's architectural layouts has called for the implementation of contemporary flowerbed planting. As appreciation of these gardens has grown, we have become much more open to the beauty and colour nuances of the best colour arrangements, rather than sneering at their artificiality.

Tatton's tree ferns (opposite)
The fernery at Tatton Park, in Cheshire, was built in the 1850s – probably by Joseph Paxton. It has recently been restored by the National Trust to provide a home for a fine collection of tender plants, including tree ferns from Australia and New Zealand, growing here above clivias and the chain fern (*Woodwardia radicans*). The tree ferns were collected by Captain Charles Randle Egerton RN, the brother of the first Lord Egerton. On a rather different scale, the invention of the Wardian case in the 1840s (see page 198) had, by the 1850s, led to "pteridomania", a craze for growing tender ferns in closely glazed cases, which protected them from gas fumes and other pollution.

CHAPTER NINE

THE
AMERICAS

New horizons in horticulture

IN THE VASTNESS OF THE AMERICAS any mention of a garden prompts the question: what is the local climate like? Before any European stepped ashore, the Incas in Peru and the Aztecs in Mexico had perfected an understanding of local growing conditions that has seldom been surpassed. Once the conquistadors had destroyed the magnificent gardening traditions of both ancient empires (those of Mexico rivalled their Persian and Mughal Indian contemporaries in splendour), it was back to square one. Colonists from Britain, France, Holland and Spain variously contended with unexpected climates and alien plants, eventually succeeding in creating pockets of gardening first along the eastern seaboard and then further west. Horticulture in those lands that were to become Canada mostly either followed a similar pattern or at this stage was non-existent.

At the end of the 19th century, gardening became universal and this part of the American story, taken up in Chapter 12, was a time when American designers truly came into their own. Here we are concerned with the earlier stepping-stones, how American regional styles gradually evolved from ideas of layout imported from Europe and how, under the guidance of such visionaries as Frederick Law Olmsted, a new, more democratic attitude to garden-making began to emerge. It becomes clear, too, along the way, how the great exchange of plants between the Americas and Europe benefited gardeners on both sides of the Atlantic.

Southern beauty
The Audubon Swamp Garden at the old Magnolia Plantation on the Ashley River in South Carolina has a romantic beauty with native southern trees, including the bald cypress (*Taxodium distichum*), growing in a natural setting. Long boardwalks have been specially designed to allow visitors close-up views of the swamps, where rice fields flourished before the Civil War.

Water beds

The Aztecs' *chiampas*, still in use today for growing crops, were created by piling up layers of mud and vegetation, which were held together by tree roots so that pockets of land appear to be floating on the water.

Discovering the dahlia

In 1570 Francisco Hernandez, physician to Spain's Philip II, was commissioned to study the "natural, ancient and political history of the New World". The 16 volumes he produced revealed valuable information on the medical traditions and botanical gardening of the Aztecs. One of the most spectacular plants first drawn and described by Hernandez was the double dahlia (right), or *cocoxochitl*, which he found growing near the Quauhnahauac mountains.

THE AZTECS AND THEIR GARDENS

At the time of the Spanish conquest of Mexico by Hernando Cortés in 1519, the Aztecs dominated southern North America, their empire comprising a mosaic of small principalities covering approximately 200,000 sq km (80,000 sq miles). Montezuma II, the last Aztec emperor (reigned 1502–20), occupied the throne. Although the Aztecs are most often remembered in images of war and brutal human sacrifice, beauty and pleasure were a significant part of their culture, as the Spaniards discovered on their march from the Gulf of Mexico along the coast and inland to the Mexican plateau and basin. Their way, as described by the historian W.H. Prescott, led them through a terrestrial paradise of tropical vegetation: "wide rolling plains covered with a rich carpet of verdure and overshadowed by groves of cocoas and feathery palms…clustering vines of the dark purple grape, variegated convolvulus".

The Aztecs were obviously sophisticated gardeners, and on the coastal plains the alternate heat and moisture stimulated every sort of growth. As the Spanish advanced towards the capital city of Tenochtitlán, they found a valley (the Mexico basin), the Spaniards' description of which inspired Prescott further: "[The valley's] picturesque assemblage of water, woodland, and cultivated plains, its shining cities and shadowy hills, was spread out like some gay and gorgeous panorama before them…stretching far away at their feet were seen noble forests of oak, sycamore, and cedar, and beyond, yellow fields of maize and the towering maguey [agave], intermingled with orchards and blooming gardens…in the midst the fair city…the far-famed Venice of the Aztecs."

One of the Aztec's most distinctive achievements was the development of "floating islands", or *chiampas*, in the lakes of the mountain-rimmed plateau 2,200m (7,200ft) above sea level (now the site of Mexico City). The *chiampas* provided fertile vegetable and flower gardens, with drainage ditches connected by artificial mud causeways. Gardening was a favourite Aztec pastime and probably an elite profession, as noted by the Spaniards in their observations of the gardens situated in and around the cities. These gardens were created by hewing rock and moving earth to make flowerbeds, ponds and water features, although many of them seem to have been constructed around existing canals, part of the *chiampa* lagoon system.

Pleasure parks were first developed in the first millennium AD at Teotihuacan, under the Mayan civilization, but by the 15th century the Aztecs in both the capitals of Tenochtitlán and Texcoco could afford more luxuriant parks. Aztec rulers and nobles created two different types of park: great imperial retreats such as those developed on sacred hills near Tenochtitlán and Texcoco; and hunting and game parks on the promontory islands of Lake Tezcuco. Parks might have luxurious palaces, with rock-cut baths, such as those at Texcotzinco, or *bas reliefs* cut into the rock face as at Chapultepec, where Montezuma II had his likeness preserved for posterity alongside other Tenochtitlán rulers. Shrines, temples, tombs and spaces for theatrical performances might also be included.

In the cities, there were urban gardens. Some of the houses, according to Prescott, had "flat roofs...protected with parapets, so that every house was a fortress. Sometimes these roofs resembled parterres of flowers, so thickly were they covered with them, but more often they were cultivated in broad terraced gardens, laid out between the edifices." Close to the palaces were amusement parks with menageries and aviaries, as well as horticultural gardens with water features, groves of trees and flowers in quantity. There was also a form of botanic garden with collections of flora, nurseries and seedbeds, the beds laid out in scientific fashion to allow study. These can be considered among the earliest known examples of a garden of botanical collections, anticipating, perhaps by half a century or more, the foundation of Pisa and Padua Botanic Gardens in Italy in 1545.

Skilled Aztec gardeners almost certainly knew how to protect and cultivate the more tender plants that came from the rainforests on the coastal plains. Some of the most decorative flowers known today, such as dahlias, zinnias, marigolds, cosmos, the Peacock tiger flower (*Tigridia pavonia*) and tuberose (*Polianthes tuberosa*) originated in Mexico. Other plants, including tobacco plants, sunflowers and marvels of Peru (*Mirabilis jalapa*), were natives of South America but had been absorbed into Aztec culture. Later, they were taken further north where native Americans were cultivating them when the early European colonists arrived.

Fast-growing native trees included the evergreen *ahuehuetl*, the Mexican cypress (*Taxodium mucronatum*), a relative of the American bald cypress (*T. distichum*), and the Californian redwood (*Sequoia sempervirens*). Both were tolerant of swamp conditions and high altitude, clothing the mountain slopes and giving gravitas to the grand parks, where they were grown in lines or even avenues. In the zoos, the gardens seem to have been arranged to accommodate the mammals and birds, with flowers on trellis edging the paths, but with a rectilinear format determined, as we have seen in the early Egyptian tomb paintings and in Muslim gardens, by the canal system of irrigation.

TROPICAL HUAXTEPEC

During the 1460s, Montezuma I of Tenochtitlán, the rival city ruled by cousins of Nezahualcoyotl, constructed a horticultural garden at Huaxtepec, 95km (59 miles) southeast of Tenochtitlán in tropical Morelos. The planting possibilities there were much greater than in the basin of Mexico. In hilly terrain, within a boundary fence of 10km (6 miles), Montezuma dammed streams to create a lake, around which he planted many tropical species, some of them brought to Tenochtitlán "in great quantities, with the earth still about the roots wrapped in fine cloth". Later Cortés, in a letter to Charles V of Spain, described the gardens "as the most beautiful and refreshing gardens ever seen...There are summerhouses

NEZAHUALCOYOTL'S GARDENS

The Aztec ruler Nezahualcoyotl (reigned *c*.1430–72) "delighted in flower gardens and aviaries". The 17th-century historian Alva Ixtilxochitl wrote of the palace Nezahualcoyotl built at Texcoco that the way "led through intricate labyrinths of shrubbery, into gardens where baths and sparkling fountains were overshadowed by tall groves of cedar and cypress. The basins of water were well stocked with fish of various kinds, and the aviaries with birds glowing in the gaudy plumage of the tropics. Many birds and animals which could not be obtained alive were represented in gold and silver so skilfully as to have furnished the great naturalist Hernandez with models for his work."

Nezahualcoyotl's favourite residence was a rural retreat at Tezcotzinco, northeast of the main city. It was "laid out in terraces or hanging gardens, having a flight of steps five hundred and twenty in number, many of them hewn in natural porphyry". In the garden on the summit of the hill, an aqueduct carried water over hill and valley for several miles to feed a reservoir. Basins below the reservoir distributed water to numerous channels, refreshing the shrubs and flowers surrounding the palace.

The most famous of Nezahualcoyotl's gardens was Chapultepec, begun at Tenochtitlán in the late 1420s – the first documented Aztec pleasure garden. By the 16th century, orchids from the coastal rainforests were being grown in the garden and the hill, terraced with wide steps, had been planted with trees.

spaced out...and very bright flowerbeds, a great many trees with various fruits, and many herbs and sweet smelling flowers." The garden is also described by Diaz del Castillo in his 1532 chronicle of the discovery and conquest of Mexico: "the orchard...so beautiful...contained such fine buildings that it was best worth beholding of anything we had seen in New Spain...certainly the orchard of a great prince".

Montezuma I died in 1468 and Nezahualcoyotl in 1472. Following an earthquake in Tenochtitlán in 1475, the ruler Axayacatl encouraged both his nobles and householders to beautify the rebuilt city with landscapes and gardens, which were later praised by the Spaniards in the time of Montezuma II. The main pleasure gardens were situated close to Axayacatl's palace in marshy ground with a major city canal flowing through it. As well as flowers, the gardens were home to countless waterfowl, other birds and reptiles, and contained a zoo-aviary complex spread over several locations. A disastrous flood in 1499 ensured further construction of pleasing gardens and fine courtyards.

By 1519, Tenochtitlán was the most important city in the Mexico basin. It was built on a grid system of narrow streets and canals, and was linked to the mainland north, west and south by three broad causeways. Satellite towns, all connected by causeways through the lagoons, ringed the city. The public services and sanitation systems had no parallel in 16th-century Europe. In each street men were constantly sweeping and sprinkling and tending burning braziers through the night. Huge barges collected all the waste matter, which went to fertilize the *chiampa* beds. A dyke 16km (10 miles) long shut off the western end of the lagoon, with its sweet, fresh waters, from the salty marshes to the east. A contemporary report by Antonio de Solis gives a description of Montezuma II's own gardens in Tenochtitlán: "All these houses had large gardens, well cultivated. There were no fruit trees nor edible plants in these places of recreation – it was said that orchards of that kind were the possessions of ordinary people and that it was more proper among princes to have delight without mixing utility therewith. Everywhere were flowers of rare diversity and fragrance, and medicinal herbs used in the stables [probably sheds for wild animals]. Every type of infirmity and pain had a plant to cure it, using either the juice as a draught or *aplicaciones*. They achieved admirable results working empirically: without identifying the cause of illness they nonetheless restored the patient to health...In all these gardens...were many fountains of fresh clean water, which they brought from the neighbouring mountains, brought in open aqueducts as far as the causeways, where the water went into pipes and was thus led into the city."

In 1521, Cortés besieged and conquered Tenochtitlán, destroying many of its most beautiful garden sites, beginning with the severance of the Chapultepec aqueduct. The Spaniards later rebuilt the city, transforming Chapultepec into a hunting park for conquistadors. Chapultepec's summit became a *castillo*, then the imperial palace of the 19th-century Hapsburg ruler Maximilian. Since 1934 it has been the palace of the presidents of the republic, and the park is one of the most important recreational sites in Mexico City, with some ancient cypresses remaining from Aztec times. Nezahualcoyotl's complex at Texcotzinco is now only an archaeological site. Cortés kept Huaxtepec for himself and Francisco Hernandez visited there in 1570. Today it is a holiday resort. As Diaz del Castillo said in 1532 of the Spanish invasion: "No future discoveries will ever be so wonderful. Alas! Today, all is overthrown and lost, nothing left standing." These gardens, paralleling those of contemporary Persia and Mughal India, were wantonly destroyed by the Spaniards and, except in the realm of ideas, seem to have had no influence on future garden development.

THE INCAS OF PERU

In 1532 in South America, the Spanish found and destroyed another thriving and sophisticated pre-Colombian civilization, the empire of the Incas of Peru in the Andes, a civilization that had developed from around 2500 BC. Unfortunately, although the rulers and high officials had elaborate gardens which were described in the earliest Spanish chronicles, there is no detail of layout or of ornamental plants. There was an intensive agricultural system around Lake Titicaca some 3,816m (12,500ft) above sea level, successful enough to lead to a high density of population as well as pockets of habitation in the valleys and those desert areas where the land could be irrigated. In the small mountain-side terraced fields, vegetables and fruit were grown as well as utilitarian plants for medicine, contraception, dyes and poisons. The Spanish botanist Hipólito Ruiz Lopez made a study of the medicinal plants used by the Incas during his expedition to South America between 1777 and 1788. The terraces on the precipitous slopes were arranged so that the lowest strip might contain hundreds of acres of cultivated crops, while those at the top could accommodate only a few rows of maize. The massive terraces also offered protected pockets of microclimate where particular varieties could flourish.

An industrious population settled along the lofty regions of the plateaux, with villages clustering among orchards and wide spreading gardens. Prescott described this in the *History of the Conquest of Peru*, his information gleaned from early Spanish chronicles. The Spaniards had found elaborate gardens belonging to Inca rulers, with water channels, pools and basins sometimes made of silver or gold. Prescott goes on to speak of "groves and airy gardens…stocked with numerous varieties of plants", and "parterres" made in gold and silver that were arranged with plants. Unfortunately, Spanish sources do not give any more useful detail.

Prescott describes the gardens of Yucay, situated near the capital Cuzco, where water was conducted through subterranean channels of silver and basins of gold. The beds were stocked with numerous varieties of plants and flowers that grew without effort in the tropical temperate climate. Far fetched though it sounds, the Peruvian mountains teemed with gold, which was expertly worked by the Incas.

Flos Solis maior.

Symbol of the sun
Generally considered to have originated in Peru, the common sunflower (*Helianthus annuus*) appears to have been in cultivation in Europe by the end of the 16th century, its enormous size contributing to its popularity. Grown as a crop today, it is all too common. This portrait is taken from Basilius Besler's great florilegium, the *Hortus Eystettensis* of 1613 (see pages 181–84).

HUMBOLDT'S AMERICAN MISSION

IN 1799, THE GERMAN Baron Alexander von Humboldt (1769–1859) and the field botanist Aimé Bonpland sailed from Spain for the Spanish territories in America. Humboldt was commissioned to study, observe and collect material, at his own expense, just at a time when colonial resentment against the Spanish Empire was fermenting. Two fruitful years were spent studying the geology, flora and fauna of the Cordillera of the Andes and the history of Inca cultivation, with another year devoted to the highlands of Mexico. Humboldt met the famous botanist José Celestino Mutis in Bogota, who since 1760 had been studying quinine and malaria control and South American flora.

Having climbed the two main volcanoes in Ecuador, Chimbarazo and Pichincha, Humboldt and Bonpland set off for Peru, examining on the way the porphyry paving stones of the great Inca highway between Quito and Cuzco. Humboldt visited the ruins of the

ALEXANDER VON HUMBOLDT

Inca Tapayupangi nearby, with its "summerhouse" cut out of solid rock, located to give a view over an enchanting landscape. A champion of the destroyed Inca nation, he reported that "our English gardens contain nothing more elegant", referring to the 18th-century garden-parks in Germany inspired by the English Landscape Movement.

In March 1803, Humboldt and his companions reached Mexico, where they spent a year. From Mexico he and Bonpland sent seeds of new species of dahlia to the Empress Josephine at Malmaison, where Bonpland would return to become curator in 1808. The expedition returned to France with more than 60,000 plant specimens. In 1804, Humboldt wrote his most popular book, *Aspects of Nature*, an "aesthetic treatment of natural history" rather than a travelogue or scientific treatise, designed for educated but non-scientific readers. One of his comments, which is of interest to gardeners, is that it is possible to create a regional look in a garden by using plants that resemble those in the area, rather than sticking to authentic regional plants – for a modern example, using phormiums from New Zealand in a Mediterranean-style garden. The results of his journeys were published in some 30 books, which took over 20 years to produce.

AQUEDUCTS AND GUANO

The Incas' artistic and technological achievements were a matter of great surprise to the conquistadors. Although a population has survived in similar environmentally harsh regions – the Kalahari Desert, the Gobi and the Arctic – at no other high altitude has there developed such a productive and sophisticated agricultural and pastoral society with a high population density. Much of the almost desert-like conditions along the sea coast could only be cultivated if irrigated, and the Incas developed an elaborate system of canals and subterranean aqueducts, as ingenious as the *qanats* in Persia (see page 24). At times they were of great length, bringing water at least 650km (400 miles) from the mountain slopes. The water came from a natural lake or reservoir in the mountains, and other basins along the route fed the ducts. This required considerable feats of engineering, similar to those employed in building their magnificent paved causeways. The watercourses were constructed from slabs of stone nearly 1.5m (5ft) high and 1m (3ft) wide.

The Incas pioneered the use of different types of manure, particularly guano – the deposit of sea birds – as fertilizer for their crops. Given the climatic situation, which involved diurnal rather than seasonal changes in temperature, they could cultivate a range of plants suitable for different altitudes, from bananas and cassava trees (*Manihot esculenta*) at sea level, to the staples maize, maguey (*Agave americana*) and tobacco. The naturalist and traveller Alexander von Humboldt was among the first to recognize that the zones of vegetation between the tropics and the polar regions are also repeated vertically, near the equator, from sea level to snow line – exactly the situations covered by the Inca empire.

NORTH AMERICA'S NATIVE PEOPLES

Unlike the Aztecs and Incas, the North American Indians were basically hunter-gatherers who supplemented their main diet of fish and game with fruit and vegetables. They had quite considerable botanical knowledge, not least in the plants they grew to cure ailments, which stimulated interest from the early colonials. But their way of life was inconsistent with the artificial conceptions of a pleasure garden: the 50 or more plants they grew provided them with food, drink, dyes, clothing and, most importantly, medicine.

Hollies such as *Ilex cassine* and *I. vomitoria* produced popular beverages, their virtues applauded by both French and Spanish writers. In the northwest, the bulbs of *Camassia* species were a vegetable food. In Mexico and Florida, early Spanish missionaries taught the native peoples to cultivate peaches, apples, cucumbers and watermelons, which had been brought from Europe. Peach trees flourished in the hot summers and peach orchards became so common that early American botanists believed they were native fruits. The native mulberry (*Morus rubra*) was fairly common and popular for its sweet black fruit. It was often planted around native settlements.

THE FIRST EUROPEAN SETTLEMENTS

The earliest settlements by Europeans in North America occurred in Florida, where, in 1565, the Spanish established themselves at St Augustine. The governor of St Augustine imported tools, seeds and plants and within 25 years the new village had gardens and orchards, laid out in rectangular enclosures according to European traditions and fenced to keep out marauders. At a number of missions

Native knowledge
An unknown artist travelling on a ship of Sir Francis Drake recorded this American native sowing seed in a cultivated plot. Although basically hunter-gatherers, many of the indigenous peoples grew plants for food, drink and medicine, their knowledge of the latter proving highly useful to the arriving settlers.

established further north, as far as the Carolinas and west into Alabama, similar gardens were established for curative plants, at first mainly brought from Europe but gradually including those used for remedies by American Indians. When James Oglethorpe, founder of Georgia, arrived in Savannah in 1733 he found plantations of olives, figs, oranges and lemons left by missionaries, and the local native peoples growing peaches, which the Spaniards had introduced.

On the east coast of Maine (then New France), French settlers under Champlain had set up a garden by 1618; a sketch of its layout was published in *Les Voyages*, showing houses and neat rectangular-patterned gardens based on contemporary French fashions. It is not certain whether it was ever completed.

During the early years, the basic elements of design of the most elementary kind were remarkably similar in all the settlements and colonies on the Atlantic shore. The enclosed garden had a simple geometric arrangement of beds, usually rectilinear, which fitted inside the fence next to a house. Such gardens were mainly utilitarian: the owners had little space for growing plants for beauty alone, and lacked time required to cultivate them. Plants included fruit trees, vegetables and a few flowers; seeds and tools came from the home country.

The main differences in emerging styles arose as a result of local climate and attitudes. In the harsh New England conditions, the settlers tended to be educated men of personal conviction, escaping England because of religious or political persecution. Some felt it a duty to carry the gospel to the New World, if only to prevent the Spanish or French Jesuits from being first in the field. The stern demands of their austere morality forbade any semblance of luxury or personal display. In the warmer south, early settlers were impelled by profit motives rather than idealism. As the large plantations for tobacco, indigo and cotton developed, landowners could afford the luxury of a pleasure garden, especially after the influx of slave labour at the beginning of the 18th century. Yet their gardens remained geometric. By the end of the 17th century, colonists locating their plantations along the rivers for ease of transport developed a whole complex: mansion, farm, farm buildings, servants or slave quarters and garden were all part of one unit, creating a whole community, comparable to the Italian villa in its conception.

Circles in the landscape
By 1900 the environmentalist designer Jens Jensen was creating landscapes in the Midwest in which only native plants were grown. One of the few architectural features used by Jensen was an adaptation of an Indian council ring, built in local stone, where groups of young people could gather around a camp fire.

Although there were a few exceptions, most documented gardens – or those revealed in recent excavations – remained of traditional geometric design throughout the 18th century. Yet up to the War of Independence (1775–83) close contacts with England ensured an up-to-date knowledge of the more natural, irregular garden developing there, even if only a few could actually implement the ideas. By the end of the century, both documentary and graphic evidence confirm that George Washington at Mount Vernon and Thomas Jefferson at Monticello (see pages 302–03) were tentatively introducing elements of the new freer style.

The English Settlements

The English managed to squeeze in their settlements between the French in the north and the Dutch in New York and south to Chesapeake Bay, and to establish bases in Virginia, where they were outside the zone of Spanish interference. In the north, the new arrivals saw themselves as settlers and not colonials: their aim was to establish new freedoms and independence from England, while in the tidelands of Virginia the mother country expected to gain from colonial expansion and to control and exploit it.

To the new arrivals in the 17th century, searching for economic material for crops or medicine, the untamed American countryside must have been overwhelming. For some, the vegetation was a source of wonder: the trees, shrubs and flowers of great beauty were to be explored and categorized for potential use. For others, it was a "hideous howling wilderness" full of swamps, rocks, predatory Indians, wolves, mosquitoes and snakes; the natural vegetation was to be hacked or burned in order to plant roots and seeds brought from Europe. The settlers had to learn to appreciate Indian skills in plant medicine, and gradually to assimilate both indigenous fruit bushes and ornamentals into their plots. The housewife from England, already skilled at brewing, fermenting and distilling a variety of flowers and roots, soon experimented with those she found around her.

There was little accurate information on conditions in the New World for the pioneer immigrants. Thomas Heroin's *Account…of Virginia*, Nicolas Monardes' *Joyfull Newes out of the Newe Founde Worlde* (1577) and William Wood's *New-England's Prospect* (1634), together with John Josselyn's two contributions, *New England's Rarities Discovered* (1672) and *An Account of Two Voyages to New England* (1673), were among the most useful books available with information about the New World. Woods and Josselyn were by far the most accurate, both speaking from experience and Josselyn having twice visited his brother in the colonies.

The Pilgrim Fathers, among them some Dutch, arrived in Plymouth in 1620; their first seeds, brought from the Old World, were sown on 7 March 1621

Image of village life
John White's views of the American native village of Secoton in North Carolina, painted in 1585, were engraved by the German Theodor de Bry in 1590 for Thomas Harriot's *A Briefe and True Report of the New Found Land of Virginia*. The work was dedicated to Sir Walter Raleigh and translated into both Latin and French by Clusius. The engraving of the garden owed much to the imagination and was more European in style than the reality as portrayed by White.

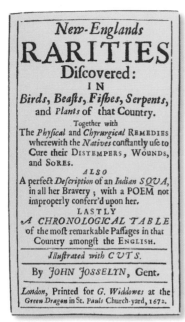

Early reference

The title page from *New-England's Rarities Discovered* by John Josselyn, published in 1672. Based on Josselyn's own experiences, the book, which discussed nuts, grains, squashes and fruit such as blueberries, and included a range of native wild flowers, proved a useful guide to settlers. Josselyn used Thomas Johnson's 1633 revised version of Gerard's *Herball* as an aid to identification.

following a severe winter. (Some of their apple trees survived until the beginning of the 20th century.) The early gardens were close to the house, replicas of the rectangular front or back gardens familiar to them in their native country, enclosed by whitewashed wooden picket fences. Very soon the settlers learned that shade was essential, and planted trees such as red maple (*Acer rubrum*) on the south side of the house, a tradition that continues to this day.

John Winthrop, the first governor of Massachusetts Bay colony, established a garden, known as the Governor's Garden, on Conant Island in Boston harbour during the 1620s. By 1630 reports speak of him growing vines as well as mulberries, raspberries, carrance (currants), chestnuts, filberts, walnuts, smalnuts, hurtleberries and haws of white-thorne. There was enough to help stock the orchard of his neighbour, George Fenwick, which was later to become one of the first fruit nurseries. In 1631, Winthrop asked his son John to bring more seeds from England – the old familiar flowers that they would have been accustomed to at home, but not the new bulb "rarities" that were all the fashion in Europe, which were too expensive for experiment. Although Winthrop's garden was not grand, it achieved a certain ambience, sufficient for it to be a place to "step out into" in the evening for rest and enjoyment.

THE DUTCH IN NEW YORK

In Europe, Dutch supremacy in agriculture and horticulture was already apparent by the early 17th century. The emigrant Hollanders and Huguenots – of which there was a large influx after the Revocation of the Edict of Nantes in 1685 – believed that only hard, solid work would bring lasting dividends. They were not lured by gold like the Spanish or like the Virginian colonists by the quick fortunes from tobacco crops. Their early settlements in New Amsterdam (later New York) and Long Island reflected their background. The climate, not so different from that of Holland, was suitable for farming and cultivating fruit trees.

The Dutch colonial administrator Peter Stuyvesant settled in New Amsterdam in 1647, bringing the celebrated Stuyvesant pear tree, a Bon Chrétien, from Holland in a tub. (It flourished in what is now the Bowery district of New York until 1866.) Cared for by 40 or 50 slaves, Stuyvesant's farm and gardens thrived. The estate was noted for its flowers, vegetables and farm crops as well as fruit trees. The plants were propagated from seed and scions and distributed to farms up the Hudson River as far as Albany and beyond. The Dutch not only brought flowers and fruit trees to the New World but also recognized the ornamental and economic value of indigenous flora. In 1655, Adrian van der Donck wrote that the Hollanders were growing red and white roses, besides several kinds of gillyflower (*Dianthus*), fine tulips, crown imperials (*Fritillaria imperialis*), anemones, violets and marigolds. He noticed various indigenous trees that were handsome and native flowers such as the morning star (*Lilium concolor*), red, white and yellow "maritoffles", which he describes as a very sweet flower, and several species of campanula. In 1652, on Shelter Island at the north end of Long Island, Nathaniel Sylvester established a plantation of box (the ordinary *Buxus sempervirens*, later called American box by Americans) introduced from Europe, probably the first box to be grown in America. Sylvester's garden still flourishes, although most of the vast box plants must be more recent replacements of the originals.

GARDEN DESIGN ON THE ATLANTIC SEABOARD

In the states of the northern seaboard, a taste for formality in garden design predominated throughout the colonial period. In general, the farms and gardens remained small – moral attitudes condemning any question of ostentatious display. The soil was hard and stony, the winters long and cold. Information on what the colonists grew has been gleaned mainly from nursery lists, with merchants emphasizing those roots and seeds still obtained from England and Holland.

Although many of the distinguished 18th-century country houses remain or have been restored, their original gardens can only be imagined. In towns, both the public open spaces and some small private gardens have survived. Village greens in Ipswich and Lexington and the famous commons of Boston and Cambridge, originally intended as common cow pasture – and for drilling the local militia – set a precedent for future town developments and the whole idea of city parks. A small private garden, the Nichols garden in Salem, Massachusetts, until recently retained a layout that must have been more than two centuries old. It was typical of the usual tight pattern, with a long straight path dividing the sloping garden in half and the side areas subdivided into rectangular flowerbeds.

THE SETTLEMENT OF VIRGINIA

By the late 1600s, a few elegant gardens based on contemporary European fashions had been laid out in Virginia, at the time the most populous and prosperous of the English colonies. But even there, prior to the influx of African slave labour in the second quarter of the 18th century, development was held back by a shortage of skilled manpower. During the next hundred years, the South continued to look to the mother country for its markets and its most luxurious supplies, but in Virginia garden design did not immediately reflect England's awakening to the charms of nature.

At least two factors ensured that the "natural style" in England did not immediately appeal to colonists. First, settlers far from home still liked to think of the traditional French or Dutch garden style as evocative of the old life. Second, the colonists were still pioneers, still fighting back the wilderness.

The governor's plan
The gardens of colonial Williamsburg were restored in the 1930s. Those of the Governor's Palace closely resemble an early 18th-century English layout with clipped topiary, a mount, a water garden and pleached arbours. These gardens were originally laid out by the ambitious Alexander Spotswood from 1716, and enormous amounts of public money were spent on them but only a few descriptions and no plans survived to help in the restoration. The Ballroom Garden shown here is laid out on a north–south axis with formal planting in the geometric beds and topiary shapes in yaupon holly (*Ilex vomitoria*). Although a contemporary of John Custis of Williamsburg, a great plant collector, Governor Spotswood seemed to be mainly interested in design.

BROTHERS OF THE SPADE

THE GARDEN AT William Byrd I's plantation at Westover, near Richmond, Virginia, was already being talked about in the early years of the 18th century. The house, facing south across the James River, is one of the finest extant examples of American colonial houses. A plan of Westover in 1701 shows three avenues radiating out from the house, but no garden detail. William Byrd II inherited the property in 1705 and started to improve it, making a collection of American plants, encouraged by a visit from the English plant collector and author Mark Catesby in 1712. In 1714 Byrd was in England, where he visited gardens such as Blenheim and the Duke of Argyll's Whitton, in Middlesex.

Although we know little of the Westover garden layout, William Byrd II revealed much of his gardening philosophy through his correspondence with English acquaintances, in which he speaks of his appreciation of "wild and uninhabited woods" and the painting-like quality of a successful landscape. If he carried out some of his ideas, Westover may have been one of the earliest picturesque gardens in America. From the 1720s, with his brother-in-law John Custis, Byrd obtained plants from England through Sir Hans Sloane and Quaker botanist Peter Collinson (see page 193). In 1738, the great American plantsman John Bartram described "new gates, gravel walks, hedges and cedars finely twined and a little green house with two or three orange trees with fruit on them".

WILLIAM BYRD II AND JOHN CUSTIS IV

Nothing remains of Williamsburg's most important private garden, the 1.6 hectares (4 acres), or 8 lots, belonging to the wealthy John Custis and gardened by him from 1717 until his death. Nor are there plans, although Custis's appreciation of "shaped" trees and bushes suggest his garden was laid out along quite formal lines and not entirely for botanical interest. His concern for colour also shows a developed aesthetic sense, but, unlike his brother-in-law, he only visited England in 1716, and it therefore seems unlikely that he developed any taste or understanding of the landscape ideal.

Both Custis and Byrd fostered the exchange of plants between the colony and the home country, receiving as many plants from England as those that crossed the Atlantic in the other direction. Custis planted numerous evergreens, including variegated forms of hollies and English boxwood (he was the first in the South to mention receiving the so-called dwarf English box, *Buxus sempervirens* 'Suffruticosa'), admitting that his taste for these was

out of fashion. He was always looking for colourful flowers, importing roses, tulips and other bulbs from the Orient through his English contacts.

Many of Custis's evergreens were clipped into pyramids, balls and other decorative shapes, some of which he lost in a year of bad drought. His imports included "handsome striped hollies and yew trees...with handsome body and not too big", but to his annoyance, until he teamed up with Peter Collinson, not all consignments arrived in good condition. "The box for my garden was all rotten as dirt," he complained in 1723. "I did not have one sprig; the gardener was either a fool or a knave."

The letters between Custis and Collinson from 1734 to 1746 document Custis's gardening opinions. Unfortunately, a list Custis compiled in 1737 of plants that he was growing in his garden has not survived, so we cannot know everything he received from England; however, his correspondence with Collinson discusses many of the American natives he dispatched.

Custis was a competitive gardener, priding himself on having the best collection of foreign plants, many new on the American coast. He was upset by bad winters, dry summers and other vagaries of the climate that led to plant losses, finding that plants from England were particularly susceptible to the heat. In 1738, Custis wrote that he kept "three Negroes continually filling large tubs of water" for evening watering.

Domestication meant order and safety, and trim, enclosed gardens were an essential contrast to the threat of unruly and little understood nature. The hard-working colonists had no time to appreciate the aesthetic merits of wild, romantic beauty or to apply it to the principles of gardening. However, as the century proceeded, many of the more prosperous Virginia gentlemen visited England, where they encountered more irregular and picturesque designs, which they could consider adopting in a modified form when they returned home. By 1779, they were certainly able to understand the principles of enlightenment, liberty and equality enough to consider abandoning the more disciplined designs linked with tyranny and oppression. Thomas Jefferson's visits to some of the English landscape parks in 1785, particularly Philip Southcote's comparatively modest *ferme ornée* at Wooburn Farm (see page 232), inspired him with ideas to implement on his farm at Monticello.

Williamsburg, the capital of Virginia, became the focal point of the developing state and was to have the first recognizable ornamental gardens in America. In 1694, John Evelyn wrote from England to a correspondent in America that George London (renowned English designer and nurseryman) was sending out a gardener, James Road, from Hampton Court "on purpose to make and plant the Garden, designed for the new Colledge, newly built in yr country". The college was that of William and Mary, the building of which began the following year. The college garden, and that at Westover (see opposite) further up the James River, was conceived as an experimental garden for the study of native plants and the effects of climate on plants introduced from the Old World.

Between 1700 and 1704, the governor, Francis Nicholson, had Williamsburg laid out on a grid system; with Philadelphia, it is an early example of American urban planning. The larger properties were on the edge of town, with common land retained for a public green. Alexander Spotswood succeeded Nicholson as governor in 1711, and began to develop a sophisticated geometric design for the garden of the Governor's Palace. It included a terraced area (now restored as a kitchen garden) overlooking a formal canal and fishpond in a deep valley, an orchard and some vistas across the swamps. The whole complex was surrounded by a ha-ha to give a park-like effect. It was the finest garden in America of the first half of the century, with terraces and canal completed in about 1717. It may well have become a model for later garden developments on Virginia plantations.

GARDENS IN 18TH-CENTURY PHILADELPHIA

As was the pattern in other Atlantic colonies, the first gardens in the more temperate climate of Pennsylvania were ancillary areas to orchards and farmland. They were enclosed, rectilinear in design and practical in use. Although the traveller Andrew Burnaby described the city of Philadelphia in 1759 as well endowed with "villas, gardens and luxuriant orchards" this style of gardening was to prevail throughout most of the colonial period. He referred to Israel Pemberton's garden of the late 1750s as "laid out in the old fashioned style...with walks and alleys nodding to their brothers", and with clipped topiary ornaments, so there must have been a recognition of the fact that something new was afoot.

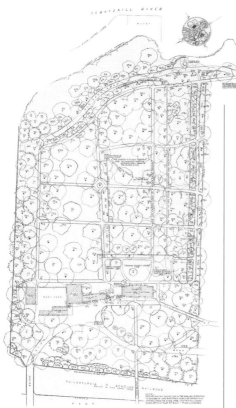

A plantsman's paradise
Quaker plant hunter John Bartram, born in Darby, Pennsylvania, in 1699 was, according to Linnaeus, "the greatest natural botanist in the world". Today, the garden-cum-nursery he created on the Schuylkill River (above) has become North America's oldest surviving botanic garden. Despite the perils of rattlesnakes and the like, Bartram devoted more than 30 years to exploring northeast America in search of new plants. His numerous finds included birches, *Rhododendron maximum*, *Lilium philadelphicum* and *L. superbum*, bee balm (*Monarda didyma*), gentians, asters and golden rod (*Solidago*). He sent many plants to fellow plant enthusiast Peter Collinson in London, and received in exchange highly prized tulips, hyacinths and various European species. Bartram also developed an arboretum, where, based on ecological theory, he tried to give his plants the same sort of site as they would have in the wild, often surrounded by weeds.

The city of Philadelphia – founded by William Penn for the Quakers in 1682 – was laid out on a grid system, with a square of 4 hectares (10 acres) for a public park at the centre, and four subsidiary public spaces of 3.2 hectares (8 acres) "for the comfort and recreation of all for ever". "Let every house," wrote Penn, "be placed...in the middle of its plot so that there may be ground on each side for Gardens and Orchards, or fields, so that there may be a green Country Towne...and will always be wholesome." He also directed that every owner should plant one or more trees before the door so that the town would be well shaded from the violence of the sun in summer, and so be rendered healthier. This practice was adopted by many of the new American cities with open public commons in the centre.

The Society of Friends established the teaching of "the nature of herbs, roots, plants and trees" in their schools and, as befitted a Quaker, Penn wished to develop his garden as much as an example to others as for his own interest. He brought gardeners from England to work on his estate at Pennsbury, his gardener James noting the speed of growth in May compared to that in England: "Seeds do come apace, for those seeds that in England take 14 days to rise, are up here in 6 or 7 days." Letters from William Penn mention terraces in front of the house, an *allée* of poplars from the front door to the landing stage, orchards and meadows. He imported 4,000 fruit trees and some Gallica roses in 1684, but other than this information, there is no further indication of the topography of the garden.

Penn's garden was one of the first to be established in what was to become the hub of American horticultural development, the valleys of the Delaware, Schuylkill and Brandywine Rivers. As the century proceeded, many prosperous Philadelphians acquired country seats in this area and needed nurseries – such as that of John Bartram on the Schuylkill River – to supply them with both native and imported plants and seeds from England for their new landscapes. These gardens were probably a well-regulated mixture of traditional formal elements softened by some early attempts to "call the country in" with plantings of naturalistic groves. Penn's grandson John Penn laid out the grounds of the Solitude on the site of what is now the Philadelphia zoo. Here he banished all formality from near the house and planned that views, with a multiplicity of natural effects, should unfold along a circuitous path from the house to a distant flower garden, with a clump of trees between the house and river giving perspective.

THE SOUTHERN COLONIES

By 1682, Thomas Ashe was able to describe the gardens of Charleston, South Carolina, and those of the plantations on the Ashley and Cooper Rivers, as beginning "to be beautified and adorned with such Herbs and Flowers, which to the Smell or Eye are pleasing and agreeable, viz. The Rose, Tulip, Carnation and Lilly, etc." Much of the late 17th- and 18th-century correspondence on gardening in Charleston dwelt almost exclusively on plants and nurseries, with little reference to garden layout – something that is explained by the suitability of the climate for growing plants from many different habitats. All that is known is that the colony's early gardens conformed to the prevailing pattern elsewhere of a "simple" formal appearance. Many of the plantation gardens were laid out as part of working farms for rice crops and indigo. In 1730 William Middleton's garden at Crowfield, on the Cooper River, was in a simplified French style, but by 1743 it was already described by Eliza Lucas Pinckney as having serpentine walks, variety of elevation, wildernesses and groves, mounts and what she calls a classical flavour. A large square bowling green sunk below the level of the rest of the garden was surrounded by flowering laurel (mountain laurel, *Kalmia*

latifolia) and catalpa, and there were large fishponds "properly disposed". Little remains at Crowfield, although archaeological finds have confirmed many of the elements mentioned, but at Middleton Place on the Ashley River, the gardens, begun in 1742, still belong to descendants of the original owner, Henry Middleton, and have recently been restored. The design belongs more to William and Mary as exemplified at Williamsburg than the less formal 18th century. The main house has gone but five graceful terraces descend to the butterfly ponds where the garden meets the low-lying rice fields, a sophisticated control of water levels

Function and beauty

The terraces and butterfly ponds at the rice plantation at Middleton Place, constructed in 1742, were part of a working farm complex, the lakes drained and flooded as required for the rice crop. Henry Middleton's terraces may have been inspired by John Aislabie's Moon Ponds at Studley Royal in Yorkshire, and perhaps, modern in spirit as they seem, Charles Jencks's double helix and curving reflecting water at Portrack (see page 421) have their roots in Studley Royal and Middleton Place.

Verdant boxwood

In the Southern states, so-called American boxwood – in reality European *Buxus sempervirens* – grows very vigorously in the heat to make distinctive mounded boxwood gardens, very different from the clipped formality of its European appearance. A number of boxwood gardens date back to 18th-century colonial times but many others have been restored, since it was a style that remained fashionable. Designers such as Charles Gillette working from the 1920s to 1960 captured the essence of the originals.

maintaining the height of the ponds and the flow to the tidal mill pond. A hundred plantation slaves worked for 10 years to build the mainly geometric garden, working in the "off-season". Most of the garden lies to the north in a curve of the river, where box-edged parterres, a bowling green and a mount are hemmed in by a canal.

Demand for plants and seeds in the region was sufficient for John Lawson to set up a nursery business as early as 1701. Mark Catesby visited Charleston between 1719 and 1726, gathering material for his great work the *Natural History of Carolina, Florida, and the Bahama Islands*. By 1730, John Bartram was corresponding about seeds and plants with a local gardener, Mrs Martha Logan, author of *The Gardener's Calendar*. The amateur botanist Dr Alexander Garden, after whom Linnaeus named the gardenia from China, started his own nursery near the city in 1754.

The most interesting nursery belonged to the famous Frenchman André Michaux, who in 1785 was sent by the French government to investigate and introduce plants of economic use to France, especially trees for reafforestation. In 1786, he purchased a tract of 45 hectares (111 acres) outside Charleston. There he grew valuable native plants found on his extensive travels through the eastern part of America and introduced plants from Europe or further afield. He is credited with bringing the first camellia to grow at Middleton Place, and the fragrant tea olive (*Osmanthus fragrans*), the pride of India (*Melia azedarach*), the ginkgo (*Ginkgo biloba*) and *Azalea indica* to American gardens.

PLANT EXCHANGE

The colonials brought with them seeds of familiar medicinal plants and herbs, grafts of useful fruit and, as a luxury, a few seeds of their favourite sweet-smelling flowers. The plants included rosemary, lavender, clary sage, hollyhock and eglantine rose. Some, such as toadflax (*Linaria vulgaris*), loosestrife (*Lysimachia* species), dandelions, ox-eye daisy (*Leucanthemum vulgare*), docks, mulleins (*Verbascum* species), Scotch thistle and even bouncing Bet (*Saponaria officinalis*) – and several which were accidentally brought in in animal feed or soil – have spread to become alien weeds, today carpeting meadows near old settlements and blocking waterways. Perhaps the most aggressive is the kudzu vine (*Pueraria lobata*), introduced in the 1900s to help with erosion problems in the Southern states and now destructively invasive, damaging native woods. More satisfactory were introductions, probably in the 18th century, of the common lilac (*Syringa vulgaris*), only introduced into western Europe a century earlier. Governor Wentworth planted lilacs on his terrace in New Hampshire, and it is said that George Washington's lilacs at Mount Vernon were slips from these.

Catesby's magnum opus
This illustration of dogwood (*Cornus florida*) and mockingbird comes from Mark Catesby's *Natural History of Carolina, Florida, and the Bahama Islands* (1797). Catesby, an English plantsman and collector, produced his magnificent study of the flora and fauna of the British colonies in America as a record of his expedition there. It took him 20 years to complete and contained 220 engravings, mostly by himself but several by such distinguished colleagues as Georg Dionysius Ehret.

The English mathematician and astronomer Thomas Harriot came to America in 1585 as "geographer" or "scientific adviser" with an unsuccessful expedition organized by Walter Raleigh to establish an English colony on Roanoke Island. He travelled through North Carolina and Virginia and recorded his observations in *A Briefe and True Report of the New Found Land of Virginia*. Harriot not only noticed native plants but even introduced some to England, including American chestnut (*Castanea dentata*, now extinct as a forest tree), the sunflower (*Helianthus annuus*) and Indian maize, the two latter already having been sent to Spain.

In addition to the American species brought to Europe through Spain, by the early 17th century plants were arriving in France from the French settlements further north in the colonies. Jean Robin, herbalist, botanist and gardener to the French kings, established a garden, the Jardin du Roi, in Paris, for the king's collections (renamed Jardin des Plantes after the Revolution). Robin shared some of his acquisitions with John Tradescant the Elder at Lambeth (see page 185), who was a member of the English Virginia Company and obtained plants through their offices. Both the French and English claim the first introduction of the false acacia or black locust (*Robinia pseudoacacia*), named after Robin. The tree soon naturalized in Europe and became a feature in hedgerows. Although from the earliest days seeds and cuttings of plants were sent back from the New World, it would be another hundred years before the colonials grew to appreciate the botanical riches that lay on their doorstep. It was America's first botanist, John Bartram (1699–1777), who, while employed to search for new plants for England and Europe, was able to introduce his contemporary fellow Americans to the wonders of the American flora in the 1730s and 1740s.

The "great exchange" transformed gardens in both the New and Old World. On the one hand, America abounds with a wealth of trees and shrubs suitable for ornamental gardening, its wild flowers far surpassing in variety and beauty European natives, although some of the greatest prairie plants and asters of the northeast were first "improved" in Europe before being re-introduced to American gardeners as cultivars. On the other hand, Europe and Asia are richer in bulbs, which contribute their beauty throughout the year.

GARDENING LITERATURE

For reference, the English authorities available to English settlers for plant identification were Gerard's *Herball* (1597), or its improved 1633 edition by Thomas Johnson, and John Parkinson's *Paradisi in Sole Paradisus Terrestris* (1629) and his second book, *Theatrum Botanicum* (1640). In an age still easily swayed by superstition, Culpeper's *Herbal*, full of astrological references, in its many late 17th-century editions was popular. The work of the Flemish herbalist Rembert Dodoens (1554), translated into English by Henry Lyte (1578) and plagiarized by Gerard, was probably brought by Governor Brewster on the *Mayflower*.

It seems possible that the settlers brought with them useful garden manuals, such as Thomas Hill's *The Gardener's Labyrinth* (first published in 1577) or even the recently published *A New Orchard and Garden* (1618) by William Lawson. The

THE GREAT TRANSATLANTIC EXCHANGE

The great exchange of plants in the late 17th and early 18th centuries between the Williamsburg gardeners William Byrd and John Custis and the English Quaker and naturalist Peter Collinson was not the first or only example of plant trading. Besides explorers such as John Clayton, John Banister and, later, Mark Catesby dispatching plants to England – to the Bishop of London at Fulham, to Collinson and to Philip Miller at the Chelsea Physic Garden – other plants went through private hands. The greatest supplier of American plants was the botanist John Bartram. As seen in Chapter 6, Bartram changed the appearance of English gardens and landscapes, his American introductions as influential in promoting the new natural style as all the theories propounded by poets and philosophers such as Shaftesbury, Milton and Pope. He also, importantly, persuaded American gardeners to appreciate the beauty of their native plants.

The path towards a new society (above)

The New World of America was a magnet for Europeans hoping to escape the evils of the Old World and create a more just society. Within a decade of its foundation in 1814 by members of a German communitarian group, the little town of New Harmony in Indiana was renowned for its prosperity and its orderly beauty. The hard-working, public-spirited Harmonists' amenities included a vineyard, an orchard and a labyrinth made of bushes, vines and flowering plants. Like the route to true social harmony, the route to the heart of the labyrinth was not easy to find. Originally, its goal was a circular log hut, but for the reconstruction, planted in concentric circles of privet between 1939 and 1941, the goal is a plain stone temple. The Harmonists planted mazes as aids to contemplation at each of their three settlements in the United States.

Aid to recuperation (right)

A group of World War II nurses and soldiers negotiate their way around the extensive 19th-century maze at Hatfield House, in Hertfordshire.

Arboreal goal (left)

The one essential of a 17th-century hedge maze was that it should offer something of a challenge and a reward. Both these Dutch designs have a single tree as their goals, but the tree on the left is on top of a mound. From there, the successful maze-trotter would have had an entertaining, grandstand view of the less fortunate, still working their way through the peripheral preliminaries.

Het fraaye Doolhof N.º 59, in de leegte met zes, en in de hoo omgangen van groene Schutten.

Door I.Vanden Avelen getek. en geëtst, en door N. Vischer uytgegeven met Privilege.

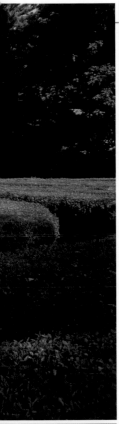

Mazes

One way or another, the concept of the maze – a web of convoluted lines leading, or not leading, to a central goal – has surfaced in every society, and in the gardens of the Western world it has generally taken the form of a network of hedges. Hedge mazes first became popular in the Renaissance gardens of 16th-century Italy. They were a way of providing an entertaining walk in a limited space and they had excellent classical credentials. The maze of the Villa d'Este, Tivoli, was a homage to the mythical minotaur's labyrinth, from which Theseus escaped with the help of Ariadne's thread, and French hedge mazes were sometimes called *dédales* after Daedalus, legendary designer of the man-bull's lair.

On reaching the heart of a maze, 16th- and 17th-century maze-trotters might be rewarded with seats and shade, drinking fountains, sun-dials, poetic inscriptions and statues. The 750m (830yd) trail of the maze at Versailles, which was destroyed in 1775, took in no fewer than 35 features inspired by Aesop's fables. Elsewhere, the twists and turns and blind alleys reflected life's ups and downs. The German Prince of Anhalt's maze was a veritable obstacle course, featuring rocks and caverns and sudden, steeply cut paths.

England's oldest surviving hedge maze, the much imitated Hampton Court maze, is in the area of garden known as the Wilderness. It was planted in the late 17th century but the original hornbeam has since been replaced by holly and yew. Cypress, juniper, lime, box, privet and laurel are also among the traditionally favoured plants. But the magic of the maze pertains more to the overall pattern of its walls and paths than to the plants used. Wood, sand and stone have served in places where hedges do not thrive, and other maze traditions provide inspiration. The only essential is that a maze should represent something of a challenge, or an invitation.

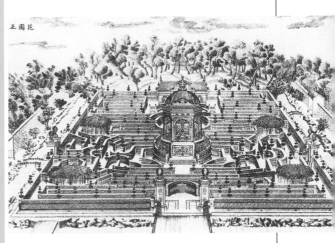

Chinese puzzle (above)
A European maze was one of the exotic features of Yuan Ming Yuan, the vast and multifarious summer park of the 18th-century Chinese emperor Qian Long. Yuan Ming Yuan (see page 344) accommodated so many themes and scenes it was called the garden of 10,000 gardens. The maze was recorded by its designer, Father Giuseppe Castiglione, who was one of the Jesuits serving at the imperial court.

Seasonal accents (above)
Winter snow delineates the web of the hedge maze at Hever Castle in Kent. Many different plants have been favoured for hedge mazes but their continuing appeal has more to do with the puzzle of the walls or paths than their plant content.

American columbine
Many native American plant species, found from the East Coast to the Mississippi River and north into Canada, have the specific epithet *canadensis* because much of the land was originally owned by the French settlers and trappers. *Aquilegia canadensis* was introduced to Europe through John Tradescant and the Virginia Company and by John Tradescant the Younger in 1637. The Louisiana Purchase of 1803, by which Thomas Jefferson acquired huge tracts originally in French hands, ensured American expansion westwards and inaugurated new plant exploration, in particular the Lewis and Clark expedition to the Pacific West Coast (see page 304).

latter included suggested layouts for workable gardens rather than the sort of grand design that would have been totally unsuitable for the New England ethos. Richard Surflet's English version of Charles Estienne's and Jean Liébault's *L'agriculture et maison rustique* (1564) was published in 1600 as *The Countrie Farm* and was part of John Winthrop III's library. In his *Paradisus* Parkinson recommends laying out a "garden of pleasant flowers" with plan illustrations, and discusses the ordering of the kitchen garden and the orchard, a model of contemporary recommendations sometimes overlooked in favour of the more entertaining Gerard. Ralph Austen's discourse on fruit trees, published in 1676, must have been a boon in a country where orchards flourished; St John de Crevecoeur's *Letters from an American Farmer* on fruit growing in America was not published until 1782 and then first in England.

Both the New England settlers and the colonists further south would, at first, have relied entirely on English works. As the 17th century proceeded there was a greater choice of gardening manuals, although none provided any experience or advice on regional climates or extremes of cold and heat. Stephen Blake's *The Compleat Gardener's Practice* (1664) and Leonard Meager's *The English Gardener* (1670) expressed contemporary fashions in design, providing patterns for knots and flowerbeds and suggestions for planting fruit trees. In a country that had yet to produce its own literature, these were useful as guides to creating gardens once circumstances became more comfortable and garden "conceits" could claim a place. Meager's very practical advice on how "to level and bring a Garden into some sort of form" makes his a handy book for gardeners in any age.

Some American agriculture and husbandry books contained useful horticultural references. *The Husbandman's Guide* (1710) by John Allen and Eleazar Phillips, and *Essays upon Field Husbandry in New England* (1760) by Jared Elliot were both published in Boston. John Smith's *Profit and Pleasure United, or the Husbandman's Magazine*, although first published in London in 1684, was reprinted in America in 1718 and besides farming matters dealt with improvements of fruit trees, plants and flowers.

As late as the 1770s, George Washington was reading Batty Langley's *New Principles of Gardening* (1728), in which "irregularity" in design is first shown in plans. The publication influenced Washington in laying out the home farm at Mount Vernon with just a hint of naturalism. Even John Bartram, in the 1730s, had to rely as far as he could on the long outdated 1597 edition of Gerard's *Herball* (he did not have Johnson's superior 1633 edition). In 1737, he received a copy of Parkinson's *Paradisus* from John Logan and Philip Miller's *Gardener's*

Dictionary – the most prized volume throughout the 18th century – from Peter Collinson. John Randolph's *Treatise on Gardening* (1788) is thought to be the first gardening book actually published in America.

The Governor of Virginia, Francis Nicholson, had a better library than most. It contained, as well as Meager's *English Gardener*, more recent publications: John Evelyn's *Sylva* (1664) and his translation of La Quintinye's *The Compleat Gard'ner*, John Worlidge's *Systema Agriculturae* (1669), Moses Cook's *Manner of Raising, Ordering and Improving Forrest-Trees* (1676) and, as a plant reference, a manuscript copy of the botanist John Banister's *Treatise on the Flora and Fauna of Virginia*, dated 1690. Except for Meager, these were either plant books or practical manuals and did not promote design ideas.

The most useful publication covering all branches of horticulture was the American *Gardener's Calendar* (1806) written by the nurseryman Bernard M'Mahon. Eighteen pages of the book cover ornamental designs and planting, much of the information cribbed from Humphry Repton's writings but presented for American conditions. It became the standard authority on American gardening for the next 50 years, going into 11 editions. Already a convert to the English naturalistic school, M'Mahon was the first to describe the principles of the natural garden especially for Americans. He recommended rural open spaces and the abolition of long, straight walks in favour of winding paths, "all bounded with plantations of trees, shrubs and flowers in various clumps". M'Mahon, an Irish immigrant, settled in Philadelphia in 1796, where he opened a seed store, which rapidly acquired an international reputation. His catalogue of plants is the most important source for determining which plants were being grown in America at the time.

THE PICTURESQUE GARDEN EXPLORED

George Washington's garden at Mount Vernon contained formal elements – the traditional patterns of colonial gardening – but also marked an essay into appreciating the beauties of nature, provided for him in abundance with lawns sloping down to the Potomac River. A view to the west of the house by Samuel Vaughan shows the regularity of Washington's layout with only a hint of compromise in the serpentine paths winding through the shrubbery. As Bernard Latrobe said, "Towards the East of the Mansion nature has lavished magnificence, nor has art interfered but to exhibit her to her advantage." Locust trees and shrubs framed the view across the river. In 1798, Latrobe made clear a shift in opinion by condemning Washington's box parterre. "For the first time since I left Germany I saw here a parterre, clipped and trimmed with infinite care into the form of a richly flourished Fleur de Lis: the expiring groans, I hope, of our grandfathers' pedantry." By the end of the century, such formal elements were no longer in vogue.

Although Thomas Jefferson (see overleaf) brought the picturesque taste to the forefront of American landscape design, he was not the first to develop the more natural garden, although he made it fashionable. In the South, the natural exuberance of romantic scenery was appreciated by William Bartram, John Bartram's

COLONIAL GARDENS AND GARDEN ARCHAEOLOGY

After the Civil War, many of the gardens in the South simply disappeared, overcome by neglect; without slave labour, plantations ceased to be economic. Early 20th-century restorations tended to conjure up box-hedged gardens based on a colonial revival style, with a formal pattern of box near the house. These have their own charm, and without sufficient records it seemed the only approach. More recently, refined archaeological techniques have made the process of recovering and reconstructing areas of America's past much more feasible. Soil stratification reveals dates and details of hard landscaping and planting, and holes for wooden posts define fence lines, unravelling the garden spaces, while pollen analysis can establish actual plant specimens.

JEFFERSON'S MONTICELLO

MOST OF THE EVIDENCE for pleasure gardening in North America in the 17th and 18th centuries comes from diaries, accounts, letters, inventories and travel writers, and from orders for plants from England. Each commentator had their own agenda and assessment of prevailing taste: a "good" garden might signify a formal, traditional layout or convey a taste for irregularity. Yet by the beginning of the 19th century, as Americans began to appreciate the beauties of their own countryside, reports tended to favour the more picturesque aspects of garden design and to consider the structured garden old-fashioned.

George Washington's home at Mount Vernon seems to belong to one era, Thomas Jefferson's at Monticello and the great campus quadrangle he conceived at the University of Virginia to another. While both men were interested in plants, Jefferson had a more modern approach to botany and horticulture. Jefferson, also an enthusiastic architect, was America's 18th-century Renaissance man.

Monticello, Jefferson's "little mountain", begun in 1771 and re-modelled in 1796 and 1809, was situated 6km (4 miles) from Charlottesville. He constructed long terraces with a promenade that formed a "U" with the mansion. This arrangement placed all the utilitarian buildings out of view of the house. Jefferson wrote of the setting: "Where has nature spread so rich a mantle under the eye?", and later wrote from Paris that he preferred the "woods, the wilds, and the independence of Monticello, to all the brilliant pleasures of this gay capital".

During his time as American minister to France in the 1780s, Jefferson took every opportunity to visit French chateaux, including Marly and Versailles. The influence of Marly can be seen in his plans for the elegant campus pavilions at the University of Virginia at Charlottesville. He also made a long trip to England in 1786, where he was inspired by the new landscapes and particularly enjoyed the modest but ingenious circuit walks at the Leasowes and Wooburn Farm (see page 232), although he was highly critical of the results in both cases.

Jefferson admired 'Capability' Brown's parks for their pastoral quality and the "variety of hill and dale", which he called the first beauty in gardening. Yet he found difficulties in re-creating similarly open scenes in America, where the sun was more violent: "Under the beaming, constant and almost vertical sun of Virginia, shade is our Elysium. In the absence of this no beauty of the eye can be enjoyed." He goes on to suggest an alternative. "Let your ground be covered with trees of the loftiest stature.

Trim up their bodies as the constitution and form of the tree will bear, but so as their tops shall still unite and yield dense shade. A wood so open below will have nearly the appearance of open grounds." He realized that in his country the "noblest gardens might be made without expense. We have only to cut out the super-abundant plants" – a point of view that influences the making of gardens in the United States even today, where many are still carved out of forest. Unfortunately, cutting a few trees, making a winding path in the woods and planting a few native perennials and shrubs is on occasion a substitute for the properly designed naturalistic garden of which Jefferson would have approved. He also felt there was a superfluity of temples, statuary and obelisks in English gardens, and that these decorative additions were unsuitable for the American landscape and the current mood for liberty and equality. Yet by 1809 he was planning to introduce a gothic temple among "ancient and venerable oaks", interspersed with "gloomy evergreens" and other buildings that would convey different moods.

The idea of the *ferme ornée* specially appealed to Jefferson's interest in the cultivation of the soil, which was the proper labour of "the chosen people of God". A plantation setting such as that at Monticello, with agricultural and vegetable crops, could be best adapted without the garden spoiling the natural advantages of the site.

America's Renaissance man
Apart from his other interests, Jefferson was a lifelong devotee of Palladio's classicism and a keen architect. He taught himself draughtsmanship at a time when America offered no professional training for an architect.

THOMAS JEFFERSON, 1789, BY JEAN-ANTOINE HOUDON

son, a botanical painter. In his writings about nature he travels through North and South Carolina, east and west Florida, and anticipates Thoreau and Audubon. He was also to inspire the romantic poetry of Coleridge and Wordsworth. Like his father, Bartram was influential in encouraging American gardeners to appreciate the superb "wilderness" in their own gardens. What was on their own doorstep needed interpretation on a more domestic basis, the Garden of Eden brought into the realm of garden design. Sadly, few 18th-century landowners grasped this opportunity, although some of the gardens near Charleston, and particularly at Magnolia Plantation, created in 1743 (pictured on page 280) caught some of the atmosphere of undeveloped nature.

Exploration: the Lewis and Clark Expedition

In 1803, President Thomas Jefferson sent the British explorer Captain Merriwether Lewis and his companion Captain William Clark on a fact-finding expedition. They were to cross the Rocky Mountains from the higher reaches of the Missouri River and travel down the Columbia River to reach the Pacific Ocean, an area only tentatively familiar even to fur traders. The expedition, conducted with astonishing bravery, has become something of a legend. Briefed to map the area, and to provide information on the flora and fauna, Lewis and Clark brought back many botanical treasures, including the Oregon grape (*Mahonia aquifolium* – named in honour of the nurseryman M'Mahon), which was to sell for $20 a plant within a few years, as well the Osage orange (*Maclura pomifera*), used for thorny hedging in its native Midwest until barbed wire was invented later in the 19th century. Jefferson was one of the first to plant it as a hedge on the Atlantic seaboard. Plants and seeds were given to William Hamilton, a plant expert at Woodlands outside Philadelphia, and to M'Mahon. Lewisias and clarkias are named after Lewis and Clark.

The botanist Frederick Pursh, employed by M'Mahon, obtained specimens of some of the plants. He took them with him to the Elgin Botanic Garden in New York and then to Europe, without permission, publishing their first description in *Flora Americae Septentrionalis* (1814), with 13 illustrations from Lewis's herbarium – one of the few instances of a botanist behaving badly.

Botanic Gardens and Nurseries

As the fashion for English gardening grew in post-federal America, with a prosperous slave-owning society in the South and a new class of well-to-do manufacturers in the North, the demand for plants increased. At the same time, American society was anxious to develop its own scientific establishments where newly discovered plants could be identified and catalogued. With Philadelphia the centre of scientific enquiry, gardeners no longer needed to depend on those in the

Old World for their expertise. Dr Benjamin Smith Barton was a most distinguished naturalist who made a lifetime's study of medicinal plants found on the American shores. New seed merchants and nurseries that were part of an expanding industry could offer American plants as well as those from the Old World.

The 18th-century botanic gardens and nurseries of John Bartram and André Michaux were rivalled, at the time, only by the more commercial nursery started by Robert Prince in Flushing on Long Island in 1735. By 1790 both American plants and those received from Europe covered a wide range.

The Elgin Botanic Garden in New York occupied the site of what is now the Rockefeller Center. When David Hosack founded it in 1801, it was almost in the country, on the edge of the swamps and ravines where Central Park would be laid out in 1858. Hosack's 2,000 plants, both natives and exotics, were arranged scientifically, classified by both the Linnean system and the more natural orders of Jussieu. A belt of forest trees and a 2m (7ft) stone wall surrounded the garden.

André Parmentier, who came to New York from Belgium in 1824, established one of the most interesting nurseries when he set up his "Botanic Garden" in Brooklyn. The garden contained almost as many exotics as could be found in London at Kew or at Loddiges' Hackney nursery. Invited to take over the flourishing Elgin Botanic Garden, Parmentier preferred to start up on his own, establishing a garden-design practice promoting the natural style. His nursery garden in Brooklyn was famous for a "rustic prospect arbor", serving the same purpose as a Tudor mount and giving views over the surrounding countryside. Before his death in 1830 he had influenced the youthful Andrew Jackson Downing, who was to become the first American writer to treat the subject of landscape gardening in a specific American way.

AN AMERICAN PERSPECTIVE ON THE PICTURESQUE

Andrew Jackson Downing (1815–52) was a knowledgeable horticulturist who based his ideas about art in the garden on his appreciation of beautiful scenery. His book *A Treatise on the Theory and Practice of Landscape Gardening Adapted to North America* (1841) was a huge success, rapidly going into six editions. It appears that by stimulating interest in "home improvements", Downing caught the prevailing mood of a public ready to expand their ideas on ornamental gardening and an appreciation of the picturesque. One of Downing's most engaging traits was his complete sincerity. In philosophic mood, he believed that human behaviour is greatly influenced by environment – anticipating theories of social wellbeing in the 20th century. He advocated the adoption of J.C. Loudon's gardenesque principles, and exploited these for the American villa owner inside a general framework of naturalistic gardening based on his own interpretation of both 'Capability' Brown and Humphry Repton.

Downing may be criticized on several grounds: that his advice is only half thought out; and that the illustrations of his ideas on landscape are only remarkable for the spottiness of the planting and lack of obvious design. Downing constantly refers to "taste" and "tastefulness" as excellent qualities only to be found in the elite, while the "mass of uncultivated minds" could be expected to have "false

Delightful prospect
The frontispiece to Andrew Jackson Downing's *A Treatise on the Theory and Practice of Landscape Gardening Adapted to North America*, published in 1841, is of Blithewood on the Hudson River. Downing, who tragically drowned in an accident on the Hudson when only 37, was a disciple of John Claudius Loudon, and encouraged American villa owners and gardeners to appreciate the "lovely prospects" of their own scenery and to use native trees and flowers in their landscapes. He recommended different sorts of specimen trees to "go" with certain architectural styles, inspiring an appreciation of the "Beautiful and Picturesque scenes" to be found in the Hudson River valley.

taste". Perhaps the content of his book mattered less than his enthusiasm for a new appreciation of the duties of a progressive homeowner.

Nevertheless, Downing encouraged Americans to appreciate their own undoubtedly picturesque native landscape at a time of great expansion, and to improve their residential properties. One of his most lasting acts was to introduce the young English architect Calvert Vaux to America in 1850. And it was Downing who, with William Cullen Bryant, agitated for the establishment of a park in New York, to ensure that public land would be developed for the benefit of all the people of the city. Eventually, in 1858, after Downing's tragic death by drowning, the Vaux partnership with Frederick Law Olmsted was to produce Central Park, the first "country park" in a city, and to usher in a new era in American town planning.

PUBLIC PARKS: GREENERY IN THE CITY

Although in the earliest settlements in America, common land had often been set aside in the centre of towns, the idea of creating a space with a rural feel, specifically for public recreation and enjoyment, was still a new one in the 1850s. The nearest approach to a public park was the innovatory design for Mount Auburn Cemetery in Cambridge, Massachusetts, created in 1831, which gave space for strolling and solitude. Town planning in Philadelphia and in Southern towns such as Savannah had open accessible squares, with plenty of trees to give shade. They were, however, part of the general ambience, rather than being envisaged as places for relaxation, just as Major L'Enfant's plan for Washington DC, executed in 1791, made ample provision for green spaces.

OLMSTED'S BREADTH OF VISION

FREDERICK LAW OLMSTED (1822–1903) had a varied career as farmer, journalist, publisher and traveller before submitting his winning design for Central Park in 1858. He was to become the best known of American landscape architects and one of the first environmentalists, yet he was by no means a visionary only. His experiences also made him a practical man, capable of managing thousands of employees in the Central Park project. Following completion of the park, Olmsted, with the architect Calvert Vaux, achieved an impressive number of commissions. They included the design of Prospect Park, Brooklyn, and the curving vista over the Long Meadow, the Capitol grounds in Washington DC and the Boston park system. Olmsted's work as a landscape architect included the Chicago World's Fair, proposals for city planning at Buffalo and the Riverside project in 1868 on the edge of gangster-ridden Chicago. The last was a suburban development along the Des Plaines River in Illinois. It was designed as a rural village of gently winding streets on a grid system, its rules including specification on building setback, tree-planting requirements, a network of community parklands and a ban on fences, anticipating Frank Scott (see page 311) by a few years. Olmsted laid out Mount Royal in Montreal and a number of other public parks in Canada as well as the Stanford campus at Palo Alto in California. He was among those involved in conservation work at Yosemite in California.

Olmsted adopted the English 18th-century landscapes as models for his naturalistic urban parks for city workers, a form of social reform close

FREDERICK LAW OLMSTED

to his heart. For him, the designs were part of a moral crusade, extended by his work in promoting the principles of American National Parks, in which he hoped to save nature for the enjoyment of American citizens.

Olmsted's last major commission was in 1888 for George Vanderbilt at Biltmore House in Asheville, North Carolina. There, around the vast French-style chateau built of Indiana limestone by Richard Morris Hunt, he laid out the 100-hectare (250-acre) estate grounds, driveways and an arboretum, and installed a forestry nursery for raising native trees and shrubs. The last developed into the Biltmore School of Forestry, with Vanderbilt ultimately owning 48,500 hectares (120,000 acres).

Biltmore, where Olmsted worked for over seven years, was one of his favourite projects, a private undertaking that could benefit from a shared vision with his employer and from the latter's limitless resources. He could achieve

the fine tuning seldom possible in a public venture. For the arboretum, he constructed a 14km (9-mile) avenue planted with trees and shrubs that could be expected to thrive in the region. The estate would also serve as a testing ground for plants in the American South. Many of the plants were natives, with 10,000 *Rhododendron maximum* providing a backdrop to rarer exotics.

The ordinary approach road was a 5km (3-mile) stretch with carefully orchestrated picturesque planting opening out onto the formal Esplanade near the house, which was flanked by tall tulip trees. Olmsted preferred an abrupt transition from the naturalistic driveway planting to "the trim, level, open, airy, spacious, thoroughly artificial Court, and the Residence", rather than any mixture of styles. He especially designed the long *allée* of the Esplanade to provide a view outward from the house to a distant statue, with vistas to the west and southwest. South of the Esplanade were two large terraces, followed by a shrubbery and walled garden and, further down the slope, by the naturalistically designed Bass Pond leading down to the river and lagoon, which reflected the house far above.

By 1894, Olmsted was in increasingly poor health and had to retire from Biltmore. His son Rick (1870–1957), who later took the name of Frederick Law Olmsted Jnr, stood in for his father for the completion of the portrait by John Singer Sargent that still hangs at Biltmore. He established his office, with his stepbrother John Charles Olmsted (1852–1920), in Boston for the next half century, achieving leadership in the fields of planning and landscape design.

Formality and informality
The aerial view of Biltmore (left) shows Olmsted's formal terrace, designed to match Hunt's French-style chateau on the ridge, and below it the elaborate walled garden, where the plants included choice fruit and vegetables as well as decorative flowers for use in the house. Between the two, the shrubbery was "a glen-like place with narrow winding paths", with a sheltered walk protected by shrubs rather than the usual specimen shade trees.

Tranquil water
Olmsted seldom chose to practise the sort of formality displayed in the geometric patterns of the walled garden, and elsewhere on the estate the planting is naturalistic, as can be seen in the shrubbery and also in trees around the lake (below), where there is an emphasis on native species.

New York's breathing space
The bird's-eye view of Central Park from the north (top) was painted by John Bachmann in 1863; above, the park at night showing one of the bridges. One of Olmsted and Vaux's most successful innovations was the traffic system, a series of sunken transverse roads, which they imposed on a pastoral setting. The scheme gave the people of New York a place for recreation, the breathing space which Olmsted wanted for all cities. Much influenced by English parks, he believed in the subconscious therapeutic powers of landscape on people's minds.

In 1851, the state of New York, recognizing the need to provide recreational space for the teeming city, passed the first Park Act, setting aside land specifically for public use. As the original site proved too small, the act was amended in 1853, granting the authority to take land between Fifth Avenue and Eighth Avenue (now Central Park West) and 59th Street and 106th Street (extended to 110th Street in 1859), an area of swamps and rocky outcrops. The board of commissioners appointed Frederick Law Olmsted as their first superintendent in September 1857. Within a month, the commissioners held a competition to choose an overall plan for the projected park. Olmsted joined the English architect Calvert Vaux to create a design that could cope with the many problems of the site. Their anonymous presentation, entitled "Greensward, plan 33", was awarded the prize in April 1858.

The Olmsted-Vaux plan envisaged a pastoral landscape and a system of sunken transverse roads with arched underpasses for pedestrians. It was inspired by the park at Birkenhead in England laid out by Joseph Paxton in 1843 and visited by Olmsted in 1850. As an innovation, the partners introduced a formal note with a double avenue of American elms framing an architectural mall. The tract of rural scenery was to be a haven "where lawn, glade, water and wilderness weave in and out to push back the turbulent metropolis".

Olmsted wrote: "It is one great purpose of the Park to supply the hundreds of thousands of tired workers, who have no opportunity to spend their summers in the country, a specimen of God's handiwork that shall be shown to them, inexpensively, what a month or two in the White Mountains or the Adirondacks is, at great cost, to those in easier circumstances." Olmsted also expressed his conviction that the park should be a single work of art throughout, in which all its parts contributed to the whole, so that "every foot of the park's surface, every tree and bush, as well as every arch, roadway and walk has been fixed where it is with a purpose". A disciple of Downing, Olmsted believed fervently in the idea of public access and in the idea of the English landscape tradition allied to American romanticism, as personified by the Hudson River school of painting (see page 382).

Although Olmsted's views on creating pastoral scenes for the relief of the workers probably far surpassed contemporary thinking, Central Park was virtually completed by 1877, in spite of various obstacles. Olmsted and Vaux resigned in 1870 but were reinstated a year later to supervise a "wilder" sort of planting. By 1875, inspired by William Robinson's *The Wild Garden* (see page 386), Olmsted was recommending its reading to his head gardeners. Today, although some recreational facilities have been added, the park retains its basic integrity and has been authentically and sympathetically restored.

THE AMERICAN FRONT LAWN

Olmsted is not only remembered for his urban parks and his pioneering of a movement to save the American wilderness. Both he and Downing also influenced the development of the smaller domestic garden landscape in America. Their ideas were translated, in part, by writers such as Frank Scott who, by the second half of the 19th century, was providing detailed and practical advice for the suburban homeowner. As Americans began to search for some sort of national identity in their gardens, many began to feel that the order and regularity imposed by geometric schemes, while necessary during the colonial period when nature was a threat, represented social values at variance with a democratic spirit. The formal layouts of the grand country estates were seen as retrogressive. Frank Scott recommended doing away with barriers between front gardens in middle-class suburbs, seeing them as exclusive and undemocratic. In his opus *The Art of Beautifying Suburban Home Grounds* (1870) Scott hoped that suburbia would become half country, half town, where one would find "streets and roads and streams, dotted with a thousand suburban homes peeping from their groves".

Scott went so far as to condemn hedging, suggesting that "the practice of hedging one's ground so that the passer-by cannot enjoy its beauty, is one of the barbarisms of old gardening, as absurd and un-Christian in our day as the walled courts and barred windows of a Spanish cloister, and as needlessly aggravating as the close veil of the Egyptian women". Instead broad sweeps of lawn and trees joining houses together would give unity, with curved walks and flowerbeds cut in the grass for annual displays producing a shared utopian outlook for all the houses. Scott's predilection for the American front lawn was to have far-reaching consequences. Over the next hundred years, the American lawn became sacrosanct. Its displacement in the last few years of the 20th century was only possible as part of a more general ecological attitude based on saving water and inhibiting the use of fertilizers and pesticides that could damage the environment.

THE LANDSCAPE OF THE CEMETERY

Before the development of city parks in the second half of the 19th century, cemeteries provided pleasant surroundings for recreation. Monuments were concealed in a landscape of paths winding through shady groves, which alternated with sweeping, open lawns. In these new parks of remembrance, the best contemporary architectural and sculptural features were displayed to add cultural and educational significance. The cemetery of Spring Grove in Cincinnati, Ohio, was founded in 1845, designed by Robert Daniels. It was modelled on Boston's Mount Auburn (1831), Philadelphia's Laurel Hill (1836) and Baltimore's Green Mount (1838). Adolph Strauch, a Prussian landscape gardener, came to Cincinnati – then the nation's sixth largest and fastest-growing city – to work on developing private estates. Advising at Spring Grove, he sought to eliminate the tangled picturesque style of the earlier cemeteries and to introduce a preponderance of gentle flowing lines. He was gradually able to reduce the "fencing barbarism" of individual plot holders and their indiscriminate mixtures of planting. With disdain for "the gaudy parterre of transitory blooming" he allowed no eye-catching flowerbeds to disturb the primarily green landscape. Spring Grove, with its sweeping lawns and stately avenues, soon outshone Mount Auburn as a model for a cemetery landscape and, by 1875, Frederick Law Olmsted was to prefer it to all other rural cemeteries for its adherence to the natural principles of landscape gardening.

The Arnold Arboretum
The aim of the Arnold Arboretum, founded in 1872, was to collect, grow and display as far as possible all the trees, shrubs and herbaceous plants, whether indigenous or exotic, that could be raised in the open in the vicinity of Boston. Professor and curator Charles Sprague Sargent asked Frederick Law Olmsted to lay out the grounds, which would form part of Olmsted's "emerald necklace" of parks around Boston. Inauguration was made possible by a gift of land from Benjamin Bussey and a legacy of $100,000 from James Arnold. The arboretum is a monument to 19th-century vision. The trees and shrubs form a living museum and provide a practical demonstration of planting possibilities. Famous plant explorers such as the Englishman Ernest Wilson (below left, with Sargent) collected many of the plants. From

1906 to 1920, Wilson introduced plants of outstanding garden worthiness, many from Asia, including the beauty bush (*Kolkwitzia amabilis*), *Lilium regale*, the tea crab (*Malus hupehensis*), the dove tree (*Davidia involucrata*) and *Magnolia wilsonii*. Today, the arboretum contains more than 7,000 types of tree and shrub and has been responsible for the introduction of over 500 ornamental species and varieties to North American gardens.

Olmsted must be credited with the first recommendation of the lawn as part of American suburban life. At his Riverside development in Illinois, each owner could have one or two trees and "a lawn that would flow seamlessly onto his neighbour's". Lawns, originally found in England on landed estates where acres of greensward would thrive in the temperate damp climate, had little relevance for the humbler English gardener, still less for the homeowner in America with its extremes of climate.

It was in America that lawns became democratized, with the grid-like system of land division making it possible to site a house with a front and back garden area. The "backyard" could be gardened in a personal way, but the front lawn became public property visually. Scott went as far as he could, branding those who wished to hedge or fence their front gardens as "selfish", "un-neighbourly", "un-Christian" and "undemocratic". Who could rebel against such castigation? Very few did, and it was only at the end of the next century that the American lawn became recognized as an environmental hazard.

THE GROWTH OF AMERICAN GARDENING JOURNALS AND SOCIETIES

Throughout the first half of the 19th century there was a new consciousness in America of the beneficial effects that came from contact with nature, as romanticized by the Hudson River school of painting, which portrayed and idealized the great sweeps of natural landscape. As gardening became more popular, a stream of journals – many aimed specifically at women – societies and shows proliferated, making gardeners feel in touch and gardening more possible.

Andrew Jackson Downing's journal *The Horticulturist*, begun in the 1840s, was aimed at the cultured reader who wished to beautify their "home grounds". Later publications such as *Country Life in America*, *House Beautiful* and *House and Garden* all catered for a rather refined taste, but other journals such as *The Magazine of Horticulture* and the *American Gardener's Magazine* had a more practical side. *Garden and Forest*, produced by Charles Sprague Sargent through the Arnold Arboretum, dealt with landscape practice as well as botany and was among the most highly regarded. The Pennsylvania Horticultural Society, founded in 1827 and based in Philadelphia, held its first public exhibition in 1829, the first important flower show in America and the forerunner of the modern annual Philadelphia Flower Show, now America's most prestigious show.

Nurserymen's catalogues such as that of Grant Thorburn of New York, published from 1805, provided ordinary gardeners with a stimulus to try new varieties. Thorburn wrote for the gardening press under the *nom de plume* of Laurie

Todd. Robert Buist, for a time the most prolific garden writer in America, was trained at the Royal Botanic Garden, Edinburgh, and came to America to work for Henry Pratt at Lemon Hill, now a part of Fairmount Park in Philadelphia. He became a florist, introducing and breeding verbenas, and was famous for his camellias and roses. Later he had a successful seed business. He published the first book on flowers for gardeners, *The American Flower-Garden Directory* (1832), which contains very practical advice, a boon to the new gardening public. Other of his publications included a book on roses and one on the family kitchen garden (1852). *The Flower Garden: or Breck's Book of Flowers* (1852) was also written by a famous seed merchant, Joseph Breck.

DEVELOPMENTS IN THE WEST

In the Midwest, as pioneers pushed across the continent and adapted to the even more extreme climate of the central plains, American gardening followed the pattern of East Coast development, albeit with a time lag. From 1534 until 1759, the French owned much of the Midwest, with fur trading stations and forts linking them with Quebec in the north. After the defeat of France by the British at Quebec (1759), the French retained only land west of the Mississippi. This was ceded to Spain in 1762, following which the rights were formally "sold" by Napoleon to Jefferson in 1803 with the Louisiana Purchase. The Americans were then free to occupy great tracts of western land extending to the Rocky Mountains. Although the heat and cold on the Great Plains at first made gardening difficult, with prosperity it became possible to make gardens comparable to those on the East Coast. By the late 1800s, gardens were of two main kinds, as in the East: natural gardens in the Olmsted tradition and the more regular formal gardens drawing on Platt and his Renaissance type architectural followers, as discussed in Chapter 12.

THE FAR WEST

California became part of the United States in 1846. The gardeners who arrived on the West Coast from 1850 onwards were more influenced by contemporary fashions on the eastern seaboard and in Europe than by the existing Hispanic traditions they found in the West. They wrestled with, or defied, the challenges of the climate, and California became the setting for the familiar debate between gardeners with an appetite for artifice and those like Olmsted who attempted to understand the climate and soil of every region.

Early explorers, like most of their Victorian successors, believed that an Arcadian society could be created in the benign and dramatic Californian landscape, but they did not find the climate easy. With severe droughts alternating with heavy rain, success depends on an elaborate system of irrigation and drainage. The topography is enormously variable and although the climate is basically Mediterranean with mild wet winters and hot dry summers, there are vast local variations. By the end of the 20th century 24 different gardening zones had been identified in California, varying between rainforest, desert, lush warm growth in the microclimate of Santa Barbara and the cold fogs that roll into San Francisco.

The Franciscan Spanish missionaries were the first gardeners to test their skills in the Californian climate. Coming from a society where water supply was a constant problem and was treated with Islamic respect, they used traditional cultivation methods, perhaps with some simple modifications. Father Juniperis Serra founded the earliest mission of San Diego de Alcala in 1769, carrying seeds of the castor-oil plant (*Ricinus communis*), wheat, vines and dates with him on foot from Mexico City. From then on a string of missions with walled courtyards was established from Mexico and Arizona up the Californian coast, each a day's brisk walk apart. The buildings were in the Spanish colonial style with thick adobe walls and overhanging tiled roofs. The missionaries planned to introduce the native Americans to both the Roman Catholic faith and to the plants and fruits of the Old World, but soon found that they themselves were also growing indigenous plants, their uses having been explained by the local tribes.

As usual the first priorities were agricultural crops, orchards, olive groves, vegetables and herbs. When Captain George Vancouver arrived off the Californian coast in 1793 he found apples, pears, plums, figs, oranges, grapes, pomegranates, and peaches besides bananas, coconut and sugar cane growing in the mission garden at San Buena Ventura, where ample water made the fertile soil even more productive. San Fernando, founded in 1797, was known for the 32,000 grapevines imported from Spain, making the mission famous for its brandy. In the gardens, South American plants such as the pepper tree (*Schinus molle*), *Nicotiana glauca* and the Chilean wine palm (*Jubaea chilensis*) grew alongside the indigenous holly-leaved cherry (*Prunus ilicifolia*) of the Los Angeles mountains – later to give the name Hollywood to the area – as well as plants that were imported from Europe, but had often originated elsewhere.

Many mission gardens fell into a state of neglect after Mexico attained independence from Spain in 1822 and secularized the extensive estates, making thousands of acres available as ranching land. However in 1846, the year California became part of the United States, Edwin Bryant visited the Mission San Fernando to find "two extensive gardens surrounded by high walls" in which there were many fruits and plants from both temperate and tropical climates. "Roses were in bloom in January, and lemons, figs and olives hung upon the trees, with blood red tuna – or prickly pear – looking very tempting." He also admired the avenue outside the mission itself, a "broad *almeda*, shaded by several rows of stately trees – elms and willows – planted by the *padres*…forming a most beautiful drive or walk for equestrians or pedestrians".

The second group of gardeners who arrived after 1850 had every intention of realizing their East Coast notions in their new home. Regardless of local conditions they imposed designs derived from Downing's recommendations, in which J.C. Loudon's gardenesque schemes, planned to display individual plants, predominated. The most successful of these gardeners had the means to introduce sufficient water to cultivate a vast range of plants, including those from temperate, subtropical and tropical countries. Nurseries, established from the 1840s, provided new plants and seed from Europe and the eastern centres of American horticulture. A typical Downing-inspired estate at Lachryma Montis in Sonoma, complete with lawn, was established in 1850 by General Mariano Vallejo, his previous adobe house transformed into a wooden villa of gothic design imported around Cape Horn. Antoine Borel from Switzerland moved to San Francisco in 1861. He made himself feel at home on his country estate in San Mateo, introducing French-style ribbon beds of flowering annuals and carpet bedding with delicate succulents. Lawns near the house were the foreground to extensive and eclectic tree planting.

Frederick Law Olmsted, one of the first easterners with a more realistic attitude to local conditions, was invited to make a proposal for a "natural" city park at San Francisco. Following a design for the Mountain View Cemetery in Oakland in 1865, Olmsted was approached by the mayor of the gold-rush town to plan a pleasure park on a windy site that would meet the needs of an expanding city. Unfortunately his ideas of suiting the park to the site, with a sunken promenade and wind-resistant indigenous trees rather than a forest of exotics, did not appeal. Within five years new plans for what was to become the Golden Gate Park were implemented by the ecologically minded William Hammond Hall. He was succeeded by John McLaren, who attempted to re-create different "natural" land-

Reminders of Spain

The garden at San Juan Capistrano Mission in California has its original arcaded courtyard and ornamental pool. The earliest Spanish missions were established towards the end of the 18th century and contained mainly flowers, fruit and vegetables from the Old World or from the Spanish in South America. Islamic-inspired Spanish traditions of water usage governed the design of the mission gardens and also of the farming communities or pueblos. Although many of the gardens have been restored with colourful and often appropriate regional and historic planting, the originals are unlikely to have had such an aesthetic content and would have mainly contained more useful plants.

The RUDBECKIA

American prairie perennials have, in recent years, discovered a new and highly fashionable place in planting schemes both in America and across the Atlantic. The various types of rudbeckia, sometimes called cone-flowers, have, in particular, shown their worth. With their velvety, intensely dark central boss, the perennial *Rudbeckia fulgida* and the shorter lived *R. hirta*, often grown as an annual, are both known as black-eyed Susan. Rudbeckias come from the Midwest and a little further east, growing in the deep rich soil that supports the corn belt of America. They thrive in open meadows and light woodland.

RUDBECKIA FULGIDA

Both *Rudbeckia fulgida* and *R.hirta* were introduced to Europe from the United States in the 18th century during the "great transatlantic plant exchange", and were named for the Swedish botanists Olaf Rudbeck and his son, early supporters of Linnaeus and his binomial system of nomenclature. (Another rudbeckia, *R. laciniata*, had arrived much earlier in Europe, first received by Vespasian Robin in Paris who sent it on to John Tradescant in London in 1632.)

The late-flowering *Rudbeckia fulgida* has bright orange daisy flowers while in its variety *R. f.* var. *sullivantii* 'Goldsturm' the flowers are more golden. Another variety, *Rudbeckia fulgida* var. *deamii*, is drought tolerant. All the rudbeckias, including short-lived *R. hirta*, are particularly suitable for massed effects to carry the garden into late summer, the perennial varieties needing little maintenance and continuing to flower for many years.

scapes within the park, adapting soil and aspect to suit a wide range of plants. In an effort to stabilize the shifting sand dunes and break the force of the wind to the west of the city, Hall planted thousands of Monterey cypresses, pines and blue gum (*Eucalyptus globulus*). There were unforeseen consequences: Australian eucalypts, introduced in the 1850s, in time colonized the surrounding countryside as weed trees.

In 1888, on the campus at Stanford University at the foot of the Santa Cruz mountains, Olmsted hoped to create something of the Hispanic style of the missions by combining Mediterranean-type planting with an arboretum of native trees and some plantings of trees from similar world habitats. Seeking an alternative to irrigated lawns, he studied the neglected mission complexes and planting choices. His client, Governor Leland Stanford, implemented only parts of the Olmsted scheme.

Californians were slow to recognize the dangers of being so dependent on an ample supply of water. By the late 19th century the gardens were full of plants from all corners of the globe that would grow in the favoured climate if sufficiently irrigated, giving the gardens a distinctly exotic look. Any type or style of landscape could be created with the help of the hosepipe. Few paused to consider the long-term ecological effects of growing so many foreign plants by such artificial means. The English garden writer A.T. Johnson was among those, with Olmsted and Hall, to express doubts after a visit to Pasadena: "It is the liberal use of the hosepipe and garden sprinkler which are turned on with such lavish generosity in the gardens and parks that is the main factor in making the wilderness bloom as the rose."

TOWARDS TRANSITION

By the middle of the 19th century, American horticultural fashions were running in tandem with those of Victorian England and Continental Europe. It was a time of consolidation, with the foundation of botanic gardens and an awareness of American plants and gardening possibilities. Downing's influence promoted the picturesque aspects of the English style, especially for the grounds of suburban villas, exploiting Loudon's gardenesque and eclectic attitudes to displaying plants, while many of the older, large gardens retained the formal elements of the earlier colonial style. By the 1870s, the suburbs of Boston and New Jersey were the playing fields of the rich, while by the turn of the century huge mansions set among grandiose gardens were being built north of Chicago along the shores of Lake Michigan and in Grossepoint, Detroit. The architect H.H. Richardson could create houses from any period, with historically inspired gardens to match.

From 1870 onwards, ideas and influences became ever more homogenized across the globe and the story of American gardening can no longer be viewed separately. When Japan opened its doors to the rest of the world Eastern attitudes to design had a profound effect, not least in America, and on both sides of the Atlantic there was a resounding call for a new naturalism in gardens – the ecological debate was about to begin in earnest. We see how it develops in America, and elsewhere, in Chapter 12.

CHAPTER TEN

GARDENS OF CHINA

A timeless tradition

THE GARDENS OF CHINA reveal the oldest and most continual civilization the world has ever seen. For thousands of years they have expressed a distinctively Chinese understanding of the universe, and alternately baffled and beguiled Western visitors. The Chinese deeply love nature – wind, water, mountains, trees and flowers – but have never sought to master it. In the Chinese garden, nature and humankind are partners in a space that is designed to "stand in" for the totality of the universe.

The relative unimportance of plants is the most immediate difference between the garden-making traditions of China and those of the West. The Chinese garden is not particularly green and it is built rather than planted. Stones and water, which both have great symbolic significance, are its prime components. Plants are accessories, yet they are charged with literary, artistic and philosphical meanings. By constantly celebrating the association of certain flowers and trees with certain sentiments and seasons, the gardens of China are a source of emotional refreshment and intellectual stimulation. And although there is no one essential model, every Chinese garden, whether it be the legendary demesne of a megalomaniacal emperor, or the modest retreat of a scholarly mandarin, has been designed to reflect and affirm the infinite rhythms of nature.

The ties that bind
Birds in the bush, as observed and painted by 12th-century Emperor Zhao Ji, who devoted much of his undeniable talent – and his realm's resources – to the creation of an artificial mountain called Gen Yue. For thousands of years the arts of painting and gardening have been inseparable in China.

THE GARDEN AS MICROCOSM OF THE UNIVERSE

China takes its name from its first emperor, Qin Shi Huang Di, a ruthless and extremely efficient tyrant who by 221 BC had established an empire that roughly corresponds to present-day mainland China. From north to south, Qin Shi Huang Di's realm extended for thousands of miles and from his capital at Changan (near present-day Xian) he could survey the mist-wreathed pinnacles of the mountains from which he derived his authority to rule it. Like Chinese kings before him, and all the emperors who came after him, Qin Shi Huang Di believed he had a mandate from Heaven, his divine ancestor, to rule the land below. Heaven governed the universe, fixed the seasons, gave fertility to humans and animals, and ordered the cycle of death and renewal. As the Sons of Heaven the emperors were closer to the Supreme Ancestor than any other human being, and they were priests as well as rulers.

Around 210 BC, while he was touring his empire in search of the Immortals — enchanted beings from whom he hoped to obtain the elixir of everlasting youth —

Land of mists and mountains
Mist rises up from a lake, and pinnacled mountains reach up to heaven in Guangxi province in southern China. Chinese gardens are miniature reproductions of natural scenes like this, with rocks standing in for mountains and ponds standing in for lakes.

Qin Shi Huang Di suddenly died. By then hundreds of thousands of labourers were already hard at work on his mausoleum near Mount Li in northern China, excavating stadium-sized pits, diverting underground rivers and constructing the massive, central mound, which was planted with trees and shrubs to make it look like a mountain. This tomb chamber was guarded by thousands of life-sized replicas of Qin Shi Huang Di's soldiers, complete with weapons, horses and chariots. They survive as the phenomenal Terracotta Army, but for an account of the first emperor's equally phenomenal park at Shanglin we have to rely on ancient records.

In prehistoric times, the plains of China's two mighty rivers, the Yellow (Huang He) and Yangzi Rivers, were richly forested. Much of this forest, with its abundance of fruit trees, including peach, pear, plum, persimmon and apricot, retreated under the impact of intensive farming, but China's early rulers sited their parks and gardens on what remained of the choice primeval landscape. Set against the cosmic mountains and sewn with eight rivers, Qin Shi Huang Di's park served as a hunting reserve, much like the great parks of the Sumerians and the Assyrians in the foothills of Persia some centuries earlier, as well as a pleasure garden. Within this landscape he amassed tributes of rare plants and animals from his far-flung subjects so that, besides being a showcase for the diversity of his realm, the scale of his wealth and the range of his power, Shanglin was a miniature, or microcosm, of the universe. A later poem recalls the plenitude of the first emperor's immense garden:

> The sun rises from the eastern ponds
> And set among the slopes of the west;
> In the southern part of the park,
> Where grasses grow in the dead of winter…
> Live Zebras, yaks, tapirs, and black oxen,
> Water buffalo, elk and antelope…
> Aurochs, elephant and rhinoceros.
> In the north, where in the midst of summer
> The ground is cracked and blotched with ice…
> Roam unicorns and boars,
> Wild asses and camels,
> Onagers and mares…

During Qin Shi Huang Di's reign, China's weights, measures, currency and script were standardized, and much of the Great Wall was completed. But these achievements were not accompanied by any major cultural or religious shifts. Continuity rather than change has been the hallmark of Chinese civilization for all but the last century of the past two and a half millennia. By the 5th century BC, centuries before Qin Shi Huang Di's lifetime, the Chinese were already understanding and managing the interplay of soil types, altitude and the water table, to the betterment of their orchards and fields, and this expertise also found applications in the splendid gardens of their rulers. The earliest description of a

Unearthly powers
An Immortal riding his three-legged toad. Since very ancient times the Chinese have been stirred by tales of an island mountain paradise inhabited by mysterious Immortals, fairy-like beings with access to the elixir of eternal youth. The legend inspired successive emperors to create lake-and-island gardens in the hope of attracting Immortal visitors.

Quest for paradise
The 16th-century artist Wen Zhengming's interpretation of an 8th-century poem about a journey to the Isles of the Immortals. At least one of the full-scale naval task forces sent by the emperors in search of this garden paradise failed to return. Real or imagined, the quest for the Immortals was a favourite subject of Chinese artists and poets, and a major theme of the garden.

Chinese pleasure garden is in a poem written in the 4th century BC. This imaginary garden belongs to a dying prince, whose retainers urge him to seek renewal in its orchid-scented air. Streams meander by peacocks and a flowering hibiscus hedge. There are loggias and covered walks "for exercising beasts." Balconied pavilions tower over the palace roofs, a lotus has just opened in a pool, and high-stepped terraces afford views of the all-important mountains.

THE MYSTIC ISLES OF THE IMMORTALS

In 206 BC Qin Shi Huang Di's incompetent son was murdered and the Han imperial dynasty, which was to last for four centuries, was established. The Han rulers inherited all the pomp and circumstance of Qin Shi Huang Di's reign – including his palaces and his park, with its microcosmic array of rare plants and animals. But when the Han Emperor Wudi (187–140 BC) built a new park he went one better than the first emperor and created habitats for the *Hsien*, or Immortals.

Like Qin Shi Huang Di before him, Wudi longed for eternal youth, and wished to make contact with the Immortals. These magical, fairy-like beings were believed to inhabit the highest points of the highest western mountains (the Himalayas), caverns deep underground and floating islands in the eastern sea. Along the shores of the eastern Isles of the Immortals, which were thought to be supported by turtles, there were pearl- and jewel-bearing trees, and pleasure halls of gold, silver and jade, which, like their denizens, dissolved into mist at the approach of humans. Instead of funding quests for the Immortals, as Qin Shi Huang Di and other rulers had, Wudi invested his considerable resources in the construction of alternative island homes for them. His hope was that on learning of the loveliness of his purpose-built islands, the *Hsien* would fly in on the backs of storks and, maybe, offer him a taste of the elixir of immortality.

Wudi's park was contoured with artificial hills, and the islands in its lakes were planted with exotic flowers, potent herbs and unusual stones. As a further visual aid to the garden's theme, tall sculptures of the *Hsien* held out dew-collecting bowls. In this context, dew symbolized *chi*, or life spirit, the spiritual essence of the universe which rose up to become Heaven and which was the major ingredient of the elixir of immortality. Sadly, the *Hsien* did not appear and Emperor Wudi died of normal old age, but his enchanting lake and island garden did achieve a kind of immortality. Wudi's strategy for attracting the Immortals gave rise to a classic element of the Chinese and Japanese garden. The old

legend survives in the form of pond and island gardens, first conceived in anticipation of a visit from the *Hsien*.

According to the historical chronicles, Wudi's garden contained 2,000 plants, including mandarins, bamboos, gardenias and lychees from the balmy south, for which heated houses were built. Han imperial gardens also benefited from contact with the world beyond China. Under Han rule the empire was extended and new trading routes were set up – including the Silk Road, which followed a chain of oases across central Asia. Out went silk, lacquer and jade, and back came wool, pearls, fur, spices, horses, orchids and rhubarb, as well as Buddhist monks. One who did well out of the boom in trade, a merchant named Yuan Guanhan, indulged himself with an amazing garden. Streams were diverted to flow through his park, where deer, oxen and Tibetan yaks grazed, and tropical parrots screeched overhead. It boasted a rockery mountain 30m (100ft) high and 43 fine halls and terraces, all linked by open galleries. Unfortunately, Yuan Guanhan's extravagance aroused the authorities' suspicions and, along with the emperor's favour, he lost his garden and his head.

PLANTS AND PAPER

The Han emperors sent ambassadors to their military allies and trading partners. One such ambassador, Chang Ch'ien, was instructed to bring back new plants for the imperial garden. In 126 BC he returned from Bactria, after an epic 12-year journey, with both the grape vine (*Vitis vinifera*) and alfalfa (*Medicago sativa*). Some chronicles suggest that Chang Ch'ien's travels took him as far west as the Greek communities of the eastern Mediterranean, so it is possible that he was also responsible for the introduction of other plants such as the cucumber, fig, sesame, pomegranate and walnut, all of which reached China before the 3rd century AD. The tea plant was another new bounty. Although tea-drinking took several more centuries to become a northern Chinese habit, it is first recorded as a feature of life in the south in AD 273.

Along with the new plants and new ideas (which included Buddhism), there were major technological advances in Han times. The wheelbarrow, which would take another millennium to find its place in

Symbolic lotus
The most favoured plants in the Chinese garden are rich in symbolic meaning, as well as literary and philosophical associations. The lotus, which emerges from mud and water to blossom so perfectly in the air above, serves as a living metaphor for the Buddhist soul's emergence from the slough of the material world to the free air of the spirit.

Fragile burden
A street porter, yoked with a variety of potted plants, and captured on paper by an 18th-century European visitor to China. The first Western visitors were astonished by the sophistication of Chinese horticultural practices.

The PEONY

Although the common herbaceous peony, *Paeonia officinalis*, is a European native, named in Greece for Paeon the Healer, we must look to China for the more sophisticated *Paeonia lactiflora* and shrubby tree peony (*Paeonia suffruticosa*), both originally grown for their curative properties. *Paeonia lactiflora* is a native of parts of Mongolia, northern China and eastern Siberia, and has been grown for centuries as a garden flower in China. During the Tang dynasty peonies became popular, and literature about them proliferated. A 1075 treatise by Wang Guan, called *Yangzhou Shaoyao Pu*, described over 30 kinds, with artists commissioned to paint the different varieties.

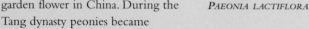

PAEONIA LACTIFLORA

In the 1780s, the French botanist Pierre-Martial Cibot was the first European to give an account of *P. lactiflora*, recommending that it should be grown in rich, moist soil, protected from strong winds. Cibot described the beauty of more than 40 kinds – singles, semi-doubles and doubles of various colours – many grown for cut flowers. In 1863, the explorer Robert Fortune saw fields of this peony along the Grand Canal near Tianjin, where it was grown for the ladies of the city. Today, there are collections in the gardens of the imperial summer palace at Chengde. Although grown in the West by the end of the 18th century, *P. lactiflora* only became freely available to English gardeners after 1808 when it was re-introduced from Canton by Reginald Whitley, a nurseryman in Fulham. During the 19th century, French breeders offered many new varieties, while by 1884, the British nursery Kelways (still specializing in peonies today) was able to offer 250 kinds.

Europe's gardens, was one such advance. A Han invention of even more import was paper. Paper was much easier to handle and store than the bulky bamboo strips it replaced, and it gave a great fillip to the production of encyclopaedias, dictionaries and handbooks. From the start, botany was an important subject: the first edition of an encyclopaedia, the *Erya*, treats of no fewer than 300 plants. More specialist works, such as *Fang Tshao Chuang* (*A Study of Plants and Trees of the Southern Regions*), written at the turn of the 3rd century AD, described the qualities and the horticultural requirements of plants such as *Hibiscus rosa-sinensis*, which, by dint of being pot-grown and seasonal, could be enjoyed in northern gardens. The *Fang Tshao Chuang* also records the recent introduction of two scented jasmines (*Jasminum offiicinale* and *J. sambac*) from faraway Arabia.

After the invention of paper Chinese horticultural literature continued to develop without interruption. Hundreds of new varieties were named in studies which referred to cultivated plants as well as species and recorded the results of hybridization. Trees, fruits, shrubs and herbs were exhaustively catalogued in terms of their ancient symbolic meanings, their ornamental value and their culinary and pharmaceutical applications. But this vast corpus of plant know-how, which was further stimulated by the invention of printing in the late 8th century, did not change the face of China's gardens. As ever, plants in the Chinese garden continued to be valued for their symbolic and moral associations and qualities that reached back to their ancient values as food, medicine and raw materials. It was by these critera that the lotus, the pine, the bamboo and the chrysanthemum were first assured of their places in the Chinese garden. It was no coincidence that the chrysanthemum, which blooms in autumn when everything else is dying off, was esteemed as a life-prolonging herb long before it became a garden ornamental; that the versatile bamboo, which bends but does not break in the storm, symbolized righteousness; or that the pine tree, the essential ingredient of the courtyard garden, was redolent of time.

YIN AND YANG

The language of the traditional Chinese garden has always spoken more of digging cavities for water and piling up rocks than planting. Tellingly, the characters that

Yin and Yang
These rocks in the Liu Yuan, a 16th-century Suzhou garden, represent mountains, the embodiment of the hard masculine quality of Yang. To be complete, a Chinese garden must also include water, representing the complementary but opposite female quality of Yin.

combine to make the Chinese word for landscape (*shanshui*) are mountains and water. The mountains that seem to touch Heaven are likened to the "bones" of the Earth's body, whose "veins" are its watercourses. In the Chinese garden, the universal bone structure of mountains, in the shape of artificial hills and rockeries, and the "blood" of water, in the shape of streams and ponds, interact as complementary opposites, just as the interaction of Yin, the soft female force, and Yang, the hard masculine force, is thought to underpin all natural happenings and all human behaviour.

Every aspect of Chinese civilization is pervaded by the harmonious relationship between these complementary opposites, the Yin and the Yang. In painting the Yin-Yang balance of the universe can be expressed in terms of light and shade; in gardening it is most decidedly expressed by mountains and water, and further developed by such plant contrasts as the delicacy of a blossom and the stark outline of a bough. In the centuries of political disunity and uncertainty that followed the collapse of the Han dynasty in the 3rd century AD, when there was a decline in the construction of great parks, this sense of nature as a balancing act between two opposite but complementary principles was further refined in the smaller and more intimate gardens of the mandarins.

THE SCHOLAR'S GARDEN

From Han times onwards Chinese society was run by mandarins – elite civil servants. Before being appointed to their jobs – as collectors of taxes, commissioners of state projects, supervisors of trade and industry, district magistrates and regional governors – these officials studied the Analects or classic texts of the philosopher

THE GARDEN CITY OF SUZHOU

China's Grand Canal, which was completed in AD 605, linked the city of Suzhou and the fertile lower basin of the Yangzi with the Yellow River system of the north. Suzhou grew so rich from trade in rice, fish and silk that it contributed one-tenth of China's annual tax revenue, but it was equally famous as the home town of a disproportionately high number of successful candidates in the examinations for the imperial service. Having served his time, and amassed a personal fortune, the Suzhou-born mandarin would return home to work on his garden. A private garden of exquisite elegance and refinement was a highly acceptable extravagance in exclusive Suzhou society.

Essential Yin (above)
This "Chinese" garden scene, imagined for an English wallpaper pattern, shows the garden's occupants all but surrounded by water. Europeans were mystified by the prestige of rocks in Chinese design, but the importance of lakes and ponds was better understood. Still water was, after all, a prime component of the landscape garden.

Peace and movement (below)
Nothing disturbs the symphony of light and cloud on the surface of this round pool by Belgian designer Jacques Wirtz. In what might seem a calm and peaceful space, the pattern of the changing sky brings animation and movement to the garden.

Twice the effect (right)
Among the perfections of Les Quatre Vents, the celebrated Quebec garden created by Francis Cabot, is the elegant three-and-a-half storey Pigeonnier – modelled on a traditional French dovecote – which contemplates itself in a long, looking-glass pool.

Tuscan tranquillity (below right)
The calm surface of an old pool at the 17th-century Villa Garzoni, near Lucca in Tuscany, makes an hospitable home to water-lilies. The plants cannot withstand the constant agitation of a fountain spray and will only thrive in still water.

Still waters

Even when they are artificial, water features in the Chinese garden are designed to look and behave like natural bodies of water. This is because, in China, water is redolent of all that is pure and noble. Like the wise man, water follows its own path, seeks its own level, and does what is completely natural. As concentrations of the vital female force of Yin, streams, ponds and lakes are crucial also to the Yin-Yang balancing act – the interplay of mountains and water, light and dark, soft and hard, stillness and motion – which is everywhere to be seen in the Chinese garden.

Although very different ecological and cosmological concerns obtain in the gardens of Islam and the West, still water enjoys a comparable place. It would seem that no garden-making society is immune to the magic of light shimmering on the surface of a canal, to the serenity of a lotus- or lily-filled pool. Even in the dry Zen gardens of Japan, the contemplative, meditative power of water is evoked by "rivers" of stone and "seas" of sand. More prosaically, water is used everywhere to make small spaces seem large and views seem endless.

But not all the benefits deriving from lakes, ponds and canals are ascetic, or philosophical. In endowing their gardens with areas of water, past owners were also thinking of the joys of bathing, boating, fishing and fireworks. The Grand Canal at Versailles was a theatre and playground for the court of Louis XIV of France. In addition to the resident flotilla of small-scale ships and barges – one of which was reserved for the royal orchestra – there were gondolas for the courtiers. A boat ride along the canal with its illuminated banks might follow a walk through the beautifully lit gardens. The gondoliers, brought from Italy, were housed near the canal, at a spot still called Little Venice.

Mirrored arches (above)
The archways and balustrades of a 17th-century pavilion are replicated in the accompanying pool at the Shalimar Bagh in Lahore, Pakistan. Water, and its capacity for reflection, was the all-pervasive theme of the gardens of the Mughal emperors, of which the Shalimar Bagh is the best preserved.

The long view (above)
A sheet of silver, this pool by British designer David Hicks "contains" the endless blankness of the overhead sky.

Imagined pleasures
In the cloud-capped mountains, the Tao hermit (above) hoped to achieve immortality and spiritual purity. Those who could not escape from the everyday world of work and family had to make do with excursions to the countryside, and the microcosmic landscapes contained within their gardens.

Confucius (d.479 BC). Although his philosophy is sometimes described as a religion, Confucius regarded himself as a teacher with a mission to remind men of the best ancient traditions, including reverence towards Heaven and ancestors, the notion of the life-spirit, *chi,* and the complementary forces of Yin and Yang.

According to Confucius, the man who wishes to live according to the will of Heaven must treat others as he would want them to treat him, but he is guided in all his deeds by the duties of four important social relationships: those between father and son, elder brother and younger, husband and wife, friend and friend. The senior member of each of these relationships must be benevolent and the junior member must be respectful and dutiful. In his own lifetime Confucius had little opportunity to see his principles in practice. He was a tutor to the sons of powerful, aristocratic families and wandered between their warring territories, hoping for the conditions in which a more just society could be created.

During interludes of isolation and disappointment, Confucius was consoled by the timeless rhythms of nature and his teachings repeatedly endorsed the landscape – mountains and streams – as a source of life-enhancing, even life-prolonging, joy: "The wise find pleasure in water; the benevolent find pleasure in mountains. The wise are active; the benevolent are tranquil. The wise are joyful; the benevolent are long-lived." (Confucius, *The Analects*, 6.23)

Fortunately for the story of China's gardens, Confucius saw no incompatibility between his rules of right behaviour and the inexpressible mysticism of another ancient sage, Lao Zi (*c.*604–517 BC), the founder of Taoism. The concept of the Tao, or the way, meaning the method or principle that directs the universe, complements the concept of *chi.* The Tao pervades and surrounds everyone and everything in existence, and it is the eternal source of all life and all beauty. It cannot be reduced to a particular rite or action because, like nature, "it acts by not acting", and to become one with it is to lose all fear and uncertainty. By appreciating and even adjusting natural forces and forms in their gardens, without presuming to control or master them, cultivated Chinese gentlemen sought oneness with the Tao.

The contrast between Confucian and Taoist values has been expressed in terms of the contrast between the mandarin's house, with its plain façade and its orderly succession of rooms and courtyards, and the apparent spontaneity of his garden, or *yuan*, with its meandering walkways, rocks, ponds and tree-bowered pavilions. But this alleged duality overlooks the overlapping of the two philosophies in the Chinese garden. The orchid is a case in point. Like the Tao, the subtle but strong scent of the orchid "acted by not acting" but the perfection of its stems and blooms was also a reward for Confucian hard work. Similarly, the banana tree symbolized Confucian self-improvement because of its association with a poor scholar of legend, who resorted to its leaves for paper, but as he sat in his garden in the rain, the Taoist side of this Chinese gentleman-gardener appreciated the pitter-patter of raindrops against the subtropical banana tree's exceptionally large leaves.

In his town garden the mandarin could find peace while still doing his duty. Such gardens were the only landscapes available to the ladies of the household. Restricted in their movements by social convention and, later, the practice of foot-binding, mandarin womenfolk were not free to commune with nature "in the wild". In the miniature garden "universes" of their country villas, intellectuals and officials were safe from the intrigues and dangers of the unstable regimes that followed the collapse of the Han dynasty. Thus, after years of onerous official duties, the poet Dao Yuanming (AD 365–427) returned to the freedom of his country estate:

> I had rescued from wilderness a patch of the Southern Moor
> And, still rustic, I returned to field and garden…
> Long I lived checked by the bars of a cage;
> Now I have returned gain to Nature and Freedom.

Similar scenes show the great scholar-gardener Sima Guang (AD 1019–89) enjoying his garden in the city of Luoyang. Sima Guang's study pavilion was surrounded by *wutong* trees (*Firmiana simplex*), favourite perches of the mythical phoenix. His fishpond was excavated in the shape of a tiger's claw, and he was especially proud of his leafy fisherman's hut, made of trained bamboo trees, which was all his own work. Sima Guang named his garden Du Le Yuan (Garden of Solitary Enjoyment) and wrote of how it refreshed his spirit. When he was weary of his studies he would go to his garden to fish and tend his flowers and herbs, and "let his eyes wander to and fro wherever he pleased".

Domestic affairs

The town gardens of successful mandarins (left), powerful officials and upright family men, were crammed with an astonishing number of buildings. A wealthy household might include pavilions for retired servants, poor relations, lesser wives and concubines, as well as libraries and studies for scholars and family tutors, and rustic huts for sages and poets. With the help of portable charcoal braziers, Chinese garden buildings were versatile spaces. They provided rooms for eating, sleeping and relaxing, for solitude and entertaining, and for composing poetry and meditating, as well as family gatherings.

Philosophical pursuits

The "scholar's hut" was a recognized institution in Chinese gardening tradition. Other pavilions were constructed for more specific intellectual activities such as music, chess and poetry.

BUDDHIST IDYLLS

Late in the 6th century AD, after three and a half centuries of short-lived regimes, unity and prosperity returned to China under the Sui dynasty. At Luoyang on the Yellow River the second Sui emperor, Yangdi, set up his court and spent vast sums on a landscape with "a thousand prospects and a variegated beauty unequalled in the world of men." Sixteen water palaces, each with its own garden, were reflected in the water of its 9.5km- (6-mile) long lake. Along with its microcosmic array of exotic and rare plants, including mature trees, there were islands for the Immortals and spectacular floating machines – giant puppets on boats – which were used for pageants on themes from China's history. A million people were said to have worked on the creation of Yangdi's park, where winter maples were decked with silk leaves and summer lotus blossoms were artificially enhanced. This was the garden that the Japanese envoy Ono no Imoko visited, with so many consequences for the development of Japanese garden-making traditions (see pages 353–54). But it cost far more than Yangdi's subjects were prepared to pay. After he raised taxes he was assassinated and his revenue-devouring park was destroyed.

Yangdi's assassin, Li Yuan, was the first Tang emperor. The success of this dynasty over the next 200 years owed much to China's first and only female Son of Heaven, the redoubtable Empress Wu. She arrived at court as a 14-year-old concubine of the Emperor Tai Tsung. He died in AD 649 but his successor, Kao Tsung, was so deeply in love with her that he allowed her to remain at the palace. When Wu gave birth to Kao Tsung's son and heir she obtained the title of empress. In AD 683, when she had been a dominant figure at court for 30 years, she deposed her own son, and ruled in her own name until, at the age of 82, she was forced to abdicate.

The Empress Wu was a profound believer in Buddhism and an active sponsor of Buddhist monasteries. (In her support, Buddhist monks forged a document which foretold that Maitreya, the future Buddha, would appear in female form.) Towards the end of her reign, Wu acted on her religious convictions by moving the entire court from Changan to an unfenced Buddhist retreat in the forested

A poet's estate
A 16th-century scroll painting, based on an 8th-century original, depicts Wang Chuan, the country villa of the influential Tang poet and artist Wang Wei. Besides the main residence, the estate contained many smaller structures, including balconied pavilions from which the best views could be enjoyed, and "rustic" cottages half-hidden by flowering fruit trees.

mountains of Shensi, 96km (60 miles) to the north. Although the Empress Wu was a unique figure in Chinese history, and her courtiers grumbled about sleeping in grass huts, she was not alone in her yearning for the Buddhist's simple life.

Since the 1st century AD, the Taoist and Confucian philosophies of ancient China had been melding with Buddhism and by the 7th century it was pervading every aspect of Chinese culture. In their mountain retreats, or in city parks, Buddhist monks preserved and created spaces for contemplation, respites from the "world's dust". The Buddhist perception of the oneness of creation complemented the Taoist sense of allegiance with creation, and added to the spiritual dimensions of the Chinese appreciation of nature in general, and plants in particular. (Some Taoists believed that their founder, Lao Zi, had left China for India in the 7th century BC and transformed himself into the historical Buddha.) The great artist Wang Wei (AD 701–761) was a devout Buddhist. He was the originator of a style of painting in which the tonality of ink on silk scrolls expressed depth, texture and atmosphere. In scroll paintings of his country garden – classics of Tang art that were endlessly copied over the years – Wang Wei expressed the Chinese Buddhist's subtle rapture with nature.

LOVE AND DEATH AND THE FALL OF THE TANG

While the artist Wang Wei was a boy, Emperor Xuan Zhong ascended to the throne of Heaven. He was a generous and cultivated lover of art and literature and of his mistress, the exquisite Yang Guifei. For her comfort and delight, and that of her sisters, he adorned the imperial capital at Changan with fabulous gardens and palaces. He is said to have gazed upon Yang Guifei from a secret peephole while she bathed in a marble pool and to have constructed an "island-mountain" of lapis lazuli, around which handmaidens sculled in boats of sandalwood and lacquer. But Changan was always vulnerable to invaders from the west and the northwest and in 755 it was raided by a Tibetan army. Xuan Zhong's generals blamed Yang Guifei for the city's weakness and while the court was in flight they forced him to have her killed.

Pictures of a poem
Wang Wei's famous garden, Wang Chuan, in Shaanxi province in central China was a gentle landscape of lake and forest, hills and streams. Each space cell of the original 8th-century painted scroll focused on a particular aspect or feature of the garden, and corresponded to a verse from Wang Wei's poem on the same subject.

Under the Tang emperors China had prospered. A network of canals was built, printing was invented and all the arts flourished. Chinese civilization spread and left its mark on neighbouring Korea and Japan. But as the economy foundered, and territory was lost, there was a backlash against Buddhism. In 845 all non-Chinese religions were outlawed and rich but unproductive Buddhist monasteries and convents were dispossessed. These measures were to no avail and in 907 the Tang dynasty was in ruins. Next came the period of the Five Dynasties, 50 years when, as one poet lamented, "states rose and fell as candles gutter in the wind". Then, in 960, a new dynasty arose, that of the Song emperors, who were to preside over the golden age of Chinese gardening.

THE IMPREGNABLE MOUNTAIN

The Song dynasty is divided into two periods, the Northern Song and the Southern Song. In the first Northern period (960–1127), the imperial capital was Kaifeng, on the Yellow River. Here, the Song Emperor Zhao Ji, who was a gifted painter, celebrated his passion for nature in a truly astonishing garden. Zhao Ji's garden at Kaifeng accommodated the time-honoured elements of imperial parks. There were islets for the Immortals, flora and fauna from all over the empire, orchards and fields to supply food for the court, "rustic" Taoist-Buddhist enclaves, and so on, but in terms of acres Zhao Ji's garden was not particularly large by previous imperial standards. What was special, and on an unprecedented scale, was the artificial mountain landscape in which his park was set.

This vast assemblage of rocks and rubble was called Gen Yue (the Impregnable Mountain). Its peaks, the highest of which rose more than 60m (200ft) above the surrounding plain, were intercepted with deep and densely planted chasms, and its foothills were laced with ponds and streams and a sluice-gated waterfall. The buildings on Gen Yue's steep slopes – which included a library and a Hall of the Flower with the Green Calyx – were accessed by winding stone steps, and all about there were extraordinary rocks: rocks that appeared to have horns, claws, beaks or noses, rocks that looked like pine trees, rocks whose

Imperial brush strokes
Nothing remains of 12th-century Gen Yue, the great mountain landscape that was the pride and ruin of Zhao Ji. But this painting by the ill-fated Song emperor survives as evidence of his love of nature, and his considerable talent as an artist.

Filial achievement
The Yu Yuan, an elaborate 16th-century Shanghai garden whose name translates as "to please the aged parent". Some of the Yu Yuan's finest rocks are said to have been salvaged from the ruins of Gen Yue.

shapes and textures were suggestive of emotions and ideas, legends and poems. Since Han times the shapes and textures of rocks had mattered a great deal to the Chinese, and curious specimens were highly acceptable as foreign tributes to the emperors. Besides their rich Yang content and their association with the heavenly mountains, rocks were monuments to the Taoist fusion of weather, water and time. In the Song period, this fascination reached fever pitch, and one famous petrophile, the poet and calligrapher Mi Fei, is said to have bowed down before his prize rock every morning, addressing it as "elder brother".

Zhao Ji hired Chu Mien to locate and deliver the finest rocks in the empire. Some came from Lake Tai, near the old city of Suzhou, the source of the most expensive and desirable, waterworn limestones. Other fine rocks were commandeered from the gardens of their owners. Normal traffic on the canals was disrupted by rock-bearing barges. Specimens that suggested human gestures and postures were engraved in gold with their "names" and displayed on the imperial carriageway into the park.

But there was more to Zhao Ji's interest in stones than connoisseurship. Work on Gen Yue had begun after he consulted his *feng shui* (wind and water) experts about his failure to beget a male heir. They had to assess how the currents of *chi* were being affected by the topography and the orientation of his capital. Negative currents were thought to travel in straight lines – hence the evil-deflecting spirit walls at the entrance to Chinese courtyards – and the ideal site for positive currents was south-facing, two-thirds of the way up a hill on dry ground, with lower hills to the east and west, and a pool to contain a reservoir of benevolent water. Since, according to Zhao Ji's *feng shui* practitioners, his capital was too flat and too northeasterly for a man who wanted sons, work began on the more auspicious topography of Gen Yue.

Before long Zhao Ji did have a son, but his garden bankrupted the state. When Kaifeng was overrun by nomads in 1126 the whole court was forced to

FENG SHUI

Feng shui literally means "wind" and "water". Put simply, it is the ancient Chinese art of surveying the "vital spirits" running through a given space. Whether these vital spirits are negative or positive depends on the directional alignment of a site, its rise and fall, its proximity to water and the shape of its dominant features. In *feng shui* terms, the ideal garden is halfway up a south-facing hill, with lesser slopes to the east and west, and a pool at the bottom to act as a reservoir of positive energy. Few traditional Chinese gardens can boast the ideal site, but each one is bounded by a wall, which preserves the positive forces within. Negative currents are thought to travel in straight lines, hence the winding walls and paths, and the evil-deflecting screens just inside a courtyard entrance. Many of the most charming attributes of the Chinese garden began as *feng shui* stratagems.

flee south. Zhao Ji ended his days as a prisoner of the barbarians and the people left behind demolished Gen Yue, resorting to its precious bamboos and trees for fuel.

THE GARDENS OF HANGZHOU

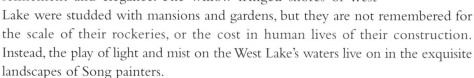

The imperial court now settled in Hangzhou (Hangchow), a city of canals and bridges lying between the mouth of the Zhijiang River and the huge man-made West Lake, with a western and southern hinterland of wooded hills. Here, the emperors of the Southern Song dynasty presided over a society of the utmost refinement and elegance. The willow-fringed shores of West Lake were studded with mansions and gardens, but they are not remembered for the scale of their rockeries, or the cost in human lives of their construction. Instead, the play of light and mist on the West Lake's waters live on in the exquisite landscapes of Song painters.

In China the art of gardening and the art of painting are inseparable. Garden-makers were also painters, as well as scholars, calligraphers and poets. Their works were created and considered with the same eye and the same sense of nature; so the white walls that rise behind the rocks and trees of a garden landscape are directly comparable with the blank silk background of a painted landscape. The Song period of Chinese civilization saw the development of mountain scrolls, paintings in which human figures are dwarfed by their spectacular landscape surrounds. More gently, this sense of the serenity and dignity of nature was evoked in detailed portraits of individual birds and blooms, and quiet riverside and mountain scenes: *Sunset Glow over a Fishing Village*, *Listening to the Wind in the Pine Trees*, *Fine Weather after a Storm in a Lonely Mountain Town*. Long after the fall of the Song dynasty, this tradition of landscape painting was continued in the work of such great masters as Wang Men (d.1385), Wu Chen (c.1354), Huang Kung-wang (d.1354) and Ni Zan (1301–74), who began the Suzhou garden called Shi Zin Lin (The Lion Grove). The gardens of old China had a relationship with Chinese literature and philosophy similar to that of 18th-century European gardens with classical antiquity.

For two- and three-dimensional artists, Hangzhou's setting was, and still is, one of the most inspirational landscapes in the world. Marco Polo, who arrived after it had been ruined by the Mongol army, repeatedly uses the word paradise in connection with West Lake: "And truly a trip on this lake is a much more charming recreation than can be enjoyed on land. For on the one side lies the city in its entire length, so that the spectators in the barges, from the distance at which they stand, take in the whole prospect in its full beauty and grandeur, with its numberless palaces, temples, monasteries and gardens, full of lofty trees, sloping to the shore." Centuries later, in honour of

The unfolding garden
A "moon gate" opening in the wall of a Suzhou garden frames the court beyond and tempts the visitor onwards. The play of light and shadow is more important than strong colour in old Chinese gardens, which are designed to unfold like a painted landscape scroll.

his mother's 60th birthday, Emperor Qian Long (1736–95) reproduced the vistas of Hangzhou in the grounds of Yi He Yuan near Beijing.

NEW GARDENS ON OLD THEMES

The rule of the Song dynasty ended when the Mongol cavalry of Genghis Khan swept over the Great Wall in 1279, but Chinese civilization and Chinese traditions of garden-making were far too well established to be disrupted by the new rulers. The Mongols soon established their own dynasty, the Yuan. Their imperial capital was just inside the Great Wall at Beijing, where, in what was the far north of old China, the climate was familiar and they were close to their steppe homelands.

Kublai Khan, Genghis' grandson, was on the throne when Marco Polo claimed to have visited Beijing. Not surprisingly, for a ruler with nomadic roots, Kublai's imperial park was more green and less rocky than the imperial parks of previous emperors. Whole trees, their native earth still clinging to their roots, were carried to the site by elephants, and transplanted on the shores of an enlarged natural lake, a "sea" whose central island was embellished with lapis lazuli rather than limestone. Marco Polo described it as "intensely green, so that trees and rock alike are as green as green can be and there is no other colour to be seen". Although nothing remains of Kublai's more northerly hunting park at

Essential elements
A 16th-century interpretation of *Peach Blossom Spring* by 8th-century artist Wang Wei. Inspired by the luminous subtlety of Wang Wei's original scroll paintings, generations of Chinese artists focused on the structure and surface textures of landscape features: the crinkles of a mountainside, the shape of a cloud and fissures in a rock.

THE YUAN YE

The classic garden-making treatise of China, the *Yuan Ye* (*Craft of Gardens*) was written between 1631 and 1634 by Ji Cheng, an artist and landscape designer of the Ming period. Its three volumes contain copious detail on the construction of artificial mountains, the design and ornamentation of buildings and walkways, and the selection of rocks and sites. In keeping with the traditional Chinese emphasis on building rather than planting, the *Yuan Ye* makes little mention of growing things. As a painter Ji Cheng appreciated both real landscape and the garden arrangements of rocks, water and bamboo through eyes educated by a thousand years of landscape painting. The garden with its changing light and atmosphere, from dawn to dusk and through the seasons, became a landscape scroll, through which it was possible to stroll as if through a three-dimensional painting.

Meaningful patterns
Chinese-style fencing, according to an 18th-century English carpenter's handbook. The names given to the shape and patterns of traditional Chinese garden features are delightfully revealing. A balustrade can have a "cracked ice" pattern, a pathway can meander like "playing cats", while five pavilions in a group make the claws of a five-toed dragon.

Chemin-fu – the inspiration for the English poet Coleridge's vision of Xanadu – the artificial hill in modern Beijing's central public garden, Beihai Park, is said to date from his reign.

But the empire was not peaceful under the Khans, and in 1368 a new Chinese dynasty, the Ming (meaning brilliant) dynasty, came to power. Although the Ming emperors modelled themselves on the great emperors of the Han, Tang and Song dynasties, they retained Beijing as the imperial capital. They endowed it with the world's most splendid palace, the Forbidden City, and embellished the man-made lakes strung out on its western side with pavilions, trees and rocky "seashores".

Ming times saw a huge expansion of book printing and learning, and of all the arts. It was via the porcelain of Ming China, which was brought to Europe by Dutch traders, that the West had its first glimpses of the land of pagodas and palanquins and peonies. But these tranquil porcelain scenes were not matched by reality, and by the mid-17th century China was once again in turmoil. In 1644 the Ming dynasty was replaced by the Qing (Manchu) dynasty, whose emperors were to rule China until 1911.

STILLNESS IN THE MIDST OF CITY TURMOIL

But while China's imperial dynasties rose and fell, Chinese garden-making ideals continued to be expressed and refined in the private gardens of merchants and mandarins. The benefits of a private garden were explained in the *Yuan Ye*, the classic gardening manual published in 1634: "If one can thus find stillness in the midst of city turmoil, why should one then forego such an easily accessible spot and seek a more distant one? As soon as one has some leisure time then one can go and wander there, hand in hand with a friend." Into these modest spaces, often of not much more than 0.4 hectares (1 acre) in extent, a great resonance of time-honoured meanings and symbols was packed. These illustrated the dictum in *Yuan Ye*: "When you have the real thing within you, it will become real."

Each garden was conceived as a microcosm of the universe whose prime components were, as ever, rocks and water, over which the rhythms of the seasons swept in the form of plants and trees. Contrasts and juxtapositions – high and low, light and dark, narrow corridors yielding to wide spaces – conspired to create the illusion of infinity. The visitor could appreciate these gardens by strolling through a series of vistas, which unfolded like a painted landscape scroll, or by pausing at designated fixed points. Openings in the garden's walled *lang* (walkway) and pavilions served as these fixed viewing points. *Ting*, the Chinese word for pavilion, literally translates as a traveller's resting place, and no garden was complete without one.

Early Western visitors to Chinese gardens were immediately struck by the relatively large number and variety of buildings. These structures were inscribed with carefully chosen names, quotations, and references from the classic poems, paintings and parables, which, in the culture of China's elite, played a role similar to that of the classics of ancient Greece and Rome in Europe.

Contrast and illusion
A quatrefoil opening in the wall of a Suzhou garden frames the composition beyond. Elsewhere, these openings, which are called "leaking windows", may be infilled with designs that enhance the hide-and-seek effect of the garden. By dint of the contrasts between high and low, light and dark – and by using playful, naturalistic designs for paths, palings and plasterwork – a small space is endlessly expanded.

Wang Shizen, a scholar and leading figure of literary and cultural society in Taicang in the 1580s, described his garden, Yan Shan, thus: "Within the garden are three mountain peaks, one mountain range, two Buddhist chapels, five towers, three halls, four studies, one side hall, ten pavilions, one long gallery, two stone bridges, six wooden bridges, five stone walkways, four grottoes, four sets of pools and rapids, and two watercourses for floating wine cups. The various rocky cliffs and rushing streams cannot be counted on one's fingers, and the varieties of bamboos, trees, flowers, and fragrant and medicinal herbs are beyond calculation." In all the garden covered about 7 hectares (17 acres).

Wang Shizen's "watercourses for floating wine cups" are a reminder that Chinese gardens were arenas for parties and festivals as well as "stillness in the midst of city turmoil". Such channels and streams facilitated a popular garden party game. While the competitors were sitting about the garden, composing their verses, cups of wine were sent floating down a nearby stream. Those who had not finished their poems when their cups came floating by had to drink them, with convivial results.

MINIATURE COMPENSATIONS

The pleasures of the garden were not restricted to the wealthy and the leisured. With the aid of small bowl or trough landscapes, known as *peng jing*, the poor and the busy were not starved of "mountains and water". *Peng jing* are the Chinese bonsai, tiny plants grown on their own, or arranged in miniature landscapes of stones and water. Scholars and officials would have *peng jing* gardens on their desks, and they were often placed in the antechambers of temples and public buildings.

The 19th-century writer Shen Fu lived in the garden city of Suzhou. Although he was too poor to own his own garden, he enjoyed designing and tending to those of his friends and relatives: "In laying out gardens, pavilions and meandering paths, layered stone mountains and flowers, try to give the sense of the small in the large and the large in the small, the real in the illusion and the illusion in the real." It saddened Shen Fu greatly that his beloved wife was unable to accompany him on his country walks. She had the idea of building a *peng jing* garden around some pretty yellow pebbles which he had brought back from a visit to the family graves in the mountains. Accordingly, they pounded the least interesting of the pebbles into dust before mixing it with putty and setting the resulting "mountain" mixture into a rectangular dish. They packed an empty corner of the dish with river mud and planted it with duckweed, then, on top of the stones, they planted morning glory. "By the mid-autumn the morning glory had grown all over the mountain, covering it like wisteria hanging from a rock face, and it bloomed a deep red. The white duckweed also flowered and letting our spirits roam among the red and white was like a visit to the Isles of the Immortals."

Shen Fu was distressed when his treasured orchid suddenly died. Then he discovered that a rival orchid-fancier, to whom he had refused a cutting, had poured boiling water over it. Orchids were but one among the many potted flowering objects of the Chinese gentleman-gardener's solicitude and erudition. Peonies and chrysanthemums were grown in pots and arranged artistically along the edges of gardens and terraces, where they could be observed at every stage of development, and enjoyed for their seasonal and literary associations.

The role of plants
Grown in pots and trays – and set out at the edges of terraces and along balustrades – flowers and foliage are accessories rather than prime components of the traditional Chinese garden.

THE GARDEN OF THE MASTER OF THE FISHING NETS

Suzhou's gems
Two views of the 800-year-old Wang Shi Yuan, the sophisticated but supremely rewarding Garden of the Master of the Fishing Nets. It is one of the garden masterpieces for which the city of Suzhou, inland from Shanghai, is famous. Many of the rocks came from Lake Tai, which is not far away.

WANG SHI YUAN IS ONE of the most ancient and famous private gardens in the serene city of Suzhou, which stands about 75km (46 miles) east of Shanghai. Hidden behind high white walls, and no more than half a hectare (1 acre) in area, it is a labyrinthine composition of more than 10 small courtyards, each of which has its own distinctive atmosphere. Some of these courts have been designed to "vanish" around corners, some are open-ended, yet others are closed off as intimate cul-de-sacs.

Everywhere at Wang Shi Yuan there is a play of contrasts – between light and shadow, high and low, and peace and liveliness. At the garden's heart is a lake-like pond of such a skilfully irregular shape that the garden cannot be viewed in its entirety, and this pond is surrounded by reception halls and shaded viewing and resting places.

Wang Shi Yuan has been a garden for 800 years but its name, which translates as the Garden of the Master of the Fishing Nets, dates from the 18th century, when its owner was an official at the court of the garden-loving Qing Emperor Qian Long. The Astor Chinese Garden in the Metropolitan Museum of Art in New York is a faithful reproduction of one of Wang Shi Yuan's exquisite and fascinating courtyards.

YUAN MING YUAN

The Emperor Qian Long (1736–95) was at pains to reconcile his passion for designing landscapes with his desire to avoid the shameful and selfish extravagance of previous emperors. He resisted the temptation to improve and expand the grounds of the imperial Summer Palace outside Beijing until he had mourned his father for a full three years and then he persuaded himself that, strictly speaking, gardens were essential for the moral health of a wise ruler: "Every emperor and ruler, when he has retired from audience, and has finished his public duties, must have a garden in which he may stroll, look around and relax his heart."

It was Qian Long's pious hope that future emperors would be spared the inconvenience and expense of making new gardens because Yuan Ming Yuan (the Garden of Perfect Brightness) was and ever would be the imperial pleasure park *par excellence*. One of the Jesuit priests employed at Qian Long's court, Father Attiret, astonished Europe with his description of Yuan Ming Yuan's intricacies. Within the immense walls of this vast "improved" landscape, which at the time of its greatest extent spread out over 25,000 hectares (60,000 acres), there were mountains, valleys and grottoes, streams, lakes and islands, halls for imperial entertainments, a monumental library, temples, gazebos, rustic farms, miniature hunting parks, reproductions of celebrated southern Chinese vistas, menageries and military drill grounds. According to Attiret, the rocks edging Yuan Ming Yuan's paths were "plac'd with so much Art that you would take it to be the work of Nature" and "in some parts the water is wide, in others narrow; here it serpentizes, and there spreads away, as if it was really pushed off by the Hills and Rocks. The banks are sprinkled with flowers: which rise up even thro' the hollows of the Rockwork, as if they had been produced there naturally."

Ironically, the Yuan Ming Yuan of Qian Long and Father Attiret's day survives in the shape of the curious ruins known as Xi Yang Lou. These, the remains of the marble buildings designed in the European baroque style by the 18th-century emperor's Jesuit servants, are a case of chinoiserie in reverse.

A foreigner's record
The east side of the Palace of the Calm of the Sea, an engraving by the 18th-century Jesuit Giuseppe Castiglione. Yuan Ming Yuan contained more than 200 pavilions and halls, some 30 of which were designed with input from Jesuit architects in the imperial service.

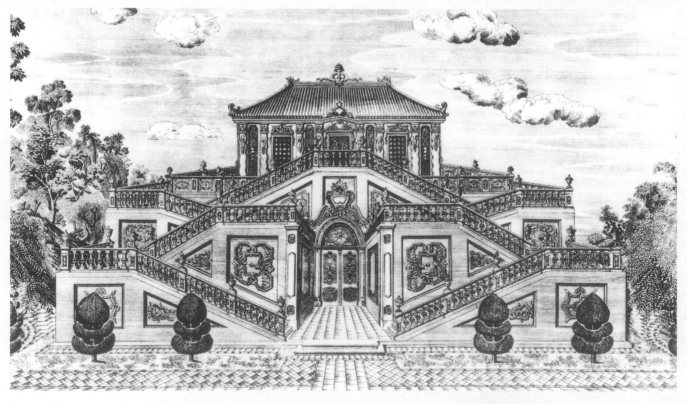

EXCHANGES BETWEEN EAST AND WEST

While mandarins and scholars constructed their garden idylls in the towns and countryside, the Qing emperors pursued rather grander designs. Like the khans, the Qing emperors came to power as warrior conquerors from the north and once a year they made a pilgrimage to their ancestral homelands, stopping over at the magnificent Chengde palace and gardens 240km (150 miles) northwest of Beijing. But they did not change Chinese civilization and their gardens continued to express ancient perceptions of art, beauty and nature. And when, in the mid-18th century, a distinctly foreign influence briefly intruded on a section of a Chinese imperial garden, it was the influence of Versailles, the suitably grandiose pleasure ground of the king of France.

Imperial China only admitted foreigners as subject tribute-bearers, and could not conceive of a superior non-Chinese religion, so the Jesuit priests who penetrated the Qing court had little hope of gaining converts to Christianity. But these sophisticated priests were accepted, and even honoured, as mathematicians, astronomers, cartographers, doctors, engineers and artists.

Father Attiret was one of the Jesuit artists patronized by Emperor Qian Long (1736–95). In letters home, published in 1749, he thrilled European readers with his account of the making of a Chinese garden masterpiece, Yuan Ming Yuan (the Garden of Perfect Brightness, opposite). In fact Yuan Ming Yuan was a complex of gardens, with much of its vast extent taken up by water. Near Beijing, it accommodated all the time-honoured microcosmic components of an imperial park, and in one of its myriad sections there are the ruins of some strange structures. Known as Xi Yang Lou, these are the remains of the Chinese baroque marble follies commissioned by Qian Long from his Jesuit courtiers. Another Jesuit, Father Cibot, who died in Beijing in 1784, studied Chinese horticultural literature and pioneered European understanding of the history and symbolism of plants in the Chinese garden.

European merchants were not as readily accepted as the Jesuits, but in the same period French, British, Dutch and Portuguese were granted extremely

CHINOISERIE AND SHARAWADGI

THE "ENLIGHTENED" ARISTOCRATS and intellectuals of 18th-century Europe were fascinated by Chinese civilization. It was a fascination which led to a fashion for chinoiserie – philosophy and art, ideas and things "in the Chinese manner".

In the homes of the rich this taste was demonstrated by porcelain tea-sets and translations of Confucian and Taoist classics; in gardens it was demonstrated by meandering streams and paths, and elegant bridges, pagodas and pavilions.

The Dutch traveller Jan Nieuhof, travelling in China between 1653 and 1657, reported on the many-storeyed artificial mountains he had seen in Beijing, but most of Europe's early information about the gardens of China was secondhand and impressionistic. Writing in the late 17th century, a period when the grand gardens of Europe were highly mathematical, formal spaces, the English commentator Sir William Temple alleged that the Chinese scorned straight lines and coined the term *sharawadgi* for the asymmetrical, irregular beauty of their garden landscapes.

Scholars are at a loss for the source of Temple's *sharawadgi*, which does not correspond to any Chinese phrase, but, regardless of this fact, the concept somehow struck a chord among influential English garden-makers – notably Stephen Switzer and Alexander Pope. Switzer was the first professional garden designer to translate *sharawadgi* into practicable, naturalistic designs, while in his garden at Twickenham, Pope accommodated Chinese-style principles of "pleasing intricacy" and "artful wildnes".

Decades later, the first detailed eyewitness description of a Chinese garden – Father Attiret's account of Yuan Ming Yuan – was the talk of fashionable Europe. A further interpretation of the principles of Chinese landscape design was put into practice by the architect William Chambers, who had visited Guangzhou (Canton) in his youth. Among the buildings Chambers designed for the garden of George III at Kew was a 10-storeyed Chinese pagoda, and in 1772 he published a celebrated *Dissertation on Oriental Gardening*.

By this time, the Landscape Movement had become so dominant in England that, in promoting his understanding of Chinese garden-making principles, Chambers was arguing against the rolling emptiness of the landscape garden and was in favour of a return to diversity and formal complexity. It was his contention that, far from scorning straight lines and formal structures, as Temple and others had alleged, the Chinese had no "aversion to regular geometrical figures".

In Germany and France, Chambers' designs were taken up more enthusiastically than they were in England. The Chinese House in the grounds of the Prussian palace of Sanssouci (see page 220), for example, was originally surrounded by a formally laid-out garden. By the late 18th century chinoiserie-fanciers were the objects of satire, and the Anglo-Irish writer Oliver Goldsmith wrote of an imaginary mandarin's astonishment at the purported origin of a fashionable aristocrat's pavilion summerhouse.

Chinoiserie never amounted to much more than winding paths and pretty pavilions. Unlike the moss, scroll and Zen Buddhist gardens of Japan, which were reproduced as entities in the 19th- and 20th-century gardens of Europe and North America, the Chinese garden as an entity was not translated in the 18th-century gardens of Europe.

The finer details
A Chinese temple, fit for a late 18th-century German garden (left). Fanciful Chinese-style buildings and features first became popular in England, where the landscape garden provided a suitable setting, but the fashion for chinoiserie lasted longer in Continental Europe.

Das chinesissche Lusthaus in Laxenburg.   Le Pavillon chinois à Laxenbourg

Wien, bey Artaria u. Comp.

Chinese style abroad

A little piece of China enlivens Vienna's Laxenberg Gardens (above), while a French catalogue (right) offers a selection of "Anglo-Chinois" temple designs. These two designs appeared in *Jardins Anglo-Chinois à la Mode* by George Louis le Rouge, published c.1776. In Europe, pattern books abounded, their pages filled with plans and ideas for all manner of oriental buildings, bridges and gates. The vogue for chinoiserie was no less evident indoors, where Chinese-inspired wallpaper, carpets and chairs furnished the rooms of the fashionable house.

Landmark pagoda

In 1757 the Prince of Wales, later to become George III, commissioned William Chambers to landscape the royal gardens at Kew. Chambers subsequently published the designs of his "eye-catchers", notably the spectacular pagoda that still stands as a monument to chinoiserie.

Temples Chinois.

Modules pour   l'Attique

limited trading facilities. Given the insatiable demand in 18th-century Europe for Chinese silk, tea, cotton and porcelain, these facilities were barely adequate. Chinese people were forbidden to teach their language to foreigners, and trading tariffs were not fixed, which encouraged bribery and corruption. By sending embassies to Beijing, the Europeans began the lengthy process of forcing China to do business with them on more favourable terms.

In 1782 the first official British embassy to China was led by Lord Macartney. He was an aficionado of the Landscape Movement in his own country, and his response to the imperial gardens was enthusiastic: "There is no beauty of distribution, no feature of amenity, no reach of fancy, which embellishes our pleasure grounds in England that is not to be found here. Had China been accessible to Mr Brown or Mr Hamilton, I should have sworn they should have drawn their happiest ideas from the rich sources, which I have tasted this day." Lord Macartney was accompanied by the Irish plant collector Sir George Staunton and two botanists. They brought back more than 200 plant specimens, including the evergreen climbing rose *Rosa bracteata* and the herbaceous perennial *Macleaya cordata*. Twenty-five years later, *Rosa banksiae*, named for Lady Banks, was procured by William Kerr from a Canton garden. Kerr introduced a number of other good plants, including kerrias and the tiger lily, *Lilium lancifolium*.

By the mid-19th century, more Westerners were travelling within China, seeking mineral resources, surveying railways and searching for new flora. Robert Fortune, collecting for the Royal Horticultural Society, brought back the first "Japanese" anemone, the first forsythia, weigela, winter-flowering honeysuckles and three viburnums. (The epithet Japanese or *japonicum* was often applied to plants actually first collected and brought to Europe from China.) Fortune's plant-hunting forays in both China and Japan are said to have resulted in the intro-

Lakeside folly
This extraordinary marble paddle-ship was built in 1889 as a tea house for the equally extraordinary Dowager Empress Cixi with funds intended for China's navy.

duction of more than 120 new garden species, so that "all Europe was obliged to him". But plant hunters were the least threatening of China's foreign explorers and travellers. Far more ominous, from the Chinese government's point of view, were the activities of British traders, who were selling opium produced in India in exchange for Chinese silks, spices and teas.

In the Opium War of 1839–42, Britain crushed an imperial attempt to stop the opium trade in Canton, then the only point of contact between China and Western finance. The resulting Treaty of Nanking was the first of a series of "unequal agreements" that legalized the opium trade and granted trade and territorial rights to Western powers. China was now opened up to Western exploitation. The civilization that had lasted for thousands of years was weak in the face of European industrial and military might, and the imperial gardens of Yuan Ming Yuan were among the first casualties. In 1860 much of Qian Long's visionary landscape – its pavilions and porticoes and fountains and trees – was put to the torch by combined British and French forces in reprisal for the torture and execution of Western hostages seized under a flag of truce.

Yi He Yuan

Six years later, the Dowager Empress Cixi, who was the effective ruler of China from 1884 until 1908, restored a section of Yuan Ming Yuan and renamed it Yi He Yuan (Garden of Happy Harmony) as an indication of her peace-making intentions. Cixi was an able and tough-minded ruler, but she was also greedy, corrupt and ruthless, and she used her power as the emperor's mother to block reform and modernization in China. In 1887 she celebrated her 60th birthday by commissioning further work at Yi He Yuan, including a theatre stage, a mile-long *lang* or walkway and a marble tea house in the shape of a paddle ship. But the money Cixi lavished on her birthday garden had been intended for the modernization of China's navy. She obtained it on the pretext of developing Yi He Yuan as the site of a new naval academy, which would use the lake for training exercises. Among her progressive subjects it was a bitter joke that the only modern boat in China was made of marble.

Today, this marble boat is enjoyed by hundreds of tourists and ordinary citizens of the People's Republic of China, and though another century may pass before the Dragon Empress is remembered with the same affection as, say, Queen Victoria, her Garden of Happy Harmony is maintained as a treasured national park.

Royal prerogative
The Dowager Empress Cixi, of whom a courtier once remarked: "It was characteristic of Her Majesty to experience a keen sense of enjoyment at the trouble of other people." Cixi also experienced a keen sense of enjoyment in her gardens, and had a railway built so that she could move easily between the various imperial pavilions.

CHAPTER ELEVEN

JAPANESE STYLE

Symbolism and restraint

THE JAPANESE GARDEN is a unique achievement, of major importance and influence in the West. More than any other people, the Japanese have succeeded in endowing the art of garden-making with transcendental meaning. They have never perceived nature as something "other" and apart, and this sense of the oneness of creation is a consistent theme in the story of their inspirational gardens.

It is a story that cannot be told as a sequence of aesthetic and religious shifts because in Japan the ancient and the old have ways of coexisting and blending with the new. The great gardens of Japan have a timeless quality, and it is possible to describe them in the past and present tense. The story opens with "the way of the gods", the ancient Shinto nature spirits whose shrines were Japan's first holy places. Then there are Chinese episodes, for the gardens of Japan's golden Heian age could not be understood without reference to the influence of Chinese civilization and the impact of Buddhism. But in Japan the triumph of imported values and teachings did not spell defeat for native traditions. Often, the holy places of Shinto times took on an extra Buddhist significance, while the Shinto consciousness of nature was further refined in the serene economy of the Zen garden. More than any other expression of the native genius for garden-making, the Zen garden exemplifies the Japanese trust that the cultivation of beauty is a profoundly spiritual business.

Winter's mantle
Kenroku-en Park under snow. Originally the private garden of a powerful clan, Kanazawa's famous park was first opened to the public in 1871. The name Kenroku translates as "combined six" and refers to the classic virtues of the perfect garden: seclusion, spaciousness, artificiality, antiquity, plentiful water and wide views. One of the park's distinctly Japanese attributes is its all-seasonality: its beauty does not depend on the flowering habits of plants.

THE ESSENCE OF THE JAPANESE GARDEN

To Western eyes the Japanese garden, whether it is the pond-and-island garden, with rocks and tightly clipped evergreen shrubs, the tea garden, the estate stroll garden, or the almost plantless dry Zen Buddhist garden of rocks and raked gravel, has an immediate "look". Since the late 19th century this look, or style, has been emulated in gardens all over Europe and North America, but, for all their charms, most of these Japanese-style gardens are a far cry from the real thing. This is because the ethos, as opposed to the look, of a true Japanese garden cannot be reproduced in terms of strict pruning, fewer plants and interesting ways with sand, gravel and stones.

Compared with Western gardeners, the Japanese are strict and comprehensive pruners. Although this results in less seasonal flower, the moulded pruning of evergreen shrubs and small trees in Japan imparts a greater sense of control. Another obvious contribution to the look of a Japanese garden is the use of a relatively small range of plants within each garden, even though Japan is rich in native flora. There is no emphasis on plant collecting or rarity in Japan. The Japanese gardener is an artist rather than a horticulturist. Each stone or plant is chosen for its contribution to the whole design, rather than its individual merit, and the whole is impeccably maintained. Leaves are swept up, gravel and sand raked or brushed, plants are manicured and trees are pruned in the interests of order, control and restraint: key components of the country's gardening ethos.

Outside Japan, modern garden design takes account of ideas, techniques and philosophies from different periods of history and different civilizations, including Japanese history and civilization. But Japanese garden design remains a distillation of Japanese history and religion. In Japan, as in no other society, the relationship between people and nature is profoundly spiritual, and garden-making is much more than a horticultural business. Deriving from Shinto – the country's most ancient religion – as well the teachings and practices of Buddhism, this ethos informs every aspect of Japanese garden-making.

For all their serenity and simplicity, and apparent timelessness, the gardens of Japan are as contrived as the formal gardens of 16th- and 17th-century Europe. But the formal structure of the Japanese garden cannot be understood in terms of geometric symmetry. Japanese gardens are essentially ungeometric, without straight lines, axes and alignments, and their very asymmetry is the result of careful placement of the main ingredients: stone, water and plants. Each of these ingredients is freighted with symbolic meanings, an understanding of which enriches not only our appreciation of Japanese garden design, but also deepens our understanding of garden meanings in general.

STONES AND WATER

There is a great deal more to the role of stones in the Japanese garden than meets the casual eye. Ancient rocks have always been esteemed in Japan: their presence in gardens can be compared with the presence of maturing trees in European landscapes. Traditionally,

Precise art
Trees and shrubs are so tightly pruned that they appear to have been moulded. As evergreen "boulders", "clouds" and "waves", they frame vistas and contribute to the formal structure of the Japanese garden.

the most coveted stones have been *sabi*, stones with a patina of age acquired through years of exposure to the elements. For the early gardens of Kyoto, stones were collected from nearby streams and hillsides, but by the 17th century vast sums were being spent on the collection of famous stones from old gardens, as well as natural sites, and stones for the gardens of the later capital of Edo (modern Tokyo) had to come from long distances. Finally, in the 19th century, such phenomenal prices were being paid for *sabi* that a government edict limited the sum payable for a single specimen.

Although individual rocks and groups of rocks may be treated as sculptures, their placement is as crucial to the intended effect as size and shape. In the first Japanese garden design book, the 11th-century *Sakuteiki* (*Treatise on Garden-making*), there are no fewer than 17 taboos related to stone setting, the most enduring of which is the requirement that stones brought into the garden should be set in the same orienta-

The path to follow

The shady entrance to the Zen Buddhist temple complex of Daitoku-ji, the precincts of which include two of Japan's garden jewels: the dry landscape of Daisen-in and the exquisite maples of Koto-in. The entrance ways to Japanese gardens give little indication of the interior.

Spiritual arrangement

The size, shape, texture and placement of rocks is a time-honoured preoccupation of the Japanese garden designer. This 20th-century arrangement, laid out by Shigemori Mirei in the spirit, if not according to the letter, of the 11th-century book *Sakuteiki*, enlivens the grounds of the medieval monastery of Tofuku-ji in Kyoto.

Petalled clouds

The spectacular spring show put on by Ueno-koen's cherry trees is captured in this early 20th-century, hand-tinted photograph. Tokyo's Ueno Park is still a popular venue for traditional *hanami* (blossom viewing). The blossom-viewing season begins with plum in February, and is followed by peach in March, and cherry in April.

tion in which they were found. Tall upright rocks are dynamic, echoing the shapes of native trees, while smooth, rounded rocks convey a sense of peace and quiet. To give the illusion of a truly enormous boulder arising from the ground, large rocks may be buried to as much as 70 per cent of their volume.

In lakes and ponds, rocks in the shape of cranes and turtles serve to evoke the Mystic Isles of the Immortals of Chinese mythology (see page 322), towards which convoys of "boat" stones, called *yo-domari* or night mooring stones, sail. Groupings of stones may represent the natural Japanese landscape of mountains and cliffs, or boulders washed by ocean waves. Pebbles of white quartz or white sand, used from the earliest times to mark out the sacred or ceremonial area in front of Shinto shrines and imperial residences, are used in Zen gardens to symbolize waves. Since the Zen garden is first and foremost a place for meditation, the ancient Shinto status of rocks and sand or gravel is further enriched by their qualities as objects of contemplation.

Although pollution and a shortage of space are problems in today's Japanese cities, the country's high rainfall and humidity means that Japanese garden-making traditions are generous with water. Some garden ponds are modelled on natural bodies of water, or celebrated stretches of coastline; some are cloud- or gourd-shaped; in other cases their flowing shapes are adapted from calligraphic renderings of the Chinese characters for water and spirit. Even when there is no actual water, artful arrangements of rocks produce dry cascades, to give the illusion that the flow of water has only just stopped, or is about to begin.

FESTIVALS OF FLOWER AND FOLIAGE

The Japanese love of nature is renowned, and it is hardly surprising given the country's spectacular landscapes. The islands of Japan boast richly forested mountains, laced with tumbling streams and shrouded in drifting mist, and magnificent meandering coastlines of steep cliffs and sandy bays. The long, slow springs are heralded by a progression of plum and cherry blossom, whose flowering is the occasion for festivals and entertainments. The autumns that follow the hot, humid summers – and the monsoons of June and July – are enriched with gold and crimson foliage from deciduous trees, such as maples and katsuras (*Cercidiphyllum japonicum*), while the darker evergreen woods, often of Japanese cedars (*Cryptomeria japonica*), glow with flowering sasanqua camellias and scented osmanthus.

To complement garden rock shapes, plants are clipped into tight rounded forms to evoke the idea of mountains, clouds and ocean waves – the background to the natural Japanese landscape – their sinuous outlines suggesting continual movement. Occasionally, they are clipped into square blocks to provide precise silhouettes, even if this restricts the flowering of favourites such as azaleas. Except for the seasonal flowering of the traditional trees and shrubs, the Japanese garden looks the same in winter as in summer, the stones and strong evergreen shapes creating a framework. Most of the traditionally favoured plants are natives – pines, plums, cherries, maples, camellias, azaleas and bamboo used for decorative fencing or trellis – still found in the secondary forests. But the plum, or Japanese apricot (*Prunus mume*), which heralds spring and rejuvenation, originally came from China. The coastal, sea-contorted black pine, *Pinus thunbergii*, represents coastal scenery, while the red pine, *Pinus densiflora*, represents hillside forests. Pine trees also represent longevity and permanence.

Pines can be trained into arched shapes to give the appearance of great age, specialist hand-pruning achieving the desired effects. The Japanese apricot is also heavily cut back, or pollarded, to produce new shoots on a thick, gnarled trunk. By contrast, the cherry, imported from the mountains for its flowering beauty and much celebrated in Japanese poetry and art, has always been allowed to grow into its natural shape. Sasanqua camellias, flowering in autumn, carpet the ground with their petals. Japanese maples, in particular the low and fine-leaved *Acer palmatum*, create light shade. In spring their leaves are translucent; in autumn they present a spectacle of scarlet and crimson to rival the colours of the eastern American fall.

Among the most popular evergreens are the Japanese cedar; osmanthus, with its sweet autumn scent; spring-flowering cleyera; and hollies and bamboos. Traditional flowering trees and shrubs include deciduous wisteria, magnolias, katsuras and, a fountain of pale yellow in spring, kerrias. Few herbaceous plants feature in traditional garden design, but, as in China, cultivated peonies and chrysanthemums are grown for show in pots and displayed on special stands, sheltered from sun and rain. Autumn leaves, especially maple leaves, and flower petals, especially cherry and camellia, are sometimes left on garden moss or grass as a decorative effect.

When the Japanese select garden plants, they consider the principle of *shakkei*, or borrowed scenery, to be of the utmost importance. By planting smaller trees at the perimeter of a garden and larger ones nearer the centre, an illusion of distance is created and views beyond the boundaries of the garden are framed within it. Another major factor in the story of Japan's gardens is housing. While the winters in Japan are mild, the summers are hot and humid, and houses are designed to cope with summer's discomforts. They tend to be better ventilated than they are insulated, and more open and outward-looking than

Cherished symbol
Golden chrysanthemums stand for the brilliance of autumn on this fan, a colour print made from wood blocks, *c.*1843–47, for the *Fashionable Flower Arrangements of the Four Seasons* series by Utagawa Hiroshige (1797–1858). In Japan, autumn is the season of the chrysanthemum – the country's national flower, it has long been an object of affection and celebration. The 11th-century romance *Genji Monogatari* (*The Tale of Genji*) mentions blooming chrysanthemums, "whose sweet perfume soothed us with its gentle influence".

Outside-in
As this old Kyoto garden shows, the boundary between inside and outside is fluid in traditional Japanese architecture, which is almost without walls. Movable screens, bamboo blinds and sliding doors mean that, in the stifling summers, every advantage can be taken from the cooling breeze and refreshing view.

Western homes, which leads to a much greater harmony between the inside and the outside.

SACRED LANDSCAPES

The Japanese veneration of nature dates back to Shinto times, when the *kami*, or spirits, which were believed to reside in mountains, trees, streams, rocks and sea, blended with the spirits of departed ancestors, and played an important part in the affairs of living humans. Exceptionally old trees and exceptionally shaped or sized boulders, inland or by the seashore, were set aside by the farming and fishing communities of ancient Japan as places for prayer and sacred rituals. Venerable stones were left in their natural sites within a roped enclosure, but others were set upright, or placed in ponds as islands, and natural pond settings were deepened and widened so that the stones stood out as island shrines.

The most important Shinto goddess is Amaterasu, Goddess of the Sun and mythical ancestress of Japan's emperors. A Shinto myth tells of Amaterasu's search for a site for a shrine. She found it at Ise, on Honshu's eastern coast, near where the Lord of Garden Making had started a garden in which he grew useful plants for food, medicine and dyes. Even today this is the most holy spot in Japan. A simple wooden building stands in an unspoilt forest, with gravel walks wandering among the great trees, allowing glimpses of hills and distant water. At such Shinto sites, trees are intermediaries between people and gods, and venerable trees are girdled by purifying ropes called *shimenawa*. The Japanese word for forest, *mori*, also means a place to which gods descend – a shrine without a building.

The shrines of Japan's Shinto gods cannot be said to have played a direct part in the story of gardening because they have never been perceived, or accessed, as pleasure gardens. Nevertheless, the practice of marking out a sacred spot with white sand or gravel began with the making of Shinto shrines, and, from the end of the 6th century, the ancient appreciation of landscape and natural forms was overlaid and complemented by Buddhist sensibilities.

THE INFLUENCE OF TANG CHINA

Traditionally, Buddhism is held to have entered Japan around 550, but it was during the regency of Prince Shotuki Taishi (574–622) that the new religion took root as part of the fabric of Japanese official life. Prince Shotuki was a young man when he began his mission to disseminate Buddhism and build a Japanese state along Chinese lines. In Prince Shotuki's Japan, Buddhism and the civilization of Tang China went hand-in-hand. The Chinese script, Chinese systems of medicine, astronomy, taxation and administration, Confucian and Taoist philosophy, and Chinese styles of architecture and garden-making permeated Japan in the 6th and 7th centuries.

Ono no Imoko was an imperial envoy to the Chinese court who returned to Japan in 607 with a delegation of Chinese scholars and experts. It is said that the Chinese emperor, Yangdi, was not too pleased at being addressed as an equal by the emperor of Japan in Ono no Imoko's letter of introduction: "The Emperor of the sunrise country writes to the Emperor of the sunset country." (The Japanese call their country Nippon, or Origin in the Sun. Indeed, Shinto's sacred emblems are the jewel, the sword and the mirror, in which the sun's rays can be caught to keep the land prosperous.) While in China, Ono no Imoko was impressed by Yangdi's magnificent garden (see page 330), which was then a work in progress

Sacred shrine
Nikko's recorded history as a sacred site stretches back to the 8th century. This well, in the grounds of one of its shrines, is adorned with the strips of white paper known as *gohei*. Shinto shrines are kept scrupulously clean, and worshippers purify themselves by washing their hands and rinsing their mouths.

Chrysanthemum party
The great 19th-century artist Hokusai Katsushika (1760–1849) captures the somewhat sedate enthusiasm of the ladies of the imperial court as they sally forth to view chrysanthemums. For centuries the chrysanthemum festival, held on 9 September, has been an occasion for poetry and outings, and it is still one of Japan's five important national festivals.

involving a million labourers. Such projects displayed the power and added to the prestige of China's government, and acted as models for Japan's ruling elite. In 710 Japan's first permanent capital, the city of Nara, was constructed along Tang Chinese lines.

The palaces, mansions and temples of Nara were linked by broad avenues and set in beautiful gardens. Although little trace of these gardens remains, surviving landscape paintings and poems show that they were closely modelled on the gardens of the Tang Chinese capital of Changan. The gardens of Nara noblemen were naturalistic and always included areas of water with islands and rock groupings. Pleasure barges modelled on dragons or phoenix heads provided amusement on garden lakes. An 8th-century anthology of poems entitled *Man'yoshu* describes the mandarin ducks and the white pieris blossom in the pond-and-island garden of the scholar nobleman Soga no Umako. One poem mourns the untimely death of Prince Kusakabe, a young protégé of Soga's: "Around the island boulders, now that you are gone, grows grass that was not there when you were here," and, "Will we see again the azalea-flooded path by the boulder-bordered flowing of the pond." Other verses celebrate the sparkle of a lake's waters, the reflection of a rock, the green of young willows and the fragrance of wisteria.

In keeping with his personal commitment to Buddhism, Prince Shotuku founded important temples, including the five-storeyed Horyuji Temple in Nara. But he saw no incompatibility between his favouring of Buddhism and his continuing support for Shinto beliefs and rituals. Buddhism is not a jealous religion. In Japan, as elsewhere, it did not require its adherents to reject their old deities, provided they gave the place of honour to the Buddha. Often, the Shinto mountain shrines took on an added Buddhist significance, and so sacred pilgrimages could combine. However, temple-building thrived at the expense of tomb-building and, by the close of the 8th century, Buddhism was such a powerful presence in Japanese society that a Buddhist priest, Dokyo, tried to seize the imperial throne. This danger led to the imperial court's decision, in 794, to leave Nara and start again in a new capital.

THE CAPITAL OF PEACE AND TRANQUILLITY

The new imperial capital was named Heian-kyo, which means the capital of peace and tranquillity, but it is better known as Kyoto. Before work commenced on a new imperial palace, geomancers cleared Kyoto as an auspicious site, and the deities of the imperial tombs and the major Shinto shrines were notified. Like Nara, Kyoto was laid out on a chequerboard pattern. It was, and is, a city on two rivers, surrounded on three sides by verdant hills, with the high peak of Mount Hiei to the northeast.

There was not enough space within the first imperial enclosure at Kyoto for a garden, but within a few years of the court's relocation a large lake-and-island park, Shinsen-in (Divine Spring Garden) was laid out. The emperor's new pleasure park covered just over 13 hectares (33 acres) and its attractions included a pavilion, low hills, and maple, willow and cherry trees. According to a contemporary admirer: "One cannot look at this garden long enough, for its beauties are

ineffable…darkness always seems to drive one home before one is ready." Except for a pool located deep in the old part of Kyoto, nothing now remains of Shinsen-in, but Saga-in, an imperial country estate of the same period, and of a similar layout and style, has survived better.

In 823 the Emperor Saga, who hosted the first imperial cherry-blossom viewing parties, retired to Saga-in. On its site, on the shores of a small lake called Osawa-no-ike, a Buddhist temple, known as Daikaku-ji, now stands amid flowering cherries and graceful maples. When Osawa-no-ike was emptied for repairs and conservation in the 20th century, the eminent landscape designer Shigemori Mirei had an opportunity to study it. He found that over the years the water level had been raised, reducing the size of the islands, and that the remaining rocky islet was one of five flat stones arranged in a straight line. The original bottom of Osawa-no-ike was made watertight by small stones tightly packed with clay. Typically for the period, the lake was created by damming a mountain stream. Rocks forming the foundations of a cascade that eventually fed into Osawa-no-ike still survive.

For the next millennium Kyoto was the imperial capital of Japan, but the emperors' power was increasingly nominal and ceremonial. Between 866 and 1160 the real powers in the land were members of the Fujiwara family, who intermarried with the imperial family, and controlled all the important political appointments. But the imperial court's loss, in terms of political and military

Saga's retreat

The 9th-century Emperor Saga is said to have hosted the first imperial cherry-blossom viewing parties at his country garden, Saga-in. The precincts of Daikaku-ji (shown here), a Buddhist foundation in Kyoto, contain the pond called Osawa-no-ike, all that remains of the Tang Chinese-style garden to which the Emperor Saga retired in AD 823.

THE TALE BEHIND THE STORYTELLER

The author of *Genji Monogatari* (*The Tale of Genji*) is known as Murasaki Shikibu, but the first of those names is that of a character in her book and the second is the title of her father's official position at the imperial court. Although Murasaki's real name is a mystery, it is known that she was born into a minor branch of the powerful Fujiwara family, who virtually ruled Japan between 866 and 1160. In about 1000 she married an officer of the imperial guard, but he died a couple of years afterwards, leaving her with a baby daughter. Through her father's influence she was made a lady-in-waiting to the teenage Empress Akiko – indeed, her short reign provides the historical background of *Genji Monogatari*.

power, was art and culture's gain. The Heian period (794–1185) is celebrated as a golden age of Japanese civilization. Gardens were a component of the Heian achievement. The cultivated, pleasure-loving aristocrats of Kyoto developed gardens as an art form and an extension of the poetry that was an integral part of court life. Excursions to the hills surrounding Kyoto, from which the courtiers brought back wild flowers to plant in the gardens, were important rituals of Heian high society.

Although the gardens of the Heian golden age do not survive in their original form, their character is revealed in the literature and paintings of the period. This literature includes the 11th-century masterpiece *Genji Monogatari* (*The Tale of Genji*), written by Murasaki Shikibu, a lady-in-waiting at the imperial court. Twice as long as *War and Peace*, Murasaki's classic blockbuster is the story of a young prince – his life, his loves, his travels, his efforts to acquire an education – and it closely reflects and recreates the Heian court life that Lady Murasaki knew.

A more practical source of knowledge about Heian gardens is the *Sakuteiki*, the oldest text on Japanese garden design. The *Sakuteiki* was written at the close of the 11th century by another courtier, Tachibana no Toshitsuna. The *Sakuteiki* contains copious advice on the design and maintenance of gardens, much of which is as relevant and practical today as it was a thousand years ago. It also reveals how, since Nara's heyday, garden design had moved on from its concern to reproduce Tang Chinese models to becoming a distinctively Japanese art. As ever, nature is the garden-maker's prime inspiration, but instead of simply miniaturizing nature, in the Tang Chinese fashion, the Heian aristocracy idealized nature. And, rather than reproduce the jagged crags of the Chinese landscape, they imitated the more gentle contours of their own landscapes.

Again, while the *Sakuteiki* accepts the Chinese principles of *feng shui* (see page 333), it offers Japanese adaptations. Trees are suggested as substitutes for the essential elements demanded by classic Chinese *feng shui*: nine willows for a river, nine Judas trees for a pond, seven maples for the highway, three cypresses for a hill, and so on. Besides these recommendations, and a great deal of information about the placement of stones and the direction of watercourses, with all due attention to myriad aesthetic, religious and practical considerations, the *Sakuteiki* details the layout of Heian noblemen's estates.

The mansion of the Heian aristocrat was constructed in a style known as *shinden*. It consisted of a set of pavilions, for his wives and members of his retinue, connected by outdoor corridors. The Kyoto grid system allowed a standard plot of about 120 sq m (140 sq yd) for an aristocrat, with larger areas at the disposal of persons of higher rank. Between the pavilions were small courtyard gardens known as *tsubo*. With space at such a premium, nature had to be miniaturized in these little gardens. They were covered with sand or moss, and planted with stones and flowering trees and shrubs, according to their owners' fancies. If a *tsubo* featured wisteria, that flower might occur as a decorative motif, stencilled on screens or embroidered on curtains, in the pavilion looking onto it. *The Tale of Genji* features a Lady Fuji-Tsubo, or She of the Wisteria Chamber. The main garden of a noble household was beyond the open space immediately to the front

The secluded garden
This painted screen, from Japan's 17th-century Edo period, shows a lovers' rendezvous on the veranda of a pavilion overlooking a garden. The mansions of Heian aristocrats contained many separate pavilions, each facing out on to its own *tsubo*, or garden unit, planted according to the occupant's taste.

of the main pavilion. This front space was covered with white sand and used as an arena for entertainments or, in the case of imperial palaces, ceremonies and official functions. The empty front courtyard, spread with white sand or gravel, was a mark of the emperor's purity and sacred status. (In the modern imperial palace at Kyoto, dating from 1855, there are two vast gravelled spaces in front of the main ceremonial halls.) The open space might be framed by a few trees to its left and right, but the landscaping of streams and hillocks was confined to areas beyond it. In imperial villas not used for state functions, these restrictions did not apply. Their gardens were reproductions of natural scenery, as can still be seen in the Shugaku-in and Katsura gardens (see page 371).

FROM KYOTO TO KAMAKURA

The Heian period in Kyoto lasted for over 350 years, reaching a pinnacle of rich cultural development in the 11th and 12th centuries. After 894 there were no more official embassies to the declining Tang Chinese empire. In the following centuries of isolation, as Chinese influence waned, a distinctively Japanese culture blossomed. Architectural styles, like gardening styles, became less flamboyant and

THE GARDENS OF PRINCE GENJI

THE GARDENS OF THE HEIAN GOLDEN AGE are brought to life in Murasaki's *The Tale of Genji*. The hero of her story is Prince Genji, of whose palace she writes: "He effected great improvement in the appearance of the grounds by a judicious handling of knoll and lake, for though such features were already there in abundance, he found it necessary here to cut away a slope, there to dam a stream, that each occupant of the various quarters might look out of her windows upon such a prospect that pleased her best. To the southeast he raised the level of the ground, and on this bank planted a profusion of early flowering trees. At the foot of this slope the lake curved with especial beauty, and in the foreground, just beneath the windows, he planted borders of cinquefoil, of red plum, cherry, wisteria, kerria, rock azalea, and other such plants as are at their best in springtime; for he knew that Murasaki [the mysterious author of *The Tale of Genji* is named after her hero's favourite] was in especial a lover of spring; while here and there, in places where they could not obstruct his main plan, autumn beds were cleverly interwoven with the rest."

To reach the spring-flowering islands visible from Murasaki's garden, Genji resorts to Chinese-style pleasure boats, "first rowing along the Southern Lake, then passing through a narrow channel straight towards a toy mountain which seemed to bar all further progress…they discovered to their delight that the shape of every little ledge and crag of stone had been as carefully devised as if a painter had traced them with his own brush. Here and there in the distance the topmost boughs of an orchard showed above the mist…and where the boats were tied, mountain kerria poured its yellow blossom over the rocky cliffs in a torrent of colour that was mirrored in the waters of the lake below."

Another of the prince's amours, Akiko-no-chugu, preferred the late summer. Accordingly, her garden "was full of such trees as in autumn time turn to the deepest hue. The stream above the waterfall was cleared out and deepened to a considerable distance; and that the noise of the cascade might carry further, he set great boulders in mid-stream, against which the current crashed and broke." A garden of winter beauty was designed for the mother of Genji's daughter, while that of yet another lady, She of the Village of Falling Flowers, focused on a cool spring, "the neighbourhood of which seemed likely to yield an agreeable refuge from the summer heat. In the borders near the house upon this side he planted Chinese bamboos, and a little further off, a tall-stemmed forest whose thick leaves roofed airy tunnels of shade, pleasant as those of the most lovely upland wood. This garden was fenced with hedges of white deutzia flower, and the orange tree 'whose scent re-awakes forgotten

A moonlit voyage
This fan print by Utagawa Hiroshige, dating from c.1854, shows Prince Genji taking his favourite, the Lady Murasaki, out for a moonlit voyage around the lake. The lake's islands of blossoming trees are a distant view from the Lady Murasaki's own little tsubo *garden.*

love', the briar rose, and the giant peony, with many sorts of bush and tall flower so skilfully spread about among them that neither spring nor autumn would ever lack in bravery."

Throughout the story of Genji's gardens there is an emphasis on poetic composition. For Murasaki's romantic hero, as for the real-life Heian courtiers who inspired him, garden design was filtered by an intensely poetic perception of nature. Plants and features are laden with poetic and romantic meanings and messages, so that, besides being a place of beauty, relaxation and flirtation, the garden acted as a poetic whole. The flowering of chrysanthemums in September, and of "sweet flags" (*Acorus calamus*) in May, were occasions for festivals and entertainments. The courtiers whose lifestyle inspired *The Tale of Genji* were intensely refined and aesthetic, and the

Images of Genji's tale
This woodblock print (above), c.1847–52, by Utagawa Kunisada (1786–1865), illustrates a scene from The Tale of Genji. *Like the pavilions of Heian courtiers, the pavilions of Murasaki's fictional ladies were joined by raised, covered walkways and verandas, on which ladies could avail themselves of the lake garden's refreshing sights and fragrances.*

The amorous visitor
Katsukawa Shunso's illustration of Genji's "Yugao" chapter. Yet another lady welcomes the indefatigable Prince Genji into her lovely garden. Like the fictional prince, Heian noblemen visited their loves at night and left in the morning.

whole work is permeated by a wistful sense of the transience of love and beauty. "The chrysanthemums in the gardens were in full bloom, whose sweet perfume soothed us with its

gentle influence: and round about us the scarlet leaves of the maple were falling, as ever and anon they were shaken by the breeze. The scene was altogether romantic."

more refined, and in literature a new, phonetic script supplemented Chinese characters. It was a mark of the new confidence that *The Tale of Genji* was written in Japanese, the language of everyday life, rather than the scholar's Chinese. This splendid isolation lasted until the period known as the Kamakura shogunate (1185–1333), when Japan renewed its interest in Chinese civilization.

Under the Fujiwara regents, Japanese aristocrats gravitated towards the imperial court at Kyoto. The power vacuum in the provinces was filled by ambitious clan leaders, not unlike the barons of feudal Europe, who maintained law and order with the help of their own armies. Their elite fighters were known as *bushi* or *samurai*, which means one who serves. In 1184 the Taira clan was defeated on land and sea by the Minamoto clan. Now the Minamoto leader, Minamoto Yoritomo, took the title Seii-Tai-Shogun, meaning Barbarian-subduing Generalissimo, and chose to rule from the city of Kamakura, which was in his own territory, hundreds of miles away from the polite and polished society of Kyoto.

As a result of his conquests in northern Japan, Yoritomo encountered the Buddhist temple of Motsu-ji. Built in the Chinese manner, with both a belltower and a drum to toll the hours, Motsu-ji is set in a lovely Heian lake garden called Hiraizumi. In 1189 work began on Yoritomo's replica of Motsu-ji and its garden, which is called Eifuku-ji, and set among the pines of Kamakura. Gardens were of little interest to tough Kamakura warlords, unless they were associated with a temple.

In the background of Kamakura rule is the peasant farmer, labouring in the rice fields; in the foreground there is a beautiful but lethal sword. Although the Kamakura elite scorned the effete lifestyles of imperial courtiers, their *samurai* code of honour meant that they were especially sympathetic to Zen, a form of Buddhism that exalts human intuition and will above the human ability to learn. Zen perceptions of existence and nature were so well received and refined in Japan that their Indian origin and Chinese filters are often forgotten. In the Kamakura period Japanese priests visited Chinese monasteries, and Zen Buddhist ideas permeated the archipelago. Zen literally means meditation, and its emphasis on calm ritual, designed to stimulate feeling for simple things, would lead, in time, to the refinement of a new gardening style.

THE MUROMACHI RENAISSANCE

In 1333 the Kamakura shogunate was replaced by the Ashikaga shogunate. The Ashikaga shoguns returned to Kyoto, to the Muromachi district that gave its name to their period of supremacy in Japan (1333–1568). This was a period when all the arts, including the art of garden-making, flourished. Under the ruling Ashikaga family Kyoto was once again the centre of government, as well as the imperial court. Muromachi Hall, the Ashikaga family's mansion in the northeast of Kyoto, was known as the Flowery Palace because of the number of cherry trees found in its grounds. The Muromachi elite had the power and wealth (the result of heavy taxation of the peasants) to be patrons and practitioners of the arts. They took lessons in poetry-writing and calligraphy and were assiduous collectors of fine art, paintings, ceramics and lacquer objects from China.

Just as the gardens of the Heian golden age tell of the influence of Tang Chinese civilization, the gardens of the Muromachi period tell of the influence of the northern Chinese Song civilization. As the conquering armies of the Mongols overran China, many of the craftsmen and artists of the Song court found patrons and pupils in Japan. The fashion for Song art complemented the new fashions in garden, in a new way.

Painting and gardening had worked together before. At the end of the 9th century, the court painter Kose no Kanaoka had developed a style of landscape painting that served as a source of inspiration for garden design. In the Heian period there were professional painters called *niwa-eshi* who could prepare drawings of projected gardens. But then, as ever, the Japanese garden did not lend itself to the discipline of a two-dimensional blueprint, because its elements were selected and arranged for so much more than appearance's sake. The shape of stones, for example, was of as much import as their placement. So although the

The perfection of Ginkaku-ji

The garden of Ginkaku-ji (the Silver Pavilion) was built by the 8th Ashikaga shogun, Yoshimasa (1436–90), as a villa for his retirement. In designing it, the artist Soami was mindful of the beauties of Saiho-ji, which Yoshimasa admired and regularly visited. Another major contributor to the garden of Ginkaku-ji was the humble "riverbank gardener" Zen'ami, acknowledged as a master of garden design and of the subtle art of stone placement.

The garden is in two parts. First is the area around the large pond by the pavilion, which is called the Silver Pavilion because of a projected but never realized silver-leafed roof. This composition of rocks, water and plants, with green hills in the background and trees silhouetted against the skyline, unfurls as a series of scenes, like a painted landscape scroll. Second is the area of the sand sculptures in the foreground of the pavilion, which were probably added in the Edo period when the garden of Ginkaku-ji was being restored. A sand sculpture in the form of a truncated cone may have been intended to represent Mount Fuji. The horizontal Sea of Silver Sand is raked into a wave pattern.

Under Yoshimasa, who was more active as a patron of the arts than a ruler, classical Japanese culture reached its zenith. Artists, poets and scholars gathered around him, creating images and gardens in which nature itself, and distinctly Japanese landscapes, were celebrated. After his death, Ginkaku-ji became a Zen Buddhist temple called Jisho-ji.

Gleam of gold
Kinkaku-ji (the Temple of the
Golden Pavilion) is one of the best-
known sights in Japan. The shogun
Yoshimitsu's retirement home, it was
built at the very end of the 14th
century and designed to be viewed
from a slowly moving boat on the
lake. The pavilion was converted
into a temple by Yoshimitsu's son. Its
name derives from the gold foil of
the interior of the top storey, which
20th-century restorers mistakenly
extended to lower storeys.

relationship between the gardens of the Muromachi era and Song Chinese paintings was not a matter of garden life imitating art, the Ashikaga shoguns' appreciation of Song subtleties was echoed, and developed, in the simpler, more ascetic
design of their gardens.

The garden of Kinkaku-ji, (the Temple of the Golden Pavilion, known today
as Rokuon-ji), in Kyoto, shows the influence of Song Chinese aesthetic values. It
was built in 1397 as the retirement palace of the third Ashikaga shogun, Yoshimitsu,
who was a fervent devotee of Zen and a generous sponsor of Chinese culture.
Although the site was an existing pond and temple garden, the former estate of a
Kamakura-era courtier, Kinkaku-ji and its immediate surroundings presented a
novel spectacle. It is framed by flowering cherries and the space between them
and the pavilion is filled with gravel of five different colours, raked into a pattern
representing ocean wavelets. Scenes similar to the Kinkaku-ji are recognizable in
Song paintings, and it is likely that its designers were knowing imitators. Under
the Ashikaga shoguns, Japanese Buddhist priests visited the Chinese monasteries
around Hangzhou, on the beautiful West Lake, and they had a sophisticated
understanding of the meanings and allusions contained within Song painted
landscapes and Song garden landscapes.

Yoshimitsu's three-storeyed pavilion later became a temple. Its name derives
from the fabulous decoration of the top storey, whose interior is entirely covered
with gold, and which served as a Zen oratory for the retired shogun. The middle
storey was probably used by Yoshimitsu for his music and poetry parties, and the
lowest storey contained his living quarters. The pavilion survived until after the

THE MOSS GARDEN AT SAIHO-JI

THE GARDEN OF SAIHO-JI TEMPLE in Kyoto has survived for nearly a thousand years. It was first laid out, in the 11th century, around a lake in the shape of the Chinese character for the heart or soul. Then, *c.*1339, it was restored and improved by the influential Zen Buddhist artist and priest Muso Soseki (1275–1351), also known as Kokushi and credited with the design of the nearby Tenryu-ji garden. Extending to 1.8 hectares (4.5 acres), Muso Soseki's Saiho-ji was designed as a stroll garden. It appears to have no boundaries. The wooded hills rising behind the central lake and a forest of giant bamboo lead the eye into the seemingly endless vistas to each side. Although the path is in deep shade, slanting sunlight plays across the water's surface.

A Korean visitor of 1443 reported on the garden works in progress at Saiho-ji. He noted that the branches of trees were tied with ropes to force them into the shapes desired, and that young trees were treated to make them look old. He also wrote of plants being shaped or pruned – the first mention of this practice in Japanese garden history – and of stones being excavated from the earth, only to be artificially re-positioned or re-arranged.

Saiho-ji comprises two distinct garden areas. The lower area, around the lake known as the Golden Pond, represents the perfect world of tranquillity and paradise. The pavilions along its shores once included the Rurikaku, the temple hall in which relics of Buddha were kept, and to which the Ashikaga shoguns Yoshimitsu and Yoshimasa, among other important personages, came to offer reverence and burn incense. Their pavilions, the Kinkaku-ji and the Ginkaku-ji (see

Serene carpet

Tidying the Moss Garden at Saiho-ji in Kyoto. The verdant slopes and lichen-covered tree trunks of this accidental masterpiece, established by nature during centuries of neglect, have inspired garden-makers all over the world.

opposite and page 361), were modelled on the Rurikaku temple hall at Saiho-ji – burned down in the war-torn 15th century and further destroyed by later flooding.

In the upper area of Saiho-ji, Soseki created a garden representing our imperfect world. Known as Mount Koin, this area is entered by an ornamental gateway, and strewn with projecting boulders. Beyond a clear spring, lined and protected with rocks, is the famous dry cascade, whose artfully tumbled boulders look as if water has just stopped running over them. Today this cascade falls into "pools" of brilliant moss. More than 120 varieties of moss, in emerald, jade and bronze, contour the hills and "flow" over the ledges of the pond. Sheltered from the north wind and from the sun, under the deep shade of broadleaved evergreens and a scattering of Japanese maples, the site, in heavy clay, is ideal for moss cultivation. Reflected in the water, the mossy hillsides and lichen-covered tree trunks add a mystical

dimension to Saiho-ji, an inspiration to gardeners from many cultures.

Today, Saiho-ji's spectacular Moss Garden is regarded as a national treasure, but it didn't grow by design. During its centuries of neglect, when the Buddhist monastery was too poor to maintain the garden as it was in its heyday, moss thrived in the shaded, heavy clay of the upper area. Late in the 19th century, when Saiho-ji became a popular park, the Moss Garden was appreciated and maintained as an accidental garden masterpiece. In spring, when the moss carpet is at its most intense green, it contrasts with flame-coloured azaleas; in summer lotus leaves adorn the pond; and in autumn the scarlet and crimson tones of maple foliage add their own magic to this extraordinary garden.

Second World War, when it was burned down by a disturbed student monk. During the rebuilding, the surfaces of the two upper storeys were accidentally faced with gold leaf, but time is softening the garish effect of this error.

The temple's 0.2-hectare (4.5-acre) garden includes a large lake rimmed by trees, with an opening to reveal a view of Mount Kinagusa. By planting smaller trees in the distance the designers increased the garden's apparent dimensions and made it blend into the woodland, controlling distant views. The lake's delights were designed to be appreciated from pleasure boats. The vertical rocks in it are shaped like mountain peaks. (One is so enormous that 17 oxen were required for its transport.) The outlines of other rocks are reflected in the water as turtles, and there is a crane island in front of the pavilion. Twisted pine trees grow on the islands. In summer the water's surface is patterned with lily-pads; in winter tall reeds fringe the lake's shore. On the hill behind the pavilion is the Dragon Gate Cascade, made for the pre-Muromachi owners of the estate, where a rock at the base of a dry waterfall – itself representing a mountain – stands for a carp thought to turn into a dragon once it succeeds in swimming to the top of the falls. Originally, the cascade was at the edge of the pond, but over the centuries the water boundaries have silted up and this area is now shaded by trees and carpeted with emerald moss. Kinkaku-ji is an integrated work of art, a garden composition of perfect balance and exquisite vistas.

Patterns for meditation

Synonymous with purity since very ancient times, white sand and gravel are raked into patterns and act as an aid to meditation in Zen Buddhist gardens. Highly controlled, and freshly raked, these serenely economical spaces usually have fixed points, such as verandas, from which to contemplate them, as here in Marc Peter Keane's Kyoto garden.

THE CONSOLATIONS OF ZEN

From Kamakura times Zen was the favourite and, therefore, the most favoured Buddhist sect of the shoguns. Zen monks were, in effect, licensed to dedicate themselves to art and learning and, surprisingly, trade. They were themselves artists, scholars and mystics, and they had many opportunities for contact with foreign cultures. The shoguns actively encouraged the monks to import goods, as well as aesthetic and religious trends, from China, and they were generous benefactors of Zen institutions. The great Japanese artist Sesshu (1420–1506), for example, was a monk who had visited China. The Muromachi period, when the Ashikaga shoguns ruled, was followed by a period of turmoil and civil war. In these troubled times Zen monasteries and temples served as spiritual and aesthetic oases.

According to a typical Zen paradox, uttered by the famous scholar Zekkai, "Great mastery is as if unskilful." This notion of mastery is expressed in the gardens of temples and monasteries of the 15th and 16th centuries, many of which still survive. Although Zen is by its very nature resistant to

the Western habit of dividing things in two —
reason/emotion, body/mind, reality/illusion, and so
on — it is easier for us to understand Zen garden-
making in terms of two philosophical or spiritual
impulses. First, the Buddhist perception of the oneness
of humanity and nature, the idea that everything in
existence is permeated by a single unifying spirit.
Second, the impulse in art and garden-making to
create images and environments in which human
beings can meditate and come to an intuitive realization
of their identity with the universe. With a few strokes
of a black-inked brush, great Zen artists such as
Sesshu and Soami (1472–1523) captured the essence
of a sublime landscape on small pieces of paper, and
the same unerring economy is the hallmark of the
classic Zen garden.

Zen *kare-sansui*, or dry landscapes, composed of
rocks and gravel or sand, are designed as an aid to
meditation. Gravel and white sand were of ancient
lineage as symbols of purity, having been used to
mark out Shinto shrines. Raked into wave patterns in
the dry Zen garden, these materials represent the
ocean. Rocks and moss add a further dimension, the
shape and directional placement of rock islands
expressing symbolic meanings. The rectangular spaces, designed to be viewed
from the veranda and framed by its pillars, are backed by a long wall, painted
white to represent the ethereal mist shrouding the mountains. In these *kare-sansui*
gardens, actual water, plants and views are replaced by abstractions of the real
landscape.

Plants are included in the Zen gardens that work as intimate landscapes. Here,
rocks represent mountains, sand or gravel represents water, and the overall effect,
in three dimensions, is of a brush-and-ink landscape. The sliding wall screens
within the temple often featured black-on-white paintings in this style and it is
no coincidence that the painter Sesshu was also a garden-maker. Just as, for the
Heian connoisseur, the garden became a poem so, for the Zen monk, the garden
became a painting. And the daily maintenance of these garden artworks was in
itself a part of a ritual cleansing conducive to meditation and self-knowledge.

TWO TIMELESS GARDENS

Daisen-in and Ryoan-ji are two of Kyoto's classic Zen gardens. The garden
of Daisen-in, which is a subsidiary temple of the 16th-century Daitoku-ji
monastery, is the finest example of a *kare-sansui*, and since World War II has been
restored by designer Nakane Kinsaku. At Daisen-in a narrow approach passage
opens into an austere landscape, a landscape of perhaps 800km (500 miles) in its
actual geographic range, which has been miniaturized in a space of less than 85 sq m

Ascetic values
The profoundly minimal garden of
Daisen-in, Kyoto, begins with a
landscape of serrated rocks from
which a river of sand rises, and
eventually flows into an open sea
containing two mounds. The Zen
Buddhist appreciation of the austere,
of imbalance and asymmetry, has
come to be reflected in many
cultural spheres, but it is in the art of
landscape design that it has been most
successfully expressed and translated.

(100 sq yd). Enormous vertical rocks represent mountain crags, while a cascade is signified by striated rock and a stream by white quartz; small trees and shrubs are used to portray a mountain grouping, and the whole adds up to a three-dimensional landscape, complementing the paintings on the sliding panels of the main room within the temple.

Other rocks floating in a sea of sand represent both the turtle and the crane. These auspicious creatures are associated with the Mystic Isles of the Immortals of Chinese mythology, but in this Japanese context they further indicate, respectively, the depths to which the human spirit can sink and the heights to which a human spirit can soar. One flat rock is a bridge, another junk-shaped rock simultaneously represents a celestial treasure ship that descended to Earth in the times of the gods and the human soul voyaging towards Buddhist enlightenment or the Mystic Isles of the Immortals. Shrubs are clipped to represent distant scenery.

Contemplative ideal

Enclosed by an earthen wall, the mysterious Garden of Crossing Tiger-Cubs at Ryoan-ji temple in Kyoto, is perhaps the best-known *kare-sansui* (dry landscape). Five groups of three rocks are adrift in a sea of sand, and whatever they represent – islands, mountain peaks or tiger cubs – the overall effect is calming. Neither the identity nor the specific vision of Ryoan-ji's designer is known, but it seems likely that he was a monk-artist and that he wished to create a garden conducive to quiet introspection.

The L-shaped gardens to the east and north, which have been slightly altered in layout over the centuries, express the human condition in symbols and stories. They wrap round the main temple building, leaving its southern view as an open rectangle of sand. Raked in horizontal lines, this is the ocean into which the white sand river empties. The ocean is backed by two lines of hedging, clipped at different heights to represent the ocean and purity, and inset with two cones of sand. The single, June-blooming tree in the southwest corner is a *shara no ki* or stewartia, representing the sal tree under which the Buddha was born.

Ryoan-ji, also in Kyoto, is the most famous and most influential Zen garden. Ryoan-ji means Dragon Peace Temple, and according to one theory the artist Soami had a hand in the restoration of its celebrated rock garden after the temple was destroyed by fire in 1488. (Sesshu worked mainly outside Kyoto, building the Joeji-ji garden near Yamaguchi, in the following years.) The temple was again destroyed in 1780, leaving the garden untouched and relatively unknown until the 1930s.

Lying behind the main hall of the temple, the garden, backed by a wall and a backdrop of trees, is intended to be viewed only from the veranda. It is never set foot in by anyone but the lay brother who keeps it raked and clean. Moss, the only living material in the garden, grows around the base of 15 rocks, cunningly arranged in five groups of five, two, three, two and three. The interest of rocks as a form of abstract art lies not in their shapes but in their relative spatial relationships. Some hold that the stones represent a mother tiger and her cubs swimming; others see the stones as metaphors for the tops of metaphysical mountains or islands in a plain or sea of consciousness. Many modern artists, including David Hockney, and modern garden designers have been influenced by the mystery of Ryoan-ji, which was completed 400 years before Europe's influential Impressionist and Modernist art movements. But the age of Ryoan-ji is not what is important. Indeed, its layout today may differ from its original conception. Ryoan-ji's success lies in its timelessness, and its enduring power as an aid to meditation.

PEACHES AND GOLD

Late in the 15th century, after a hundred years of civil war and social turmoil, three great military leaders brought peace and stability to Japan. The first of these was Oda Nobunaga (1534–82), and the second was Toyotomi Hideyoshi (1537–98). Hideyoshi was a man of humble birth who rose through the ranks to become Nobunaga's greatest general. He was considered ineligible for the title of shogun because of his humble birth, but the era of his supremacy, the Momoyama period, takes its name from his lavishly decorated palace. Momoyama means Peach Hill, which was the name of Hideyoshi's castle at Fushimi, south of Kyoto.

In Hideyoshi's heyday if you had it, you flaunted it. Accordingly, the pure Zen gardens of sand and rock began to lose favour to designs in which a few trees, shrubs and rocks were spaced out in sand, not to represent a whole landscape or a three-dimensional painting but to give a suggestion of one. These more colourful and impressionistic gardens coincided with the vogue for a rich and colourful new style of painting, named the Kano style after Kano Eitoku (1573–1616). He invented the use of gold leaf as a background to screen painting in strong opaque colours. Art of this style, which featured in the homes of Japan's new magnates, was produced by professional artists, as opposed to contemplative monk-scholars. A similar extravagance accompanied new developments in the tea ceremony and its setting, the tea garden (see page 369).

Since the Muromachi period, tea-drinking had been a Zen rite, designed to induce wakefulness in preparation for meditation. One of the earliest buildings associated with the tea ceremony, which often took place at night and always happened indoors, was in the garden of the last Ashikaga shogun's Ginkaku-ji. But, under the patronage of Hideyoshi, the tea ceremony and its surroundings lost some of their spiritual qualities, and became instead the focus of lavish and ostentatious hospitality. In October 1587 Hideyoshi announced publicly in Kyoto, Osaka and other cities that he would hold a great tea ceremony in the next month. Everyone, from the poorest peasant to the richest vassal, was invited, and asked to bring a kettle, a cup and a mat to sit upon. For another of Hideyoshi's monster parties, the ancient temple of Sambo-in was restored and enlarged along suitably splendid Momoyaman lines. The great tea master Sen No Rikyu was a central figure at Hideyoshi's court until, for reasons that are not

KANO SCHOOL OF JAPANESE PAINTING

By the end of the 15th century Japan had begun to develop its own tradition of landscape painting, breaking away from the austere, Chinese-inspired Song style. This rich and distinctively Japanese style, which has some similarities to European baroque art, is known as the Kano school. It originated with Kano Masanobu (1434–1530), the first of a long line of Japanese artists that included his son and grandson (Motonubu and Eitoku) and lasted for centuries.

Floral splendour
White chrysanthemums blossom against the vivid gold background of this screen. The 16th-century Momoyama period was a time of huge gardens, brilliant textiles and rich screen paintings.

understood, he fell out of favour and was obliged to kill himself by *hare-kiri*, the ritual form of suicide that was the exclusive privilege of the *samurai* class.

THE RISE AND RISE OF EDO

After Hideyoshi's death it was the turn of Tokugawa Ieyasu, another of Nobunaga's brilliant generals, to take control of Japan. In 1603 Tokugawa Ieyasu became shogun, and the Tokugawa dynasty was to rule Japan until 1868. Although Tokugawa Ieyasu treated the emperor at Kyoto with all due respect, he kept the imperial court under strict surveillance and chose to rule Japan from his own castle at Edo, 300km (480 miles) northeast of the old capital.

By 1700 the village of Edo (later renamed Tokyo) had become one of the largest cities in the world, with a population of more than a million. Since the unswerving aim of the Tokugawa clan was to maintain their own power and influence, and prevent another civil war, they kept a close eye on rival families. All the important lords or *daimyos* (literally, great names) were obliged to spend time in the new capital every other year, sometimes more frequently, and when they were away in their country estates their families had to remain in Edo as hostages. Before long the captive *daimyos* were installing large stroll-garden parks on the edge of the city. Similar to the imperial villas of Katsura and Shugaku-in in Kyoto, these landscaped parks included more intimate tea gardens, which were used for entertaining.

Without the springs so plentiful in Kyoto, Edo's garden builders made the most of the open marshlands found along the bay and tidal river. Neither did they have Kyoto's splendid background scenery, although, 80km (50 miles) away, Mount Fuji provided a distant view, and many of the new gardens of the Tokugawa era faced out onto views of the sea and sailing boats in Edo Bay. Among the most impressive is Koraku-en, constructed by the gardener Tokudaiji Sahe'e. Koraku-en contains tree-covered hills and a large lake with islands. The

Evolving pleasures
Now one of Tokyo's most popular parks, Koraku-en began as one of the first aristocratic pleasure gardens to be laid out in the new capital of Edo. Its enduring attractions include reproductions of some of Kyoto's celebrated temple gardens and a large lake with islands.

THE TEA CEREMONY OR CHA-NO-YU

Late in the 12th century a Zen monk who had studied in China brought tea plant seeds and the tea ceremony to Japan. Essentially, the ceremony consisted of a gathering of friends in a small room, bare of all but a few beautiful things in which to boil water and make tea before drinking it. The principles that governed everything associated with the ceremony – the tea house, the utensils, the conversation and the surrounding garden – were purity, cleanliness and tranquillity.

By the 15th century the art of tea-drinking had moved away from the mountain huts of Zen monks to become a feature in the lifestyle of the *samurai* elite. The tea house built near the Ginkaku-ji, or Silver Pavilion (see page 361), by the Zen monk Murata Juko (who died in 1502), was designed to accommodate four-and-a-half *tatami* mats, and became the model for all future tea rooms. Within the simple and scrupulously clean tea room and its ceremonial alcove, the *tokonoma*, there might be a scroll painting or a flower arrangement. The tea house's garden setting would contain a stone basin filled with water, with which participants in the ceremony could wash their hands and rinse out their mouths before proceeding along the *roji*, or dewy path, a term taken from a Buddhist *sutra*, to the tea house.

The founder of the tea ceremony as it is still performed today was Sen No Rikyu (1522–91) – an arbiter of taste, and an authority on cultural matters at Hideyoshi's court. Under his auspices, the stone basin, where guests could cleanse their senses from contamination, the flat stepping stones that preserved the garden's mossy carpet and the

Ceremonial duties
Ladies clean up the antechamber to the tea house in this painting by Mizuno Tôshikata, c.1890–1900. Courtiers and the wives of samurai were expected to learn the art and rituals of the tea ceremony, in which the emphasis is on simplicity, purity, serenity, composure and melancholy. Wabi, the Japanese word for this ethos, literally translates as worn or humble.

lanterns that lit their way at night became accepted elements of the ceremony. Among its wealthy practitioners the cult soon lost much of its original austerity. Connoisseurs paid huge prices for flower vases and paintings, and for porcelain bowls and caddies, which were handed down as family heirlooms. The requirements of the tea ceremony stimulated developments in ceramic art, as well as architecture and garden design – the latter, of course, an especially important factor in the development of our story.

There are many humorous tales about the relationship between Hideyoshi, the rough and ready general, and Rikyu, the educated and ascetic tea master. One such tale tells of how, when Hideyoshi heard about the beautiful morning glories blooming in Rikyu's garden, he determined to see them. On entering the garden, however, he saw none. He then stepped into the tea

house and beheld a single flowering morning glory. Hideyoshi's love of display and extravagance was at odds with the tea ceremony's true purpose, a purpose which Rikyu himself never lost sight of.

In Rikyu's own garden at Sakai, the sea view was obstructed and the tea garden's stone basin was positioned so that, as a guest raised his face, he caught a glimpse of the ocean beyond the garden – experiencing a moment of connection between the water of the basin and the water of the sea, and, therefore, himself and the universe.

rocks that adorn its hillsides, as well as providing stepping stones and cascade components, came from distant parts of the country. Scenes from well-known temple gardens in Kyoto were reproduced at Koraku-en, as well as miniature versions of familiar scenes from art and literature.

The gardens of Edo tended to be more literal and less open to individual interpretation than earlier Japanese gardens. This conformity was in keeping with the principles of Chinese Confucian philosophy, which the Tokugawa shoguns encouraged at the expense of Buddhism. Even the name Koraku-en, meaning ease and garden, derives from the Confucian axiom that a ruler should be the first to bear the hardships of existence and the last to taste its joys (it is now translated as the Garden of Philosophy). A famous Confucian scholar, Chu Shun-sui, supervised the inclusion at Koraku-en of landscape details adapted from the romantic lake-side gardens of Hangzhou in south China (see page 334). He designed the much copied Bridge of the Round Moon, a half-circle bridge that forms a perfect circle when united with its reflection in the stream.

FOREIGNERS FROM THE WEST

A Confucian code of ethics – stressing the importance of qualities such as self-discipline, deference and hard work, based on the Chinese philosophy of Confucius (see page 328) – was promoted by the Tokugawa shoguns, from Ieyasu's shogunate onwards. Confucianism provided the ideological glue for strong, stable government, and after the fall of China's Ming dynasty the Tokugawas welcomed refugee Chinese scholars. But after 1641 Japan was virtually closed to all other foreigners and foreign influences, except for a few Dutch traders at Deshima island near the port of Nagasaki.

A hundred years before, when Japan was divided by civil war, Europe had begun to get first-hand information about Japan through Portuguese sailors shipwrecked off the coast of Kyushu. The first Spanish Jesuit missionaries arrived in 1549, and they were swiftly followed by Portuguese, Dutch and English traders. But the numbers of Japanese converts to Christianity grew so fast that the Tokugawa shoguns, fearing colonization by a European power, began to persecute them. After the 37,000 Christian defenders of Hara Castle were massacred in 1637–38, Christianity went underground for the rest of the Edo period and Japan was closed to foreigners for the next two centuries.

Once a year, the Dutch traders allowed to remain at Nagasaki were expected to send an embassy with gifts to the shogun at Edo. This was the Westerners' only lawful opportunity to observe life on mainland Japan and some of them ventured beyond the law to provide Europe with further glimpses of Japan's botanical treasures. The German Engelbert Kaempfer (1651–1716) came to Japan in 1690 as chief surgeon to the governor of the Dutch East India Company and remained for two years. Kaempfer's book *Amoenitates Exoticae*, which was published in 1712, was the first description of Japanese trees, shrubs and flowers –

Treasure trove
The title page from Kaempfer's influential book *Amoenitates Exoticae.* Published in 1712, it offered Europe the first descriptions of such Japanese horticultural treasures as skimmia, hydrangea and camellia.

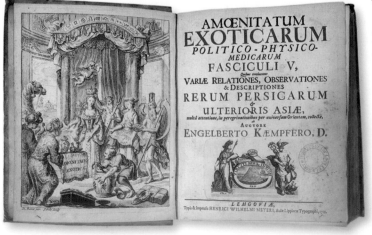

KATSURA AND SHUGAKU-IN IMPERIAL ESTATES

THE KATSURA AND SHUGAKU-IN are 17th-century imperial gardens. Their features and vistas, designed to unfold before a visitor making a circuit of the garden, served as models for the stroll gardens of the Edo period.

Katsura was given to Prince Toshihito, the younger brother of Emperor Goyozei, by his adoptive father Hideyoshi. Covering about 4.5 hectares (11 acres), it is in the Katsura riverside district, where many of the Heian nobles had their pleasure gardens. The landscape, on which work began *c.*1620, includes a large lake and walks that wind over bridges and around rockwork. The focal area is the tea garden, with its stepping stones in patterns, basins, lanterns and rustic huts.

It is said that Prince Toshihito, who was already 40 when work began at Katsura, was advised by his friend, the tea master Kobori Enshu. Between 1620 and 1625 there was ceaseless activity at Katsura: hundreds of workmen dug out the lake, constructed hillsides with the spoil and built "jewel-like pavilions".

In the mid-17th century the 54-hectare (133-acre) hillside estate of Shugaku-in, to the northeast of Kyoto, was turned into a vast landscape by the retired Emperor Gomizunoo (1596–1680). Here, views of the surrounding mountain peaks act as *shakkei* (borrowed scenery), blending into the garden's wooded scenery and glimpsed as vistas from special points.

Shugaku-in's smaller, intimate gardens, with their tightly clipped shrubs, stone bridges and carpets of moss, are typically Japanese, but there is a Western feel to the wider landscaped areas, with their reflecting water, sloping banks of trees and shrubs, green manicured lawns and blended distant vistas. In the central, flat area, terraced rice and vegetable gardens lend an informal rustic air, but the most remarkable part of Shugaku-in is the Upper Garden, which is entered by the Imperial Gate. Here, multiple clipped hedges of 40 different shrub varieties repeat the pattern of the rice terraces below, and cover the western embankment of the lake. Pruned in horizontal tiers, they give a modernist twist to the design, and have been copied in modern gardens such as Professor Yoshida's Japan Academy garden in Tokyo. Neglected for many years the great stroll garden, now restored, is exquisitely maintained.

Illusions of space
The gardens of the 17th-century imperial villa of Shugaku, Kyoto, make impressive use of the principle of shakkei *or borrowed scenery. Skilful planting and winding paths create the illusion of great distance, and the surrounding hills are incorporated as vistas.*

New leaves
Acer japonicum from Siebold's *Flora Japonica*, which was illustrated with reproductions of botanical drawings by Japanese artists. The cultural impact in the West of Siebold's book was reinforced by the horticultural impact of his nursery at Leiden, which acted as a conduit for the introduction of Japanese plants to Europe.

plants now familiar to every keen gardener — to reach Europe. These included aucuba, skimmia, hydrangea, chimonanthus, magnolias, ginkgo, prunus, azaleas, tree peonies and nearly 30 varieties of camellia, as well as *Lilium speciosum* and *L. tigrinum*. Kaempfer also wrote a history of Japan that became the major source for Europe's perception of Japanese civilization during the centuries of isolation. Unfortunately, Kaempfer's sympathy and sensitivity to Japanese culture was rather lost in the first English translation by Johann Gaspar Scheuchzer, a Swiss employed by Sir Hans Sloane. (Today, Kaempfer's herbarium specimens are held in the British Museum in London.)

Kaempfer was fortunate enough to join two annual expeditions from the trading station at Nagasaki to the shogun's headquarters at Edo, during which he collected wild flower specimens in "a shabby Javanese box made of bark", in which he also concealed a compass. He was not allowed to gather plants himself, but had to rely on his Japanese escorts. Fortunately, his guards were interested in plants and ready to discuss their properties with the locals. Kaempfer visited Japan during the exceptionally peaceful and prosperous period of the fifth Tokugawa (Tsunayoshi) shogun's rule. The quality of the roads, restaurants and inns impressed Kaempfer, who compared them favourably with the primitive facilities encountered on his previous travels through Russia, Persia, Ceylon, Batavia and Siam.

While he was stopping over at Kyoto, the old imperial capital, Kaempfer was able to visit the monastery garden of Chion-in. "At the foot of a wooded tall mountain (where there were still other pleasant small temples hidden among the shrubbery of the slopes, and which was levelled with boulders more than one fathom high) was a small Japanese pleasure or miniature garden. That is to say a narrow space, or piece of flat ground, covered with river sand or stones, where the existing uniformity is carefully broken up with artistically made overgrown small, and neat cliffs, rare rocks, and well pruned and twisted trees and turned into a pretty garden…there was a winding, shallow stream of water, running round man-made cliffs in a maze-like pattern to give the impression of a wilderness lake in a narrow gorge, spanned with various ornamental stone bridges." So much for a European's first view of a Japanese temple garden.

Kaempfer's own direct observations were supplemented by information received from local Japanese spies, who were sometimes rewarded from his "cordial and plentiful supply of European liquors". Over 80 years later, the next intrepid naturalist to feed Europe's fascination with Japan's botanical gems was the Swedish Carl Peter Thunberg (1743–1828). Thunberg arrived in Japan in 1775 as a physician to the governor of the Dutch traders' settlement, but he was also a trained botanist. Linnaeus, no less, had been Thunberg's mentor and for his work in Japan Thunberg is regarded as one of the great Swedish naturalist's apostles.

By Thunberg's day, the restrictions on the movements and activities of foreigners in Japan had eased slightly. He was permitted to visit a nursery and spend as much as he could spare on a collection of "the scarcest shrubs and trees planted in pots". Thunberg succeeded in establishing a garden in the foreign compound, from which he despatched living specimens, via Batavia, to the Hortus Medicus in Amsterdam. Thunberg's specimens included *Thujopsis dolabrata*, ornamental maples, two plants of *Cycas revoluta* and the popular *Berberis thunbergii*. This was no mean feat, coming as it did before the invention of the Wardian case (see pages 198–99) in the 1840s, which improved by 100 per cent the survival chances of plants exported by long sea journeys. Thunberg spared no efforts to obtain plants and seeds, but his book, *Flora Japonica*, which was published in 1784, did not have the same impact as Kaempfer's best-selling *Amoenitates Exoticae*.

The third pioneering European botanist and collector in Tokugawa Japan was Philipp Franz von Siebold (1796–1866) from Wurzburg, a Bavarian eye-specialist who was appointed as a physician to the Dutch governor in 1826. Although the restrictions on foreigners were still in force, Siebold managed to extend his plant-hunting forays further and further afield on the pretext of visiting patients. While he in was in Tokyo, as a member of the annual Dutch embassy to the shogun, he persuaded the court astronomer to provide him with maps, which were strictly forbidden to foreigners. On discovery, the astronomer and several intermediaries were tortured or committed suicide. Siebold himself was imprisoned for more than a year, until December 1829, when he was released and expelled from Japan.

In spite of this ordeal Siebold managed to send a consignment of plants to Europe before he left Japan, and he took with him another 485 plants, which were already established at Deshima. With the 80 plants, including bamboos, azaleas, camellias, lilies and hydrangeas, that survived his return voyage, Siebold set up a nursery in the Leiden Botanic Garden. There is still a Siebold collection of Japanese plants at Leiden, as well as in the Okogarden at Würzburg. His two-volume *Flora Japonica* was published between 1835 and 1842, with coloured plates after drawings by anonymous Japanese artists. On his second visit to Japan, Siebold fell foul of the authorities again, but he returned with *Hydrangea paniculata*, *Malus floribunda*, *Spiraea thunbergii* and *Prunus sieboldii*.

The HOSTA

Hostas, plantain lilies or *giboshi* in Japanese, were first known to Europeans as funkias. They were finally named for Austrian botanist Nicolaus Thomas Host (1761–1834), physician to the emperor in Vienna. There are about 70 species distributed between China, Japan, Korea and eastern Russia, and today these have been improved to provide hundreds of cultivars with varying leaf shapes and textures. Mainly grown for their ribbed, green and variegated foliage, many hostas also have scented white or lilac flowers. Hostas have a long history of cultivation in Japan, thriving in the wild in mist and high humidity, in meadows and damp woodland. They adapt well to garden conditions – especially if their magnificent leaves can be protected from slugs and snails – and are useful as ground-cover plants under tree or shrub canopies. *Hosta sieboldiana* was introduced from Japan in 1876, and named in honour of the intrepid Philipp Franz von Siebold.

HOSTA SIEBOLDIANA

The nomenclature of hostas is much confused, many of them being named from Japanese clones and hybrids and not from original species. *Hosta sieboldiana*, and its variety *H. sieboldiana* var. *elegans*, normally come true from seed, but others confuse attempts for exact classification, with many hybrids of uncertain origin appearing in American breeding programmes. In Japanese gardens, where planting is kept simple, the hostas that are used tend to be close to original species. *H. sieboldiana* has heart-shaped, thick, puckered leaves (glaucous grey-green, almost blue above and paler below), with flowers fading from pale lilac to white. Its variegated form 'Frances Williams' is particularly popular with flower-arrangers. *Hosta sieboldiana* var. *elegans* is the finest form of the species, with even larger crinkled leaves of blue-grey.

THE OPENING OF JAPAN

Up to 1853 Japan had been closed to all foreigners, except for a few Dutch and Chinese traders, for more than 200 years. This was the year when Commodore Matthew Perry steamed into Edo Bay with four United States warships, and demanded a trade and supply treaty, and more humane treatment of shipwrecked American whaling crews. After a year's delay, the shogun granted the American requests, and before long agreements had been reached with Britain, France, the Netherlands and Russia.

Now that the plants and gardens that had tantalized Europeans for so long were accessible, a botanical gold rush began. After the treaty of 1854 the first plant collectors were Americans, but they only sent home herbarium specimens. In 1861 a keen amateur, Dr George Rogers Hall, sent back the first living plants to Boston, by dint of a Wardian case. Among the plants entrusted by Hall to the care of the horticulturist Francis Parkman were the hardy Japanese yew, *Taxus cuspidata*, 10 garden forms of *Chamaecyparis obtusa*, three magnolias, *Magnolia stellata*, *M. kobus* and *M. halleana*, the Japanese dogwood, *Cornus kousa*, *Wisteria floribunda* and various forms of *Acer palmatum*. Many of these plants have become popular on both sides of the Atlantic, with the Japanese yew and box, and their cultivars, proving more reliable in the extremes of the North American climate than their European relatives.

By 1860 other botanists and collectors were at work in Japan. John Gould Veitch (1839–70), a grandson of the famous English nurseryman based at Exeter, and

Shades of Japan
The oriental garden at Heale House in Wiltshire. With the collaboration of weeping willows, a thatched tea house and a vermilion bridge, this English garden speaks with a beguiling, if not entirely convincing, Japanese accent.

the Scot Robert Fortune (1812–80) were able to obtain plants from flourishing Japanese nurseries and send them home by steamship in Wardian cases. They also obtained the seeds of rare trees, now almost extinct in the wild, from temple gardens. At the same time, the Russian botanist Carl Maximowicz was busy sending huge collections of plants back to St Petersburg and recording many more. Maximowicz, who spent three and a half years in Japan, became such an authority on the flora of eastern Asia that St Petersburg became the centre for its scientific study.

NOTHING LIKE IT IN JAPAN

These collectors and explorers inaugurated a new era in Western gardening. The late 19th century saw a proliferation of naturalistic-style gardens with specially prepared water-fringed sites, where acid-loving Japanese plants could thrive. Many of the first Japanese-style gardens in Europe and America were made with little understanding of the meanings behind traditional Japanese garden elements. In their infatuation with newly available Japanese plants, Western gardeners tended to disregard a central tenet of Japanese garden design, that less is more. To give their water and bog gardens a Japanese twist, these early enthusiasts decked them with rocks and stone lanterns, red lacquer bridges and tea houses. The results were at best pastiches and at worst parodies of Japanese garden design.

Several English pioneers of the Japanese-style garden had seen the real thing. A.B. Freeman-Mitford, later Lord Redesdale, an English aristocrat who was attached for a while to the British embassy in Tokyo, made a collection of bamboos for his country house garden at Batsford in Gloucestershire. There he also sited the stone lanterns that were to become a ubiquitous prop of the Japanese garden abroad, but, interestingly, the Japanese gardens of Japan were not to Lord Redesdale's personal taste. He considered them too "spick and span" and "intensely artificial and a monument to wasted labour".

English interpretation
A tea house nestles in the green and pleasant shade of the recently restored Japanese garden at Tatton Park in Cheshire.

Lacquered image
The gateway to a Japanese garden is captured in gold and silver on this lacquered writing box, *c.*1900. Lacquer is a kind of natural varnish, tapped as a resin from trees. Practised to perfection in Japan, the art of lacquering went admired but untried by Europeans.

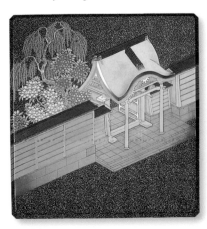

Meanwhile, at Heale House in the water meadows of Wiltshire, Louis Greville, who was also a former British diplomat, was seeking to create a more authentically Japanese garden. His garden, with its informal grouping of Japanese maples and its vermilion bridge, curving over an English stream, boasted a thatched tea house built by Japanese craftsmen. In 1910 Japanese craftsmen were also enlisted for the Moss Garden at Tatton Park in Cheshire – a Shinto shrine, a half-moon bridge and a tea house on an island are carpeted with moss and shaded by Japanese maples. Trees and shrubs are reflected in the water, although the colourful rhododendrons and azaleas are not pruned into typical Japanese shapes.

Even when Japanese craftsmen and Japanese materials were involved, these early Japanese-style gardens were more fanciful than faithful to Japanese garden-making principles. As Lawrence Weaver observed in 1915: "The disposition of a few typical ornaments, of a bronze stork here and stone lantern there, does not make a Japanese garden; it only makes an English garden speak with a Japanese accent." This truth is evident in the story of the proud owner showing off his newly completed Japanese garden to a visitor from Japan. The visitor admires it, saying, "We have nothing like it in Japan."

The early picture in North America was similar. Many of the first Japanese-style gardens created in the United States were associated with exhibitions or city parks. As with other Japanese gardens abroad, they tended to include a medley of Japanese-style garden designs and features. Today, Japanese-style gardens are almost commonplace in North American cities, and offer, in botanical gardens and arboreta, a precise location for Asian plants. Some of the early private gardens, commissioned by wealthy individuals at the turn of the 19th century, are now regularly accessible to public visitors. Built with great skill, often with Japanese participation, these gardens offer invaluable insights into the history of the Japanese garden abroad, as well as a respite from modernist influences.

In recent years an important influence on Western gardens, especially those in the United States, Canada, Australia and parts of Europe, has been the Japanese tradition of using and developing native flora rather than making gardens into collections of exotics. The idea of echoing native and regional landscapes appeals to 21st-century environmentalists intent on saving water and eliminating unnecessary herbicides and pesticides.

Since World War II, Japanese-style gardens have tended to concentrate on abstract sand and stone gardens, modest and uncontroversial creations that can be appreciated as modern art. As early as 1934 the landscape designer Christopher Tunnard, then in the forefront of modernist thought, suggested in his *Gardens in the Modern Landscape* that a contemporary garden, made to complement asymmetrically aligned modern architecture and expressing an affinity with nature, could seek inspiration from the gardens of Kyoto. Once discovered, the underlying principles of these classic Japanese gardens could offer the basis for a modern technique. In 1982 the Kyoto designer Nakane Kinsaku built the Tenshin-en garden

Venerable roots
Tree roots clothed in brilliant moss provide a spectacle in the Japanese-style garden of the Bloedel Reserve at Bainbridge Island, Washington.

The timeless view (opposite)
Unlike the landscapes of Italian palazzi, French chateaux and English country houses, this scene of stone and gravel at Terry Welch's garden in Seattle is unchanging. There are no flowers to fade, no leaves to fall. Change happens in the mind and perception of the onlooker.

next to the Boston Museum of Fine Arts' new west wing, designed by Chinese-American architect I.M. Pei, as well as the small stone and gravel garden of the east wing of the National Gallery in Washington in 1988.

PLANT CRAFT

After the treaties of the 1850s the mood in Japan was one of crisis and uncertainty. Fearing colonization by a European power, the Tokugawa government built warships and began to modernize the economy, but many Japanese looked to the past for inspiration on how to deal with the future. In 1868 the Tokugawa era ended with the Meiji Restoration, when warriors from the western provinces restored the emperor's political power. Sixteen-year-old Emperor Mutsuhito (1852–1912) moved his court to Edo, and renamed it Tokyo.

Although, in the interests of peace and prosperity, the Tokugawa shoguns tended to foster Confucian conventionalism at the expense of Buddhist visions, Japanese culture in general, and Japanese garden design in particular, were far from stagnant in the Edo period. Respect for old-time crafts and traditions is evinced by the continuing importance of the *Sakuteiki*, the garden-making handbook of the Heian era (see page 356), and the popularity of the *Tsukiyama Teizoden*, a book on traditional garden design by Kitamura Enkinsai.

By the early 16th century there was a flourishing nursery trade in Japan, and by the 17th century treatises on the cultivation of chrysanthemums and azaleas were being published, the latter already naming more than 400 varieties. Specialist societies for peonies, morning glories, camellias and cherries existed in Japan before foreign botanists and horticulturists arrived. During the centuries of authoritarian government and isolation from the rest of the world, the arts of miniature tray or dish gardens called *hachi-niwa* and bonsai flourished. Siebold described the practice of dwarfing trees in his *Flora Japonica*: "The Japanese have an incredible fondness for dwarf trees, and…the cultivation of the Ume or plum, is one of the most general and lucrative employments of the country. Such plants are increased by in-arching, and by this means specimens are obtained which have the peculiar habit of the Weeping Willow. A nurseryman offered me for sale in 1826 a plant in flower which was scarcely three inches high: this *chef d'oeuvre* of gardening was grown in a little lacquered box of three tiers, similar to those filled with drugs which the Japanese carry in their belts: in the upper tier was this Ume, in the second row a little Spruce Fir, and at the lowest a bamboo scarcely an inch and a half high."

ANCIENT WAYS, NEW MATERIALS

Since the Second World War, garden designers in Japan have been aware of their heritage without feeling constrained by it. Instead of copying the protoypes, or slavishly following traditional rules, they have been more inclined to use new materials in imaginative and distinctly Japanese ways. In the late 1930s the celebrated garden designer Shigemori Mirei made a study of the old garden masters and the extant gardens. The resulting 26 volumes of research are an invaluable source of information and inspiration. Discouraged by the lack of new

Nature in miniature
The finest bonsai are produced using plants, such as this Japanese red maple, which have tapering trunks, naturally twisted branches and small leaves. The art of dwarfing woody trees and shrubs, by pruning and restraining root growth, has been popular for centuries in Japan.

vitality displayed in contemporary gardens, Shigemori began to build gardens
himself. He liked to explain his approach with a quotation from the *Sakuteiki*:
"While we are influenced by the past and must consider the desires of the garden
owner, we should still strive to create something different whenever we undertake a new piece of work."

Some of Shigemori's best-known achievements are showcased in his *Japanese
Gardens*, which was published in 1964, and features some 47 of the 120 gardens
created by this modern master. Three of the most highly regarded are in the
precincts of the medieval Tofuku-ji monastery at Kyoto. In the first rectangle he
made a series of green mounds, with three-quarters of the garden a series of vertical and horizontal stone groups to represent mountains and islands. At the west
end, shrubs are cut into low chequerboard patterns, recalling the rectilinear grid of
land division, while in the north garden, the most famous of Shigemori's designs,
squared granite slabs are set into a sea of moss.

CHAPTER TWELVE

A time of change

FROM
NATURALISM
TO
MODERNISM
1870 – 1950

THE YEAR 1870 WAS A WATERSHED. By the last quarter of the 19th century the developments in garden styles could almost cease to be considered in terms of separate continents and civilizations. Britain, Europe and the United States were all now open to similar influences, with cultural movements effecting a cross-fertilization of garden ideas. By the turn of the century both continents were influenced by Japanese philosophies bringing new aesthetic and intellectual stimulation. Also from the Far East came a new influx of hardy gardenworthy plants to boost the reaction against Victorian artificiality. The spirit of naturalism has pervaded the story of gardening ever since, although it manifests itself differently in different areas of the world and occasionally assumes some unlikely guises. During these eight decades it became evident that nature was now very much on the move.

Classicism at Renishaw
Sir George Sitwell, the eccentric baronet and author of *On the Making of Gardens*, transformed the garden at Renishaw, near Sheffield, into a classic Italian landscape, with terraces descending from the house to frame the distant Brown-style landscape and lake.

THE RISE OF NATURALISM

The year of 1870 – the year at which this chapter opens – marks the publication of *The Wild Garden* by William Robinson. It is a symbolic watershed in a longer process that evolved from the 18th-century Landscape Movement and which has not yet spent its force. Over the years this natural approach has developed into a full-scale ecological attitude to planting, the importance of saving plants threatened in the wild, and the development of regional gardening styles in which plants appropriate to climate and soil conditions are selected. The new American garden style of Wolfgang Oehme and James van Sweden (see page 442) of the 1980s, which incorporates native prairie plants and East Asian grasses, and the new German and Dutch-style perennial planting of the 1990s have evolved through a hundred years of "naturalism". Today, in the 21st century, whether we choose a formal or a more natural style for our gardens, we have absorbed the lessons of naturalism in much of our actual planting. During those 130 years or so other styles have come and gone, leaving valuable legacies, but most, even with some degree of formality, have had undertones of more relaxed planting styles. The Arts and Crafts Movements on both sides of the Atlantic, the unparalleled influence of the Jekyll/Lutyens partnership on Edwardian flower gardening and its potency today, the rise and fall of modernism, the post-World War II fashions for useful ground-covers driven by a shortage of money and skilled labour and a parallel interest in mixed and shrub beds and borders all reflect Robinsonian teaching.

WILDNESS OR WILDERNESS?

Europe and North America shared a common garden tradition and seemed set on a common path of development. However, there was a quite fundamental difference

A reverence for nature
The Course of Empire: the Savage State by Thomas Cole (1801–48). Cole, an English-born painter, settled in New York State and became the founder of the Hudson River school of landscape painters who "discovered" the beauties of the untouched American wilderness. While in 19th-century Europe the "wild" no longer existed, in the United States Americans could marvel at the genuine beauty of nature and seek to emulate it in their gardens by using regional native plants arranged in naturalistic ways. As Americans explored the wilderness they became increasingly aware of the need to save parts of it for posterity and to conserve indigenous plants in their habitats.

llljl l.,h,.,,.l,,,.,.

in their emerging attitude to nature. In Europe by the late 19th century the landscape was old, managed and altered by man over centuries, with no real "wild" still in existence. Attempts at planting in imitation of nature reflected the artificiality of the existing countryside. In America the "wilderness" idea, promoted by painting schools such as the Hudson River artists, could be a genuine search for a new beginning. Saving native plants in their habitats and generally working with and sustaining the landscape could coincide with dreams of a still-existing wilderness.

American contemporaries of Robinson, largely independent of his influence, also explored the possibilities of using plants in more natural ways, developing their own mode of naturalistic planting, making use, in regional planting schemes, of the huge range of gardenworthy plants found in North America. Pioneer environmentalists such as the Scotsman John Muir and the great American park designer Frederick Law Olmsted, who first introduced Americans to their wilderness areas, the Danish Jens Jensen working in tune with Frank Lloyd Wright's Prairie School of architecture in the Midwest, the designer Warren Manning who persuaded his clients to use native plants suitable for their sites, and various subsequent landscape designers and naturalists have established the need to work with nature. They aimed not only to save plants but also to save water and to prevent pollution and the spread of disease, themes which have assumed even more importance today. For both Muir and Olmsted the wilderness acquired a sacred quality, evoking a reverential mood, but they still appreciated that nature needed manipulating.

Olmsted himself, following in the footsteps of Andrew Jackson Downing (see page 306), was first inspired in his appreciation of the need to provide public recreation spaces in cities by a visit in 1850 to Joseph Paxton's new park at Birkenhead, near Liverpool. From this beginning, and from his successful partnership with the English architect Calvert Vaux in creating New York's Central Park, he became the most famous advocate of city parks, the "green lungs" of the people, his influence spreading throughout the civilized world. At a time when few landlords were creating vast-scale designs, city parks were now being developed for public enjoyment and, especially in the United States, park-like cemeteries. During the last hundred years or so landscape architecture training has become

The BLUE POPPY

MECONOPSIS BETONICIFOLIA

Among the most exciting finds of the late 19th century was the famous blue poppy, *Meconopsis betonicifolia*, first observed by the French missionary the Abbé Delavay in 1886, growing in Yunnan Province, China. It was also recorded by Colonel Frederick Bailey and George Forrest before being finally introduced into Europe by Frank Kingdon Ward from Tumbatse in south Tibet in 1926. "Suddenly I looked and there, like a blue panel dropped from heaven – a stream of blue poppies dazzling as sapphires in the pale light," wrote Kingdon Ward of his first sighting. The seeds, which he later harvested in 40 degrees of frost, then had to endure a temperature of 90 degrees in India, from where they were shipped to Britain. Nevertheless, within little more than a month seedlings had germinated at Kew, Edinburgh, Wisley and a hundred other gardens to which Kingdon Ward had sent consignments.

Meconopsis betonicifolia, which requires an acid soil and high humidity, was soon being grown in the wild gardens and planted woodlands advocated by William Robinson. In fact, most wild gardens need skilful management and, in its special soil requirements, this blue meconopsis was just as demanding as many of the American woodland plants introduced in previous centuries. It proved easy to grow from seed, but flowered less successfully, although Kingdon Ward saw it massed in display beds in London's Hyde Park and Glasgow's Ibrox Park within two years of its introduction to Britain.

The blue poppy was not the first meconopsis to be introduced into Britain. The light blue, Himalayan *M. simplicifolia* had flowered in England as early as 1848, forging a pre-Ice Age generic link with the little yellow or orange Welsh poppy, *M. cambrica*, a hardy self-seeding British native.

Gravetye example (opposite)
William Robinson tried out many
of his theories at his home at
Gravetye Manor, West Sussex, and
wrote about it in *Gravetye Manor, or
Twenty Years' Work Around an Old
Manor House*, published in 1911. His
garden became a model for his ideas
on the naturalization of bulbs and
hardy plants. Landscape designer and
plantsman Edouard André
dispatched 400 autumn-flowering
cyclamen to him from France, while
friends in America sent trilliums and
the moccasin flower (*Cypripedium
acaule*), which were difficult to find
in the quantities he needed. His
interests also covered the
acclimatization of hardy trees and
shrubs, many of which can still be
seen at Gravetye (the house is now
run as a hotel, with the garden open
to guests). The restored garden
reflects Robinson's lifetime's work in
encouraging a more natural style of
gardening.

Irish interpretation
The gardens of Anne's Grove (right)
in County Cork, Ireland, are
renowned for their Robinsonian-
style planting. Both the woodland
and water garden are awash with
hardy plants suitable for the terrain,
acid soil and soft, humid Irish
weather.

not only a vocation but a whole science involved with preserving nature, its
disciplines both embracing aesthetics and emphasizing self-sustaining scientific
horticulture and the conservation of natural environments such as wetlands,
woodland and meadow.

ROBINSON'S REVOLUTION

For all that the delightful "cottage-style" planting dependent on a wide mix of
both woody and herbaceous plants was invented in England, its prophet was an
Irishman, William Robinson (1838–1935). Long acclaimed as the father of
the English flower garden, in Europe he is still considered the originator of the
natural tradition. Before all the scientific jargon of ecology, habitats and plant
communities, Robinsonian planting meant choosing plants suitable for a garden
site and working with nature, rather than imposing a style based on visual aesthetic values. Gertrude Jekyll in England, Willy Lange and Karl Foerster in Germany, Jacques P. Thijsse in Holland and more recently Richard Hansen at
Weihenstephan, near Munich, together with a host of modern gardeners have
developed Robinson's ideas into a scientific gardening mode consistent with an
ecological approach.

Although by no means the first to recommend working with nature in the
garden, William Robinson somehow captured the moral high ground in his
books and magazines. *The Wild Garden* was published in 1870 and his *English*

THE GROWING MESSAGE OF THE WILD GARDEN

I N *THE WILD GARDEN*, written in 1870 when he was only 32, William Robinson recommended gardening with hardy plants in woods, at the wood's edge and in meadows. In this one short book Robinson managed to revolutionize attitudes to gardening. It struck many chords with those who disliked the flamboyant and wasteful practice of twice-annual bedding out in formal flowerbeds. Where other writers, such as Shirley Hibberd, had merely suggested growing hardy perennials in borders, Robinson went a great deal further by announcing a whole new gardening philosophy. He suggested that "vast numbers of beautiful hardy plants from other countries…might be naturalized…in many situations in our plantations, fields and woods – a world of delightful plant beauty". Unhappily his message is often misunderstood. Basically what he was recommending was giving plants the type of soil and aspect that they would enjoy, rather than forcing them into a mould to satisfy aesthetic considerations based on colour or season.

It is important to remember that Robinson did not insist on native-plant gardening; instead he recommended using any wild or exotic flower that

WILLIAM ROBINSON, PHOTOGRAPHED IN ABOUT 1900

would thrive in a given situation. "The idea of the wild garden is placing plants of other countries, as hardy as our hardiest wild flowers, in places where they will flourish without further care or cost." He thoroughly appreciated what he saw on his travels in America: "It is that which one sees in American woods in late summer and autumn when the Golden Rods and Asters are seen in bloom together. It is one of numerous aspects of the vegetation of other countries which the 'wild garden' will make possible in gardens."

Properly understood and applied, this philosophy is of low-maintenance gardening with self-sustaining and self-perpetuating plant associations thriving together. *The Wild Garden* does not offer ideas on actual garden design – as his *English Flower Garden* does – but it contains ideas for a transitional zone between the garden proper and the surrounding landscape – ideas followed up by Gertrude Jekyll and an important part of any naturalistic gardening scheme today.

In advocating the idea of naturalizing spring bulbs such as narcissi, snowdrops, bluebells, anemones and crocus in grass, Robinson was an innovator; in his recommendations of woodland and woodland edge plantings he was a prophet.

The Wild Garden is still highly readable, although we take with a pinch of salt statements such as that in a wild garden "an owner might go away for ten years and find it more beautiful than ever on his return". Most of us find that although a "wild" garden may not need many hours of labouring maintenance, it calls for a constant programme of skilled editing and manipulation in order to retain its natural beauty.

Revolutionary vision

The publication of William Robinson's book The Wild Garden *heralded a new attitude to gardening, and the book itself, which was illustrated by Alfred Parsons (frontispiece below), remained in print for nearly 70 years, until after his death.*

Flower Garden in 1883, both going into many editions during his lifetime. What had been a trend in late Victorian gardening became avant-garde fashion under Robinson, and an aesthetically sophisticated planting style used by his disciple Gertrude Jekyll in her border schemes. His plea for choosing hardy plants suitable for the site (though they did not necessarily have to be native) not only influenced gardening on a grand scale at a time when the new introductions from Asia were enhancing fine collections and arboreta, but also had a direct appeal for the ordinary home gardener. For the plantsman-collector the Robinsonian recommendations for self-sustaining horticulture encouraged mixed planting of trees, shrubs, perennials and bulbs from all corners of the world as long as they were suitable for the site: the "layered" style which is still a feature of all so-called naturalistic schemes. And these schemes could be readily adapted for smaller spaces.

Robinson's way of planting came to represent a new ideal in gardening practice. Rather different from the great environmentalists such as Olmsted – or, indeed, the makers of the English 18th-century parks – Robinson altered the emphasis from the grand scale of landscape to the detail of specific plants and plantings, very much as Jens Jensen was to do in his prairie schemes in the American Midwest. It was the possibility of adapting Robinson's ideas to quite small-

Naturalism in America
On the East Coast of America, artistic gardeners such as Henry du Pont pursued their own aesthetic renderings of Robinson's recommendations. At Winterthur, in Delaware, du Pont wove exotic pink and white azaleas under a canopy of native tulip trees (*Liriodendron tulipifera*), underplanted with American native woodland plants, such as blue-flowered *Phlox divaricata* and Virginian bluebell (*Mertensia virginica*).

scale gardens that ultimately revolutionized 20th-century gardening, both confirming a new awareness of plant requirements and making an interest in the art of gardening universal instead of the prerogative of the wealthy.

Imperious, and with a difficult and argumentative personality, Robinson towered above his less forceful contemporaries. Unfortunately, his sometimes almost reckless assaults on those who disagreed with him, although drawing an avid readership at the time, have led to some historic misinterpretation of his true intentions. From a distance of over a hundred years it is now easier to assess his importance – and to be entertained by the colourful nature of the debate.

Robinson's viewpoint, derived in part from John Ruskin, and much in sympathy with views expressed by William Morris and the Arts and Crafts Movement, developed as a moral crusade, as fervent as the current 21st-century American dedication to growing native plants. He attacked his contemporaries for the artificiality of the bedding system and for their dependence on architects of garden design who were not themselves horticulturists. As his ideas crystallized, he opposed any type of formal gardening. When he referred to Victorian bedding as "the pastry cook's garden", had he perhaps been reading Francis Bacon, who in 1625 was complaining that knot gardens had an affinity to tarts? He despised any form of topiary or "vegetable sculpture" and, exaggerating as ever, suggested that "clipping yews leads to leprous disfigurement, disease and death". Certainly some of his appeal was emotional rather than rational, and his ideas were not always consistent. Recognizing the desirability of giving a house a platform, at his own garden at Gravetye Manor, an imposing Elizabethan mansion in Sussex acquired in 1885, he terraced the slopes around the house and introduced structured flowerbeds and a pergola, although his planting elsewhere on his estate reflected his naturalistic views.

THE NATURALISTIC BANDWAGON UNDER ATTACK

Although the ideas of William Robinson largely prevailed, in his day not everyone (and especially not every architect) believed that gardens should be "natural". Reginald Blomfield's *The Formal Garden in England* (1892) recommended that a house should have a proper architectural setting, praising the "refinement and reserve" of the 17th-century garden. Closer in spirit to the Arts and Crafts protagonists who advocated house and garden as an integrated unit, Blomfield concentrated on design rather than plants. He condemned both the mindless patterns of Victorian bedding and the woolly-minded romanticism of Robinson's naturalistic bandwagon. His book has minor historical inaccuracies but is still highly readable, a useful antidote to those who scorn any form of garden geometry. At the time it helped to shape the undefined boundaries of the Arts and Crafts gardens. Together with J.D. Sedding's *Garden Craft, Old and New* (1891), it also made Robinson blow his top.

Seeing these books as a criticism of all he had spent 20 years working for, Robinson fired off insults with a vitriolic review in

The garden-architect's view
Sir Reginald Blomfield (1846–1942), author of the controversial *The Formal Garden in England* with drawings by Inigo Thomas, designed the grand gardens at Mellerstain in Berwickshire, illustrated here in a bird's-eye view perspective by Adrian Berrington. Blomfield's book instigated controversy over the appropriate roles of architect and gardener in design, his views implacably opposed by William Robinson, nature's prophet. At Mellerstain, Blomfield applied Le Nôtre-like ideas of grandeur, with terraces, parterres and water features. Not everything was done as drawn, but the scheme is still comprehensive, with magnificent central views to the lake and distant Cheviot Hills.

A Renaissance voice
Inigo Thomas, who illustrated
Blomfield's *The Formal Garden in
England*, was himself a landscape
architect of genius. He tended to
make revivalist gardens, often
including topiary features harking
back to the late 17th or early 18th
centuries. His gardens at
Athelhampton, Dorset (left),
designed in 1891, demonstrate his
mastery of spatial conceptions. The
elegant stonework and sunken
garden, overlooked by a terrace and
pavilions with cross-axial views,
seem a perfect example of
Renaissance planning. Yet in their
relative simplicity, Thomas's plans
also have a modern flavour,
incorporating the low-lying water
meadows as a foil to the more
architectural features. In 1893,
when Athelhampton was finished,
Thomas went on to make a study
of Italian gardens.

Garden Design and Architects' Gardens to start one of the most famous of garden controversies. Gardeners lined up behind the outspoken Robinson, architects supported the equally opinionated Blomfield. Today if you analyse the points in question there seems very little between the opposing schools of thought. Just as in his own garden Robinson recognized the need for an architectural platform to link house and garden, so both Blomfield and Sedding, although committed to the more architectural context, were firmly on Robinson's side about the worst extravagances of bedding out. It all seems largely irrelevant now – although its rhetoric is amusing. Sedding held the middle ground and may in the end have had the most influence on contemporary garden styles, encouraging both an architectural framework and a freedom in planting – a style honed and perfected by Gertrude Jekyll in the lasting triumph of the Edwardian garden.

THE NATURAL MOVEMENT IN EUROPE

Robinson's ideas soon spread to Continental Europe, especially Germany and Scandinavia. By the 1900s the German garden architect Willy Lange (1864–1941) further developed the idea of natural gardening by taking an ethical standpoint, borrowing some of his ideas from Robinson, and even drawing on Goethe's garden theories and Alexander von Humboldt's ideas of association of plants with similar appearance (see page 286). Lange is of particular interest because he anticipated the function of the garden as a nature preserve, not so much with the intention of protecting threatened plants, but with an almost religious veneration of nature – ideas in harmony with some of the more extreme native-plant fanatics of today. His interpretation was stricter than Robinson's generalization about hardy plants; he preferred German natives to foreign ones and interpreted the garden as part of the surrounding landscape. Later Lange's concept of the "nature garden", in which he

Continental drift
In Germany, Karl Foerster extended the use of natural planting theories both in his own garden (below) and by introducing "natural-looking" plants which he distributed through his nursery.

Ideological planting

Twentieth-century discussion for
and against natural gardening often
became polemical. Willy Lange, in
Germany, took on Robinson's
mantle, turning the "nature garden"
into an almost entirely "design-less"
entity based on political ideology.
He saw the "artistic nature garden"
as the highest form of garden design.

Holland's heem parks

In Holland, a country where
preserving any form of indigenous
planting was vital, J.P. Thijsse taught
principles of natural landscaping to
his compatriots, and at Haarlem,
outside Antwerp, he laid out a series
of *heem* parks (right and far right).
The layout and planting of the parks
(*heem* means homestead) was
determined on strict ecological
lines, with only native plants
included. By the 1980s, the term
"ecological" was often used instead
of "natural", indicating the
importance of environmental issues.
The *heem* parks work as an inspiring
landscape concept, closely related to
Ian McHarg's teaching in the
United States during the 1970s (see
page 441), but they need a large
canvas, not often available to private
gardeners.

accorded plants and animals equal rights to those of the
garden owner, was extended as if it was typical of the
German people. By the 1930s the idea was used as a form
of discrimination against Jewish people who, according to
the National Socialists, could not grasp the idea of nature
preservation. Lange's ideas coincided with other Nazi ideals
in a search for a Germanic identity, with forest themes
invading both art and politics. Lange's approach to naturalism may have been debased by political ideology. The
demand during the Fascist period for German plants for
German gardens set in the German landscape was echoed
in part by the Danish-born Jens Jensen's almost racist recommendations for native plantings in the American Midwest, which condemned
the oriental or Latin styles that seemed to be encroaching on the Germanic spirit
of much of settled America. Interestingly, if in Germany the identification with
wilderness and original forest was part of 1930s totalitarian ideology, in the
United States the idea of wilderness became an emblem of democracy. However,
this did not prevent a genuine appreciation of the principles involved in the idea
of the designed garden being fitted appropriately into its surrounding landscape,
with plants chosen for their appropriateness for the site. None of these theories
seems so important now, just as it hardly matters who first formulated the "natural" ideas. Karl Foerster in Germany, J.P. Thijsse in Holland and many others
have followed in more or less extreme ways. Today, to the "natural" gardeners, a
country garden is generally seen as a part
of its surrounding landscape, with an
implication that it should not attract
attention as an alien element but should
have planting corresponding to the typical
indigenous vegetation.

AMERICA'S NATURE MOVEMENT

In the second half of the 19th century,
Americans, inspired in part by the romantic poetry of Wordsworth and Emerson
and the experiences of Thoreau at Walden
Pond, awoke to the aesthetics of their own
natural landscape. In the 1840s Andrew
Jackson Downing was among the first to
attempt to define garden beauty for Americans, encouraging them to make gardens
appropriate to the surrounding landscape.
By the end of the 19th century the environmental movement, although not
strictly relevant to gardening, was having a
considerable influence on how garden

THE PAINTERLY VISION OF CHARLES PLATT

CHARLES A. PLATT (1861–1933) was first a painter and etcher, mainly of landscapes. While studying for five years in Paris he visited Italy. He began his career as an architect and garden designer while living with a colony of artists at Cornish, New Hampshire, attracted there by the sculptor Augustus Saint-Gaudens and his circle. In spring 1892 he returned to Italy to study the villa gardens, taking with him his brother William, who was working in Frederick Law Olmsted's office. Platt wanted to introduce William to a more disciplined tradition of gardening. The next year Platt published articles in *Harper's* magazine, which in 1894 were expanded into his book *Italian Gardens*. From then on clients were never lacking, one of his most important being Charles F. Sprague at Faulkner Farm, Brookline, where work commenced in 1897.

Among Platt's best-known projects is the mansion and garden at Gwinn for the entrepreneur William Gwinn Mather (1857–1951) on the shores of Lake Erie near Cleveland. Here, in 1906, Platt built the house – modelled in part on the White House in Washington DC – and, in an uneasy collaboration with Warren Manning, the garden of the 11-hectare (27-acre) estate. Manning, who had already worked for Mather on previous projects and came from the Olmsted school, was the leading proponent of the informal landscape approach, devoted to using native plants when appropriate. But he was no fanatic and accepted that gardens immediately around a house should have an architectural basis. Like Olmsted he believed in the spiritual benefits of a naturalistic approach. (Manning was one of the founder members of the American Society of Landscape Architects.)

Platt's plans for the 2-hectare (5-acre) garden were in two parts. To the north, Lake Erie was theatrically framed by the pillars of a semicircular portico with a complex system of stairways, terraces and fountains. Box-edged beds framed a lawn on the south and west, flanked by a wild garden to the east. Manning was influential in establishing the cathedral-like avenue of American elms, silvery spires of Lombardy poplars and wildflower carpets in the woodland.

Whatever the stresses and strains in the relationship, Platt and Manning achieved a masterpiece, the geometric complex in the home grounds complementing the relaxed beauty of the wilder areas, an example of how formal and informal approaches can be combined in one great landscape without detriment to either. In fact rather the reverse, art and nature working in accord. In 1914 Mather called in Ellen Biddle Shipman to "soften" some of Platt's too rigid planting in the formal beds.

Platt never wrote a book expressing his theories of landscape design, but in 1931 he stated his principles in an article: "The essential truth in country house architecture is that house and gardens together form one single design. They cannot be separated." He was responsible for re-establishing landscape design as one of the fine arts. His painter's training led him to believe that creating architecture and gardens was governed by the same principles as that of landscape painting – the skilful handling of perspective, a balanced composition and a unity of conception. (We follow up the Italian influence and the role played by Platt on page 409.)

Serene geometry
At Gwinn, Platt's designs for the formal parts of the garden achieved a beauty that perfectly complemented the more naturalistic areas.

styles developed. In the early 1900s landscape architecture matured as a science. Through the century it was to develop into something much more than rearranging the topography of a site and placing plants artistically. Within the next hundred years it was to become a discipline embracing the whole ecological system in which geology, topography, land use, vegetation, wildlife and climate are all critical elements in design practice. The saving of native plants in their habitats has become a crucial part of all conservation and teaching landscape architects to work with an existing landscape rather than damaging it is an essential part of a new ecological gardening ethic. The danger of such a strategy is an implied assumption that nature itself is the only possible model for landscape design, something with which many of us would not agree.

In the last years of the 19th century, Americans were as fully involved in the dialogue between what was thought of as Olmsted's ideological framework for landscaping and the more formal approaches advocated by architects as Robinson and Blomfield were in Britain. At the time Charles Platt's alternative structured gardens (see opposite) were equally popular. The debate is closely akin to the nature and art controversy that continues today. Both styles were derivative, with the natural ideal more easily adapted to America, where great stretches of wilderness still existed. It was not until nearly the end of the 20th century that any attempt to define an American style was recognized as dependent on a garden's location.

JENS JENSEN AND THE PRAIRIE SCHOOL

Jens Jensen (1860–1950), a Danish immigrant working in the Midwest from the 1880s, encouraged Americans – often new arrivals like himself – to appreciate the beauty of the rolling prairies and the distant horizons. His interest in naturalism in the landscape is said to have begun from a visit to the Englischer Garten in Berlin in his youth. His American landscape designs were characterized by broad open meadows bordered by wooded peninsulas and woodland trails that curved out of sight in the forests. Although passionate about saving the native prairie plants, including horizontal spreading hawthorns, crab apples and perennials, he recognized the necessity of retaining more formal areas around the house, in which he planted traditional plants, many from the Old World.

Jensen's genius lay in his appreciation of the Midwestern light and the character of the untouched countryside. Long before environmental activists, he foresaw the need to preserve the native heritage, the dunes, forests, prairies and wetlands of

Harmonious landscapes
Danish-born Jens Jensen, working in the American Midwest, was one of the first garden environmentalists. In his book *Siftings*, published in 1939, Jensen sums up his attitude to garden-making: "Landscaping has just been born, and its birthright is the soul of the out-of-doors. The world is rich in landscapes in harmony with soil and climatic conditions. In the virgin forest you can read the story of creation…there are a multitude of ideas for the fertile mind to work with and shape into something that will inspire the race with a spiritual force for real accomplishments in the realm of art."

Natural vista (opposite)
Warren Manning's designs at Stan Hywet in Akron, Ohio (1911), for the industrialist F.A. Sieberling, famously include this birch alley, underplanted with periwinkle and lily-of-the-valley. There is also an alley of European plane trees, as well as a naturalistic planting of American natives in the woodland. Manning (1860–1938) had worked for Olmsted before setting up his own office in 1896, where he was later to employ Fletcher Steele and Dan Kiley (see pages 432 and 434), forging a continuity between Olmsted and the modern era. Working in the mainly wooded American landscape, Manning applied English picturesque features such as stony crags and waterfalls inside the much more enclosed forests, but allowed long views into the countryside. He combined domestic orchards and meadows with his visionary views of the American wilderness.

the Midwest, and became increasingly aware of the need to use plants ecologically suitable to a site. Even by the early 1900s the supply of water was beginning to be a problem.

Jensen became increasingly concerned by the destruction of the native flora – so much so that for his Lincoln Memorial Garden in Springfield, Illinois, he sent out school parties to collect native trees, shrubs and perennials that were threatened by agricultural and commercial development for inclusion in his scheme. From 1913 he worked for Mr and Mrs Henry Ford at Fair Lane and in the 1920s and 30s for Edsel and Eleanor Ford at Gaukler's Point outside Detroit. His work for the Henry Fords ended when he refused to incorporate a formal garden into one of his meadow landscapes, the "path of the setting sun", in which he had arranged native sugar maples, dogwood, shadbush, paper birch and hawthorns underplanted with wild flowers.

Jensen worked on schools, playgrounds, parks, hospitals and government buildings, besides making landscapes for wealthy businessmen such as the Ford family. Each of his projects reflected the nature of the site and the individual needs of the client, but Jensen established some of his own trademarks, including symbolic plants species and council rings (see page 288).

The Prairie Movement in garden design was described by Wilhelm Miller in *The Prairie Spirit in Landscape Gardening* in 1915. He gave Jensen and Ossian Cole Simonds the credit for celebrating the openness and flatness of the natural Midwest landscape, as well as opening out the steep ravines and forests found in the North Shore region of Chicago. Their designs were idealizations of nature rather than literal re-creations, emphasizing the spirit of the regional landscape. In his *Siftings* Jensen emphasizes his view that man can never satisfactorily mimic nature: "nature is not to be copied – man cannot copy God's out-of-doors. He can only interpret its message in a composition of living tones." Like Olmsted earlier, following the tenets of the 18th-century English landscape "improvers", Jensen argued that his work was art rather than an imitation of natural scenery. Modern native plant enthusiasts, often followers of Jensen, tend to overlook his crucial understanding that the best work was an interpretation rather than a copy. Re-establishing prairies in suitable locations and saving plants in their wild habitat would have been among his priorities today, rather than collecting them in an artificial environment. In the 1930s, writing for German garden magazines, Jensen developed his unfortunate ideological ideas that "Germanic-type" gardening better expressed the American spirit than those styles subject to Latin or oriental influences.

ORIGINS OF THE ARTS AND CRAFTS MOVEMENT

The Arts and Crafts Movement evolved in England as a recognizable style during the 1880s and 1890s, and a few years later in America in more regional interpretations. In England its origins can be traced to John Ruskin (1819–1900), who believed that real quality in design was possible only if a craftsman's imagination and creative powers were integrated in the product – the antithesis of the inhuman character of mass-produced factory goods that was rapidly gaining momentum.

Outside-inside
The trelliswork in the garden at William Morris's Red House in Kent was to inspire *Trellis*, one of his first three wallpaper designs, in 1864. The two other patterns, *Daisy* and *Fruit*, were also inspired by plants in his garden. The whole Arts and Crafts Movement, both in Europe and in America, however individualistically practised, can be said to owe its origins to Morris's original impulse towards organic art and architecture. The movement's nostalgia for a pre-industrial age was prompted not by the introduction of machines, but by the way they were used in tasteless mass production.

ARTS AND CRAFTS GARDENS IN EUROPE

The Arts and Crafts Movement was not confined to Britain but extended into Europe as well as North America. The German architect Hermann Muthesius studied architecture in England and published his *Landhaus and Garten* in 1907. In it, he insisted that "house and garden are a unit of which the main features must be thought out by the same genius".

The movement also looked to nature for guidance. As early as 1838 Ruskin castigated Victorian bedding plants as "an assembly of unfortunate beings, pampered and bloated above their natural size, stewed and heated into diseased growth", his polemic as violent as anything Robinson contributed later in the century. William Morris, too, emphasized the importance of genuine craftsmanship, readily joining Robinson in expressing his horror of the contemporary bedding system. Morris – poet, pioneering socialist, dyer, weaver and designer, a passionate believer that all creative work must have a practical side – first employed Philip Webb in 1859 to help him build Red House in an orchard site in Kent, where they were able to construct their ideal. It was described by Hermann Muthesius, the German architect, as "the first private house of the new artistic culture…conceived and built as a unified whole inside and out", linked with the surrounding countryside by the use of vernacular building traditions. (Muthesius here gives a just definition of what the Arts and Crafts Movement was all about.) Nature did not have it all its own way. The Arts and Crafts garden was inspired by medieval formality, with old-fashioned fruit growing in the orchards and old-fashioned flowers in the beds – "roses on trellises, hollyhocks, great spires of pink, orange and white with their soft downy leaves" – and it established a formula to be explored, extended and made fashionable by Gertrude Jekyll in her expression of the Edwardian garden.

Even today, in a less sentimental age, we can be moved by the romanticization of the past. The Arts and Crafts Movement has had a significant influence on all garden development since 1900. By no means in total sympathy with Robinson's plea for gardening in more natural ways with hardy plants, its advocates did share with him an emphasis on simplicity, traditional plants and vernacular materials, together with a reverence for nature. To this they added a nostalgic searching for a past era before styles were debased by over-sophistication. As advocated by Robinson, plants were encouraged to break free from formal control, to spill across pathways and over walls, to seed in unexpected places, to blur the straight lines made by a strong structure so that, superficially at least, nature seemed to have the upper hand. Above all, for the mass of the people, it was a style suitable for all sizes of garden and its ready adaptation to low-maintenance techniques has given it an enduring quality. But whereas Robinson advocated that the garden should be outside the control of the architect of the house, the Arts and Crafts practitioners believed that house and garden should be designed as one integrated whole, the garden a logical extension of the house, extending around it as a series of linked spaces.

In 1883 Robinson quoted from William Morris in his frontispiece to *The English Flower Garden*: "Another thing also much too commonly seen, is an aberration of the human mind, which otherwise I would have been ashamed to warn you of. It is technically called carpet-gardening. Need I explain it further? I had rather not, for when I think of it, even when I am quite alone, I blush with shame at the thought." Morris and his followers encouraged the use of traditional and regional crafts, a simplicity of design depending on skills passed down from father to son, its principles readily applied to the more intimate garden rather than the grand estates. The revival of the idea of the pre-18th-century English garden, with clipped hedges, alleys and flowerbeds filled with old English flowers, although mostly in the mind, set the scene for a closer relationship with the simplicities of nature. It is ironic that in a search for an escape from Victorian excesses, the Arts and Crafts partisans returned to the more intimate English styles which had been abandoned in the 18th century in exchange for the naturalistic Landscape Movement.

By romanticizing historical myths and the rural idyll in painting, architecture and gardening, the Arts and Crafts Movement liberated culture. In their paintings the Pre-Raphaelites had associated wild nature with a type of feminine beauty unfettered by conventions. Their work signified nostalgia for a pre-industrial age. In their gardens, the Arts and Crafts designers exploited similar cravings for an uncluttered and romantic past. Clipped hedges and trelliswork screens were acceptable because, although formal and structural, they seemed to relate to a period before industrialization. The Edwardian garden, with a series of terraces, pergolas, sunken gardens and herbaceous borders, although superficially almost as architectural and geometric as its Victorian equivalent, was seen as something

Kelmscott's inspiration

After the sale of Red House, William Morris moved to Kelmscott Manor in Oxfordshire, his country retreat from 1871 to 1876. It was here he "discovered" the Cotswolds. In *News from Nowhere*, published in 1892, Kelmscott represented an archetypal old house that had grown organically "out of the soil". The garden – as it is today – is quite formal, with its stone-flagged approach lined with standard roses, reminiscent of a 17th-century English garden.

quite different, as the actual planting styles expressed a much more direct affinity to the Arts and Crafts ideal and a harmony with natural form.

ARTS AND CRAFTS GARDENS IN AMERICA

In America, Arts and Crafts gardens have more regional context and vary according to available vernacular materials, climatic conditions and historical context. As in Britain, the Arts and Crafts Movement here had its origins in the evils of industrial development, in which individual workmen ceased to have freedom of design in the interest of mass production. In Europe, where real wildness had long ceased to exist, Arts and Crafts protagonists looked back in history to the period when local gardens seemed to have been laid out with a firm eye on appropriate planting and prevailing culture. In America, where the wilderness still existed without such cultural loading, the Arts and Crafts garden could be developed with greater freedom. In searching for the pre-industrial pleasures found in the productions of true craftsmen, it was possible to emphasize the regional building materials available to the first colonists and the westward-moving pioneers.

Until World War I and the financial crash of 1929, during the affluent golden age, many of the grand gardens in Europe and America tended to be almost lookalikes, designed with scant regard to regional suitability. The best designers, however, had a more sensitive approach, inspired by a common interest in natural objects. A Lutyens and Jekyll garden, making use of old traditions in Surrey in England, might ostensibly have little resemblance to the garden at Cranbrook Academy in Michigan, designed by the great Finnish architect Eliel Saarinen, or the work of Charles and Henry Greene in Pasadena in California, all of which had a strong regional bias. There was, nevertheless, a constant interchange of ideas between England and America. Magazines kept the Arts and Crafts designers in touch on both sides of the Atlantic. In England *The Studio* and *Country Life* matched America's *House Beautiful*, *House and Garden* and *Country Life in America*. Just as Lutyens's designs and use of materials for the Mughal Garden in New Delhi looked back in time to the great tradition of the Islamic gardens made by the Emperor Babur's descendants, so the gardens by Irving Gill (1870–1936) in southern California echoed the earliest Hispanic designs in which the walled mission courtyards provided a haven from the hottest sun – oases in desert conditions. Designers in Virginia such as Charles Gillette (1886–1969) found his inspiration in the boxwood gardens of the colonial era. This style could make size irrelevant, with large gardens split up into a series of outdoor rooms, each with its own character. With an almost Renaissance use of space, indoor and outdoor "rooms" could be united in one integrated overall design. The hedged garden compartments at Hidcote in Gloucestershire, planned from 1907, provide one example (see page 404); another is the gardens of Filoli in California (see page 406), created during World War I. Both gardens have a distinct Italian flavour, but strong lines are softened by luxuriant planting.

Based on ideas rather than a unifying code, Arts and Crafts gardens in America developed alongside houses of very variable architectural style, which could be gothic, Tudor, Spanish-mission courtyard, low ranch-type or log cabin. They were

True to the vernacular
The house and gardens at Rodmarton Manor, near Cirencester, Gloucestershire, were made over a 20-year period, between 1909 and 1929, by Ernest Barnsley, the head gardener William Scrubey and Margaret Biddulph, the wife of the owner. The garden layout is quite sharp and formal – a series of outdoor rooms containing long walks, clipped yew hedges, topiary pieces in box and attractive cottage-style planting. Both house and garden were inspired by the local vernacular. The work of skilled craftsmen helped to forge a coherent entity. Barnsley was a disciple of Philip Webb (Morris's architect for his Red House), who had built his own house in nearby Sapperton.

At the cutting edge (right)
Edwin Budding, the inventor in the 1830s, and John Ferrabee, the manufacturer, are said to have tested their brainchild, the first mechanical grass-cutter, in the dead of night. Although it was made of cast-iron and quite an effort to operate, they recommended it to "country gentlemen" as a means of obtaining "amusing, useful and healthy exercise".

The rustic charms of the old technology (above)
The 18th-century park depended for its effect on expanses of smooth grassland. Keeping it trim, until the lawnmower's advent, was a matter of men toiling with scythes, as in this painting of Chiswick House by Balthasar Nebot, or having it grazed by sheep or deer.

Players' sward (below)
With the availability of the mower (simple enough, advertisments usually made clear, for women to use), and the simultaneous rise in popularity of grass-based sports such as tennis and golf, the face of the land changed in countries all around the world.

Green circles (right)
One way or another, green grass has long been a characteristic ingredient of the English garden. A marriage of tradition and innovation, this turf labyrinth forms the sublime heart of the Shropshire garden designed by Dr Katherine Swift.

RANSOMES' Lawn Mowers
THE BEST in the WORLD

THE AUTOMATONS AND ANGLO-PARIS

On the lawn

When the 17th-century philosopher and scientist Francis Bacon wrote that "nothing is more pleasant to the eye than green grass kept closely shorn" he was expressing an unusually common and popular opinion. Green grass was so synonymous with England that French garden designers referred to lawns as *parterres à l'Angloise* (English sections).

To make the lawns of the 18th-century landscape garden at Painshill, in Surrey, the Honourable Charles Hamilton began by having the ground "cleansed" of weeds and levelling it: "if any ground was very foul, I generally employed a whole year in clearing it, by ploughing it sometimes five, but at least four times and harrowing it very much after each ploughing...this harrowing brings up all the couch grass and weeds to the surface; which after every harrowing I have raked up in heaps and burned". Then and only then were Mr Hamilton's acres sown with the "cleanest hayseed" available, plus quantities of Dutch clover seed.

Small armies of men with scythes, and flocks of sheep and deer, kept these aristocratic lawns smooth. The inventor of the first lawnmower, Edwin Budding, was inspired by a machine used to trim the pile on factory-made velvet cloth, and hoped that his machine would eliminate the "circular scars, irregularities and bare patches" produced by scythes. The new smooth lawn stimulated the rise of popular sports: notably golf, tennis, cricket and football. The 20th century saw such an alliance between sport and the science of grass horticulture that in recent times the place of the perfect lawn in the average garden has become less asssured. Environmental concerns have contributed to the popularity of the wildflower meadows and a new tolerance of such "enemies" as daisies and moss.

Rough with the smooth (above and below)
The triumph of the science and technology of grass cultivation has given rise to environmental concerns and a new appreciation of the "untidy" species-rich lawn. Besides offering a scene of great beauty, the flower-strewn orchard at Great Dixter in East Sussex serves as an asylum for wild flowers and butterflies threatened by modern farming practices. For some, the appeal of a patch of grass lies in the gadgetry used to cut it. The average lawn depended on hand-pushed cylindrical mowers until the arrival of motor-powered machines in the mid-20th century, but the idea of a remote-controlled mower still seems a remote possibility.

Individualistic approach
The Arts and Crafts Movement in
the United States depended on a
functional approach and superb
craftsmanship, using local materials.
It remained highly individualistic. At
the oriental-style Gamble House in
Pasadena, California, built from 1907
by the brothers Charles Sumner
Greene and Henry Mather Greene,
the design of house and garden are
so integrated that the house seems
almost organic, as if it grew out of its
site. Wide, partly shaded terraces,
with sleeping quarters above, link
interior and exterior seamlessly. The
garden's design incorporates
borrowed views of the Californian
landscape, with mountains
containing the further vistas, while
features include walls of locally
made brick and stone found in the
neighbouring arroyos.

united by a respect for the nature of a site. Many of the principles of the movement are reflected in the work of modern landscape architects. House and garden
needed to flow together with formal enclosed spaces near the house, opening out
into more natural landscape. Materials such as local stone for walls, steps, pavements and gravel helped settle a garden into its surroundings. Nature was a primary source of inspiration, its patterns and functional qualities incorporated
indoors as ornament and wallpaper, and in the garden in plant selection. The use
of old-fashioned plants rather than highly bred varieties expressed rural garden
traditions and a search for simplicity, with plants self-seeding naturally to create
unplanned effects. Flower colours tended to be muted, with an emphasis on paler
hues and the greens and greys of foliage, following nature's seasonal colourings
into autumnal shades.

EDWARDIAN STYLES

For many the Edwardian garden represents the best in British gardening, a
collaboration between architect and gardener that is hard to surpass. Edwardian
gardeners developed their own combination of naturalistic planting inside a
strongly structured axial layout, often quite Italian in its definition of space.

From 1900 onwards, in both Britain and America, there was a growing appreciation of the possibilities of combining formal and informal ideals in quite

Cottage idyll
The idealization of the cottage garden inspired a whole genre of paintings, including *The Flower Garden* (left) by Abbott Fuller Graves and scenes by Helen Allingham. The pictures were evocative of an imaginary past age, when roses and hollyhocks grew by the doors of labourers' cottages to make romantic, eminently paintable scenes. The reality was somewhat different, with many agricultural workers impoverished by earlier enclosures and the farming depression at the end of the 19th century. Nevertheless, cottage-garden-style planting became a requisite theme in upper- and middle-class gardens, implying a sort of careless rapture of happily associated plants. It is still very much in vogue today.

modest gardens by creating a strong regular structure and then filling it with a bold, relaxed planting of mixed shrubs, perennials and bulbs that disguised the geometry. Terraces, sunken gardens, arbours, alleys and enclosures could be planted to convey simplicity rather than to demonstrate the possession of wealth. This cottage-garden planting, as we call the style today, originated in late 19th-century England and was refined by William Robinson and Gertrude Jekyll, to be adopted in gardens such as Lawrence Johnston's Hidcote, in Gloucestershire. In America Beatrix Farrand was one of its exponents, her designs a blend of Charles Platt's architectural approach and Olmsted's appreciation of landscape. Women designers such as Ellen Biddle Shipman, Louise King (Mrs Francis King) and Louise Beebe Wilder were particularly good at interpreting the style for smaller gardens. In intimate garden design as opposed to the creation of whole landscapes, this is still the preferred taste of middle-class England, even if dismissed by the more conceptual landscape architects.

A LUTYENS HOUSE WITH A JEKYLL GARDEN

The collaboration between architect Edwin Lutyens and gardener Gertrude Jekyll became the Edwardian symbol of good taste, the epitome of excellence for a generation on the brink of extinction. Architectural and planting expertise worked together to produce aesthetic and horticultural compositions, and although few survive in their original state their influence is still felt in countless modern gardens. In the hands of the sensitive Lutyens the formal structure, changes of level, directional axes, stonework, pergolas and water tanks and rills provided the perfect complementary framework for Gertrude Jekyll's planting

PORTRAIT OF AN ERA

The description "Edwardian" makes a useful shorthand term for a "golden afternoon" period in Western gardening as in other arts. Edward VII sat on the British throne for less than a decade – from 1901 to 1910 – but the style borrowing his name seems to encompass both the *fin-de-siècle* last years of Queen Victoria's long reign and an Indian summer on into the 1914–18 World War. In America the good times continued in many cases until 1929.

The genius of Hidcote

Lawrence Johnston's Hidcote, in Gloucestershire – the most influential of the compartmented gardens, and "parent" of Sissinghurst (see page 427) and Tintinhull, in Somerset – has become an icon of 20th-century garden design. Its hedged rooms, planted with mixed beds of shrubs, roses, peonies, perennials and bulbs in quiet cottage-garden style, represented all that was considered best and most sensitive in English gardening in the early 20th century. The garden was started after 1907, when American-born Johnston acquired the land. Much of Hidcote's success depends on his sophisticated sense of space and his development of interlocking axes which define the garden areas. These are separated by several layers of hedging. The geometry of box-edged beds, pillars of yew, topiary, straight lines, right angles and circles confirms the garden's Italian nuances. Inside this framework, Johnston's planting was informal and luxurious, rare plants jostling with traditional favourites. His masterpiece was the installation of the aerial hornbeam hedges, the Stilt Garden, which extended the view from the house through the Scarlet Borders to frame a view of sky above the escarpment. The White Garden (right) was originally called the Phlox Garden. Sometimes Hidcote has been called a collection of cottage gardens, but Johnston's genius ensured that the overall design concept was coherent and disciplined.

A Californian oasis

Filoli, at Woodside near San Francisco, owes little of its character to the surrounding Californian landscape. Italianate in conception, Filoli's formal, compartmented layout evokes echoes of Hidcote. But its lush irrigated lawns and manicured perfection amid the arid Californian landscape give Filoli the semblance of an oasis in a desert, borrowing something in spirit from the earliest gardens known to mankind. Its central reflecting pool, formal walks of Irish yew (dark sentinels resembling staccato cypresses) and olive trees recall the gardens of Islam. Ornamental flowering cherries and magnolias soften the straight lines of walls, hedges and pathways, just as fruitful orchards added the more natural elements in Islamic designs. Instead of plane trees, great evergreen oaks – the coastal live oak (*Quercus agrifolia*) – provide canopies of shade. The garden was created from 1916 for William Bourn by designer Bruce Porter, though its subsequent owners made some changes. Porter intended Filoli to have vivid splashes of seasonal colour throughout the garden – camellias, rhododendrons and begonias in shade, and tulips, roses and petunias in sun. These have been maintained and today Filoli remains one of the most beautiful gardens in North America.

schemes. For many visitors interested in flower gardening the great English landscape parks, although of world importance, are not real gardens; it is the Edwardian ideal which represents English gardening at its best and most memorable. The ideas behind the Lutyens/Jekyll partnership, illustrated and described in issues of *Country Life* from the 1900s, have been exploited all over the world, from the French and Italian Rivieras to the American Midwest and West Coast.

The famous and creative partnership between Gertrude Jekyll (1843–1932) and Edwin Lutyens (1869–1944) lasted some 20 years, during which they designed over a hundred gardens. Jekyll first met Lutyens in spring 1889 when she was 45 and he was 20. Having trained as an artist but early abandoned painting because of bad eyesight, she was already an established figure in the gardening world, but had yet to launch herself into her writing career. Lutyens was talented but almost untrained, with just a few commissions from friends for cottages and lodges. The pair established an immediate rapport, finding that they shared a deep interest in the landscape and country ways of old Surrey and in vernacular materials. From the start they worked together, with Lutyens designing the house, the garden layout a joint effort and the detailed planting all Jekyll's. One of their most important concepts was Munstead Wood, where Lutyens designed a house for Jekyll herself inside the partially completed garden that she had begun a few years earlier. During the next two decades, the golden age before World War I, Lutyens graduated from the Jekyll circle to a much grander clientele, but it was their combined talents that ensured the magic of the gardens, the naturalistic Jekyll planting softening Lutyens's inspired stonework, pergolas and water rills.

Few of Jekyll's planting schemes survive intact, although there have been outstanding restoration schemes at Hestercombe, in Somerset, and Upton Grey, in

Hampshire (the latter designed without Lutyens's involvement): her type of cottage-garden exuberance was too fragile in content and spirit to survive long without her presence and that of the skilled gardeners who understood and implemented her designs. Her thoughts on colour arrangement and appreciation of texture of leaf, flower and bark must have been partly engendered by her artistic training. Her insistence on appropriate planting – the right plants for the right spot – showed her horticultural knowledge and sensitivity; Robinson's influence showed in her naturalistic schemes and use of hardy plants – he was a friend and mentor who employed her to write for his journals. Jekyll's attention to detail in her carefully orchestrated border schemes complemented Lutyens's layouts. Happily many of her own copies of her original plans have been preserved, thanks to Beatrix Farrand, and are safely held in Berkeley, California (in the Reef Point Collection). Her teaching,

Architect of the partnership
Sir Edwin Lutyens (a contemporary of Frank Lloyd Wright) was much influenced by his working partnership with Gertrude Jekyll, whom he met while in his twenties. He considered that the designs for a house and garden should be intertwined, so that each conveyed a similar theme to complement the other.

Jekyll's Munstead Wood
Helen Allingham painted the main border at Gertrude Jekyll's garden at Munstead Wood (left) in 1900 and again in 1902 at its peak. The border, was carefully orchestrated, with strong "hot" colours at the centre, tapering off to "cooler" pale blues and silvery foliage plants at either end, with sharp yucca leaves flanking the doorway. Jekyll (inset, walking in her garden, aged 80) believed in harmonies of flower colour – the reds, yellows and oranges – but used blues and yellows for contrasting effects. She loved to use flower and foliage spikes to offset the more rounded forms of many perennials. A high wall at the border's back supported a curtain of climbers. Today the main garden has been restored using the original plants.

Edwardian masterpiece

The gardens at Hestercombe, in Somerset, are, for many, the epitome of the Lutyens/Jekyll partnership. Commissioned in 1906, Edwin Lutyens produced a design of great complexity that upstaged the existing ugly Victorian house. On a meadow below the terrace, he constructed his Great Plat. Via intricate changes in level and a succession of open and closed vistas, the visitor can descend to the Plat, passing the long rills (opposite) which carry water to the end of the garden. These travel from domed tanks under the walls of the house to pools beside the pergola, a distance of some 43m (140ft). Lutyens's stonework, perhaps Hestercombe's greatest triumph, provided the perfect background for Gertrude Jekyll's planting. In the Great Plat her combination of bergenias — a Jekyll favourite — with pink roses and lilies does not quite reach a high note. The more sensitive silver border, however, along the higher edge of the Plat shows her in better form. Lutyens's massive pergola (left), today planted with climbing roses, vines and honeysuckles — again all Jekyll favourites — is one of the garden's most successful features and expresses all that is best in their long collaboration.

set down in her books and in many articles, has lived on to inspire generations of gardeners. Fortunately architecture is less vulnerable to time's erosion and many of Lutyens's houses and garden stonework, although in need of repair, survive.

THE ITALIAN INFLUENCE

Many gardens of the period in both Europe and America overtly reflected a revived interest in the Italian Renaissance garden. Sir Harold Peto (1854–1933) was another remarkable Edwardian designer working in Britain and on the Riviera, his best work executed between 1890 and 1914. With a strong bent towards the gardens of Italy, Peto designed with architectural features such as colonnades, temples, terraces and statuary. His style and influence can be compared with that of his contemporary Charles Platt working in America. Both brought back from Italy a true appreciation of the spirit and elegance of the Italian garden and of the Italian landscape, and in their work introduced a series of geometric units in the garden that linked terraces, alleys and flowerbeds on axial views from the house. This they managed without over-indulging in formal parterre arrangements and extravagances typical of Victorian England or the East Coast gardening of late 19th-century America. Peto may or may not have known of Platt's work, his visit to America in 1887 pre-dating Platt's emergence as an influential figure. But by

BEATRIX FARRAND AND DUMBARTON OAKS

BORN IN 1872 AS BEATRIX JONES, Beatrix Farrand came from an established old New York family. Her aunt was Edith Wharton, and Henry James was a personal friend, as was (perhaps more importantly to her career) Charles Sprague Sargent, the professor in charge of the Arnold Arboretum since its inception in 1872. She gained a formidable knowledge of plants training under Sargent for a year, then travelled to Europe in 1895 to visit gardens. In her mature work she was able to incorporate both Italianate concepts and the kind of wild garden proposed by William Robinson, whom she met at his home at Gravetye. Throughout her career she never forgot Sargent's advice to "make the plan fit the ground and not twist the ground to fit a plan".

Farrand was to become one of America's pre-eminent landscape gardeners, designing the Italianate gardens at Dumbarton Oaks in Washington DC and the Princeton and Yale campuses, where she introduced rural schemes inside classical layouts. In England, she worked for the Elmhirsts, the American philanthropist owners of Dartington Hall, in Devon. Through her own social contacts she established a client base that included many eminent names. In 1899 she was one of the founder members of the American Society of Landscape Architects.

Farrand's designs were quite formal in origin but softened by Arts and Crafts influences. One of her favourite reference books was Liberty Hyde Bailey's *Standard Encyclopaedia of Horticulture*, published in three volumes in 1900. Almost comparable to J.C.

Design lines
Beatrix Farrand greatly admired the gazebos in the garden at Traquair in Scotland, with their distinctively shaped roofs, and designed copies for the garden at Dumbarton Oaks.

Loudon's *Encyclopaedia of Gardening* of 1822, Bailey's book is still a pleasure to peruse.

One of Farrand's most revered works is the Eeyrie, the Abby Aldrich Rockefeller garden at Seal Harbor in Mount Desert in Maine. Here she not only designed the perennial beds with woven colour sequences – perhaps influenced by Gertrude Jekyll – but also introduced the Spirit Walk through the woods, an evocative pathway lined with antique stone figures from Korea. It is shaded by tall native pines and spruce and underplanted with more indigenous plants from the region, such as mosses and ferns. For a visitor, the entrance or Spirit Walk is still one of the most moving of garden experiences. Unfortunately much of the perennial planting has been replaced by garish annuals.

At Dumbarton Oaks, where work started in 1922, her garden designs included architectural features such as a planting of Carolina hornbeam to create a hedge on stilts in the form of an ellipse, mounds of box lining the stairways and a separate garden room for roses. A sheltering wooden arbour in a secret garden with fragrant herbs was inspired by du Cerceau's 16th-century designs for trelliswork at Montargis (see page 142). Her client Mildred Barnes Bliss was especially delighted by one of the plantings, which she described as "the great billowing mass of forsythia tumbling down two hillsides turned to gold".

Unlike many designers, Beatrix Farrand left explicit instructions for future management of her plantings: her *Plant Book for Dumbarton Oaks* is being used today for restoration work, but could also serve as an instructive manual for any garden. Of the masses of box she planted flanking the garden's steep stairways, she wrote in 1941:

"Nothing will ever be quite so beautiful as the rumpled masses of Box as they follow the slope of the hill." For a British visitor to America, the mounded shapes made by box plants is one of the first revelations about American gardens. So-called American box (actually European *Buxus sempervirens*) grows fast in the heat and is difficult to keep trimmed as a hedge – hence the origins of the splendid colonial-style boxwood gardens of Virginia.

Ellipse of hornbeam
*Dumbarton Oaks's hedge on stilts, in the form of an ellipse, was possibly inspired by Lawrence Johnston's Stilt Garden at Hidcote. The tree used is the Carolina hornbeam (*Carpinus caroliniana*).*

Farrand had hoped to make a foundation at her own garden at Reef Point in Bar Harbor on Mount Desert, but this was not accomplished. Her papers are now held at the University of Berkeley in California. The major part of Dumbarton Oaks was given to Harvard University in 1941.

THE PERFECTION OF IFORD MANOR

IFORD MANOR, NEAR BATH, the home and garden of Sir Harold Peto, is arguably the most beautiful ensemble of buildings and garden in England. The house was Peto's home from 1899 until his death in 1933. In many ways Peto is England's answer to Charles Platt. They both shared a love of Italian architecture, obvious in their gardens, but managed to include the softening effects of flower and foliage in their stone-led designs.

An architect turned landscape architect after training in the offices of Ernest George until 1892, Peto worked on the French and Italian Rivieras until the turn of the century. He was to become known and revered for his masterly formula for combining architectural formality with a degree of naturalistic planting. In spite of his emphasis on classical formulae, his work was greatly admired by Gertrude Jekyll, who included illustrations of various designs by Peto in her book *Garden Ornament* in which she especially recommended his use of pergolas and open-air loggias for his villas on the Riviera. Many of his designs for gardens in Britain, such as Buscot Park in Oxfordshire (see pages 414–15), Easton Lodge in Essex, Heale House in Wiltshire and Garinish in western Ireland, are almost equally successful, but it is to his own garden that we must turn for the detail.

The limestone manor house at Iford is Elizabethan in origin but has an elegant early Georgian front. In the narrow valley of the River Frome, it nestles under hanging beech woods, probably planted early in the 19th century. Peto constructed a series of terraces reached from the east end of the house. A succession of staircases leads up to an oval lily pool, and a sloping lawn leads on up to the main terrace, which dates back to the 18th century. Peto added an octagonal summerhouse at the eastern end of this terrace, which is laid with carefully raked gravel, and bordered it with classical sculptures and architectural fragments collected on his travels. To the west, a loggia with columns of pink Verona marble (*c.*1200) stands back from the main promenade, which

Measured steps
The most important view in the garden looks up the terraces from the east end of the house. Peto's manipulation of space was masterly.

terminates with a well-head and a circular stone bench overlooking the orchard below.

Although we know that Peto liked flowers, the most important planting at Iford is of evergreen shrubs: hollies, phillyreas, rosemary, choisya, cypress, juniper and yew, the perfect foils to the stonework on the steep terraces. The borders are planted with glossy-leaved acanthus, scented herbs, spiky irises and agapanthus.

A Tuscan colonnade contains the south side of the terrace walk to create a romantic ruin as it frames the view into the countryside across the river valley. Today the garden is kept in perfect order. Renewals of the planting carefully interpret Peto's wishes without conveying a museum-like atmosphere, and the stonework is kept pristine and sparkling.

Edwardian terrace
An octagonal summerhouse closes the vista at the eastern end of Iford Manor's main terrace.

the turn of the century he would probably have read Platt's *Italian Gardens*. By interpreting a site on the spot, Peto made use of all its characteristics. Sir George Sitwell also interpreted the pure spirit of Italy at his home at Renishaw (see pages 380–81) in northern England. There, in a design composed according to precepts expressed in his masterly book *On the Making of Gardens* (1909), he introduced green yew-hedged enclosures, massive 18th-century statues, a central pool and a marine theatre inspired by the remains of the Roman Emperor Hadrian's villa at Tivoli.

In America, Charles Platt reintroduced Renaissance values to garden design, infusing his own strong sense of structure into what was still a new profession in search of a way forward and with a desire to formulate measurable standards. One of the dangers of too much affluence was that, without principles and rules, the whim of a wealthy employer could buy bad-quality design as easily as good. Platt reintroduced some basic order into the free-for-all (provided you were rich) American garden patterns of the late 19th century.

At first through his *Italian Gardens*, Platt introduced Americans to the visual strengths of a typical Italian villa in its setting, the role it played in the cultural life of its time, and its positive integration of architecture and landscape design, with indoor and outdoor spaces linked together. Invitations to design both houses and gardens soon followed, with clients asking Platt to adapt the Italian ideal to the American way of living. Seen as a radical alternative to the fashionable naturalistic designs of Olmsted, Platt's appeal lay in his organization of space around a series of sightlines which linked the various spaces, with house and grounds treated as one integrated composition. He guided a style that already existed in the country house era into a disciplined and logical event, leaving nothing to chance – American landscaping controlled by an Italian ethic. Beyond the immediate vicinity of the house both Platt and his successors adhered to the more pastoral park-like style that has remained a feature of American landscape architecture, using the superlative background scenery to provide more picturesque aspects.

Writers such as Edith Wharton helped to foster the new American interest in Italian styles. "The American landscape has no foreground and the American mind no background," wrote the cosmopolitan Wharton dismissively to a friend in Boston as she completed her own garden, the Mount, in Lenox, Massachusetts. For her the magnificent natural scenery, in her case the Berkshire Hills, was only truly effective when contrasted with the controlled geometry of a formal layout near the house, a lesson she had gleaned during her Italian journeys. Wharton spent the spring of 1903 travelling by train, carriage and motor car to explore some 80 Italian estates for her book *Italian Gardens* (1904), illustrated with watercolours by Maxfield Parrish. For Americans, Wharton's book brought glamour to Charles Platt's earlier treatise, reminding gardeners of the importance of relating a garden both to the architecture of the house and to its setting.

DESIGN FOR A HILLSIDE GARDEN . WINDERMERE .

Mawson's Italianate approach
Edwin Lutyens and Gertrude Jekyll were not the only practitioners of an Edwardian style. Thomas Mawson (an almost exact contemporary of Harold Peto) worked in a more self-conscious Italianate way. Many of his greatest schemes involved giving old gardens a facelift. This design for a hillside in the Lake District was published in his book *The Art and Craft of Garden Making* (1900). By the early 1900s Mawson (1861–1933), a self-styled landscape architect from Lancashire, had built up a substantial practice and was recognized as one of the foremost designers of the day. Although he was knowledgeable about plants, his work tended more towards a monumental interpretation of Renaissance architectural gardens. He liked to link house and garden, creating terraces and steep steps descending to wide lawns with views to distant shrubberies, woodland or hills, as in this design. He lacked Lutyens's flair for detailing in stonework and was totally unsympathetic to the more naturalistic schemes of Robinson or Jekyll.

THE BEGINNINGS OF THE MODERNIST MOVEMENT

The Modernist Movement in gardening, as much as in architecture, came from a growing impatience with historical themes and styles and as a reaction to established garden formulas. It reflected a love of nature and the countryside, and the "sense of place" fundamental to successful garden design, but rejected any form of traditional approach, looking instead to the world around the site for inspiration. Borrowing from other art forms – modernism applied to literature and music as well as to the visual arts – modernist garden schemes were conceived as logical geometric structural arrangements, involved with progress and technology, with a wholly functional relationship with the house or adjacent buildings. The austerity of a design was relieved by an emphasis on natural planting.

The movement's leading force, the architect Walter Gropius, believed in the indivisibility of "art, industry, nature, practicality and pleasant living". There was to be no more copying of styles; instead things should be thought out from scratch. Modernism was not just a matter of seeing space in cubist modules applied to the landscape; it gave an almost holistic ethos to environmental design, satisfying people's needs by providing liveable spaces for individuals as well as social groups, in an effort to escape the horrors of the man-made monotony appearing in an age of concrete and bulldozers. At the same time, the modernists were dedicated to exploring the potentialities of new techniques, new materials and how new concepts of space could be utilized. Christopher Tunnard's *Gardens in the Modern Landscape*, written in 1938 before he moved from Britain to the United States, where he taught city planning at Harvard University, was one of the few books to try to define the movement. He stressed that a garden was meant to be used – that was its purpose – and objected to the abundant semi-wild styles of the post-Robinson age as romantic and sentimental, preferring the more objective view of the Japanese. But at the time his teaching fell on deaf ears: modernism failed to find an audience for another half century. During the years after World War II both ordinary gardening and landscape architecture continued to pay homage to old formulas.

As an historical gardening movement, European and British modernism was never influential. Few designers had the opportunity to develop its potential in the 1920s and 1930s, and any further progress was halted by the outbreak of war in 1939. Private clients were in general either too conservative to try something new, or had old estates in which tradition remained of relevance. What was important, however, was the fact that for the first time in the 20th century, garden design was seriously analysed and discussed. Ironically, by removing the crutches of the past, modernist principles led to a feeling of panic and ultimately a greater retreat into historical precedent. Immediately after World War II, a shortage of skilled gardeners and the expense of employing them meant that more and more of the larger gardens, which would in the past have been trendsetters, settled for a

GAMBERAIA

Memories of Italy

Edith Wharton's *Italian Gardens*, published in 1904, was illustrated with watercolours by Maxfield Parrish. She included some 80 estates, many of which can still be visited today. Her book, as a follow-up to Charles Platt's, caught the reader's imagination and led to a renewed interest in Italian styles.

A Mughal theme (opposite)

At Buscot Park, in Oxfordshire, Harold Peto designed a grand water garden in 1904 for the financier and art collector, Lord Faringdon (then Alexander Henderson), with a vista to an 18th-century lake and temple. The water features are framed by box and Irish yews and the ensemble has a strong Mughal ambience, resembling some of the gardens laid out around Lake Dal in Kashmir by the Emperors Akbar and Jahangir. Another of Peto's gardens on Garinish Island, in County Cork, repeats the Islamic theme with a central water rill and viewing pavilion.

A planner's per
Frederick Gibber
architect and town
modernist and fur
to garden design.
personal garden, M
the new town of
designed, was mac
from 1956. It cov
hectares (6 acres)
meadows sloping
woodland glade, h
collection of colu
(above), salvaged f
Coutts Bank in th
which he had mo
water rill (opposit
architectural featu
between groves ar
progression amon
planting. Althoug
formal hedges, qu
evergreens – yew,
box – divide the
separate spaces, w
open areas Gibbe
trees. The garden
posterity as a cha

Elegance and ecology
Mien Ruys, the distinguished Dutch designer, working at her father's nursery at Moerheim in Dedemsvaart, grouped a series of 25 small gardens around an open lawn to introduce people to different aspects of design. In one swamp area, known as the Marsh Garden, she used recycled, non-slip black plastic to create "stepping-stones", giving a modernistic twist to a simple and naturalistic arrangement of bog plants. Mien Ruys's functional planting has echoes of the work of designers such as Sylvia Crowe (see page 423) and Brenda Colvin, who often worked on improving industrial sites in England.

She had an outstanding knowledge of plants and was to become one of the most sensitive of garden designers, a follower of Karl Foerster and German-school naturalism and modern Dutch architecture. Her own development went through several phases. After a visit to England, where she worked for a nursery, she designed a classic English border at Moerheim in 1927; this still survives. Later, having studied landscape architecture at Delft, she moved beyond Jekyllean influences to appreciate Mondrian's grid-like paintings and Christoper Tunnard's writings. She became an expert at achieving an uncluttered look, analysing a site to use its message in planting shapes. At Moerheim she made 25 demonstration gardens, all self-contained and suitable for different environments. Many of the gardens, designed to inspire nursery visitors, were arranged around a large lawn. The circular Yellow Garden, defined by a narrow brick walkway, formed the centrepiece; another garden was designed around container-filled plants, and another around some modern sculpture. Each took just a single theme, which was perhaps the most important lesson of all. Often she used square or rectangular planting blocks, eliminating curves that had no relationship to the garden space.

It was not until the 1980s that Martha Schwartz finally rescued modernism from oblivion – at first mainly in North America and then by the end of the century in Europe, too. Her work is discussed in the next and final chapter.

CHAPTER THIRTEEN

TODAY and TOMORROW

A world of opportunity

WHERE WILL OUR STORY LEAD NEXT? As we begin the 21st century there is a wider interest in gardening and a greater diversity of design ideas than ever before. Gardening is no longer the preserve of the few; it is there to be enjoyed by us all. The planting palette is extending all the time, as is the range of materials that can be used for the garden's "hardware". But as our story has so often shown, seldom are the ideas of the day truly original. Instead a fresh spin is put on concepts whose roots lie in earlier centuries. Though they may make innovative use of plastic, glass and stainless steel, today's designers still apply spatial theories first formulated in 16th-century Italy, and adapt Islamic-style layouts developed more than a thousand years ago in Iran and Iraq. Some are keen to meet the challenge of working in unpropitious sites where they have to devise schemes that do not rely on soil and plants. For many others, the ecological aspect is all important; they carry on the crusade started by the plant conservation pioneers of the 19th and early 20th centuries. There are those, too, who seek to engage the mind as well as the emotions and put a new twist on allegorical themes.

In the concluding chapter of this history we look at the work of those designers, gardeners and landscape architects who, since the 1950s, have helped to shape the present and future look of our gardens, but in so doing have nearly always kept one eye on the past.

New dimensions
The garden landscape made by Maggie Keswick and Charles Jencks near Dumfries in Scotland, with moulded contours, steep-sided double-wave earthworks and curved reflecting ponds, is visually captivating. A deeper interpretation, however, reveals Keswick's interest in Chinese *feng shui* and Jencks's fascination with the theory of chaos.

The EUPHORBIA

The genus *Euphorbia*, the spurge or milkweed, which includes sun and drought-loving species as well as those tolerant of shade and damp, is of great interest to modern gardeners. The stems all exude a milky juice which, when cut, especially on hot days, can damage the skin. All the garden euphorbias, excluding the desert varieties, bear a strong family likeness, with narrow leaves crowding the stem. The flowers themselves are inconspicuous but are surrounded by lime-green-to-yellow bracts which look extremely handsome for many weeks. One of the most beautiful is the evergreen Mediterranean *Euphorbia characias*, with narrow spikes of brown-eyed green flowers on arching stems. Its sub-species E*uphorbia characias* subsp. *wulfenii* is even more spectacular, with larger heads of similar flowers, though with yellow-green centres. There are several forms, such as 'Lambrook Gold', from Margery Fish's garden at East Lambrook, and 'John Tomlinson', which have broader, flatter flowerheads.

Euphorbia characias was known to Greek naturalist Theophrastus and to Dioscorides, who was well aware of its irritant, thick milky sap. Pliny the Elder, in his *Naturalis Historia*, warns against letting it touch the eyes. The sub-species *wulfenii* is taller than the species and found in the wild in Slovenia, through Croatia, Bosnia-Herzegovina and Albania, into Greece and western Turkey, but it and *Euphorbia characias* freely self-hybridize in cultivation to confuse the taxonomists. Although short-lived and not altogether hardy in temperate gardens, especially if the soil is poorly drained, *E. characias* will self-seed prolifically *in situ* once established. Cuttings from young shoots can also be easily rooted. The euphorbia is a splendid architectural plant with a distinctive flowering habit. At the end of winter, the floral heads bend over like a shepherd's crook, the stem only straightening out as the flower truss finally develops.

EUPHORBIA CHARACIAS

CHANGING DYNAMICS

The "ideal" garden has always been in the mind, a way of thinking about nature and culture and how they influence each other. The garden is a balancing point between human control and "wild" nature. In ancient times the garden was at first an oasis, a refuge, an escape from the threat of nature or from marauders, human or animal. Over the centuries emperors and kings developed fantastic parks to express their power and personality, the Chinese Han emperors often bankrupting themselves or their nation in the process. The parks of the Assyrian kings are legendary, tempting emulation as Europe emerged from the Dark Ages. Louis XIV's 17th-century Versailles, still to be admired, expressed the king's triumph over nature's freedom. Much more recently the wealthy William Randolph Hearst created something almost as legendary at San Simeon in California.

In the Renaissance architects played with the manipulation of space and studied optics to produce academic gardens to satisfy the intellect – geometry and repetition applied to nature. In the 18th century, garden and nature became philosophically intertwined, with schemes to emulate nature in her natural state, in reality as contrived and designed as the formal layouts of earlier periods. These natural landscapes were the forerunners of the public recreational parks of today, first evolving in the 19th century, with Olmsted's Central Park in New York setting an ideal, and were also the "parents" of Robinsonian gardening and the modern Dutch ecological *heem* gardens around Amsterdam, based entirely on indigenous planting (see pages 390–91). Although Edwardian garden styles embraced structured layouts, as exemplified by the Lutyens/Jekyll gardens, much of the planting inside reflected the naturalistic idea, which was to hold the horticultural imagination for the rest of the 20th century. The large landscape style, beyond the means of most private individuals, had a new lease of life as landscape architects, in search of the lost countryside, created park-like settings for modern blocks of flats and corporate buildings and amended industrial sites.

Today, landscapes and gardens play many different public and private roles and contain many different themes. There are two extremes of modern design: the projects in the public domain which concern the wider landscape and are almost outside the realm of gardening, but which by providing a new vision stimulate more modest projects, and the intimate compositions, often flower-dominated, which are attainable on a private level. There are also community gardens, shopping mall gardens, healing gardens at hospitals and hospices, roundabouts, window boxes and hanging baskets to be enjoyed by the passing public, organic gardens, wildlife gardens and edible gardens (including allotments). Above all, by the last years of the 20th century the understanding and respect for the intrinsic nature of a site has become fundamental to design thinking. Alexander Pope's advice to "consult the genius of the place in all" could be extended to include history and geology, and elements invisible to the naked eye, so that the design evolves from the landscape rather than being imposed on it.

Through garden visiting and television programmes the public enjoy great historic gardens in both Europe and America. They discover the more intimate personal tastes of previous owners and acquire an understanding of the layers of history. In England, especially, many private gardens have traditionally been open to a visiting public – the National Garden Scheme was introduced in 1927 – but in Continental Europe and in America there was no such custom until quite recently. In Holland certain gardens are in a scheme that allows membership visits and, in the last 10 years, the Garden Conservancy in the United States has encouraged opening of private gardens.

By the 1960s, landscape architecture and ordinary horticulture for gardeners seemed to be moving in different directions. The gap between the requirements of individuals for the use and enjoyment of a private space and those of public landscaping – the needs of a crowd – widened. Landscape architecture had become an academic and technical subject to such an extent that it was on a different plane to ordinary gardening.

The private gardener, even if the garden would ultimately be shared with an interested public, looked for different personal rewards and experiences, and could formulate personal iconographical and symbolic features as well as indulging personal preferences for suitable plants. Quite modest gardeners had the chance to introduce new planting schemes and exploit new plants, mainly by following the route suggested by William Robinson with any attempts at formality and garden structure elbowed out by naturalistic curves and free-flowing plants. Until 1975 it was rare to find any elements of geometry in new owner-made private gardens. The word formal was seldom used, and even traditional recommendations of hedges in straight lines to back borders were regarded with suspicion. In America this trend was even more pronounced and longer lasting. Old ideas from Europe, considered a relic of aristocratic landlord domination, were increasingly despised in favour of gardens which reflected the idea of the American wilderness.

For each owner the garden provided an escape from the modern world – albeit without the spiritual dimension of the Islamic enclosed garden. As Sylvia Crowe says in her *Garden Design* (1958), "no space is too small to be developed as an oasis of peace, privacy and plants". By the last quarter of the century many young, reasonably affluent owners were beginning to implement more structured schemes. In doing so, they were following the example of gifted

Voice of wisdom
Dame Sylvia Crowe (1901–97) – whose book *Garden Design* (1958) is still one of the best and most comprehensive guides on the subject – was a British landscape architect of considerable influence. Although she drew up some private designs, she was best known for her interest in the greater landscape. From 1964 she was landscape consultant to the Forestry Commission, and she was also involved in landscaping the new towns of Harlow and Basildon, in Essex, and the land around reservoirs and factories.

Distinctive potager

During the last quarter of the 20th century, Rosemary Verey's garden at Barnsley House, Gloucestershire, became a mecca for garden visitors, for its design – with strong historical nuances – its planting and colour themes and, more recently, for its French-style potager. Verey's writings, together with her garden, inspired many. A self-taught horticulturist and designer, she scorned the dullness of labour-saving, weed-suppressing planting and instead chose to garden excitingly, conveying the joy of gardening to her disciples. Her books and the many gardens she made for clients, which live on both in Britain and in America, will be a lasting testament to her genius.

designers such as Rosemary Verey, who gardened at Barnsley House in Gloucestershire with a strong sense of history, introducing axial paths and symmetry combined with an exuberance of planting far removed from rationalization of labour costs.

Such garden owners were quick to realize that clipping hedges and topiary could be done by relatively inexperienced staff using modern tools, while naturalistic gardening schemes required a deep knowledge of plants and their needs as well as an eye for painting a picture. There was a new vogue for knots and parterres, straight lines and vertical hedges. In designing a landscape it is impossible not to be influenced by the past so that inevitably all new garden schemes have an element of tradition, appealing to preconceived images. Restoration of historic gardens, with the aid of researched archives and garden archaeology, has become ever more authentic, stimulating further interest in the history of gardens and plants, and extending the historic revivalism of the late Victorian period. In Britain, the Garden History Society was founded in 1965 and today has an expanding membership of scholars and interested gardeners. Many modern gardens during the last years of the 20th century base their appeal on a combination of historical elements with areas of naturalistic planting. The best gardens combine these ingredients with Alexander Pope's sense of place.

On the other hand, the landscape architects worked inside a set of rules established by their training; they had to conform to preconceived notions of how space around blocks of flats and industrial buildings should be organized within a budget and their horticultural vocabulary was limited to a few recommended trees and shrubs, underplanted with useful ground-cover plants. As Sir Geoffrey Jellicoe put it at a much later date in a foreword to *Designing New Landscapes* by Sutherland Lyall (1991), "a civil park [had] potential power to calm, refresh, satisfy and inspire the soul of Everyman in the tradition of church and temple". Sadly, much of the time the inspirational public work now being done to improve the environment is enjoyed but largely ignored by average gardeners and the work of modern landscape architects such as Sir Geoffrey Jellicoe, Dan Kiley, Roberto Burle Marx and Martha Schwartz, although recognized by the *cognoscenti*, has had little impact outside the professional world.

Another style of gardening, which became increasingly influential, took a middle road, and ultimately provided personal and public stimulus. In National Trust properties in Great Britain and North America, old gardens, long neglected while in their original owners' hands due to rising labour costs and high death duties, were restored and increasingly visited by a new public whose own standards of horticulture were correspondingly raised. It is impossible to over-emphasize the encouragement to good gardening made in Britain by the National Trust during the second half of the 20th century. The Trust, ably led by Graham Stuart Thomas as Gardens Adviser from the 1950s to the 1970s, produced lessons in rationalization whilst achieving high aesthetic standards. America's National Trust is organized rather differently, with properties run on a local level.

After World War II there was a strong emphasis on economy of both money and manpower. With many new technical aids – including herbicides and improved mowing machines – gardens which had once required a large team could be kept tidy, if not always very interesting, by very few. Stuart Thomas was able to recommend that a single-handed gardener could maintain three or four acres of garden, where earlier three or four gardeners would have been employed. As a great horticulturist he could introduce economies of effort without sacrificing the finer nuances of gardening. Sissinghurst (see overleaf) and Hidcote (see page 404) are the supreme examples of successful Trust gardens which maintain the spirit and genius of their original owners, while at the same time educating their many annual visitors. On the large estates still in private hands economies often led to less satisfactory results, with gardens getting minimum attention. However by the 1980s, owners realized that the financial rewards to be gained from garden

The adventurous plantsman
Under Christopher Lloyd's ownership, the gardens at Great Dixter in East Sussex – their layout executed by Lutyens for his parents in the 1920s – have become a British gardening icon. Gardened intensively by Lloyd, a skilled plantsman, with vibrant colour schemes, Dixter is not only familiar to many visitors but known through his books and journalism. *The Well-Tempered Garden* (1970), perhaps Lloyd's most influential book, introduced readers to relaxed but effective gardening practices, and eye-opening methods of seasonal gardening. His amusing, rather sharp, writing has endeared him to the horticultural world. One of his latest innovations has been an area of half-hardy, large-foliaged tropical plants, with flowers in bright, eye-catching hues.

Inimitable Sissinghurst

The garden at Sissinghurst in Kent, designed by Vita Sackville-West and her husband Harold Nicolson, but now owned by the National Trust, must be the best-known garden in England, flocked to by visitors from the Continent and America. With quite a formal design, the planting is strictly cottage-style – very similar to that of Hidcote. The high pink brick walls, long axial walks, pleached limes and dark yew hedges, establish a framework for relaxed compartmental planting. During Vita Sackville-West's lifetime (1892–1962) the garden reflected her informal approach. More recently, because there is now a vast number of visitors to control, the Trust's schemes are more ordered, but Sissinghurst retains its magic. One of the most beautiful "rooms" is the White Garden (shown here), dominated by a huge rose, *Rosa mulliganii*, growing over a central arbour, set off by clipped box and silver and grey foliage plants.

Home territory

John Brookes's garden at Denmans, in West Sussex, reflects his interest in natural gardening. In the Walled Garden, instead of borders to match its formal outline, trees, shrubs and self-sown perennials and annuals give it a relaxed but very carefully planned coherence. At the centre, gravel changes to heat-reflecting paving for the aromatic Herb Garden. Native plants such as self-seeding mulleins are repeated through the garden to draw the design together, and more natives take it into the landscape beyond. Famous as a modern designer, John Brookes works all over the world, in Europe, Asia and North and South America, one of his most successful gardens being an English garden at the Chicago Botanic Garden in Wisconsin.

visitors could make a garden viable and attracting the public became a competitive exercise. Stimulated by the excellence of National Trust gardens, this initiative led to a vast improvement in maintenance and in horticulture, with the result that by the turn of the century many "old" gardens had been completely rejuvenated, often with the aid of college-trained head gardeners.

In historical terms, although there was a continual search among both garden designers and amateur gardeners for a way out of the Robinson/Jekyll legacy into something more modern and innovative there was also a complacency about accepting the English contribution of the Edwardian garden to world horticulture. By the 1960s and 1970s the "English garden" had become, in the eyes of the rest of the world, instead of the green 18th-century park, a sort of watered-down version of the Jekyll and Lutyens partnership. Often, as at Hidcote, Sissinghurst, Great Dixter and later at Barnsley House, it had been made by inspired gardeners who had an innate sense of spatial design combined with a painter's eye and a deep knowledge of plants. To Americans and Europeans with a more extreme continental climate coming in search of inspiration to this English garden, it all seemed like perfection. The charm of Sissinghurst, as garden writer and historian Jane Brown has pointed out, partly depends on the close relationship of Vita Sackville-West with the place. Her writing as much as her gardening style permeates everywhere, evoking memories as potent as those in any modern garden vision.

EUROPEAN GIANTS OF DESIGN

In Europe there are a number of outstanding figures who have dominated landscape design during the last years of the 20th century. Two, both British, Russell Page (1906–85) and Sir Geoffrey Jellicoe (1900–96), died before the century's end. The Belgian Jacques Wirtz carries the flag into the new century; he is involved, today, in a grand scheme for Alnwick Castle in Northumberland. In their approach to design, these designers could belong to any age. They have many messages for the future. Belonging to no identifiable school of design, their works speak for themselves.

The designs of Page, Jellicoe and Wirtz, steeped in European history and culture, reflect their understanding of how classicism worked, with plenty of axial views, sculptural terraces and stonework. Their work goes far beyond any sterile reproduction of historic features. To English eyes their work is readily under-

Structured exuberance
At La Mortella, on the island of Ischia near Naples, Russell Page designed the lower garden with Islamic-type pools and water rills, around which Lady Susana Walton has used semitropical plants and tree ferns to create a luxuriant but controlled jungle. It is a perfect example of a talented client enhancing the work of a great designer.

Strength of vision
The Belgian Jacques Wirtz has often been described as a modern-day André Le Nôtre. Some of his work has been the restoration of great historic layouts such as the Tuileries in Paris, but often Wirtz designs for private and public clients, weaving his strong architectural themes to make a setting for modern innovations. At the Banque de Luxembourg, a serpentine water canal silhouettes bare tree trunks.

SIR GEOFFREY JELLICOE: AN INTELLECTUAL VIEW

IN MANY WAYS Sir Geoffrey Jellicoe (1900–96) was as much an academic as a modern designer. As a young man he spent nine months in 1923 with a fellow student from the Architectural Association, J.C. Shepherd, studying and measuring Renaissance gardens in Italy. Although he never consciously imitated a specific garden, it was an experience which grounded him in the proportions of classical design and taught him to appreciate the fundamental importance of the relationship between the villa and its supporting garden. It also resulted in his book *Italian Gardens of the Renaissance*, published in 1925. Later both Greek philosophy and the works of the Roman poets, as studied by the humanists in 15th-century Italy, became a fundamental part of his thinking and his new "cosmic" approach to landscape design. His classical reading and an understanding of the Renaissance mind led to his firm conviction that, by looking at the past, we can find a way forward in all landscape design. As he put it: "Ponder on the past not as the past but as a pointer to the future."

Jellicoe's first major commission was at Ditchley House, Oxfordshire, where he composed a formal Italianesque garden with a long terrace and water gardens. The movement he created between the open and closed spaces was a concept he repeated in many of his designs. Although he based his preliminary ideas for a project on Renaissance philosophy, he would then often enrich them with "in-filling" dependent on medieval allegory and 20th-century art. His Kennedy Memorial (1965–66) at Runnymede, in Berkshire, a simple woodland glade with seats for contemplation along a path, recalls the allegory of John Bunyan's *The Pilgrim's Progress*.

From 1981 Jellicoe had the opportunity to link a great 16th-century house at Sutton Place near Guildford, Surrey, with a modern garden. Here, he could introduce the formality of a classical garden, the naturalism of an 18th-century park and a series of "unseen" symbolic elements of fantasy that help to link Tudor man with the present and future. The garden traces humankind's evolution and gradual civilization and search for fulfilment. A large and a small island in the lake represent a mother and child, the first steps in evolution. At first Jellicoe invites a hazardous journey across stepping stones in the moat to a paradise garden through which you can proceed to a primitive moss garden shaded by a plane tree. In the Magritte Walk, huge Roman vases are purposefully arranged at random to invoke disorder in the midst of order. After a walk through a dark wood, Ben Nicholson's White Wall, reflected in a dark pool, represents Aspiration.

Jellicoe found his stimulation in the visual and in philosophy, rather than in nature. His wife, Susan, or another colleague was usually responsible for the planting plans and other horticultural considerations. Jellicoe was primarily interested in the conceptual and in his later gardens worked with symbolic subjects, asking the viewer to penetrate to the "idea" behind what they could actually see, to look beyond the visible plan to the invisible idea.

Roman heroes
At Shute House near Shaftesbury, on the Dorset and Wiltshire border, Jellicoe designed the garden for Michael and Anne Tree between 1969 and 1988, with water as its primary element. The River Nader provides the water source. Shown here is the view down the canal, flanked by arum lilies, towards three classical busts of Ovid, Virgil and Lucretius.

standable or at least comprehensible without undue intellectual effort. It might be easy to dismiss Page, especially as so many of his gardens are no longer maintained or have been subdivided. Self-taught, he began with little except a love of plants and an interest in modern art and the contemporary world. In his work, although untrained, he seemed to have an intuitive sense of space manipulation, the basics of "cut" and "fill". He worked mainly for wealthy clients in Europe and America, but, as a gifted traditionalist and expert plantsman, he evolved sensitive lively schemes while using many of the basic rules of both French and Italian Renaissance design. Page sought always to establish harmony between the natural terrain of the site and the architectural style of the house, paying considerable attention to detail. Although many of his gardens have a sculptural "green" quality, Page also excelled in making perennial borders. At first he worked with an interior designer in Paris, creating new gardens around old properties, but soon he had commissions all over Europe as well as in the United States. His book *The Education of a Gardener* (1962), in which he describes his own odyssey, is one of the most stimulating testaments of all time, for the amateur and professional alike, its ideas and hints perfectly adaptable to gardens of any dimension. By reading his book it is possible to extract much of his intuitive philosophy.

THE NEW DESIGNERS IN AMERICA

By the middle of the 20th century, Europe no longer dominated the practice of landscape architecture. Until the outbreak of World War II traditional American teaching, taking a much more prominent role following the foundation of the American Society of Landscape Architects in 1899 with Beatrix Farrand, Jens Jensen and the younger Olmsted as charter members, was still based on the Beaux Arts tradition with an emphasis on naturalism. By the 1950s it had to respond to the challenge of extending its relationship with modern architecture. But by far the most interesting ideas for private gardens or public spaces depended on individual landscape architects and designers following their own intuition. Any mainspring gardening in most of the country was limited by the climatic extremes of cold winters and hot, dry or humid summers. Only on the West Coast were gardening possibilities almost as favourable as in the Gulf Stream countries of Europee and people able to garden without great expenditure.

To many Americans Olmsted, with his innovative ideas about the design and social aspects of green spaces, has become an almost legendary figure, as important as William Robinson has been in the European naturalist tradition. Just as Olmsted's inspiration came from parks he first saw in England, most of those who practised landscape architecture successfully in the United States could trace their talent to an interest in tradition and garden history. The development of estate gardens followed a similar pattern. The rich not only collected paintings, furniture and architectural styles from Europe, they also imported ideas for gardens.

THE WEST COAST: LANDSCAPES FOR LIVING

On the West Coast of the United States, in the favourable climate of California, the modern garden could develop to please a new society. Although site specific

THE BEAUX ARTS TRADITION

The Beaux Arts style, which originated in late 19th-century France, influenced many American architects who attended the Ecole des Beaux Arts in Paris before 1914. In the United States this richly ornamented classical style, apart from being used for many buildings, became incorporated into the teaching of garden design in schools such as Harvard and Berkeley. Emphasis was placed on an analytical approach which could be strictly formal or interpreted in the English landscape style. From 1950, however, individual designers were no longer content with traditional symmetry and began to adapt gardening styles to suit modern architectural themes and the new outdoor lifestyles of their clients.

Design for living (opposite)
The most revered of Thomas
Church's gardens is El Novillero,
which he created for the Donnells
at Sonoma, in California, between
1947 and 1949. Here, the swooping
lines of pool and garden reflect the
surrounding hillside and the
winding salt marshes in the valley
below. Designed on a hilltop
encircled by Californian live oaks
(*Quercus agrifolia*), the garden feels
safely poised while having distant
views. A pioneer in Californian
styles, Church marked out a path
mid-way between the polarity of
Beaux Arts formality and the
picturesque landscape approach, as
taught at Harvard University, by
establishing a new vocabulary of
garden design to cope with the
needs of modern life. In particular,
he catered to the relaxed Californian
style of outdoor living. He designed
in small irregular spaces, often on
steep hillsides, to blend his gardens
with the low ranch-type houses and
the natural scenery beyond the
garden perimeter, his concepts
unfettered by old-fashioned ideas
of repetition and symmetry.

and based on a thorough knowledge of indigenous flora, the designs swung
between adaptations of Hispanic and Italian-inspired gardens, and are best
described in the work of individual designers. The greatest was Thomas Church
(1902–78), who worked mainly in California from the 1930s, and who, by the
1950s, had become one of the leading landscape architects in the United States.
The bulk of his practice was on a domestic scale: he laid out gardens to surround
low ranch-type houses, with fluid abstract shapes for pools, hard landscape and
planting. Above all he evolved a new style to match the requirements of his clients
in an all-season environment, with the garden acting as an extension of the house.
Trained at Berkeley and at Harvard he still considered his development as a
designer motivated by his first tour of Europe in 1927, when he visited Spain and
Italy, which have similar climates to California. At first Church's gardens reflected
Italianate influence but after 1937 he became obsessed with modern art, abandoning a central axis in favour of a multiplicity of viewpoints and flowing abstract
lines, with texture, colour, space and form manipulated in ways reminiscent of
cubist painters. As Michael Laurie said in *An Introduction to Landscape Architecture*:
"Church developed a theory based on cubism, that a garden should have no
beginning and no end and that it should be pleasing when seen from any angle,
not only from the house". Not only did Church respect the site and the wishes of
a client, including functional areas in his overall plan, but he was also a keen
plantsman, choosing plants that would thrive in the Californian climate, and thus
able to take his designs through to completion. His *Gardens are for People* (1955),
although seldom explicit about his philosophy, is immensely practical and sets out
his aim of providing a green oasis for each individual. Until his death, Church was
regarded as the doyen of landscape architects.

Another designer of the Californian school is Garrett Eckbo (b. 1910).
Brought up, like Church, in California, but in a less prosperous environment,
Eckbo spent a formative six months with an uncle in Norway when he was 19,
which gave him a new slant on nature. He went to Harvard in 1936 with a scholarship and studied at the same time as James Rose and Dan Kiley. The three
reacted angrily to the current historically orientated teaching of landscape architecture in the Beaux Arts style and in their subsequent work they virtually
invented modern American landscape architecture. Eckbo and Kiley, however,
travelled different roads. They found the insistence on a choice between formal
and informal anachronistic and divisive and sought to devise a new approach to
landscape architecture by uniting man and nature. They were influenced by
Walter Gropius, by now teaching in Harvard's architecture department, and the
fresh breezes blowing in across the Atlantic from the Bauhaus movement in Germany. Eckbo recognized the difficulties of integrating the ordered geometry of
architecture with the fluid organic form of the natural site and plant shapes, and
encouraged a blending of styles. In his *Landscape for Living* (1950) he speaks of his
philosophy: "Outdoors and indoors are inseparable, they are complementary and
supplementary, two sides of the same door…we think of 'house' and 'garden', but
seldom of 'home' as a unit greater than mere house and garden." Both Eckbo and
Church redefined the garden for relatively wealthy clients as a place to live in

with all the baggage of modern recreation, including swimming pools and barbe-cues, vegetables and cutting gardens. To date, Eckbo has designed more than 300 private gardens and worked on many urban housing projects and community centres, his chief interest being in focusing on the design challenges set by social and environmental problems, such as urban sprawl and low-cost housing for migrant workers.

Dan Kiley, who attended Harvard University's Graduate School from 1936 to 1938, was born in Boston (in 1912) but spent many happy vacations on his grandparents' farm in New Hampshire, exploring the fragrant pinewoods. Reared on Thoreau's *Walden*, Kiley felt a great affinity and nostalgia for the American landscape. Employed in the office of Warren Manning (see page 394), Kiley worked on grand estate gardens, often using native plants. After Manning's death in 1938 he went to work for Louis Kahn in Washington DC on housing projects. At the end of World War II he visited the classical Le Nôtre gardens of France and discovered that the formal *allées* and reflecting mirrors were far more impressive than the sterile teaching at Harvard had led him to expect. Saturated with Le Nôtre's ideas, Kiley applied a grid system to his modern designs, using its disci-pline to work with the changing dynamics of nature and seasonal change, and making use of light and shadow to enhance trees, shrubs and ground-cover. His most famous modern garden was made in 1957 for the Irwin Miller House in Columbus, Indiana, where he worked with the architects Eero Saarinen and Roche. The avenue of honey locusts with a Henry Moore sculpture at its end has become an icon in garden history.

CULTURAL INFLUENCES

Perhaps the most inspired of all the designers whose ideas could be applied to ordinary gardening as well as adjusted to the demands of modern architecture, were the Brazilian Roberto Burle Marx (1909–94), the Mexican Luis Barragán (1902–88) and the Japanese-American Isamu Noguchi (1904–88). These highly educated, cultured men were able to bring depth to their projects and invest them with mystery and beauty. Although superficially their gardens may seem to have little relevance to the ordinary gardener, closer study provides extraordinary insight into possibilities in design, and particularly the ideas behind the design. All three drew their inspiration from tradition and culture in Brazil, Mexico and Japan respectively. Burle Marx first grasped the beauty of his own native Brazilian flora while studying painting in Germany, and Barragán's ideas were stimulated by a visit to the Alhambra and villa gardens in Spain and Italy. Noguchi, a sculptor, partly brought up and educated in Japan, was able to produce a fusion of garden styles suitable for America but with a strong overtone of Japanese philosophy; many of his projects were based on carved or cut stone, which he considered the essential bones of the garden.

One of the most important and influential garden designers of the Modernist Movement, Burle Marx brought a touch of the exotic to 20th-century garden design. His abstract "paintings" created by massing coloured foliage plants in amoeba-like shapes are modern art on a vast scale. He has influenced many other

Colourful canvas
The Brazilian landscape architect Roberto Burle Marx designed the garden at São José dos Campos for Olivo Gomes from 1950, incorporating abstract patterns of foliage plants as well as trees and shrubs to relieve the flat landscape. A row of tall trees (*Schizolobium parahybum*) frames distant views, their trunks reflected in water. Burle Marx described an individual plant as being "a form, a colour, a texture, a scent, a living being with needs and preferences, with a personality of its own", and compared plants to notes in music, which could be played in more than one way to get different effects.

designers, including Wolfgang Oehme and James van Sweden, whose scrolls of densely planted prairie plants and waving grasses have revolutionized the American landscape scene. Burle Marx studied painting, architecture and landscape design in Rio de Janeiro. He combined a painter's eye with a sound knowledge of landscape design principles and an encyclopaedic knowledge of Brazilian flora, beginning his career by redesigning parks for the city of Recife, where he replaced foreign plants with natives to create almost jungle effects. His particular influential style involved a series of curvilinear interlocking patterns of contrasting colours and textures, although by the 1950s he was experimenting with more traditional geometric compositions. He not only fought for the preservation of natural habitats in Brazil but as a botanist studied plants *in situ*, introducing several new species which bear his name. In his compositions Burle Marx insisted on providing conditions for plants similar to their natural habitats. As a young man he found the glasshouses in the Dahlem Botanic Garden in Berlin a revelation. The wonders of his native Brazil were encapsulated there for his study, realizing as he drew and painted that "one may think of a plant as a brushstroke…but one must never forget that it is an individual living plant".

Equally interested and inspired by his own vernacular culture and environment, Luis Barragán had no formal training in landscape architecture, coming to it through his interest in the arts and visits to Europe, particularly the Moorish gardens of the Alhambra. Barragán's designs reflected the walled refuges that in traditional Mexican and Spanish buildings provide privacy and shelter in the hot climate. His work appears to be a synthesis of architecture and sculpture with an underlying ecological theme of man's relationship to his environment.

Isamu Noguchi's interest in the Zen qualities of traditional Japanese garden design left very little room for horticultural interest. His symbolic gardens, incorporating Western ideas but with an oriental aesthetic, are composed mainly of stone and water.

GIFTED INNOVATORS

While professional landscape architects and garden designers were searching for modern formulas, many gardeners, without considering style or fashion, continued to develop the themes which interested them, producing something unique and very personal. These gardens had style but remained strongly individualistic. Madame Ganna Walska's Lotusland in California was developed between 1941 and 1984, in much the same period as Vita Sackville-West and her husband Harold Nicolson were extending their own garden paradise at Sissinghurst. Both gardens have a hint of Robinsonian naturalism and depend on stylized colour or plant themes in separate enclosures. In both gardens the plants are chosen for their suitability for the site. But there the resemblance ends. Lotusland was flamboyant even for California; Sissinghurst seems the epitome of English garden traditions, a translation of Edwardian splendour into a personal odyssey. In the early part of the century at Hidcote, Lawrence Johnston developed a style that was to

Japan meets America
Isamu Noguchi, half Japanese and half American, is best remembered as a sculptor. His garden designs achieved a synthesis of sculpture and space using a minimum of different elements. In a career directed towards artistic achievement and self-expression, his life's work was a bridge between Japanese and American cultures. Noguchi explored the problem of space as it relates to both sculpture and landscape design. He once said that he liked "to think of gardens as sculpturing of space...scale and meaning enter when some thoughtful object or line is introduced". His California Scenario at Costa Mesa (right), designed between 1980 and 1982, illustrates his sense of theatre and also embodies a contemplative Zen influence. Tall mirror-glass office towers and a blank wall create a neutral space where Noguchi used a number of elements, including large single stones and a "desert" sparsely planted with cacti.

deeply influence gardeners in Britain, Europe and America. It allowed the traditionalist to create an integrated architectural framework with axial views to focal points and into the landscape beyond, while for enthusiasts there were hidden compartments where plant passions could be indulged without disturbing the balance of the design. As well as plant diversification, plant themes and colour schemes could be introduced. The idea of compartmentalism was hardly new but the relaxed cottage-style planting inside each enclosure at Hidcote may well have inspired Vita Sackville-West and Harold Nicolson when, in 1932, they began their development of Sissinghurst, a garden set among ancient farm buildings with a moat and a tall Elizabethan tower.

A CHANGE IN ATTITUDE

During the last 50 years there have been enormous changes in attitudes to garden design and improvements in horticultural aids. As the grander country estates faltered and gardening help became erratic and often unskilled, the practice of gardening on a smaller scale began to be taken very seriously. For the middle and upper classes without skilled paid help it was necessary to grasp the rules of horticulture. More and more information was available, with garden centres stocking a wide range of gardening aids. In the British Isles, National Trust and National Trust for Scotland gardens set a high standard of upkeep, and mounting visitor numbers showed there was considerable public interest. Visiting good gardens has

Element of theatre
The Mexican Luis Barragán, influenced by a visit to the Alhambra in Spain, saw the house and garden as a refuge – part of an ancient tradition of walled privacy that began with the Persian or Islamic garden and travelled west with Spanish missionaries. From the painter Ferdinand Bac he absorbed the bold use of colour, which he exploited in his austere architecture, where paint creates a series of stage sets, bringing a theatrical element into his designs. The stables at San Cristobal (above) in the suburbs of Mexico City, created between 1967 and 1969, consist of a house, swimming pool, horse pool and stables, with both grooms and horses as actors on the stage.

Role model
Margery Fish died in 1969, having
created her cottage-style garden at
East Lambrook, in Somerset, with a
collection of both usual and
extremely unusual plants, available to
the public from her nursery. During
the 1950s and 1960s the garden
became famous for its particular
form of relaxed planting. This and
the popularity of her books ensured
a following among a new sort of
owner-gardener who sought
interesting plants and interesting
ways of using them. Robinsonian in
her use of hardy plants, Margery
Fish addressed herself to a postwar
generation who did the gardening
themselves and looked beyond
planting clichés.

proved more valuable than reading books and magazines or any
academic study. The spin-off was a number of new small-scale
gardens, adapted to modern living but drawing on centuries of
experience in style and horticultural skills.

Radio and television gardening programmes began to reach
a wide audience. Environmental concerns also became important. Native plant and xeriscape gardens were developed to save
water, at first in the deserts of the United States and in dry California, but soon they spread in popularity across the country
and across the Atlantic to Europe and to Mediterranean countries. Even as herbicides and pesticides of remarkable effective-
ness were being introduced to help gardeners, there was a strong
reaction against their use and the pollution of the countryside.
In America, especially, native plant gardening became an extension of Robinsonian gardening. As labour became both scarce
and expensive, modern machinery took the place of manpower.
Gardens have become smaller and, in place of the great estate
gardens, have themselves become trendsetters, with ideas often
emanating from the gifted owner rather than from a trained
designer. However, from the 1950s, the gap between the world
of the qualified landscape architect (often mainly working on
public or corporate schemes) and the visionary but amateur
designer of domestic gardens has continued to widen.

In the last half century, new species continued to be introduced with plant
hunting in western China again a political possibility. Intensive plant breeding
programmes were led by American specialists who sought cultivars that could
survive extremes of heat or cold, and cope with the difficult humidity and heat of
gardens in the southeast of the United States. Less desirable was the sustained
breeding of perennials with shorter stalks and bigger, long-lasting flowers which
inevitably lost something of the plants' original grace. Container-grown plants
introduced in the early 1960s made all-year-round planting possible. This was a
huge boon to many, but encouraged impulsive plant acquisitions, to the detriment of good design and proper planning for the future. A vast range of plants
that could be grown in containers on a large commercial scale soon became available to the casual shopper. Plants that were less amenable to the production line,
however, became difficult to find. Small specialist nurseries, often not making a
viable income but surviving as a family interest, fulfilled this need and continue
to supply plant enthusiasts. Furthermore, in Great Britain, Europe and the United
States, annually produced guides list all plants and their specialist suppliers.

THE MODERN ARCADIAS

During the last years of the 20th century, a full-scale native plant movement in
the United States took naturalistic garden design and "using native plants only"
onto a high moral plane, regardless of the fact that rare and threatened wild flowers are best preserved in their natural habitat and not necessarily in small gardens.

Nevertheless the spread of alien "weeds" justified the native plant movement and gave it momentum. The wild woods and fields were increasingly colonized by introduced plants – kudzu vine, Hall's honeysuckle, celastrus, *Ampelopsis brevipedunculata*, multiflora roses and loosestrife to name but a few – which could thrive and multiply in summer heat, seriously disturbing ecological balance. Even regional areas found it necessary to prevent the incursion of "foreign" plants from other areas, as cross-fertilization between similar species led to genetic pollution. Native plant enthusiasm may go over the top but it has stimulated the development of American regional styles. It has also helped to cut down on the use of herbicides, pesticides and artificial fertilizers, with native plants needing fewer preventative treatments. Native plants, well adapted to their environment, also require less watering.

In Europe, and especially in the British Isles with its more limited flora, exotic plants are too highly prized to have been eliminated entirely from most garden schemes. In Germany, Professor Richard Hansen at Weihenstephan has taken the lead in detailed experiment and research into habitat requirements of perennials, with the result that many are using prairie and steppe plants from around the world in new ecological, meadow-like border schemes.

Plantsman's paradise
At Heronswood, near Seattle, Dan Hinkley, plant explorer, lecturer and nurseryman, has established his garden in a dense woodland of Douglas firs, opening out into glades of light around the house. Hinkley's eye for a good plant is remarkable and many of his introductions have proved extremely gardenworthy, expanding the horizons of American gardeners. Even today new plants are being discovered in many parts of the world, and it is people like Dan Hinkley who both bring them home and make them available to an enthusiastic gardening public. He is the best sort of new American gardener: inspiring and articulate, he encourages his customers, at the nursery and on lecture tours, to experiment and learn about plants.

Professor Richard Hansen, originally a disciple of Karl Foerster, experimented with perennial breeding and habitat planting at Weihenstephan. His *Perennials and their Garden Habitats* (published in German in 1981 and translated into English in 1993) has become a bible for all those perennial gardeners who seek to create long-lasting and self-sustaining plant communities. Going far beyond Robinson, Hansen's gardening is scientific, aimed at creating and sustaining plant associations which are site specific. Not completely naturalistic in his teaching, Hansen recommends manipulating the site to provide exactly the right conditions of soil and drainage for success, and to ensure minimum future maintenance. Plants could be selected for their "sociability" – their ability to thrive with their neighbours.

The present vogue, inspired originally by Robinson but given practical viability by Foerster and Hansen, in which hardy perennials and grasses thrive in meadow-like borders, has a large following. Work by garden designers such as Piet Oudolf in Holland and Dan Pearson in Britain is extending the meadow concept in new and exciting ways. In many cases although almost self-perpetuating, these schemes work best on a large public scale, where a certain "shagginess" is more acceptable than in a private oasis.

In the United States, influential landscape architect and academic Darrel Morrison encourages gardeners to observe nature and appreciate the beauty of fading flowers and seedheads, developing a new aesthetic appreciation. The Oehme, van Sweden partnership continues to develop its original 1980s designs with subtle meadow-like schemes. These artists are painting pictures with flowers with a strong environmental twist, a skill that requires a sound knowledge of plant needs and management as well as a keen sense of the visual. In Great Britain, over many years and partly through her nursery and books, Beth Chatto has pioneered the introduction of modern ecological concepts into gardening, stressing the importance of matching plants to site.

SKILLS OF LANDSCAPE ARCHITECTS

There have been many changes over the last half century. Today's landscape architects, trained to understand such important environmental factors as soil, geology and the water table, have virtually become scientists, in danger, in the search for ecologically sound solutions in accord with nature, of overlooking aesthetic demands. They also have to confront social issues on a level unimagined by Frederick Law Olmsted in his visionary plans for "places for people". Although Ian McHarg, Professor of Landscape Architecture at Pennsylvania University in the 1970s, reasoned that "if nature is respected the design aspects will look after themselves", this did not satisfy those who felt design was an art form. Throughout the 1970s McHarg encouraged his students to see a landscape as a whole environment. His book *Design with Nature*, published in 1969, emphasized the immutable scientific rules of ecological landscape design. If the rules worked the aesthetics would work too. More than 30 years later McHarg's innovations in teaching landscape design are still largely relevant. In his emphasis on environmental matters Olmsted would have approved of McHarg's work, although he

Plant painting (opposite, top)
Tall filipendulas frame the bench and dark water canal at the Dutch painter Ton ter Linden's garden near Ruinen, in northern Holland. The garden combines an air of naturalism with his intense appreciation of colour composition. Unlike traditional borders with solid repetitive blocks of colour, Ton ter Linden's borders are abstract patterns of colour harmonies woven from flowers and foliage. As a young man he was familiar with the "nature" gardens being developed at Amstelveen, near Amsterdam, just when he was starting to paint. As a gardener, he developed his own style, with borders seen against backgrounds of dark yew – hedges planted for wind protection – so that the spaces become rooms in which colours fade into each other and shapes of plants and their foliage are as important for final effects as flower colour.

The sociable border (opposite, below)
At Weihenstephan's horticultural college, at Freising near Munich, the borders are outstanding. Soil is specially prepared to suit the plants and plants are chosen for their suitability to the site and their "sociability" with each other. In *Perennials and their Garden Habitats*, Professor Richard Hansen studies perennials and their habitats in depth showing how self-perpetuating borders, the planting style somewhere between a traditional border and a meadow, are possible. With very skilful maintenance, the planting and colour schemes at Weihenstephan are superb, but similar schemes in experimental gardens elsewhere have demonstrated the necessity for plant knowledge and annual editing, without which even the most carefully prepared borders deteriorate quickly.

Degrees of control

Working from Washington DC, the firm of Oehme, van Sweden has established its own style over the last 20 years, in which perennials and tall swaying grasses are planted in broad swathes (above) in interlocking patterns. In spring, scrolls of bulbs, massed in one variety, create the same effect. Although naturalistic in appearance, the planting is in fact very formal and controlled. By choosing compatible plants for his schemes, Dan Pearson achieves in a quite different way a natural look (right) in which he seems to let nature have a free rein. Basically, he allows an ecosystem to develop, and interferes as little as possible, having provided suitable plants. However, it still obviously needs a controlling hand and an artist's eye to develop an ever-changing and evolving garden scene. Unlike the Oehme, van Sweden gardens, which are set in their mould, Dan Pearson's designs recognize that making a garden is a constant process, and produces a continually changing product.

Supreme plant skills

Beth Chatto, in England, and Piet Oudolf, in Holland, are both highly knowledgeable nursery growers of herbaceous perennials. They also have a genius for design. Always working within the limits imposed by her ecological attitude to gardening, Beth Chatto in her Gravel Garden (left), in Essex, has shown how creating beauty can work hand in hand with using plants appropriately. Planting with nature does not have to be untidy or dull. In the Gravel Garden, plants, chosen for their drought-resistance, weave patterns in the dry, well-drained soil. Piet Oudolf, now an international designer, has also developed his own style (below), using statuesque grasses and tall perennials, that is equally dependent on understanding plants' needs. Chatto and Oudolf carry on the Karl Foerster tradition, and inspire new gardeners to choose plants appropriate to their site.

The city park Paris-style

Parc André Citröen, on the banks of the River Seine in southwest Paris, is one of a growing number of imaginative new parks found in Continental Europe, created on industrial waste land and aimed at reinvigorating run-down city areas. Designed by Alain Provost and Gilles Clément around a central grass area, it reflects the French interest in history, combining water displays, inspired by Renaissance cascades and Islamic _chadars_ (as above), with enlivening themed flower gardens.

might have questioned his assertion that if you followed the hallowed environmental rules the results, through nature, would be beautiful. Ecology as a science is, indeed, recognized in creating an understanding of the complex relationships of the natural world, but an aesthetic defined only in ecological terms will not always work. Just as natural and beautiful cannot always be equated in gardening, so schemes determined only by ecological rules can lack vision. They will be satisfactory if the landscape is handled by a visionary designer.

Today Darrel Morrison, now at the University of Georgia, is encouraging American gardeners to re-examine their attitudes to ornamental gardening. His message is to observe nature, and to garden to conserve it and its natural resources.

CLASSICISTS, MINIMALISTS AND VISIONARIES

Through the centuries garden styles have borrowed heavily from other eras and other cultures, sometimes in details of structural layout and sometimes in buildings and follies which introduce an exotic element. Dan Kiley, Sir Geoffrey Jellicoe, Jacques Wirtz and Fernando Caruncho (see page 448) all share echoes of Renaissance principles in their designs. Kiley was primarily influenced by Le Nôtre's linear landscapes and Wirtz and Caruncho by classical Greek and Roman literature. But, rather than adapting actual Renaissance patterns, all these designers use or have used elements taken directly from the grammar of formality, which are then applied in novel ways more suitable for contemporary life. By imposing a grid system on an outline plan it is possible to introduce balance, whether the design is ultimately formal or informal.

The minimalists, unlike the modernists and their attempts to break with tradition, also find their roots in the past. Whether influenced by the enclosed spiritual gardens of Islam, by the geometric cubic spaces of Renaissance architects, by contemplative religions from the Far East as interpreted by Isamu Noguchi, or by the genius of the Mexican Luis Barragán, designers such as Fernando Caruncho, Martha Schwartz, Christopher Bradley-Hole and Kathryn Gustafson look at the land in a new way, their schemes more nearly akin to "land art" than to landscape architecture. Uncluttered, clean, often geometric lines, vernacular colours, indigenous planting and an

Garden of the mind
The garden of Little Sparta, created by the poet and artist Ian Hamilton Finlay in Lanarkshire, Scotland, is intensely personal, a philosopher's garden in a wild bleak landscape where the visitor moves from groves of trees to moorland beside the lake. Quotations inscribed on stone are open to interpretation by the viewer, and columns and statuary are of greater importance than plants. It is, perhaps, the most original garden made since 1945, reflecting Hamilton Finlay's art and philosophy.

The way the wind blows

Topher Delaney, partner in Delaney, Cochran and Castillo, based in San Francisco, is an innovative designer who uses her art to blur the lines between architecture and horticulture. Delaney, who grew up in the art world, is influenced by the past. She not only considers historic styles in gardening, but also examines earlier social, political and cultural perceptions of nature and reinterprets them in a way that makes them relevant to modern-day clients. She endows each location, whether public or private, with a narrative that becomes site specific, and often combines traditional and modern materials. In her roof garden created for the employees of the Bank of America in San Francisco she produced a bold design of climber-covered spheres, huge palm trees and multicoloured windsocks, generating movement and life.

FERNANDO CARUNCHO'S PARTERRES OF WHEAT

THE SPANISH DESIGNER Fernando Caruncho came to design while studying classical philosophy at the University of Madrid. Working mainly in Spain, he seems inspired by a search for a particular relationship between the history of the land and its agricultural tradition. The implementation of his designs relies on a basic grid system that is applicable to both productive and decorative landscaping and unites all the individual elements.

Best known for his repetitive groves of silver-grey olive trees, wheat fields, avenues of slender, tall cypresses and water parterres (see page 54), Caruncho brings a basic purity to design, using straight lines and right angles on a large landscape scale, emphasizing light and shadow, movement, form, leaf colour and texture, with little reference to flowers. He believes that the mind craves the reassurance of geometry and his schemes are the antithesis of the popular romantic Jekyll-style English garden, in which plant shapes disguise any formality in structure.

Caruncho's work can be described as a fusion of the Moorish gardens of the Alhambra and Italian and French Renaissance gardens, particularly as evidenced in his native Spain, in the royal gardens of Aranjuez, in Madrid, and La Granja, in Segovia, the latter largely inspired by Louis XIV's Versailles. Also much influenced by the Mexican architect Luis Barragán, Caruncho uses walls of sienna-coloured stucco to create his spaces – volumes of space in the Renaissance sense – sometimes clothing the walls with rippling ivy.

At Mas de les Voltes in northern Spain, Caruncho made an entirely new garden, around the house, with wheat fields and carp pond parterres enclosed by groves of evergreen oaks, orchards of cherry, apple, pomegranate and fig, and stands of rustling bamboo. He described the garden himself in a recent book: "This is an agricultural garden…here a flower – any flower – would look out of place. For flower-filled borders one can go to Sissinghurst, but the landscape of the Mediterranean needs something quite different. This is a garden of forms, geometry and light…In the summer, the wheat is tall and golden and the great plots sway gently in the wind. There is fruit in the orchard. Autumn brings the grape harvest and the cutting of the wheat. In the winter the earth is ploughed and sown and marked by wonderful patterns. And in the spring once again, all is a sea of green. What could be more enobling than producing flour from the wheat, wine from the vines, oil from the olives, and fruit from the trees? In a sense this is the first garden with all the purity of a Platonic ideal."

Spanish inheritance
At Mas de les Voltes, Fernando Caruncho has melded his enthusiasm for the geometry of Renaissance design with his love of the agricultural landscape of his native Spain.

1. GLYNDEBOURNE 2. TERRACE 3. YEW GARDEN 4. TORTE'S GARDEN 5. SPRING GARDEN 6. THE FLORA GLADE 7. THE KNOT GARDEN 8. FOUNTAIN-COURT 9. ARABELLA ORCHARD 10. SCHÖNBRUNN ORCHARD 11. SILVER JUBILEE GARDEN 12. PIERPONT MORGAN ROSE GARDEN 19. ASHTON ARBOUR 20. COVENT GARDEN 21. V. & A. TEMPLE 22. NUTCRACKER GARDEN 23. RANDOM HOUSE 13. SCANDANAVIAN GROVE 14. HILLIARD GARDEN 15. THE BIRTHDAY GARDEN 16. THE BEATON STEPS 17. SHAKESPEARE MONUMENT 18. HEARNE'S OAK

The LASKETT *Herefordshire* Created by SIR ROY STRONG & DR JULIA TREVELYAN OMAN

aura of tranquillity are characteristics of a minimalist approach, with form and function in perfect balance. These new designers are history orientated but also concerned with maintaining a balanced ecology. Outwardly modern in appearance, the minimalist garden appears to break with the past but in its historical nuances is also intensely derivative. In an age of immense technical possibilities and with an extensive range of plants from which to choose, minimalist gardens are best exemplified by the power of restraint in both architectural features and in choice of plants. The famous words of Ludwig Mies van der Rohe in 1959, "less is more", seem entirely appropriate.

Some of the most inspirational gardens made since 1970, however – those which carry us into the future – have been created by talented owner-gardeners, who have always played a role in the development of garden history. They, too, like professional designers, borrow ideas and features from the past.

Rosemary Verey's garden at Barnsley House, Ian Hamilton Finlay's Little Sparta, Francis Cabot's Les Quatre Vents in Quebec and Charles Jencks's garden in the borders of Scotland all have a visionary quality. While all contain elements of the past, of necessity, the designs reflect the realities of contemporary life. These personal gardens are as important and influential as the writings and theories of the greatest landscape architects and it is because of this personal element that they outshine gardens made by a designer for a client.

A life laid out

This plan of the Laskett demonstrates an obsession with structure and control, but the garden of Sir Roy Strong and his wife, Dr Julia Trevelyan Oman, a theatre designer, has many hidden nuances. Begun in the 1960s, it is an autobiographical garden, each of its ingredients commemorating an event in one of their distinguished lives – the Victoria and Albert Temple, for instance, referring to Sir Roy's time as director of the renowned museum. Highly formal and architectural in layout, the garden also reflects their mutual love of plants, evidenced by a collection of crab apples and other fruits. The plan was painted by Jonathan Myles-Lea in 1995.

High ideals

In this roof garden by Christopher Bradley-Hole tall grasses grow in raised beds, contrasting with the stark surrounding architecture. Bradley-Hole, already well known among fellow designers, came into the public eye when the garden he created for *The Daily Telegraph* at the Chelsea Flower Show in 2000 won the award for the best garden in the show. It demonstrated how a rigidly geometric layout could have a strong modernist appeal, although the inspiration was found in Virgil's 1st-century pastoral poems and the plants were Mediterranean in origin.

THE GARDEN AS ART

Gardening as an art form remains quite different from more exact disciplines such as architecture and painting owing to the time element. The architect, sculptor or painter makes a finished product; the gardener must peer into the future to project his or her plan into another era. Gardening is a process, not necessarily a product. A garden's four-dimensional quality, involving development, change and growth, gives it a dynamic quality which bricks and mortar cannot match. Gardens also develop at different paces. The trees in the great 18th-century landscapes of 'Capability' Brown took two hundred years to mature, while ephemeral flower gardens reach their peak in 10 years and need restoration after 15. Some of the garden icons of the late 20th century may already be in need of revision.

Gardening is big business. In Britain and the United States a vast amount is spent every year on plants and garden-related products, and gardening now ranks among the top leisure activities. Indeed, a well-planned garden has become a status symbol. In the past, history was written in terms of the great estates, their garden fashions evaluated for each period. Today, with so many fine old gardens open for visiting, ordinary gardeners can admire grander schemes and adapt them for their own use. With books, magazines and "makeover" and "hands-on" television programmes providing inspiration, a huge range of equipment at garden centres supplying the means of implementation and containerized plants enabling instant gratification, it is now the age of the small, intimate garden.

MARTHA SCHWARTZ: DESIGNER-PROVOCATEUR

A FIRM MODERNIST, Martha Schwartz believes in functional art and that modern life is the justification for artistic endeavour. Influenced by Pop Art, she is able to introduce humour and provocation as well as vibrant colour into her work, without any cosiness. She is often commissioned for sites where little planting is possible. Instead of using plants she finds a theme to connect with the history of the site. At the Rio Shopping Centre in Atlanta, gold plastic frogs are arranged in a quincunx pattern (like trees in a Renaissance orchard), each frog-face directed towards the source of water, a giant sphere, inspired by the *Bassin de Latone* at Versailles. Her Davis Garden at El Paso in Texas, designed for a private client, reflects a Barragán influence in her use of colour, with a series of box-like compartments, their walls colour-washed in sumptuous shades of pink, purple and dark yellow.

Working since the 1980s, Schwartz has been a necessary catalyst for change but is too individualistic and shocking to have a following of other designers. Her pioneering role – perhaps now coming to its end – has been to awaken sensibilities to alternative ways of gardening and allow modern garden design to progress. One of her most appealing gardens, full of light-hearted wit but also serious and almost chilling, is the Splice Garden she made for the Whitehead Institute for Biomedical Research in Cambridge, Massachusetts. Here, the garden is in two parts, one basically formal French, the other Japanese, separated by a sharp line. In the version of a Zen garden, gravel radiates from the "rocks", actually plastic shrubs, while in the

French garden, blocks in geometric shapes, some topped with a basket of plastic flowers, are covered with Astroturf. Trunks of plastic trees have protrusions like pruned branches.

Schwartz has irritated, amazed, shocked, amused and enlightened her public, with a style of gardening that is a deliberate liberation from links with the past.

Within these walls
At the Davis Garden (left) at El Paso, Texas, Schwartz constructed a series of painted walls, sombre on the outside and vibrant and startling on the inner surface, with a conical mound of pebbles as the only decoration.

Creative edge
Surrounded by green walls and anchored by green gravel, Schwartz's design for the Splice Garden (below) has a sinister nuance related to gene-splicing and the creation of artificial life.

Australian realism (right)

Australian designer Vladimir Sitta has strong views on humankind's necessarily interventionist role – which he sees as an act of violence – in making a garden. "If nature is allowed to survive in a garden at all, it is only in fragments. The continuing presence of man is, of course, a condition of a garden's existence." Sitta understands the centuries-old dialogue between man and nature, and the respective roles of each in a garden, but feels the designer should always offer something out of the ordinary or ordinarily predictable. In this garden he designed at Bellevue Hill in Sydney, a black pool fed by a brightly walled channel reflects the vast Australian sky.

Cypress spires (opposite, top)

At Las Navas, near Toledo in Spain, Arabella Lennox-Boyd has made a fortress garden, an oasis with a cascade and octagonal pool, around the hilltop house. Tall cypresses, ghostly olive trees underplanted with lavenders and irises with a matrix of box hedging link the garden with the surrounding agricultural countryside. Lennox-Boyd, working in many different climates all over the world, likes to relate her landscape to the house and to the surrounding countryside, and shows an acute awareness and sense of place.

Enduring Islamic appeal (opposite, below)

In Ireland, at her Dublin garden, Helen Dillon has recently replaced the central lawn with a long canal fed by a rill. Influenced by her visits to Morocco, India and the Alhambra in Spain, Dillon, as a fitting example of design at the end of this book, has captured the essence of the Islamic garden, which has its origins in the paradise gardens of the desert. She has, however, used stark Irish limestone with a polished edge to give a very contemporary look.

BIBLIOGRAPHY

I found the following titles invaluable in writing this book, and for those readers who would like to take their interest in the history of gardening further, these are the books and journals I would recommend they read.

GENERAL

Bazin, Germain. *Paradeisos*. London, 1990.

Bisgrove, Richard. *The National Trust Book of the English Garden*. London, 1990.

Dixon Hunt, John. *Garden and Grove*. London, 1986.
– *Greater Perfections: the Practice of Gardening Theory*. London, 2000.

Goody, Jack. *The Culture of Flowers*. Cambridge, 1993.

Gothein, Maria Luise. *A History of Garden Art*, translated by Laura Archer-Hind. New York, 1928 (reprinted 1979).

Hobhouse, Penelope. *Plants in Garden History*. London, 1992.

Hussey, Christopher. *English Gardens and Landscapes 1700–1750*. Country Life, 1967.

Jellicoe, Geoffrey and Susan; Goode, Patrick; and Lancaster, Michael, editors. *The Oxford Companion to Gardens*. Oxford, 1986.

Mosser, Monique; and Teyssot, Georges, editors. *The History of Garden Design*. London, 1991.
– Also published as *The Architecture of Western Gardens*. Boston, 1991.

Schama, Simon. *Landscape and Memory*. Vintage Press, 1996.

Thacker, Christopher. *The History of Gardens*. Croom Helm, 1979.

Periodicals

Garden History (the journal of the Garden History Society), 1972–

Journal of Garden History, published by Taylor & Francis, 1981–1998

Studies in the History of Gardens and Designed Landscapes, Taylor & Francis, 1998–

CHAPTER ONE

Hepper, F. Nigel. *Pharaoh's Flowers*. London, 1990.

Jellicoe, Geoffrey and Susan. *The Landscape of Man*. London, 1975.

Mann, William. *Landscape Architecture: an Illustrated History in Timelines, Sites, Plans and Biography*. John Wiley and Sons, 1993.

Manniche, Lise. *An Ancient Egyptian Herbal*. London, 1993.

Wilkinson, Alix. *The Garden in Ancient Egypt*. The Rubicon Press, 1998.

Xenophon. *Oeconomics*, translated by E.C. Marchant. London and New York, 1923.

CHAPTER TWO

Baumann, Hellmut. *Greek Wild Flowers*, translated by W.T. and E.R. Stearn. Herbert Press, 1993.

Blunt, Wilfrid; and Raphael, Sandra. *The Illustrated Herbal*. London, 1979.

Burr Thompson, Dorothy, editor. *Garden Lore of Ancient Athens*. American School of Classical Studies, Princeton, 1968.

Columella. *On Agriculture and Trees*, translated by H.B. Ash, E.S. Forster, and E.H. Heffner. London and Cambridge, Massachusetts, 1951–55.

de la Riuffinière du Prey, Pierre. *The Villas of Pliny from Antiquity to Posterity*. Chicago, 1994.

Farrar, Linda. *Ancient Roman Gardens*. Sutton Publishing, 1998.

Huxley, Anthony. *An Illustrated History of Gardening*. London, 1988.

MacDougall, E.B.; and Jashemski, W.F., editors. *Ancient Roman Gardens*. Dumbarton Oaks, Washington DC, 1981.

Pliny the Younger. *The Letters of the Younger Pliny*, translated by Betty Radice. Harmondsworth, 1967.

Raven, John. *Plants and Plant Lore in Ancient Greece*. Leopard's Head Press, 2001.

Virgil. *The Georgics*, translated by Robert Wells. Manchester, 1982.

Periodicals

Jashemski, W.F. "The Gardens of Pompeii, Herculaneum and the Villas Destroyed by Vesuvius". *Journal of Garden History*, Vol. 12, No. 2, 1992.

Littlewood, A.R. "Gardens of Byzantium". *Journal of Garden History*, Vol. 12, No. 2, 1992.

Plant Lore of Ancient Athens, edited by Maureen Carroll-Spillecke. *Journal of Garden History*, Vol. 12, No. 2, April–June 1992.

CHAPTER THREE

Babur. *The Babur-nama in English*, translated by A.S. Beveridge. London, 1922.

Bernus-Taylor, Marthe; and others, editors. *Arabesques et Jardins de Paradis: Collections Français d'Art Islamique*. (Catalogue of exhibition at the Louvre, Paris, 1989–90). Paris, 1989.

Brookes, John. *Gardens of Paradise*. London, 1987.

Chardin, Sir John. *Travels in Persia*, translated by E. Lloyd. London, 1927.

Clark, Emma. *Underneath Which Rivers Flow: the Symbolizm of the Islamic Garden*. Prince of Wales's Institute of Architecture, 1997.

Dixon Hunt, John, editor. *Garden History: Issues, Approaches, Methods*: "The medieval Islamic garden: typology and hydraulics", Yasser Tabbaa. Dumbarton Oaks, Washington DC, 1992.

Foster, William. *Sir Thomas Herbert Travels in Persia 1627–29*. Routledge, 1928.

Heavenly Art, Earthly Beauty. (Catalogue of exhibition at the Nieuwe Kerk, Amsterdam, 2000). Amsterdam, 2000.

Khansari, Mehdi. *The Persian Garden: Echoes of Paradise*. Mage Publishers, 1998.

Koran, The.

L. Tjion Sie Fat & E. de Jon, editors. *The Authentic Garden*: "The culture of gardens and flowers in the Ottoman Empire", Nevzat Ilhan; "The

Abbasid garden in Baghdad and Samarra", Qasim Al-Sammarrai; "Botanical foundations for the restoration of Spanish-Arabic gardens", Esteban Hernandez Bermejo; "The botanic gardens in Muslim Spain 8th-16th centuries", Angel Lopez y Lopez. Clusius Foundation, 1991.

Lehrman, Jonas. *Earthly Paradise*. London, 1980.

MacDougall, E.B.; and Ettinghausen, R., editors. *The Islamic Garden*. Dumbarton Oaks, Washington DC, 1976.

MacDougall, E.B.; and Wilber, Donald N.. *Persian Gardens and Garden Pavilions*. Dumbarton Oaks, Washington DC, 1979.

Moynihan, Elizabeth. *Paradise as a Garden in Persia and Mughal India*. New York, 1979.

Olearius, Adam. *Vermehrte Newe beschreibung der Muskowitischen und Persischen*. Germany, 1656.

Pavord, Anna. *The Tulip*. London, 1999.

Sackville-West, Vita. *Passenger to Teheran*. Hogarth Press, 1926.

Titley, Norah; and Wood, Frances. *Oriental Gardens*. London, 1991.

Periodicals

Harvey, John. "Gardening books and plant lists of Moorish Spain". *Journal of Garden History*, Vol. 3, No. 2, Spring 1975.
– "Turkey as a source of garden plants". *Journal of Garden History*, Vol. 4, No. 3, Autumn 1976.

Stronach, David. "Pasargadae". *Journal of Garden History*, Vol. 14, No. 1, Spring 1994.

CHAPTER FOUR

Harvey, John. *Medieval Gardens*. Batsford, 1981.

L. Tjion Sie Fat & E. de Jon, editors. *The Authentic Garden*: "Some strip of herbage", Hans de Bruijn. Clusius Foundation, 1991.

Landsberg, Sylvia. *The Medieval Garden*. London, 1998.

MacDougall, E.B., editor. *Medieval Gardens*: "Reality and Literary Romance in the Park of Hesdin", Anne Hagopian Van Buren; "Pietro de' Crescenzi and the Medieval Garden", Robert G. Calkins; "The Medieval Monastic Garden", Paul Meyvaert. Dumbarton Oaks, Washington DC, 1986.

McLean, Theresa. *Medieval English Gardens*. Collins, 1981

Stokstad, Marilyn; and Stannard, Jerry. *Gardens of the Middle Ages*. (Catalogue of exhibition at the Spencer Museum of Art, Lawrence, Kansas). Lawrence, Kansas, 1983.

Strabo, Walafrid. *Hortulus*, translated by Raef Payne, with a commentary by Wilfrid Blunt. Pittsburgh, 1966.

CHAPTER FIVE

Alberti, Leon Battista. *The Ten Books of Architecture*, translated by J. Leoni. London, 1755 (reprinted New York, 1986).

Batey, Mavis. *Oxford Gardens*. Scolar Press, 1982.

Colonna, Francesco. *Hypnerotomachia Poliphili*,

translated by Joscelyn Godwin. London, 1999.

de Caus, Salomon. *Hortus Palatinus*. Frankfurt, 1624.

Dezallier d'Argenville, Antoine-Joseph. *La Théorie et la Pratique du Jardinage*. Paris 1709.
– *The Theory and Practice of Gardening*, translated by John James. London, 1712.

Dixon Hunt, John; and De Jong, Eric. *The Anglo-Dutch Garden in the Age of William and Mary*. (Catalogue of exhibition, also *Journal of Garden History*, No. 2 & 3, Vol. 8, 1988). London, 1988
– As editor. *The Italian Garden*. Cambridge, 1996.

du Cerceau, Jacques Androuet. *Les plus excellents bâtiments de France*. Paris, 1576–1607.

Estienne, Charles. *L'Agriculture et maison rustique*, translated by J. Liébault. Paris, 1570 (later editions augmented and revised by Liébault, 1586, 1598).
– *Maison Rustique or the Countrie Farme*, translated by Richard Surflet. London, 1600.

Fiennes, Celia. *Illustrated Journeys 1685–1712*, edited by Christopher Morris. London, 1988.

Gaunt, W., editor and translator. *Lives of the Painters, Sculptors and Architects*. London, 1963.

Green, David. *Queen Anne*. Oxford, 1956.

Gurrieri, Francesco; and Chatfield, Judith. *The Boboli Gardens*. Florence, 1972.

Harris, Walter. *A Description of the King's Royal Palace at Het Loo*. London, 1699.

Jacques, David; and van der Horst, Arend, editors. *The Gardens of William and Mary*. London, 1988.

Lazzaro, Claudia. *Italian Renaissance Garden*. Yale, 1990.

Masson, Georgina. *Italian Gardens*. London, 1961.
– "Italian Flower Collectors' Gardens in Seventeenth Century Italy". *The Italian Garden*, edited by David R. Coffin. Dumbarton Oaks, Washington DC, 1972.

Strong, Roy. *The Artist and the Garden*. Yale, 2000.
– *The Renaissance Garden in England*. London, 1979.

Weiss, Allen. *Mirrors of Infinity: the French Formal Garden and Seventeenth Century Metaphysics*. Princeton, 1995.

Woodbridge, Kenneth. *Princely Gardens: the Origins and Development of the French Formal Style*. London, 1986.

Whalley, Robin; and Jennings, Anne. *Knot Gardens and Parterres*. Barn Elms Publishing, 1998.

Periodicals

Andrew, Martin. "Theobalds Palace: the gardens and park". *Journal of Garden History*, Vol. 21, No. 2, Winter 1993.

Henderson, Paula. "Sir Francis Bacon's water gardens at Gorhambury". *Garden History*, Autumn 1999.

CHAPTER SIX

Arber, Agnes. *Herbals: their origin and evolution*. Second edition. Cambridge, 1938.

Aymonin, Gerard. *The Besler Florilegium: Plants of the Four Seasons*. New York, 1987.

Barker, Nicholas. *Hortus Eystettensis*. London, 1994.

Besler, Basilius. *Hortus Eystettensis*. Nuremburg, 1613.

Chambers, Douglas. *The Planters of the English Landscape Garden*. Yale, 1993.

Coats, Alice. *The Quest for Plants*. Studio Vista, 1969.

Dixon Hunt, John; and Peter Willis. *The Genius of Place: the English Landscape Garden*. Elek, 1975.

Evelyn, John. *Sylva, or a Discourse of Forest-trees*. London, 1664.
– *Sylva, or a Discourse of Forest-trees*, with notes by Alexander Hunter. York, 1776.
– *The Diary of John Evelyn*, edited by Esmond de Beer. Oxford, 1955.

Fairchild, Thomas. *The City Gardener*. London, 1722.

Gerard, John. *The Herball or General Historie of Plants*. London, 1597.
– Second edition amended by Thomas Johnson. London, 1633.
Leaves from Gerard's Herball, arranged by Marcus Woodward. Second edition, London, 1931 (reprinted London, 1985).

Hanmer, Sir Thomas. *The Garden Book of Sir Thomas Hanmer*. London, 1933.

Henrey, Blanche. *British Botanical and Horticultural Literature Before 1800*. London, 1975.

Hill, Thomas. *The Gardener's Labyrinth*. London, 1577.
– Edited by Richard Mabey. Oxford, 1987.

Kastner, Joseph. *A World of Naturalists*. John Murray, 1978.

L.Tjion Sie Fat & E.de Jon, editors. *The Authentic Garden: "Clusius' garden – a reconstruction"*. Clusius Foundation, 1991.

Lawson, William. *A New Orchard and Garden*. London, 1618.
– *The Countrie Housewife's Garden*. London, 1617.

Leapman, Michael. *The Ingenious Mr Fairchild*. Headline, 2000.

Leith-Ross, Prudence. *The John Tradescants*. London, 1984.

Mattioli, P.A.. *Commentarii in sex libros Pedacii Dioscoridis*. Venice, 1565.

O'Brian, Patrick. *Joseph Banks: a Life*. Harvill Press, 1987.

Parkinson, John. *Paradisi in Sole Paradisus Terrestris*. London, 1629.

Rea, John. *Flora Ceres & Pomona*. Second edition. London, 1976.

Rix, Martyn. *The Art of Botanical Illustration*. Lutterworth Press, 1981.

Turner, William. *A New Herball*. London, 1551.

van de Pass, Crispin. *Hortus Floridus*. Utrecht, 1614 (reprinted London, 1974).

Veendorp, H.; and Bass Beckling, L.G.M.. *Hortus Academicus Lugduno-Batavus 1587–1937*. Leiden, 1938 (reprinted 1990).

Whittle, Tyler. *The Plant Hunters*. Heinemann, 1969.

Periodicals

Leith-Ross, Prudence. "The garden of John Evelyn at Deptford". *Journal of Garden History*, Vol. 25, No. 2, Winter 1997.

CHAPTER SEVEN

Batey, Mavis. *Alexander Pope: the Poet and the Landscape*. Barn Elms Publishing, 2000.

Cobbett, William. *The English Gardener*. London, 1829 (reissued 1833, reprinted Oxford, 1980).

Daniels, Stephen. *Humphry Repton*. Yale, 1999.

Dixon Hunt, John. *William Kent*. Zwemmer, 1987.

Humphry Repton: Landscape Gardener. (Catalogue of exhibition, Victoria and Albert Museum, London, 1982.)

Hussey, Christopher. *Picturesque: Studies in a Point of View*. F. Cass, 1967.

Jacques, David. *Georgian Gardens: the Reign of Nature*. London, 1983.

Laird, Mark. *The Flowering of the English Landscape: English Pleasure Grounds 1720–1800*. University of Pennsylvania Press, 1999.

Loudon, John Claudius. *Arboretum et Fruticetum Britannicum*. London, 1835–38.

Malins, Edward. *English Landscaping and Literature*. Oxford, 1966.

Pevsner, Nicolaus, editor. *The Picturesque Garden and its Influence Outside the British Isles*. Dumbarton Oaks, Washington DC, 1974.

Philips, Henry. *Sylva Florifera: The Shrubbery Historically and Botanically Treated*. London, 1823.

Olin, Laurie. *Across the Open Field: Essays Drawn from English Landscapes*. Pennsylvania, 1999.

Repton, Humphry. *Fragments on Landscape Gardening and Architecture as Connected with Rural Scenery*. 1816.
– *Sketches and Hints*. 1793.
– *Theory and Practice*. 1803.
– *The Art of Landscape Gardening*, reprinted Houghton Mifflin, Boston and New York, 1907

Shaftesbury, Earl of. *The Moralists*. London, 1709.

Stroud, Dorothy. *Capability Brown*. London, 1975.
– *Humphry Repton*. London, 1962.

Swinden, Nathaniel. *The Beauties of Flora Display'd*. London, 1778.

The Palladian Revival. (Catalogue of exhibition at the Royal Academy of Arts.) London, 1995.

CHAPTER EIGHT

Batey, Mavis; and Lambert, David. *The English Garden Tour*. J. Murray, 1990.

Boniface, Priscilla, editor. *In Search of English Gardens*. London, 1990.

Brooke, E. Adveno. *The Gardens of England*. London, 1858.

Carter, Tom. *The Victorian Garden*. London, 1984.

Devonshire, Deborah, Duchess of. *The Garden at Chatsworth*. Frances Lincoln, 1999.

Elliott, Brent. *Victorian Gardens*. London, 1986.

Hayden, Peter. *Biddulph Grange, Staffordshire: a Victorian Garden Rediscovered*. London, 1989.

Hughes, John Arthur. *Garden Architecture and Landscape Gardening*. London, 1866.

MacDougall, E.B., editor. *John Claudius Loudon and the Early Nineteenth Century in Great Britain*. Dumbarton Oaks, Washington DC, 1980.

Loudon, John Claudius. *Encyclopaedia of Gardening*. Third edition. London, 1825.
– *The Suburban Gardener and Villa Companion*. London, 1838.

Musgrave, Toby. *The Plant Hunters*. London, 1999.
Simo, Melanie Louise. *Loudon and the Landscape*. New Haven and London, 1988.
Stearn, William, editor. *John Lindley: 1799–1865*. London, 1998.

Periodicals
Laurie, Ian. "Landscape at Eaton Park". *Journal of Garden History*, Autumn 1985.
Ridgway, Christopher. "W.A. Nesfield". *Journal of Garden History*, Vol. 13, 1993.
The Gardener's Magazine. 1826–43.

CHAPTER NINE
Bartram, William. *Travels Through North and South Carolina, Georgia, East and West Florida*. Philadelphia, 1791, and London, 1792.
– Facsimile edited by Robert McCracken Peck. Salt Lake City, 1980.
Berkeley, Edmund and Dorothy Smith. *The Life and Travels of John Bartram*. Florida, 1982.
Birnbaum, Charles; and Karson, Robin. *Pioneers of American Landscape Design*. McGraw-Hill, 2000.
Botting, Douglas. *Humboldt and the Cosmos*. London, 1973.
Catesby, Mark. *The Natural History of Carolina, Florida, and the Bahama Islands*. London, 1729–47.
Downing, Andrew Jackson. *A Treatise on the Theory and Practice of Landscape Gardening*. Sakonnet, 1977 (first published 1841).
Griswold, Mac. *Washington's Gardens at Mount Vernon: Landscape of the Inner Man*. Houghton Miflin, 1999.
– With Eleanor Weller. *The Golden Age of American Gardens*. Harry N. Abrahams, 1992.
Harriot, Thomas. *A Briefe and True Report of the New Found Land of Virginia*. London 1588 (reprinted by Dover, 1972).
Hedrick, U.P.. *A History of Horticulture in America to 1860*. New York, 1950 (reprinted Portland, 1988).
Jefferson, Thomas. *Garden Book 1766–1824*, edited by Edwin Morris Betts. Philadelphia, 1944.
Josselyn, John. *New-England's Rarities Discovered*. London, 1672.
Leighton, Anne. *American Gardens in the Eighteenth Century*. Massachusetts, 1976.
– *American Gardens of the Nineteenth Century*. Massachusetts, 1987.
– *Early American Gardens*. Massachusetts, 1986.
Lockwood, Alice. *Gardens of Colony and State*. Scribners, 1931 (reprinted by the Garden Club of America, 2000).
Maccubin, Robert; and Martin, Peter, editors. *Eighteenth Century Life: British and American Gardens*. Williamsburg, 1983.
– *British and American Gardens of the Eighteenth Century*. Virginia, 1988.
MacDougall, E.B., editor. *Prophet with Honor: The career of Andrew Jackson Downing 1815–52*. Dumbarton Oaks, Washington DC, 1989.
Martin, Peter. *The Pleasure Gardens of Virginia*. Princeton, 1991.
Mitchell, Ann Lindsay; and House, Syd. *David Douglas: Explorer and Botanist*. Aurum, 1999.
Newton, Norman. *Design on the Land*. Harvard, 1971.

Nichols, Frederick Doveton; and Griswold, Ralph. *Thomas Jefferson Landscape Architect*. Virginia, 1978.
Prentice, Helaine Kaplan. *Gardens of Southern California*. San Francisco, 1990.
Prescott, W.H. *The Conquest of Mexico*. Gibbings and Company, 1896.
– *History of the Conquest of Peru*. Gibbings and Company, 1896.
Punch, Walter, editor. *Keeping Eden*. Massachusetts Horticultural Society. Bullfinch, 1992.
Reveal, James. *Gentle Conquest*. Starwood, 1992.
Rybczynski, Witold. *A Clearing in the Distance: Frederick Law Olmsted and America in the Nineteenth Century*. Scribner, 1999.
Sanger, Marjory Bartlett. *Billy Bartram and His Green World*. Farrar, Straus and Giroux, 1972.
Scott, Frank Jesup. *The Art of Beautifying Suburban Home Grounds*. New York, 1870 (reprinted New York, 1982).
Streatfield, David. *California Gardens*. Abbeville Press, 1994.
Swem, E.B., editor. *Brothers of the Spade: Correspondence of Peter Collinson of London and of John Custis of Williamsburg, Virginia 1734–1746*. Worcester, Massachusetts, 1949.
Wilkinson, Norman. *E.I. du Pont, Botaniste*. Charlottesville, Virginia, 1972.

Periodicals
Evans, Susan Toby. "Aztec Royal Pleasure Parks". *Studies in the History of Gardens and Designed Landscapes*, Vol. 20, No. 3, July–September 2000.
Journal of the New England Garden History Society.
Magnolia (the journal of the Southern History Society).

CHAPTER TEN
Attiret. *A Particular Account of the Emperor of China's Gardens near Peking*, translated by Sir Henry Beaumont. 1749.
Birch, Cyril, editor. *The Songs of Ch'u: an Anthology of Chinese Literature*. 1975.
Cheng, Ji. *The Craft of Gardens*. Yale, 1988.
Confucius. *The Analects*.
Fu, Shen. *Chapters from a Floating Life*, translated by S. Black. 1960.
Keswick, Maggie. *The Chinese Garden*. Academy Editions Architecture Series, 1986.
L. Tjion Sie Fat & E. de Jon, editors. *The Authentic Garden*: "Insight into Chinese traditional botanical knowledge" by Georges Metailie. Clusius Foundation, 1991.
Needham, Joseph. *Science and Civilisation in China*, Vol. 1 & Vol. 6. Cambridge, 2000.
Siren, Osvald. *China and the Gardens of Europe in the 18th Century*. Dumbarton Oaks, Washington DC, 1990 (reprinted edition).
Valder, Peter. *The Garden Plants of China*. Timber Press, 1999, Weidenfeld Illustrated, 1999.

Periodicals
Hammond, Kenneth. "Wang Shizen's Garden Essays". *Studies in the History of Gardens and Designed Landscapes*. Vol. 19 July–December 1999.

CHAPTER ELEVEN
Itoh, Teiji. *The Gardens of Japan*. Kodansha International. 1998.
Kaempfer, Engelbert. *Kaempfer's Japan*, edited by Beatrice Bodart-Bailey. Hawaii, 1999.
Keane, Marc Peter. *Japanese Garden Design*. Tuttle Publishing, 1997.
Kuck, Lorraine. *The World of the Japanese Garden*. Weatherhill Publishers, 1980.
Shikibu, Murasaki. *The Tale of Genji*, translated by Arthur Waley. London, 1935.
Treib, Marc; and Herman, Ron. *A Guide to the Gardens of Kyoto*. Shufunotomo, Japan, 1980.

CHAPTER TWELVE
Allan, Mea. *William Robinson*. Faber & Faber, 1982.
Balmori, Diana; McGuire, Diane; and McPeck, Eleanor. *Beatrix Farrand's American Landscapes*. New York, 1985.
Bisgrove, Richard. *The Gardens of Gertrude Jekyll*. Frances Lincoln, 1992.
Blomfield, Reginald; and Thomas, Inigo. *The Formal Garden in England*. Macmillan, 1892.
Brown, Jane. *Gardens of a Golden Afternoon*. Allen Lane 1982.
– *The Art and Architecture of English Gardens*. Weidenfeld and Nicolson, 1989.
– *The English Garden in Our Time*. Antique Collectors' Club, 1986.
Darke, Rick. *In Harmony with Nature*. Friedman/Fairfax. 2000.
Dunster, David, editor. *Edwin Lutyens* Architectural Monograph 6. Academy Editions 1979
Farrand, Beatrix. *Beatrix Farrand's Plant Book for Dumbarton Oaks*, edited by Diane McGuire. Washington DC, 1980.
Hitchmough, Wendy. *Arts and Crafts Gardens*. Pavilion, 1997.
Hood Museum of Art. *Shaping an American Landscape: the Art and Architecture of Charles A. Platt*. New England, 1995.
Karson, Robin. *The Muses of Gwinn*. Harry N. Abrahams, 1996.
Lutyens. (Catalogue of the exhibition at the Haywood Gallery, Arts Council of Great Britain, London, 1981.) London, 1981.
Morgan, Keith. *Charles A. Platt: the Artist as Architect*. New York, 1985.
O'Neill, Daniel. *Lutyens' Country Houses*. Lund Humphries, 1980.
Platt, Charles A.. *Italian Gardens*. Saga/Timber Press, 1993.
Robinson, William. *The Wild Garden*. John Murray, 1870.
– *The English Flower Garden*. John Murray, 1883.
Ruskin, John. "The Poetry of Architecture". *The Architectural Magazine* (1837–38).
Sitwell, Sir George. *On the Making of Gardens*. London, 1909.
Shelton, Louise. *Beautiful Gardens in America*. Scribner, 1915.
Tankard, Judith. *The Gardens of Ellen Biddle Shipman*. Harry N. Abrahams, 1996.

Wharton, Edith. *Italian Villas and their Gardens.* The Bodley Head, 1904.

CHAPTER THIRTEEN

Adams, William Howard. *Grounds for Change.* Bullfinch, 1993.

Boyden, Martha; Vinciguerra, Alessandra, editors. *Russell Page: Ritratti di Giardini Italiani.* American Academy in Rome, Electra, 1998.

Bradley-Hole, Christopher. *The Minimalist Garden.* Mitchell Beazley, 1999.

Brown, Jane. *The Modern Garden.* London, 2000.

Church, Thomas. *Gardens are for people.* New York, 1955.

Clément, Gilles. *Les Libres Jardins de Gilles Clément.* Editions du Chêne, 1997.

Cooper, Guy; and Taylor, Gordon. *Gardens for the Future.* Conran Octopus, 2000.
– *Paradise Transformed: the Private Garden for the Twenty-first Century.* Monacelli Press, 1996.
– *Mirrors of Paradise: the Gardens of Fernando Caruncho.* Monacelli Press, 2000.

Crowe, Sylvia. *Garden Design.* Country Life, 1958.

Eckbo, Garrett. *Landscape for Living.* F.W. Dodge

Corporation, 1950.

Eliovson, Sima. *The Gardens of Roberto Burle Marx.* London, 1991.

Spens, Michael. *Jellicoe at Shute.* Academy, 1993.
– *The Complete Landscape Designs and Gardens of Geoffrey Jellicoe.* London, 1994.

Streatfield, David. *California Gardens.* Abbeville Press, 1994.

Sutherland, Lyall; and Jellicoe, Geoffrey. *Designing the New Landscape.* London, 1991.

Walker, Peter; and Simo, Melanie. *Invisible Gardens.* MIT Press, 1994.

PICTURE ACKNOWLEDGEMENTS

Abbreviations:
l=left, r=right, t=top, b=bottom, c=centre, bkgd=background, i=inset

KEY TO SOURCES:

AAA	The Ancient Art and Architecture Collection
AL	Andrew Lawson
BAL	The Bridgeman Art Library
BAL/STC	The Bridgeman Art Library/The Stapleton Collection
BL	The British Library
BM	The British Museum
EH	English Heritage Photographic Library
GPL	Garden Picture Library
IA	The Interior Archive
ILN	Illustrated London News
IP	Impact Photos
JH	Jerry Harpur
LF	Life File
MH	Marcus Harpur
MK	Mehdi Khansari
MM	Marianne Majerus
NT	The National Trust
RHS	Royal Horticultural Society, Lindley Library
V&A	V&A Picture Library
WF	Werner Forman Archive

Dorling Kindersley would like to thank the following sources for their kind permission to reproduce their photographs and illustrations:

Page 1 Paul Rocheleau; **2** GPL/John Ferro Sims; **3** JH/Topher Delaney; **4/5** JH/Bob Dash, Long Island, USA; **6** V&A; **7** Peter Anderson; **8** BL (Ms. Or. 338. F.110a); **10** © Photo RMN/Arnaudet; **11** MM/des: Piet Oudolf

CHAPTER ONE 16/17 Egyptian Expedition of The Metropolitan Museum of Art, Rogers Fund, 1930. (30.4.56) Photograph © 1978 The Metropolitan Museum of Art; **18** AAA; **20** BM (WAA 124939); **21** RHS; **22** BAL/STC/Private Collection; **23** BM (WAA 124920); **24** BAL/STC/Private Collection; **25** BAL/Deir el-Medina, Thebes, Egypt; **26** RHS; **27** The Metropolitan Museum of Art, Rogers Fund and Edward S. Harkness Gift, 1920 (20.3.13) Photograph © 1992 The Metropolitan Museum of Art; **28** BAL/British Museum, London, UK

CHAPTER TWO 30/31 Corbis/Roger Wood; **32** V&A; **33t** Patrick Taylor; **33br** BAL/Archaeological Museum of Heraklion, Crete, Greece; **34** AAA/Ronald Sheridan; **35** BAL/Ashmolean Museum, Oxford, UK; **36** RHS; **37bl** Corbis/Roger Wood; **37t** Corbis/Paul Almasy; **37br** RHS; **38b** BAL/Eton College Library, Windsor; **38tl** Corbis/Bettmann; **40** WF/Topaki Palace Library, Istanbul; **41r** RHS; **41 l** RHS;

43 BAL/Biblioteca Marciana, Venice, Italy; **44bl** Corbis/Mimmo Jodice; **44t** WF; **45** WF; **46** BAL/Musée National du Bardo, Le Bardo, Tunisia; **47** BAL/Bibliothèque Nationale, Paris/Giraudon; **50tl** AL/Levens Hall, Cumbria; **50b** BAL/STC/Private Collection; **50/51t** Corbis/Elio Ciol: **50/51c** BAL/STC/Private Collection; **51br** MH; **51tr** © Photo RMN/Gerard Blot; **51bc** ILN; **52** Corbis/Archivo Iconografico S.A. **54t** IA/Eduardo Munoz; **54/55c** Corbis/Archivo Iconografico S.A.

CHAPTER THREE 56/57 WFA; **58** MK; **59t** Corbis/Roger Wood; **59cr** Musée des Arts Decoratifs, Paris/Laurent-Sully Jaulmes; **60** V&A; **61l and r** V&A; **63** WF; **64** Aerofilms; **66/67** Corbis/Sheldan Collins; **66l** Corbis/Macduff Everton; **68** RHS; **70tr** WF; **70cl** BAL/STC/Private Collection; **70bl** BAL/STC/Private Collection; **71** Corbis/Angelo Hornak; **72** V&A; **73** BL (27257 f44b); **75** BAL/STC/Private Collection; **76/77** MK, **77r** MK; **78** RHS; **79b** MK; **79i** MK; **80** V&A; **81** V&A; **82** BAL/British Library, London, UK; **83l** V&A; **83r** V&A, **84/85** BAL; **86tl** GPL/John Ferro Sims; **86bl** JH/William Pye, Antony House, Cornwall; **86/87t** BAL/STC/Private Collection, **86/87b** Corbis/Dave G. Houser; **87tr** BAL/STC/Private Collection; **87br** NT/John Hammond; **88** RHS; **89cr** BAL/Ashmolean Museum, Oxford, UK; **89br** BAL/Victoria & Albert Museum, London, UK; **90** WF; **91** Christie's Images; **92** BM (1983.66); **93** BL (Or. 7094 f.7a); **94** JH/Penelope Hobhouse, Walmer Castle; **95** JH/Les Quatre Vents, Canada

CHAPTER FOUR 96/97 BAL/Musée National du Moyen Age et des Thermes de Cluny, Paris, France/Lauros/Giraudon; **98** BAL/Städelsches Kunstinstitut, Frankfurt-am-Main, Germany; **100** AKG London, **101** BAL/British Library, London, UK; **102bl** BL (Royal MS. 6E.ix f.15v); **102r** BAL/Musée Condé, Chantilly, France/Lauros/Giraudon; **104t** Corbis/Archivo Iconografico S.A.; **104b** Foto Toso/Biblioteca Nazionale, Venice; **105** The Bodleian Library, University of Oxford (MS Canon Misc.482 f.62v); **106** BL (Add. MS 19720 f.117); **107** BAL/Château de Versailles, France; **108** BAL/Victoria & Albert Museum, London, UK, **109** RHS; **110/111** Trinity College Library, Cambridge; **111tr** Corbis/Archivo Iconografico S.A.; **112** BAL/British Library, London, UK; **113** BAL/British Library, London, UK; **114** BAL/British Library, London, UK; **115** BAL/British Library, London, UK; **116** BL (MS Add 38126 f.110); **117** BAL/Musée Condé, Chantilly, France/Lauros/Giraudon

CHAPTER FIVE 118/119 AL/Villa d'Este, Italy; **120** Scala/Gabinetto dei Disegni e delle Stampe, Firenze; **121** Alex Ramsay; **122t** BAL/Palazzo Vecchio, Florence, Italy; **122b** RHS; **123** BAL/Villa Lante della Rovere, Bagnaia, Italy; **124cl** Corbis/Archivo Iconografico S.A.; **124br** Corbis/Archivo Iconografico S.A.; **125** BAL/STC/Private Collection; **126** BAL/Museo de Firenze Com'era, Florence, Italy; **127** Corbis/Massimo Listri; **128cl** BAL/STC/Private Collection, **128br** Villa d'Este, Italy; **129** BAL; **130tl** Graphische Sammlung Albertina, Wien; **130br** BAL/STC/Private Collection; **131** BAL/Villa Lante della Rovere, Bagnaia,

Wooster; **385** MH/Gravetye Manor; **386l** Gravetye Manor; **386r** RHS; **387** AL/Winterthur Gardens, USA, **388** British Architectural Library, Drawings Collection; **389t** RHS; **389br** Anita Fischer; **390tl** RHS; **390/391b** Steven Wooster; **391** Steven Wooster; **392** Smithsonian Institution, Archives of American Gardens, The Garden Club of America Collection; **393** Jensen Papers, Library, The Moreton Arboretum, Lisle, Illinois.; **395** JH/Stan Hywett Hall; **396** V&A; **397** V&A; **398** JH/Rodmarton Manor; **400tl** EH; **400/401t** RHS; **400bl** The Advertising Archives; **400/401b** AL/des: Kathy Swift; **401tr** JH/Great Dixter; **401br** The Advertising Archives; **402** The Gamble House, Greene and Greene Archives; **403** BAL/David Findlay Jr. Fine Art, NYC, USA/Private Collection; **404/405** JH/Hidcote; **406** JH/Filoli, CA; **407tr** Corbis/Bettmann; **407bl** BAL/Mallett & Son Antiques Ltd., London, UK; **407br** Country Life Picture Library; **408** AL/Hestercombe, Somerset; **409** AL/Hestercombe, Somerset; **410** JH/Dumbarton Oaks; **411** JH/Dumbarton Oaks; **412tr** Penelope Hobhouse; **412bl** JH/Iford Manor; **413** BAL/STC/Private Collection; **414** AL/Buscot Park; **415** RHS;

416 MH/Frederick Gibberd, Essex; **417** MH/Frederick Gibberd, Essex; **418/419** Marijke Heuff; **419r** Marijke Heuff

CHAPTER THIRTEEN 420/421 Charles Jencks; **422** RHS; **423** RHS/The Landscape Institute; **424** AL/Barnsley House, Gloucestershire; **425** JH/Christopher Lloyd; **426/427** NT/Andrew Lawson; **428** JH/Denmans, Sussex; **429t** JH/La Mortella; **429b** MM/Jacques Wirtz; **430** AL/Shute House; **433** Garden Matters; **434** Tim Street-Porter; **435tl and b** Michael Moran; **436** Tim Street-Porter; **437** Tim Street-Porter; **438** RHS; **439** JH/Dan Hinkley, 'Heronswood', Seattle; **440t** JH/Ton ter Linden; **440b** JH/Weihenstephan, Munich, Germany; **442t** James van Sweden; **442b** AL/Dan Pearson; **443t** MH/Beth Chatto Gardens, Essex; **443b** AL/Piet Oudolf, Hummelo; **444/445** Garden Matters; **445 r** AL/Ian Hamilton Finlay, Little Sparta; **446/447** JH/Topher Delaney; **448** Fernando Caruncho/Laurence Toussant; **449** Jonathan Myles-Lea; **450** JH/Christopher Bradley-Hole; **451t** JH/Martha Schwartz; **451b** Martha Schwartz; **452** Terragram Pty./Vladimir Sitta; **453t** AL/des: Arabella Lennox-Boyd; **453b** AL/des: Helen Dillon.

INDEX

Page numbers in *italic* refer to illustrations

A

'Abbas I, Shah 61, 74–75, 78, 79
'Abbas II, Shah 75
'Abd al-Rahman I 65, 68
'Abd al-Rahman III 65, 66
Abies procera (noble fir) 272
Abu Bakr 62
Abu Hanifah al-Dinawari 63
acanthus/*Acanthus* 37, 47, 55; *A. mollis* 34, 36, *36*; *A. spinosus* 36
Acer japonicum 372, *372*; *A. palmatum* 351; *A. rubrum* 290
Achaemenians 22–23, 58
Acorus calamus (sweet flag) 39
Acts of Enclosure 46, 218
Addison, Joseph 206, 207, 212
agora 35
Agra 83, 84, 88
agronomes 49, 110
Ahmed III 91, 92
Ailanthus altissima (tree of heaven) 200
Aislabie, John 295
Aiton, William 201
Akbar 84, 415
Akiko, Empress 356
Alberti, Leon Battista 46, 47, 112, 116, 120, 131, 132, 143, 158; *De re aedificatoria* 46, 122, 125; *Della pittura* 120
Albertus Magnus 49, 99, 103–105, 117; *De vegetabilibus et plantis* 103
al-Biruni 63
al-Buhturi 64
Albury 166, 188
Aldrovandi, Ulisse 186
Alexander the Great 23, 36, 38–39

Alexandria 39, 48, 64, 119, 130; *see also* Hero
Alfonso X 69, 72
Alhambra *56*, 57, 69, 70–71, *70*, 72, *247*, 434, 435, 437, 448, 452
Allen, John 300
Allingham, Helen 403, 407
al-Ma'mun 68
aloe (*Aloe sine floribus*) 174, *174*
Alnwick Castle 428
Alphand, J.C.A. 273
Alphonso II 140
al Sabi 64
Alton Towers 249, 260
al-Ya'qubi 64
Amaryllis josephinae 202, *202*
Amboise 141, 143
Ameratsu 352
American Gardens 194, 200, *200*, 227, 276
American Indians 287ff
Ammannati, Bartolomeo 128
Amstelveen 441
anemone/*Anemone* 41, 74, 90, 134, 178, 181, *181*, 186, 256, 263; *A. coronaria* 33; *A.* 'Sermoneta' 186
Anet 142, *142*, 147, 158
angelica/*Angelica sylvestris* 34, 37, *37*
Anhalt-Dessau, Prince Franz von 232, 240, 299
Anne, Queen 206
Anne of Brittany 141
Anne of Denmark 160, *160*
Anne's Grove 384, *384*
Antony House 86, 226
Apennines 47, 126, 128
Apennino 126, *127*
Apollo 33, 53, 126, 146, 153, 219, 221, 240
Apuleius Platonicus Herbarium 38, 38
aqueducts 45, 48, 58, 66, 128, 156, 283, 284, 286
aquilegia/*Aquilegia* 181; *A. canadensis*

300, *300*
Aranjuez 448
Araucaria araucana (monkey puzzle, Chile pine) 255, *255*, 274
Arbutus (strawberry tree) 35, 44, *44*, 55; *A. unedo* 173; trailing arbutus (*Epigaea repens*) 200
archaeology 33, 34–35, 42, 44, 54, 109, 301
Archimedes 130
Argyll, Duke of 197
Aristophanes 34
Aristotle 33, 35, 36, 38, 124, 130; Lyceum 35, 36
Arnold Arboretum 312, *312*, 408
Arruzafa 68
Arts and Crafts Movement 382, 388, 396–99; in America 399–402
Arundel House 160
Ashe, Thomas 294
Ashmolean Museum 185
Ashridge Park 228, 255
Ashurbanipal II 18, *18*, 23, *23*
Assyrians 19, 21–22, *22*, 62, 63, 321
Astor Chinese Garden (NYC) 339
Athelhampton 389, *389*
Athens 33, 34, 35, 38, 48
Attiret, Fr. 241, 242, 340, 341, 342
Aubrey, John 162, 166
Aubriet, Claude 169, 173
aubrieta 169
Audley End 233, 237, 238, 276
Audubon, J.J. 304
Audubon Swamp Garden, Magnolia Plantation *280*, 281, 304
Augusta, Princess 201
Augustus, Emperor 45
Aurangzeb 84
auriculas 186, 187, *187*
Austen, Jane 226
Austen, Ralph 300
Axayacatl 284
Aztecs 174, 281, 282–85, 287

B

Babur, Emperor 72, *72*, 73, 74, 81, 82–83, *82–83*, 84, *87*, 399
Babylon 21, 39, 62, 63; Hanging Gardens 21, *21*
Bac, Ferdinand 437
Bachmann, John 310
Bacon, Sir Francis 162, 206, 388, 401
Bagatelle 202, 241
Baghdad 59, 63, 64, 71, 73 *see also* Ctesiphon
Bagh-e 'Adalat 71
Bagh-e Fin 78, 79, *79*
Bagh-e Vafa (Garden of Fidelity) 82, 83, *83*
Bagh-i-Babur Shah 87, *87*
Bailey, Col. Frederick 383
Bailey, Liberty Hyde 410
Balkuwara Palace 64, *64*, 65
Ballymaloe *133*
Bampfylde, Copleston Warre 219
Banister, John 189, 297, 301
Banks, Sir Joseph 195, 197, 201, *201*, 246, 255, 277; Lady 344
Banque de Luxembourg 429, *429*
Barbarigo, Zuane Francesco 121
Barillet-Deschamps, J.P. 273
Barnsley, Ernest 399
Barnsley House 139, *139*, 424, *424*, 428, 449
Barragán, Luis 434, 437, 445, 448, 451
Barry, Sir Charles 245, 246, 256–59, 279
Bartholomew the Englishman (de Glanville) 103, 117
Barton, Dr Benjamin Smith 306
Bartram, John 193, 194, 197, 231, 236, 292, 294, 296, 297, 300, 304, 306
Bateman, James 248, 249, 255, 274

Battersea Park 273, *273*
Bauer, Ferdinand 41, 174
Bauhin, Caspar, *Pinax* 184
bay laurel (*Laurus nobilis*) 35, 55, 66, 69, 126; sweet bay 110
Bayreuth 220
Beaton, Donald 259, 261, 264, 266, 269, 273
Beaux Arts style 431, 432
Beckford, William 200
bedding schemes 246, 251, 256, 262-66, *264*, 276, 388, 389, 396
Bede, the Venerable, St 52, 104, 114
Bedford, sixth Duke of 222, 227, 229
Beihai Park 336, 341, *341*
Bélanger, Francois-Joseph 132
Bellevue Hill 452, *452*
Belon, Pierre 41, 88, 89, 173
Berrington Hall 223
Berthault, Louis 202
Besler, Basilius 170, 173, 181ff, 184, 285
Bible: Genesis 20, 184; New Testament 20, 104, 116; Old Testament 20, 104; Song of Solomon 104
Bicton 255
Biddulph Grange 247, 248, *248*, 249, 255, 274, 277
Biltmore House 308, 309, *309*
birch alley 394, *395*
Birkenhead Park 242, 267, 383
Birmingham Botanic Garden 253, 279
Blaikie, Thomas 241, 277
Blake, Stephen 300; *The Compleat Gardeners' Practice* 139
Blenheim Palace 43, 222, 223, *224-25*, 292
Bliss, Mildred Barnes 411
Bloedel Reserve 377, *377*
Blois 141, 143
Blomfield, Sir Reginald 388-89, 393
Bobart, Jacob 180
Boboli (Medici/gardens) 122, 128, 129, 134, 148
Boccaccio 174; *Decameron* 101, 116
Bologna 186; botanical garden 176
Bomarzo (now Sacro Bosco) 121, 124, *124*
Bonpland, Aimé 202, 286
bonsai 378, *378*
Book of Mechanical Devices 107
Borel, Antoine 315
Bosschaert, Ambrosius 181
botanic gardens 39, 66, 117, 171, 174, 175-76, 180, *180*, 203, 283, 304-306; *see also under* Bologna; Birmingham; Edinburgh; Elgin; Florence; Heidelberg; Kew; Leiden; Montpellier; Oxford; Padua; Paris; Pisa
botany 31, 33, 38, 39, 60, 63, 324
Botany Bay 201
Bourdichon, Jean 141
Bowood 223, 251, 258, *258*

box, boxwood *see Buxus*
Bradley-Hole, Christopher 445, 450
Bramante, Donato 120, 121
Breck, Joseph 313
Brenna, Vincenzo 240
Bridgeman, Charles 208, 210, 211, 212, 223
Bridgewater, Earl of 228
Brighton Pavilion 239, *239*, 263
Brompton Park Nursery 206
Brooke, H. Adveno 245, 247, 258
Brookes, John 428
Broughton, Lady 277
Broughton Hall 261
Brown, Jane 416, 428
Brown, Lancelot 'Capability' 163, 167, 205, 210 211, 212, 215-22, 223, *223*, 238, 241, 243, 261, 276, 302, 306, 344, 450
Brueghel, Jan the Elder 181
Brunfels, Otto 176
Bryant, Edwin 314
Bryant, William Cullen 307
Buddhism 323, 330-31, 332, 347, 348, 353, 354, 365
Budding, Edwin 401
Buist, Robert 313
Bulstrode Park 132, 222
Bunyan, John 430
Buontalenti, Bernardo 126, 129, 133
Burghley 223
Burke, Edmund 222, 229
Burlington, Lord 206, 208, 209
Burnaby, Andrew 293
Burton, Decimus 261, 268
Busbecq, Ogier Ghiselin de 40-41, 89, 90, 90, 178
Buscot Park 412, *414*, 415
Bussey, Benjamin 311
Bute, Lord 197
Buxus sempervirens (box, boxwood, American box) 47, 50, *50*, 55, 69, 134, 136, 148, 166, 190, 206, 251, 290, 295, *295*, 301, 393, 399, 404, 411; *B.s.* 'Suffruticosa' (dwarf box) 139, 149, 164, 248, 292
Byrd, William I & II 292, *292*, 297
Byron, Robert 74

C

Cabot, Francis (Frank) 71, 95, 449
Caccini, Matteo 178, 184-86
Caetani, Francesco, Duke of Sermoneta 186, 263
Caie, John 265
calceolarias 261, 263, 265, 267, 269
Calypso 33, 206
Calystegia sepium (bell-ivy/morning glory) 45, 69
camellia/Camellia 199, 253, 274, 304, 313, 350, 351, 372; *C. japonica* 194
Camerarius, Joachim 170, 178, 184

Cameron, Charles 240
canals 24, 43, 74, 143, 151, 152, 161, 163, 165, 267, 279, 293, 296, 325, 429
Candolle, A.P. de 195
canna 181, 273
Canons Ashby 166
canopus 31, 48
Caprarola 130
carnation 36, 92, 112, 116, *116*, 185
Caroline, Queen 212
carpet bedding 264, *264*, 315, 396
Carpinus caroliniana (American hornbeam) 411, *411*
Caruncho, Fernando 54, 120, 445, 448
cascades and chutes 75, 84, 86, 87, 121, *121*, 130, 157, 161, 214, 267; dry cascade 363; *catena d'acqua* 130, 131, *131*; *see also chadars*
Caserta: English Garden 240
Cassiano dal Pozzo 135
Cassiodorus, *Institutions* 110
Castanea dentata (American chestnut) 297
Castell, Robert, *The Villas of the Ancients Illustrated* 47
Castiglione, Fr. Giuseppe 299, 340
Castillo, Diaz del 284, 285
Castle Ashby 262
Castle Howard 221
Castle Kennedy 255
Catesbieae spinosa 203, *203*
Catesby, Mark 191, 193, 194, 197, 203, 292, 296, 297
Catherine of Braganza 163
Catherine the Great 240
Cato the Elder, 35, 44, 52, 55, 110; *De re agricultura* 46; *De re rustica* 35, 49
Catullus 46
Cecil, Robert (first Earl of Salisbury) 162, 185
Cecil, William (Lord Burghley) 160, 179
cedars 21, 69, 81, 131; *Cedrus libani* (cedar of Lebanon) 192, 193; Japanese cedar (*Cryptomeria japonica*) 351
Celebi, Evliya 92
cemeteries 39, 68, 241, 311, 315, 383
Central Park 242, 253, 307, 308, 310, *310*, 311, 383, 422
Cercidiphyllum japonicum (katsura) 350, 351
Certosa di Pavia 111, *111*, 114
Cesalpina, Andrea 195
chadar (cascade) 62, 86, 87
chahar bagh (fourfold garden) 20, 58, 60, *60*, 62, 77, 83, *83*, 85
Chamaecyparis 276; *C. lawsoniana* (Lawson's cypress) 274; *C. obtusa* 374
Chamaerops humilis (palmetto, fan palm) 26, 242
Chambers, Sir William 201, 222, *222*, 233, 241, 342, 343

Champlain, Samuel de 288
Chang Ch'ien 323
Chantilly 151, *151*
Chapultepec 283, 284
Chardin, Sir John 75, 78-79
Charlemagne, Emperor 99, 100; *Capitulare de villis* 100, 117
Charles II 149, 162-63, 164
Charles V of France 117
Charles V, Holy Roman Emperor 71, 107, 143
Charles VIII 140-41
Charles IX 142
Charles X 241
Charleston 197, 294, 296, 304
Charleval 142
Chartres Cathedral 109
Chatsworth 43, 163, *163*, 223, 267, 264, 266, 267, 268, *268*, 270, 277
Chatto, Beth 441, 443
Chaucer, Geoffrey 109, 116
Chehel Sutun 75, 77, *78*
Chelsea Flower Show 221, 450
Chelsea Physic Garden 191, 192, *192*, 277, 297
chenar 35, 62, 74; *see also* Plane tree
Chenonceaux 146, 147
cherry 351, 354, 358, 406; blossom 350, *350*, 355
cherry laurel (*Prunus laurocerasus*) 149, 178, 193, 219
Chevreul, M.E. 266; colour wheel 266, *266*
chi 328, 333, *335*
chiampas 282, *282*
Chicago Botanic Garden 428
Chicago World's Fair 308
Chile 255
Chile pine *see Araucaria*
China 22, 51, 63, 65, 200, 209, 241 243, 277, 296, 319-45, 438; Immortals (*Hsien*) 20, 320, 321, *321*, 322, 323, 330, 332, 350, 366; landscape (*shanshui*) 319, 325
chinoiserie 221, 342-43, *342-43*
Chionanthus virginicus (Virginian fringe tree) 231
Chion-in 372
Chiswick House 208, *208*, 210, 214, 241, 267, 400, *400*
Chotek, Count 232
Christ Church, Canterbury 110, *110*
Christianity/Christendom 97-117, 341, 370
Christina, Queen 149
Christ's thorn (*Paliurus spina-christi*) 49
chrysanthemum 45, 324, 338, 351, *351*, 353, 359, 367, *367*, 378
Chu Mien 333
Chu Shun-sui 370
Church, Thomas 120, 432
Cibot, Fr. Pierre-Martial 324, 341
Cicero 46
Cimon 34
Cisterna 186
citron *see Citrus*

Citrus aurantium (bitter orange) 68; *C. limon* (lemon) 44, *135*, 135; *C. medica* (citron) 44, 55, 135; *C. x meyeri* 'Meyer' 135

Cixi, Dowager Empress 344, 345, *345*

Claremont 210, *210*, 214, 223

Clarendon 107

Clark, Capt. William 304

clarkia 263

Claude Lorraine 32, 33, 213, 219

Clavijo, Ruy González de 72

Clayton, John 297

Clément, Gilles 444

Clifford, George 195

Cliveden 251, 256, *257*, 264, 266, 268

Clusius, Carolus (Charles de l'Ecluse) 173, 174, 175, 176, 178, *178*, 184, 186, 289

Cobbett, William 233, 236

Cobham, Lord 211, *212*, *223* (Viscount) 221

Codex Neapolitanus 41

Codex Vindobonensis 40

Colchester, Maynard 166

Cole, Thomas 382

Coleridge, Samuel 304

Collinson, Peter 193, 194, 231, 236, 292, 294, 297, 301

Colonna, Francesco, *Hypnerotomachia Poliphili* 125, *125*, 138, 143, 158

Colosseum 48

Columella 49-52, 55, 110, 134, 189; *De re rustica* 112

Colvin, Brenda 418

Compton, Henry, Bishop of London 187-89, 191, 297

Confucius/Confucianism 328, 329, 331, 342, 353, 370

Conimbriga/Coimbra 54, *54*

Constable, John 219

Constantinople 40, 60, 64, 88, 89, 90, 92, 173, 178, 181, 186

Cook, Capt. James 200, 201

Cooke, Edward 248

Cooper, Anthony Ashley (third Earl of Shaftesbury) 209

Cordoba 59, 62, 63, 65, 84

Corinthian order 34, 36, 37, *37*

Cornus florida (dogwood) 296, *296*; *C. kousa* (Japanese dogwood) 374

Corsham Court 226

Cortés, Hernando 282, 283, 284, 285

Cortile del Belvedere 120, *120*, 121, 147

Coryate, Thomas 135, 166

Cos 36, 173

Cotelle, Jean 152

cottage gardens 403, *403*; cottage style 384, 399, 404, 407, 427

cottage orné 227

Cotton, Sir Dodmore 74

Cowell, Fiona 231

Crescenzi, Pietro de' 49, 99, 106, 116; *Liber ruralium commodorum* 103-105, *105*, 112, 117, 125, 131; *Livre des Proffits Ruraux* 112, *112*, 117, *117*

Crete 33, 34, 35

Crisp, Frank 277

crocus/*Crocus* 55, 181; *C. sativus* (saffron crocus) 34

Croome Court 223

Crowe, Sylvia 418, 423, *423*

Crowfield 295

Cryptomeria/Cryptomeria 350; *C. japonica* (Japanese cedar) 276, 351

Crystal Palace 199, 265, 267, 270-71, *270*, 279

Ctesibius 39

Ctesiphon (modern Baghdad) 58, 59

Culpeper, Nicholas, *English Physician* 193; *Herbal* 297

x *Cupressocyparis leylandii* (Leyland's cypress) 274

Curtis, William 200-3, 254

Custis, John 292, *292*, 297

Cyclamen hederifolium 181, *182*

Cyperus papyrus (papyrus) *16*, 17, 26, 28, 33, 34

cypress (Cupressus) 22, 33, 35, 39, 47, 55, 60, 61, *61*, 62, 66, 69, 73, 79, 82, 92, 95, 124, 131, 149, 167, 188, 190, 247, 256, 259, 356, 406, 452; Monterey cypress (*C. macrocarpa*) 274, 276 316; mourning cypress (*C. funebris*) 276; Lawson's cypress *see Chamaecyparis lawsoniana*; Leyland's cypress *see* x *Cupressocyparis leylandii*; swamp/bald cypress *see Taxodium*

Cypripedium acaule 384

Cyrus I 20

Cyrus the Great 22-23, 57, 58, *58*

Cyrus the Younger 20, 38

D

Dahlen Botanic Garden (Berlin) 435

dahlia 202, 282, *282*, 283

Daikaku-ji 355, *355*

Daisen-in 349, 365, *365*

Daitoku-ji temple 349, *349*

Daniel, Henry 117

Daniell, Thomas 239

Dante Alighieri 124

Danvers, Henry 180

Dao Yuanming 329

Darius III 39

Dark Ages 49, 55, 97, 98

Dartington Hall 410

Dashwood, Sir Francis 205

date palm *see Phoenix dactylifera*

Davidia involucrata (dove tree) 312

Davis Garden 451, *451*

de Bry, Theodor 289

de Caus, Isaac 158, 160, 161

de Caus, Salomon 144, 160, 161, 162

de Crevecoeur, St John 300

Deepdene 233

Defoe, Daniel 164

Delaney, Topher 447

Delavay, Abbé 383

de l'Orme, Philibert 142, 157; *Le premier tome de l'architecture* 147

Delos 39

Demosthenes 35

Dendariarena, Francisco 255

Denmans 428, *428*

d'Entrecolles, Père 200

Descartes, René 150, 152

Devonshire, sixth Duke of 251, 267, 268

Dezallier d'Argenville, Antoine Joseph, *La Théorie et la Pratique du Jardinage* 150

Diana 53, 129

Dillenius, J.J. 180, 193

Dillon, Helen 452

d'Incarville, Pierre 200

Diodorus 21

Dionysius of Syracuse 39

Dioscorides 38, 40-41, *40*, 43, 54, 63, 88, 173, 174, 177, 178; *De Materia Medica* 32, 33, 40-41, 52, *63*, 88, 173

Ditchley Hall 223

Ditchley House 430

Dixon Hunt, John 167

Dodoens, Rembert (Dodonaeus) 176, 184, 297; *Crüÿdeboeck* 176, 179

dogwood (*Cornus*) 200, 231, 296, *296*, 374, 394

Douglas, David 263, 272

doum palm *see Hyphaene thebaica*

Downing, Andrew Jackson 306-307, 312, 314, 316, 383, 390

Downton 229

Drake, Sir Francis 287

Drottningholm 219, 220, 221

Drummond Castle 251, *251*, 252

du Cerceau, Jacques Androuet 140, 141, 142, 144, 151, 157, 411

Du Le Yuan 329

Du Pérac, Etienne 147, 149

du Pont, Henry 387

Duchêne, Achille 152

Dumbarton Oaks 410-11, *410-11*

Dürer, Albrecht 174-75; *The Large Piece of Turf* 175, *175*

Dutch East India Company 195, 197

E

East Lambrook 422, 438, *438*

Easton Lodge 412

Easton Piercy 166

Eaton Hall 261

Eckbo, Garrett 432, 434

Eden Project 271, *271*

Edinburgh, Royal Botanic Garden 313

Edward VII 403

Edwardian styles 396, 402-403, 416, 422

Edwards, Sydenham 203

Egypt 17, 18, 19, 23-29, 34, 38, 48, 62, 63, 68, 173

Ehret, Georg Dionysius 194, 195, 296

Eichstätt 184

Eifuku-ji 360

El Novillero 432, *433*

Eleanor of Castile 117

Elgin Botanic Garden 304, 306

Elizabeth I 158, 159, 160

Elizabeth, HRH the Queen Mother 95

Elizabeth Stuart 144, 161

Ellacombe, Canon Henry Nicholson 246, 269, *269*

Elvaston Castle 246, 247, *247*

Elysium/Elysian gardens 20, 211, 218, 234, 237, 303, 383

Emerson 390

Endsleigh 222, 227-28, 229, *229*

Englischer Garten 393

English Garden 239-42; at Caserta 240

English Landscape Movement *see* Landscape Movement

Enville Hall 265

Epic of Gilgamesh 20-21

Epicurus 36; Epicurean creed 46

Epigaea repens (trailing arbutus) 200

Erddig 251, *251*

Erechtheum 48

Esarhaddon 22

Estienne, Charles and Liébault, Jean 300

estrade 102, 112, 116

Eucalyptus globulus (blue gum) 316

Euclid, *Optics* 152

Euphorbia characias 422, *422*

euripes 43

Evans, Sir Arthur 33

Evelyn, John 39, 79, 129, 130, 135, 141, 148, 166, 167, 177, 186, 188, *188*, 190, 293, 301

F

Fairchild, Thomas 191

Fairchild's mule 191, *191*

Fairmount Park 313

Falda, Giovanni Battista 184; *Le Fontane di Roma* 128, 130

Fang Tshao Chuang (Study of plants…) 324

Farrand, Beatrix 403, 407, 410-11, 431

Farrer, Reginald 277

Faulkner Farm 392

feng shui 333, 356, 421

Fenwick, George 290
Ferdinand I 41, 90, 178
ferme ornée 215, 231, 232, 293, 302
Ferrari, Giovanni Battista, *Flora* 190, *190*; *Hesperides* 122, 135
Ferula communis 269, *269*
Fiennes, Celia 165
Filippino Lippi 104
Filoli 399, 406, *406*
Fiorenzuola, Girolamo, *La grande arte della agricultura* 131, 134
Firdausi, *Shah-nameh* (Book of Kings) 73, *73*
Firmiana simplex 329
firs 197, 234; balsam fir 194; Douglas fir (*Pseudotsuga menziesii*) 272, 439; noble fir (*Abies procera*) 272
Fish, Margery 422, 438, *438*
fishponds 27, 28, 111, 112, 134, 293, 295, 329
Fleming, George 256, 265, 273
Fleming, John 256, 259, 264, 266, 268
Flitcroft, Henry 219
Flora 53, 161, 221, 240
Florence 119, 122, 126, 128, 136; botanic garden 176
florilegium or *hortus floridus* 39, 170, 173, 180, 184, 189, 202
florists 313; societies 184, 186
flowerbeds 70, 73, 84, 90, 92, 99, 117, 122, 125, 129, 134-35, 138-39, *138-39*, 140, 149, 152, 157, 161, 188, 190, 206, 218, 233, 234, 237-39, *238*, 245, 246, 251, 284, 311, 388, 397, 409
flower borders 265
flower gardens 68, 149, 166, 210, 231, 294, 450
flowery mead 72, 96, *97*, 98, 102, *102*, 116
Foerster, Karl 384, 389, 390, 419, 441, 443
Fontainebleau 140, *140*, 143, 146, 148, 149, 158, 159, 199
Fonthill Abbey 200, *200*
Ford, Edsel & Eleanor 394
Ford, Henry 394
Forestier, J.C.N. 241
Forrest, George 383
Fortune, Robert 248, 274-76, 324, 344, 375
Fothergill, Dr John 277
fountains 39, 43, 44, 45, 48, 54, *54*, 60, 62, 66, 72, 74, 79, 84, 86-87, 101, *101*, 102, 103, 111, 116, *118*, 119, 122, 123, 124, 126, 128, 129, 130, 136, 149, 151, 152, *152*, 156, 156, 158, *160*, 162, 165, 166, 167, 255, 259, 260, 267, 279, 392
Fouquet, Nicolas 152, 153
fourfold garden *see chahar bagh*
Foxley 229, 231
France 51, 88, 99, 107, 119, 138-39, 140-56, 157, 159, 162-64, 207, 241, 281, 287, 288, 296, 297, 302, 313, 434

Francini family 147, 148
François I 140, 143, 147, 157, 159
François II 146
frankincense (*Boswellia sacra*) 26
Frederick the Great 220
French Revolution 140, 241, 297
frescoes 33, *33*, 34, *34*, 44, *44*, 53, 77, 97
Friar Park 277
Friedrich V (Elector Palatine) 144, 161
Fuchs, Leonhart 169, 176, 177, *177*; *De Historia Stirpium* 176, *176*
fuchsia 169, 177
Fujiwara family 355, 356, 360
Fulham Palace 187
Furber, Robert 191
Furttenbach, Joseph, *Architectura Privata* 171, *171*

G

Gaillon 141, 142, 143, 158
Galen 38, 43
Gambara, Cardinal 131
Gamble House 402, *402*
Garden, Dr Alexander 296
gardenesque style 231, 236, 246, *246*, 249, *249*, 253, 306, 314, 316
Garden of Eden 20, 104, 107, 113, 179, 184, 237, 304
Garinish 412, 415
Gartenreich *see* Wörlitz
Gaukler's Point 394
Gen Yue (Impregnable Mountain) 319, 332, 332, 333
Generalife 69, 70, *70*, 72
Genghis Khan 65, 71-73, 335
Genji Monogatari (Tale of Genji) 351, 356, 358-59, *358-59*, 360
Geoffrey de Montbray, Bishop of Coutances 109
George II 211, 212
George III 201, 220, 342, 343
George, Ernest 412
geranium *see Pelargonium*
Gerard, John 179; *Herball 179*, 179, 290, 297, 300
Germany 49, 99, 150, 171, 286
Gesner, Conrad 177
Getty Museum 50-51, *50-51*
Ghazan Khan 71
Ghini, Luca 177
Giambologna 126, 126, 128
Gibberd, Sir Frederick 416, 417
Gibson, John 173
Gilbert of Hoyland 113
Gilbert, Rev. Samuel 263
Gill, Irving 399
Gillette, Charles 295, 399
Gilpin, Rev. William 229
Ginkaku-ji (Silver Pavilion) 361, *361*, 363, 367
Ginkgo biloba 296 372
giochi d'acqua (water jokes) 86, 161

Girtin, Thomas 223
gloriette 102, 103, 107
Goethe, Johann Wolfgang von 240, 242, 266
Golden Gate Park 271, *271*
Goldsmith, Oliver 218, 237, 342
Gomes, Olivo 435
Goodwood 194, 197
Goose or Barnackle tree 179, *179*
Gorhambury 162
Gozzoli, Benozzo 109
Grand Tour 125, 135, 167, 209, 234
grapevine (*Vitis vinifera*) 23, *23*, 28, 33, 34, 39, 45, 323
Graves, Abbott Fuller 403
Gravetye Manor 384, *385*, 388, 410
Gray, Christopher 191-93
Great Dixter 401, *401*, 425, *425*, 428
Greece 22, 31-42, 43, 48, 53, 55, 133
Green Mount Cemetery 311
Greene, Charles Sumner 399, 402
Greene, Henry Mather 399, 402
Greenwich 161, 163
Greville, Louis 377
Grew, Nehemiah 191
Grimani Breviary 104, *104*
Gronovius, Johann 193
Gropius, Walter 415, 432
grottoes 33, 39, 121, 123, 124, 125, 126, 129, 130, 132-33, *132-33*, 135, 143, 144, 147, 149, 158, 159, 160, 161, 163, 166, 206, 219, 221, 232, 337
guano 286-87
Guerra, Giovanni 130
Guillaume de Lorris 114, 116
Guillaume de Machaut, *Remede de Fortune* 107
Gustafson, Kathryn 445
Gwinn 392, *392*

H

Hadrian 48; Villa *30*, 31, 43, 48, 413
Haga Park 92, 219
ha-ha 212, *212*, 231
Hall, Dr George Rogers 374
Hall, William Hammond 315, 316
Hamilton, Charles 133, 215, 221, 234, 344, 401
Hamilton, William, 304
Hamilton Finlay, Ian 232, 445, 449
Hampton Court 159, 163, 164-65, *164-65*, 223, 293, 299
Han Yanzhi, *Ju Li* 135
hanami (blossom viewing) 350, *350*
Hangzhou 334
Hanmer, Sir Thomas 186-87
Hannan, William 205
Hansen, Prof. Richard 384, 439, 441
Harcourt, Earl 218, 237, 238
Harewood House 223, *223*, 227, 256, 259, 261, 279
Harmonists 298
Harrington, Lucy 161

Harriot, Thomas 289, 297
Hartweg, Theodor 272
Hartwell 233, 237, 238-39, *238*
Harun al-Rashid 62, 63
Hasht Behesht (Eight Paradises) 75, 78
Hatfield House 159, 162, 185, 298, *298*
Hathor (Nut) 27, 29
Hatshepsut 26
Hatton, Sir Christopher 161
Hazar Jarib 74
Heale House 374, *374*, 377, 412
Hearst, William Randolph 422
heem gardens/parks 390, *391*, 422
Heidelberg 144, 161; botanic garden 176
Helianthus annuus (sunflower) 134, 285, *285*, 297
Hellbrunn 124, 126
Henri II 142, 146, 147
Henri III 142, 146, 147
Henri IV 126, 139, 140, 143, 147, 149
Henrietta Maria 149, 160, 162
Henry II 105
Henry III 109
Henry III of Castile and Leon 72
Henry VIII 105, 157, 159, *159*
Henry Prince of Wales 126, 161
Hentzner, Paul 162
herbaceous border 269, 397
herbals 39, 40-41, 173, 175, 189
herbarium (winter garden/*hortus siccus*) 27, 89
herber 102
Herbert, Sir Thomas 74
herbularis (herb garden) 96, 110
Herculaneum 42, 44
Hercules 53, 128, 129, 153, 219
Hernandez, Francisco 174, 282, 283, 285
Hero of Alexandria 39, 160; *Pneumatica* 53, 130
Herodotus 19, 38
Heroin, Thomas 289
Heronswood 439, *439*
Hesdin 107, *107*, 117
Hesiod 38
Hestercombe 87, *87*, 219, 406, *408-409*, 409
Het Loo 139, 156-57, 260
Hever Castle 299, *299*
Hibberd, Shirley 265, 269
Hibiscus rosa-sinensis 190, *190*, 324
Hicks, David 327
Hidcote 399, 403, 404, *405*, 406, 411, 425, 428, 436, 437
Hideyoshi, Toyotomi 367, 368, 369, 371
Hieron 39
Hildegard of Bingen 110
Hill, Thomas 189; *The Gardener's Labyrinth* 49, 139, 189, *189*, 297
Hinckley, Dan 439
Hippocrates 36, 173
Hoare, Henry 132, 213, 215, 219, 220, 232, 234, 274

Hobhouse, Penelope 95
Hoboken 197
Hockney, David 367
Hoefnagel, Joris 173
Hokusai Katsushika 353
Holdenby 161, 162
Holford, Sir Robert 274, 276
Holkham Hall 222
Holland 143, 149, 150, 159, 164, 173, 281, 290, 291; *see also* Netherlands
Homer 32, 33-34, 36, 207, 237; *Iliad* 34; *Odyssey* 33, 34, 206
Honsholredyk 157
Hooker, Sir Joseph 276
Hooker, Sir William 201
Hoole House 277, *277*
hornbeam 143, 149, 156, 157, 190, 206, 247, 404; American hornbeam (*Carpinus caroliniana*) 411, *411*
horse-chestnuts 176, 178, 193, 206
Horti Farnesiani 122, *122*, 184, *184*
Horticultural Society of London 266, 272
Hortus (garden) 43, 55
hortus conclusus 98, *98*, 102-103, 104, *104*, 113, 116
Hortus Eystettensis 170, 173, 181, *182-83*, 285, *285*
Hortus Palatinus 144, *144-45*, 161
hortus sinus 176, 177
Horyuji Temple 354
Hosack, David 306
Host, Nicolaus Thomas 373
Hosta (plantain lily) 373; *H.* 'Frances Williams' 373; *H. sieboldiana* 373, *373*; *H.s.* var. *elegans* 373
Hôtel de Saint Pol 117
Houdon, Jean-Antoine 302
Huang Kung-wang 334
Huaxtepec 283
Hudson River 290, 307, *307*; artists/school 311, 312
Huerta del Rey 68, 69, 117
Hughes, J.A. 249
Huis ten Bosch 138, *138*
Humayun 72, 83, 84
Humboldt, Alexander von 202, 286, *286*, 287, 389
Hunt, Richard Morris 308, 309
hunting parks *see* Parks
Hussein Baikara 74
Hyacinthus orientalis 186
Hydrangea paniculata 372, 373
hydraulic devices 53, 64, 126, 130; *see also* Water
Hyphaene thebaica (doum palm) 26, 28, 29

I J

Iberian peninsula 48, 62, 99
Ibn al-'Awwam 69
Ibn Arabshah 72

Ibn Bassal 72; *Book of Agriculture* 68, 69
Ibn Madrun 68
Ibn Wafid 68, 72
Idstein 173, *173*
Iford Manor 412, *412*
Ilex cassine 287; *I. vomitoria* (yaupon holly) 287, 291
Incas 281, 285-86, 287
India 39, 63, 64, 65, 174, 452; Mughal gardens 57, 81-88, 281, 285
Ira Keller complex (Portland) 62, 87, *87*
Iran/Iranian plateau 24, 58, 65, 73, 74, 421; *see also* Persia
Iraq 21, 421
iris 33, 34, 55, 90, 110, 181; flag iris 98, *98*
irrigation 18, 19-20, 23, 24, 29, 35, 49, 53, 64, 65, 74, 102, 112, 130, 286, 316
Irving, Washington 71
Irwin Miller House 434
Isfahan 24, 61, 62, 74, 75, 77, 78, *78*, 95
Islam 20, 22, 55, 57-95, 97, 98, 103, 104, 197, 151, 315, 399, 406, 415, 421, 423, 429, 436, 444, 445, 452
Isma'il 69
Isolotto gardens, Boboli, 31, 48; Isolotto Basin 128
Italianate styles 251, 254ff, 262, 406, 409-13, 432
Italy 39, 60, 86, 99, 119-140, 399, 402, 421, 434
Jacquemont, Victor 274
Jahan, Shah 66, *80*, 81, 84, 85, 88
Jahangir, 60, 72, *80*, 81, 84, 415
James I of Scotland 106
James I of UK 161, 162
James, Henry 410
Japan 22, 50, 75, 197, 200, 277, 317, 323, 327, 330, 332, 342, 344, 347-79, 434, 436
jardin anglais 202
Jardin des Plantes 274
Jardin du Roi (later Jardin des Plantes) 197, 202, 297
jardins anglo-chinois 241
Jasminum officinale 324; *J. sambac* 324
Jean de Meun 116
Jean Duc de Berry 108
Jefferson, Thomas 240, 289, 293, 300, 301, 302, *302*, 304, 313
Jekyll, Gertude 219, 265, 269, 279, 382, 384, 387, 389, 396, 399, 403, 406-409, *407*, 411, 412, 413, 414, 422, 428
Jellicoe, Sir Geoffrey 120, 136, 424, 428, 430, 445
Jencks, Charles 295, 421, 449
Jensen, Jens 288, 383, 387, 390, 393-94, *393*, 431; Prairie School 393
Jesuit missionaries 200, 248, 340, 341, 370
Ji Cheng, *Yuan Ye* (Craft of Gardens) 336
Joeji-ji 366

John of Gaunt 106
Johnson, A.T. 316
Johnson, Dr Samuel 132, 232
Johnson, Thomas 179, 290, 297, 300
Johnston, Lawrence 403, 404, 411, 436
Jones, Inigo 160, 180
Josephine, Empress 199, 202, 240, 267, 286
Josselyn, John 289, 290
Judaism 20
Judas tree 356
jubes 24
Jussieu, A.L. 195, 306

K

Kaempfer, Engelbert 75-78, 200, 370, 372, 373; *Amoenitates Exoticae* 370, *370*
Kâgithane 92, *93*
Kallimachos 37
Kalm, Pehr 197
Kalmia/*Kalmia* 200; *K. angustifolia* (mountain laurel) *196*, 197; *K. latifolia* 295
Kanazawa 347
Kano Eitoku 367
Kano Masanobu 367
Kano Motonubu 367
Kao Tsung 330
Kara Mutafa Pasha 89
kare-sansui (dry landscapes) 365, 366, *366*
Karnak 23, 27
Kashmir 81, 84, 415
Katsukawa Shunso 359
Katsura 357, 368, 371
katsura (*Cercidiphyllum japonicum*) 350, 351
Keane, Marc Peter 364
Kelmscott Manor 397, *397*
Kemp, Edward 242, 248
Kenilworth 161
Kennedy, George 250, 258
Kennedy, Lewis 202, 250
Kennedy Memorial 430
Kenroku-en Park 346, 347
Kent, William 33, 71, 167, 206, 207, 209, 210, 212, 214, 215, 218, 223, 233, 241
Kephissos 35
kepos 35
Kerr, William 344
kerria 351, 358
Keswick, Maggie 421
Kew (Royal Botanic Gardens) 92, 201, 222, 252, 255, 261, 264, *264*, 272, 306
Kew House 197, 201, 342, 343
Khorasabad 22, *22*
Kiley, Dan 394, 424, 432, 434
King, Louise 403
Kinkaku-ji (Golden Pavilion), now Rokuan-ji 362, *362*, 363, 364

Kinkaku-ji 50, *51*
Kip, Johannes 163, 163, 164, 166, 212
Kitamura Enkinsai, *Tsukiyama Teizoden* 378
Knight, Richard Payne 222, 229, 230, 231, 272
Knight, Thomas Andrew 272
Knossos 33, 34, 35
knots 138-39, *139*, 148, 158, 160, 162, 190, 209, 388, 424; *entrelacs* 142
Knyff, Leonard 163, 166, 212
Kobori Enshu 371
Kokushi *see* Muso Soseki
Koraku-en 368, *368*, 370
Kolkwitzia amabilis (beauty bush) 312
Koran 20, 57, 58, 59, 73, 85, 88
Kose no Kanaoka 361
Koto-in 349
Kublai Khan 335
kudzu vine (*Pueraria lobata*) 296, 439
Kusakabe, Prince 354

L

La Brède 241
labyrinths 117, 124, 125, 126, 141, 160, 162, 400
Lachryma Montis 314
La Granja 448
Laird, Mark 231, 234
La Mortella 429, *429*
Landscape Movement 32, 42, 51, 102, 140, 159, 167, 190-91, 286, 342, 344
Lange, Willy 384, 389, 390, *390*
Langley, Batty 194, 209, 241, 262, 300
Lao Zi 328, 331
lakes 140, 153, 162, 205, 210, 211, 218, 219, 222, 223, *224-25*, 234, 239, 309, *309*, 319, 323, 326-27, 330, 334, 354, 358, 362, 363, 364, 368, 371, 388, 430, 445
La Quintinye, Jean Baptiste de 141; *Le Parfait Jardinier* 141, *141*
Larix kaempferi 276
Las Navas 452, *452*
Laskett, the 449, *449*
Lassels, Richard 167
Latania borbonica 199, *199*
laurel (bay laurel: *Laurus nobilis*) 36, 44, *44*, 47, 49, 131; *see also under Kalmia, Prunus*
Laurel Hill Cemetery 311
Laurentium 47, 48
Laurie, Michael 432
Lavandula stoechas 181, *182*
lawns 71, 72, 79, 105, *105*, 116, 152, 166, 202, 232, 234, 239, 254, 301, 310, 311-12, 316, 371, 400-401, *400-401*, 413
Lawson, John 296
Lawson, William 190; *The Country Housewife's Garden* 139, *139*; *A New Orchard and Garden* 189, 297

Lawsonia inermis (henna) 63, *63*
Laxenberg Gardens 343, *343*
Le Comte, Louis 200
Le Moyne de Morgues, Jacques 180
Le Nôtre, André 140, 148, 149, 150–
56, 163, 241, 261, 388, 429, 434, 445
Le Rouge, Georges Louis, *des Jardins Anglo-Chinois* 132, 343
Lear, Edward 32
Leasowes, the 215, 231, 232, *232*, 241, 243, 302
Lee, James 202
Lee, Lady Elizabeth 238–39
Leiden 89, 176, 178, 372, 373; botanic garden 176, 178, 373
lemon 36, 44, 135, *135*; *see also Citrus limon*
Lemon Hill 313
Lennox-Boyd, Arabella 258, 452
Leonardo da Vinci 174
Les Quatre Vents 71, 95, *95*, 326, *326*, 449
Levens Hall 50, *50*, 212
Lewis, Capt. Merriwether 304, *304*
Lewis and Clark expedition 300, 304
Li Yuan, Emperor 330
Liberale, Giorgio 175, 176
Ligorio, Pirro 46, 128
lilac (*Syringa*) 170, 176, 178, 193, 233, 296
lily/*Lilium* 34, 55, 66, 74, 90, 92, 110, 181; *L. bulbiferum* var. *croceum* 181, *183*; *L. candidum* (Madonna lily) 22, 45, 98, *98*, 104; *L. chalcedonicum* 22, 34, *34*; *L. lancifolium* (tiger lily) 344; *L. philadelphicum* 294; *L. regale* 312; *L. speciosum* 372; *L. superbum* 294; *L. tigrinum* 372
Limbourg, Pol de, *Très Riches Heures* 103, 108, *108*
Limnanthes douglasii 256
Lincoln Memorial Garden 394
Linden, Ton ter 441
Lindley, John 266, 268
Linnaeus (Carl von Linné) 176, 193, 195, *195*, 200, 201, 294, 296, 306, 316
Linnean Society 195, 252
liquidambar 200
Liriodendron tulipifera (tulip tree) 185, *185*, 193, 200, 387
Little Sparta 232, 445, *445*, 449
Liu Yuan 325, *325*
Llanthony Priory 106
Lloyd, Christopher 425
Lobb, William 255
l'Obel, Matthias de (Lobelius) 169, 176, 177, *177*, 179
lobelia/*Lobelia* 169, 177, 262, 265, 267; *L. cardinalis* 187; *L. speciosa* 273
locus amoenus 116
Loddiges's nursery 199, 254, 263, 306
Logan, John 300
Logan, Martha 296
London, George 165, 188, 206, 212, 293

Longleat 223, 239
Lopez, Hipólito Ruiz 255, 285
lotus 17, 26, 84, 323, 324, 363; blue-flowered/sacred (*Nymphaea caerulea*) 22, 26
Lotusland 436
Loudon, Jane 252, 263
Loudon, John Claudius 69, 200, 203, 226, 230, 233, 234, 236, 246, 249, 251, 252, *252*, 253, 306, 314
Louis of Blois (Blosius), *Statuta monastica* 114
Louis XII 141, 142
Louis XIII 147, 148, 186
Louis XIV 51, 119, 143, 144, 146, 147, 152, 153–56, *153*, 162, 163, 173, 327, 422, 444
Louis XVI 197
Lucullus 43
Lutyens, Sir Edwin 219, 382, 399, 403, 406–409, *407*, 413, 416, 422, 428
Luxembourg 147, 148, 157
Lyall, Sutherland 424
Lyte, Henry 297

M

Macartney, Lord 344
Macedonia 38
McHarg, Ian 390, 441
M'Intosh, Charles, *Practical Gardener* 246, *246*
McLaren, John 315
Macleaya cordata 344
Maclura pomifera (Osage orange) 304
M'Mahon, Bernard 301, 304
Madraseh-e Shah 74
magnolia/*Magnolia* 200, 276, 351, 372, 406; *M. grandiflora* 236, *236*; *M. halleana* 374; *M. kobus* 374; *M. stellata* 374; *M. wilsonii* 312
Magnolia Plantation *280*, 281, 304
mahonia/*Mahonia* 264, 276; *M. aquifolium* (Oregon grape) 304
Malaspina, Alessandro 272
Malmaison 202, 267
Malpighi, Marcello 191
Malus hupehensis 312
mandrake (*Mandragora officinalis*) 40, *40*, 177
mannerism 121, 124, 143, 159, 160, 161
Manning, Warren 383, 394, 434
maples 276, 350, 351, 354, 356, 359, 363; red maple (*Acer rubrum*) 290; sugar maple 394
marigold (*Tagetes*) 181, *181*, 263, 283
Marine Theatre 48
Marly 153, 156, *156*, 302
Marot, Daniel 156 157, 164, 247, 260
Marshal, Alexander 185
Marsh Lane 416, *416, 417*
marvel of Peru *see Mirabilis jalapa*

Marx, Roberto Burle 424, 434, 435
Mary Stuart (Mary II) 157, 163, 164
Mary Tudor (Mary I) 159
Mas de les Voltes 448, *448*
Mason, William 222, 237, 238
Masson, Francis 197–99
Mather, William Gwinn 392
matthiola (stocks) 169, 177, 185
Mattioli, Pierandrea 41, 169, 176, 177, *177*; *Commentarii in sex libros Pedacii Dioscoridis* 174, *174*, 177
Mawson, Thomas 413
Maximilian II 41, 126, 178
Maximowicz, Carl 375
Mayan civilization 282
mazes 121, 144, 262, 298–99, *298-99*
Meager, Leonard 300, 301
Meconopsis betonicifolia 383, *383*; *M. cambrica* 383; *M. simplicifolia* 383
Medes 21, 22
Medici family 46, 47, 126, 128–29
Medici, Catherine de' 142, 143, 146, *146*
Medici, Cosimo de' (the Elder) 121–22, *122*, 133
Medici, Ferdinando 134
Medici, Francesco I 122, 126
Medici, Lorenzo (the Magnificent) 147
Medici, Marie de' 148
Medici Palace chapel 109
Medina Azahara 65, 66, *66*, 84
Mehmed II 90, *90*
Mehmed IV 91
Melia azedarach (Persian lilac, pride of India, Chinese bead tree) 68, *68*, 69
Mellerstain 388, *388*
Melrose Abbey 114
Memphis 23
menagerie 63, 107, 146, 227, 283
Ménagier de Paris, le 117
Mendel, Gregor 272
Mentuhotpe I 27
Mentuhotpe II 26, 27
Menzies, Archibald 255, 272
Mesopotamia 17, 18, 19, 20, 21, 22, 23, 29, 48, 205
Methen 26
Mexico 156, 281, 282–84, 286, 287, 314
Meyer, Albrecht 176
Meyerpeck, Wolfgang 175, 176
Mi Fei 333
Michaux, André 197, 296, 306
microscope 170, 180, 190
Middleton, Henry 295
Middleton, William 295
Middleton Place 197, 295, *295*, 296
Mies van der Rohe, Ludwig 449
Miller, Philip 191, 192, 193, 194, 263, 297; *Dictionary* 193
Miller, Wilhelm 394
Milner, Edward 279
Minamoto Yoritomo 360
Minoans 33, 34, 35
Mirabilis jalapa (marvel of Peru) 74, 134, 174, 181, 186, 263, 283

mission gardens 60, 288; San Diego de Alcala 314; San Fernando 314; San Juan Capistrano 315, *315*
Mizuno Toshikata 369
moats 140, 143, 146, 161, 437
Modernism/Modernist Movement 377, 415–19, 434
Moerheim 416, 418–19, *418-19*
Mollet family 149
Mollet, André 138–39, 149, 163; *Le Jardin du Plaisir* 149
Mollet, Claude 147, 149; *Théâtre des plans et jardinage* 149, *149*
monarda/*Monarda* 169, 294; *M. didyma* (bee balm) 294
Monardes, Nicolas 169; *Joyfull News out of the Newe Founde World* 174, 178, 285
monasteries 110–14
Mongols 65, 71–73
monkey puzzle *see Araucaria*
Montagu, Lady Mary Wortley 92
Montaigne, Michel de 124, 126, 130, 133, 135
Montargis 142, *142*, 411
Montesquieu, Baron 241
Montezuma I 283, 284
Montezuma II 282, 283, 284
Monticello 289, 293, 302, *302*
Montpellier 110, 156, 175, 177, 178; botanic garden 176
Mont Ventoux 102
Moore, Henry 434
Moor Park 161, 166
Morin, Pierre 186, 188
Morison, Fynes 126, 135, 166
Morris, William 388, 396, 397, 399
Morrison, Darrel 441, 445
Motsu-ji temple 360
Mount, the 413
Mountain View Cemetery 315
Mount Auburn Cemetery 307, 311
Mount Royal, Montreal 308
Mount Vernon 289, 296, 300, 301, 302
mounts 129, *129*, 158, 160, 162, 291, 295, 296, 306
Mughal empire 57, 73, 81–88, 281, 285, 415; Garden, New Delhi 399; miniatures 60
Muhammad (Prophet) 20, 57, 58, 62
Muhammad V 69, 70
Muir, John 274, 383
Mumtaz Mahal 85, 88
Munstead Wood 406, 407, *407*
Murad III 90
Murad IV 91, 92
Murasaki Shikibu, *Genji Monogatari* 356, 358–59, *358-59*
Murato Juko 369
Muskau 263, *263*
Muso Soseki (Kokushi) 363
Muthesius, Hermann 396
Mutis, José Celestino 286
myrrh (*Commiphora myrrha*) 26
myrtle 34, 35, 44, 49, 55

N

Nakane Kinsaku 365, 378
Napoleon Bonaparte 203, 241, 313
narcissi 74, 90, 92, 134, 186
Nash, John 226, 236, 239, 260
nasturtium 170, *170*
National Trust 210, 248, 256, 279, 424, 425, 427, 428, 437
Nasim Bagh 84
Nebamun 27, 28
Nebot, Balthasar 239, 400
Nebuchadnezzar II 21
Neckam, Alexander *De Naturis Rerum* 36
Neckar 144
Nero 38, 45, 48
Nesfield, Markham 260
Nesfield, William Andrews 246, 259, 260 62, 276, 279
Netherlands 89, 99, 156-57, 170, 178, 185; *see also* Holland
nettle tree (*Celtis australis*) 55
Neugebaude 126
New York 289, 290, 304, 307, 308, 339, 422
New Zealand 286
Newcastle, Duke of 210
Nezahualcoyotl 283, 284
Ni Zan 334
Nichols Garden 291
Nicholson, Ben 430
Nicholson, Francis 293, 301
Nicolson, Harold 427, 436, 437
Nieuhof, Jan 342
Nikko 353, *353*
Nile 18-19, 23, 24, 39
Nimla 82
Nimrud 18
Nineveh 20, 21, 22, 23
Nizami 73
Noguchi, Isamu 434, 436, 445
Nonsuch 159, 160
Normandy 103, 109
Northampton, Marquis of 262
Nourse, Timothy 207
Nuneham Courtney 218
Nuneham Park 233, 237, 238, *238*, 239
Nuremburg 174, 175
Nur Jahan *80*, 81
Nut *see* Hathor
Nymphaea caerulea (sacred lotus/blue-flowered water-lily) 26, 29; *N. lotus* (white water-lily) 29
nymphaeum 33, 46, 129

O

oasis 17, 21, 26, 92, 166, 406, 432
Odo Nobunaga 367, 368
Oehme, van Sweden partnership 441, 442
Oehme, Wolfgang 382, 435
Oglethorpe, James 288
Olmsted, Frederick Law 242, 253, 267, 281, 307, 308-309, *308*, 310, 311, 312, 315, 316, 383, 387, 392, 393, 394, 403, 413, 422, 431, 441
Olmsted, Frederick Law Jr. 308
Olmsted, John Charles 308
Oman, Julia Trevelyan 449
Ono no Imoko 330, 353
opium poppy *see Papaver somniferum*
Oplontis 45
orangery 163, 165, 167, 270
orchards 8, *8*, 52, 62, 68, 72, 92, 98, 100, 105, 106, *106*, 109, 110, 111, 116, 120, 190, 284, 287, 293, 294, 321, 401
Origo, Marchesa Iris 136
Orsini, Count Vicino 124
Osawa-no-ike 355
Osbeck, Peter 200
Ottoman empire 57, 60, 88-92
Oudolf, Piet 11, 441, 443
Ovid 42, 132, 209, 430; *Metamorphoses* 128, *128*, 129
Oxford, Earl of 212
Oxford: botanic garden 176, 180, *180*

P Q

Padua 121, 130; botanic garden 39, 135, 138, *176*, 177, 180, *180*, 283
Paeonia/peony 89, 324, 338, 351, 359, 378; *P. lactiflora* 324, *324*; *P. officinalis* 324; *P. suffruticosa* 324
Paestum 49, 55
Page, Russell 120, 428, 429, 431
Painshill 92, 133, *133*, 215, 221, 234, *234-35*, 401
pairidaeza 19; *see also* paradise
Palazzo Doria 135
Palermo 107
Palissy, Bernard 147
Palladio, Andrea 47, 158, 302
Palladius 49, 52, 110, 134
palmetto/fan palm (*Chamaerops humilis*) 26, 242
palm tree 18, 22, 23, *23 see also Chamaerops, Dactylifera*
Palo Alto 308
Papaver somniferum (opium poppy) 45, 88, *88*
papyrus (*Cyperus papyrus*) *16*, 17, 26, 28, 33, 34
paradise/paradise gardens 9, 17, 19, 20, 58, 81, 88, 100, 109, 113, 129, 321, 322, 334, 430, 452
Parc André Citroën, Paris 444, *444*
Parc Monceau 241, 273
Parennin, Dominique 200
Paris 126, 141, 143, 273, 316, 429, 431, 444; botanic garden 176; *see also* Jardin du Roi

Parkinson, John 88, 179; *Paradisus* 138, 179, 185, 190, 193, 263, 300
Parkinson, Sydney 201
parks 16, 29, 65, 109, 293, 321, 323, 325, 330, 341, 368, 413, 422, 431; city/public parks 205, 239, 251, 253, 279, 307-11, 315, 331, 336, 383, 422; deer parks 107, 109, 205; *heem* parks 390, 422; hunting parks 19, 21-22, 63, 98, 109, 205, 242, 283, 321, 335-36, 340; land-scape parks 29, 46, 109, 117, 215, 218, 231, 406; nature parks 276; Persian-style "paradise"/ pleasure parks 39, 89, 109, 282, 341; royal/ imperial parks 29, 107, 149, 406
Parmentier, André 306
Parnassus 41, 129, *129*, 146, 160, 161
Parnell, Sir John 234
Parrish, Maxfield 413, 415
Parsons, Alfred 386
parterres 123, 125, 138-39, *138-39*, 146, 147, 148, 149, 153, 163, 164, 167, 206, 233, 251, 256, *256*, 260-61, 262, 267, 276, 279, 296, 301, 424, 448; *parterre de broderie* 138, 147, 148, 149, 156, 157, *157*, 164, 209; water parterre 136, 448
Parthenon 48
Pasargadae 20, 23, 58, *58*
Passe, Crispin van de, *Hortus Floridus* 180-81, 187, *187*
Patel, Pierre 153
Paul III, Pope 184
Pavlovsk 240, *240*
Paxton, Joseph 163, 242, 246, 251, 252, 254, 266-68, *267*, 279, 310, 383
peach (*Prunus persica*) 36, 54, 105, 287
Pearson, Dan 441, 442
Pei, I.M. 378
Pelargonium (geranium) 250, 256, 258, 259, 261, 262, 263, 265, 269, 272, 310; *P. zonale* 269, *P. inquinans* 269
Pemberton, Israel 293
peng jing (Chinese bonsai) 338
Penn, John 294
Penn, William 294
peony *see Paeonia*
Perelle, Adam 151
peripatoi 36
peristyle gardens 33, 39, 42, 43, 125
Perry, Commodore Matthew 374
Persepolis 39
Persia 17, 18, 22, 24, 29, 39, 52, 57, 58, 60, 61, 62, 63, 65, 68, 78-81, 117, 281, 285, 321, 436; Persian garden carpets 58, 59, *59*; miniatures 73, *81*, 88; *see also* Iran
Peru 170, 281, 285-87
Peter the Great, Tsar 188
Peto, Sir Harold 409, 412, 413, 415
Petraia 122
Petrarch, Francesco Petrarca 102, 116, 174
Petre, Lord 194, 197, 200

Petworth 223
phacelia 263
Philadelphia 293, 304, 312, 313
Philip II 174, 282
Philip the Good, Duke of Burgundy 107
Philippa, Queen 117
Philips, Henry 233, 236
Phoenix dactylifera (date palm) *16*, 17, 18, 26, *26*, 28, 33, 34, 35, *35*
Phoenix Park 265
Phragmites australis (giant reed) 19
Picturesque style 92, 228, 229ff, 253-54, 272, 276, 306, 316
Pincian Hill 43
Pinckney, Eliza Lucas 295
pine trees (*Pinus*) 23, 26, 69, 92, 197, 234, 276, 316, 324; lacebark pine (*P. bungeana*) 276; Monterey pine (*P. radiata*) 272, 276; sugar pine (*P. lambertiana*) 272, umbrella pine 95; Virginia pitch pine 194; Chile pine *see Araucaria*
Pini, Girolamo 169
Pinsent, Cecil 136
Pinus bungeana (lacebark pine) 276; *P. lambertiana* (sugar pine) 272; *P. radiata* (Monterey pine) 272
Piper, Frederik Magnus 219, 234
Pisa: botanic garden 39, 176, 180
Pitti Palace 122, 148
Pius II, Pope, *Commentaries* 102
plane trees (*Platanus*) 35, 36, 47, 52, 55, 73, 74, 77, 78, 82, 83, 129, 406; London plane (*P. x hispanica*) 191; oriental plane (*P. orientalis*) 35, 43, 44, 191; *see also* chenar
Plantin, Christophe 176, 179
Platanus x hispanica (London plane) 191; *P. occidentalis* 191; *P. orientalis* (oriental plane, *chenar*) 191
Plato's Academy 35
Platt, Charles A. 392, 393, 403, 409, 412, 413
Platt, William 392
Platter, Thomas 159
pleasance 102, 107
Pliny the Elder 31, 43, *43*, 44, 48, 49, 51, 52, 55, 178; *Naturalis Historia* 43, 52, *52*, 54, 422
Pliny the Younger 36, 42, 47, *47*, 48, 69, 100, 123, 134, 209; two villas of 47
Plutarch 35
Poggio Reale 140, 141
Polianthes tuberosa (tuberose) 74, 134, 153, 156, 186, 283
Polo, Marco 334, 335
pomegranates 26, 35, 44, 55, 66, 68, 69, 74, 82, 92, 134, 194, *194*
Pompeii 42, 43, 44-45, *44-45*, 53, 54, 135; House of the Marine Venus *44*; House of Vetti *45*; Villa Julia Felix *44*
Pompey 43
pools and ponds 28, *28*, 43, 45, 48,

54, *54*, *56*, 57, 64, 66, 69, 71, 73,
75, 77, 121, *121*, 126, 161, 162,
214, 228, 319, 326-27, *326-27*,
328, 339, 352, 406, 412, 413, 420,
421; swimming pools 432, *433*,
437, *437*
Pope, Alexander 33, 92, 132, 206,
206, 207, 208, 209, 210, 212, 214,
297, 342, 423, 424
poplars 33, 36, 73, 74, 95, 294; black
35; Lombardy 234, 243, *243*
poppies 55, 73, 74; opium (*Papaver
somniferum*) 45, 88, *88*; *see also
Meconopsis*
Portland, Duchess of 132
Portland, Duke of 222
Portrack 295, *295*
Portugal 54, 163 135, 178
Portugal laurel (*Prunus lusitanica*) 193,
256, 259, 264
potager 424, *424*
Poussin, Nicolas 32, 33, 213, 214
Prairie School 393-94
Pratt, Henry 313
Praxiteles 53
Prescott, W.H. 282, 285
Price, Sir Uvedale 222, 229, 230, 231
Primaticcio 143, 146, 147
Prospect Park, Brooklyn 308
Provost, Alain 444
Prunus laurocerasus (cherry laurel) 89,
149; *P. lusitanica* (Portugal laurel)
259; *P. persica* (peach) 36, 54, 105,
287
Pseudotsuga menziesii (Douglas fir)
272
Pückler-Muskau, Prince 236, 240,
242, 263
Pueraria lobata (kudzu vine) 296, 439
Pursh, Frederick 304
Pye, William 86
qanats 24, 60, 74, 78, 79, 286
Qian Long, Emperor 299, 335, 339,
340, 341, 345
Qin Shi Huang Di, Emperor 320-
21, 322
Qiongdao (Jade Islet) *341*
Quercus agrifolia (Californian/coastal
live oak) 406, 432; *Q. ilex* (holm
oak) 173; *Q. suber* (cork oak) 173
quincunx 122, 126, 190, 451
Quincy, Quatremère de 253

R

Rae, John 263
Raleigh, Sir Walter 289, 297
Ram Bagh 83
Ramelli, Agostino 130
Ramzi 74
Randolph, John 301
Rauwolf, Leonhardt 41, 89
Ray, John 191, 193, 195
Raymond, John 167

Rea, John 187
Redesdale, Lord 375
Red Fort, Agra 66, 84
Red House 396, 397, 399
Redouté, Pierre-Joseph 197, 202
redwood *see Sequoia, Sequoiadendron*
Reef Point 411
Refik, Ahmet 90
Regent's Park 237, 260, *260*, 265
Renaissance 31, 40, 42-43, 46, 47,
51, 86, 97, 103, 119-67, 242, 246,
399, 413, 430, 444, 445, 448, 451
Renishaw 31, *380*, 381, 413
Repton, George 226
Repton, Humphry 200, 210, 212,
222, 226, 233, *233*, 249, 251, 253,
255, 305; Red Books 222, 227,
227, 239, 256, 263, 306
Repton, John 226
rhizotomists 36, 38, *38*
Rhodes 34, 39
Rhododendron 200, 219, 231, 234,
245, 250, 267, 274, *274*, 276, 406;
R. arboreum 274; Ghent azaleas
274; *R. catawbiense* (rosebay) *196*,
197; *R. fortunei* 276; *R. luteum*
173-74, 197; *R. maximum* 294,
308; *R. ponticum* 173
ribbon bedding/borders 265, 266, 315
Richardson, H.H. 317
Richardson, Samuel 234
Richelieu, Cardinal 147, 148
Richmond, Duke of 194, 200
Richmond Lodge 206
Richmond Palace 126, 161
rills and watercourses 57, 58, 60, 69,
70, 71, 214, 215, *215*, 337, 356, 403,
406, *408*, 409, 415, 416, 452, *452*
Ripa, Fr. Matteo 209
Road, James 293
Robert of Artois 107
Robin, Jean 148, 169, 186, 297
Robin, Vespasien 316
Robinia pseudoacacia (black locust,
false acacia) 186, 193, 297
Robinson, William 246, 252, 261,
265, 269, 273, 279, 311, 383, 384,
386-89, 386, 393, 396, 403, 408,
423, 431, 438; *English Flower
Garden* 386, 387, 396; *Wild Garden*
382, 386, *386*
rockwork 121, 248, 267, 277, *277*,
324-25, 326, 328, 333, 334, 340,
348, 349-50, 364, 365-66, 371
Rodmarton Manor *398*, 399
Rokuan-ji, see Kinkaku-ji
Roman de la Rose 101, *101*, 109, 114,
114, *115*, 116
Romano, Jacob 157
Rome 31, 42-55, 132, 205, 209, 214,
242; Roman Empire 97, 99, 109
Rondelet, Guillaume 175, 178
Rosa, Salvator 230
Rosamund's Bower 105
Rose, James 432
rose/*Rosa* 33, 34, 44, 47, 49, 62, 66,

68, 73, 74, 90, 91, 92, 95, 101, 104,
109, 110, 180, 181, *181*, 233, 272,
313; *R. x alba* 55, *113*; *R. banksiae*
(Banksian) 272, 344; *R. bracteata*
(Macartney rose) 200, 344; *R.
canina* (dog) 34, 55; *R. centifolia*
(cabbage) 34; *R. damascena* var.
semperflorens (autumn damask) 55;
R. x damascena var. *bifera* (of
Paestum) 55; *R. gallica* 55, *109*,
294; *R.g.* var. *officinalis* 109; *R.g.*
'Versicolor' 109, *113*; rosa mundi
109; *R. mulliganii* 427, *427*; *R.
phoenicia* 55; *R. x richardii*
(Abyssinian) 34, 109; *R. roxburghii*
304; *R. sempervirens* 63; *R.*
'Tuscany Superb' 109
Rosedown 304, *305*
rosemary 117, 138, 141
Rothschild, Alfred de 262
Rousham, 71, 128, 210, 212, 214,
215, *215*, *216-17*, 221, 233, 239
Rousseau, Jean-Jacques 237, 240,
241, 243
Royal Botanic Gardens, *see* Kew
Royal Horticultural Society 201, 344
Royal Society 188, 192, 272
Rudbeck, Olaf 316
Rudbeckia 316; *R. fulgida* 316, *316*;
R. hirta 316
Rudolph II 173, 186
Rueil 148
Rukh, Shah 73
Ruskin, John 388, 394-6
Russia 150, 185, 239
Ruys, Mien (Wilhelmina Jacoba)
416-19
Ryoan-ji (Dragon Peace Temple)
365, 366, *366*, 367
Rysbrack, Pieter 208

S

Sa'adatabad 74
Saarinen, Eliel 399, Eero 434
sabi stones 349
Sackville-West, Vita 79-81, 427, 428,
436, 437
Sacro Bosco *see* Bomarzo
Saga-in 355, *355*
sage (*Salvia officinalis*) 100, *100*
Saiho-ji 363, *363*
St Augustine 287
St Benedict 111
St Bernard of Clairvaux 111
St Gall 99, 100, 105, 111
Saint-Germain-en-Laye 126, 138,
142, 147, 148, *148*, 149
Saint-Simon, Duc de 150
Sakuteiki (Treatise on garden-
making) *see* Tachibana no
Toshitsuna
Salerno 110
Saling Hall (Essex) 51, *51*

salvia/*Salvia* 267; *S. officinalis* (sage)
100, *100*; *S. splendens* 263
Salvin, Anthony 260
Samarkand 24, 71-73, 73, 82
Samarra 24, 64, *64*
Sandby, Paul 237
San Mateo 315
San Simeon 422
Sanssouci, Potsdam 220, *220*;
Chinese House 342
Santorini (Thira) 33, 34
São José dos Campos 435, *435*
Sardis 38
Sargent, Charles Sprague 312, *312*,
408
Sargent, John Singer 308
Sargon II 22
Sayes Court 186, 187, 188
Scandinavia 99
Scheuchzer, Johann Gaspar 372
Schickhardt, Heinrich 130
Schizolobium parahybum 435
Schuylkill river 294
Schwartz, Martha 419, 424, 445, 451
Scilla peruviana 187, *187*
Scopas 53
Scott, Frank 308, 311
Scott, Geoffrey *Architecture of
Humanism* 136
sea daffodil (*Pancratium maritimum*)
33, 34
Searle, John 207
Secoton 289, *289*
Sedding, J.D. 388-89
Selim II 91
Sen No Rikyu 369
Sennacherib 22, 23
Sennadjem 25
Sennufer 27
Sequoiadendron giganteum
(wellingtonia, giant redwood) 248,
274
Sequoia sempervirens
(Californian/coastal redwood)
272, 283
Serlio, Sebastiano 138, 143, 158; *Tutte
l'opere d'architettura* 147
Servilius 53
Sesshu 364, 365, 366
shaduf 24, *24*
shakkei (borrowed scenery) 351, 371
Shalimar Bagh 84, 88, 327, *327*
Shanglin park 321
sharawadgi 166, 207, 209, 342
Sheffield Park 223
Shen Fu 338
Shenstone, William 215, 232, 241,
243
Sheringham Park 228, *228*
Shi Zin Lin (Lion Grove) 334
Shigemori Mirei 349, 355, 378-79, *379*
Shinto 347, 348, 352, 353
Shipman, Ellen Biddle 392, 403
Shiraz 22, 24, *75*, 95
Shisen-in (Divine Spring Garden)
354-55

Shotuki Taishi, prince 353
Shrewsbury, sixteenth Earl of 249, 260
shrubbery 231, 233, 236, 237, 245, 301, 308, 309, 413
Shrubland Park 259, 266
Shugaku-in 357, 368, 371, *371*
Shugborough 213
Shute House 430, *430*
Sibthorp, John 33, 41, 174, 180; *Flora Graeca* 41, *41*, 174, 195
Sicily 39, 52, 55, 60, 65, 68, 103, 117, 135
Sieberling, F.A. 394
Siebold, Philipp Franz von 200, 372, 373
Sima Guang 329
Simonds, Ossian Cole 394
Sissinghurst 404, 425, *426*, 427, 428, 436, 437, 448
Sitta, Vladimir 452
Sitwell, Sir George 381, 413
Sloane, Sir Hans 191, 292, 372
Smith, James Edward 195
Smith, John 300
Sneferu 26
Soami 361, 365, 266
Society of Gardeners 191, 193
Soderini, Giovanvittorio, *Trattata della Cultura* 131
Soga no Umaka 354
Solander, Daniel 201
Solari, Santino 126
Solis, Antonio de 284
Solitude, the 294
Somalia (Land of Punt) 26
Somerset House 161
Southcote, Philip 215, 232, 293
Sowerby, James 203
Spain 57, 60, 65, 99, 117, 135, 150, 178, 281, 282, 284, 285, 286, 297, 313-15, 434, 448; Moorish/ Muslim rule 57, 65-71, 72
Speckle, Veit Rudolf 176
Spence, Joseph 206, 232, 234
Spotswood, Alexander 291, 293
Sprague, Charles F. 392
Spring Grove Cemetery 311
Stanford, George Leland 316
Stan Hywet 394, *395*
Staunton, Sir George 344
Steele, Fletcher 394
stewartia 366
Stirling Castle 106
Stoke Edith 167, *167*
Stourhead 132, *132*, 213, 215, 219, *219*, 221, 232, 234, 239, 272, 274, *274*
Stowe 54, 128, 210, 211, *211*, 212, 214, 221, 223, 226, 234, 239
Strauch, Adolph 311
strawberry tree *see Arbutus*
stroll gardens 368
Strong, Sir Roy 159, 449
Stuart-Smith, Tom 221
Studley Royal 295
Stuyvesant, Peter 290

Süleyman I 75, 178
Süleyman the Magnificent 40, 92
Sumerians 19, 21, 62, 321
sunflower (*Helianthus annuus*)134, 174, 178, 181, 283, 285, *285*, 297
Surflet, Richard 300
Sutherland, Duke and Duchess of 256, 264
Sutton Place 430
Suzhou 325, 334, 339
swamp cypress (*Taxodium distichum*) 200
Sweden 149, 220, 221, 239
Sweert, Emmanuel 184-86, 187
Swift, Dr Katherine 400
Swinden, Nathaniel 237
Switzer, Stephen 209, 232, 62
sycamore fig (*Ficus sycomorus*) 17, 26, 27, 173; sycamore goddess 27, 28; *see also* Hathor
Sylvester, Nathaniel 290-91
Syon House 223
Syracuse 39
Syria 68, 91

T

Tachard, Guy 200
Tachibana no Toshitsuna, *Sakuteiki* (Treatise on garden-making) 349, 356, 378, 379
Tacuinum sanitatis 100, *100*
Tagetes (marigold) 174; *T. erecta* 263; *T. patula* 263
Tai Tsung, Emperor 330
Taj Mahal 84, 85, *85*, 88
Tamerlane *see* Timur
Tang Yin 335
Taoism 328, 331, 342, 353
Tatton Park *278*, 279, 375, *375*, 377
Taxodium distichum (bald/swamp cypress) 281, 283; *T. mucronatum* (Mexican cypress) 283
Taxus cuspidata 374
tea garden/house 220, *220*, 240, 344, *344*, 368, 369, 377
Temple, Sir William 166, 207, 342
temple gardens 26-27, 370; temples as landscape features 210, 219, 220-21, *220-21*, 302, 338; Amun, Karnak 23; Apollo Epicurius, Bassae 37; Daitoku-ji 349, *349*; Deir-el-Bahari, Thebes 23, 26, 27; Hephaistos, Athens 35, 36; Horyuji 354; Motsu-ji 360; Ryoan-ji (Dragon Peace Temple) 365, 366, *366*, 367
Tenochtitlán 282, 283,
Tenryui-ji 363
Tenshin-en garden 378
Teotihuacan 282
Texcoco 282
Thebes 17, 23, 25, 26, 27, 39
Theobalds 160, 179

Theophrastus 33, 36, 38, *38*, 39, 41, 131, 422; *Enquiry into Plants* 36, 38
Thijsse, Jacques P. 384, 390
Thira (Santorini) 33
Thomas, Francis Inigo 388, 389
Thomas, Graham Stuart 256, 425
Thomas, William, *Historie of Italie* 135
Thomson, George 264
Thorburn, Grant 312
Thoreau, Henry David 390, 434
Thorndon 194, 197
thujas 197, 200
Thunberg, Carl Peter 197, 200, 372-73
Tigridia pavonia (peacock tiger flower) 283
Tigris 19, 22, 59, 63, 64
Tijou, Jean 164-65
Timur (Tamerlane) 71, 72, *72*, 74
Tintinhull 404
Tofuku-ji monastery 349, *349*, 379, *379*
Tokudaiji Sah'e 368
Tokugawa Ieyasu 368, 370
tomb gardens 39
tomb paintings 19, 23, 25, *25*, 26, 29
Tomkins, William 238
tools 52
topiary 50-51, *50-51*,103, 117, 120, 124, 143, 156, 159, 162, 166, 167, 189, 190, 206, 291, 293, 388, 399, 404, 424
Topkapi Saray 90, 92
Tournefort, Joseph Pitton de 173, 193
Toshihito, Prince 371
Tradescant family 185, 186
Tradescant, John the Elder 185, *185*, 297, 300
Tradescant, John the Younger 169, 185, *185*, 300, 316
Tradescantia virginiana 169, 185, *185*
Traquair 410
tree of life 18, *18*, 67, 112
Trentham Park *244*, 245, 256, *256*, 265, 273
tuberose (*Polianthes tuberosa*) 74, 134, 153, 156, 186, 283
Tuileries, the 48, 149, 429
tulip/*Tulipa* 73, 82, 83, 89, 90, 91, *91*,134, 167, 170, 171, *171*, *172*, 173, 181, *181*, 185, 199, 263, 292, 294; *T. clusiana* 178, *178*, 186
tulipomania 173, 178
tulip tree (*Liriodendron*) 185, *185*, 200, 234, 308
Tunnard, Christopher 377, 415, 419
Turf 111; turf bench/seat 101, *101*, 102, 116, 117; *gazon coupé* 165; *see also* Lawns
Turkey (Ottoman Empire) 57, 88-92; Turkish-style buildings 92, 234
Turnbull, Daniel 304
Turnbull, Martha 304
Turner, J.M.W. 219
Turner, Richard 261
Turner, William 177, 193

Tusculum 47, 48
Tuthmosis 27, 28
Twickenham 33, 207, 342

U V W

Ueno Park 350, *350*
Underwood, Catherine Fondren 304
Upton Grey 406
Utagawa Hiroshige 351
Utagawa Kunisada 359
Utens, Giusto 122, 126, 134
Vaccinium vitis-idaea 149
Vallejo, Gen. Mariano 315
Van der Donck, Adrian 290
Van der Groen, Jan, *Den Nederlandtsen Hovenier* 138, 157
Van Eyck, Jan 107; *Adoration of the Lamb* 109
Van Sweden, James 382, 435
Vanbrugh, John 211, 222
Vancouver, Capt. George 255, 314
Vanderbilt, George 308
Varro 49, 52, 110
Vaughan, Samuel 301
Vaux, Calvert 307, 308, 310, 383
Vaux-le-Vicomte 150-52, 153
Veitch, John Gould 374
Veitch & Co, nurserymen 255, 274, 276
Veitshöccheim, Bavaria 129
Veltrusy 232
Ventenat, Etienne Pierre 202
Venus 53, 129, 130, 240
verbena/*Verbena* 261, 267, 313; *V. chamaedrifolia* 263; *V. venosa* 264
Verey, Rosemary 139, 424, 424, 449
Verneuil 142
Versailles 10, *10*, 51, 87, *87*, 119, 143, 146, 150, 152, *152*, *154-55*, 156, 279, 299, 302, 327, 341, 422, 444, 451
Vespasian 38
Vesuvius 42, 43, 44
Victoria amazonica 267
Vienna 41, 60, 89, 126, 178, 343
Vignola 47, 131, 143, 184
Villa Aldobrandini 160
Villa Barbarigo (Pizzoni Ardemani) 2, 121, *121*, 214
Villa Borghese 256
Villa Castellazzo 50, *50*
Villa Castello (Villa Medici, Medici gardens) 122, 124, 128, 133, *133*, 135, 142
Villa d'Este, Tivoli 39, 40, 86, *118*, 119, 123, 128-29, 130, 135, 147, 158, 255, 299
Villa della Petraia 134, *134*
Villa di Artimino 122, 126
Villa Gamberaia 136, *136*
Villa Garzoni 160, 326, *326*
Villa Julia Felix, Pompeii 44, *44*
Villa la Foce 136, *137*

Villa Lante 47, 86, 123, *123*, 125, 129, 130, 131, *131*
Villa La Rotonda 47
Villa Pratolino 121, 122, 124, 126, *126-27*, 128, 129, 130, 130, 133, 148, 160, 161
villas 46; country 46, 122-24; Pliny's 47; Roman 42
violet 49, 55, 92, 104, 110, 114
Virgil 42, 46, 100, 124, 430, 450; *Aeneid* 219; *Eclogues* 46, 134; *Georgics* 42, 46-48, 49, 55, 100, 112, 134, 209
Virginia 179, 185, 289, 290, 291, 302
Virgin Mary *96*, 97, 98, *98*, 104, *104*, 109, 116
virgultum 103
viridarium 102, 106, *106*, 107
Vitruvius 120, 130, 160; *De Architectura* 53
Voltaire, François Marie Androuet de 240
von Gemminger, Johann Conrad, Prince-Bishop of Eichstätt 173, 181-85
von Sckell, Friedrich Ludwig 236
Vredeman De Vries, Jan 142, 157
Waddesdon Manor 262, 276
Wager, Sir Charles 236
Walafrid Strabo 39, 100 *De cultura hortulorum* 100
Walden Pond 390, 434
Waldstein, Baron 160, 162
Wallich, Nathaniel 267, 274
Walmer Castle 95, *95*
Walpole, Horace 212, 214
Walpole, Sir Robert 211, 212
Walska, Mme Ganna 436
Walton, Lady Susana 429
Wang Chuan 330-31, *330-31*
Wang Guan, *Yangzhou Shaoyao Pu* 324
Wang Men 334
Wang Shi Yuan 339, *339*

Wang Shizen 337
Wang Wei 330, 331, 331, 335
Ward, Frank Kingdon 383
Ward, Nathaniel Bagshaw 198, *198*; Wardian case 198, *198*, 199, 273, 279, 373, 375
Washington, George 289, 296, 300, 301, 302
water clock 68; watercourses *see* Rills; waterfalls 232, 332, 394; dry 364; water jets and spouts 70, *70*, 78, 86, 107, 121, 126, 267; water jokes and devices 53, 107, 121, 129-30, 160; *see also giochi d'acqua*; wine-cooling trough 47; *see also* Cascades, Fountains, Lakes, Pools
water-lily 179, *179*, 326, *326*; *see also Nymphaea*
waterwheel 24, 64, 68, 83, 156
Webb, Philip 396, 399
Weiditz, Hans 176
Weihenstephan 384, 439, *440*, 441
Welbeck Abbey 222
Welch, Terry 377
wellingtonia or giant redwood (*Sequoiadendron giganteum*) 248, 274
Wen Zhenming 322
Wentworth, Governor 296
Westbury Court 163
Westminster, Duke of 261
Westonbirt Arboretum 274, *275*, 276
Westover 292, 293
West Wycombe Park *204*, 205
Wharton, Edith 410, 413, 415
Whately, Thomas 233, 241
wheelbarrows 116, *116*, 188, 323
White, John 289
Whitehall Palace 158, *158*, 159, 163, 164
Whitehead Institute 451
Whitton 197, 292
Wilder, Louise Beebe 403
wilderness 130, 149, 160, 161, 163,

165, 188, 200, 209, 212, 233, 295, 310, 342, 382-84, 390, 399
Wilhelm IV of Hesse 178
Wilhelmshoe, Kassel 202
William and Mary College 293
William of Orange (William III) 157, 163,164
William the Conqueror 109
Williamsburg 291, *291*, 292, 293, 295
Willmott, Ellen 269
Wilson, Ernest 312, *312*
Wilton House 158, 160, *160*, 161, *161*, 167
Wimbledon House 160, 162
Wimpole Hall 212
Windsor Castle 106, 135
winter garden/*hortus siccus* 135 (herbarium)
Winterthur 387, *387*
Winthrop, John 290, 300
Wirtz, Jacques 120, 326, 428, 429, 445
Wise, Henry 165, 206, 212, 263
wisteria/*Wisteria* 351, 354, 356, 358; *W. floribunda* 374; *W. sinensis* 200
Woburn Abbey 222, 227, *227*
Wolley-Dod, Rev 269
Wolsey, Cardinal 159
Wooburn Farm 215, 231, 232, 293, 302
Wood, William 289
Woodlands 304
Woods, Richard 238, 239
Woodstock Park 105-106, 107
Woodwardia radicans 279
Wordsworth, William 390
Worlidge, John 207, 301
Wörlitz (now Gartenreich) 232, *232*, 240, 242, 243
Wotton 166, 188
Wren, Sir Christopher 164, 188
Wright, Frank Lloyd 383, 407
Wright, Thomas 213
Wu Chen 334

Wu, Empress 330-31
Wudi, Emperor 322-23
Wyatt, James 228
Wyatville, Jeffry 227-28, 267

XYZ

Xenophon 19, 20 38; *Oeconomicus* 38
xeriscape gardens 438
Xi Yang Lou 340, 341, 345
Xuan Zhong, Emperor 331
Yan Shan 337
Yang Guifei 331
Yangdi, Emperor 330, 353
yew 50, 51, 95, 165, 166, 190, 206, 233, 256, 399, 404, 413, 427; Irish 258, 259, 406, 415; Japanese 374
Yi He Yuan (Garden of Happy Harmony) 335, 345
Yin/Yang 319, 325, 324-25, 327
Yosemite 308
Yoshida, Prof. 371
Yoshimasa, Shogun 361, 363
Yoshimitsu, Shogun 362, 362, 363
Young, Sir Arthur 234
Yuan Guanhan 323
Yuan Ming Yuan (Garden of Perfect Brightness) 340, *340*, 341, 345, 342
Yuan Ming Yuan maze 299, *299*
Yuan Ye see Ji Cheng
Yucay 285
yuccas 407, *407*
Yusuf I 70
Yu Yuan 333, *333*
Zekkai 364
Zen 327, 347, 348, 364-67, 369, 436, 451; Zen Buddhism 342, 348
Zen'ami 361
Zhao Ji, Emperor 319, 332-34
ziggurat 21
zinnias 283

AUTHOR'S AND PUBLISHER'S ACKNOWLEDGEMENTS

AUTHOR'S ACKNOWLEDGEMENTS

Almost three years ago I was fortunate to meet Christopher Davis, the Publisher of Dorling Kindersley, at a lunch party given by my agent Felicity Bryan. I had been thinking of writing a book about the history of garden design and, to my joy and amazement, he was interested. Within a few weeks after meetings with David Lamb the project was agreed. I knew I was in safe hands at Dorling Kindersley.

I would like to thank the team at Dorling Kindersley: David Lamb, who has been of unfailing support, the extraordinary Pamela Brown, who became the editor in charge, Ursula Dawson, the designer who has made the book beautiful, besides Penny David and Margaret Mulvihill, who have made significant editorial improvements. Many others have been at the end of the telephone to answer queries. Sandra Raphael, Patrick Taylor and the staff at the Lindley Library have been unfailingly patient. Emily Hedges took on the gigantic task of matching pictures to the text and has given the book an extra visual dimension.

Above all, of course, I owe a vast debt to garden historians. Mine is a general garden history but it is their illuminating research on the detail of different periods which has made my book possible. Perhaps I can single out the scholars who have contributed to the Dumbarton Oaks publications, contributors to the *Journal of Garden History* (since 1998 *Studies in the History of Gardens and Designed Landscapes*) and to *Garden History*, the journal of the Garden History Society. The work of two individuals stands out as sources, the late medievalist John Harvey and John Dixon Hunt, now Professor of Landscape Architecture at Pennsylvania University.

PUBLISHER'S ACKNOWLEDGEMENTS

Dorling Kindersely would like to thank Anne Askwith and Casey Horton for additional editorial help and Penny David for the index.

Extracts from *The Tale of Genji* by Lady Murasaki, translated by Arthur Waley, copyright © 1935 by Arthur Waley, are reprinted by kind permission of Houghton Mifflin Company.